C000212671

1 MONTH OF
FREE
READING

at
www.ForgottenBooks.com

By purchasing this book you are
eligible for one month membership to
ForgottenBooks.com, giving you
unlimited access to our entire
collection of over 1,000,000 titles via
our web site and mobile apps.

To claim your free month visit:
www.forgottenbooks.com/free260512

* Offer is valid for 45 days from date of purchase. Terms and conditions apply.

ISBN 978-0-656-52892-9
PIBN 10260512

This book is a reproduction of an important historical work. Forgotten Books uses
state-of-the-art technology to digitally reconstruct the work, preserving the original format
whilst repairing imperfections present in the aged copy. In rare cases, an imperfection in
the original, such as a blemish or missing page, may be replicated in our edition. We do,
however, repair the vast majority of imperfections successfully; any imperfections that
remain are intentionally left to preserve the state of such historical works.

Forgotten Books is a registered trademark of FB &c Ltd.
Copyright © 2018 FB &c Ltd.
FB &c Ltd, Dalton House, 60 Windsor Avenue, London, SW19 2RR.
Company number 08720141. Registered in England and Wales.

For support please visit www.forgottenbooks.com

NEVADA LEGISLATURE---SENATE.

THIRD SESSION.

FIRST DAY.

CARSON CITY, January 7th, 1867.

Pursuant to the provisions of Section 12, Article 17, of the Constitution of the State of Nevada, the Senate was called to order by the Hon. J. S. Crosman, President, at 12 o'clock, noon.

The following named Senators answered to their names at roll call:

Messrs. Carpenter, Doron, Eastman, Edwards, Geller, Grey, Haines, Hastings, Hutchins, Linn, Mason, Meder, Monroe, Nelson, Proctor, Stevenson, Sumner, Terry, Welty.

The President appointed D. J. Gasherie, Sergeant-at-Arms *pro tempore.*

Mr. Proctor, of Nye, offered the following:

"SENATE CHAMBER, January 7th, 1867.

" *To the President of the Senate:*

"I object to the admission of George T. Terry to a seat in the Senate of Nevada, on the ground that at the time of his pretended election he was holding a lucrative office under the Government of the United States, and is therefore, under the Constitution of Nevada, ineligible to hold the office of State Senator now claimed by him."

Mr. Proctor contended that action thereon should be had before the oath of office was administered to Senators elect.

Mr. Welty raised the point of order, that the credentials of a claimant to a seat were *prima facie* evidence of his right to such seat.

The Chair ruled the point well taken, and that the Senate could only properly determine the right to a contested seat after full organization.

Messrs. C. Carpenter, of Lyon County, Lewis Doron and B. S. Mason, of Esmeralda, C. H. Eastman and Sol. Geller, of Washoe, T. D. Edwards and B. H. Meder, of Ormsby, O. H. Grey, John Nelson, and C. C. Stevenson, of Storey, J. J. Linn, of Humboldt, W. G. Monroe, of Churchill, and George T. Terry and D. W. Welty, of Lander, presented their certificates of election, and each took the oath of office and of secrecy, administered by the Hon. H. O. Beatty, Chief Justice.

Mr. Hutchins moved to proceed to the election of a President *pro tempore.* Carried.

Mr. Haines placed in nomination Senator Lewis Doron.
Mr. Edwards placed in nomination Senator C. A. Sumner.
Nominations were declared closed.
The roll was called, with the following result:
For Mr. Doron: Messrs. Haines, Hastings, Mason, Meder, Sumner and Welty—6.
For Mr. Sumner: Messrs. Carpenter, Doron, Eastman, Edwards, Geller, Grey, Hutchins, Linn, Monroe, Nelson, Proctor, Stevenson and Terry—13.
Whole number of votes cast—19.
Necessary to a choice—10.
Mr. Sumner, having received a majority of all votes cast, was declared elected President *pro tem.*

On motion, the Senate proceeded to the election of Secretary.
Mr. Welty nominated B. C. Brown.
Mr. Hastings nominated Wm. M. Cutter.
The roll was then called, with the following result:
For Mr. Brown: Messrs. Doron, Eastman, Edwards, Geller, Grey, Haines, Hutchins, Mason, Meder, Monroe, Nelson, Proctor, Stevenson, Sumner, Terry and Welty—16.
For Mr. Cutter: Messrs. Carpenter, Hastings and Linn—3.
Whole number of votes cast—19.
Necessary to a choice—10.
Mr. Brown, having a majority of all votes cast, was declared duly elected.

The Senate then proceeded to the election of a Sergeant-at-Arms.
Mr. Nelson nominated Mr. Vandewater.
Mr. Grey nominated Mr. Gaige.
Mr. Hastings nominated Mr. Munckton.
Mr. Edwards nominated Mr. Gasherie.
The roll was then called, with the following result:
For Mr. Vandewater: Mr. Linn and Mr. Nelson—2.
For Mr. Gaige: Messrs. Carpenter, Doron, Edwards, Geller, Grey, Haines, Mason, Meder, Monroe, Proctor, Stevenson, Sumner, Terry and Welty—14.
For Mr. Gasherie: Messrs. Eastman, Hastings and Hutchins—3.
Whole number of votes cast—19.
Necessary to a choice—10.
Mr. M. M. Gaige, having received a majority of all votes cast, was declared duly elected.

The Senate then proceeded to the election of Enrolling Clerk.
Mr. Welty nominated John R. Williamson.

There being no other nominations, Mr. Williamson was, by acclamation, declared unanimously elected.

The Senate then proceeded to the election of Engrossing Clerk.
Mr. Hutchins nominated Wm. H. Williams.
Mr. Doron nominated John D. Gorin.
The roll was then called, with the following result:
For Mr. Gorin: Messrs. Carpenter, Eastman, Edwards, Geller, Gray, Haines, Mason, Meder, Monroe, Stevenson, Sumner, Terry, Welty—13.
For Mr. Williams: Messrs. Doron, Hastings, Hutchins, Linn, Nelson, Proctor—6.
Whole number of votes cast—19.
Necessary to a choice—10.
Mr. Gorin, having received a majority of all votes cast, was declared duly elected.

The Senate then proceeded to the election of Chaplain.
Mr. Edwards nominated the Rev. Mr. Stump. No other nominations being made, Mr. Stump was declared duly elected by acclamation.

Mr. Sumner offered the following resolution:

Resolved, That Wm. M. Cutter be, and he is hereby elected Official Reporter of the Senate.

Unanimously adopted.
Mr. Welty offered a concurrent resolution relative to the ceremonies of inauguration of the 8th inst.
Laid on the table temporarily.
B. C. Brown, Secretary; M. M. Gaige, Sergeant-at-Arms; J. R. Williamson, Enrolling Clerk; and John D. Gorin, Engrossing Clerk, took the oath of office and of secrecy administered by Chief Justice H. O. Beatty.
The Secretary read the following notices of appointments:

To the Hon. the Senate:

I have this day appointed C. C. Wallace, Assistant Sergeant-at-Arms of the Senate. Respectfully,

M. M. GAIGE,
Sergeant-at-Arms.

To the Hon. the Senate:

I have this day made the following appointments:
Assistant Secretary ....John R. Eardley
Minute Clerk ....J. P. Coolidge
Journal Clerk ....D. P. Walters
Copying Clerk ....John C. Medley
Respectfully,
B. C. BROWN,
Secretary of Senate.

John R. Eardley, Assistant Secretary; C. C. Wallace, Assistant Sergeant-at-Arms; J. P. Coolidge, Minute Clerk; and John C. Medley, Copying Clerk, took the oath of office and of secrecy.

The Senate took a recess of fifteen minutes.

Senate called to order—President in the chair. Roll called; quorum present.

On motion, Senate Concurrent Resolution No. 1, relative to the ceremonies of inauguration, was taken from the table. The roll was called on the passage thereof, with the following result:

YEAS—Messrs. Carpenter, Doron, Eastman, Edwards, Geller, Grey, Haines, Hastings, Hutchins, Linn, Meder, Nelson, Proctor, Stevenson, Sumner, Terry and Welty—17.

Passed.

Mr. Terry offered a concurrent resolution, relative to a joint committee, to wait on the Governor.

Laid on the table.

In pursuance of the requirements of Senate Concurrent Resolution No. 1, relative to the ceremonies of inauguration, the President appointed Messrs. Welty, Stevenson and Hastings a committee to make arrangements for the inauguration.

Mr. Hutchins offered the following resolution:

Resolved, That a Committee of two be appointed to inform the Governor that the Senate is now fully organized, and ready to receive any communication he may desire to make.

Adopted.

The President appointed Messrs. Hutchins and Eastman as such committee.

NOTICE OF BILLS.

Mr. Welty gave notice of his intention to introduce a bill entitled "An Act to amend an Act entitled an Act to redistrict the State of Nevada into Judicial Districts, and to fix the salaries of Judges and the terms of Court therein." Also, a bill entitled "An Act concerning incomplete service by publication of writs and process in certain cases." Also, a bill entitled "An Act to provide for the release of sureties on official bonds."

Also, a bill entitled "An Act defining the jurisdiction of the Courts in this State, where the venue is brought in question."

MESSAGES FROM THE ASSEMBLY.

The following messages were received from the Assembly:

ASSEMBLY CHAMBER, January 7th, 1867.

To the Hon. the Senate :

I am instructed to inform your honorable body that the Assembly have fully organized, by the election of the following officers, to wit:

Speaker,	R. D. Ferguson
Speaker pro tem.,	T. V. Julian
Chief Clerk,	A. Whitford
Assistant Clerk,	W. Darling
Sergeant-at-Arms,	Wm. Woodhurst
Assistant Sergeant-at-Arms,	S. A. Moulton

Enrolling Clerk,	A. D. Brill
Engrossing Clerk,	R. L. Thomas
Minute Clerk,	T. S. Davenport
Journal Clerk,	W. G. Gates
Copying Clerk,	Samuel Hyatt

Respectfully,

A. WHITFORD,
Clerk.

ASSEMBLY CHAMBER, January 7th, 1867.

To the Hon. the Senate:

I am requested to inform your honorable body that the Assembly have this day passed a resolution appointing a Committee, consisting of Messrs. Munckton, Walton and Mitchell, to act with a like Committee from the Senate, to inform the Governor that the two Houses are now organized and ready to receive any communications that he may have to make.

Respectfully,

A. WHITFORD,
Chief Clerk.

Mr. Proctor moved that a Senate Committee be appointed, in pursuance of the above communication.

Carried.

The President appointed Messrs. Proctor, Carpenter and Doron as such committee.

Mr. Hutchins, of the Committee appointed to wait on the Governor, reported that the Committee had performed their duty, and had been informed by the Governor that he would have no communication to make to the Senate until after the inauguration.

Adopted.

At three o'clock and thirty minutes, on motion of Mr. Hutchins, the Senate adjourned.

J. S. CROSMAN,
President.

Attest—B. C. BROWN,
Secretary.

————

IN SENATE—SECOND DAY.

CARSON CITY, January 8th, 1867.

The Senate met pursuant to adjournment, the President in the chair.

The roll was called, and the following Senators answered to their names:

Messrs. Carpenter, Doron, Eastman, Edwards, Grey, Haines, Hastings, Linn, Mason, Meder, Monroe, Proctor, Stevenson, Sumner, Terry, Welty—16.

The following Senators were noted absent:

Messrs. Geller, Hutchins and Nelson—3.

Prayer by the Chaplain.

The Journal of the first day was read and approved.

2

Mr. Proctor, of the Joint Committee appointed to wait on the Governor, reported that the Committee had performed their duty, and had been informed by the Governor that he would probably send in a communication to the Senate during the day.

Adopted.

Mr. Linn gave notice that he would, on some subsequent day of the session, introduce a joint resolution concerning the acception of the territory ceded by the United States to the State of Nevada.

The Secretary read the following :

To the Honorable the Senate :

Mr. D. P. Walters, the appointee as Journal Clerk, being unable to attend to his duties as such, I hereby appoint Mr. Rich. R. Parkinson as Journal Clerk.

Respectfully,

B. C. BROWN,
Sec'y Senate.

Mr. Hutchins introduced the following resolution :

Resolved, That the Sergeant-at-Arms of the Senate be, and hereby is, authorized to supply the members and attachés of the Senate with stationery, postage, expressage, and newspapers, on which the yeas and nays were called, with the following result :

YEAS—Messrs. Carpenter, Doron, Eastman, Edwards, Geller, Haines, Hastings, Hutchins, Linn, Meder, Stevenson, Terry and Welty—13.

NAYS—Messrs. Grey, Mason, Monroe, Proctor and Sumner—5.

Mr. Edwards gave notice of motion to reconsider on Monday.

The following message was received from the Assembly :

To the Honorable the Senate :

I herewith transmit to your honorable body Senate Concurrent Resolution No. 1, concerning inauguration of Governor and Lieutenant Governor, the same having passed the House this day: yeas, 34; nays, none; and Messrs. Wheeler, Bence and Huse were appointed as such committee, to act with Senate Committee.

Respectfully,

A. WHITFORD,
Clerk.

On motion of Mr. Welty, at 11 o'clock 30 minutes the Senate took a recess until 1 : 30 P.M.

AFTERNOON SESSION.

At one o'clock 30 minutes P.M. the Senate reassembled.

Upon a quorum being found present, the Senate was called to order pursuant to adjournment.

The roll was called, and the following Senators noted present :

Messrs. Doron, Eastman, Edwards, Geller, Grey, Hastings, Mason, Monroe, Nelson, Stevenson and Sumner—Total, 12.

Absent—Messrs. Carpenter, Haines, Hutchins, Linn, Meder, Terry and Welty—Total, 7.

Mr. Hastings moved a call of the House.
Carried.

Messrs. Carpenter, Haines, Hutchins, Linn, Terry and Welty appearing, were, on motion, excused.

Mr. Grey moved that further proceedings under call be dispensed with.
Carried.

Mr. Welty, Chairman of Joint Committee on Inauguration Ceremonies, submitted the following report:

To the Senate and Assembly of the State of Nevada:

Your Joint Committee appointed to make arrangements for the inaugural of the Governor and Lieutenant Governor elect, submit the following report:

The two Houses will meet in Joint Convention at the hour provided for by the joint resolution, and be formed in procession by the Marshal of the day, and march in a body in the order hereinafter mentioned, to the Governor's residence, and after receiving the Governor and Lieutenant Governor, return to the Assembly Chamber, where the oath of office shall be administered, and the Inaugural Address of the Governor received; after which the members of the Joint Convention will escort the Governor to his residence, and return again to the Hall of the Assembly.

The following programme has been adopted:

First.—Music.
Second.—Members of Assembly and officers.
Third.—Members of the Senate and officers.
Fourth.—Governor and Lieutenant Governor.
Fifth.—Staff Officers of the Governor.

Order of proceedings at the Hall:

1st. Prayer by the Chaplain of the Senate.
2d. Oath of office to the Governor by Chief Justice Beatty.
3d. Oath of office to the Lieutenant Governor by Chief Justice Beatty.
4th. Inaugural Address by the Governor.
5th. Benediction by the Chaplain of the Assembly.

The Committee have appointed Brigadier General A. L. Page as Marshal of the day.

(Signed)
                                        D. W. WELTY,
                                        D. L. HASTINGS,
                                        C. C. STEVENSON,
                                        J. A. WHEELER,
                                        S. E. HUSE,
                                        H. H. BENCE.

The report was unanimously adopted.

The following communication was received from the Assembly:

STATE OF NEVADA, ASSEMBLY CHAMBER,
Carson City, January 8th, 1867.

To the Honorable the Senate :

I am instructed to inform your honorable body that the Assembly are now ready to go into Joint Convention for the purpose of performing the inaugural services as per concurrent resolutions.

Respectfully,

A. WHITFORD,
Clerk.

On motion of Mr. Welty, the members of the Senate and attachés proceeded to the Assembly Chamber, according to the arrangements made by Joint Convention.

IN JOINT CONVENTION.

The Convention met and was called to order by the President, J. S. Crosman.

Prayer by the Chaplain.

On motion of Senator Welty the report of the Joint Committee was read.

Brigadier General A. L. Page, Marshal of the day, formed the members and attachés of both Houses in procession, according to the arrangements of the Joint Committee.

The procession returning to the Assembly Chamber, the following Oath of Office was administered to the Governor elect, HENRY G. BLASDEL, and to the Lieutenant Governor elect, JAMES S. SLINGERLAND, by Chief Justice Beatty:

I, ——————— do solemnly swear that I will support, protect, and defend the Constitution and Government of the United States, and the [Constitution] and Government of the State of Nevada, against all enemies, whether domestic or foreign, and that I will bear true faith, allegiance and loyalty to the same, any ordinance, resolution, or law of any State, Convention, or Legislature to the contrary notwithstanding; and further, that I do this with a full determination, pledge, and purpose, without any mental reservation or evasion whatever. And I do further solemnly swear, that I have not fought a duel, nor sent or accepted a challenge to fight a duel, nor been a second to either party, nor in any manner aided or assisted in such duel, nor been knowingly the bearer of such challenge or acceptance, since the adoption of the Constitution of the State of Nevada; and that I will not be so engaged or concerned, directly or indirectly, in or about any such duel, during my continuance in office. And, further, that I will well and faithfully perform all the duties of the office on which I am about to enter. So help me God.

The Governor then delivered his Inaugural Address, for which see Appendix.

On motion of Senator Doron, a vote of thanks was tendered to Brigadier General A. L. Page, Marshal of the day, for the very able manner in which he had conducted the procession.

On motion of Mr. Bence, at 3 o'clock 15 minutes P.M., the Convention adjourned.

IN SENATE.

The Senate was called to order, the President in the chair.

On motion of Mr. Hastings, Senator Sumner, President *pro tem.*, was appointed a committee of one to escort the Lieut. Governor, James S. Slingerland to the chair; the which being done, he was introduced to the Senate, and made the following address:

Senators—

The convening of this body heralds the approach of business to be by you transacted, that is of a most grave and solemn import. You have been chosen by an intelligent people, and intrusted by them to speak their voice.

During life, none of you may ever be called upon to discharge duties of graver import than are now lodged with you. Feeling assured from my personal knowledge of many of you, that you all feel duly impressed with the responsibility of the charge you hold; and having firm faith that those duties will be faithfully and fearlessly performed by you, I assume my position as your presiding officer, with great doubts of my own worthiness to do my duties ably and well; yet with a fixed purpose in all things to act impartially and justly with you. I ask of you in turn that you will be patient as friends, and courteous as Senators, if in any or many things that I do, I may in your opinion err.

The Senate will now come to order for the transaction of business.

The President appointed

Messenger, ...John F. Craddoc
Porter, ...William Skeen
Pages, ...Llewellyn Meder
" ....Furman Barclay

The President appointed the following Committees:

Committee on Mileage.—Messrs. Linn, Eastman and Doron.
Committee on Election.—Messrs. Grey, Mason and Monroe.

On motion of Mr. Proctor, at 3 o'clock and 30 minutes the Senate adjourned.
JAMES S. SLINGERLAND,
President.

Attest—B. C. BROWN,
Secretary.

IN SENATE—THIRD DAY.

WEDNESDAY, January 9th, 1867.

The Senate met pursuant to adjournment.
President in the chair.
Roll called.
Present—Messrs. Carpenter, Doron, Eastman, Edwards, Geller, Grey,

The Senate took a recess of fifteen minutes.

Senate called to order—President in the chair. Roll called; quorum present.

On motion, Senate Concurrent Resolution No. 1, relative to the ceremonies of inauguration, was taken from the table. The roll was called on the passage thereof, with the following result:

YEAS—Messrs. Carpenter, Doron, Eastman, Edwards, Geller, Grey, Haines, Hastings, Hutchins, Linn, Meder, Nelson, Proctor, Stevenson, Sumner, Terry and Welty—17.

Passed.

Mr. Terry offered a concurrent resolution, relative to a joint committee, to wait on the Governor.

Laid on the table.

In pursuance of the requirements of Senate Concurrent Resolution No. 1, relative to the ceremonies of inauguration, the President appointed Messrs. Welty, Stevenson and Hastings a committee to make arrangements for the inauguration.

Mr. Hutchins offered the following resolution :

Resolved, That a Committee of two be appointed to inform the Governor that the Senate is now fully organized, and ready to receive any communication he may desire to make.

Adopted.

The President appointed Messrs. Hutchins and Eastman as such committee.

NOTICE OF BILLS.

Mr. Welty gave notice of his intention to introduce a bill entitled " An Act to amend an Act entitled an Act to redistrict the State of Nevada into Judicial Districts, and to fix the salaries of Judges and the terms of Court therein." Also, a bill entitled " An Act concerning incomplete service by publication of writs and process in certain cases." Also, a bill entitled " An Act to provide for the release of sureties on official bonds."

Also, a bill entitled " An Act defining the jurisdiction of the Courts in this State, where the venue is brought in question."

MESSAGES FROM THE ASSEMBLY.

The following messages were received from the Assembly :

ASSEMBLY CHAMBER, January 7th, 1867.

To the Hon. the Senate :

I am instructed to inform your honorable body that the Assembly have fully organized, by the election of the following officers, to wit:

Speaker,..R. D. Ferguson
Speaker pro tem.,...T. V. Julian
Chief Clerk, ...A. Whitford
Assistant Clerk,..W. Darling
Sergeant-at-Arms,.......................................Wm. Woodhurst
Assistant Sergeant-at-Arms, ...S. A. Moulton

Enrolling Clerk, ...A. D. Brill
Engrossing Clerk, ...R. L. Thomas
Minute Clerk, ...T. S. Davenport
Journal Clerk, ...W. G. Gates
Copying Clerk, ...Samuel Hyatt

Respectfully,

A. WHITFORD,
Clerk.

ASSEMBLY CHAMBER, January 7th, 1867.

To the Hon. the Senate:

I am requested to inform your honorable body that the Assembly have this day passed a resolution appointing a Committee, consisting of Messrs. Munckton, Walton and Mitchell, to act with a like Committee from the Senate, to inform the Governor that the two Houses are now organized and ready to receive any communications that he may have to make.

Respectfully,

A. WHITFORD,
Chief Clerk.

Mr. Proctor moved that a Senate Committee be appointed, in pursuance of the above communication.

Carried.

The President appointed Messrs. Proctor, Carpenter and Doron as such committee.

Mr. Hutchins, of the Committee appointed to wait on the Governor, reported that the Committee had performed their duty, and had been informed by the Governor that he would have no communication to make to the Senate until after the inauguration.

Adopted.

At three o'clock and thirty minutes, on motion of Mr. Hutchins, the Senate adjourned.

J. S. CROSMAN,
President.

Attest—B. C. BROWN,
Secretary.

IN SENATE—SECOND DAY.

CARSON CITY, January 8th, 1867.

The Senate met pursuant to adjournment, the President in the chair.

The roll was called, and the following Senators answered to their names:

Messrs. Carpenter, Doron, Eastman, Edwards, Grey, Haines, Hastings, Linn, Mason, Meder, Monroe, Proctor, Stevenson, Sumner, Terry, Welty—16.

The following Senators were noted absent:

Messrs. Geller, Hutchins and Nelson—3.

Prayer by the Chaplain.

The Journal of the first day was read and approved.

2

Also, Senate Bill No. 7, entitled "An Act concerning incomplete Service, by publication of writs and processes, in certain cases."

Read first and second time by title, and referred to Committee on Judiciary.

Mr. Monroe rose to a question of privilege, excepting as a member of the Democratic party to an article appearing in the "Carson Appeal" of this morning, which states that John B. Winters was the choice of the Democratic members of the Legislature of the State of Nevada, for United States Senator.

The President [announced] his appointment of the following Standing Committees:

On Judiciary—Messrs. Welty, Edwards, Proctor, Sumner and Nelson.

On Ways and Means—Messrs. Sumner, Hutchins, Proctor, Hastings and Eastman.

On Corporations—Messrs. Carpenter, Eastman, Haines, Stevenson and Monroe.

On Supplies and Expenditures—Messrs. Terry, Geller and Linn.

On Rules and Joint Rules—Messrs. Haines, Doron and Hutchins.

On Engrossment—Messrs. Hastings, Meder and Welty.

On Enrollment—Messrs. Linn, Carpenter and Mason.

Mr. Edwards, by leave of the Senate, declined serving on the Judiciary.

The President, by leave of the Senate, withdrew his appointment of the Judiciary Committee.

At 11:30 A.M., on motion of Mr. Proctor, the Senate adjourned.

JAMES S. SLINGERLAND,
President.

Attest—B. C. BROWN,
Secretary.

IN SENATE—FOURTH DAY.

CARSON CITY, January 10th, 1867.

Senate met at eleven o'clock, and was called to order by the President.

Roll called.

Present—Messrs. Carpenter, Doron, Eastman, Edwards, Geller, Grey, Haines, Hastings, Hutchins, Linn, Mason, Meder, Monroe, Sumner, Proctor, Stevenson, Terry and Welty—18.

Absent—Mr. Mason—1.

Prayer by the Chaplain.

The Journal of the third day read and corrected, to show that the introduction of Senate Concurrent Resolution concerning the adoption of Constitutional Amendments of the United States was made under the head of "Motions and Resolutions," instead of Notice of Bills, as appears in the Journal. After this correction, the Journal was approved.

The first biennial message of the Governor, accompanied by the first biennial reports of the State Mineralogist, and the State Superintendent of Public Instruction, also by the report of the Commissioners on Losses by Indian Depredations, were received, and temporarily laid on the table.

REPORTS OF COMMITTEES.

Messrs. Linn and Eastman, of the Committee on Mileage, submitted the following report:

Mr. President:

Your Standing Committee on Mileage beg leave to report that they have had the matters committed to them under consideration, and find that the members of the Senate are entitled to mileage in the following amounts, to wit:

	No. Miles.	Amount.
Mr. Carpenter	24	$ 9 50
Mr. Doron	220	88 00
Mr. Eastman	50	20 00
Mr. Geller	50	20 00
Mr. Grey	30	12 00
Mr. Haines	34	13 60
Mr. Hastings	30	12 00
Mr. Hutchins	320	128 00
Mr. Linn	300	120 00
Mr. Mason	220	88 00
Mr. Monroe	340	136 00
Mr. Nelson	30	12 00
Mr. Proctor	460	184 00
Mr. Stevenson	30	12 00
Mr. Sumner	30	12 00
Mr. Terry	400	160 00
Mr. Welty	400	160 00
Mr. President	50	20 00

All of which is respectfully submitted.

J. J. LINN, Chairman.
C. H. EASTMAN.

Mr. Haines, Chairman of Committee on Rules and Joint Rules, submitted the following report:

Mr. President:

Your Committee appointed to act conjointly with a like Committee of the House, in drafting and submitting Joint Rules for the government of the two Houses in the transaction of business between them, unanimously recommend the adoption of the Joint Rules as amended by the last session.

J. W. HAINES,
Chairman of Senate Committee.
T. V. JULIEN,
Chairman of House Committee.

The President announced his appointment of the following Standing Committees:

3

On Judiciary—Messrs. Welty, Proctor, Sumner, Nelson, and Hutchins.
On Mines and Mining—Messrs. Stevenson, Linn, Doron, Nelson, and Terry.
On Federal Relations—Messrs. Mason, Monroe, and Edwards.
On State Affairs—Messrs. Doron, Meder, and Monroe.
On Agriculture and Manufactures—Messrs. Haines, Eastman, and Meder.
On Education—Messrs. Grey, Edwards, and Terry.
On Public Printing—Messrs. Doron, Carpenter, and Meder.
On Counties and County Boundaries—Messrs. Proctor, Hutchins, Grey, Terry, and Eastman.
On State Prison—Messrs. Geller, Sumner, and Proctor.
On Public Morals—Messrs. Meder, Mason, and Welty.

COMMUNICATION FROM THE GOVERNOR.

The following communication from the Governor was received:

STATE OF NEVADA, EXECUTIVE DEPARTMENT, }
Carson City, January 1st, 1867.   }

Gentlemen of the Senate and Assembly:
I have this day appointed Thomas Wells my private Secretary.
H. D. BLASDEL,
Governor of Nevada.

BIENNIAL MESSAGE OF GOVERNOR.

The biennial Message of the Governor was now read.   (See Appendix.)

Mr. Proctor introduced Senate Concurrent Resolution No. 8, providing for the printing of one thousand copies of the Governor's Message.   The roll was called, with the following result:

YEAS—Messrs. Carpenter, Doron, Eastman, Edwards, Geller, Grey, Haines, Hastings, Hutchins, Linn, Meder, Monroe, Proctor, Stevenson, Sumner, Terry, and Welty—17.
NAYS—None.

Adopted.
The second annual report of Superintendent of Public Instruction was, on motion of Mr. Proctor, referred to the Committee on Education.
The report of State Mineralogist was referred to the Committee on Mines and Mining.
Mr. Hutchins moved that the several committees be instructed to report to the Senate, at their earliest convenience, what portions of documents accompanying the Governor's Message were desirable to be ordered printed.
Carried.
Mr. Welty offered the following resolution:

Resolved, That the Message of the Governor, and accompanying documents, be referred to a select committee, to report what subjects therein require legislation, and to what standing committees the subjects therein treated of ought to be referred.

Mr. Doron moved, as a substitute, that so much of the Governor's Message as refers to ways and means be referred to the Committee on Ways and Means;

so much as refers to the judiciary, be referred to Judiciary Committee; so much as refers to corporations, to Committee on Incorporation; so much as refers to mines and mining, to Committee on Mines and Mining; so much as refers to Federal relations, to Committee on Federal Relations; so much as refers to State affairs, to Committee on State Affairs; so much as refers to agriculture and manufactures, to Committee on Agriculture and Manufactures; so much as refers to education, to Committee on Education; so much as refers to elections, to Committee on Elections; so much as refers to printing, to Committee on Printing; so much as refers to counties and county boundaries, to Committee on Counties and County Boundaries; so much as refers to State Prison, to Committee on State Prison; so much as refers to militia and Indian affairs, to Committee on Militia and Indian Affairs; so much as refers to roads and bridges, to the Committee on Roads and Bridges; so much as refers to State Library, to Committee on State Library; so much as refers to internal improvements, to Committee on Internal Improvements; so much as refers to public lands, to Committee on Public Lands; so much as refers to supplies and expenditures, to Committee on Supplies and Expenditures.

Carried.

Mr. Grey, by leave, without previous notice, introduced Senate Bill No. 9, entitled "An Act authorizing the issuance and sale of certain State bonds, and levying a tax to provide means for the payment thereof." Read first time, and (rules suspended) read second time, by title, and referred to Committee on Ways and Means.

Mr. Welty, by leave, and without previous notice, introduced Senate Bill No. 10, entitled "An Act to provide compensation to citizens of this State for losses and damages sustained from hostile Indians." Read first time, and (rules suspended) read second time by title, and referred to Committee on Militia and Indian Affairs.

Also, introduced Senate Bill No. 11, entitled "An Act to provide revenue for the support of the government of the State of Nevada, and the Acts amendatory thereof." Read first time, and (rules suspended) read second time by title, and referred to Committee on Ways and Means.

Also, Senate Bill No. 12, entitled "An Act to amend an Act entitled an Act to regulate proceedings in criminal cases in the courts of justice in the (Territory) State of Nevada." Read first time, and (rules suspended) read second time by title, and referred to Committee on Judiciary.

Mr. Welty introduced Senate Concurrent Resolution No. 13, concerning the appointment of a Military Governor over the Territory of Utah, and raising troops for the protection thereof. Read first time, and (rules suspended) read the second time by title, and referred to Committee on Federal Relations.

Mr. Proctor, by leave, introduced Senate Bill No. 14, entitled "An Act for the relief of S. L. Baker." Read first time, and (rules suspended) read second time by title, and referred to Committee on Counties and County Boundaries.

Mr. Hastings introduced the following resolution:

Resolved, That the Sergeant-at-Arms be instructed to obtain suitable rooms for the use of the Enrolling and Engrossing Clerks of the Senate, and supply them with the necessary furniture.

Adopted.

Mr. Proctor presented the following communication:

To the Honorable the Senate of the Third Session
of the Legislature of the State of Nevada:

The undersigned respectfully represents, that on the sixth day of November, 1866, and for some time prior thereto, he was a qualified elector of the County of Lander, State aforesaid, and has since continued to be, and now is such elector.

2d. That at the general election, held in said County of Lander on said sixth day of November, A.D. 1866, for State and county officers, he received seven hundred and fifty-five (755) votes for the office of State Senator, to fill the alleged vacancy created by the absence from this State of the Hon. M. D. Larrowe, which was the highest number of votes cast at said election for any person then eligible to said office.

3d. That George T. Terry was also voted for at said election, for said office of State Senator; and, as he is informed, received from the County Clerk of the said County of Lander County a certain writing, purporting to certify in substance that said Terry had been duly elected to said office, upon the faith of which writing, he is informed, said Terry has been admitted to and is now occupying a seat in said Senate.

4th. That some time prior to said election, the said Terry was duly appointed by S. T. Gage, Esq., United States Tax Collector of the Fourth Collection District, State of Nevada, to the office of United States Deputy Tax Collector, in and for said collection district, the same being a lucrative office under the Government of the United States; that said Terry entered upon the discharge of the duties of said assistant office immediately after his appointment thereto, and continued to hold said office and exercise the duties of the same during and until after the general election, held on the sixth day of November, 1866, by reason of which he, the said Terry, was then, on said sixth day of November, 1866, ineligible to the office of State Senator, aforesaid.

Wherefore the undersigned contests the right of said George T. Terry to the aforesaid office of State Senator, and prays that he, the said Terry, be excluded from said office, and that he, the contestant, be admitted to the same.

Respectfully submitted,
C. H. PACHEN.

Mr. Hutchins moved to refer to Committee on Elections. The yeas and nays were called for by Messrs. Welty, Hutchins, and Hastings, with the following result:

YEAS—Messrs. Carpenter, Eastman, Geller, Grey, Hastings, Hutchins, Linn, Monroe, Proctor, Stevenson, and Sumner—11.

NAYS—Messrs. Doron, Haines, Meder, and Welty—4.

Carried.

Mr. Proctor introduced the following resolution:

Resolved, That the Secretary be instructed to furnish the Sergeant-at-Arms with a copy of the resolution instructing him to supply the members of the Senate with stationery.

Adopted.

On motion of Mr. Proctor, the Senate, at 1 o'clock P.M., adjourned.

JAMES S. SLINGERLAND.
President.

Attest—B. C. BROWN,
Secretary.

IN SENATE—FIFTH DAY.

CARSON CITY, January 11th, 1867.

The Senate met at eleven o'clock A.M., and was called to order by the President.

Roll called.

Present—Messrs. Carpenter, Doron, Eastman, Edwards, Geller, Grey, Haines, Hastings, Hutchins, Linn, Mason, Meder, Monroe, Proctor, Stevenson, Sumner, Terry, and Welty—18.

Absent—Mr. Nelson.

Prayer by the Chaplain.

The Journal of the Fourth day was read and approved.

The following communication, with documents, was received:

STATE OF NEVADA.

[Seal of State.]

OFFICE OF SECRETARY OF STATE,
Carson City, January 10th, 1867.

To the Senate of Nevada:

GENTLEMEN—I have the honor to transmit herewith, for your consideration, the claim of Andrew Whitford, in the sum of one hundred dollars, for clerical services performed for the Senate at the First Session of the Nevada Legislature, the same having been passed upon and approved by the Board of State Examiners, but for the payment of which no appropriation has been made.

Very respectfully,

C. N. NOTEWARE,
Secretary of State.

Referred to Committee on Claims.

Mr. Sumner offered the following resolution:

Resolved, That the Committee on Judiciary, and the Committee on Ways and Means, be, and they are hereby authorized respectively, to employ a clerk.

Adopted.

Mr. Edwards introduced Senate Bill No. 15, entitled "An Act to Repeal an Act entitled 'An Act to Establish a Standard of Weights and Measures,' approved February 28, 1866." Read first time; rules suspended; read second time by title, and referred to Committee on State Affairs.

Mr. Monroe introduced Senate Bill No. 16, entitled "An Act to Repeal an Act, entitled 'An Act concerning the Location and Possession of Mining Claims.'"

Read first time; rules suspended; read second time by title, and referred to Committee on Mines and Mining.

Mr. Welty, by leave, (no previous notice having been given) introduced Senate Bill No. 17, entitled "An Act in relation to Fines."

Read first time; rules suspended; read second time by title, and referred to Committee on State Affairs.

Mr. Welty introduced Senate Concurrent Resolution No. 18, memorializing the Commander of the Department of the Pacific to establish a fort at Gravelly Ford.

Read first time; rules suspended; read second time by title, and referred to Committee on Military and Indian Affairs.

Mr. Linn introduced Senate Concurrent Resolution No. 19, in relation to the boundaries of the State of Nevada, and the acceptance of the additional territory ceded by the United States to this State.

Read first time; rules suspended; read second time by title, and referred to Committee on Counties and County Boundaries.

The President announced his appointment of the following Committees:

On Militia and Indian Affairs—Messrs. Hutchins, Nelson, and Carpenter.
On State Library—Messrs. Nelson, Haines, and Hastings.
On Internal Improvements—Messrs. Eastman, Carpenter, and Mason.
On Public Lands—Messrs. Edwards, Doron, and Grey.
On Claims—Messrs. Monroe, Nelson, and Edwards.

NOTICES OF BILLS.

Mr. Sumner gave notice of the introduction of a bill entitled "An Act to Fund the Outstanding Indebtedness of Virginia City."

Mr. Sumner moved to adjourn.

Mr. Hastings moved to amend by adjourning until Monday, at eleven o'clock.

Yeas and nays called for by Messrs. Grey, Proctor, and Mason, which resulted as follows:

YEAS—Messrs. Carpenter, Eastman, Edwards, Haines, Hastings, Hutchins, Stevenson, Terry, and Welty—9.

NAYS—Messrs. Geller, Grey, Doron, Linn, Mason, Meder, Monroe, Proctor, and Sumner—9.

Tie vote.

Mr. President cast his vote in the negative.

Amendment lost.

The yeas and nays were called for on the original motion by Messrs. Mason, Hastings, and Proctor, which was recorded as follows:

YEAS—Messrs. Carpenter, Doron, Eastman, Edwards, Geller, Grey, Haines, Linn, Mason, Meder, Monroe, Proctor, Sumner, and Terry—14.

NAYS—Messrs. Hastings, Hutchins, Stevenson, and Welty—4.

At 11 : 45 A.M., the Senate stood adjourned.

JAMES S. SLINGERLAND,
President.

Attest—B. C. BROWN,
Secretary.

IN SENATE—SIXTH DAY.

CARSON CITY, January 12th, 1867.

The Senate met at 11 o'clock A.M., and was called to order by the President.

Roll called.

Present—Messrs. Carpenter, Doron, Eastman, Edwards, Geller, Grey, Haines,

23

Hastings, Hutchins, Linn, Mason, Meder, Proctor, Stevenson, Sumner, Terry, and Welty—17.

Absent—Messrs. Monroe and Nelson—2.

Prayer by the Chaplain.

The Journal of the Fifth day was read and approved.

Mr. Proctor reported that the Committee on Counties and County Boundaries had had under consideration the Senate Concurrent Resolution No. 19, in relation to the boundaries of the State, and had directed their chairman to report the same back to the Senate and recommend its passage. F. M. Proctor, Chairman.

Mr Sumner reported that the Committee on Ways and Means had had under consideration Senate Bill No. 11, entitled " An Act to amend an Act to provide Revenue for the support [of the Government] of the State of Nevada, and have come to a favorable conclusion thereon, but had directed their chairman to report the same to the Senate, and recommend its reference to the Committee on Judiciary, as it pertains to the issuance of summonses in certain cases.

Mr. Doron from the Standing Committee on State Affairs, to which was referred the bill entitled "An Act in relation to Fines," reported, that they had had the same under consideration, had come to a favorable conclusion thereon, and directed their chairman to report the same to the Senate without amendments, and recommend its passage.

Mr. Proctor reported that the Committee on Counties and County boundaries had had under consideration the Senate Bill No. 14, entitled "An Act for the relief of S. L. Baker," and had directed their chairman to report the same back to the Senate and recommend its passage.

Mr. Stevenson reported that the Committee on Mines and Mining had had under consideration the Senate Bill No. 16, entitled " An Act to repeal an Act entitled' An Act concerning the Location and Possession of Mining Claims,' " and had directed their chairman to report the same to the Senate and recommend its passage.

Mr. Hutchins, from the Committee on Military and Indian Affairs, reported that they had had under consideration "An Act to provide Compensation to citizens of this State for Losses and Damages sustained from hostile Indians," and recommend that the same be indefinitely postponed.

Mr. Stevenson reported that the Committee on Mines and Mining had had under consideration the Annual Report of the State Mineralogist, and believing it to be a valuable document, had directed their chairman to recommend that two thousand copies be printed.

The Annual Report of the Warden of the State Prison was received. Mr. Edwards introduced Senate Concurrent Resolution No. 20, ordering the printing of the Report of the Warden of the State Prison.

Read and passed unanimously.

Mr. Grey introduced Senate Concurrent Resolution No. 21, in relation to the printing of the Report of the State Mineralogist.

Read and passed unanimously.

NOTICES OF BILLS.

Mr. Haines gave notice that he will, on some future day, introduce a bill concerning the office of Public Administrator, and his duties.

Also, a bill entitled " An Act to amend an Act entitled ' An Act to provide Revenue for the Support of the Government of Nevada.' "

Mr. Welty gave notice that he would, on some future day, introduce a bill entitled : " An Act to accept the donations of Public Lands by Congress to the State of Nevada for certain purposes."

Mr. Geller gave notice that he would, at an early day, introduce a bill entitled " An Act to reduce the Compensation of the Officers of Storey County."

Mr. Edwards gave notice that he would, at some future day, ask leave to introduce a bill entitled " An Act to define the duties of the Attorney General of the State of Nevada.

Mr. Carpenter, by leave, (without previous notice) introduced Senate Bill No. 22, entitled " An Act to define the powers and duties of Grand Juries in the State of Nevada; read first time ; rules suspended; read second time by title, and referred to Committee on Judiciary.

Mr. Welty, by leave, (without previous notice) introduced Senate Bill No. 23, entitled " An Act to amend an Act entitled ' An Act to regulate Proceedings in Criminal Cases in the Courts of Justice in the Territory of Nevada,' approved November 26, 1861." Read first time ; rules suspended; read second time by title, and referred to the Committee on Judiciary.

GENERAL FILE.

Senate Bill No. 11, entitled " An Act to amend an Act entitled 'An Act to provide Revenue for the Support of the Government of the State of Nevada, and Acts amendatory thereof.' "

Senate Concurrent Resolution No. 19, in relation to the Boundaries of the State of Nevada, and the acceptance of the additional Territory, ceded by the Government of the United States to this State, ordered engrossed.

Senate Bill No. 17, an Act in relation to Fines, ordered engrossed.

Senate Bill No. 16, " An Act to repeal an Act entitled 'An Act concerning the location and possession of mining claims.' " ordered engrossed.

Senate Bill No. 14, an Act for the relief of S. L. Baker, ordered engrossed.

Senate Bill No. 10, an Act to provide compensation to citizens of this State for losses and damages sustained from hostile Indians.

Indefinitely postponed.

MESSAGE FROM THE ASSEMBLY.

The following Message was received from the Assembly :

CARSON CITY, January 10th, 1867.

To the Honorable the Senate :

I herewith transmit to your honorable body, House Concurrent Resolution No. 3, relative to printing Rules and Joint Rules of both Houses, the same having passed the Assembly this day, unanimously.

Respectfully,

A. WHITFORD,
Clerk.

The Resolution above referred to was read and passed unanimously.
On motion of Mr. Hastings, at 11 : 45 A.M. the Senate adjourned.

Attest—B. C. BROWN,
Secretary.

JAMES S. SLINGERLAND,
President.

IN SENATE—EIGHTH DAY.

CARSON CITY, Jan. 14th, 1867.

The Senate met at 11 o'clock A.M., and was called to order by the President.
Roll called.

Present—Messrs. Carpenter, Doron, Eastman, Edwards, Geller, Grey, Haines, Hastings, Hutchins, Linn, Mason, Meder, Monroe, Proctor, Stevenson, Sumner, and Welty—17.

Absent—Messrs. Nelson and Terry—2.

Prayer by the Chaplain.

The Journal of the Sixth day was read and approved.

Mr. Hutchins, Chairman of Committee on Military and Indian affairs, reported Senate Concurrent Resolution No. 25, in regard to Indian claims in Humboldt County.

Read first time; rules suspended; read second time by title, and ordered engrossed.

Mr. Welty introduced Senate Concurrent Resolution No. 26, in relation to the Practice Act to be reported by the Hon. J. Neely Johnson.

Read and passed unanimously.

Mr. Edwards introduced Senate Concurrent Resolution No. 27, in relation to printing the report of the Superintendent of Public Instruction.

Read and passed unanimously.

REPORTS OF COMMITTEES.

Mr. Grey, from the Committee on Education, to which was referred the Report of the Superintendent of Public Instruction, reported that they had had the same under consideration, and had come to a favorable conclusion thereon, and they recommend that five hundred copies thereof be printed.

NOTICE OF BILLS.

Mr. Hutchins gave notice that he would at some future day ask leave to introduce a Bill for an Act, entitled " An Act in regard to assessment work upon Mining Claims."

Mr. Mason gave notice that he would, at some future day, ask leave to introduce a Bill for an Act, entitled " An Act defining the duties of County Commissioners in the several counties of the State of Nevada, and fixing their compensation."

Mr. Grey gave notice that he would, at some future day, ask leave to introduce a Bill for an Act, entitled " An Act in relation to the segregation and location of School Lands donated to the State of Nevada."

Mr. Haines gave notice that he would, at some future day, introduce a Bill entitled " An Act to amend an Act regulating marriages."

MESSAGES FROM ASSEMBLY.

The following Message was received from the Assembly:

ASSEMBLY CHAMBER, CARSON CITY, }
Jan. 14th, 1867.

To the Hon. the Senate:

I herewith transmit to your honorable body for your consideration, Assembly

4

Joint Resolution No. 2, relative to the Constitutional Amendment; the same having passed the House January the 11th, 1867.

Respectfully,

A. WHITFORD,
Clerk.

The Assembly Joint Resolution No. 2, above referred to, was read a first time; rules suspended; [read] second time by title, and referred to Committee on Federal Relations.

On motion of Mr. Hutchins, at 11:25 A.M. the Senate adjourned.

JAMES S. SLINGERLAND,
President.

Attest—B. C. BROWN,
Secretary.

IN SENATE—NINTH DAY.

CARSON CITY, January 15th, 1867.

The Senate met pursuant to adjournment, the President in the chair.

Roll called. All present.

Prayer by the Chaplain.

The Journal of the Eighth day was read and approved.

Mr. Sumner, by leave, introduced the following resolution:

Resolved, That the Senate proceed immediately to the naming of candidates for United States Senator, from this State, for the term of six years, commencing March 4th, 1867.

Adopted.

In accordance with the above resolution, and in pursuance of an Act of Congress, entitled "An Act to regulate the time and manner of holding elections for Senators in Congress, approved July 25th, 1866," the Senate proceeded to

NOMINATION OF UNITED STATES SENATOR.

Mr. Monroe nominated Thomas H. Williams, of Storey.

Mr. Meder nominated James W. Nye, of Ormsby.

Mr. Welty seconded the nomination.

Mr. Grey nominated Charles E. De Long, of Storey.

Mr. Mason seconded the nomination.

Mr. Eastman nominated Thomas Fitch, of Washoe.

Mr. Hastings nominated John B. Winters, of Storey.

Mr. Hutchins seconded the nomination.

The roll was then called, which resulted as follows:

For Mr. Williams—Messrs. Geller, Monroe and Proctor—3.

For Mr. Nye—Messrs. Carpenter, Doron, Edwards, Haines, Linn, Meder, and Welty—7.

For Mr. DeLong—Messrs. Grey, Mason, Nelson, Stevenson, and Sumner —5.

For Mr. Fitch—Messrs. Eastman and Terry—2.

For Mr. Winters—Messrs. Hastings and Hutchins—2.

Whole number of votes cast—19.

Necessary to a choice—10.

Mr. Williams received 3 votes.

Mr. Nye received 7 votes.

Mr. DeLong received 5 votes.

Mr. Fitch received 2 votes.

Mr. Winters received 2 votes.

No election.

On motion of Mr. Hastings, the Senate proceeded with the regular order of business.

MESSAGE FROM ASSEMBLY.

The following Message was received from the Assembly:

ASSEMBLY CHAMBER, CARSON CITY, }
January 15th, 1867. }

To the Hon. the Senate:

I am directed to return to your honorable body the following Senate Concurrent Resolutions, the same having passed the Assembly by the following vote, to wit:

Senate Concurrent Resolution in relation to Practice Act to be reported by Hon. J. Neely Johnson.

YEAS—34.

NAYS—1.

Senate Concurrent Resolution in relation to printing report of Superintendent of Public Instruction.

YEAS—34.

NAYS—1.

Respectfully,

A. WHITFORD,
Clerk.

REPORTS OF STANDING COMMITTEES.

Mr. Hastings reports that the Standing Committee on Engrossment had carefully compared the following entitled Bills with the originals, and found the same correctly engrossed:

Senate Bill No. 14, an Act for the relief of S. L. Baker.

Also, Senate Bill No. 16, an Act to repeal an Act entitled " An Act concerning the location and possession of Mining Claims."

Also, Senate Bill No. 17, an Act in relation to Fines.

Also, Senate Concurrent Resolution No. 19, in relation to the boundaries of the State of Nevada, and the acceptance of additional territory ceded by the United States to this State:

And herewith reports the same back to the Senate.

Mr. Geller, from the Standing Committee on State's Prison, to which was referred the annual report of the Warden of the State Prison, reported that they have had the same under consideration ; and had directed their chairman to report the same to the Senate, with a recommendation that 750 copies be ordered printed.

Mr. Monroe, from the Standing Committee on Claims, to which was referred the claim of A. Whitford for one hundred dollars, reported that they had had the same under consideration, and had come to a favorable conclusion thereon, and had directed their chairman to report the same to the Senate without amendment, and to recommend its passage.

Mr. Welty, from the Judiciary Committee, to which was referred the Bill entitled " An Act relating to the release of sureties on official bonds and under-takings," reported that they had had the same under consideration, and had come to a favorable conclusion on the subject matter, and had directed their chairman to report to the Senate a substitute therefor, and recommend that it be printed.

Mr. Welty reported that the Committee on Judiciary had had under consideration the Senate Bill entitled " An Act to amend an Act entitled ' An Act to provide revenue for the support of the Government of the State of Nevada,' " and had directed their chairman to report the same without amendment, and recommend its passage, and that it be printed.

Mr. Linn, Chairman Committee on Enrollment, reports that Senate Concurrent Resolution relative to the inauguration of the Governor and Lieutenant Governor had been carefully compared with the original, found correctly enrolled, and has this day been deposited with the Secretary of State.

Mr. Doron in the chair.

INTRODUCTION OF BILLS.

Mr. Hutchins introduced Senate Concurrent Resolution No. 29, in relation to a joint convention for the election of a United States Senator.

Read and passed.

Mr. Welty introduced Senate Bill No. 30, entitled " An Act in relation to, and accepting the lands granted to the State of Nevada by the Government of the United States."

Read first time ; rules suspended ; read second time by title, and referred to the Committee on Public Lands.

Mr. Haines introduced Senate Bill No. 31, " An Act concerning Public Administrators."

Read first time ; rules suspended ; read second time by title, and referred to Committee on Judiciary.

At 12 : 40 A.M., on motion of Mr. Grey, the Senate adjourned.

JAMES S. SLINGERLAND,
President.

Attest—B. C. BROWN,
Secretary.

IN SENATE—TENTH DAY.

CARSON CITY, January 16th, 1867.

The Senate met, pursuant to adjournment, the President in the chair.
Roll called.
Present—Messrs. Carpenter, Doron, Eastman, Edwards, Geller, Grey,
Hastings, Hutchins, Linn, Mason, Meder, Monroe, Nelson, Proctor, Stevenson,
Sumner, Terry, and Welty—19.
Prayer by the Chaplain.
The Journal of the Ninth day was read and approved.

REPORTS OF STANDING COMMITTEES.

Mr. Hutchins, from the Standing Committee on Military and Indian Affairs,
to which was referred Senate Concurrent Resolution No. 18, in regard to
establishing a military post at the junction of the north fork with the Humboldt
River, reported that they had had the same under consideration, had come to a
favorable conclusion thereon, and directed their chairman to report the same to
the Senate with amendments, and recommend its passage.
Mr. Hastings reported that the Standing Committee on Engrossment had
carefully compared the following entitled bill, and found the same correctly
engrossed, viz: Senate Joint Resolution No. 25, in regard to Indian claims in
Humboldt County; and herewith report the same back to the Senate.

MESSAGES FROM THE ASSEMBLY.

The following Messages were received from the Assembly:

ASSEMBLY CHAMBER, CARSON CITY,
January 15th, 1867.

To the Honorable the Senate:

I am directed to return to your honorable body Senate Concurrent Resolution
No. 20, ordering the printing of the Report of Warden of State Prison; also,
Senate Concurrent Resolution No. 21, in relation to printing Report of State
Mineralogist, the same having passed the Assembly this day unanimously.
I also transmit to your honorable body for your consideration Assembly Joint
Resolution No. 4, relative to daily mail from Virginia City, Nevada, to Boise
City, Idaho.
Also, Assembly Joint Concurrent Resolution No. 10, relating to the election
of United States Senator, the same having passed the Assembly this day.
Respectfully,

A. WHITFORD,
Clerk.

ASSEMBLY CHAMBER, CARSON CITY,
January 15th, 1867.

To the Honorable the Senate:

I herewith transmit to your honorable body for your consideration Assembly
Bill No. 2, entitled "An Act to repeal an Act entitled 'An Act concerning the
Location and Possession of Mining Claims,'" the same having passed the Assem-
bly this day—yeas, 24; nays, 8. I also return Senate Concurrent Resolution

relative to printing Governor's Message, the same having passed the Assembly this day unanimously.

Respectfully,

A. WHITFORD,

Clerk.

NOTICES OF BILLS.

Mr. Welty gave notice that he would, on some future day, introduce a Bill entitled " An Act to provide for the Selection and Sale of the Public Lands donated to this State for various purposes, and for the proper application of the proceeds of the sale thereof."

Mr. Mason gave notice that he would, on some future day, ask leave to introduce a Bill for an Act entitled " An Act to amend an Act entitled ' An Act to regulate the settlement of the Estates of Deceased Persons,' approved November 29th, 1861."

INTRODUCTION OF BILLS.

Mr. Welty, by leave, introduced Senate Bill No. 35, entitled " An Act to amend an Act entitled ' An Act concerning Fines and Punishments.' " Read first time; rules suspended; read second time by title, and referred to Committee on Judiciary.

GENERAL FILE.

Senate Bill No. 14, entitled " An Act for the relief of S. L. Baker."
Read third time, and passed by the following vote :

YEAS—Messrs. Carpenter, Doron, Eastman, Edwards, Geller, Grey, Haines, Hastings, Hutchins, Linn, Mason, Meder, Monroe, Nelson, Proctor, Stevenson, Sumner, Terry, and Welty—19.

Senate Bill No. 16, entitled " An Act to repeal an Act entitled ' An Act concerning the location and possession of Mining Claims.' " Read third time, and passed by the following vote :

YEAS—Messrs. Carpenter, Doron, Eastman, Edwards, Geller, Grey, Haines, Hastings, Hutchins, Linn, Meder, Monroe, Nelson, Proctor, Stevenson, Sumner, Terry, Welty—18.
NAYS—Mr. Nelson—1.

Senate Bill No. 17, " An Act in relation to Fines." Read third time, and passed by the following vote :

YEAS—Messrs. Carpenter, Doron, Eastman, Edwards, Geller, Grey, Haines, Hastings, Hutchins, Linn, Mason, Meder, Monroe, Nelson, Proctor, Stevenson, Sumner, Terry, and Welty—19.

Senate Concurrent Resolution No. 19, in relation to the boundaries of the State of Nevada, and the acceptance of additional territory, ceded by the United States to this State. Read third time, and passed by the following vote :

YEAS—Messrs. Carpenter, Doron, Eastman, Edwards, Geller, Grey,

Haines, Hastings, Hutchins, Linn, Mason, Meder, Monroe, Nelson, Proctor, Stevenson, Sumner, Terry, and Welty—19.

Mr. Hutchins, by leave, introduced Senate Concurrent Resolution No. 36, in relation to joint convention for election of United States Senator.

Read and passed unanimously.

Senate Joint Resolution No. 25, in regard to Indian claims, in Humboldt County, read third time, and passed by the following vote:

YEAS—Messrs. Carpenter, Doron, Eastman, Edwards, Geller, Grey, Hastings, Hutchins, Linn, Mason, Meder, Monroe, Nelson, Proctor, Stevenson, Sumner, Terry, and Welty—18.

Senate Bill No. 5, entitled "An Act providing for the Release of Sureties on official bonds and undertakings."

A substitute therefor was reported by the Committee on Judiciary, which was adopted, and two hundred and forty copies ordered printed.

Senate Bill No. 11, entitled "An Act to amend an Act, entitled ' An Act to Provide Revenue for the Support of the Government of the State of Nevada, and the Acts amendatory thereof.' "

The usual number of copies ordered printed.

Senate Concurrent Resolution No. 18, memorializing the Commander of the Department of the Pacific to establish a fort at Gravelly Ford.

Ordered engrossed.

Assembly Joint Resolution No. 4, relative to a daily mail from Virginia City, Nevada, to Boise City, Idaho.

Read first time; rules suspended; read second time by title.

Rules further suspended, and the resolution placed on its third reading, and final passage.

Passed by the following vote:

YEAS—Messrs. Carpenter, Doron, Eastman, Edwards, Geller, Grey, Hastings, Hutchins, Linn, Mason, Meder, Monroe, Proctor, Stevenson, Sumner, Terry, and Welty—17.

NAYS—Mr. Nelson—1.

Assembly Joint Concurrent Resolution No. 10, in relation to the election of a United States Senator, read, and on motion of Mr. Hutchins, laid on the table.

MESSAGE FROM THE ASSEMBLY.

The following Message was received from the Assembly:

ASSEMBLY CHAMBER, CARSON CITY, }
January 16th, 1867. }

To the Hon. the Senate:

I hereby return to your hon. body Senate Concurrent Resolution No. 29, in relation to joint convention for the election of United States Senator, the same having passed the Assembly this day unanimously.

Respectfully,

A. WHITFORD,
Clerk.

At 11 : 50 A.M., on motion of Mr. Proctor, the Senate took a recess, to meet at twelve o'clock in the Assembly Chamber, in joint convention.

IN JOINT CONVENTION.

Proceedings of Joint Convention, to elect a United Senator to succeed the Hon. James W. Nye, whose term of office will expire on the third day of March, 1867.

The Convention was called to order by the President of the Senate, in conjunction with the Speaker of the Assembly.

The Roll of the Senate, and also of the Assembly, was called, and all the members were present.

Such portions of the Journals of each House of the preceding day as pertained to the election of United States Senator, were read.

Mr. Edwards moved that the rule be suspended, and that the official Reporters of both Houses be admitted to seats within the bar.

Carried unanimously.

The following nominations were before the Convention: James W. Nye, Charles E. De Long, John B. Winters, Thomas Fitch, and Thomas H. Williams.

Mr. Monroe, by leave, withdrew the name of Thomas H. Williams.

Mr. Hastings, by leave, withdrew the name of John B. Winters.

The roll was then called, with the following result:

For James W. Nye—Senators Carpenter, Doron, Edwards, Haines, Hastings, Hutchins, Linn, Meder, Welty; Assemblymen Brown, Bence, Cary, Cullen, Caldwell, Folsom, Horton, Julien, Jones, Jacobs, Mallory, Mayhugh, Munckton, Poor, Tennant, Wingate—25.

For Charles E. DeLong—Senators Geller, Grey, Mason, Monroe, Nelson, Stevenson, and Sumner; Assemblymen Dorsey, Dana, Grimes, Groves, Huse, Koneman, Lissak, Lammon, Mitchell, Parker, Potter, Roney, St. Clair, Stampley, Swaney, Strother, Walton, Welch, Wheeler, Mr. Speaker—27.

For Mr. Thomas Fitch—Senators Eastman and Terry; Assemblymen Parmater and Prince—4.

For Mr. Williams—Senator Proctor—1.

Whole number of votes cast	57
Necessary to a choice	29
Mr. Nye received	25
Mr. DeLong received	27
Mr. Fitch received	4
Mr. Williams received	1

No election.

At 12 : 40 P.M., Mr. Haines moved to adjourn.

The yeas and nays were called for by Messrs. Grey, Monroe, and Mayhugh, and recorded as follows:

YEAS—Senators Carpenter, Doron, Eastman, Edwards, Haines, Hastings, Hutchins, Linn. Meder, Proctor, Sumner, Terry, and Welty; Assemblymen Brown, Bence, Cary, Cullen, Caldwell, Folsom, Horton, Julien, Jones, Jacobs, Lissak, Mallory, Munckton, Poor, Parmater, Prince, Stampley, Swaney, Tennant, and Wingate—33.

NAYS—Senators Geller, Grey, Mason, Monroe, Nelson, Stevenson; Assemblymen Dorsey, Dana, Grimes, Groves, Huse, Koneman, Lammon, Mayhugh, Mitchell, Parker, Potter, Roney, St. Clair, Strother, Walton, Welch, Wheeler, and Mr. Speaker—24.

The Convention stood adjourned.

IN SENATE.

Roll called. All present.
At 12 : 50 P.M., on motion of Mr. Grey, the Senate was adjourned.

JAMES S. SLINGERLAND,
President.

Attest—B. C. BROWN,
Secretary.

IN SENATE—ELEVENTH DAY.

CARSON CITY, January 17th, 1867.

The Senate met pursuant to adjournment, Mr. Sumner, President *pro tem.*, in the chair.
Roll called.
Present—Messrs. Carpenter, Doron, Eastman, Geller, Grey, Haines, Hastings, Hutchins, Linn, Mason, Meder, Monroe, Nelson, Stevenson, Terry, and Welty—17.
Absent—Messrs. Edwards and Proctor—2.
Prayer by the Chaplain.
The Journal of the Tenth day was read and approved.
The President in the chair.

REPORTS OF STANDING COMMITTEES.

Mr. Linn, chairman of Committee on Enrollment, reported that Senate Concurrent Resolution No. 26, relative to the Practice Act, and Senate Concurrent Resolution No. 27, relative to printing the Report of the Superintendent of Public Instruction, have been carefully compared with the original copies, found correctly enrolled, and had this day been deposited with the Secretary of State.

MESSAGES FROM THE ASSEMBLY.

The following Messages were received from the Assembly:

ASSEMBLY CHAMBER, CARSON CITY,
January 16th, 1867.

To the Honorable the Senate:

I am instructed to transmit to your honorable body, for your consideration, Assembly Bill No. 1, entitled " An Act to create Legislative Funds," the same having passed the Assembly this day.

YEAS—37.
NAYS—0.

Respectfully,
A. WHITFORD,
Clerk.

ASSEMBLY CHAMBER, CARSON CITY, }
January 16th, 1867. }

To the Honorable the Senate:

I am instructed to return to your honorable body Senate Concurrent Resolution No. 36, in relation to Joint Convention for election of United States Senator, it having passed the Assembly by the following vote:

YEAS—30.
NAYS—6.

A. WHITFORD,
Clerk.

Assembly Bill No. 1, entitled "An Act to create Legislative Funds," above referred to, read first time; rules suspended; read second time by title, and referred to the Committee on Ways and Means.

NOTICES OF BILLS.

Mr. Mason gave notice that he would, at some future day, ask leave to introduce a Bill for an Act entitled "An Act concerning the Office of Public Administrator."

Mr. Welty gave notice that he would, at some future day, ask leave to introduce a Bill for an Act entitled "An Act providing for the payment of James Cochran, Sheriff of Trinity County, California, for certain services rendered and expenses incurred."

INTRODUCTION AND FIRST READING OF BILLS.

Mr. Haines introduced Senate Bill No. 38, "An Act concerning Marriages;" read first time; rules suspended; read second time by title, and referred to Committee on State Affairs.

Mr. Welty, by leave, without previous notice, introduced Senate Bill No. 39, entitled "An Act to amend an Act entitled 'An Act relating to the manner of commencing Civil Actions,' approved December 20th, 1862;" read first time; rules suspended; read second time by title, and referred to Committee on Judiciary.

Also, Senate Bill No. 40, entitled "An Act to amend an Act entitled 'An Act empowering the Governor to appoint Commissioners of Deeds, and to define their duties;'" read first time; rules suspended; read second time by title, and referred to the Committee on State Affairs.

GENERAL FILE.

Assembly Bill No. 2, entitled "An Act to repeal an Act concerning the location and possession of Mining Claims," approved February 27th, 1866; read first time; rules suspended; read second time by title, and referred to Committee on Mines and Mining.

Mr. Welty, by leave, introduced Senate Bill No. 41, entitled "An Act providing for the payment of George [James] Cochran, Sheriff of Trinity County, California, for certain services rendered and expenses incurred;" read first time; rules suspended; read second time by title, and referred to Committee on Claims.

At 11:40 A.M., on motion of Mr. Hutchins, the Senate took a recess until 11:50.

The Senate met pursuant to adjournment at 11:50 A.M., Mr. Sumner, President *pro tem.*, in the chair.

The following Message was received from the Assembly:

ASSEMBLY CHAMBER, CARSON CITY, }
January 17th, 1867. }

To the Honorable the Senate:

I herewith transmit to your honorable body, for your consideration, Assembly Concurrent Resolution relating to the Editor of *Carson Appeal*, the same having passed the Assembly this day unanimously.

Respectfully,

A. WHITFORD,
Clerk.

The Assembly Joint Resolution No. 13, above referred to, was read.

Mr. Doron moved to amend so as to allow the admission of the Editor of the *Virginia Daily Union.*

Carried.

The Joint Resolution as amended was passed unanimously.

IN JOINT CONVENTION.

The Convention met at 12 o'clock M., and was called to order by the President of the Senate, in conjunction with the Speaker of the Assembly.

Roll called.

All present.

That portion of the Journal of the Senate of yesterday, relating to the proceedings in Joint Convention, was read and approved.

Mr. Eastman, by leave, withdrew the name of Thomas Fitch as a candidate for United States Senator.

The roll was then called and recorded as follows:

For James W. Nye—Senators Carpenter, Doron, Eastman, Edwards, Haines, Hastings, Hutchins, Linn, Meder, Terry, and Welty: Assemblymen Brown, Bence, Cary, Cullen, Caldwell, Folsom, Horton, Julien, Jones, Jacobs, Lissak, Mallory, Mayhugh, Munckton, Poor, Parmater, Parker, Prince, Swaney, Tennant, and Wingate—32.

For Charles E. DeLong—Senators Geller, Grey, Mason, Monroe, Nelson, Sumner, Proctor, and Stevenson: Assemblymen Dorsey, Dana, Grimes, Groves, Huse, Koneman, Lammon, Mitchell, Potter, Roney, St. Clair, Stampley, Strother, Walton, Wheeler, and Mr. Speaker—25.

Whole number of votes cast...............................57

Necessary to a choice 29

James W. Nye received 32

Charles E. DeLong..25

Mr. Lissak asked leave to explain his vote, which was, on motion, granted.

Mr. Swaney also asked leave to explain his vote, which was, on motion, granted.

James W. Nye having received the majority of all votes cast by the Convention, was declared duly elected United States Senator for the term commencing March 4th, 1867, and ending March 3d, 1873.

Mr. Hutchins moved that a Special Committee, consisting of one Senator and two Assemblymen, be appointed to wait on the Honorable James W. Nye, Senator elect, and inform him of his election to the United States Senate for a term of six years, commencing March 4th, 1867, and escort him to the Convention. Carried.

The President appointed Messrs. Hutchins, Lissak, and Cullen. .

Mr. Lissak declined serving on the Committee.

The President appointed Mr. Swaney in his stead.

The Committee reported to the Convention the presence of the Honorable James W. Nye, Senator elect.

On motion of Mr. Hastings, at 12 : 40 P.M. the Convention adjourned *sine die.*

IN SENATE.

The President in the chair.
Roll called.
Quorum present.
On motion of Mr. Hastings, at 12 : 45 P.M. the Senate adjourned.

JAMES S. SLINGERLAND,
President.

Attest—B. C. BROWN,
        Secretary.

IN SENATE—TWELFTH DAY.

CARSON CITY, January 18th, 1867.

The Senate met pursuant to adjournment, Mr. Sumner, President *pro tem.*, in the chair.

Roll called.

Present—Messrs. Carpenter, Doron, Eastman, Edwards, Geller, Haines, Hastings, Hutchins, Linn, Mason, Meder, Monroe, Proctor, Stevenson, Sumner, Terry, and Welty—17.

Absent—Messrs. Grey and Nelson.

Prayer by the Chaplain.

The Journal of the Eleventh day was read and approved.

REPORTS OF STANDING COMMITTEES.

Mr. Sumner, Chairman of the Committee on Ways and Means, submitted the following Report:

To the President and Members of the Senate:

Your Committee on Ways and Means, to whom was referred Assembly Bill No. 1, " An Act to create Legislative Funds," report the same, with the recommendation that it do pass.

MOTIONS AND RESOLUTIONS.

Mr. Hutchins introduced Senate Concurrent Resolution No. 43, in relation to Lieutenant Governor Slingerland.
Read and passed unanimously.

MESSAGE FROM THE ASSEMBLY.

The following Message was received from the Assembly :

ASSEMBLY CHAMBER, CARSON CITY,
January 17th, 1867.

To the Honorable the Senate :

I am instructed to inform your honorable body that the Assembly have concurred in the amendment of the Senate to Assembly Concurrent Resolution No. 13, in relation to the editors of the " Carson Appeal," and " Virginia Daily Union."

Respectfully,

A. WHITFORD,
Clerk.

Mr. Doron asked leave of absence for the Chaplain of the Senate, Mr. Stump, for Tuesday and Wednesday next.   Granted.

NOTICES OF BILLS.

Mr. Linn gave notice that he would, at some future day, ask leave to introduce a bill regulating fees of County Clerks.

INTRODUCTION OF BILLS.

Mr. Carpenter, by leave, and without previous notice, introduced Senate Bill No. 44, entitled "An Act to provide for the removal of civil officers, other than State officers, for Malfeasance or Nonfeasance in Office." Read first time by title ; rules suspended; read second time by title, and referred to Committee on Judiciary.
Mr. Sumner, by leave, and without previous notice, introduced Senate Bill No. 45, entitled "An Act appropriating money for the benefit of the Orphan Asylum, conducted by the Sisters of Charity, at Virginia City." Read first time; rules suspended; read second time by title, and referred to the Committee on Ways and Means.

GENERAL FILE.

On motion of Mr. Edwards, the Senate went into a Committee of the Whole, President *pro tem.* in the chair, for the consideration of Assembly Bill No. 1, entitled " An Act to create Legislative Funds." The Committee rose and reported favorably. The report was adopted, and the bill passed by the following vote:

YEAS — Messrs. Carpenter, Doron, Eastman, Edwards, Geller, Hastings, Haines, Hutchins, Linn, Mason, Meder, Monroe, Proctor, Stevenson, Sumner, Terry—16.

NAYS—Mr. Welty—1.

The report of the State Treasurer was read, and on motion of Mr. Proctor, was referred to the Committee on Ways and Means.

Mr. Proctor, by leave, introduced Senate Concurrent Resolution No. 46, in relation to adjournment on January 26th. Read, and on motion of Mr. Proctor, it was made the special order for Saturday, the 19th, at 12 o'clock M.

Mr. Stevenson rose to a question of privilege relative to his name not being recorded in the "Gold Hill News" of yesterday, as voting for Charles E. De Long, for United States Senator.

Mr. Sumner rose to the same question of privilege.

At 11 : 40 A.M., on motion of Mr. Carpenter, the Senate adjourned.

JAMES S. SLINGERLAND,
President.

Attest—B. C. BROWN,
Secretary.

IN SENATE—THIRTEENTH DAY.

CARSON CITY, January 19th, 1867.

The Senate met pursuant to adjournment, Mr. Sumner, President *pro tem.*, in the chair.

Roll called.

Present—Messrs. Carpenter, Doron, Eastman, Edwards, Geller, Grey, Haines, Hastings, Hutchins, Linn, Mason, Meder, Monroe, Proctor, Sumner, Terry, and Welty—17.

Absent—Messrs. Nelson and Stevenson—2.

Prayer by the Chaplain.

The Journal of the Twelfth day was read and approved.

REPORTS OF STANDING COMMITTEES.

Mr. Sumner, Chairman of Committee on Ways and Means, submitted the following report:

Mr. President:

The Committee on Ways and Means, to which was referred Senate Bill No.

9, "An Act authorizing the Issuance and Sale of certain State Bonds, and levying a Tax to provide means for the Payment thereof," have had the same under consideration, report the same back with the following amendments, and recommend its passage as amended:

Amend section 1, line 26, by striking out the word "two," and inserting the word "three." Also, in the same section, line 30, insert the words "and one-fourth" after the word one. Also, in line 37 of the same section, strike out the word "two," and insert the word "three."

Amend section 3, line 13, by inserting after the word "one" the words "and one-fourth."

Mr. Grey, from the Standing Committee on Elections, to which was referred the resolutions contesting the seat occupied by Mr. Terry, have had the same under consideration, and report the same back without recommendation, other than to ask that the contestants be admitted to the floor of the Senate, with consent to discuss their relative claims before the Senate.

REPORTS OF COMMITTEES.

Mr. Hastings reported that the Standing Committee on Engrossment have carefully compared the following entitled Bill with the original, and found the same correctly engrossed, viz:

Senate Concurrent Resolution No. 18, memorializing the Commander of the Department of the Pacific to establish a Fort at Gravelly Ford, and herewith reports the same back to the Senate.

Mr. Doron, from the Standing Committee on State Affairs, to which was referred the Bill entitled "Senate Bill No. 40, An Act to amend an Act empowering the Governor to appoint Commissioners of Deeds, and to define their duties," reported that they had had the same under consideration, had come to a favorable conclusion thereon, and had directed their chairman to report the same to the Senate without amendments.

Mr. Sumner, from the Committee on Ways and Means, reported that the Committee recommended that two hundred and forty copies of the State Treasurer's Report be printed.

MOTIONS AND RESOLUTIONS.

Mr. Grey offered the following resolution:

Resolved, That a Committee of seven be appointed by the chair, whose duty it shall be to propose such amendments to the State Constitution as they may on consideration deem proper and necessary.

Adopted.
Mr. Doron in the chair.
Mr. Grey also introduced the following resolution:

Resolved, That a per diem of sixteen dollars be and is hereby allowed the Official Reporter of this body, payable out of the Contingent Fund of the Senate.

Adopted.

MESSAGES FROM THE ASSEMBLY.

The following Message was received from the Assembly:

ASSEMBLY CHAMBER, CARSON CITY,
January 18th, 1867.

To the Honorable the Senate:

I am instructed to return to your honorable body Senate Concurrent Resolution No. 19, in relation to the boundaries of the State of Nevada, and acceptance of additional territory ceded by the United States to this State.

Also, Joint Resolution No. 25, in regard to Indian claims in Humboldt County, the same having passed the Assembly this day.

YEAS—35.
NAYS—0.

Respectfully,

A. WHITFORD,
Clerk.

INTRODUCTION OF BILLS.

Mr. Haines, by leave, introduced Senate Concurrent Resolution No. 47, in relation to amending Joint Rule No. 7 of the Senate and Assembly.
Read and passed.

NOTICES OF BILLS.

Mr. Meder gave notice that he would, at some future day, ask leave to introduce a Bill entitled "An Act to repeal an Act to provide for the appointment of a Deputy State Controller."

GENERAL FILE.

The Senate Concurrent Resolution No. 18, in relation to memorializing the Commander of the Department of the Pacific to establish a Fort at Gravelly Ford.
Title amended to read as follows: Senate Concurrent Resolution No. 18, in relation to memorializing the Commander of the Division of the Pacific to establish a Fort at or near the Junction of the North Fork with the Humboldt River. Read third time, and passed by the following vote:

YEAS—Messrs. Carpenter, Doron, Eastman, Edwards, Geller, Grey, Haines, Hastings, Hutchins, Linn, Mason, Meder, Monroe, Proctor, Sumner, Terry, and Welty—17.
NAYS—None.

Senate Bill No. 5, entitled "An Act providing for the release of sureties on Official Bonds and Undertakings." Made special order for Monday, the 21st instant, at 11 : 30 A.M.
Senate Bill No. 11, entitled "An Act to amend an Act entitled 'An Act to provide Revenue for the support of the Government of the State of Nevada,' and the Acts amendatory thereof." Made the special order for Monday, 21st instant, at 11 : 30 A.M.

Senate Bill No. 9, entitled " An Act authorizing the Issuance and Sale of certain State Bonds, and levying a Tax to provide means for the Payment thereof."
Ordered engrossed.

Senate Concurrent Resolution No. 46, in relation to the adjournment of the Legislature.

Special order postponed until Monday, 21st instant, at 12 o'clock M.

Mr. Sumner, by leave, introduced Senate Concurrent Resolution No. 48, in relation to printing the State Treasurer's Report.

Read and passed unanimously.

At 12 : 20 P.M. Mr. Hutchins offered the following resolution :

Resolved, That as a mark of our sympathy with Lieut.-Governor J. S' Slingerland in his bereavement in the death of his infant son, this Senate do now adjourn.

Adopted unanimously.

JAMES S. SLINGERLAND,
President.

Attest—B. C. BROWN,
Secretary.

IN SENATE—FIFTEENTH DAY.

CARSON CITY, January 21st, 1867.

The Senate met pursuant to adjournment, the President in the chair.

Roll called.

Present—Messrs. Carpenter, Doron, Eastman, Edwards, Geller, Grey, Haines, Hastings, Hutchins, Linn, Mason, Meder, Monroe, Proctor, Stevenson, Terry, and Welty—17.

Absent—Mr. Nelson—1.

Prayer by the Chaplain.

The Journal of the Thirteenth day was read, corrected, and approved.

The President appointed the following special Committee to report amendments to the State Constitution :

> Mr. Grey, of Storey.
> Mr. Welty, of Lander.
> Mr. Monroe, of Churchill.
> Mr. Hutchins, of Humboldt.
> Mr. Hastings, of Lyon.
> Mr. Eastman, of Washoe.
> Mr. Stevenson, of Storey.

REPORTS OF STANDING COMMITTEES.

Mr. Linn, Chairman of Committee on Enrollment, reported that Senate Concurrent Resolution No. 8, " Concerning Printing Governor's Message," Senate Concurrent Resolution No. 20, "Ordering the Printing of Report of the Warden of the State Prison ;" Senate Concurrent Resolution No. 21, "In relation to Printing Report of State Mineralogist ;" Senate Concurrent Resolution No. 29, " In relation to Joint Convention for the Election of United States Senator;" also, Senate Concurrent Resolution No. 36, " In relation to Joint Convention for the election of United States Senator," had been carefully compared with the engrossed resolutions, as passed by the two Houses, found correctly enrolled, and that the same had this day been deposited with the Secretary of State. Also, that Senate Joint Resolution No. 25, " In regard to Indian Claims in Humboldt County;" also, Senate Joint Resolution No. 19, " In relation to the Boundaries of the State of Nevada, and the acceptance of additional Territory ceded by the United States to this State," had been carefully compared with the engrossed resolutions, as passed by the two Houses, found correctly enrolled, and that the same had this day been delivered to the Governor for his approval.

Mr. Mason, from the Standing Committee on Federal Relations, reported that they had had Assembly Joint Resolutions No. 2, Senate Concurrent Resolution No. 2, and Senate Concurrent Resolution No. 3, each in relation to the adoption of the Constitutional Amendments, under consideration, had come to a favorable conclusion thereon, and recommended the passage of Assembly Resolutions. That the Committee failed to discover any material difference in the three foregoing sets of resolutions, all alike abounding in National Patriotism toward our legislative duties; recognizing alike the high and noble patriotism prompting the action of each of the authors of the three sets of resolutions, their reasons for recommending the first-named were simply that they have been legislated upon, and passed the Assembly, and to save time and unnecessary delay; and inasmuch as the discussion of the merits or demerits of these amendments are the current history of the day, the Committee deem it time thrown away to enter into such discussion, and ask their immediate passage.

Mr. Hastings, Chairman of Standing Committee on Engrossment, reported that they had carefully compared the following entitled bill with the original, and had found the same correctly engrossed, viz: Senate Bill No. 9, "An Act authorizing the Issuance and Sale of certain State Bonds, and levying a tax to provide means for the payment thereof," and herewith reports the same back to the Senate.

Mr. Welty, from the Judiciary Committee, to which was referred the bill entitled "An Act to Provide for the Removal of Civil Officers, other than State Officers, for Malfeasance or Nonfeasance in Office," reported that they had had the same under consideration, had come to a favorable conclusion thereon, and had directed their chairman to report the same to the Senate with an amendment, adding another section to the bill, and to recommend its passage. Also, the bill entitled " An Act concerning the office of Public Administrator," reported that they had had the same under consideration; had come to a favorable conclusion thereon, and had directed their Chairman to report the same to the Senate without amendments, and to recommend its passage.

NOTICES OF BILLS.

Mr. Proctor gave notice that he would, at some future day, ask leave to introduce a bill for an Act entitled "An Act to reapportion the Representation in the Legislature of the State."

Mr. Grey gave notice that he would, at some future day, ask leave to introduce a bill for an Act entitled "An Act to Provide for the Appointment of a Commission to Revise and Codify the Statutes of the State."

Mr. Welty gave notice that he would, at some future day, ask leave to introduce a bill for an Act entitled " An Act to amend an Act entitled ' An Act for the appointment of Senators and Assemblymen in the different Counties of the State.'" . .

Also, that he would, at some future day, introduce a Concurrent Resolution proposing to amend Section One of Article Fifteen, and Section One of Article Fourteen of the Constitution of this State.

Also, a bill entitled "An Act to amend an Act entitled 'An Act to provide for the Registration of the names of Electors, and for the ascertainment by proper proofs, who shall be entitled to the right of Suffrage,' approved February 24th, 1866."

Also, a bill entitled "An Act to provide Printed Poll Books and Blanks to be used in holding Elections in the different Counties of this State."

INTRODUCTION OF BILLS.

Mr. Proctor introduced Senate Bill No. 49, entitled "An Act to change the County Seat of Nye County."

Read first time; rules suspended; read second time by title, and referred to the Committee on Counties and County Boundaries.

Mr. Welty introduced Senate Bill No. 50, entitled "An Act to provide for the sale of certain Lands belonging to this State, and for the application of the proceeds of the sale thereof."

Read first time; rules suspended; read second time by title, and referred to the Committee on Public Lands.

Mr. Hutchins introduced Senate Bill No. 51, entitled "An Act in regard to Assessment Work upon Mining Claims."

Read first time; rules suspended; read second time by title, and referred to Committee on Mines and Mining.

Mr. Mason introduced Senate Bill No. 52, entitled "An Act to amend an Act entitled 'An Act to regulate the Settlement of the Estates of Deceased Persons,' approved November 29th, 1861."

Read first time; rules suspended; read second time by title, and referred to Committee on Judiciary.

Mr. Sumner, by leave and without previous notice, introduced Senate Bill No. 53, "An Act to authorize the State Librarian to distribute copies of the Nevada Constitutional Debates among Newspaper Proprietors in this State."

Read first time; rules suspended; read second time by title, and referred to the Committee on State Library.

Mr. Welty introduced Senate Bill No. 54, entitled "An Act to amend an Act entitled 'An Act to provide for the Registration of the names of Electors, and for the ascertaining by proper proofs who shall be entitled to the right of Suffrage,' approved February 24th, 1866."

Read first time; rules suspended; read second time, and referred to Committee on Elections.

Also, Senate Concurrent Resolution No. 55, proposing amendments to Section First of Article Fifteen and Section First of Article Fourteen of the Constitution of this State.

Read first time, and referred to the Committee on Judiciary *for* [with] instructions.

Also, Senate Bill No. 56, entitled "An Act to amend an Act entitled 'An Act for the Apportionment of Senators and Assemblymen in the different Counties of this State,' approved February 27th, 1866."

Read first time; rules suspended; read second time by title, and referred to Committee on State Affairs.

Also, Senate Bill No. 57, entitled "An Act to provide necessary printed Poll Books and Blanks to be used in holding Elections in the different Counties of this State."

Read first time; rules suspended; read second time by title, and referred to Committee on Elections.

The Senate went into Committee of the Whole, Mr. Hutchins in the chair, for the consideration of Senate Bill No. 9, entitled "An Act authorizing the issuance and sale of certain State Bonds, and levying a Tax to provide means for the payment thereof."

The Committee rose and reported that they had had the Bill under consideration, and recommended its passage.

The Bill was read the third time, and passed by the following vote:

YEAS—Messrs. Carpenter, Doron, Eastman, Edwards, Geller, Grey, Haines, Hastings, Hutchins, Mason, Meder, Monroe, Proctor, Stevenson, Sumner, Terry, and Welty—17.

NAYS—None.

On motion of Mr. Proctor, all Bills on the General File were referred to a Committee of the Whole.

Mr. Grey, by leave, introduced the following resolution:

Resolved, That the consideration of the Report of the Committee on Elections, touching the right of Mr. Terry to his seat, be made the special order for Monday, the 21st instant, at 2 o'clock P.M.

Adopted.

Senate Concurrent Resolution No. 46, in relation to the adjournment of the Legislature, which was made the special order for Monday, 12 o'clock M., was, on motion of Mr. Edwards, indefinitely postponed.

On motion of Mr. Doron, the Senate went into a Committee of the Whole, for consideration of the General File.

The Committee arose, and reported having had under consideration Substitute Senate Bill No. 5, entitled "An Act providing for the release of Sureties on Official Bonds and Undertakings," having made amendments thereto, and recommended its engrossment:

Report adopted, and the Bill ordered engrossed.

At 1 o'clock P.M., on motion of Mr. Proctor, the Senate took a recess until 2 o'clock P.M.

IN SENATE.

At 2 o'clock, P.M. the Senate reassembled—President in the chair.

Roll called—quorum present.

SPECIAL ORDER.

Mr. Edwards moved that the consideration of the report of the Committee on Elections, touching the right of Mr. Terry to a seat, be indefinitely postponed.

The yeas and nays were called for by Messrs. Sumner, Proctor and Hastings, with the following result:

YEAS—Messrs. Carpenter, Doron, Eastman, Edwards, Geller, Haines, Hastings, Hutchins, Linn, Meder, Sumner, and Welty—12.

NAYS—Messrs. Grey, Mason, Monroe, Proctor, and Stevenson—5.

Mr. Grey, by leave, introduced Senate Concurrent Resolution No. 8, relative to the admittance of the Hon. J. Neely Johnson to a seat within the Bar.

Read and passed.

At 2 : 20 P.M., on motion of Mr. Hutchins, the Senate adjourned.

JAMES S. SLINGERLAND,
President.

Attest—B. C. BROWN,
   Secretary.

IN SENATE—SIXTEENTH DAY.

CARSON CITY, January 22d, 1867.

The Senate met pursuant to adjournment, the President in the chair.

Roll called.

Present—Messrs. Carpenter, Doron, Eastman, Edwards, Geller, Grey, Haines, Hastings, Hutchins, Linn, Mason, Meder, Monroe, Proctor, Stevenson, Sumner, Terry, and Welty—18.

Absent—Mr. Nelson—1.

The Journal of the Fifteenth day was read and approved.

PRESENTATION OF PETITIONS.

Mr. Proctor presented petitions from residents of Nye County, praying for the removal of the county seat thereof.

Received, and referred to the Committee on Counties and County Boundaries.

Mr. Sumner presented Senate Memorial and Joint Resolution No. 59, asking Government aid in the construction of the Sutro Tunnel. Read first time ; rules suspended ; read second time by title, referred to Committee on Federal Relations, and two hundred and forty copies ordered printed.

Mr. Hastings introduced Senate Joint Memorial and Resolution No. 60, in relation to the United States Branch Mint located at Carson City, State of Nevada. Read first time ; rules suspended ; read second time by title, referred to the Committee on Mines and Mining, and two hundred and forty copies ordered printed.

MESSAGES FROM THE ASSEMBLY.

The following Messages were received from the Assembly :

ASSEMBLY CHAMBER, CARSON CITY,
January 21st, 1867.

To the Honorable the Senate :

I am instructed to return to your honorable body Senate Concurrent Resolution No. 43, relative to the Hon. James S. Slingerland, the same having passed the Assembly this day unanimously.

I also transmit to your honorable body, for your consideration, Assembly

Concurrent Resolution No. 19, relative to the printing of the Governor's Inaugural Address, the same having passed the Assembly this day.

Yeas—18.
Nays—9.

Respectfully,

A. WHITFORD,
Clerk.

Assembly Chamber, Carson City,
January 21st, 1867.

To the Honorable the Senate:

I am instructed to return to your honorable body Senate Concurrent Resolution No. 47, in relation to amending Joint Rule No. 7.

Also, Senate Concurrent Resolution No. 48, in relation to printing State Treasurer's Report; they having passed the Assembly this day unanimously.

I also transmit to your honorable body, for your consideration, Assembly Bill No. 4, entitled "An Act to amend an Act entitled 'An Act to provide for the incorporation of religious, charitable, literary, scientific, and other associations,' approved December 7th, 1862," the same having passed the Assembly this day.

Yeas—29.
Nays—0.

Respectfully,

A. WHITFORD,
Clerk.

Assembly Concurrent Resolution in relation to printing the Governor's Inaugural Address. Read and laid upon the table.

Assembly Bill No. 4, "An Act entitled an Act to amend an Act entitled 'An Act to provide for the incorporation of religious, charitable, literary, scientific, and other associations,' approved December 7th, 1862." Read first time; rules suspended; read second time by title, and referred to Committee on State Affairs.

Senate Bill No. 50, entitled "An Act to provide for the sale of certain lands belonging to this State, and for the application of the proceeds of the sale thereof." Two hundred and forty copies thereof were ordered to be printed.

On motion, the Senate went into a Committee of the Whole for the consideration of the General File, Mr. Doron in the chair.

The Committee arose, and submitted the following report:

Mr. President:

The Senate, as Committee of the Whole, have had under consideration Senate Bill No. 10, "An Act to amend an Act entitled 'An Act to provide Revenue for the support of the Government of the State of Nevada, and the Acts amendatory thereof,'" report progress thereon, and recommend its postponement for ten days.

Also, Senate Bill No. 40, "An Act to amend an Act entitled 'An Act empowering the Governor to appoint Commissioners of Deeds, and to define their duties,'" and recommend its engrossment.

Also, Assembly Joint Resolution relating to Constitutional Amendments, and recommend that it do pass.

Also, Senate Bill No. 44, "An Act to provide for the Removal of Civil Officers, other than State Officers, for malfeasance and nonfeasance in Office," report progress, and recommend that it be made a special order for February 1st, to be considered in a Committee of the Whole.

Also, Senate Bill No. 31, "An Act concerning the office of Public Administrator," which they report back, with the recommendation to print two hundred and forty copies.

Senate Bill No. 11, entitled "An Act to amend an Act entitled 'An Act to provide Revenue for the support of the Government of the State of Nevada, and the Acts amendatory thereof.'" Postponed for ten days.

Senate Bill No. 40, entitled "An Act to amend an Act entitled 'An Act empowering the Governor to appoint Commissioners of Deeds, and to define their duties.'" Ordered engrossed.

Assembly Joint Resolution No. 2, entitled "An Act relating to Constitutional Amendments." Read third time, by sections, and passed, by the following vote:

YEAS—Messrs. Carpenter, Doron, Eastman, Grey, Hastings, Hutchins, Mason, Meder, Stevenson, Sumner, and Terry—11.

NAYS—Messrs. Geller, Monroe, and Proctor—3.

Mr. Edwards, appearing, requested to have his vote recorded on the passage of Assembly Joint Resolution No. 2.

On motion, leave was granted, and he voted "Yea."

Senate Bill No. 44, "An Act to provide for the Removal of Civil Officers, other than State officers, for malfeasance or nonfeasance in office," was made special order for February 1st, to be considered in Committee of the Whole.

On motion, the Senate went into Committee of the Whole for consideration of the balance of the General File.

The Committee arose, and reported having had under consideration Senate Concurrent Resolution No. 2, concerning the adoption of the Constitutional Amendments of the United States, and recommended that it be laid on the table.

Also, Senate Concurrent Resolution No. 3, same title as the above, recommended that it also be laid on the table.

The resolutions above referred to were laid on the table.

The following Message was received from the Assembly:

ASSEMBLY CHAMBER, CARSON CITY, }
January 22d, 1867. }

To the Honorable the Senate:

I am instructed to return to your honorable body Senate Bill No. 9, entitled "An Act authorizing the Issuance and Sale of certain State Bonds, and Levying a Tax to provide means for the Payment thereof," the same having passed the Assembly this day.

AYES—30.

NAYS—1.

Respectfully,

A. WHITFORD,
Clerk.

On motion of Mr. Meder, at one o'clock P.M. the Senate adjourned.

JAMES S. SLINGERLAND,
President.

Attest—B. C. BROWN,
Secretary.

IN SENATE—SEVENTEENTH DAY.

CARSON CITY, January 23d, 1867.

The Senate met pursuant to adjournment, the President in the chair.
Roll called.
Present—Messrs. Carpenter, Doron, Eastman, Edwards, Geller, Grey, Haines, Hastings,. Hutchins, Linn, Mason, Meder, Monroe, Proctor, Stevenson, Sumner, Terry, and Welty—18.
Absent—Mr. Nelson—1.
The Journal of the Sixteenth day was read and approved.
Messrs. Welty, Haines and Linn asked leave to record their votes on the passage of Assembly Joint Resolution No. 2, entitled "An Act relative to Constitutional Amendments." On motion they were granted leave, and their names being called, they each voted yea.

REPORTS OF STANDING COMMITTEES.

Mr. Hastings reported that the Standing Committee on Engrossment had carefully compared the following entitled Bills with the original, and found the same correctly engrossed, viz:
Substitute Senate Bill No. 5, "An Act providing for the Release of Sureties on Official Bonds and Undertakings."
Also, Senate Bill No. 40, "An Act to amend an Act, entitled 'An Act empowering the Governor to appoint Commissioners of Deeds, and to define their Duties.'" And herewith reports the same back to the Senate.
Mr. Welty, from the Judiciary Committee, to whom was referred Senate Concurrent Resolution No. 55, relating to proposed amendments to the Constitution, reported that they had had the matter under consideration, and had come to the conclusion that resolutions of that character ought to be in form joint, and not concurrent, and that the Resolution No. 55 ought to be so amended as to be in form a joint resolution.
Mr. Linn, Chairman Committee on Enrollment, reported that Senate Bill No. 9, entitled "An Act authorizing the Issuance and Sale of certain State Bonds and Levying a Tax to provide means for the Payment thereof," had been carefully compared with the Engrossed Bill, as passed by the two Houses, found correctly enrolled, and that the same had this day been delivered to the Governor for his approval.
Mr. Mason, from the Committee on Federal Relations, submitted the following favorable report in relation to Joint Memorial and Resolution No. 59, asking Government aid in the construction of the Sutro Tunnel.
(See Appendix.)
Mr. Stevenson reported that the Committee on Mines and Mining had had under consideration the Assembly Bill No. 2, entitled "An Act to repeal an Act entitled, 'An Act concerning the location and possession of Mining Claims,' approved February 27th, 1866," and had directed their chairman to report the same back with the following amendment:
Add section 2. All rights acquired under the Act hereby repealed shall remain valid, and all assessment-work done, or assessments paid, shall hold the possession of the claims on which the same was done or paid, as in said Act provided; and in all mining districts wherein the provisions of the said Act were adopted as the mining laws, or regulations of the District, the same shall be made the laws thereof until repealed or amended by such districts, except the

requirement to cause the record of claims to be made in the County Recorder's office. And recommended its passage, as amended.

Mr. Proctor, from the Standing Committee on Counties and County Boundaries, to which was referred Senate Bill No. 49, entitled "An Act to change the County Seat of Nye County," report that they had had the same under consideration; have come to a favorable conclusion thereon, and had directed their Chairman to report the same to the Senate with some amendments, and to recommend its passage. Amend section 1 by striking out April, and insert May. Also, in section 2, last line, strike out April and insert May.

Mr. Doron, from the Standing Committee on State Affairs, to which was referred Assembly Bill No. 4, entitled "An Act to amend an Act entitled 'An Act to provide for the incorporation of religious, charitable, literary, scientific, and other associations,' approved Dec. 7th, 1862," reported that they had had the same under consideration; had come to a favorable conclusion thereon, and directed their chairman to report the same to the Senate without amendments, and to recommend its passage.

Mr. Doron, from the Standing Committee on State Affairs, to which was referred Senate Bill No. 56, entitled "An Act to amend an Act entitled 'An Act for the apportionment of Senators and Assemblymen in the different counties of this State,' approved Feb. 27th, 1866," report that they had had the same under consideration; have come to an unfavorable conclusion thereon, and directed their chairman to report the same to the Senate, with a recommendation that the same be indefinitely postponed.

Mr. Doron, from the Standing Committee on State Affairs, to which was referred Senate Bill entitled "An Act to repeal an Act entitled 'An Act to establish a Standard of Weights and Measures,' approved Feb. 28th, 1866," reported that they had had the same under consideration; had come to a favorable conclusion thereon, and directed their chairman to report the same to the Senate without amendments, and to recommend its passage.

The following communication was received from the Secretary of State:

OFFICE OF SECRETARY OF STATE,
Carson City, January 23d, 1867.

To the Senate of the State of Nevada:

GENTLEMEN—I have the honor to transmit herewith for your consideration the claim of John S. Child, with accompanying papers in support of the same. This claim was examined by the Board, August 3d, 1865, and disapproved, and from which action the claimant appeals to the Legislature. This claim was rejected for the reason that there is no law authorizing its payment; the indebtedness of Carson County, Utah Territory, never having been assumed by the Territory or State of Nevada, except as to individual cases, and then by special enactment.

Very respectfully,
C. N. NOTEWARE,
Secretary of Board of Examiners.

On motion of Mr. Doron, the above was referred to the Committee on Claims.

MOTIONS AND RESOLUTIONS.

Mr. Grey introduced the following resolution:

Resolved. That two thousand copies of Senate Joint Memorial and Resolution, in reference to the Sutro Tunnel, and the report of the Committee on Federal Relations thereon, be ordered printed.

Adopted, unanimously.
Mr. Proctor offered the following resolution:

Resolved, That C. H. Patchin be allowed the sum of $160 mileage and $111 per diem; and that the Controller of State be and he is hereby instructed to draw his warrants for the same, payable out of the Contingent Fund of the Senate.

Mr. Meder moved to indefinitely postpone the above, on which the yeas and nays were called by Messrs. Proctor, Meder and Hutchins, which resulted as follows:

YEAS—Messrs. Carpenter, Doron, Eastman, Edwards, Grey, Hastings, Hutchins, Meder, Terry, and Welty—10.
NAYS—Messrs. Geller, Haines, Mason, Monroe, Proctor, Stevenson, and Sumner—7.

The resolution was indefinitely postponed.
Mr. Hutchins introduced the following resolution:

Resolved, That the Standing Committee on Printing be, and hereby are, instructed to inquire into the reasons for the delay in printing the various papers ordered printed by the Senate.

Adopted.

MESSAGE FROM THE ASSEMBLY.

ASSEMBLY CHAMBER, CARSON CITY, }
January 22d, 1867.

To the Honorable the Senate:

I am instructed to transmit to your honorable body for your consideration, Assembly Concurrent Resolution No. 7, relating to the establishment of a weekly mail from Dayton, in Lyon County, *via* Hot Springs, to Pine Grove, Esmeralda County, the same having passed the Assembly on yesterday.

YEAS—26.
NAYS—0.

I also return to you Senate Bill No. 17, entitled "An Act in Relation to Fines," the same having passed the Assembly this day without amendment.

YEAS—23.
NAYS—5.

Respectfully,

A. WHITFORD,
Clerk.

Assembly Concurrent Resolution No. 7, relating to the establishment of a weekly mail from Dayton, in Lyon County, *via* Hot Springs, to Pine Grove, Esmeralda County. Read first time; rules suspended; read second time by title, and referred to the Committee on Federal Relations.

Mr. Terry gave notice that he would, at some future day, ask leave to introduce a bill to amend an Act entitled "An Act to Incorporate the City of Austin, approved February 20th, 1864," and the Acts amendatory thereof.

Also, a bill for an Act entitled "An Act to amend an Act to provide for the maintenance and supervision of Public Schools."

Also, a bill for an Act entitled "An Act to amend an Act to provide Revenue for the support of the State of Nevada."

Mr. Welty gave notice that he would, at some future day, ask leave to introduce a bill for an Act entitled "An Act to regulate and make effectual the power of the Governor, the Judges of the Supreme Court and Attorney General, to remit fines and forfeitures, to commute punishments, and to grant pardons after conviction."

Also, a bill for "An Act to amend an Act entitled ' An Act relating to Officers, their qualification, times of election, terms of office, official duties, resignations, etc., etc.,' approved March 9th, 1866."

Also, a bill for an Act entitled "An Act to regulate Vacancies in the offices of Senators and Members of the Assembly of this State."

Mr. Hastings, by leave, and without previous notice, introduced Senate Bill No. 64, "An Act to amend an Act entitled ' An Act to provide for the formation of Corporations for certain purposes.'" Read first time; rules suspended; read second time by title, and referred to Committee on Corporations.

Mr. Proctor, by leave, and without previous notice, introduced Senate Bill No. 65, "An Act to further amend an Act entitled 'An Act to provide Revenue for the support of the Government of the State of Nevada,' approved March 1st, 1866." Read first time; rules suspended; read second time by title, and referred to Storey County delegation.

Mr. Mason introduced Senate Bill No. 66, "An Act concerning the office of Public Administrator." Read first time; rules suspended; read second time by title, and referred to Committee on Judiciary.

On motion of Mr. Proctor, the Senate went into a Committee of the Whole for the consideration of the General File, the President in the chair.

The Committee arose, and submitted the following report:

Mr. President:

The Senate in Committee of the Whole, have had under consideration Senate Bill No. 55, proposing amendments to Section 1st, Art. 15th, and Section 1st, Art. 14th, of the Constitution of this State, which they report back with recommendation to refer to the Special Committee on amendments to the Constitution of the State. Also, Senate Memorial and Joint Resolution No. 59, asking Government aid in the construction of the Sutro Tunnel, which they report back, and recommend its passage.

Also, Assembly Bill No. 2, "An Act to repeal an Act entitled ' An Act concerning the location and possession of Mining Claims,' approved February 27th," which they report back, with a recommendation to adopt the amendment as proposed by the Committee on Mines and Mining.

Also, Senate Bill No. 49, "An Act to change the county seat of Nye County," which they report back with a recommendation to adopt the amendments as reported by the Committee on Counties and County Boundaries, and that it be engrossed.

Also, Assembly Bill No. 4, entitled "An Act to amend an Act entitled ' An Act to provide for the incorporation of Religious, Charitable, Literary, Scientific and other Associations,' approved December 7th, 1862," which they report back, and recommend its passage.

Also, Senate Bill No. 56, "An Act to amend an Act entitled 'An Act for the apportionment of Senators and Assemblymen in the different Counties of this State,' approved February 27th, 1867," which they report back, and recommend its indefinite postponement.

At 1:15 P.M., on motion of Mr. Hutchins, the Senate took a recess until 2 P.M.

IN SENATE.

The Senate convened at 2 o'clock P.M., Mr. Sumner, President *pro tem.*, in the chair.

Roll called.

Quorum present.

GENERAL FILE.

Senate Concurrent Resolution No. 55, proposing amendments to Sec. 1, Art. 15, and Sec. 1, Art. 14, of the Constitution of this State.

Referred to Special Committee on Constitutional Amendments.

Senate Memorial and Joint Resolution No. 59, asking Government aid in the construction of the Sutro Tunnel.

Ordered engrossed.

Assembly Bill No. 2, "An Act to repeal an Act entitled 'An Act concerning the location and possession of Mining Claims,' approved February 27th, 1866."

The amendments were adopted; the bill read third time by sections, and passed by the following vote:

YEAS—Messrs. Carpenter, Doron, Eastman, Edwards, Grey, Hastings, Hutchins, Meder, Monroe, Proctor, Stevenson, Sumner, Terry, and Welty—14.

NAYS—Mr. Mason—1.

Senate Bill No. 49, "An Act to change the County Seat of Nye County."

Amendments concurred in, and ordered engrossed.

Assembly Bill No. 4, entitled "An Act to amend an Act entitled 'An Act to provide for the incorporation of Religious, Charitable, Literary, Scientific and other Associations,' approved December 7th, 1862." Read the third time by sections, and passed by the following vote:

YEAS—Messrs. Carpenter, Doron, Eastman, Edwards, Grey, Hastings, Hutchins, Meder, Monroe, Proctor, Stevenson, Sumner, Terry, and Welty—14.

NAYS—Mr. Nelson—1.

Senate Bill No. 56, "An Act to amend an Act entitled 'An Act for the apportionment of Senators and Assemblymen in the different Counties of this State,' approved February 27th, 1866."

Indefinitely postponed.

Senate Substitute Bill No. 5, "An Act providing for the Release of Sureties on Official Bonds and Undertakings." Read third time by sections, and passed by the following vote:

YEAS—Messrs. Carpenter, Doron, Eastman, Geller, Grey, Haines, Hastings, Hutchins, Linn, Meder, Monroe, Proctor, Stevenson, Sumner, Terry, and Welty—16.

NAYS—Mr. Mason—1.

Senate Bill No. 15, " An Act to repeal an Act entitled ' An Act to establish a Standard of Weights and Measures,' approved February 28th, 1866."
Ordered engrossed.
At 2 : 25 P.M., on motion of Mr. Hutchins, the Senate adjourned.

JAMES S. SLINGERLAND,
President.

Attest—B. C. BROWN,
      Secretary.

IN SENATE—EIGHTEENTH DAY.

CARSON CITY, January 24th, 1867.

The Senate met pursuant to adjournment, Mr. Sumner, President *pro tem.*, in the chair.
Roll called.
Present—Messrs. Carpenter, Doron, Eastman, Edwards, Geller, Grey, Haines, Hastings, Hutchins, Linn, Mason, Meder, Monroe, Proctor, Stevenson, Sumner, Terry, and Welty—18.
Absent—Mr. Nelson—1.
Prayer by the Chaplain.
The Journal of the Seventeenth day was read and approved.

REPORTS OF STANDING COMMITTEES.

Mr. Mason, from the Standing Committee on Federal Relations, to which was referred Assembly Concurrent Resolution No. 7, relating to the establishing of a Weekly Mail from Dayton to Pine Grove, reported that they had had the same under consideration ; had come to a favorable conclusion thereon, and had directed their chairman to report the same to the Senate without amendments, and to recommend its passage.

Mr. Carpenter, from the Standing Committee on Corporations, to which was referred Senate Bill No. 64, entitled "An Act to amend an Act entitled 'An Act to provide for the formation of Corporations for certain purposes," reported that they had had the same under consideration, had come to a favorable conclusion thereon, and had directed their chairman to report the same to the Senate without amendments, and to recommend its passage.

Mr. Hastings reported that the Standing Committee on Engrossment had carefully compared the following entitled bills with the originals, and found the same correctly engrossed, viz : Senate Bill No. 15, " An Act to repeal an Act entitled 'An Act to establish a Standard of Weights and Measures,' approved February 28th, 1866 ;"

Also, Senate Bill No. 49, " An Act to change the County Seat of Nye County ;"

Also, Senate Memorial and Joint Resolution No. 59, asking Government aid in the Construction of the Sutro Tunnel ; and herewith report the same back to the Senate.

Mr. Linn, Chairman Committee on Enrollment, reported that Senate Concurrent Resolution No. 43, " In relation to Lieut. Governor Slingerland ;"

Also, Senate Concurrent Resolution No. 48, "In relation to Printing State Treasurer's Report;"

Also, Senate Concurrent Resolution No. 47, "In relation to amending Joint Rule No. 7, of the Senate and Assembly," had been carefully compared with the original resolutions as passed by the two Houses, found correctly enrolled, and the same had this day been deposited with the Secretary of State.

Mr. Doron, from the Standing Committee on State Printing, submitted the following report:

SENATE CHAMBER, January 24th, 1867.

Mr. President.

Your Standing Committee beg leave to report that they have, as per instruction of the Senate, made inquiry as to the delay in printing bills and other matter ordered printed by the Senate; your Committee found that there has been no unreasonable delay in the printing of the bills and resolutions ordered printed by the Senate. The Message of the Governor has been printed, and will be ready for distribution this day; the Reports of the Superintendent of Public Instruction, State Treasurer, and Warden of the State Prison, have been sent, as heretofore, to San Francisco to be printed, and will probably be returned here in about five or six days from this time. The Report of the State Mineralogist has been copied so far as the same has been received; but because of its incompleteness, has not been delivered to the State Printer.

Mr. Hutchins, from the Committee on Ways and Means, submitted the following report:

In relation to Senate Bill No. 9, "An Act authorizing the Issuance and Sale of certain Bonds, and levying a Tax to provide means for the Payment thereof," (see Appendix) 240 copies ordered printed.

MOTIONS AND RESOLUTIONS.

Mr. Doron introduced the following resolution:

Resolved, That five hundred copies of the Memorial and Resolution in reference to the Sutro Tunnel, and the Report of the Committee on Federal Relations thereon, be delivered to A. Sutro, for distribution at the seat of Government of the United States.

Adopted.

Mr. Haines submitted the following resolution:

Resolved, That all extra copying required to be done, shall be compensated at the rate of fifteen cents per folio, and shall be under the supervision of the Secretary of the Senate; and upon such accounts being audited and certified to by the Chairman of the Committee on Claims, the Sergeant-at-Arms shall draw his warrant on the Contingent Fund of the Senate in payment thereof.

Adopted.

MESSAGES FROM THE ASSEMBLY.

The following Message was received from the Assembly:

ASSEMBLY CHAMBER, CARSON CITY, }
January 23d, 1867.

To the Honorable the Senate:

I am instructed to return to your honorable body Senate Concurrent Resolution No. 58, in relation to admitting Hon. J. Neely Johnson to a seat within the Bar of each House of the Legislature, the same having passed the Assembly unanimously.

I also transmit to you for consideration Assembly Bill No. 8, entitled "An Act authorizing Married Women to transact business in their own name, as Sole Traders," the same having passed this day:

YEAS—29.
NAYS—4.

Respectfully,

A. WHITFORD,
Clerk.

Mr. Doron introduced Senate Joint Resolution No. 67, in relation to Weights and Measures.

Read first time; rules suspended; read second time by title, and referred to the Committee on Federal Relations.

Mr. Stevenson, by leave and without previous notice, introduced Senate Bill No. 69, entitled "An Act supplementary to an Act entitled 'An Act to create a Board of County Commissioners, in the several Counties of this State, and to define their Duties and Powers,' approved March 8th, 1865."

Read first time; rules suspended; read second time by title, and referred to the Committee on Judiciary.

GENERAL FILE.

Senate Bill No. 40, entitled "An Act to amend an Act entitled 'An Act empowering the Governor to appoint Commissioners of Deeds, and to define their Duties.'"

Laid temporarily on the table.

Senate Bill No. 15, "An Act to repeal an Act entitled 'An Act to establish a Standard of Weights and Measures,' approved February 28th, 1866."

Bill read third time by sections. The yeas and nays being called, on the final passage of the bill, were recorded as follows:

YEAS—Messrs. Carpenter, Doron, Eastman, Edwards, Geller, Haines, Hastings, Hutchins, Linn, Mason, Meder, Monroe, Proctor, Stevenson, and Terry—15.

NAYS—None.

So the bill passed.

Mr. Hutchins in the chair.

Senate Bill No. 49, entitled "An Act to change the County Seat of Nye County."

Read third time by sections. The yeas and nays being called, on the final passage of the bill, were recorded as follows:

YEAS—Messrs. Carpenter, Doron, Eastman, Edwards, Grey, Hastings, Hutchins, Linn, Mason, Meder, Monroe, Proctor, Stevenson, Sumner, and Terry—16.
NAYS—Mr. Haines—1.

So the bill passed.
Senate Memorial and Joint Resolution No. 59, asking Government aid in the construction of the Sutro Tunnel.
Read third time by sections. The yeas and nays being called, on the final passage of the resolution, were recorded as follows:

YEAS—Messrs. Carpenter, Doron, Eastman, Edwards, Geller, Grey, Haines, Hastings, Hutchins, Linn, Mason, Meder, Monroe, Proctor, Stevenson, and Terry—16.
NAYS—None.

So the resolution passed.
Assembly Concurrent Resolution No. 7, relating to the establishment of a weekly mail from Dayton, in Lyon County, via Hot Springs to Pine Grove, in Esmeralda County.
Read third time. The yeas and nays being called upon the final passage of the resolution, were recorded as follows:

YEAS—Messrs. Carpenter, Doron, Eastman, Edwards, Geller, Grey, Haines, Hastings, Hutchins, Linn, Mason, Meder, Monroe, Proctor, Stevenson, and Terry—16.
NAYS—None.

So the resolution passed.
Senate Bill No. 64, "An Act to amend an Act entitled 'An Act to provide for the formation of Corporations, for certain purposes.'"
Ordered engrossed.
On motion, Mr. Carpenter was granted indefinite leave of absence.
On motion, Mr. Stevenson was granted leave of absence for two days.
At 12 : 15 P.M., on motion of Mr. Haines, the Senate adjourned.

JAMES S. SLINGERLAND,
President.

Attest—B. C. BROWN,
Secretary.

IN SENATE—NINETEENTH DAY.

CARSON CITY, January 25th, 1867.

The Senate met pursuant to adjournment, the President in the chair.
Roll called.
Present—Messrs. Doron, Eastman, Edwards, Geller, Grey, Haines, Hast-

ings, Hutchins, Linn, Mason, Meder, Monroe, Proctor, Sumner, Terry, and Welty—16.

Absent—Messrs. Nelson and Stevenson—2.

Prayer by the Chaplain.

The Journal of the Eighteenth day was read and approved.

REPORTS OF STANDING COMMITTEES.

Mr. Linn, Chairman of Committee on Enrollment, reported that Senate Bill No. 17, entitled "An Act in relation to Fines," had been carefully compared with the engrossed bill, as passed by the two Houses, found correctly enrolled, and that the same had this day been delivered to the Governor for his approval.

Also, Concurrent Resolution No. 58, "In relation to admitting J. Neely Johnson to a seat within the Bar of each House of the Legislature," had been carefully compared with the original resolution as passed by the two Houses, found correctly enrolled, and that the same had this day been deposited with the Secretary of State.

Mr. Hastings reported that the Standing Committee on Engrossment had carefully compared the following entitled bill with the original, and found the same correctly engrossed, viz :

Senate Bill No. 64, "An Act to amend an Act entitled 'An Act to provide for the formation of Corporations for certain purposes," and herewith reports the same back to the Senate.

Mr. Doron, from Standing Committee on Mines and Mining, to which was referred Senate Memorial and Resolution No. 60, in relation to the United States Mint located at Carson City, in the State of Nevada, reported that they had had the same under consideration, had come to a favorable conclusion thereon, and directed their chairman to report the same back to the Senate without amendments, and to recommend its passage.

The Senate took a recess for five minutes, for the purpose of contributing for the relief of R. C. Gridley, the Flour-Sack Man.

Senate called to order.

NOTICES OF BILLS.

Mr. Mason gave notice that he would, at some future day, ask leave to introduce a bill for an Act entitled "An Act to amend an Act to 'Provide for the Registration of the names of Electors, and for ascertainment by proper proofs of the persons who shall be entitled to the Right of Suffrage,' approved February 24th, 1866."

Mr. Eastman gave notice that he would, at some future day, ask leave to introduce a bill for an Act entitled "An Act to declare so much of the Truckee River as lies within the State of Nevada, navigable, and to Prevent Obstructions in the same."

MOTIONS AND RESOLUTIONS.

Mr. Sumner introduced Concurrent Resolution No. 70, in relation to Adolph Sutro, for services, etc., in originating the Sutro Tunnel, on which the yeas and nays were called for by Messrs. Sumner, Meder, and Hastings, with the following result :

AYES—Messrs. Doron, Eastman, Edwards, Geller, Grey, Hastings, Hutchins, Linn, Mason, Meder, Monroe, Proctor, Sumner, Terry, and Welty—15.

NAYS—0.

8

So the resolution passed.

Mr. Hutchins introduced the following resolution:

Resolved, That the papers accompanying the Report of the Indian Commissioners in Humboldt County, which are now in the hands of the Senate, be returned to the Governor, and that he be requested to forward the same to, and for the use of our Representatives in Congress.

Adopted.

Mr. Grey introduced the following resolution:

Resolved, That two hundred and forty additional copies of the Special Report of the Committee on Ways and Means presented on yesterday, be ordered printed, making four hundred copies ordered.

Adopted.

INTRODUCTION OF BILLS.

Mr. Welty introduced Senate Bill No. 71, "An Act to regulate vacancies in the office of Senators and Members of the Assembly of this State." Read first time; rules suspended; read second time by title, and referred to Committee on State affairs.

Also, Senate Bill No. 72, "An Act to amend an Act entitled ' An Act relating to Officers, their qualifications, times of election, terms of office, official duties, resignations, removals, vacancies in office, and the mode of supplying the same, misconduct in office, and to enforce official duty,' approved March 9th, 1866." Read first time; rules suspended; read second time by title, and referred to the Committee on State Affairs.

Also, Senate Bill No. 73, "An Act to regulate and make effectual, the power of the Governor, the Judges of the Supreme Court, and Attorney General, to remit fines and forfeitures, to commute punishments, and to grant pardons after convictions." Read first time; rules suspended; read second time by title, and referred to Committee on State Affairs.

Also, Senate Substitute Bill No. 40, entitled "An Act to repeal an Act of the Legislative Assembly of the Territory of Nevada, entitled ' An Act authorizing the Private Secretary of the Governor to demand and receive certain Fees,' approved Nov. 29, 1861."

Also, to repeal an Act of the Legislature of the State of Nevada, entitled "An Act in relation to the collection of certain Fees, heretofore collected by the Governor's Private Secretary, approved February 17th, 1866." Read first time; rules suspended; read second time by title, and referred to the Committee on Ways and Means.

GENERAL FILE.

Senate Bill No. 64, entitled "An Act to amend an Act entitled ' An Act to provide for the formation of Corporations for certain purposes.'"

Read third time by sections. The yeas and nays were called on the final passage of the bill, and recorded as follows:

YEAS—Messrs. Doron, Eastman, Geller, Grey, Hastings, Hutchins, Linn, Mason, Meder, Monroe, Proctor, Sumner, Terry, and Welty—15.

NAYS—0.

So the bill passed.

On motion of Mr. Hutchins, the Senate went into Committee of the Whole, the President in the chair, for the consideration of the General File.

The Committee arose, and submitted the following report:

The Senate, in Committee of the Whole, have had under consideration the following bills and resolution:

Senate Bill No. 31, "An Act concerning Public Administrator," which they report back, with amendments, and recommend it be engrossed.

Also, Senate Memorial and Joint Resolution No. 60, in relation to the United States Branch Mint, located at Carson City, in the State of Nevada, which they report back, and recommend it be engrossed.

Mr. Doron in the chair.

Senate Bill No. 31, "An Act concerning Public Administrator." The amendments of the Committee of the Whole were adopted, and ordered engrossed.

Senate Memorial and Joint Resolution No. 60, in relation to the United States Branch Mint, located at Carson City, in the State of Nevada. Ordered engrossed.

The following communication was received from the Executive Department:

STATE OF NEVADA, EXECUTIVE DEPARTMENT, }
Carson City, January 25th, 1867. }

To the Honorable the Senate of Nevada:

I herewith transmit the annual reports of the Directors of the State Library, and the State Librarian, for the year A.D. 1866.

Respectfully submitted,

H. G. BLASDEL.

The above reports were referred to the Committee on State Library.

MESSAGE FROM THE ASSEMBLY.

The following Message was received from the Assembly:

ASSEMBLY CHAMBER, CARSON CITY, }
January 25th, 1867. }

To the Honorable the Senate:

I am instructed to return to your honorable body Senate Joint Resolution No. 18, memorializing the Commander of the Division of the Pacific to establish a fort at or near the junction of the North Fork with the Humboldt River, the same having been amended as follows: In first resolution, strike out the words "point where the North Fork joins the main Humboldt," and insert in lieu thereof the words "junction of the Reese River with the Humboldt." Also amending the title to conform to the resolution as amended; and passed the same yesterday. Yeas—35. Nays—3.

Also, Senate Memorial and Joint Resolution No. 59, asking Government aid in the construction of the Sutro Tunnel, which passed the Assembly yesterday without amendment. Yeas—34. Nays—0.

I also transmit to your honorable body, for your consideration, the following Assembly Bills:

No. 5, entitled "An Act to create two additional Commissioners to represent the State of Nevada at the World's Fair, to be held at Paris, France, A.D. 1867."

Also, No. 7, entitled "An Act conferring jurisdiction upon Justices' Courts concurrent with the District Court in actions to enforce Mechanics' Liens;" the same having passed the Assembly yesterday.

Respectfully,

A. WHITFORD,
Clerk.

The yeas and nays being called on the concurrence by the Senate to Assembly amendments to Senate Joint Resolution No. 18, were recorded as follows:

YEAS—Mr. Mason—1.
NAYS—Messrs. Doron, Eastman, Edwards, Geller, Grey, Hastings, Hutchins, Linn, Meder, Monroe, Proctor, Sumner, Terry, and Welty—14.

So the Senate refused to concur.
Assembly Bill No. 5, "An Act to create two additional Commissioners to represent the State of Nevada at the World's Fair, to be held at Paris, France, A.D. 1867." Read first time; rules suspended; read second time by title, and referred to Committee on State Affairs.
Assembly Bill No. 7, entitled "An Act conferring jurisdiction upon Justices' Courts concurrent with the District Court, in actions to enforce Mechanics' Liens." Read first time; rules suspended; read second time by title, and referred to Committee on Judiciary.
At 12:40 P.M., on motion of Mr. Edwards, the Senate adjourned.

JAMES S. SLINGERLAND,
President.

Attest—B. C. BROWN,
Secretary.

IN SENATE—TWENTIETH DAY.

CARSON CITY, January 26th, 1867.

The Senate met pursuant to adjournment, the President in the chair.
Roll called.
Present—Messrs. Doron, Eastman, Edwards, Geller, Grey, Haines, Hastings, Hutchins, Linn, Mason, Meder, Monroe, Proctor, Sumner, Terry, and Welty—16.
Absent—Messrs. Nelson and Stevenson—2.
Prayer by the Chaplain.
The Journal of the Nineteenth day was read and approved.

REPORTS OF STANDING COMMITTEES.

Mr. Linn, Chairman of the Committee on Enrollment, reported that Senate Memorial and Joint Resolution No. 59, asking Government aid in the construction of the Sutro Tunnel, had been carefully compared with the Engrossed Memorial and Joint Resolution, as passed by the two Houses, found correctly enrolled, and that the same had this day been delivered to the Governor for his approval.
Mr. Hastings reported that the Standing Committee on Engrossment had

carefully compared the following entitled Bill and Joint Resolution with the original, and found the same correctly engrossed, viz : Senate Bill No. 31, "An Act concerning the office of Public Administrator ;"

Also, Senate Memorial and Joint Resolution No. 60, in relation to the United States Branch Mint, located at Carson City, in the State of Nevada; and herewith report the same back to the Senate.

Mr. Mason reported that the Committee on Federal Relations had had under consideration Senate Joint Resolution No. 67, in relation to Weights and Measures ; had come to a favorable conclusion thereon ; had directed their chairman to report the same back to the Senate, and recommend its passage.

Mr. Grey, from the Special Committee, composed of the Storey County delegation, to which was referred the bill entitled "An Act to amend an Act to provide Revenue for the Support of the Government of the State of Nevada," (Senate Bill No. 65) reported that they had had the same under consideration ; had come to an unfavorable conclusion thereon, and directed their chairman to report the same to the Senate, and recommend its indefinite postponement.

Mr. Doron, Chairman of Committee on State Affairs, to which was referred Assembly Bill No. 5, "An Act to create two additional Commissioners to represent the State of Nevada at the World's Fair, to be held at Paris, France, A.D. 1867," reported that they have had the same under consideration, had made no amendments thereto, had come to a favorable conclusion thereon, and recommend its passage.

Also, Senate Bill No. 73, "An Act to regulate and make effectual the Power of the Governor, the Judges of the Supreme Court, and Attorney General, to remit fines and forfeitures, to commute punishment, and grant pardons after conviction," which they had amended, and recommend its passage as amended.

Also, Senate Bill No. 71, "An Act to regulate Vacancies in the office of Senators and Members of the Legislature of this State," which they had also had under consideration, and herewith beg leave to offer a substitute therefor, and recommend the passage of the substitute.

GENERAL FILE.

Mr. Hastings in the chair.

Senate Bill No. 31, entitled "An Act concerning the Office of Public Administrator." Read third time, by sections. The yeas and nays being called on the final passage of the bill, were recorded as follows :

YEAS—Messrs. Doron, Eastman, Edwards, Geller, Grey, Hastings, Hutchins, Linn, Mason, Meder, Monroe, Proctor, Sumner, Terry, and Welty—16.
NAYS—0.

So the bill passed.

Senate Memorial and Joint Resolution No. 60, in relation to the Branch Mint located at Carson City, in the State of Nevada. Read third time. The yeas and nays were called on the final passage of the resolution, and recorded as follows:

YEAS—Messrs. Doron, Eastman, Edwards, Geller, Grey, Haines, Hastings, Hutchins, Linn, Mason, Meder, Monroe, Proctor, Sumner, Terry, and Welty—16.
Nays—0.

So the resolution passed.

On motion of Mr. Hutchins, the Senate went into a Committee of the Whole, for the consideration of the General File.

Mr. Hutchins in the chair.

The Committee arose, and submitted the following report:

Mr. President:

The Senate, in Committee of the Whole, have had under consideration Assembly Bill No. 5, "An Act to create two additional Commissioners, to represent the State of Nevada at the World's Fair, to be held at Paris, France, A.D. 1867," which they report back to the Senate, and recommend its passage as amended. Also, Senate Bill No. 23, "An Act to regulate and make effectual the Power of the Governor and Judges of the Supreme Court and Attorney General to remit fines and forfeitures, to commute punishments and grant pardons after convictions," which they report back to the Senate, and recommend that it be printed with amendments.

Also, Senate Substitute Bill No. 71, "An Act to regulate Vacancies in the office of Senators and Members of Assembly of this State," which they report back to the Senate, and recommend that it be indefinitely postponed.

Also, Senate Joint Resolution No. 67, in relation to Weights and Measures, which they report back to the Senate, and recommend its engrossment.

Also, Senate Bill No. 65, "An Act to further amend an Act entitled 'An Act to Provide Revenue for the Support of the Government of the State of Nevada,' approved March 1st, 1866;" which they report back to the Senate, and recommend it be indefinitely postponed.

President in the chair.

Assembly Bill No. 5, entitled "An Act to create two additional Commissioners to represent the State of Nevada at the World's Fair, to be held at Paris, France, A.D. 1867."

Read third time by sections.

The yeas and nays were called on the final passage of the bill, and recorded as follows:

YEAS—Messrs. Geller, Grey, Hastings, Hutchins, Linn, Monroe, Proctor, Sumner, Terry, and Welty—10.

NAYS—Messrs. Doron, Eastman, Haines, Mason, and Meder—5.

So the bill passed.

Senate Bill No. 73, "An Act to regulate and make effectual the Power of the Judges of the Supreme Court and Attorney General to remit Fines and Forfeitures, to commute Punishment, and grant Pardons after Convictions," ordered to be printed with amendments.

Senate Substitute Bill No. 71, "An Act to regulate Vacancies in the Office of Senators and Members of the Assembly of this State."

Indefinitely postponed.

Senate Joint Resolution No. 67, in relation to Weights and Measures, ordered engrossed.

Senate Bill No. 65, "An Act further amending an Act entitled 'An Act to Provide Revenue for the Support of the State of Nevada,' approved March 1st, 1866."

Indefinitely postponed.

Mr. Grey, by leave, introduced the following resolution:

Resolved, That the Controller be authorized to prepare a copy of the Controller's Annual Report, to be made for publication in the " Enterprise" of Tuesday next, at a cost of not exceeding thirty dollars, payable out of the Contingent Fund of the Senate; for which sum the Controller is authorized to draw his warrant in compensation of said work.

Adopted.

The following communication was received from the Executive Department:

STATE OF NEVADA, EXECUTIVE DEPARTMENT, }
Carson City, January 26th, 1867. }

To the Honorable the Senate of Nevada :

I herewith transmit the Annual Report of the Controller, for the fiscal year 1866.

Respectfully submitted,

H. G. BLASDEL.

On motion of Mr. Sumner, the Report of the State Controller was referred to the Committee on Ways and Means, and ordered printed.

MESSAGES FROM THE ASSEMBLY.

ASSEMBLY CHAMBER, CARSON CITY, }
January 25th, 1867. }

To the Hon. the Senate :

I am instructed to transmit to your honorable body, for your consideration, the following Assembly Bills, the same having passed the Assembly this day, viz:

No. 19, entitled "An Act to amend an Act entitled 'An Act to provide for Reporting the Decisions of the Supreme Court of the State of Nevada,' approved March 14th, 1865."

YEAS—34.
NAYS—0.

No. 20, entitled "An Act to amend an Act entitled 'An Act in relation to the Distribution of the Reports of the Supreme Court of the State of Nevada,' approved March 14th, 1866."

YEAS—34.
NAYS—0.

I also return to you Senate Concurrent Resolution No. 70, in relation to Adolph Sutro, the same having passed the Assembly this day unanimously.

I am also directed to inform you that the Assembly have refused to recede from their amendments to Senate Joint Resolution No. 18, " Memorializing the Commander of the Division of the Pacific to establish a Fort at or near the junction of the North Fork with the Humboldt River;" and have appointed a Conference Committee, consisting of Messrs. Mayhugh, Tennant, and Walton.

Respectfully,

A. WHITFORD,
Clerk.

Assembly Bill No. 20, "An Act to amend an Act entitled 'An Act in relation to the Distribution of Reports of the Supreme Court of the State of Nevada,' approved March 14th, 1866."

Read first time; rules suspended; read second time by title, and referred to the Committee on Judiciary.

Assembly Bill No. 19, "An Act to amend an Act entitled 'An Act to provide for Reporting the Decisions of the Supreme Court of the State of Nevada,' approved March 14th, 1866."

Read first time; rules suspended; read second time by title, and referred to Committee on Judiciary.

On motion of Mr. Hutchins, a Committee of Conference was appointed, consisting of two.

The Chair named Messrs. Hutchins and Mason as such committee.

At 1:30 P.M., on motion of Mr. Proctor, the Senate adjourned.

JAMES S. SLINGERLAND,
President.

Attest—B. C. BROWN,
Secretary.

IN SENATE—TWENTY-SECOND DAY.

CARSON CITY, January 28th, 1867.

The Senate met pursuant to adjournment, the President in the chair.

Roll called.

Present—Messrs. Doron, Eastman, Edwards, Geller, Grey, Haines, Hastings, Hutchins, Linn, Mason, Monroe, Proctor, Stevenson, Sumner, Terry, and Welty —16.

Absent—Messrs. Meder and Nelson—2.

Prayer by the Chaplain.

The minutes of the Twentieth day were read and approved.

REPORTS OF STANDING COMMITTEES.

Mr. Mason, from Standing Committee on Federal Relations, to whom was referred Senate Joint Resolution in relation to the appointment of a Military Governor over the Territory of Utah, reported that they had had the same under consideration; and from the fact that Congress having, in their superior wisdom, taken initiatory steps to divide Utah between Nevada, Colorado, and Idaho, by giving Nevada the first slice, besides fearing any encroachment of the military over the civil power, having the most implicit confidence in the patriotism, wisdom, and loyalty of Congress to so act in the premises that our equal laws shall be so enforced that our virtuous conduct may be examples worthy of imitation by surrounding nations. Notwithstanding your Committee deprecate the abominable practice of polygamy as highly immoral, unnatural, and degrading in its tendency and end, in violation of the natural, moral, social, and physical laws, still your Committee, failing to see any advantages that might arise from our suggestions to Congress, decline doing so.

Our indignation at any standard of morals, disregard or violation of law, that but exhibit the realization of the history of past barbarism, and stands condemned by all enlightened nations, cannot be reduced by the creation of a power the benefits of which, in the minds of your Committee, are doubtful. Notwithstanding the distinguished ability characterizing the Mormon elders furnishes proof conclusive that that power, capable of producing the greatest good, when diverted from its proper course, is the cause of the greatest evils; and, notwithstanding the high attainments in arts, science, political economy, and learning, characteristic of the great progress of the age, proves positively, in the language of a modern author, that "Man is frail." And further, the Chairman of your Committee would most respectfully suggest to the author of these resolutions, that a memorial to Congress, asking a law fully establishing Universal Suffrage, ignoring the aristocracy of both color and sex, an abstract right, and consequently the highest expediency, morals would be improved, justice secured, equality in truth be established, and without one remaining doubt, polygamy be soon among the "things that were."

Most respectfully submitted, and an indefinite postponement asked.

Mr. Hastings reported that the Standing Committee on Engrossment had carefully compared the following entitled resolution with the original, and found the same correctly engrossed, viz: Senate Joint Resolution No. 67, "In relation to Weights and Measures," and herewith reports the same back to the Senate.

Mr. Edwards, from the Standing Committee on Public Lands, to which was referred Senate Bill No. 30, entitled "An Act in relation to, and accepting the Lands granted to the State of Nevada by the Government of the United States," reported that they had had the same under consideration, had come to a favorable conclusion thereon, and had directed their chairman to report the same to the Senate, without amendments, and to recommend its passage.

MESSAGE FROM THE ASSEMBLY.

ASSEMBLY CHAMBERS, CARSON CITY,
January 26th, 1867.

To the Hon. the Senate:

I am instructed to transmit to your honorable body, for your consideration, the following resolutions, which passed the Assembly this day unanimously:

A Concurrent Resolution No. 26, granting leave of absence to W. K. Parkinson.

A Concurrent Resolution No. 27, relating to Constitutional Debates.

I also transmit to you, for your consideration, Assembly Bill No. 24, entitled "An Act authorizing the Official Publication of the Laws and Resolutions passed by the Third State Legislature in a Newspaper," the same having passed the Assembly this day.

YEAS—22.
NAYS—18.

Respectfully,

A. WHITFORD,
Clerk.

Assembly Bill No. 24, entitled "An Act authorizing the Official Publication of the Laws and Resolutions passed by the Third State Legislature in a Newspaper."

Read first time; rules suspended; read second time by title; rules further suspended, and placed on its third reading.

The yeas and nays were called on its final passage, and recorded as follows:

YEAS—Messrs. Edwards, Geller, Grey, Hutchins, Mason, Monroe, Proctor, Stevenson, Sumner, and Welty—10.

NAYS—Messrs. Doron, Eastman, Haines, Hastings, Linn, and Terry—6.

9

So the bill passed.

Mr. Welty gave notice, that on to-morrow he would move a reconsideration of the vote, whereby the above bill passed.

Assembly Concurrent Resolution No. 26, granting leave of absence to W. K. Parkinson, read and passed unanimously.

Assembly Concurrent Resolution, relating to Constitutional Debates, read and passed.

Senate Bill No. 44, "An Act to Provide for the Removal of Civil Officers other than State Officers, for Malfeasance or Nonfeasance in Office."

On motion of Mr. Hastings, the special order for Friday was postponed to February 4th, at 12 o'clock.

The following Message was received from the Executive Department:

STATE OF NEVADA—EXECUTIVE DEPARTMENT,
Carson City, January, 1867.

To the Hon. Senate of Nevada :

I have this day approved Senate Bill No. 17, "An Act in relation to Fines."

Also, " Senate Memorial and Joint Resolution No. 59, asking Government Aid in the Construction of the Sutro Tunnel."

H. G. BLASDEL.

At 12 : 35 P.M., on motion of Mr. Sumner, the Senate abjourned.

JAMES S. SLINGERLAND,
President.

Attest—B. C. BROWN,
    Secretary.

IN SENATE—TWENTY-THIRD DAY.

CARSON CITY, January 29th, 1867.

The Senate met pursuant to adjournment.

The President in the chair.

Roll called.

Present—Messrs. Doron, Eastman, Edwards, Geller, Grey, Haines, Hastings, Hutchins, Linn, Meder, Mason, Monroe, Proctor, Stevenson, Sumner, Terry, and Welty—17.

Absent—Mr. Nelson—1.

Prayer by the Chaplain.

The Journal of the Twenty-second day was read and approved.

At 11 : 10 A.M., on motion of Mr. Proctor, the Senate adjourned.

JAMES S. SLINGERLAND,
President.

Attest—B. C. BROWN,
    Secretary.

IN SENATE—TWENTY-FOURTH DAY.

CARSON CITY, January 30th, 1867.

The Senate met pursuant to adjournment.
The President in the chair.
Roll called.
Present—Messrs. Doron, Eastman, Edwards, Geller, Grey, Haines, Hastings, Hutchins, Linn, Mason, Meder, Monroe, Nelson, Proctor, Stevenson, Sumner, Terry, and Welty—18.
Absent—None.
The Journal of the Twenty-third day was read and approved.

REPORTS OF STANDING COMMITTEES.

Mr. Linn, Chairman Committee on Enrollment, reported that Senate Concurrent Resolution No. 70, in relation to Adolph Sutro, had been carefully compared with the engrossed Concurrent Resolution, as passed by the two Houses, found correctly enrolled, and that the same had this day been deposited with the Secretary of State.

Mr. Nelson reported that the Committee on State Library had had under consideration the report of the State Librarian ; had directed their chairman to report the same back, and recommend that it be printed.

Also, reported that the Committee on State Library had had under consideration the Senate Bill No. 53, entitled " An Act to authorize the State Librarian to distribute copies of Nevada Constitutional Debates among Newspaper Proprietors in the State," and had directed their chairman to report favorably thereon.

Mr. Welty, from the Judiciary Committee, to which was referred Assembly Bill No. 8, " An Act authorizing Married Women to transact business in their own names, as Sole Traders," reported that they had had the same under consideration, and a majority thereof had directed their chairman to report the same back to the Senate, and recommend its passage.

Also, Senate Bill No. 69, entitled " An Act supplementary to an Act entitled ' An Act to create a Board of County Commissioners in the several Counties of this State, and to define its duties and powers,' " reported that they had had the same under consideration, had come to a favorable conclusion thereon, and had directed their chairman to report the same to the Senate, with the following amendments, and recommend its passage :

By striking out the words " One Hundred," and inserting " Five Hundred ;" and after the word " character," strike out the words " the plans, specifications, conditions, and requirements of the contract in full," and insert the words " thereof, and when plans and specifications are to constitute part of such contract, it shall be stated in the notice, where the same may be seen."

Also, Assembly Bill No. 7, entitled "An Act conferring jurisdiction upon Justices' Courts concurrent with the District Court, in actions to enforce Mechanics' Liens," reported that they had had the same under consideration, had come to a favorable conclusion on the subject matter thereof, directed their chairman to report a substitute therefor to the Senate, and to recommend the passage of the substitute.

The President stated that he had before him a bill and accompanying Message from his Excellency the Governor, which had been handed to him after the adjournment of the Senate.

A Message was received from the Assembly, and laid temporarily on the table.

Mr. Sumner moved that the President of the Senate be instructed to file upon the bill, to which he referred, a certificate stating: That, it not having been received within the constitutionally prescribed time in which the Executive of this State must present his objections to a bill or resolution to the body in which the same originated, it has become a law; and direct the Secretary to affix his signature thereto; and transmit the same to the proper officers of the other House for their certificate.

The yeas and nays were called for by Messrs. Welty, Sumner, and Haines, on the passage of the above, and recorded as follows:

YEAS—Messrs. Edwards, Geller, Grey, Hastings, Monroe, Proctor, and Sumner—7.

NAYS—Messrs. Doron, Eastman, Haines, Hutchins, Mason, Meder, Nelson, Stevenson, Terry, and Welty—10.

So the motion was lost.

MOTIONS AND RESOLUTIONS.

Mr. Grey introduced the following resolution:

Resolved, That the Secretary of the Senate be authorized and required to prepare a handsomely engrossed copy of the Senate Concurrent Resolutions, No. —, relative to Adolph Sutro, signed by the officers of the two Houses, and forward the same to the person therein named.

Adopted unanimously.

A Message was received from the Assembly, and temporarily laid on the table.

Mr. Hutchins introduced the following resolutions:

Resolved, That all Committees of the Senate having in their employ clerks, be and hereby are instructed to discharge such clerks.

Resolved, That for all writing that Senate Committees may have done for them in future, they shall be allowed to pay fifteen cents per folio, payable from the Senate Contingent Fund.

The yeas and nays were called for by Messrs. Doron, Hutchins and Haines, and recorded as follows:

YEAS—Messrs. Doron, Eastman, Edwards, Haines, Hutchins, Meder, Nelson, and Stevenson—8.

NAYS—Messrs. Geller, Grey, Hastings, Linn, Mason, Monroe, Proctor, Sumner, Terry, and Welty—10.

So the resolution was lost.

At 1:25 P.M., on motion of Mr. Hutchins, the Senate took a recess until 2 P.M.

IN SENATE.

The Senate met at 2 o'clock, Mr. Sumner, President *pro tem.*, in the chair.

Roll called.

Quorum present.

Mr. Mason moved that the Senate now go into consideration of the Governor's Message.

The President ruled the motion out of order, there being no Message from the Governor before the Senate.

Mr. Edwards introduced the following resolution:

Resolved, That the Committees on Federal Relations, Public Lands, Education, Agriculture and Manufactures, Public Morals and Claims, be authorized conjointly to employ a clerk.

The yeas and nays were called for on the passage of the resolution by Messrs. Hutchins, Haines and Mason, and recorded as follows:

YEAS—Messrs. Eastman, Edwards, Geller, Grey, Linn, Mason, Monroe, Proctor, Sumner, and Terry—11.
NAYS—Messrs. Doron, Haines, Hastings, Hutchins, Meder, Nelson, and Stevenson—7.

So the resolution passed.
Mr. Grey in the chair.
Mr. Welty introduced the following resolution:

Resolved, That the Attorney General be and he is hereby requested on tomorrow to furnish the Senate with his opinion in writing, in answer to the following questions:
Must the Governor return a bill delivered to him for his approval, to the House wherein it originated, if on the fifth day after he received it, with his objection, if any, while the House is in session?
If he fail to deliver to the House while in session with his objection, if any, but after the House shall have adjourned, but on the same day after the adjournment he deliver the same to the presiding officer of the body, or its Secretary or Clerk, must the House consider the bill again, or does it become a law, as upon a failure to make any return, or attempt at a return within the five days from the time of the delivery to him of the bill?
Resolved, That the Secretary furnish the Attorney General a copy of the foregoing.

Referred to the Committee on Judiciary, to report to-morrow morning.
Mr. Welty moved that the President and Secretary be requested not to certify to any enrolled bill before Friday, February 1st, 1867.
President *pro tem.* in the chair.

MESSAGES FROM THE ASSEMBLY.

The following Messages were received from the Assembly:

ASSEMBLY CHAMBER, CARSON CITY, }
January 28th, 1867. }

To the Honorable the Senate:

I am instructed to transmit to your honorable body for your consideration, Assembly Memorial to Congress No. 18, asking a reduction of freight and fare upon the Central Pacific Railroad of California, the same having passed the Assembly this day: Yeas, 31; Nays, 3.

I also return to you, Senate Bill No. 15, entitled "An Act to repeal an Act entitled 'An Act to Establish a Standard of Weights and Measures,' approved February 28th, 1866," the same having passed the Assembly this day: Yeas, 31; Nays, 0.

I am also instructed to inform you that the Assembly have this day refused to concur in the amendments made by the Senate to Assembly Bill No. 5, entitled "An Act to create two additional Commissioners to represent the State of Nevada at the World's Fair, to be held at Paris, France, A.D., 1867," and request that the Senate do recede from their amendments.

Respectfully,

A. WHITFORD,
Clerk.

ASSEMBLY CHAMBER, CARSON CITY,
January 29th, 1867.

To the Honorable the Senate:

I am instructed to transmit to your honorable body for your consideration, the following Assembly Bills and Resolutions, viz:

No. 3, entitled "An Act supplementary to 'An Act for securing Liens to Mechanics and others,' approved November 21st, 1861," the same having passed the Assembly yesterday: Yeas, 33; Nays, 0.

No. 27, entitled "An Act to amend an Act entitled 'An Act concerning District Attorneys,' approved February 26th, 1866," the same having passed the Assembly this day: Yeas, 33; Nays, 0.

No. 45, entitled "An Act to provide for the payment of Outstanding Warrants against the Transcript Fund of Churchill County," the same having passed the Assembly this day: Yeas, 29; Nays, 0.

No. 41, entitled "An Act for the relief of James Leffingwell, Ex-Sheriff of Lander County," the same having passed the Assembly this day: Yeas, 30; Nays, 0.

A Joint Resolution, No. 22, "Appointing a Commission to negotiate for the extension of the time for payment of certain Bonds therein named," the same having passed the Assembly this day: Yeas, 25; Nays, 8.

A Concurrent Resolution No. 29, "Instructing the Secretary of State to deliver copies of the Constitutional Debates to the Secretary and Assistant Secretary of the Constitutional Convention," the same having passed the Assembly this day.

I also return to you Senate Bill No. 64, entitled "An Act to amend 'An Act to provide for the formation of Corporations for certain purposes,'" the same having passed this day: Yeas, 29; Nays, 0.

Respectfully,

A. WHITFORD,
Clerk.

ASSEMBLY CHAMBER, CARSON CITY,
January 30th, 1866.

To the Honorable the Senate:

I am instructed to transmit to your honorable body, Assembly Bill No. 15, entitled "An Act to amend an Act entitled 'An Act to regulate proceedings in Civil Cases in Courts of Justice of the Territory of Nevada,' approved November 29th, 1861," which passed the House this day: Yeas 29; Nays, 0.

Also Senate Memorial and Joint Resolution No. 60, in relation to the United States Branch Mint, located at Carson City, in the State of Nevada, which passed the House this day without amendments: Yeas, 30; Nays, 4.

Respectfully,

A. WHITFORD,
Clerk.

Assembly Memorial No. 18, a memorial to Congress, " Asking a reduction of freights and fare, upon the Central Pacific Railroad of California."

Read first time ; rules suspended ; read second time by title, and referred to the Committee on Federal Relations.

Assembly Bill No. 3, "An Act supplementary to 'An Act for Securing Liens to Mechanics and others,' approved November 21, 1861."

Read first time ; rules suspended ; read second time by title, and referred to the Committee on Agriculture and Manufactures.

Assembly Bill No. 27, "An Act to amend an Act entitled 'An Act concerning District Attorneys, approved March 11th, 1865,' approved February 26th, 1866."

Read first time ; rules suspended ; read second time by title, and referred to the Committee on Judiciary.

Assembly Bill No. 45, "An Act to provide for the Outstanding Warrants against the Transcript Fund of Churchill County."

Read first time ; rules suspended ; read second time by title, and referred to the Churchill County delegation.

Assembly Bill No. 41, "An Act for the Relief of James Leffingwell, Ex-Sheriff of Lander County."

Read first time ; rules suspended ; read second time by title, and referred to the Lander County delegation.

Assembly Joint Resolution No. 22, appointing a Commissioner to negotiate for the extension of the time for payment of certain Bonds therein named.

Read first time ; rules suspended ; read second time by title, and referred to the Committee on Ways and Means.

Assembly Concurrent Resolution No. 29, instructing the Secretary of State to deliver Copies of the Constitutional Debates to the Secretary and the Assistant Secretary of the Constitutional Convention.

Read and passed.

Assembly Bill No. 15, "An Act to amend an Act entitled 'An Act to regulate proceedings in Civil Cases in the Courts of Justice of the Territory of Nevada,' approved November 29th, 1861."

Read first time ; rules suspended ; read second time by title, and referred to the Committee on Judiciary.

Assembly Bill No. 5, "An Act to create two additional Commissioners to represent the State of Nevada at the World's Fair, to be held at Paris, France, A.D. 1867."

Mr. Welty moved that the Senate adhere to its amendments thereto.

Carried.

Mr. Grey moved the appointment of a Committee of Conference, to confer with a like committee on the part of the Assembly.

Carried.

The President appointed Messrs. Grey, Proctor, and Hutchins.

NOTICES OF BILLS.

Mr. Haines gave notice that he would, at some future day, introduce "An Act to make Compensation to the Hon. John Cradlebaugh, late United States District Judge, the same as that of the late United States District Judges of the State of Nevada."

Also, a Bill for an Act entitled "An Act to amend an Act entitled 'An Act to provide Revenue for the Support of the Government of the State of Nevada,' approved March 9th, 1865."

INTRODUCTION OF BILLS.

Mr. Edwards, by leave (without previous notice) introduced Senate Bill No. 89, "An Act relating to Criminal Prosecution." Read first time; rules suspended; read second time by title, and referred to the Committee on Judiciary.

Mr. Nelson (without previous notice) introduced Senate Bill No. 90, "An Act to regulate the business of Assaying within the State of Nevada." Read first time; rules suspended; read second time by title, and referred to the Committee on Mines and Mining.

GENERAL FILE.

Senate Joint Resolution No. 67, "In relation to Weights and Measures." Read third time by sections; the yeas and nays were called on the final passage of the resolution, and recorded as follows:

YEAS—Messrs. Doron, Eastman, Edwards, Geller, Haines, Hastings, Linn, Mason, Meder, Monroe, Nelson, Proctor, Stevenson, Terry, and Welty—16.
NAYS—0.

So the resolution passed.

Senate Bill No. 30, "An Act in relation to, and accepting the Land granted to the State of Nevada, by the Government of the United States."

Referred to a Committee of the Whole.

Senate Bill No. 73, "An Act to regulate and make effectual the power of the Governor, the Judges of the Supreme Court, and Attorney General, to remit Fines and Forfeitures, to commute Punishment, and grant Pardons after Convictions."

Referred to a Committee of the Whole.

Senate Bill No. 21, "An Act to authorize the State Librarian to distribute copies of the Nevada Constitutional Debates among newspaper proprietors in this State."

Ordered engrossed.

Assembly Bill No. 8, "An Act authorizing Married Women to transact business in their own names as Sole Traders."

Referred to a Committee of the Whole.

Senate Substitute Bill No. 75, "An Act conferring jurisdiction upon Justices' Courts, concurrent with the District Court in actions to embrace [enforce] Mechanics' Lien."

Referred to Committee of the Whole.

Senate Bill No. 69, "An Act supplementary to an Act entitled 'An Act to create a Board of County Commissioners in the several counties of this State, and to define their duties and powers,' approved March 8th, 1865."

In accordance with previous notice, Mr. Welty called up Assembly Bill No. 24, "An Act authorizing the official publication of the Laws and Resolutions passed by the Third State Legislature, in a Newspaper," and moved to reconsider the vote whereby said bill passed. The President ruled the motion out of order, on the ground that the motion was not made on the day following the passage of the bill.

Mr. Welty appealed from the decision of the Chair.

The yeas and nays were called for, by Messrs. Hastings, Haines and Grey, and recorded as follows:

YEAS—Messrs. Eastman, Edwards, Geller, Grey, Linn, Mason, Monroe, Nelson, Proctor, and Stevenson—10.
NAYS—Messrs. Doron, Haines, Hastings, Meder, Terry, and Welty—6.

So the decision of the Chair was sustained.
At 3 : 40 P.M., on motion of Mr. Hastings, the Senate adjourned.

JAMES S. SLINGERLAND,
President.

Attest—

Secretary.

IN SENATE—TWENTY-FIFTH DAY.

CARSON CITY, January 31st, 1867.

The Senate met pursuant to adjournment.
The President in the chair.
Roll called.
Present—Messrs. Doron, Eastman, Edwards, Geller, Grey, Haines, Hastings, Hutchins, Linn, Mason, Meder, Monroe, Nelson, Proctor, Stevenson, Sumner, Terry, and Welty—18.
Absent—None.
Prayer by the Chaplain.
The Journal of the Twenty-fourth day was read, and corrected to show that Mr. Welty moved to reconsider, instead of calling up Assembly Bill No. 24, "An Act authorizing the official publication of the Laws and Resolutions passed by the Third State Legislature, in a Newspaper." Also, that Mr. Mason raised the point of order that the motion could not be then considered; which point the Chair decided well taken. After which the Journal was approved.
On motion of Mr. Mason, the Chaplain was excused for absence on the Twenty-fourth day.

REPORTS OF STANDING COMMITTEES.

Mr. Edwards, Chairman of the Committee on Public Lands, to which was referred Senate Bill No. 50, entitled "An Act to provide for the sale of certain Lands belonging to the State, and for the application of the proceeds of the sale thereof," reported that they had had the same under consideration, have come to an unfavorable [conclusion] thereon; and have directed their chairman to report a substitute therefor, with the recommendation that the same do pass; which substitute is herewith reported.
The Committee find the bill referred to them cumbrous in its provisions, and so expensive to purchasers of public lands by its provisions, that, in their opinion, settlers would purchase from the General Government, under the preëmption and homestead laws, rather than from the State.
In drawing the bill herewith submitted, they have had in view the selection of lands granted by the United States to this State, in advance of settlement, so that purchasers will be obliged to purchase of the State. They have further endeavored to make a simple and economical system of selecting and selling State lands, and submit their work to the Senate, with only these explanations:

First. That by the bill, the State Surveyor General must keep an office at the seat of Government, wherein shall be kept the plats and records of and concerning all lands of the State. The rent of the office is paid by the State, and one hundred and fifty dollars per month is allowed for a clerk.

Second. The surveys are to be pushed ahead, under United States authority, with all possible dispatch, that lands may be selected by the State before homestead or preëmption settlers reach them. This is done by advancing the expenses of survey, trusting to reimbursement by Congressional legislation.

Third. The Board of Regents have general supervision of school land matters, and decide contests between contesting applicants to purchase.

Fourth. The Governor issues patents for lands sold, to be registered and countersigned by the State Surveyor General.

All of which is respectfully submitted.

Mr. Hastings, Chairman of Committee on Engrossment, reported that they had carefully compared the following entitled bill with the original, and found the same correctly engrossed, viz : Senate Bill No. 53, "An Act to authorize the State Librarian to distribute Copies of the Nevada Constitutional debates among Newspaper Publishers in this State." And herewith report the same back to the Senate.

Mr. Sumner, Chairman of the Committee on Ways and Means, reported Senate Bill No. 91, "An Act authorizing a State Loan, and levying a Tax to provide means for the Payment thereof."

Read first time ; rules suspended ; read second time by title.

Mr. Doron moved that the bill be printed, and referred to a Committee of the Whole to-morrow at 12 o'clock.

The yeas and nays were called on the motion, by Messrs. Grey, Hastings and Hutchins, and recorded as follows :

YEAS—Messrs. Doron, Eastman, Haines, Mason, Stevenson, and Welty—6

NAYS—Messrs. Edwards, Geller, Grey, Hastings, Hutchins, Linn, Meder, Monroe, Nelson, Proctor, Sumner, and Terry—12.

So the motion was lost.

On motion of Mr. Hutchins, the Senate went into a Committee of the Whole, President in the chair, for the consideration thereof.

The Committee of the Whole arose, and submitted the following report :

Mr. President :

The Senate, in Committee of the Whole, have had under consideration Senate Bill No. 91, " An Act authorizing a State Loan, and levying a Tax to provide means for the Payment thereof ;" which they report back, and recommend that it be engrossed.

Mr. Sumner offered the following amendment to Section 4 : add the words, " Provided that no portion of any tax whatsoever, levied on the proceeds of the mines, shall be construed to form any part of the revenue appropriated and placed to this section for the redemption of the said bonds, but shall be paid, if any such tax be levied, into the General Fund for general State purposes."

The report of the Committee was adopted, and the bill ordered engrossed as amended.

A Message was received from the Assembly, and temporarily laid on the table.

On motion of Mr. Edwards, at 1 : 15 P.M., the Senate took a recess until two o'clock.

IN SENATE.

The Senate met at two o'clock, Mr. Proctor in the chair.

Roll called.   Quorum present.

Mr. Linn, Chairman of Committee on Enrollment, reported that Senate Memorial and Joint Resolution No. 60, " In relation to the United States Branch Mint, located at Carson City, in the State of Nevada;" Senate Bill No. 64, "An Act to amend an Act entitled 'An Act to provide for the Formation of Corporations for certain purposes;'" Senate Bill No. 15, "An Act to repeal an Act entitled 'An Act to establish a Standard of Weights and Measures,' approved Feb. 28th, 1866," had been carefully compared with the engrossed bills, as passed by the two Houses, found correctly enrolled, and that the same had this day been delivered to the Governor for his approval.

Mr. Monroe reported that the Select Committee composed of the Churchill Delegation, had had under consideration Assembly Bill No. —, entitled " An Act to provide for Payment of Outstanding Warrants against the Transcript Fund of Churchill County," had come to a favorable conclusion thereon, report the same back to the Senate, and recommend its passage without amendments.

Mr. Welty, from Judiciary Committee, to whom was referred Mr. Welty's resolution relative to certain questions to be asked of the Attorney General, requested further time.

Granted.

Mr. Nelson introduced Senate Concurrent Resolution No. 9, in relation to printing 240 copies of [the Report of the] State Librarian and [Directors of the] State Library.   Read and passed.

MESSAGES FROM THE ASSEMBLY.

The following Messages were received from the Assembly :

ASSEMBLY CHAMBER, CARSON CITY,
January 31st, 1867.

To the Honorable the Senate:

I am instructed to transmit to your honorable body for your consideration [Substitute] Assembly Bill No. 2 [22], entitled " An Act to provide for the Organization of the Assembly at the commencement of each Session," the same having passed the House on yesterday.

YEAS—25.
NAYS—4.

I also return to you Senate Bill No. 49, entitled " An Act to Change the County Seat of Nye County," the same having passed the Assembly yesterday without amendment.

YEAS—23.
NAYS—9.

Respectfully,

A. WHITFORD,
Clerk.

ASSEMBLY CHAMBER, CARSON CITY, }
January 31st, 1867. }

To the Honorable the Senate:

I am instructed to transmit to your honorable body for your consideration, Assembly Concurrent Resolution No. 30, relative to Constitutional Debates, the same having passed the Assembly this day.

I also return to your honorable body Senate Joint Resolution No. 67, in relation to Weights and Measures, the same having passed the Assembly this day.

YEAS—35.
NAYS—0.

Respectfully,

A. WHITFORD,
Clerk.

Substitute Assembly Bill No. 22, "An Act to provide for the Organization of the Assembly at the commencement of each Session." Read first time; rules suspended; read second time by title, and referred to the Committee on State Affairs.

Assembly Concurrent Resolution No. 30, relative to Constitutional Debates. Read and referred to Committee on State Library.

INTRODUCTION OF BILLS.

Mr. Nelson, by leave, and without previous notice, introduced Senate Bill No. 94, "An Act to compensate J. F. Hatch for services in the State Library."

Read first time; rules suspended; read second time by title, and referred to the Committee on Claims.

Mr. Welty, by leave, and without previous notice, introduced Senate Bill No. 95, "An Act conferring further powers on the County Commissioners of the several Counties of this State, in reference to County Hospitals."

Read first time; rules suspended; read second time by title, and referred to Committee on Counties and County Boundaries.

Mr. Haines introduced Senate Bill No. 196, "An Act making the compensation of the Hon. John Cradlebaugh, late United States District Judge, the same as was paid to each of the late United States District Judges of the late Territory of Nevada."

Read first time; rules suspended; read second time by title, and referred to the Committee on Claims.

Mr. Edwards introduced Senate Bill No. 97, "An Act defining the Duties of the Attorney General of the State of Nevada."

Read first time; rules suspended; read second time by title, and referred to the Committee on Judiciary.

Mr. Haines introduced Senate Bill No. 98, "An Act to amend an Act, entitled ' An Act to provide Revenue for the support of the Government of the State of Nevada,' approved March 9th, 1865."

Read first time; rules suspended; read second time by title, and referred to the Committee on Ways and Means.

Mr. Welty, by leave, moved that 240 copies of Substitute Senate Bill No. 50, entitled "An Act to provide for the selection of Lands granted by the United States to the State of Nevada," be ordered printed.

Carried.

Senate Bill No. 53, "An Act to authorize the State Librarian to distribute copies of the Nevada Constitutional Debates among Newspaper Proprietors in this State."

Recommitted to Committee on State Library, with instructions to strike out "State Librarian," and insert "Secretary of State."

On motion of Mr. Welty, the Senate went into Committee of the Whole, President *pro tem.* in the chair.

The Committee arose, and submitted the following report:

Mr. President:

The Senate, in Committee of the Whole, have had under consideration Senate Bill No. 30, "An Act in relation to, and accepting the Lands granted to the State of Nevada by the Government of the United States," which they report back, and recommend that it be engrossed.

Also, Senate Bill No. 73, "An Act to regulate and make effectual the Power of the Governor, the Judges of the Supreme Court, and Attorney General, to remit Fines and Forfeitures, to commute Punishment and grant Pardons after Conviction," which they report back with amendments, and recommend that it be ordered engrossed as amended.

Also, Assembly Bill No. 8, "An Act authorizing Married Women to transact business in their own names, as Sole Traders," which they report back, and recommend its passage.

Also, Assembly Bill, No. 7, "An Act conferring Jurisdiction upon Justices' Courts, concurrent with the District Court, in actions to enforce Mechanics' Liens," which they report back, and recommend the adoption of the substitute report from the Judiciary Committee, as amended.

Senate Bill No. 30, "An Act in relation to accepting the Lands granted to the State of Nevada by the Government of the United States."

Ordered engrossed.

Senate Bill No. 73, "An Act to regulate and make effectual the Power of the Governor, and Judges of the Supreme Court, and Attorney General, to remit Fines and Forfeitures, to commute Punishment, and grant Pardons after Conviction."

Mr. Meder offered the following amendment:

Add to Section No. 4, "the Fines and Forfeitures herein mentioned, shall not be so construed as to include the remittance or discharge from liability on any Bail Bond and Bails."

Adopted as amended, and ordered engrossed.

Assembly Bill No. 8, "An Act authorizing Married Women to transact business in their own name as Sole Traders." Read third time by sections; the yeas and nays were called on the final passage of the bill, and recorded as follows:

YEAS—Messrs. Doron, Eastman, Geller, Grey, Hutchins, Linn, Meder, Monroe, Nelson, Stevenson, Sumner, and Welty—12.

NAYS—Messrs. Edwards, Haines, Proctor, and Terry—4.

So the bill passed.

Assembly Bill No. 7, "An Act conferring Jurisdiction upon Justices' Courts, concurrent with the District Court, in actions to enforce Mechanics' Liens."

Substitute Senate Bill No. 75, as reported from the Committee on Judiciary was adopted, and also the amendments thereto, and the bill ordered engrossed.

At 4 o'clock P.M., on motion of Mr. Meder, the Senate adjourned.

JAMES S. SLINGERLAND,
President.

Attest—

        Secretary.

IN SENATE—TWENTY-SIXTH DAY.

CARSON CITY, February 1st, 1867.

The Senate met pursuant to adjournment, Mr. Sumner, President *pro tem.*, in the chair.

Roll called.

Present—Messrs. Doron, Eastman, Edwards, Geller, Haines, Hutchins, Linn, Mason, Meder, Monroe, Nelson, Proctor, Stevenson, Sumner, Terry, and Welty —16.

Absent—Messrs. Grey and Hastings—2.

Prayer by the Chaplain.

The Journal of the Twenty-fifth day was read and approved.

On motion, Mr. Hastings was granted leave of absence for two days.

REPORTS OF COMMITTEES.

Mr. Stevenson, from Standing Committee on Mines and Mining, to which was referred Senate Bill No. 90, "An Act to regulate the business of Assaying within the State of Nevada," reported that they had had the same under consideration ; had come to a favorable conclusion thereon, and had directed their chairman to report the same to the Senate without amendments, and recommend its passage.

Mr. Doron, from Standing Committee on State Affairs, to which was referred Assembly Bill No. 22, " An Act to provide for the Organization of the Assembly at the commencement of each Session," reported that they had had the same under consideration ; had come to a favorable conclusion thereon ; had directed their chairman to report the same to the Senate without amendments, and recommend its passage.

Mr. Linn, Chairman Committee on Enrollment, reported that Senate Joint Resolution No. 67, " In relation to Weights and Measures ;" Senate Bill No. 49, "An Act to change the County Seat of Nye County," had been carefully compared with the engrossed bill and resolution, as passed by the two Houses, found correctly enrolled, and had this day been delivered to the Governor for his approval.

Mr. Meder, from the Committee on Engrossment, reported that the following bills had been carefully compared with the originals, and found to be correctly engrossed :

Senate Bill No. 91, " An Act authorizing a State Loan and levying a Tax to provide means for the Payment thereof."

Also, Senate Bill No. 78, " An Act to regulate and make effectual the Power of the Governor, the Judges of the Supreme Court, and Attorney General, to remit Fines and Forfeitures, to commute Punishment, and grant Pardons after Conviction."

Also, Senate Bill No. 30, "An Act in relation to land accepting the Lands granted to the State of Nevada by the Government of the United States."

Also, Senate Bill No. 75, substitute for Assembly Bill No. 7, "An Act conferring Jurisdiction upon Justices' Courts concurrent with the District Court in actions to enforce Mechanics' Liens."

A Message was received from the Assembly, and laid temporarily on the table.

Mr. Hutchins moved a suspension of the rules, and that Senate Bill No. 91, "An Act authorizing a State Loan, and levying a Tax to provide means for the Payment thereof," be taken up and placed upon its third reading and final passage.

Carried.

The bill was read the third time by sections; the yeas and nays were called on its final passage, and recorded as follows:

YEAS—Messrs. Doron, Eastman, Edwards, Geller, Grey, Haines, Hutchins, Linn, Mason, Meder, Monroe, Nelson, Proctor, Stevenson, Sumner, Terry, and Welty—17.

NAYS—0.

So the bill passed.

The Sergeant-at-Arms was granted leave of absence for the day.

The President in the chair.

Mr. Mason, from Standing Committee on Federal Relations, to which was referred "Assembly Memorial to Congress, asking a Reduction of Freight and Fare upon the Central Pacific Railroad of California," reported that they had had the same under consideration, had come to a favorable conclusion thereon, had directed their chairman to report the same back to the Senate, and to recommend its passage.

Mr. Edwards, of the above Committee, was, on motion, granted until Monday, February 4th, to present a minority report.

NOTICES OF BILLS.

Mr. Sumner gave notice that he would, at some future day, introduce a bill entitled "An Act to provide for the Election of two Associate Justices to the Supreme Court."

INTRODUCTION OF BILLS.

Mr. Terry, by leave, and without previous notice, introduced Senate Bill No. 100, "An Act to amend an Act entitled ' An Act to provide Revenue for the Support of the Government of the State of Nevada.' " Read first time; rules suspended; read second time by title, and referred to the Committee on Ways and Means.

Mr. Welty, by leave, and without previous notice, introduced Senate Bill No. 101, "An Act to amend an Act entitled ' An Act to regulate Fees and Compensation for Official and other Services in the State of Nevada,' approved March 9th, 1865." Read first time; rules suspended; read second time by title, and referred to the Committee on State Affairs.

Mr. Linn, by leave, and without previous notice, introduced Senate Bill No. 102, "An Act to transfer certain Moneys in the hands of the County Treasurers of the several counties of this State to the School Fund of their respective

Counties." Read first time; rules suspended; read second time by title, and referred to Committee on Counties and County Boundaries.

The following communication was received from the Secretary of State:

OFFICE OF SECRETARY OF STATE, }
Carson City, January 30th, 1867. }

To the Senate of Nevada:

GENTLEMEN—I have the honor to transmit herewith for your consideration, the claim of the Hon. John Cradlebaugh, for services rendered as Judge of the United States District Court, from August 1st, 1859, to March 15th, 1861, the action of the State Board of Examiners thereon having been appealed from.

This claim came before the Board of Examiners this day, and after due consideration was rejected, for the reason that no law exists which would warrant its approval by the Board.

Very respectfully,

C. N. NOTEWARE,
Secretary of State.

Referred to Committee on Claims.

OFFICE OF SECRETARY OF STATE, }
Carson City, February 1st, 1867. }

To the Senate of Nevada:

GENTLEMEN—I have the honor to transmit herewith a copy (the original being filed with the State Controller) of the claim of S. H. Marlette; this claim was examined and passed upon by the Board of Examiners on April 30, 1866, and approved in part only. The claimant feeling aggrieved by the action of the Board, takes an appeal to the Legislature. I also transmit the original bill filed, a transcript of the record of the Board, together with the notice of appeal.

Very respectfully,

C. N. NOTEWARE,
Secretary of State, and ex-officio Secretary
of the Board of Examiners.

Referred to the Commmittee on Claims.

GENERAL FILE.

Senate Bill No. 73, entitled "An Act to Regulate and make Effectual the Power of the Governor, the Judges of the Supreme Court, and Attorney General, to remit Fines and Forfeitures, to commute Punishment, and grant Pardons after Convictions."

Mr. Sumner moved to strike out the word "Judges," and insert the word "Justices."

Carried.

Read the third time by sections; the yeas and nays were called on the final passage of the bill, and recorded as follows:

YEAS—Messrs. Doron, Eastman, Edwards, Geller, Grey, Haines, Linn, Mason, Meder, Monroe, Nelson, Proctor, Stevenson, Sumner, Terry, and Welty —16.

NAYS—0.

So the bill passed.

Senate Bill No. 30, "An Act in relation to and accepting the Lands granted to the State of Nevada by the Government of the United States." Read third time by sections ; the yeas and nays were called on the final passage of the bill, and recorded as follows :

YEAS—Messrs. Doron, Edwards, Eastman, Geller, Grey, Haines, Mason, Meder, Monroe, Nelson, Proctor, Stevenson, Sumner, Terry, and Welty—15. NAYS—0.

So the bill passed.
Senate Bill No. 75, substitute for Assembly Bill No. 7, " An Act conferring Jurisdiction upon Justices' Courts, concurrent with the District Court, in actions to enforce Mechanics' Liens."
Mr. Welty moved to amend by inserting " when the amount does not exceed three hundred dollars, exclusive of interest."
Adopted.
Read third time by sections.
The yeas and nays were called for on the final passage of the bill, and recorded as follows :

YEAS—Messrs. Doron, Eastman, Grey, Linn, Mason, Meder, Nelson, Proctor, Stevenson, Sumner, Terry, and Welty—12.
NAYS—Messrs. Edwards, Geller, and Monroe—3.

So the bill passed.
Assembly Bill No. 45, " An Act to provide for the Payment of outstanding Warrants against the Transcript Fund of Churchill County."
Read third time by sections.
The yeas and nays were called on the final passage of the bill, and recorded as follows :

YEAS—Messrs. Doron, Eastman, Edwards, Geller, Grey, Haines, Linn, Mason, Meder, Monroe, Nelson, Proctor, Stevenson, Sumner, Terry, and Welty—16. NAYS—0.

So the bill passed.
Substitute Senate Bill No. 50, "An Act to provide for the Selection of Lands granted by the United States to the State of Nevada."
On motion of Mr. Welty, the above bill was made the special order for Tuesday, February 5th, at 12 o'clock.
Senate Bill No. 90, "An Act to regulate the business of Assaying within the State of Nevada."
Ordered engrossed.
Substitute Assembly Bill No. 22, "An Act to provide for the Organization of the Assembly at the Commencement of each Session."
Read third time by sections. The yeas and nays were called on the final passage of the bill, and recorded as follows :

YEAS—Messrs. Doron, Eastman, Geller, Grey, Haines, Linn, Mason, Meder, Monroe, Nelson, Proctor, Stevenson, Sumner, Terry, and Welty—15. NAYS—Mr. Hastings—1.

So the bill passed.
Assembly Bill No. 3, "An Act supplementary to 'An Act for Securing Liens to Mechanics and others,' approved November 21st, 1861."
Read third time by sections.
11

The yeas and nays were called on the final passage of the bill, and recorded as follows:

YEAS—Messrs. Doron, Eastman, Geller, Haines, Hutchins, Linn, Mason, Meder, Monroe, Nelson, Proctor, Terry, and Welty—13.
NAYS—Messrs. Grey, Stevenson, and Sumner—3.

So the bill passed.
A Message was received from the Assembly, and laid temporarily on the table.
On motion, the Senate went into Committee of the Whole for the consideration of the General File, Mr. Proctor in the chair.
The Committee arose, and submitted the following report:

Mr. President:

The Senate in Committee of the Whole have had under consideration Senate Bill No. 69, "An Act supplementary to an Act entitled 'An Act to create a Board of County Commissioners in the several counties of this State, and to define their duties and powers,' approved March 8th, 1865;" which they report back with amendments, and recommend it be ordered engrossed.
Senate Bill No. 69, "An Act supplementary to an Act entitled 'An Act to create a Board of County Commissioners in the several counties of this State, and to define their duties and powers;' approved March 8th, 1865."
The amendments of the Committee of the Whole to the bill were adopted, and the bill ordered engrossed.

SPECIAL ORDER OF THE DAY.

Senate Bill No. 11, "An Act to amend an Act entitled 'An Act to provide Revenue for the Support of the Government of the State of Nevada,'" and the Acts amendatory thereof.
Ordered engrossed.
At 1:10 P.M., on motion of Mr. Edwards, the Senate adjourned until Monday, February 4th, at eleven o'clock.

CHARLES A. SUMNER,
President *pro tem.*

Attest—B. C. BROWN,
Secretary.

IN SENATE—TWENTY-NINTH DAY.

CARSON CITY, February 4th, 1867.

The Senate met pursuant to adjournment, Mr. Sumner, President *pro tem.,* in the chair.
Roll called.
Present—Messrs. Eastman, Edwards, Geller, Grey, Haines, Hastings, Hutchins, Linn, Mason, Meder, Monroe, Proctor, Stevenson, Sumner, Terry, and Welty—16.
Absent—Messrs. Doron and Nelson—2.
Prayer by the Chaplain.

The Journal of the Twenty-sixth day was read and approved.

President in the chair.

Mr. Welty offered a petition from the residents of Lander County, protesting against the passage of the bill for the relief of James Leffingwell, ex-Sheriff of Lander County.

Received, and referred to the Lander County delegation.

A Message from the Governor was received, and laid temporarily on the table.

On motion of Mr. Haines, Mr. Doron was granted indefinite leave of absence.

Mr. Mason asked leave to withdraw the Report of the Committee on Federal Relations, in regard to Assembly Memorial and Joint Resolution No. 18, "A Memorial to Congress asking a reduction of Freight and Fare upon the Central Pacific Railroad of California."

Granted.

REPORTS OF STANDING COMMITTEES.

Mr. Hastings reported, that the Standing Committee on Engrossment had carefully compared the following bills with the originals, and found the same correctly engrossed, viz:

Senate Bill No. 11, "An Act to amend an Act entitled 'An Act to provide Revenue for the Support of the Government of the State of Nevada,' and the Act amendatory thereof."

Also, Senate Bill No. 69, "An Act supplementary to an Act entitled 'An Act to create a Board of County Commissioners in the several Counties of this State, and to define their Duties and Powers,' approved March 8th, 1865."

Also, Senate Bill No. 90, "An Act to regulate the business of Assaying within the State of Nevada:"

And herewith report the same back to the Senate.

• Mr. Edwards, from a minority of Standing Committee on Federal Relations, to which was referred Assembly Memorial No. 18, "A Memorial to Congress asking a reduction of Freight and Fare upon the Central Pacific Railroad of California," submitted the following minority report:

At the granting of the charter to the Central Pacific Railroad Company, the Congress of the United States established the tariff rates of charges for freight and passage which should not be exceeded by the Company without a forfeiture of their charter; in order to secure the early completion of this gigantic work—which is a national necessity—Congress realized the importance of liberal legislation to secure the investment of the requisite amount of capital for its early completion; and now, in the darkest hours of that Company's existence, it would be strange legislation indeed, should Congress so stultify her earlier interest and action by taking from that Company one-half of her present income from the small portion of the road now completed—and this, too, in the face of the fact that, in addition to the enormous cost of building the road [over and through the rugged Sierra Nevadas, that some twenty miles of the road] must be, in a great measure, rebuilt, because of its destruction from slides from the mountain sides during the past winter.

These hindrances and obstructions, doubtless, will continue until the Company shall have secured protection to the more exposed parts of the road.

The Company is now engaged in prosecuting the work with unparalleled energy; and although not yet within our borders, still with a fair prospect that, early in the coming season, they will have in our midst several thousand employés engaged in building the road through our State; and believing that it is the duty and interest of our citizens to render them every aid and encouragement, we are compelled to oppose any character of legislation that tends only to harass and annoy the Railroad Company, and retard the completion of the road to and within the borders of our State, and this, too, without securing any benefit to our own citizens.

This system of unfriendly legislation cannot but affect the value of the bonds of the Company, in that it creates distrust in the minds of capitalists, creating a want of confidence in the stability of our State legislation, which will greatly retard the progress and early completion of this work, so essential to the interests of our people.

We believe that the future greatness and prosperity of our State, to a great extent, depends upon the completion of the Central Pacific Railroad across our borders; for with it, capital will come as surely as effect follows cause. Let this work be once completed across our State, and a hundred cities will have sprung into existence upon our barren sage-brush plains and sandy deserts. Mills and manufactories will be established, while many localities, valuable for their extensive mineral deposits, will be made accessible—adding greatly to the wealth of the State and the Nation. But without the Railroad, a large portion of our State, rich in mineral deposits, must continue to remain in an undeveloped condition—practically worthless—and the few millions of taxable property will be compelled to continue to pay ruinous rates of taxation for the support of the State Government, the practical effect of which must result in drawing capital from our midst, and preventing other capital from coming here to seek investment.

In view, therefore, of these few facts briefly stated, the minority committee deem it unwise and impolitic to take such legislative action as is recommended in the majority report of this committee.

Mr. Grey, from the Senate Committee of Conference, appointed to confer with a like Committee on the part of the Assembly, in relation to the disagreement of the two Houses, with reference to the Assembly Bill No. 5, entitled "An Act to create two additional Commissioners to represent the State of Nevada, at the World's Fair, to be held at Paris, France, A.D. 1867," reported that they had conferred with the Assembly Committee of Conference, and the said committees unanimously recommend that the Senate adhere to their amendments.

MESSAGE FROM THE GOVERNOR.

The following Message was received from the Governor:

EXECUTIVE DEPARTMENT, CARSON CITY, {
February 1st, 1867. }

To the Hon. Senate of Nevada:

I have this day approved Senate Bill No. 15, "An Act to repeal an Act entitled 'An Act to establish a Standard of Weights and Measures,' approved February 28, 1866."

Also, Senate Bill No. 64, "An Act to amend an Act entitled 'An Act to provide for the formation of Corporations for certain purposes,' approved March 10, 1865."

H. G. BLASDEL.

MESSAGES FROM THE ASSEMBLY.

The following Messages were received from the Assembly:

ASSEMBLY CHAMBER, CARSON CITY, }
February 1st, 1867.

To the Hon. the Senate:

I am instructed to transmit to your honorable body, Assembly Concurrent Resolution No. 32, relating to the State Prison, the same having passed the Assembly this day unanimously.

Also, Assembly Concurrent Resolution No. 33, relating to State Prison, the same having passed the Assembly this day unanimously.

I also return to your honorable body Senate Concurrent Resolution No. 92, the same having passed the Assembly this day unanimously.

Respectfully,

A. WHITFORD,
Clerk.

ASSEMBLY CHAMBER, CARSON CITY, }
February 1st, 1867.

To the Hon. the Senate:

I am instructed to transmit to your honorable body, for your consideration, the following Assembly Bills, viz:

No. 28, entitled "An Act to amend an Act entitled an Act to revise an Act entitled an Act to amend section 219 of an Act entitled an Act to regulate proceedings in Civil Cases in the Courts of Justice in the Territory of Nevada," approved November 29th, 1861, approved March 6th, 1865, and to amend section 243 of an Act entitled "An Act to regulate proceedings in Civil Cases in the Courts of Justice of the Territory of Nevada," approved November 29th, 1861, approved March 3d, 1866, the same having passed the Assembly yesterday. Yeas, 31; Nays, 3.

No. 38, entitled "An Act Authorizing the Issuance, Sale, and Exchange of certain State Bonds, levying a Tax to provide means for their Payment, and providing for the Surrender of Bonds now outstanding, and to repeal all Laws in conflict therewith," the same having passed the Assembly yesterday. Yeas, 28; Nays, 4.

I am also instructed to inform you that the Assembly on yesterday appointed Messrs. Horton, Prince, Potter and Dorsey, as a Conference Committee, to act with a like committee appointed by your honorable body, in relation to Assembly Bill No. 5, relating to Commissioners to the World's Fair, to be held at Paris, France, A.D. 1867.

Respectfully,

A. WHITFORD,
Clerk.

Mr. Hutchins in the chair.

Assembly Concurrent Resolution No. 32, entitled "An Act relating to the State Prison."

Read and referred to the Committee on State Prison.

Assembly Concurrent Resolution No. 33, relating to State Prison.

Read and Referred to Committee on State Prison.

INTRODUCTION OF BILLS.

Mr. Linn introduced Senate Bill No. 107, entitled "An Act in relation to County Clerks." Read first time; rules suspended; read second time by title, and referred to Committee on Counties and County Boundaries.

Mr. Linn, by leave and without previous notice, introduced Senate Bill No. 108, "An Act to repeal an Act entitled 'An Act in regard to Currency,' approved March 3d, 1866." Read first time; rules suspended; read second time by title, and referred to the Committee on Ways and Means.

Assembly Bill No. 28, "An Act to amend an Act entitled an Act to revise an Act to amend section 219 of an Act entitled an Act to regulate proceedings in Civil Cases in the Courts of Justice in the Territory of Nevada, approved November 29th, 1861, approved March 6th, 1865;" and to amend section 243 of an Act entitled "An Act to regulate proceedings in Civil Cases in the Courts of Justice of the Territory of Nevada, approved November 29th, 1861, approved March 3d, 1866." Read first time; rules suspended; read second time by title, and referred to the Committee on Judiciary.

Assembly Bill No. 38, "An Act authorizing the Issuance, Sale and Exchange of certain State Bonds; levying a Tax to provide means for their Payment, and providing for the Surrender of Bonds now outstanding, and to repeal all Laws in conflict therewith." Read first time; rules suspended; read second time by title, and laid on the table.

Mr. Welty, by leave and without previous notice, introduced Senate Bill No. 109, "An Act to provide for taking an Enumeration of the Inhabitants of this State during the year 1867." Read first time; rules suspended; read second time by title, and referred to Committee on State Affairs.

GENERAL FILE.

Senate Bill No. 11, "An Act to amend an Act entitled 'An Act to provide Revenue for the Support of the Government of the State of Nevada,' and the Acts amendatory thereof."

Read third time, by sections. The yeas and nays were called on the final passage of the bill, and recorded as follows:

YEAS—Messrs. Eastman, Edwards, Geller, Grey, Haines, Hastings, Hutchins, Linn, Meder, Monroe, Proctor, Stevenson, Sumner, Terry, and Welty—15.

NAYS—0.

So the bill passed.

Senate Bill No. 69, "An Act supplementary to an Act entitled 'An Act to create a Board of County Commissioners in the several Counties of this State, and to define their duties and powers,' approved March 8th, 1865."

On motion, the bill was referred to a Committee of one, with instructions to amend by striking out the word "therein" in the fifth line, and inserting the word "thereof." The President appointed Mr. Hastings.

Messages were received from the Assembly, and laid temporarily on the table.

On motion of Mr. Proctor, the Senate went into a Committee of the Whole for consideration of Senate Bill No. 44, which was the special order for this hour, viz: 12 o'clock M.

The Committee arose, and submitted the following Report:

Mr. President :

The Senate, in Committee of the Whole, have had under consideration Senate Bill No. 44, "An Act to provide for the Removal of Civil Officers, other than State Officers, for Malfeasance or Nonfeasance in Office;" which they report back with amendments, and recommend it be engrossed as amended.

Senate Bill No. 44, "An Act to provide for the Removal of Civil Officers other than State Officers, for Malfeasance or Nonfeasance in Office."

Ordered engrossed.

Mr. Hastings, Special Committee, to whom was referred Senate Bill No. 69, with instructions to amend, reported amendment made as instructed.

At 1 : 20 P.M., on motion of Mr. Proctor, the Senate took a recess until two o'clock.

IN SENATE.

The Senate met at 2 P.M., President *pro tem.* in the chair.

Roll called.

Quorum present.

Senate Bill No. 69, " An Act supplementary to an Act entitled 'An Act to create a Board of County Commissioners in the several Counties of this State, and to define their duties and powers,' approved March 8th, 1865."

Read third time by sections.

The yeas and nays were called on the final passage of the bill, and recorded as follows :

YEAS—Messrs. Eastman, Grey, Hastings, Hutchins, Linn, Mason, Monroe, Proctor, Stevenson, Sumner, Terry, and Welty—12.

NAYS—0.

So the bill passed.

Senate Bill No. 90, "An Act to regulate the business of Assaying within the State of Nevada."

Read third time by sections.

The yeas and nays were called on the final passage of the bill, and recorded as follows :

YEAS—Messrs. Eastman, Geller, Grey, Hastings, Hutchins, Linn, Mason, Meder, Monroe, Proctor, Stevenson, Sumner, Terry, and Welty—14.

NAYS—0.

So the bill passed.

The following Messages were received from the Assembly :

ASSEMBLY CHAMBER, CARSON CITY, }
February 4th, 1867. }

To the Hon. the Senate :

I am instructed to transmit to your honorable body, for your consideration, Assembly Bill No. 43, entitled " An Act to provide for properly taking care of the Indigent Insane of the State of Nevada, and to create a Fund for that purpose," the same having passed the Assembly this day.

YEAS—29.

NAYS—0.

Respectfully,

A. WHITFORD,
Clerk.

ASSEMBLY CHAMBER, CARSON CITY, }
February 4th, 1867. }

To the Hon. the Senate:

I am instructed to inform your honorable body, that the Assembly have this day concurred in the amendments of the Senate to Assembly Bill No. 5, entitled "An Act to create two additional Commissioners to represent the State of Nevada at the World's Fair, to be held at Paris, France, A.D. 1867."

Respectfully,

A. WHITFORD,
Clerk.

Mr Hastings, by leave, introduced the following resolution:

Resolved, That two hundred and forty copies of the Report of the State Mineralogist, for the year 1866, be set apart for the use of Adolph Sutro, to be used as he may deem advisable for the advancement of the Sutro Tunnel project.

Adopted.

Assembly Bill No. 43, "An Act to provide for the properly taking care of the Indigent Insane of the State of Nevada, and to create a fund for that purpose."

Read first time; rules suspended; read second time by title, and referred to the Committee on State Affairs.

At 2:15 P.M., on motion of Mr. Monroe, the Senate adjourned.

CHARLES A. SUMNER,
President *pro tem.*

Attest—B. C. BROWN,
Secretary.

———

IN SENATE—THIRTIETH DAY.

CARSON CITY, February 5th, 1867.

The Senate met pursuant to adjournment, Mr. Sumner, President *pro tem.,* in the chair.

Roll called.

Present—Messrs. Eastman, Edwards, Geller, Grey, Haines, Hastings, Hutchins, Linn, Mason, Meder, Monroe, Proctor, Stevenson, Sumner, Terry, and Welty—16.

Absent—Mr. Nelson—1.

Prayer by the Chaplain.

The Journal of the [Twenty-ninth] day was read and approved.

Mr. Terry offered a petition, from the citizens of Lander County, in relation to a Bill for the relief of James Leffingwell. Referred to the Lander County delegation.

REPORTS OF STANDING COMMITTEES.

Mr. Hastings reported that the Standing Committee on Engrossment had carefully compared the following entitled bill with the original, and found the same correctly engrossed, viz:

Senate Bill No. 44, "An Act to provide for the Removal of Civil Officers, other than State Officers, for Malfeasance or Nonfeasance in Office," and herewith report the same back to the Senate.

Mr. Welty, from the Committee on Judiciary, reported, that they had had under consideration Senate Bill No. 97, entitled "An Act defining the duties of the Attorney-General of the State of Nevada," had come to a favorable conclusion thereon, and had directed their chairman to so report to the Senate.

Mr. Sumner introduced the following report:

Mr. President:

The Committee on Ways and Means, to whom was referred Assembly Joint Resolution No. 22, relative to the appointment of Commissioners to negotiate for an extension of the time of payment of State bonds, beg leave to report the same back with a recommendation that it be indefinitely postponed.

Also, report substitute for Senate Bill No. 40, "An Act to repeal an Act of the Legislative Assembly of the Territory of Nevada, entitled 'An Act authorizing the Private Secretary of the Governor to demand and receive certain Fees,' approved Nov. 29th, 1861;" also, to repeal an Act of the Legislature of the State of Nevada, entitled "An Act in relation to the collection of Fees heretofore collected by the Governor's Private Secretary," approved Feb. 17th, 1866, with a recommendation that the same do pass.

Also, report from the majority of the Committee: Senate Bill No. 98, "An Act to amend an Act entitled 'An Act to provide Revenue for the Support of the Government of the State of Nevada,' approved March 9th, 1865," with the following amendment, and recommend its passage:

Amend section first by striking out the word "four" before the word "boarders," and inserting the word "six" in lieu thereof.

Mr. Welty, from Judiciary Committee, to which was referred Senate Bill No. 89, entitled "An Act relating to Criminal Prosecutions," reported that they had had the same under consideration, had come to a favorable conclusion thereon, had directed their chairman to report the same to the Senate with amendments, and recommend its passage as amended.

Mr. Meder, from Committee on State Affairs, reported that they had had under consideration Senate Bill No. 72, entitled "An Act to amend an Act entitled 'An Act relating to Officers, their qualifications, times of election, terms of office, official duties, resignations, removals, vacancies in office and the mode of supplying the same, misconduct in office, and to enforce official duty,' approved March 9th, 1866," and had found that the statute above named covers all points necessary in law, that further legislation is uncalled for, and that said bill ought not to pass.

Mr. Linn, Chairman Committee on Enrollment, reported that Senate Concurrent Resolution No. 92, "In relation to printing the Reports of Directors of State Library and State Librarian," had been carefully compared with the Engrossed Concurrent Resolution, as passed by the two Houses, found correctly enrolled, and that the same had this day been deposited with the Secretary of State.

MOTIONS AND RESOLUTIONS.

Mr. Edwards, by leave, introduced Senate Concurrent Resolution No. 111, in relation to printing 240 copies of Practice Act prepared by Hon. J. Neely Johnson. Read and referred to Committee on Printing.

Mr. Proctor offered the following resolution:

12

Resolved, That the Practice Act Commissioner be instructed to Senate, the draft of a Practice Act on Wednesday, Feb. 6th, 1867, M., or show cause why he does not so report.

Passed.

Mr. Haines gave notice that he would, on some future day, in entitled "An Act amendatory of 'An Act relating to Roads and Hi

Mr. Edwards, by leave, and without previous notice, introdu 112, "An Act concerning the Mining School Fund collected for t ending December 31st, 1866."
Read first time; rules suspended; read second time by title, and Committee on Counties and County Boundaries.
Mr. Welty, by leave and without previous notice, introduced S(113, "An Act to amend an Act entitled 'An Act to regulate Fees tion for official and other services in the State of Nevada,' approv 1865."
Read first time; rules suspended; read second time by title, an the Committee on State Affairs.

Senate Bill No. 44, "An Act to provide for the Removal of Civil than State officers for Malfeasance or Nonfeasance in Office."
On motion, the bill was referred to the Committee on Engross structions to amend by striking from the first line, the words ' thereof."
Mr. Hastings, from Committee on Engrossment, reported tl made to Senate Bill No. 44, as directed, and reported the sa Senate.
Read third time by sections.
The yeas and nays were called on the final passage of the bill, as follows:

YEAS—Messrs. Eastman, Edwards, Geller, Hastings, Hutchins, Meder, Terry, and Welty—10.
NAYS—Messrs. Grey, Proctor, Stevenson, and Sumner—4.

So the bill passed.
Assembly Joint Resolution No. 22, appointing a Commission for the extension of the time for payment of certain bonds therei third time and indefinitely postponed.
Substitute Senate Bill No. 40, "An Act to repeal an Act of t Assembly of the Territory of Nevada, entitled 'An Act authorizi Secretary of the Governor to demand and receive certain Fees,' vember 20th, 1861. Also, to repeal an Act of the Legislature Nevada entitled 'An Act in relation to the collection of certain l collected by the Governor's Private Secretary,' approved Februai Ordered engrossed.
Senate Bill No. 98, "An Act to amend an Act entitled 'An

Revenue for the Support of the Government of the State of Nevada,' approved March 19th, 1865," ordered engrossed.

On motion of Mr. Hutchins, the Senate went into a Committee of the Whole for the consideration of the General File, Mr. Hutchins in the chair.

The Committee rose, and submitted the following report:

Mr. President :

The Senate, in Committee of the Whole, have had under consideration Substitute Senate Bill No. 50, " An Act to provide for the selection of Lands granted by the United States to the State of Nevada," on which they report progress, and ask leave to sit again at 2 : 5 P.M.

Report adopted.

Mr. Sumner, by leave, and without previous notice, introduced Senate Joint Resolution No. 114, in relation to the annexation of Utah to the State of Nevada for State jurisdiction purposes.

Read first time; rules suspended; read second time by title, and referred to a Committee of the Whole.

At 1 : 35 P.M., on motion of Mr. Sumner, the Senate took a recess until 2 o'clock P.M.

IN SENATE.

The Senate met at 2 P.M., President *pro tem.* in the chair.

Roll called. Quorum present.

A Message was received from the Assembly, and laid temporarily on the table.

On motion, the Senate went into a Committee of the Whole for the further consideration of Substitute to Senate Bill No. 50, Mr. Hutchins in the chair.

The Committee rose, and submitted the following report:

Mr. President :

The Senate, in Committee of the Whole, have had under further consideration Substitute Senate Bill No. 50, "An Act to provide for the selection of Lands granted by the United States to the State of Nevada," which they report back with amendments, and recommend it be ordered engrossed.

Substitute Senate Bill No. 50, "An Act to provide for the selection of Lands granted by the United States to the State of Nevada." The amendments of the Committee of the Whole were adopted.

Mr. Meder moved to amend section four, line two, by inserting after the word " thereof " the words "not exceeding two hundred and fifty dollars per annum."

Carried, and the bill ordered engrossed.

MESSAGE FROM THE ASSEMBLY.

The following Message was received from the Assembly:

ASSEMBLY CHAMBER, CARSON CITY,
February 5th, 1867.

To the Honorable the Senate :

I am instructed to return to your honorable body Senate Bill No. 92, entitled " An Act authorizing a State Loan and levying a Tax to provide means for the Payment thereof," the same having passed the Assembly to-day with the following amendment:

Strike out all of section eight, and insert the following as a substitute in lieu thereof:

"Section 8. Nothing contained in this Act shall be so construed as to prevent the State Treasurer from exchanging the bonds issued by virtue of this Act for any of the outstanding bonds and interest or other evidence of indebtedness provided to be paid or retired by section first of this Act; but such exchange may be made at their coin value; *provided*, no exchange shall be made until after all the bonds issued under the Act of January 19th, 1866, shall have been first exchanged or taken up."

YEAS—21.
NAYS—11.

Respectfully,

A. WHITFORD,
Clerk.

The yeas and nays were called on the question of the Senate's concurring in Assembly amendments to Senate Bill No. 91, above referred to, and recorded as follows:

YEAS—Messrs. Eastman, Edwards, Geller, Grey, Haines, Hutchins, Linn, Meder, Monroe, Proctor, Stevenson, Sumner, Terry, and Welty—14.
NAYS—None.

So the Senate concurred in the amendments of the Assembly.

On motion of Mr. Hutchins, Senate Joint Resolution No. 114, in relation to the annexation of Utah to the State of Nevada for State jurisdiction purposes, was made the special order for Wednesday, February 6th, 1867, at 12 o'clock M.

At 4:40 P.M., on motion of Mr. Hutchins, the Senate adjourned.

CHARLES A. SUMNER,
President *pro tem.*

Attest—B. C. BROWN,
Secretary.

––––

IN SENATE—THIRTY-FIRST DAY.

CARSON CITY, February 6th, 1867.

The Senate met pursuant to adjournment, President in the chair.

Roll called.

Present—Messrs. Eastman, Edwards, Geller, Grey, Haines, Hastings, Hutchins, Linn, Mason, Meder, Monroe, Proctor, Stevenson, Sumner, Terry, and Welty—16.

Absent—Mr. Nelson—1.

Prayer by the Chaplain.

The Journal of the Thirtieth day was read and approved.

REPORTS OF STANDING COMMITTEES.

Mr. Hastings reported that the Standing Committee on Engrossment had carefully compared the following entitled bills with the originals, and found the same correctly engrossed, viz:

Substitute Senate Bill No. 40, "An Act to repeal an Act of the Legislative

Assembly of the Territory of Nevada, entitled 'An Act authorizing the Private Secretary of the Governor to demand and receive certain Fees,' approved November 29th, 1861." Also, to repeal an Act of the Legislature of the State of Nevada, entitled "An Act in relation to the collection of certain Fees heretofore collected by the Governor's Private Secretary, approved February 17th, 1866."

Also, Senate Bill No. 98, "An Act to amend an Act entitled 'An Act to provide Revenue for the Support of the Government of the State of Nevada,' approved March 9th, 1865."

And herewith report the same back to the Senate.

Mr. Monroe, Chairman of Committee on Claims, to which was referred Senate Bill No. 41, entitled "An Act providing for the payment of James Cochran, Sheriff of Trinity County, for certain Services and Expenses incurred," reported as follows :

Your Committee have had under consideration the claim of James Cochran, Sheriff of Trinity County, California, who seeks compensation for arresting one W. F. Broadwater, a fugitive from justice, charged with the crime of murder committed at Cortez, in the County of Lander, and State of Nevada. Also, have examined Senate Bill No. 41, introduced by Senator Welty, providing for the payment of $2,000 to said Sheriff Cochran, which bill was referred to Committee on Claims, January 17th.

Your Committee would respectfully report, that they have given the matter careful consideration, have had before them a number of witnesses and a large amount of written statements concerning the same.

We find, from the evidence, that Sheriff Cochran did arrest in Trinity County, California, the said fugitive from justice, W. F. Broadwater, and convey and deliver him to the Sheriff of Lander County, at Austin ; that he paid his own and prisoner's expenses during the journey ; that he received the sum of Four Hundred and Eighty-two Dollars in currency, from the County Commissioners of Lander County—the amount they settled upon as being a fair compensation for his services and expenses within the limits of the State of Nevada; that he borrowed of Judge Wells, the Private Secretary of the Governor, the sum of $190.$\frac{50}{100}$ in coin, to defray his expenses on the way to Austin, and which amount of money was agreed upon the part of Cochran to be returned to said Wells whenever the State should pay a reward for the capture of said Broadwater.

We find, from reliable evidence, that at the time the County Commissioners of Lander County paid the $482, he, the said Cochran, stated that $500 more, in currency, would fully compensate him for all services performed and expenses incurred outside of the State of Nevada, to wit: in California. Also, from the testimony before the Committee in relation to the amount that should be paid, (in all) the sum of one thousand dollars in currency was testified to as being an ample sum to compensate said Cochran for all services performed and expenses incurred by him. Also, the Committee have in their possession a communication from said Cochran stating that all he asks or expects from the State, is $1,000 curency, and $190.$\frac{50}{100}$ coin, to reimburse Judge Wells for the amount advanced by him. It seems that there has never been a reward offered or papers issued for the arrest of Broadwater while in California, but that Cochran arrested him on the ground of a Telegraphic Dispatch from the Sheriff of Lander County, stating that there was or would be a reward offered. This proved to be an error. Your Committee, though, are of the opinion that no advantage should be taken of the informality of the proceedings, but that justice should be done in awarding said Cochran a just and equitable compensation for services rendered and expenses incurred ; and would, therefore, recommend that Sections Nos. 1 and 2, in Senate Bill No. 41, be so amended as to strike out the words two thousand dollars, and insert the words one thousand dollars in lieu thereof.

Mr. Linn, Chairman Committee on Enrollment, reported that Senate Bill No. 92, entitled "An Act authorizing a Loan, and levying a Tax to provide means for the Payment thereof," had been carefully compared with the engrossed bill, as passed by the two Houses, found correctly enrolled, and that the same had this day been delivered to the Governor for his approval.

MOTIONS AND RESOLUTIONS.

Mr. Monroe introduced the following resolution:

Resolved, That Standing Rule Number 19 be so amended as to increase the number of Senators on the Standing Committee on Claims, from three to five.

Laid over for one day.
Mr. Proctor offered the following resolution:
Senate Concurrent Resolution No. 115, That Joint Rule No. 20 be and the same is hereby rescinded.
Rules suspended, and passed.
Mr. Hutchins moved that Senate Bill No. 97, defining the duties of the Attorney General, reported by the Judiciary Committee on February 5th, 1867, be referred back to the same Committee.
Carried.

MESSAGE FROM THE ASSEMBLY.

The following Message was received from the Assembly:

ASSEMBLY CHAMBER, CARSON CITY,
February 4th, 1867.

To the Honorable the Senate:

I am instructed to transmit to your honorable body, for your consideration, Assembly Bill No. 42, entitled "An Act to authorize District Judges in certain cases to sign Records and settle Statements," the same having passed the Assembly on the first day of February instant.

YEAS—27.
NAYS—0.

I also return to you Substitute Senate Bill No. 5, entitled "An Act providing for the release of Sureties on Official Bonds and Undertakings," the same having been amended as follows:
In Section 2, 17th line, strike out the word "Auditor," and insert the words "County Clerk;" also, in 18th line, same section, strike out the word "Auditor," and insert the words "County Clerk;" also, in 20th line, same section, strike out the word "Clerk," and insert the word "Auditor." In Section 3, 14th line, after the word "filed," and before the word "separate," insert "and serve." At the end of Section 3, add the following:
Whenever by operation of this Act, the functions of any Sheriff shall become suspended, it shall be the duty of the Clerk with whom the statement, as hereinbefore provided, shall have been filed, to notify the acting Coroner of the County, forthwith, of such suspension; and upon being so notified, such Coro-

ner shall succeed to all the powers, and discharge all the duties of Sheriff of his County, pending such suspension of the functions of the Sheriff.

Respectfully,

A. WHITFORD,

Clerk.

Assembly Bill No. 42, "An Act to authorize District Judges, in certain cases, to sign Records and settle Statements."

Read first time; rules suspended; read second time by title, and referred to Committee on Judiciary.

INTRODUCTION OF BILLS.

Mr. Hastings, by leave without previous notice, introduced Senate Bill No. 117, "An Act to amend an Act entitled 'An Act in relation to Public Highways.' "

Read first time; rules suspended: read second time by title, and referred to the Committee on Corporations.

On motion of Mr. Proctor, J. Craddock, " Messenger," was granted leave of absence for one day.

GENERAL FILE.

Substitute Senate Bill No. 40, " An Act to repeal an Act of the Legislative Assembly of the Territory of Nevada, entitled 'An Act authorizing the Private Secretary of the Governor to demand and receive certain Fees,' approved November 29th, 1861.' Also, to repeal an Act of the Legislature of the State of Nevada, entitled 'An Act in relation to the Collection of Certain Fees heretofore collected by the Governor's Private Secretary,' approved February 17th, 1866."

Read third time by sections. The yeas and nays were called on the final passage of the bill, and recorded as follows:

YEAS—Messrs. Eastman, Edwards, Geller, Haines, Hastings, Hutchins, Linn, Mason, Meder, Monroe, Proctor, Stevenson, Sumner, and Welty—14.

NAYS—0.

So the bill passed.

Senate Bill No. 98, "An Act to amend an Act entitled 'An Act to provide Revenue for the Support of the Government of the State of Nevada,' approved March 9th, 1865."

On motion of Mr. Haines, a Committee of one was appointed, with instructions to amend by striking out the word "six" before the word " boarders " wherever it occurs, and inserting the word "four."

Carried.

The President appointed Mr. Haines.

The Committee reported the amendment made as directed. The report was adopted.

Read third time by sections.

The yeas and nays were called on the final passage of the bill, and recorded as follows:

YEAS—Messrs. Eastman, Edwards, Haines, Meder, Stevenson, Terry, and Welty—7.

NAYS—Messrs. Geller, Hastings, Hutchins, Linn, Mason, Monroe, Proctor, and Sumner—8.

So the bill was lost.

On motion of Mr. Proctor, the Senate went into a Committee of the Whole, for the consideration of the General File, Mr. Proctor in the chair.

The Committee arose, and submitted the following report :

Mr. President :

The Senate, in Committee of the Whole, have had under consideration Senate Bill No. 89, "An Act relating to Criminal Prosecutions," which they report back, with amendments, and recommend that it be engrossed.

Also, Senate Joint Resolution No. 114, " In relation to the Annexation of Utah to the State of Nevada, for State Jurisdiction purposes," made special order for twelve b'clock, which they report back with amendments, and recommend that it be considered engrossed.

Senate Bill No. 89, " An Act relating to Criminal Prosecution."

The amendments of the Committee of the Whole adopted, and the bill ordered engrossed.

Senate Joint Resolution No. 114, " In relation to the Annexation of Utah to the State of Nevada, for State Jurisdiction purposes."

The amendments of the Committee of the Whole were adopted.

Mr. Welty moved to amend by striking out the words " each of " before the words " our Senators."

Carried.

Rules suspended, and the resolution considered engrossed.

The yeas and nays were called on its final passage, and recorded as follows :

YEAS—Messrs. Edwards, Geller, Grey, Haines, Hastings, Hutchins, Linn, Meder, Monroe, Proctor, Stevenson, Sumner, Terry, and Welty—14.

NAYS—Messrs. Eastman and Mason—2.

So the resolution passed.

The following communication was received from the Hon. J. Neely Johnson, Civil Practice Act Commissioner :

CARSON CITY, February 6th, 1867.

To the Legislature of the State of Nevada :

An Act of this State, approved March 1st, 1866, appointed me a Commissioner to prepare and report to the Legislature, at the present Session, a Civil Practice Act. In pursuance of that duty, I herewith transmit one hundred and seventy-three pages of manuscript, which embraces the first three hundred and sixty-one sections of this work. The residue, or greater part thereof, I will submit to the Legislature on to-morrow. and will make my final report within the present week.

In the absence of any direction contained in the Act referred to, I have deemed it proper to submit my reports to the Senate.

Respectfully,

J. NEELY JOHNSON.

Referred to Committee on Judiciary.

At one o'clock P.M., on motion of Mr. Edwards, the Senate adjourned.

JAMES S. SLINGERLAND,
President.

Attest—B. C. BROWN,
Secretary.

IN SENATE—THIRTY-SECOND DAY.

CARSON CITY, February 7th, 1867.

The Senate met pursuant to adjournment, President in the chair.
Roll called.
Present—Messrs. Doron, Eastman, Edwards, Geller, Grey, Haines, Hastings, Hutchins, Linn, Mason, Meder, Monroe, Proctor, Stevenson, Terry, and Welty—17.
Absent—Mr. Nelson—1.
Prayer by the Chaplain.
The Journal of the Thirty-first day was read and approved.

PRESENTATION OF PETITIONS.

Mr. Welty presented petition of residents of Lander County in relation to a Bill for the relief of James Leffingwell.
Read and referred to the Lander County delegation.

REPORTS OF STANDING COMMITTEES.

Mr. Hastings reported that the Standing Committee on Engrossment had carefully compared the following entitled bills with the originals, and found the same correctly engrossed, viz:
Substitute Senate Bill No. 50, "An Act to provide for the Selection of Lands granted by the United States to the State of Nevada."
Also, Senate Bill No. 89, "An Act relating to Criminal Prosecutions;" and herewith report the same back to the Senate.
Mr. Doron, Chairman of Committee on State Affairs, to which was referred Assembly Bill No. 43, entitled "An Act to provide for the properly taking care of the Indigent Insane of the State of Nevada, and to create a Fund for that purpose," reported that they had had the same under consideration, had come to a favorable conclusion thereon, had directed their chairman to report the same back to the Senate, and to recommend its passage.
Also, Senate Bill No. 113, entitled "An Act to amend an Act entitled 'An Act to regulate Fees and Compensation for official and other services in the State of Nevada,' approved March 9th, 1865," which they report back to the Senate with an amendment, and recommend its passage as amended.
Also, Senate Bill No. 101, entitled "An Act to amend an Act entitled 'An Act to regulate Fees and Compensation for official and other services in the State of Nevada,' approved March 9th, 1865," which they herewith report back to the Senate, with the recommendation that the same be indefinitely postponed.
Mr. Meder, from Committee on State Affairs, to which was referred Senate Bill No. 109, entitled "An Act to provide for taking an Enumeration of the Inhabitants of the State during the year 1867," reported that in view of the fact that the taking of such enumeration of inhabitants would be attended with a considerable outlay of money which the counties are so illy able to expend in the present depleted state of their treasuries; that the advantages of such enumeration would not compensate for the expense and trouble thus incurred; that the taking the census of the United States will so soon follow the proposed enumeration by counties, the Committee deem legislation on the subject inexpedient, and recommend the indefinite postponement of the bill.
Mr. Hutchins, from Committee of Conference, submitted the following report:

13

Mr. President:

The undersigned, Conference Committee on the subject matter of difference between the two Houses on Senate Joint Resolution memorializing the Commander of the Division of the Pacific to establish a fort at or near the junction of the Reese River Valley and Humboldt River, beg leave to report that they have met with a like Committee on the part of the House, and, after duly considering the matter of difference, come to the following conclusion: In the first resolution strike out all after the last word in line four, and insert in lieu thereof the following: "Humboldt River, at or near the junction of the Reese River Valley with the Humboldt River;" and recommend that said bill do pass as agreed upon.

FRED. HUTCHINS,
B. S. MASON.

JOHN S. MAYHUGH,
Chairman on the part of the House.

MOTIONS AND RESOLUTIONS.

The resolution introduced February 6th, 1867, by Mr. Monroe, in relation to amending Standing Rule No. 19, to increase the number of Senators on the Standing Committee on Claims from three to five, was adopted. The Chair appointed Messrs. Eastman and Stevenson as additional members of the Committee.

MESSAGES FROM THE ASSEMBLY.

The following Message was received from the Assembly.

ASSEMBLY CHAMBER, CARSON CITY,
February 5th, 1867.

To the Honorable the Senate:

I am instructed to transmit to your honorable body, for your consideration, Assembly Bill No. 44, entitled "An Act amendatory of and supplementary to an Act defining the time of commencing Civil Actions, approved November 21st, 1861, and to repeal Acts amendatory of said Acts," the same having passed the Assembly this day.

YEAS—25.
NAYS—4.

I also return to your honorable body the following Senate Bills, which passed the Assembly this day, viz:

No. 30, entitled "An Act in relation to and accepting the Lands granted to the State of Nevada by the Government of the United States."

YEAS—23.
NAYS—0.

No. 73, entitled "An Act to regulate and make effectual the Power of the Governor, the Justices of the Supreme Court, and Attorney General, to remit Fines and Forfeitures, to commute Punishment, and grant Pardons after Conviction."

YEAS—22.
NAYS—4.

No. 75, Substitute for Assembly Bill No. 7, entitled "An Act conferring jurisdiction on Justices' Courts concurrent with the District Court in actions to enforce Mechanics' Liens, wherein the amount does not exceed three hundred dollars exclusive of interest."

YEAS—25.
NAYS—0.

All of which is respectfully submitted.

A. WHITFORD,
Clerk.

Assembly Bill No. 44, entitled "An Act amendatory of and supplementary to an Act defining the time of commencing Civil Actions, approved November 21, 1861, and to repeal Acts amendatory of said Acts." Read first time; rules suspended; read second time by title, and referred to the Committee on Judiciary.

INTRODUCTION OF BILLS.

Mr. Sumner introduced Senate Bill No. 119, "An Act to Fund the Public Debt of Virginia City." Read first time; rules suspended; read second time by title, and referred to the Storey County delegation.
On motion of Mr. Sumner, 480 copies were ordered printed.

GENERAL FILE.

Substitute Senate Bill No. 50, "An Act to provide for the Selection of Lands granted by the United States to the State of Nevada." Read third time by sections; the yeas and nays were called on the final passage of the bill, and recorded as follows:

YEAS—Messrs. Doron, Eastman, Edwards, Geller, Grey, Hastings, Hutchins, Linn, Mason, Monroe, Proctor, Stevenson, Sumner—13.
NAYS—Messrs. Meder, Terry, and Welty—3.

So the bill passed.
On motion of Mr. Edwards, the title of the bill was amended as follows: after the words "for the selection," insert words "and sale."
Senate Bill No. 89, "An Act relating to Criminal Prosecutions." Read third time by sections; the yeas and nays were called on the final passage of the bill, and recorded as follows:

YEAS—Messrs. Eastman, Edwards, Geller, Grey, Hastings, Hutchins, Mason, Meder, Monroe, Proctor, Sumner, Terry, and Welty—14.
NAYS—Mr. Doron—1.

So the bill passed.
Mr. Welty moved to amend the title of the bill by inserting after the words "An Act," the words "to enable a defendant to testify in."
Carried.
On motion of Mr. Doron, the Senate went into a Committee of the Whole, President in the chair, for the consideration of the General File.
The Committee arose, and submitted the following report:

Mr. President:

The Senate in Committee of the Whole have had under consideration, Senate Bill No. 41, " An Act providing for the payment of James Cochran, Sheriff of Trinity County, California, for certain services rendered, and expenses incurred," which they report back with amendments, and recommend it be ordered engrossed.

A Message was received from the Governor, and laid temporarily on the table.

A Message was received from the Assembly, and laid temporarily on the table.

Senate Bill No. 44, " An Act providing for the Payment of James Cochran, Sheriff of Trinity County, California, for certain services rendered and expenses incurred." The amendment of the Committee of the Whole was adopted, and the bill ordered engrossed.

Mr. Hutchins was granted leave of absence until Monday, February 11th.

Mr. Linn, Chairman Committee on Enrollment, reported that Senate Bill No. 73, entitled " An Act to regulate and make effectual the Power of the Governor, the Justices of the Supreme Court and Attorney General, to remit Fines and Forfeitures, to commute Punishment and grant Pardons after Conviction," had been carefully compared with the engrossed bill as passed by the two Houses, found correctly enrolled, and that the same had this day been delivered to the Governor for his approval.

Also, Substitute for Assembly Bill No. 7, " An Act conferring Jurisdiction upon Justices' Courts concurrent with the District Court, in actions to enforce Mechanics' Liens wherein the amount does not exceed three hundred dollars, exclusive of interest," had been carefully compared with the engrossed bill, as passed by the two Houses, found correctly enrolled, and that the same had this day been delivered to the Governor for his approval.

At one twenty P.M., on motion of Mr. Meder, the Senate took a recess until 2 o'clock.

IN SENATE.

The Senate met at 2 o'clock P.M., Mr. Sumner, President *pro tem.*, in the chair.

Roll called.

Present—Messrs. Eastman, Edwards, Haines, Hastings, Linn, Meder, Monroe, Proctor, Stevenson, Sumner—10.

Absent—Messrs. Mason, Geller, Grey, Nelson, Terry, and Welty—6.

Mr. Proctor moved a call of the Senate.

Messrs. Mason, Terry, Geller, Grey, and Welty appearing, were excused.

On motion of Mr. Proctor, further proceedings under call of the House were dispensed with.

The following communication was received from Hon. J. Neely Johnson, Civil Practice Act Commissioner:

CARSON CITY, February 7th, 1867.

To the Legislature of the State of Nevada:

In further performance of duty, under the Act of this State, appointing a Commissioner to prepare and report to the Legislature a Civil Practice Act, I herewith submit manuscript pages one hundred and seventy-four to three hundred and fourteen, which embrace sections three hundred and sixty-two to six hundred and seventy-one, inclusive.

Further and final report will be submitted on or before Monday next.

Respectfully,

J. NEELY JOHNSON.

Mr. Monroe introduced Senate Concurrent Resolution No. 120, in relation to the Civil Practice Act. Read and made the special order for 12 o'clock M., on February 8th, 1867.

Mr. Doron introduced Substitute Senate Concurrent Resolution in relation to printing the Civil Practice Act. Read and made the special order for February 8th, 1867, at 12 o'clock M.

On motion of Mr. Doron, the Senate went into Committee of the Whole, for the consideration of the General File.

President in the chair.

The Committee arose, and submitted the following report:

Mr. President:

The Senate, in Committee of the Whole, have had under consideration Assembly bill No. 43, "An Act to provide for the properly taking care of the Indigent Insane of the State of Nevada, and to create a Fund for that purpose," which they report back, with amendments, and recommend its passage.

Also, Senate Bill No. 113, "An Act to amend an Act entitled ' An Act to regulate Fees and Compensation for Official and other Services in the State of Nevada,' approved March 9, 1865," which they report back, with amendments, and recommend it be ordered engrossed.

Also, Senate Bill No. 101, "An Act to amend an Act entitled ' An Act to regulate Fees and Compensation for Official and other Services in the State of Nevada,' approved March 9th, 1865," which they report back, and recommend the bill be made the special order for February 11th.

Also, Senate Bill No. 109, "An Act to provide for taking an Enumeration of the Inhabitants of this State during the year A.D. 1867," which they report back, and recommend it be indefinitely postponed.

Also, Senate Joint Resolution No. 18, memorializing the Commander of the Division of the Pacific to establish a fort at or near the junction of the North Fork with the Humboldt River, which they report back, and recommend the adoption of the amendment as proposed by the Committee of Conference.

Also, Senate Bill No. 72, "An Act to amend an Act entitled ' An Act relating to Officers, their qualification, times of election, terms of office, official duties, resignations, removals, vacancies in office, and the mode of supplying the same, misconduct in office, and to enforce official duty,' approved March 9th, 1866," which they report back, and recommend the bill be indefinitely postponed.

Assembly Bill No. 43, "An Act to provide for properly taking care of the Indigent Insane of the State of Nevada, and to create a Fund for that purpose." The amendments of the Committee of the Whole were adopted. Bill read third time by sections. The yeas and nays were called on its final passage, and recorded as follows:

YEAS—Messrs. Doron, Eastman, Edwards, Geller, Haines, Hastings, Linn, Mason, Meder, Monroe, Proctor, Stevenson, Sumner, Terry, and Welty—15.

NAYS—Mr. Grey—1.

So the bill passed.

Senate Bill No. 113, "An Act to amend an Act entitled ' An Act to regulate

Fees and Compensation for Official and other Services in the State of Nevada,'
approved March 9th, 1865." Amendments of the Committee of the Whole
adopted, and ordered engrossed.

Senate Bill No. 101, " An Act to amend an Act entitled ' An Act to regulate
Fees and Compensation for Official and other Services in the State of Nevada,'
approved March 9th, 1865." Made special order for Monday, February 11, at
12 o'clock M.

Senate Bill No. 109, " An Act to provide for taking an Enumeration of the
Inhabitants of this State during the year A.D. 1867." Indefinitely postponed.

Assembly Joint Resolution No. 18, memorializing the Commander of the
Division of the Pacific to establish a fort at or near the junction of the North
Fork with the Humboldt River. The report of the Committee of Conference
was adopted.

At 4:5 P.M., on motion of Mr. Grey, the Senate adjourned.

JAMES S. SLINGERLAND,
President.

Attest—

Secretary.

IN SENATE—THIRTY-THIRD DAY.

CARSON CITY, February 8th, 1867.

The Senate met pursuant to adjournment, Mr. Sumner, President *pro tem.*, in
the chair.

Roll called.

Present—Messrs. Doron, Eastman, Edwards, Geller, Grey, Haines, Hastings, Linn, Mason, Meder, Monroe, Proctor, Stevenson, Sumner, Terry, and
Welty—16.

Absent—Mr. Nelson—1.

Prayer by the Chaplain.

The Journal of the Thirty-second day was read and approved.

REPORTS OF COMMITTEES.

Mr. Hastings reported that the Standing Committee on Engrossment had
carefully compared the following entitled bills with the originals, and found the
same correctly engrossed, viz:

Senate Bill No. 41, "An Act providing for the payment of James Cochran,
Sheriff of Trinity County, for certain services rendered and expenses incurred."

Also, Senate Bill No. 113, "An Act to amend an Act entitled ' An Act to
regulate Fees and Compensation for Official and other Services in the State of
Nevada,' approved March 9, 1865," and herewith reports the same back to the
Senate.

Mr. Proctor, from the Standing Committee on Counties and County Boundaries, to which was referred Senate Bill No. 95, entitled "An Act conferring
further powers on the County Commissioners of the several counties of this
State, in reference to County Hospitals," report that they had had the same
under consideration ; had come to a favorable conclusion thereon ; had directed
their chairman to report the same to the Senate, without amendments, and recommend its passage.

Mr. Eastman, from the Committee on Corporations, to which was referred Senate Bill No. 117, entitled "An Act to amend an Act entitled 'An Act in relation to Public Highways,'" report that they had had the same under consideration, had come to a favorable conclusion thereon, and directed their chairman to report the same to the Senate, without amendments, and recommend its passage.

Mr. Welty, from the Committee on Judiciary, to which was referred Assembly Bill No. 28, "An Act to amend an Act entitled an Act to revise an Act entitled an Act to amend Section 219 of an Act entitled 'An Act to regulate Proceedings in Civil Cases in the Courts of Justice in the Territory of Nevada,' approved November 29th, 1861, approved March 6th, 1865," and to amend Section 243 of "An Act entitled 'An Act to regulate Proceedings in Civil Cases in the Courts of Justice of the Territory of Nevada,' approved November 29th, 1861, approved March 3d, 1866," reported that they had had the same under consideration, and recommend that it be indefinitely postponed.

Also, that Assembly Bill No. 42, entitled "An Act to authorize District Judges, in certain cases, to sign Records and settle Statements," be amended by striking out section five; and recommend its passage.

Also, Assembly Bill No. 27, entitled "An Act to amend an Act entitled 'An Act concerning District Attorneys,' approved March 11, 1865, approved February 26th, 1866," is reported back, without amendments, and recommend its passage.

Also, Senate Bill No. 35, entitled "An Act to amend an Act entitled 'An Act concerning Crimes and Punishments,'" which they report favorably, and recommend its passage.

MESSAGE FROM THE GOVERNOR.

The following Message from the Governor was received:

EXECUTIVE DEPARTMENT, CARSON CITY, }
February 7th, 1867. }

To the Honorable Senate of Nevada:

I approved, on the 6th instant, Senate bill No. 92, "An Act authorizing a State Loan, and levying a Tax to provide means for the payment thereof."

Also, Senate Bill No. 49, "An Act to change the County Seat of Nye County."

Though I approved the last named bill, I do not consider it a conclusive criterion by which to be governed in future cases of like character. I believe that, as a rule, county seats should be changed by the popular vote of the qualified electors of the county interested; but being convinced, that had the question of the change made by this Act been submitted to such vote, it would have been carried by a large majority, I have made this case an exception to the rule suggested, and for that reason approved the bill.

H. G. BLASDEL,
Governor.

MESSAGE FROM THE ASSEMBLY.

The following Message was received from the Assembly:

ASSEMBLY CHAMBER, CARSON CITY, }
February 6th, 1867. }

To the Honorable the Senate:

I am instructed to inform your honorable body that the Assembly have this day concurred in Senate amendments to Assembly Bill No. 2, entitled " An Act to repeal an Act entitled 'An Act concerning the Location and Possession of Mining Claims,' approved February 27th, 1866."

I also return to you Senate Bill No. 16, entitled " An Act to repeal an Act entitled ' An Act concerning the Location and Possession of Mining Claims,'" the same having been indefinitely postponed by the Assembly, this day.

Respectfully,

A. WHITFORD,
Clerk.

INTRODUCTION OF BILLS.

Mr. Proctor, by leave without previous notice, introduced Senate Bill No. 121, "An Act to regulate the Recording of Mining Claims."

Read first time; rules suspended; read second time by title, and referred to Committee on Mines and Mining.

Mr. Edwards, by leave without previous notice, introduced Senate Bill No. 122, "An Act to further prescribe Rules and Regulations for the execution of the Trust arising under the Act of Congress, approved May 23d, 1844, entitled ' An Act for the relief of Citizens of Towns upon Lands of the United States, under certain circumstances.' "

Read first time; rules suspended; read second time by title, and referred to the Ormsby and Washoe County delegations.

Mr. Stevenson, by leave without previous notice, introduced Senate Bill No. 123, "An Act amendatory of an Act entitled 'An Act relating to the Support of the Poor.'"

Read first time; rules suspended; read second time by title, and referred to Committee on Counties and County Boundaries.

GENERAL FILE.

Senate Bill No. 11, "An Act providing for the payment of James Cochran, Sheriff of Trinity County, for certain services rendered, and expenses incurred."

Read third time by sections. The yeas and nays were called on the final passage of the bill, and recorded as follows:

YEAS—Messrs. Eastman, Haines, Hastings, Linn, Mason, Monroe, Proctor, Terry, and Welty—9.

NAYS—Messrs. Doron, Grey, Meder, Stevenson, and Sumner—5.

So the bill passed. "Mr. Edwards not voting."

Senate Bill No. 113, " An Act to amend an Act entitled ' An Act to regulate Fees and Compensation for Official and other Services in the State of Nevada,' approved *May* [March] 9th, 1865."

Read third time by sections. The yeas and nays were called on the final passage of the bill, and recorded as follows:

YEAS—Messrs. Doron, Eastman, Edwards, Grey, Haines, Hastings, Linn, Mason, Meder, Monroe, Proctor, Stevenson, Sumner, Terry, and Welty—15.

NAYS—0.

So the bill passed.

Senate Bill No. 95, "An Act conferring further powers on the County Commissioners of the several Counties of this State, in reference to County Hospitals."

Ordered engrossed.

Assembly Bill No. 28, "An Act to amend an Act entitled 'An Act to revise an Act entitled "An Act to amend Section 219 of an Act entitled 'An Act to regulate Proceedings in Civil Cases in the Courts of Justice in the Territory in Nevada, approved November 29th, 1861,' approved March 6th, 1865;'" and to amend Section 243 of an Act entitled 'An Act to regulate Proceedings in Civil Cases in the Courts of Justice of the Territory of Nevada, approved November 29th, 1861,' March 3d, 1866."

Indefinitely postponed.

Assembly Bill No. 42, "An Act to authorize District Judges, in certain cases, to sign Records and settle Statements."

The amendment of the Judiciary Committee was adopted.

Read third time by sections. The yeas and nays were called, on the final passage of the bill, and recorded as follows:

YEAS—Messrs. Eastman, Geller, Grey, Haines, Hastings, Linn, Mason, Meder, Monroe, Proctor, Stevenson, Sumner, Terry, and Welty—14.

NAYS—Mr. Doron—1.

So the bill passed.

Mr. Edwards, by leave, offered the following resolution:

Resolved, That the Controller of State, at his earliest convenience, be and he is hereby requested to furnish to the Senate a certified copy of the last settlement made by his office, with the Auditor and Treasurer of Humboldt County.

Adopted.

Assembly Bill No. 27, "An Act to amend an Act entitled 'An Act concerning District Attorneys, approved March 11th, 1865,' approved February 26th, 1866."

On motion of Mr. Hastings, the above bill was made the special order for Monday, February 11th, in Committee of the Whole, at 12 o'clock M.

Senate Bill No. 35, "An Act to amend an Act entitled 'An Act concerning Crimes and Punishments.'"

Ordered engrossed.

Senate Bill No. 117, "An Act to amend an Act entitled 'An Act in relation to Public Highways.'"

Ordered engrossed.

A Message was received from the Assembly, and laid temporarily on the table.

Senate Bill No. 72, "An Act to amend an Act entitled 'An Act relating to Officers, their qualifications, times of election, terms of office, official duties, resignations, removals, vacancies in office, and the mode of supplying the same, misconduct in office, and to enforce official duty,' approved March 9th, 1866."

Indefinitely postponed.

Senate Concurrent Resolution No. 120, also Substitute Senate Concurrent Resolution No. 120, being special order, set for 12 o'clock M., was, on motion, postponed until 2 o'clock P.M.

A Message was received from the Governor, and laid temporarily on the table.

Substitute Senate Bill No. 5, "An Act providing for the Release of Sureties on Official Bonds and Undertakings."

Mr. Welty moved that the Assembly amendments be concurred in.

The yeas and nays were called, on concurrence with the Assembly amendments, and recorded as follows:

YEAS—Messrs. Doron, Eastman, Edwards, Geller, Grey, Haines, Hastings, Linn, Mason, Meder, Monroe, Proctor, Stevenson, Sumner, and Welty—15.

NAYS—0.

So the Senate concurred in the amendments.

On motion of Mr. Welty, Hon. J. Neely Johnson was invited to address the Senate on the subject of the Civil Practice Act.

Mr. Edwards moved that 100 copies of the Report of Hon. J. Neely Johnson, Civil Practice Act Commissioner, be ordered printed.

Carried.

Senate Concurrent Resolution No. 120, which was made the special order for 2 o'clock, was on motion of Mr. Sumner, postponed for ten minutes.

Mr. Terry was granted leave of absence for two days.

Mr. Sumner moved that the Commissioner of Civil Practice Act be authorized and instructed to furnish the Chairman of Committee on Public Printing with headings to the several subdivisions of the Code, which he has submitted to this Senate.

Carried.

At 2:15 P.M., on motion of Mr. Mason, the Senate adjourned until Monday, February 11th, at 11 o'clock A.M.

CHARLES A. SUMNER,
President [*pro tem.*]

Attest—B. C. BROWN,
Secretary.

IN SENATE—THIRTY-SIXTH DAY.

CARSON CITY, February 11th, 1867.

The Senate met pursuant to adjournment, President in the chair.

Roll called.

Present—Messrs. Doron, Eastman, Edwards, Geller, Grey, Haines, Hastings, Hutchins, Linn, Mason, Meder, Monroe, Nelson, Proctor, Stevenson, Terry, and Welty—17.

Absent—Mr. Sumner—1.

Prayer by the Chaplain.

The Journal of the Thirty-third day was read and approved.

A Message was received from the Assembly, and laid temporarily on the table.

On motion of Mr. Grey, Mr. Sumner was granted leave of absence for one day.

REPORTS OF COMMITTEES.

Mr. Hastings reported that the Standing Committee on Engrossment had carefully compared the following entitled bills with the original, and found the same correctly engrossed, viz:

Senate Bill No. 95, "An Act conferring further powers on the County Commissioners of the several Counties of this State in reference to County Hospitals."

Also, Senate Bill No. 117, "An Act to amend an Act entitled 'An Act in relation to Public Highways,' approved March 9th, 1866."

Also, Senate Bill No. 35, "An Act to amend an Act concerning Crimes and Punishments;" and herewith reports the same back to the Senate.

Mr. Linn, Chairman Committee on Enrollment, reported that Senate Bill No. 89, entitled "An Act to enable a Defendant to testify in Criminal Prosecutions;" Substitute Senate Bill No. 5, entitled "An Act providing for the Release of Sureties on Official Bonds and Undertakings;" Senate Bill No. 30, "An Act in relation to and accepting the Lands granted to the State of Nevada by the Government of the United States;" also, Senate Joint Resolution No. 18, memorializing the Commander of the Pacific to establish a fort at or near the junction of the Reese River Valley with the Humboldt River—had been carefully compared with the engrossed bills as passed by the two Houses, found correctly engrossed, and that the same had this day been delivered to the Governor for his approval.

MESSAGE FROM THE GOVERNOR.

The following Message was received from the Governor:

EXECUTIVE DEPARTMENT, }
Carson City, February 8th, 1867. }

To the Hon. Senate of Nevada:

I have this day approved Senate Bill No. 78, "An Act to regulate and make effectual the Power of Governor, Justices of the Supreme Court, and Attorney General, to remit Fines and Forfeitures, commute Punishments, and grant Pardons after Conviction."

Also, Senate Bill No. 75, "An Act conferring Jurisdiction upon Justices' Courts, concurrent with the District Court, in actions to enforce Mechanics' Liens."

H. G. BLASDEL,
Governor.

MESSAGES FROM THE ASSEMBLY.

The following Messages were received from the Assembly:

ASSEMBLY CHAMBER, CARSON CITY, }
February 7th, 1867. }

To the Hon. the Senate:

I am instructed to transmit to your honorable body for your consideration, Assembly Bill No. 60, entitled "An Act to amend an Act entitled 'An Act relating to Sheriffs,' approved November 28th, 1861," the same having passed the Assembly this day.

YEAS—28.
NAYS—0.

I also return to you Senate Bill No. 44, entitled "An Act to provide for the removal of Civil Officers, other than State Officers, for Malfeasance or Nonfeasance in Office," the House having refused to pass the same this day.

YEAS—9.
NAYS—23.

Also, return Senate Bill No 31, entitled "An Act concerning the office of Public Administrator," the same having passed the House this day, amended as follows:

In section one, third line, after the word "Coroner," and before the word "in," the following words were inserted: " and shall also act as Sheriff."

Also, in same section, same line, after the word "County," and before the word "each," the words "Whenever by operation of law the right of such Sheriff to discharge the duties of his office, shall be suspended," were inserted.

Also, in section two, eleventh line, after the word "relation," and before the word "for," the following words were inserted: "It shall be within the power and discretion of the Court or Judge to grant letters of administration, after failure of relatives as aforesaid, to any creditor of the estate whose claim shall be of such undisputed character and magnitude as shall give evidence to the Court that such letters are not sought for any other purpose than the faithful and economical administration of the estate."

I am also instructed to inform you that the Assembly adopted the Report of the Conference Committee appointed in relation to the differences between the two Houses upon the Joint Resolution memorializing the Commander of the Division of the Pacific, etc.

All of which is respectfully submitted.

A. WHITFORD,
Clerk.

ASSEMBLY CHAMBER, CARSON CITY, }
February 9th, 1867. }

To the Hon. the Senate:

I am instructed to transmit to your honorable body for your consideration, the following Assembly Bills, which have passed the House this day, viz:

No. 51, "An Act for the Incorporation of Hospitals and Asylums in certain cases."

No. 58, entitled "An Act to amend Section 24 of an Act to amend an Act entitled 'An Act to regulate proceedings in the Courts of Justice in this Territory,' approved February 20th, 1864."

No. 56, entitled "An Act [to amend an Act] entitled 'An Act in relation to the Compensation of Members of the Legislature and State Officers,' approved January 16th, 1865."

No. 63, entitled "An Act amendatory of and supplementary to an Act of the Legislative Assembly of the Territory of Nevada, entitled 'An Act to Incorporate the City of Austin, approved February 20th, 1864,' approved March 8th, 1865."

I also return to you Senate Bill No. 90, entitled "An Act to regulate the business of Assaying within the State of Nevada," the same having passed the House, Feb. 8, without amendment.

Also, Senate Bill No. 89, entitled "An Act to enable a Defendant to testify in Criminal Proceedings," the same having passed the House this day without amendment.

Also, Senate Concurrent Resolution, No. 115, "Suspending Joint Rule No. 20," which passed the House this day unanimously.

I am also instructed to inform you that the House have this day refused to concur in Senate amendments to A. B. No. 43, entitled " An Act to provide for taking care of the Indigent Insane of the State of Nevada, and to create a Fund for that purpose," and request that the Senate do recede from their amendments.

I am also instructed to inform you that the House have this day refused to receive A. B. from the Senate which have been amended by you, unless the amendments are attached in the form of Riders, and not interlineated.

All of which is respectfully submitted.

A. WHITFORD,
Clerk.

Senate Bill No. 31, " Concerning the office of Public Administrator."

The yeas and nays were called on concurring in the first Assembly amendment to the bill, and recorded as follows:

YEAS—Messrs. Doron, Eastman, Edwards, Geller, Grey, Haines, Hastings, Hutchins, Linn, Mason, Meder, Monroe, Nelson, Proctor, Stevenson, Terry, and Welty—16.
NAYS—0.

So the Senate concurred.

The yeas and nays were called on the second amendment to the bill, and recorded as follows:

YEAS—0.
NAYS—Messrs. Doron, Eastman, Edwards, Geller, Grey, Haines, Hastings, Hutchins, Linn, Mason, Meder, Monroe, Nelson, Stevenson, Proctor, Terry, and Welty—16.

So the Senate refused to concur.

On motion, a Committee of Conference was appointed by the President, consisting of Messrs Edwards, Doron, and Mason.

Assembly Bill No. 60, " An Act to amend an Act entitled ' An Act relating to Sheriffs,' approved November 28th, 1861."

Read first time; rules suspended; read second time by title, and referred to the Committee on Corporations.

Assembly Bill No. 51, "An Act for the Incorporation of Hospitals and Asylums in certain cases."

Read first time; rules suspended; read second time by title, and referred to Committee on Corporations.

Assembly Bill No. 58, "An Act to amend Section 21 of an Act to amend an Act entitled 'An Act to regulate proceedings in the Courts of Justice in the Territory of Nevada,' approved February 20th, 1864."

Read first time; rules suspended; read second time by title, and referred to Committee on Judiciary.

Assembly Bill No. 56, "An Act to amend an Act entitled 'An Act in relation to the Compensation of the Legislative and State Officers," approved January 16th, 1865."

Read first time; rules suspended; read second time by title, and referred to the Committee on State Affairs.

Assembly Bill No. 63, "An Act amendatory of an Act entitled 'An Act amendatory of and supplementary to an Act of the Legislative Assembly of the Territory of Nevada, entitled an Act to Incorporate the City of Austin,' approved February 20th, 1864, approved March 8th, 1865."

Read first time; rules suspended; read second time by title, and referred to Lander County delegation.

Assembly Bill No. 43, entitled "An Act to provide for properly taking care of the Indigent Insane of the State of Nevada, and to create a· Fund for that purpose."

Mr. Doron moved that the Secretary be instructed to request the Assembly to return Assembly Bill No. 43, "An Act to provide for properly taking care of the Indigent Insane of the State of Nevada, and to create a Fund for that purpose," for its further consideration.

Carried.

Mr. Welty offered the following resolution:

Resolved, That the Secretary be authorized to request the Assembly to return "A. B.," referred to in the Assembly Message, dated February 9th, 1856, to the end that the same may be put in form, agreeably to the Assembly Message.

Adopted unanimously.

Mr. Mason, by leave, submitted the following report:

Mr. Mason, from the Standing Committee on Federal Relations, to which was referred Assembly Memorial to Congress, asking a reduction of freight and fare upon the Central Pacific Railroad, reports they have had the same under further consideration, and recommend the adoption of the resolution. The majority of your Committee have ever been favorable and warm in their advocacy of the Pacific Railroad, and equally favorable to some other railroad to connect our State with the navigable waters of California; believing that a multiplicity of improvements of this character act as guards against monopolies, and protection to the people. In the great controversies of the past between the power and the people, and chartered monopolies—of equality against privilege—experience has proven that there is danger in granting too extensive legislative favors to such monopolies. Believing that President Jackson, whose patriotism is undoubted, spoke wisely and well when he said, "It is not in a splendid Government supported by powerful monopolies that the people find happiness, or their liberties protection, but in a plain system, void of pomp, granting equal favors to all, and special privileges to none; dispensing its blessings, like the dews of Heaven, unseen, unfelt, save in the richness of the verdure it is seen to produce." Considering the fact, that the General Government has poured the waters of nurture so bountiful, and to an unparalleled extent, under the *just* pretext that it was a "war measure," the unusual rates of fare and freight exacted, seem to the minds of your Committee not only ungrateful but unjust. This great monopoly already shows the danger by showing favoritism to friends in its attempts to exercise influence upon *even* the primary elections in our State; we fear its power, and ask every check that strict justice may warrant to shield with vigilance the liberties of the people in their sovereign power. When we consider, again, that the present age has been, *perhaps* styled *unjustly,* "An era of universal barter," that nearly every politician "has his price," that nearly all are bent by an undivided aim upon schemes of gain and personal aggrandizement,—if this "leaven of a sordid selfishness" does run through all the channels of society, infecting the whole lump, is not this vast concentration of power alarming? And your Committee think they are, and demand the candid consideration of Senators on this floor. All of which is most respectfully submitted.

B. S. MASON,
W. G. MONROE.

INTRODUCTION OF BILLS.

Mr. Proctor, by leave, without previous notice, introduced Senate Concurrent Resolution No. 129, in relation to printing the Civil Practice Act.

Read and passed.

Mr. Grey, by leave, without previous notice, introduced Senate Bill No. 130, " An Act for the organization of a Board of Education in Counties that polled three thousand votes, or more, at the General Election of the State of Nevada, November, A.D. 1866, or that may hereafter at any general election cast that number of votes, and amendatory of, and supplemental to an Act to provide for the Maintenance and Support of Public Schools, approved March 20th, 1865."

Read first time; rules suspended; read second time by title, and referred to Committee on Education and Storey County delegation.

Mr. Haines, by leave without previous notice, introduced Senate Bill No. 131, " An Act to prohibit the carrying of Concealed Weapons."

Read first time; rules suspended; read second time by title, and referred to Committee on Public Morals.

Mr. Welty, by leave without previous notice, introduced Senate Bill No. 132, " An Act concerning Crimes against the Revenue Laws of this State, and for the punishment thereof."

Read first time; rules suspended; read second time by title, and referred to Committee on Ways and Means.

Mr. Linn, by leave without previous notice, introduced Senate Bill No. 133, " An Act to repeal an Act entitled ' An Act to provide for establishing and maintaining a Mining School, and create the office of State Mineralogist,' approved March 9th, 1866."

Read first time; rules suspended; read second time by title, and referred to Committee on Mines and Mining.

Mr. Edwards, by leave without previous notice, introduced Senate Bill No. 134, " An Act to provide for the Recording of certain papers affecting the Titles or Claims of Real Property."

Read first time; rules suspended; read second time by title, and referred to Committee on Judiciary.

On motion of Mr. Haines, the Senate went into a Committee of the Whole, Mr. Hutchins in the chair, for the consideration of the special orders of the hour, 12 o'clock M.

The Committee rose, and submitted the following report:

Mr. President:

The Senate in Committee of the Whole have had under consideration Assembly Bill No. 27, " An Act to amend an Act entitled ' An Act concerning District Attorneys,' approved March 11th, 1865, approved February 26th, 1866," have made amendments thereto, and recommend its passage as amended.

Also, Senate Concurrent Resolution No. 120, relative to printing Civil Practice Act, which they recommend be laid on the table.

Also, Substitute Senate Concurrent Resolution No. 120, in relation to printing Civil Practice Act, which they recommend be laid on the table.

GENERAL FILE.

Senate Concurrent Resolution No. 120, relative to printing the Civil Practice Act.

Laid on the table.

Substitute Senate Concurrent Resolution No. 120, in relation to printing Civil Practice Act.

Laid on the table.

Senate Bill No. 95, "An Act conferring farther Powers on the County Commissioners of the several Counties of this State in reference to County Hospitals." Read third time by sections; the yeas and nays were called on the final passage of the bill, and recorded as follows:

YEAS—Messrs. Hastings, Mason, Proctor, and Terry—4.

NAYS—Messrs. Doron, Eastman, Geller, Grey, Hutchins, Meder, Monroe, Nelson, Stevenson, and Welty—10.

So the bill did not pass.

Senate Bill No. 117, "An Act to amend an Act entitled 'An Act in relation to Public Highways,' approved March 9th, 1866." Read third time by sections; the yeas and nays were called on the final passage of the bill, and recorded as follows:

YEAS—Messrs. Doron, Eastman, Geller, Grey, Hastings, Hutchins, Mason, Meder, Monroe, Nelson, Proctor, Stevenson, Terry, and Welty—14.

NAYS—0.

So the bill passed.

Senate Bill No. 35, "An Act to amend an Act entitled 'An Act concerning Crimes and Punishments." Read third time by sections; the yeas and nays were called on the final passage of the bill, and recorded as follows:

YEAS—Messrs. Doron, Eastman, Geller, Grey, Haines, Hastings, Hutchins, Linn, Mason, Meder, Monroe, Nelson, Proctor, Stevenson, Terry, and Welty —16.

NAYS—0.

So the bill passed.

On motion of Mr. Welty, at 2:40 P.M. the Senate adjourned.

JAMES S. SLINGERLAND,
President.

Attest—B. C. BROWN,
Secretary.

IN SENATE—THIRTY-SEVENTH DAY.

CARSON CITY, February 12th, 1867.

The Senate met pursuant to adjournment, the President in the chair.

Roll called.

Present—Messrs. Doron, Eastman, Edwards, Geller, Grey, Haines, Hastings, Hutchins, Linn, Mason, Meder, Monroe, Nelson, Proctor, Stevenson, Sumner, Terry, and Welty—18.

Absent—0.

Prayer by the Chaplain.

The Journal of the Thirty-sixth day was read and approved.
A Message was received from the Assembly, and laid temporarily on the table.

REPORTS OF COMMITTEES.

Mr. Monroe, Chairman of Committee on Claims, submitted the following report :

Mr. President :
Your Committee on Claims have had presented to them (through the report of the Secretary of State to the Legislature) the claim of John S. Childs, who seeks to obtain $3,450 as compensation for performing the services of Probate and District or County Judge of the County of Carson, Utah Territory, from August 1st, 1858, to the 30th day of July, 1861.

This claim is a peculiar one, and has required a good deal of examination for the Committee to come to a satisfactory conclusion. We find that said Childs held the office of Probate Judge of the County of Carson, Territory of Utah, under authority of commissions from Governor Cumming, from August 1st, 1858, to July 30th, 1861, and that he held Court regularly and performed the duties pertaining both to the Probate and District or County Courts during this time, and that from the evidence, he has received no pay as salary for such service. Your Committee also find that the records made in his Court are of some present value to the State of Nevada. Said Childs presented to the Committee as evidence, warrants issued to him out of the County Court of Carson County, dated in June and July, 1861, amounting to the sum of $3,450, and accepted by the County Treasurer of Carson County, but not paid for want of funds. We find that there has never been a law passed, either by the Territory of Nevada or the State of Nevada, assuming the indebtedness of Carson County, (then a portion of Utah Territory) but that in the exceptional case of John L. Blackburn, the Territorial Legislature of Nevada, under date of October 31st, 1861, passed an Act compensating him and others for services performed in part in Carson City [County] and while it was in Utah Territory, but the following words, being Section 4, are found in this Act:

" All unpaid warrants heretofore issued to John L. Blackburn, by a body styling themselves the County Court of Carson County, are hereby declared void, and the Auditor shall not issue the bonds provided in this Act, until all such unpaid warrants issued by a body styling themselves the County Court as aforesaid, shall have been filed in his office."

We are unable to find any law fixing the salary of the office held by said Childs, and are therefore unable to determine that the warrants were issued by competent authority. We also find that in the laws of the Territorial Legislature of 1861, is an Act approved November 29th, entitled " An Act creating the office of and defining the duties of Territorial Auditor." The following language occurs in Section 7 :

" All persons having claims against the Territory, shall exhibit the same with the evidence in support thereof, to the Auditor, to be audited, settled and allowed within two years after such claims shall occur, and not afterwards."

This claim was presented to the Board of State Examiners, and refused on the ground of no law being in existence allowing the payment of claims arising in the Territory of Utah, and also we find that it has been presented to a former Legislature, and by them disallowed.

While your Committee find that Childs was duly commissioned, and discharged the duties of the office of Judge in Carson County, and that the records of his Court are of value to the State, yet we can find no authority in law or positive precedent to warrant us in recommending the relief asked for, and for the following reasons :

1st. There is no law authorizing the Territory of Nevada or State to assume the indebtedness of Carson County, Territory of Utah.

2d. There was no law fixing the salary of the Judge of Carson County.

3d. There is nothing to show that the County Court of Carson had the authority to issue warrants to pay the salary of officers of said Court.

4th. The precedent in the case of Blackburn, coupled with the language used, would convey the impression that the Legislature at that day regarded the County Court of Carson County as "self styled," and not real, and

5th. The Statute of Limitations passed in 1861, cuts off the relief asked for.

We are therefore of the opinion that the claim should not be allowed, but would suggest (if proper to do so here) that said Childs might be entitled to a reasonable compensation for services rendered from the organization of the Territory of Nevada to the time of relinquishing his office, and that if a bill be introduced to that effect it will meet with some favor from at least a portion of your Committee. All of which is respectfully submitted.

Mr. Proctor reported that the Committee on Counties and County Boundaries had had under consideration Senate Bill No. 102, entitled "An Act to transfer certain Moneys in the hands of the County Treasurers of several Counties of this State to the School Fund of the several Counties."

Also, Senate Bill No. 105, "An Act concerning the Mining School Fund, collected for the year ending December 31st, 1866," and had directed their chairman to report a substitute for the two bills.

Mr. Monroe, from Standing Committee on Claims, to which was referred Senate Bill No. 94, entitled "An Act to Compensate J. F. Hatch, for services in the State Library," report that they have had the same under advisement, and recommend that it do pass without amendments.

Mr. Welty, from the Committee on Judiciary, to which was referred Senate Bill No. 97, entitled "An Act defining the Duties of the Attorney General of the State of Nevada," report that they have had the same under consideration; had come to a favorable conclusion thereon, and had directed their chairman to report the same to the Senate with the following amendments, and to recommend its passage as amended :

Sec. 1, 5th line after the word State, insert "exceeding sixty consecutive days."

Sec. 4, on 1st line, strike out all except "The Attorney General"; strike out lines 2, 3, 4, 5, 6, 7, 8, 9, 10 and 11, and counting from bottom of section, lines 1, 2, 3, 4, and all of 5, except the word "sentence."

Sec. 5. Strike out lines 9, 10, 11 and 12.

Sec. 6. Line 2, after the word "General," insert as follows: "In actions to which the State is a party in interest ;" also strike out balance of line 2 ; all of line 3, and the words "service or," on line 4, and insert the word "and," in lieu of the word "or," previous to the word "when ;" also, as a substitute for Section 6, the following:

Sec. 6. Whenever the Governor shall direct, or in the opinion of the Attorney General, to protect and secure the interests of the State it is necessary that a suit be commenced or defended in any Court, it is hereby made the duty of the Attorney General to commence such action or make such defense, and such actions may be instituted in any District Court in the State, or in any Justice's Court of the proper county.

Mr. Stevenson, from the Standing Committee on Mines and Mining, to which was referred Senate Bill No. 121, entitled "An Act to regulate the recording of Mining Claims," reported that they had had the same under consideration ; had amended the same by striking out all after Section 2 of said bill, and had directed their chairman to report the same to the Senate, and to recommend its passage as amended.

Mr. Linn, Chairman Committee on Enrollment, reported that Senate Bill No. 90, entitled "An Act to Regulate the business of Assaying within the State of Nevada;" also, Concurrent Resolution No. 115, "Suspending Joint Rule No. 20," had been carefully compared with the engrossed Bill and Resolution, as passed by the two Houses, found correctly enrolled, and that the same had this day (the Bill) been delivered to the Governor for his approval, (the Resolution) deposited with the Secretary of State.

MOTIONS AND RESOLUTIONS.

Mr. Sumner offered the following resolution:

Resolved, That the Sergeant-at-Arms of the Senate be, and he is hereby instructed to furnish each member of the Senate and Assembly, and their official reporters, with one copy each of the Code of Civil Procedure, and to furnish the Secretary of the Senate with twenty copies—the latter to be forwarded by the Secretary (one each) to the Governor, Supreme Judges, District Judges, and newspaper offices in this State; the balance of the printed copies of the Code to be by the Sergeant-at-Arms kept for distribution as the Senate may hereafter determine.

Adopted.

Resolved, That one copy each of the Code of Civil Procedure be, by the Sergeant-at-Arms, forwarded to the following named law firms of Virginia City: Hillyer & Whitman, Williams & Bixler, Aldrich & DeLong, Crittenden & Sunderland, and Seeley & Campbell.

Adopted.

Also, by Mr. Grey: That two hundred and forty copies of Senate Bill No. 130, in relation to a Board of Education in certain counties, be ordered printed. Adopted.

MESSAGE FROM THE ASSEMBLY.

The following Message was received from the Assembly:

ASSEMBLY CHAMBER, CARSON CITY, }
February 11th, 1867. }

To the Honorable the Senate:

I am instructed to transmit to your honorable body, for your consideration, the following Assembly Bills, which passed the House this day, viz:

No. 57, entitled "An Act to amend an Act entitled 'An Act to provide Revenue for the Support of the Government of the State of Nevada,' approved ——."

. No. 49, entitled "An Act for the Protection of Proprietors of Hotels and Lodging-houses."

I also return Senate Bill No. 69, "An Act supplementary to an Act entitled 'An Act to create a Board of County Commissioners in the several Counties of this State, and to define their Duties and Powers,' approved March 5, 1866."

Substitute Senate Bill No. 40, "An Act to repeal an Act of the Legislative

Assembly of the Territory of Nevada, entitled 'An Act authorizing the Private Secretary of the Governor to demand and receive certain Fees,' approved Nov. 29th, 1861."

Also, to repeal an Act of the Legislature of the State of Nevada, entitled "An Act in relation to the Collection of certain Fees heretofore collected by the Governor's Private Secretary," approved February 17th, 1866, the same having passed the Assembly this day without amendment.

I also return to you Senate Bill No. 14, entitled "An Act for the Relief of S. L. Baker," which passed the House this day, amended as follows : In section one, second line, by inserting after the word " to," and before the word " draw," the word "immediately." Also, in same section, fourth line, by striking out after the word " of," and before the word " hundred " the word " eighteen " and inserting in lieu thereof the word " twelve ;" also, in same section, fifth line, by inserting after the word " dollars " and before the word " due " the words " in United States currency ;" also, by adding after the word " county " in last line of section one, the words " provided that any money, or other compensation which the said Baker may have received, if any, under and by virtue of the provisions of section one of an Act entitled 'An Act for Relief of S. L. Baker and Alfred James, late Probate Judges of Nye and Churchill Counties, approved January 20th, 1865,' shall be deducted from said sum of twelve hundred dollars."

I am also instructed to inform your honorable body that the House have this day concurred in Senate amendment to Assembly Bill No. 42, entitled "An Act to authorize District Judges in certain cases to sign Records and settle Statements." All of which is

Respectfully submitted,

A. WHITFORD,
Clerk.

Assembly Bill No. 49, entitled " An Act for the Protection of Proprietors of Hotels and Lodging Houses."

Read first time ; rules suspended ; read second time by title, and referred to Committee on Judiciary.

Assembly Bill No. 57, entitled " An Act to amend an Act entitled ' An Act to provide Revenue for the Support of the Government of the State of Nevada,' approved March 9th, 1865."

Read first time ; rules suspended ; read second time by title, and referred to Committee on Ways and Means.

Senate Bill No. 14, " An Act for the Relief of S. L. Baker." Referred to Nye County delegation.

INTRODUCTION OF BILLS.

Mr. Doron, by leave, (without previous notice) introduced Senate Bill No. 137, " An Act to provide for the Publication of Laws and Resolutions passed during the Third Session of the Legislature of Nevada."

Read first time ; rules suspended ; read second time by title, and referred to Committee on State Printing.

Mr. Nelson, by leave, (without previous notice) introduced Senate Bill No. 138, " An Act authorizing the Secretary of State to employ a Clerk in the State Library and Adjutant General's office."

Read first time ; rules suspended ; read second time by title, and referred to Committee on State Library.

Pursuant to notice, Mr. Welty moved to reconsider the vote by which Senate Bill No. 95, " An Act conferring further powers on the Board of County Commissioners in reference to Hospitals," was lost.

Carried.

The yeas and nays were called on the final passage of the bill, and recorded as follows:

YEAS—Messrs. Geller, Haines, Hastings, Hutchins, Linn, Mason, Proctor, Terry, and Welty—9.

NAYS—Messrs. Doron, Eastman, Edwards, Meder, Monroe, Nelson, Stevenson, and Sumner—8.

So the bill did not pass.

Mr. Sumner introduced Senate Bill No. 139, "An Act to Increase the Number of Justices of the Supreme Court, and to fix their Compensation."

Read first time; rules suspended; read second time by title, and referred to Committee on Judiciary.

Mr. Grey, by leave, submitted the following resolution:

Resolved, That in view of this being the birthday of our late Martyr President, Abraham Lincoln, to whose memory a grateful people can never pay too high a tribute of respect, this Senate do now adjourn.

Adopted.

At 11 : 40 A.M., the Senate adjourned.

JAMES S. SLINGERLAND,
President.

Attest—B. C. BROWN,
Secretary.

IN SENATE—THIRTY-EIGHTH DAY.

CARSON CITY, February 13th, 1867.

The Senate met pursuant to adjournment, President in the chair.

Roll called.

Present—Messrs. Doron, Eastman, Edwards, Geller, Grey, Haines, Hastings, Hutchins, Linn, Mason, Meder, Monroe, Nelson, Proctor, Stevenson, Terry, and Welty—17.

Absent—0.

Prayer by the Chaplain.

The Journal of the Thirty-seventh day was read and approved.

REPORTS OF COMMITTEES.

Mr. Linn, Chairman Committee on Enrollment, reported that Substitute Senate Bill No. 40, entitled "An Act to repeal an Act of the Legislative Assembly of the Territory of Nevada, entitled 'An Act authorizing the Private Secretary of the Governor to demand and receive certain Fees,' approved November 29th, 1861."

Also, to repeal an Act of the Legislature of the State of Nevada, entitled

"An Act in relation to the Collection of certain Fees heretofore collected by the Governor's Private Secretary, approved February 17th, 1866."

Also, Senate Bill No. 69, "An Act supplementary to an Act to create a Board of County Commissioners in the several Counties of this State, and to define their Duties and Powers, approved March 8th, 1865;" had been carefully compared with the engrossed bills as passed by the two Houses, found correctly enrolled, and that the same had this day been delivered to the Governor for his approval.

Mr. Proctor, from the Standing Committee on Counties and County Boundaries, to which was referred the bill entitled "An Act amendatory of an Act entitled 'An Act relative to the Support of the Poor,' approved November 29th, 1861," reported that they had had the same under consideration, had come to a favorable conclusion thereon, and directed their chairman to report the same to the Senate without amendments, and recommend its passage.

Mr. Doron, from the Standing Committee on State Affairs, to which was referred Assembly Bill No. 56, entitled "An Act to amend an Act entitled 'An Act in relation to the Compensation of Members of the Legislature and State Officers,' approved January 16th, 1865," reported that they had had the same under consideration, had come to an unfavorable conclusion thereon, and directed their chairman to report the same to the Senate, with the recommendation that it do not pass.

Mr. Doron, from Standing Committee on Public Printing, to which was referred Senate Bill No. 137, entitled "An Act to provide for the Publication of Laws and Resolutions passed during the Third Session of the Legislature of Nevada," reported that they had had the same under consideration, have come to a favorable conclusion thereon, and directed their chairman to report the same to the Senate without amendments, and to recommend its passage.

Mr. Eastman, from the Standing Committee on Corporations, to which was referred the bill entitled "An Act for the Incorporation of Hospitals and Asylums in certain cases," reported that they had had the same under consideration, had come to a favorable conclusion thereon, and directed their chairman to report the same to the Senate without amendments, and to recommend its passage.

Mr. Nelson reported that the Committee on State Library had had under consideration the Senate Bill No. 53, entitled "An Act to authorize the State Librarian to distribute Copies of the Constitutional Debates among Newspapers published in this State," and had directed their chairman to recommend that it be indefinitely postponed. Also, that the Committee had had under consideration the Assembly Concurrent Resolution No. 30, relative to Constitutional Debates, had come to a favorable conclusion thereon, and had directed their chairman to recommend it be adopted.

Mr. Proctor, from the Special Committee, consisting of the Nye County delegation, to which was referred the bill entitled "An Act for the Relief of S. L. Baker," reported that they had had the same under consideration, had come to a favorable conclusion thereon, and recommend the Senate do concur in the Assembly amendments.

MOTIONS AND RESOLUTIONS.

Mr. Welty offered the following resolution :

Resolved, That the Code of Civil Procedure be made the Special Order in Committee of the Whole for each day at two o'clock P.M. till disposed of, and each member desiring to do so, shall offer his amendments thereto upon reading the number of the section without further reading ; and as fast as separate divisions or chapters thereof are passed upon, the same be ordered engrossed and communicated to the Assembly; and as fast as amendments are adopted by both Houses a copy thereof showing the sections where the amendments apply shall be furnished to the Governor under the certificate of the Secretary of the Senate.

Adopted.

On motion of Mr. Grey, Mr. Sumner was granted indefinite leave of absence.

INTRODUCTION OF BILLS.

Mr. Hutchins, by leave without previous notice, introduced Senate Bill No. 140, "An Act to amend an Act to provide for Organizing and Disciplining the Militia of this State, approved March 4th, 1865." Read first time; rules suspended; read second time by title, and referred to Committee on Military and Indian Affairs.

Mr. Welty, by leave without previous notice, introduced Senate Bill No. 141, "An Act to provide for the payment of James Cochran for certain services rendered, and expenses incurred."

Read first time; rules suspended; read second time by title. Mr. Hastings moved to amend by striking out the words "one thousand," and inserting "seven hundred and fifty."

Carried.

On motion of Mr. Hutchins, the bill was ordered engrossed.

Mr. Terry introduced Senate Bill No. 142, "An Act amendatory of an Act entitled 'An Act to provide for the Maintenance and Supervision of Public Schools,' approved March 20th, 1865."

Read first time; rules suspended; read second time by title, and referred to Committee on Education.

Mr. Edwards, by leave, without previous notice, introduced Senate Bill No. 143, "An Act for the Relief of John S. Childs."

Read first time; rules suspended; read second time by title, and referred to Committee on Claims.

Mr. Eastman introduced Senate Bill No. 144, "An Act to declare navigable that portion of the Truckee River which is in the State of Nevada."

Read first time; rules suspended; read second time by title, and referred to the Committee on Internal Improvements.

Mr. Hastings moved that an addition of one be added to the Committee on Internal Improvements in place of Mr. Carpenter, absent.

Carried.

The President appointed Mr. Proctor.

A Message was received from the Governor, and laid temporarily on the table.

A Message was received from the Assembly, and laid temporarily on the table.

On motion of Mr. Edwards, the Senate went into Committee of the Whole for the consideration of the General File, Mr. Meder in the chair.

The Committee rose, and submitted the following report:

Mr. President:

The Senate, in Committee of the Whole, have had under consideration Assembly Bill No. 27, "An Act to amend an Act entitled 'An Act concerning District Attorneys, approved March 11th, 1865,' approved February 26th, 1866," which they report back with amendments, and recommend its passage as amended.

Also, Assembly Memorial No. 18, asking a reduction of Freight and Fare upon the Central Pacific Railroad of California, which they report back, and ask leave to sit again on Friday, February 15th, at 12 o'clock M.

At 1:35 P.M., on motion of Mr. Hutchins, the Senate took a recess until 2:15 P.M.

IN SENATE.

The Senate met at 2:15 P.M., President in the chair.
Roll called.
Quorum present.
Mr. Monroe, by leave, offered the following resolution:

Resolved, That the Judiciary Committee be and are hereby requested to invite Messrs. Hillyer, Aldrich, Bixler, Seeley, Sunderland, [and Keyser to appear before them and give their opinion in relation to the " Code of Civil Procedure," as reported by the Commission.

Adopted.
Mr. Monroe moved that the special order, the Code of Civil Procedure, be referred to the Judiciary Committee, and made the special order for Wednesday, February 20th, 1867, at 12 o'clock M.
Carried.
Mr. Doron moved that Assembly Bill No. 27, " An Act to amend an Act entitled ' An Act concerning District Attorneys, approved March 11th, 1865,' approved February 26th, 1866," be now placed on its final passage.
Carried.
Read third time by sections. The yeas and nays were called, on the final passage of the bill, and recorded as follows:

YEAS—Messrs. Doron, Geller, Grey, Hastings, Hutchins, Linn, Monroe, Proctor, Stevenson, and Terry—10.
NAYS—Messrs. Eastman, Haines, and Meder—3.

So the bill passed.
On motion of Mr. Proctor, the Senate went into Committee of the Whole for the consideration of the General File, Mr. Hastings in the chair.
The Committee rose, and submitted the following report:

Mr. President:
The Senate, in Committee of the Whole, have had under consideration Substitute Senate Bill No. 102, " An Act to transfer certain Moneys in the State Treasury to the County School Funds," which they report back, and recommend the substitute be ordered engrossed.
Also, Senate Bill No. 94, " An Act to compensate J. F. Hatch for services in the State Library," which they report back, and recommend it be ordered engrossed.
Also, Senate Bill No. 97, " An Act defining the Duties of the Attorney General of the State of Nevada," which they report back with amendments, and recommend it be ordered engrossed as amended.
Also, Senate Bill No. 121, " An Act to regulate the Recording of Mining Claims," on which they report progress, and ask leave to sit again.

Substitute Bill No. 102, "An Act to transfer certain Moneys in the State Treasury to the County School Fund."
Ordered engrossed.
Senate Bill No. 94, "An Act to compensate J. F. Hatch for Services in the State Library."
The yeas and nays were called for by Messrs. Meder, Doron, and Haines, on the bill being ordered engrossed, and recorded as follows:

YEAS—Messrs. Doron, Eastman, Edwards, Hastings, Linn, Monroe, Nelson, and Stevenson—8.
NAYS—Messrs. Haines, Meder, Proctor, Terry, and Welty—5.

So the bill was ordered engrossed.
Senate Bill No. 97, "An Act defining the Duties of the Attorney General of the State of Nevada."
The amendments of the Committee of the Whole were adopted, and the bill ordered engrossed.
Senate Bill No. 121, "An Act to regulate the Recording of Mining Claims."
The Committee reported progress, and asked leave to sit again.
Granted.
Mr. Monroe, by leave, submitted the following resolution:

Resolved, That the Judiciary Committee be authorized and directed to proceed to Virginia, as soon as practicable, and submit the Report of the Practice Act Commissioner to the attorneys named in the resolution adopted this day.

Adopted.
At 4:10 P.M., on motion of Mr. Stevenson, the Senate adjourned.

President.

Attest—B. C. BROWN,
Secretary.

———

IN SENATE—THIRTY-NINTH DAY.

CARSON CITY, February 14th, 1867.
The Senate met pursuant to adjournment, the President in the chair.
Roll called.
Present—Messrs. Doron, Eastman, Edwards, Geller, Grey, Haines, Hastings, Hutchins, Linn, Mason, Meder, Monroe, Nelson, Proctor, Stevenson, Terry, and Welty—17.
Absent—None.
Prayer by the Chaplain.
The Journal of the Thirty-eighth day was read and approved.

Mr. Monroe, from Standing Committee on Claims, to which was referred Senate Bill No. 143, "An Act for the Relief of John S. Childs," reported that they have had the same under consideration, and recommend that the blank in first and second lines be filled by inserting "one thousand dollars," and when so amended, they recommend that the bill do pass.

Mr. Welty, from the Judiciary Committee, to which was referred Assembly Bill No. 49, entitled "An Act for the Protection of Hotel and Lodging-house Keepers," reported that they had had the same under consideration ; had come to a favorable conclusion thereon, and directed their chairman to report the same to the Senate, without amendments, and recommend its passage.

Also, Assembly Bill No. 19, entitled "An Act to amend an Act entitled ' An Act to provide for Reporting the Decisions of the Supreme Court of the State of Nevada ;' " which they had under consideration, and had directed their chairman to report unfavorably, and to recommend that it do not pass.

Mr. Hastings reported that the Standing Committee on Engrossment had carefully compared the following entitled bills with the originals, and found the same correctly engrossed, viz :

Substitute Senate Bill No. 102, "An Act to Transfer certain Moneys in the State Treasury to the County School Funds."

Also, Senate Bill No. 141, "An Act to provide for the payment of James Cochran for certain services rendered and expenses incurred in arresting and conveying one W. S. Broadwater, a refugee from justice, from Trinity County, California, to this State."

Also, Senate Bill No. 94, entitled "An Act to compensate J. F. Hatch, for services in the State Library ;" and herewith report the same back to the Senate.

MESSAGE FROM THE GOVERNOR.

The following Message was received from the Governor:

EXECUTIVE DEPARTMENT, CARSON CITY, }
February 13th, 1867. }

To the Honorable the Senate of Nevada :

I have this day approved the following Senate Bills : No. 5 (by substitute), "An Act providing for the release of Sureties on Official Bonds and Undertakings."

No. 30, "An Act in relation to and accepting the Lands granted to the State of Nevada by the Government of the United States."

[No. 90.] "An Act to regulate the business of Assaying within the State of Nevada."

H. G. BLASDEL,
Governor.

Mr. Welty, from the Standing Committee on Judiciary, to which was referred Assembly Bill No. 20, entitled "An Act to amend an Act entitled 'An Act in relation to the Distribution of the Reports of the Supreme Court of the State of Nevada,' approved March 14th, 1866," reported that they had had the same under consideration, had come to a favorable conclusion thereon, and directed their chairman to report the same to the Senate with amendments, and to recommend its passage as amended.

Amend as follows: Strike out " County Treasurer ; " also, strike out all after the words on the fourth line from the bottom of the first page, "Treasurer each one copy."

Mr. Meder submitted the following resolution:

Resolved, That the Librarian be, and he is hereby requested to furnish the Senate answers to the following interrogations, to wit:

1st. What number of books have been taken from the State Library by the Governor and other officers of the Executive Department during the time intervening between the 6th day of March, 1866, and the 6th day of January, 1867?

2d. What number have been taken by the Justices of the Supreme Court and Attorney General?

3d. What number, if any, have been taken by persons not authorized by section three of "An Act in relation to the State Library," approved February 14, 1865, and to whom such books, if any, were delivered?

MESSAGES FROM THE ASSEMBLY.

The following Messages were received from the Assembly:

ASSEMBLY CHAMBER, CARSON CITY, }
February 13th, 1867.

To the Hon. the Senate:

I am instructed to return to your honorable body Senate Message of February 11th, requesting your honorable body to inform the House if the said Message properly embodies the action of the Senate on the subject matter contained therein?

And whether the Senate desires to have Assembly Bill No. 43 returned to them for their further consideration, or whether they desire a Conference Committee appointed by the House in relation to said bill?

Respectfully,

A. WHITFORD.

ASSEMBLY CHAMBER, CARSON CITY, }
February 12th, 1867.

To the Honorable the Senate:

I am instructed to transmit to your honorable body, for your consideration, the following Assembly bills which passed the House on yesterday, viz:

No. 71, entitled "An Act to repeal all Acts or parts of Acts so far as they conflict with an Act of Congress entitled 'An Act to protect all Persons in the United States in their Civil Rights, and furnish the means of their vindication,' passed April 9th, 1866."

No. 74, entitled "An Act to provide for the Transfer of certain Moneys from the Indigent Sick Fund of Churchill County, to the General Fund of said County."

No. 76, "An Act granting additional Authority to the Board of County Commissioners."

Respectfully,

A. WHITFORD.

Assembly Bill No. 76, entitled "An Act granting additional Authority to the Board of County Commissioners."

Read first time; rules suspended; read second time by title, and referred to Committee on Counties and County Boundaries.

Assembly Bill No. 71, entitled " An Act to repeal all Acts or parts of Acts, so far as they conflict with an Act of Congress entitled 'An Act to protect all persons in the United States in their Civil Rights and furnish the means of their vindication,' passed April 9th, 1866."

Read first time; rules suspended; read second time by title, and referred to Judiciary Committee.

Assembly Bill No. 74, entitled " An Act to provide for the Transfer of certain Moneys from the Indigent Sick Fund of Churchill County, to the General Fund of said County."

Read first time; rules suspended; read second time by title, and referred to Churchill County delegation.

GENERAL FILE.

Substitute Senate Bill No. 102, "An Act to transfer certain Moneys in the State Treasury to the County School Funds."

Mr. Linn moved that the bill be committed to a Committee of one, with special instructions to strike out all after the enacting clause, and insert: "Section 1. In order to refund to the several Counties of the State, for the use of the School Funds thereof, moneys collected thereon and paid into the State Treasury, under and by virtue of an Act entitled 'An Act concerning the Location and Possession of Mining Claims,' approved February 27th, 1866; and the State Controller is hereby authorized and required to draw his warrant on the General Fund in favor of the respective Treasurers of the Counties paying the same, for the amount paid."

Adopted.

The President appointed Mr. Linn as such Committee.

Mr. Linn, to whom was referred Substitute Senate Bill No. 102, "An Act to transfer certain Moneys in the State Treasury to the County School Funds," reported the bill back amended as ordered.

Report concurred in.

The yeas and nays were called, on the final passage of the bill, and recorded as follows:

YEAS—Messrs. Doron, Eastman, Edwards, Geller, Haines, Hastings, Hutchins, Linn, Mason, Meder, Monroe, Proctor, Terry, and Welty—14.

NAYS—Messrs. Grey, and Nelson—2.

So the bill passed.

Mr. Doron, by leave, offered the following resolution:

Resolved, That the Secretary be instructed to inform the Assembly that, inasmuch as the Assembly have received Assembly Bill No. 43, " An Act to provide for properly taking care of the Indigent Insane of the State of Nevada, and to create a fund for that purpose," as amended by the Senate, without the Senate amendments being attached, in the form of riders, the cause which necessitated its [return] is removed.

Adopted.

Mr. Doron in the chair.

A Message was received from the Assembly, and laid temporarily on the table.

Senate Bill No. 141, "An Act to provide for the payment of James Cochran for certain services rendered and expenses incurred in arresting and conveying one W. S. Broadwater, a refugee from justice, from Trinity County, California, to this State."

Read third time by sections. The yeas and nays were called, on the final passage of the bill, and recorded as follows:

YEAS—Messrs. Doron, Eastman, Geller, Grey, Haines, Hastings, Hutchins, Linn, Mason, Meder, Monroe, Nelson, Proctor, Stevenson, Terry, and Welty —16.

NAYS—Mr. Edwards—1.

Senate Bill No. 94, "An Act to compensate J. F. Hatch for Services in the State Library."

Recommitted to Committee on State Library.

Mr. Haines, by leave, offered the following resolution:

Resolved, That the Committee on State Affairs be instructed to examine into laws making appropriations of money, and to report whether the moneys have been disbursed conformably with such laws.

Adopted.

At 12:40 P.M., on motion of Mr. Meder, the Senate took a recess until 2 o'clock P.M.

IN SENATE.

The Senate met at 2 o'clock, President in the chair.

Roll called. Quorum present.

In consideration of the necessity requiring the absence of the President on to-morrow, Mr. Welty moved the election of a President *pro tem.* to hold office until his return.

Carried.

Mr. Doron was placed in nomination and unanimously elected.

On motion, the Senate went into Committee of the Whole, Mr. Hutchins in the chair, for the consideration of the General File.

The Committee rose, and submitted the following report:

Mr. President:

The Senate in Committee of the Whole have had under consideration Senate Bill No. 123, "An Act [amendatory of an Act entitled 'An Act relating to the Support of the Poor,'" which they report back, and recommend it be ordered engrossed.

Also, Assembly Bill No. 56, "An Act to amend an Act entitled 'An Act in relation to the Compensation of Members of the Legislature and State Officers,' approved January 16th, 1865," which they report back, and recommend it do not pass.

Also, Senate Bill No. 137, "An Act to provide for the Publication of Laws and Resolutions passed during the Third Session of the Legislature of Nevada," which they report back with amendments, and recommend it be ordered engrossed as amended.

Also, Assembly Bill No. 51, "An Act for the Incorporation of Hospitals and Asylums in certain cases," which they report back, and recommend that it do pass.

Also, Senate Bill No. 53, "An Act to authorize the State Librarian to distribute copies of the Nevada Constitutional Debates among Newspapers published in this State," which they report back, and recommend that it be indefinitely postponed.

Also, Assembly Concurrent Resolution No. 30, relative to Constitutional Debates, which they report back, and recommend that it do pass.

Also, Senate Bill No. 14, "An Act for the relief of S. L. Baker," which they report back, and recommend that the Assembly amendments thereto be concurred in.

Also, Senate Bill No. 121, "An Act to regulate the Recording of Mining Claims," which they report back, and recommend that it be ordered engrossed as amended.

GENERAL FILE.

Senate Bill No. 123, "An Act amendatory of an Act entitled 'An Act relating to the Support of the Poor.'"
Ordered engrossed.

Assembly Bill No. 56, "An Act to amend an Act entitled 'An Act in relation to the Compensation of Members of the Legislature and State Officers,' approved January 16th, 1865."

The yeas and nays were called on the final passage of the bill, and recorded as follows:

YEAS—0.
NAYS—Messrs. Doron, Eastman, Edwards, Geller, Haines, Hastings, Meder, Monroe, Nelson, Proctor, Stevenson, Terry, and Welty—13.

So the bill did not pass.

Senate Bill No. 137, "An Act to provide for the Publication of Laws and Resolutions passed during the Third Session of the Legislature of Nevada."

The yeas and nays were called for by Messrs. Welty, Proctor, and Terry on the bill being ordered engrossed, and recorded as follows:

YEAS—Messrs. Doron, Eastman, Geller, Haines, Hastings, Linn, Meder, Monroe, Nelson, Proctor, and Stevenson—11.
NAYS—Messrs. Edwards, Terry, and Welty—3.

So the bill was ordered engrossed.

Assembly Bill No. 51, "An Act for the incorporation of Hospitals and Asylums in certain cases."
Read third time by sections.

The yeas and nays were called on the final passage of the bill, and recorded as follows:

YEAS—Messrs. Eastman, Edwards, Geller, Haines, Hastings, Linn, Monroe, Proctor, Stevenson, and Terry—10.
NAYS—Messrs. Doron, Mason, Nelson, and Welty—4.

So the bill passed.

Senate Bill No. 53, "An Act to authorize the State Librarian to distribute Copies of the Nevada Constitutional Debates among the Newspapers published in this State."
Indefinitely postponed.

Assembly Concurrent Resolution No. 30, relative to Constitutional Debates.
Read, and adopted unanimously.

Senate Bill No. 14, "An Act for the Relief of S. L. Baker."

The yeas and nays were called on concurrence with the Assembly amendments, and recorded as follows:

YEAS—Messrs. Doron, Eastman, Edwards, Geller, Haines, Hastings, Linn, Meder, Monroe, Proctor, Stevenson, Terry, and Welty—13.
NAYS—Mr. Nelson—1.

So the Assembly amendments were concurred in.
Senate Bill No. 121, "An Act to regulate the Recording of Mining Claims."
Placed at the foot of the General File.
At 4:15 P.M., on motion of Mr. Monroe, the Senate adjourned.

JAMES S. SLINGER LAND,
President.

Attest—B. C. BROWN,
Secretary.

IN SENATE—FORTIETH DAY.

CARSON CITY, February 15th, 1867.

The Senate met pursuant to adjournment, Mr. Doron, President *pro tem.*, in the chair.
Roll called.
Present—Messrs. Doron, Eastman, Edwards, Geller, Grey, Haines, Hastings, Hutchins, Linn, Mason, Meder, Monroe, Nelson, Proctor, Stevenson, Terry, and Welty—17.
Absent—0.
Prayer by the Chaplain.
The Journal of the Thirty-ninth day was read and approved.

REPORTS OF COMMITTEES.

Mr. Hastings reported that the Standing Committee on Engrossment had carefully compared the following entitled bills with the originals, and found the same correctly engrossed, viz:
Senate Bill No. 137, "An Act to provide for the Publication of the Laws and Resolutions passed at the Third Session of the Legislature of Nevada."
Also, Senate Bill No. 123, "An Act amendatory of an Act entitled 'An Act relating to the Support of the Poor,' approved November 29, 1861."
Also, Senate Bill No. 97, "An Act defining the Duties of the Attorney General of the State of Nevada;" and herewith report the same back to the Senate.
Mr. Monroe, from the Special Committee consisting of the Churchill County delegation, to which was referred the bill entitled "An Act to provide for the Transfer of certain Moneys from the Indigent Sick Fund of Churchill County, to the General Fund," reported that they had had the same under consideration, had come to a favorable conclusion thereon, and report the same to the Senate without amendments, and recommend its passage.
Mr. Proctor, from the Committee on Counties and County Boundaries, had

had under consideration Assembly Bill No. 76, entitled " An Act granting additional Authority to the Boards of County Commissioners," had come to an unfavorable conclusion thereon, and had directed their chairman to report the same back without amendments, and recommend that it do not pass.

Mr. Grey, from the Standing Committee on Education, to which was referred the bill entitled " An Act amendatory of an Act entitled ' An Act to provide for the Maintenance and Supervision of Public Schools,' approved March 20th, 1865," reported that they had had the same under consideration, had come to a favorable conclusion thereon, and had directed their chairman to report the same to the Senate without amendments, and to recommend its passage.

Mr. Hutchins, from Standing Committee on Military and Indian Affairs, reported that they had had under consideration Senate Bill No. 140, " An Act entitled ' An Act to amend an Act to provide for Organizing and Disciplining the Militia of this State,' [approved] March 4th, 1865," and herewith report the same back without recommendation.

MOTIONS AND RESOLUTIONS.

Mr. Meder offered the following resolution :

WHEREAS, A certain bill for thirty days' services rendered by Andrew Whitford, as Clerk of Joint Committee on Railroads, Session 1864 and 1865, was duly audited and allowed by the Board of Examiners, and by Resolve of March 2d, 1866, the sum of one hundred dollars was ordered to be paid out of the Contingent Fund of the Senate of 1866, but which Contingent Fund having been exhausted before presentation, said bill has not been paid ; therefore,

Resolved, That the Controller of State be and he is hereby authorized to draw his warrant in favor of Andrew Whitford for the sum of one hundred dollars, payable out of the Contingent Fund of the Senate in such moneys as was due and payable to said Whitford, under said Resolve of March 2d, 1866.

Adopted.

MESSAGE FROM ASSEMBLY.

The following Message was received from the Assembly :

ASSEMBLY CHAMBER, CARSON CITY,
February 14th, 1867.

To the Hon. the Senate :

I am instructed to transmit to your honorable body for your consideration, Assembly Bill No. 79, " An Act for the Relief of A. Ranney, Sheriff of Nye County," the same having passed this House February 13th: Ayes, 26 ; Nays, 0.

Respectfully,

A. WHITFORD,
Clerk.

Assembly Bill No. 79, " An Act for the Relief of A. Ranney, Sheriff of Nye County."

Read first time ; rules suspended ; read second time by title, and referred to the Nye County delegation.

INTRODUCTION OF BILLS.

Mr. Terry introduced Senate Bill No. 149, "An Act amendatory of and supplementary to an Act entitled an Act to amend an Act entitled an Act amendatory of and supplementary to an Act of the Legislative Assembly of the Territory of Nevada, entitled 'An Act to Incorporate the City of Austin,' approved February 20th, A.D. 1864, approved March 8th, A.D. 1865, approved February 27th, A.D. 1866."

Read first time ; rules suspended ; read second time by title, and referred to Lander County delegation.

A Message was received from the Assembly, and laid temporarily on the table.

GENERAL FILE.

Senate Bill No. 97, "An Act defining the Duties of the Attorney General of the State of Nevada."

Read third time by sections ; the yeas and nays were called on the final passage of the bill, and recorded as follows :

YEAS—Messrs. Doron, Eastman, Edwards, Geller, Grey, Haines, Hastings, Hutchins, Linn, Mason, Meder, Monroe, Nelson, Proctor, Stevenson, Terry, and Welty—17.

NAYS—0.

So the bill passed.

Senate Bill No. 137, "An Act to provide for the Publication of the Laws and Resolutions passed during the Third Session of the Legislature of Nevada."

Read third time by sections ; the yeas and nays were called on the final passage of the bill and recorded as follows :

YEAS—Messrs. Geller, Grey, Hastings, Mason, Meder, Monroe, Nelson, Proctor, and Stevenson—9.

NAYS—Messrs. Doron, Eastman, Edwards, Haines, Hutchins, Linn, Terry, and Welty—8.

So the bill did not pass.

Mr. Hutchins in the chair.

Mr. Hastings moved that Special Order Assembly Memorial No. 18, asking a reduction of Freight and Fare upon the Central Pacific Railroad of California, set for 12 o'clock, be postponed until Wednesday, February 20th, 12 o'clock M.
Carried.

Senate Bill No. 123, "An Act amendatory of an Act entitled 'An Act relating to the Support of the Poor.' "

Read third time by sections.

Yeas and nays were called on the final passage of the bill, and recorded as follows :

YEAS—Messrs. Doron, Eastman, Edwards, Geller, Grey, Haines, Hastings, Hutchins, Linn, Monroe, Nelson, Proctor, Stevenson, Terry, and Welty—15.

NAYS—Mr. Meder—1.

So the bill passed.

17

At 12:30 [P.]M., on motion of Mr. Hastings, the Senate took a recess until 1 o'clock P.M.

IN SENATE.

The Senate met at 1 P.M., Mr. Doron, President *pro tem.*, in the chair.
Roll called.
Quorum present.
Mr. Terry introduced the following resolution :

Resolved, That two hundred and forty copies of an Act amendatory of an Act entitled " An Act to provide for the Maintenance and Supervision of Public Schools," approved March 20th, 1865, be and hereby are ordered printed.

Adopted.
A Message was received from the Assembly, and laid temporarily on the table.
Mr. Hutchins, by leave without previous notice, introduced Senate Bill No. 150, "An Act to amend an Act entitled ' An Act authorizing a State Loan, and levying a Tax to provide means for the Payment thereof,' approved February 6th, 1867."
Read first time ; rules suspended ; read second time by title.
Mr. Hutchins moved that the rules be suspended, and the bill be considered engrossed, read third time by sections, and placed on its final passage.
The Chair ruled the motion out of order.
Mr. Grey appealed from the decision of the Chair.
The ruling of the Chair was sustained.
On motion, the bill was referred to the Committee on Ways and Means.
The following communication was received from the Hon. C. N. Noteware, Secretary of State and ex-officio State Librarian, in answer to interrogatories from the Senate. (See Appendix.)
Read and referred to Committee on State Library.
On motion of Mr. Edwards, the Senate went into Committee of the Whole for the consideration of the General File, President in the chair.
The Committee rose, and submitted the following report :

Mr. President:
The Senate in Committee of the Whole have had under consideration Senate Bill No. 143, "An Act for the relief of John S. Childs," which they report back with amendments, and recommend it be ordered engrossed as amended.
Also, Assembly Bill No. 20, " An Act to amend an Act entitled 'An Act in relation to the Distribution of the Reports of the Supreme Court of the State of Nevada,' approved March 14th, 1866," which they report back, and recommend that the amendments of the Judiciary Committee be adopted.
Also, Assembly Bill No. 49, " An Act for the Protection of Proprietors of Hotels and Lodging-houses," which they report back, and recommend it do not pass.
Also, Assembly Bill No. 19, "An Act to amend an Act entitled ' An Act to provide for Reporting the Decisions of the Supreme Court of the State of Nevada,' approved March 14th, 1865," which they report back, and recommend it do not pass.
Also, Assembly Bill No. 74, "An Act to provide for the Transfer of certain Moneys from the Indigent Sick Fund of said [Churchill] County," which they report back, and recommend it do pass.

Also, Senate Bill No. 140, " An Act to amend an Act entitled ' An Act to provide for the Organizing and Disciplining the Militia of this State,' " which they report back, and recommend that it be placed at the foot of the General File.

Also, Assembly Bill No. 76, " An Act granting additional Authority to the Board of County Commissioners," which they report back with amendments, and recommend it do pass as amended.

Also, Senate Bill No. 121, " An Act to regulate the Recording of Mining Claims," which they report back, and recommend the bill be placed at the foot of the General File.

GENERAL FILE.

Senate Bill No. 143, " An Act for the Relief of John S. Childs."

The amendments of the Committee of the Whole were adopted, and the bill ordered engrossed.

Assembly Bill No. 20, "An Act to amend an Act entitled 'An Act in relation to the Distribution of the Reports of the Supreme Court of the State of Nevada,' approved March 14th, 1866."

Read third time by sections.

The yeas and nays were called on the final passage of the bill, and recorded as follows:

YEAS—Messrs. Doron, Eastman, Geller, Haines, Hastings, Linn, Meder, Monroe, Proctor, Stevenson, Terry, and Welty—12.

NAYS—0.

So the bill passed.

Assembly Bill No. 49, " An Act for the Protection of Proprietors of Hotels and Lodging-houses."

Read third time by sections; the yeas and nays were called on the final passage of the bill, and recorded as follows:

YEAS—Messrs. Doron, Eastman, Geller, Haines, Hastings, Linn, Meder, Monroe, Proctor, Stevenson, Terry, and Welty—12.

NAYS—0.

So the bill passed.

Assembly Bill No. 19, " An Act to amend an Act entitled ' An Act to provide for Reporting the Decisions of the Supreme Court of the State of Nevada,' approved March 14th, 1865."

Read third time by sections.

The yeas and nays were called on the final passage of the bill, and recorded as follows:

YEAS—0.

NAYS—Messrs. Doron, Eastman, Geller, Hastings, Linn, Meder, Monroe, Proctor, Stevenson, Terry, and Welty—11.

So the bill did not pass.

Assembly Bill No. 74, " An Act to provide for the Transfer of certain Moneys from the Indigent Sick Fund of Churchill County to the General Fund of said county."

Read third time by sections.

The yeas and nays were called on the final passage of the bill, and recorded as follows:

YEAS—Messrs. Doron, Eastman, Geller, Haines, Hastings, Linn, Meder, Monroe, Proctor, Stevenson, Terry, and Welty—12.
NAYS—0.

So the bill passed.

Senate Bill No. 140, "An Act to amend an Act entitled 'An Act to provide for Organizing and Disciplining the Militia of this State,' approved March 4th, 1865."

Placed at the foot of the General File.

Assembly Bill No. 76, "An Act granting additional Authority to the Board of County Commissioners."

The amendments of the Committee of the Whole were adopted, and the bill placed at the foot of the General File.

Senate Bill No. 121, "An Act to regulate the Recording of Mining Claims."

Placed at the foot of the General File.

Senate Bill No. 101, "An Act to amend an Act entitled "An Act to regulate Fees and Compensation for Official and other Services in the State of Nevada,' approved March 9th, 1865."

Placed at the foot of the General File.

Mr. Welty, Chairman of Judiciary Committee, by leave without previous notice, introduced Senate Bill No. 151, "An Act to amend an Act entitled 'An Act to regulate Proceedings in Criminal Cases in the Courts of Justice in the (Territory) State of Nevada,' and making further provisions relating thereto."

Read first time; rules suspended; read second time by title, and referred to Committee of the Whole, and ordered printed.

On motion of Mr. Monroe, at 4:40 P.M. the Senate adjourned till Monday, February 18th, at 11 o'clock A.M.

LEWIS DORON,
President *pro tem.*

Attest—B. C. BROWN,
Secretary.

IN SENATE—FORTY-THIRD DAY.

CARSON CITY, February 18th, 1867.

The Senate met pursuant to adjournment.

President in the chair.

Roll called.

Present—Messrs. Doron, Eastman, Geller, Grey, Haines, Hastings, Hutchins, Linn, Mason, Meder, Monroe, Proctor, Stevenson, Sumner, Terry, and Welty —16.

Absent—Messrs. Edwards and Webster—2.

Prayer by the Chaplain.

The Journal of the Fortieth day was read and approved.

On motion, Mr. Edwards was granted leave of absence for one day.

Mr. Doron in the chair.

Messages were received from the Governor, and laid temporarily on the table.

Messages were received from the Assembly, and laid temporarily on the table.

Mr. Proctor rose to a point of order: that the Message of the Governor announcing his disapproval of a bill not being presented within the time required by the Constitution, could not be received.

The Chair ruled that inasmuch as the Message was presented on the fifth session day of the Senate, the point was not well taken.

Mr. Proctor appealed from the decision of the Chair.

The yeas and nays were called for on the question by Messrs. Meder, Haines, and Welty, and recorded as follows:

YEAS—Messrs. Eastman, Edwards, Grey, Haines, Hastings, Hutchins, Linn, Mason, Meder, Monroe, Stevenson, Terry, and Welty—13.

NAYS—Messrs. Geller, Proctor, and Sumner—3.

So the decision of the Chair was sustained.

REPORTS OF COMMITTEES.

Mr. Grey, from Standing Committee on Education, to which was referred the bill entitled "An Act for the Organization of a Board of Education in certain counties, amendatory of and supplementary to an Act to provide for the Maintenance and Support of Public Schools, approved March 20th, 1865," reported that they had had the same under consideration, had come to an unfavorable conclusion thereon, had directed their chairman to report a substitute bill, and recommend its passage.

Mr. Hastings reported that the Standing Committee on Engrossment had carefully compared the following entitled bill with the original, and found the same correctly engrossed, viz:

Senate Bill No. 143, "An Act for the Relief of John S. Childs," and herewith report the same back to the Senate.

Mr. Proctor, from the Committee on Counties and County Boundaries, to which was referred Senate Bill No. 107, "An Act relating to the Compensation of County Clerks," reported the same back without recommendation.

Mr. Linn asked permission to withdraw the bill.

Granted.

Mr. Welty, from the Committee on Judiciary, to which was referred Assembly Bill No. 58, entitled "An Act to amend Section 24 of an Act to amend an Act entitled 'An Act to regulate Proceedings in the Courts of Justice in this Territory,' approved February 20, 1864," reported that they had had the same under consideration, had come to a favorable conclusion thereon, and recommend that it pass without amendment.

Also, that Senate Bill No. 139, entitled "An Act to increase the number of Justices of the Supreme Court, and to fix their Compensation," together with Senate Bill No. 134, entitled "An Act to provide for the Recording of certain Papers affecting the Titles or Claims to Real Property," be indefinitely postponed.

Assembly Bill No. 71, entitled "An Act to repeal all Acts or parts of Acts, so far as they conflict with an Act of Congress entitled "An Act to protect all Persons in the United States in their Civil Rights, and furnish the means of their Vindication,' passed April 9, 1866," reported that they had had the same under consideration, and a majority of the Committee recommend that it pass without amendments.

Granted.

Mr. Proctor, from minority of Committee on Judiciary, asked one day to present a minority report.

Mr. Sumner, from minority of Committee on Judiciary, asked leave to make a report on Wednesday next, on Senate Bill No. 139, "An Act to increase the Number of Justices of the Supreme Court, and to fix their Compensation."

Granted.

Mr. Meder, from the Committee on Public Morals, to which was referred Senate Bill, No. 131, "An Act to prohibit the Carrying of Concealed Weapons," reported that they had had the same under consideration, had come to a favorable conclusion thereon, and recommend its passage.

MESSAGES FROM THE GOVERNOR.

The following Messages were received from the Governor:

EXECUTIVE DEPARTMENT, CARSON CITY, }
February 18th, 1867. }

To the Hon. Senate of Nevada:

I herewith transmit to your hononorable body the Annual Report of the Surveyor General of this State for the year A.D. 1866.

Respectfully,

H. G. BLASDEL.
Governor.

Referred to Committee on Public Lands.

EXECUTIVE DEPARTMENT, CARSON CITY, }
February 15th, 1867. }

To the Honorable Senate of Nevada:

I herewith return to your honorable body without approval, Senate Bill No. 89, entitled "An Act to enable a Defendant to Testify as a Witness in Criminal Prosecutions."

This bill proposes to confer on defendants in criminal actions, the right to testify in self-defense, though the Constitution emphatically shields them from the operation of any law requiring them to give evidence against themselves.

Under our system of Criminal Practice and Jurisprudence, every just guard is thrown around the life and liberty of the citizen. The framers of the Fundamental and Statutory law have tested their ingenuity to secure impartial trials ; have reduced the rule to such stringency that twelve men must unanimously concur in a verdict, in order to find a defendant guilty of any felony, and then not until after being instructed by the Court, that if any reasonable doubt exists in their minds as to the guilt of the defendant, they must give him the benefit thereof, by a verdict of "not guilty." Peremptory requirements of the statutes guarantee, regardless of public expense, fair and unbiased trial juries. Yet in many instances parties guilty of grave offenses are acquitted, and go unpunished. Besides offering the highest premium for perjury, this bill, if it become a law, will certainly add greatly to the number of improper acquittals, and cause our criminal laws and Courts to be less feared and less respected than before, especially as the people are unsettled, and to a great extent, unrestrained by that well established morality which prevails in the older States, where the population is settled and fixed in their purposes for life.

I am aware that it is urged in behalf of this bill, that such a law is humane ; that in all instances, if defendants be not so permitted to testify, their mouths are sealed until called up for final sentence. It may be true that the absence of such a law may work hardships in isolated cases ; these occur under all laws.

But the mouths of criminal defendants are not closed as suggested, for it is a right of which no man can be deprived, to speak in his own defense, by counsel, or in person, as he may choose; and the *statement*, not under oath, of a defendant, if bearing the mighty impress of *truth*, will avail him as much as his sworn evidence, given under circumstances known to the jury to be incentive of perjury; the commission of one crime, to escape punishment for another.

Feeling satisfied, as I do, that such a law would subvert public justice rather than promote its administration, I return the bill for your further action.

H. G. BLASDEL,
Governor.

The question being, shall the bill pass notwithstanding the objections of the Governor, the yeas and nays were called and recorded as follows:

YEAS—Messrs. Doron, Eastman, Edwards, Geller, Grey, Haines, Hastings, Hutchins, Linn, Mason, Meder, Monroe, Proctor, Stevenson, Sumner, Terry, and Welty—17.

NAYS—0.

So the bill passed.

MOTIONS AND RESOLUTIONS.

Mr. Sumner introduced the following resolution:

Resolved, That the Storey County delegation be and they are hereby authorized to send for persons and papers in furtherance of their investigations concerning the indebtedness of Virginia City, and to administer oaths to witnesses called; and

Resolved, That said delegation be and they are hereby authorized to employ a clerk for three days.

Adopted.

MESSAGES FROM THE ASSEMBLY.

The following Messages were received from the Assembly:

ASSEMBLY CHAMBER, CARSON CITY,
February 14th, 1867.

To the Hon. the Senate:

I am intructed to transmit to your honorable body, for your consideration, the following:

Assembly Concurrent Resolution No. 39, "Relating to a Weekly Mail from Aurora to the Lower Crossing of the Truckee."

Assembly Bill No. 13, "An Act amendatory of and supplemental to an 'Act to create the County of Lincoln and provide for its organization,' approved February 26th, 1866," the same having passed the Assembly this day.

I also return to you Senate Bill No. 117, "An Act to amend an Act entitled 'An Act in relation to Public Highways,' approved March 9th, 1866," the same having been defeated by the House this day.

Respectfully,

A. WHITFORD,
Clerk.

ASSEMBLY CHAMBER, CARSON CITY, }
February 15th, 1867.

To the Honorable the Senate:

I am instructed to transmit to your honorable body, for your consideration, Assembly Bill No. 47, entitled "An Act to prescribe the number of Hours which shall constitute a Legal Day's Labor in certain cases," the same having passed the House this day.

I also am instructed to inform you that the House have appointed a Conference Committee, consisting of Messrs. St. Clair, Poor, and Cullen, on Senate Bill No. 31, entitled "An Act concerning the Office of Public Administrator."

Also, the House have appointed a Conference Committee, consisting of Messrs. Julien, Mallory, and Parker, on Assembly Bill No. 48, entitled "An Act to provide for properly taking care of the Indigent Insane of the State of Nevada, and to create a Fund for that purpose."

Also, that the House has this day refused to concur in Senate amendments to Assembly Bill No. 27, entitled "An Act to amend an Act entitled 'An Act concerning District Attorneys, approved March 11th, 1865,' approved February 26th, 1866."

I also return to you Senate Concurrent Resolution No. 129, "In relation to Printing the Practice Act," the same having been indefinitely postponed this day.

Respectfully,

A. WHITFORD,
Clerk.

ASSEMBLY CHAMBER, CARSON CITY, }
February 18th, 1867.

To the Honorable the Senate:

I am instructed to transmit to your honorable body, for your consideration, Assembly Bill No. 87, entitled "An Act to appropriate Moneys to defray the Civil Expenses of the State Government, up to the close of the Fourth Fiscal Year," the same having passed the Assembly on the 16th instant.

Respectfully,

A. WHITFORD,
Clerk.

Assembly Bill No. 47, entitled "An Act to prescribe the number of Hours which shall constitute a Legal Day's Labor in certain cases."

Read first time; rules suspended; read second time by title; and referred to Committee on Mines and Mining.

Assembly Concurrent Resolution No. 39, "Relating to a Weekly Mail from Aurora to the Lower Crossing of the Truckee."

Read, and referred to Committee on Federal Relations.

Assembly Bill No. 13, "An Act amendatory of and supplemental to an Act to create the County of Lincoln, and provide for its organization," approved February 26th, 1866.

Read first time; rules suspended; read second time by title, and referred to Committee on Counties and County Boundaries.

Assembly Bill No. 87, "An Act to appropriate Moneys to defray the Civil Expenses of the State Government, up to the close of the Fourth Fiscal Year."

Read first time; rules suspended; read second time by title, and referred to the Committee on Ways and Means.

Assembly Bill No. 43, entitled "An Act for properly taking care of the Indigent Insane of the State of Nevada, and to create a Fund for that purpose."

Mr. Proctor moved that a Committee of Conference, consisting of three, be appointed.

Carried.

The Chair appointed Messrs. Edwards, Proctor, and Mason.

Senate Bill, No. 143, "An Act for the Relief of John S. Childs."

Bill read third time [by] sections.

The yeas and nays were called on its final passage, and recorded as follows:

YEAS—Messrs. Doron, Eastman, Geller, Haines, Hutchins, Linn, Meder, Monroe, Proctor, Stevenson, and Sumner—11.

NAYS—Messrs. Grey, Hastings, Mason, Terry and Welty—5.

So the bill passed.

Senate Bill No. 140, "An Act to amend 'An Act to provide for Organizing and Disciplining the Militia of this State,' approved March 4th, 1865."

Referred to Committee of the Whole.

Assembly Bill No. 76, "An Act granting additional Authority to the Board of County Commissioners.

Mr. Welty moved that the bill be referred to a Committee of one, with instructions to strike out the second section.

Carried.

The Committee reported the bill back, amended as per instructions.

Report adopted.

Read third time by sections.

The yeas and nays were called on the final passage of the bill, and recorded as follows:

YEAS—Messrs. Eastman, Haines, Hastings, Linn, Stevenson, and Welty—6.

NAYS—Messrs. Doron, Geller, Grey, Hutchins, Mason, Meder, Monroe, Proctor, and Terry—10 [9].

So the bill did not pass.

Senate Bill No. 121, "An Act to regulate the Recording of Mining Claims."

Laid upon the table.

Senate Bill No. 101, "An Act to amend an Act entitled ' An Act to regulate Fees and Compensation for Officials, and other Services in the State of Nevada,' approved March 9th, 1865."

Indefinitely postponed.

Senate Bill No. 131, "An Act to prohibit the Carrying of Concealed Weapons."

Ordered engrossed.

Assembly Bill No. 58, " An Act to amend Section twenty-four of an Act to amend an Act entitled 'An Act to regulate Proceedings in the Courts of Justice in this Territory,' approved February 20th, 1864."

Read third time by sections.

The yeas and nays were called on the final passage of the bill, and recorded as follows:

YEAS—Messrs. Doron, Eastman, Geller, Grey, Haines, Hastings, Hutchins, Linn, Mason, Meder, Monroe, Proctor, Stevenson, Sumner, and Welty—15.

NAYS—0.

So the bill passed.

Senate Bill 139, "An Act to increase the number of Justices of the Supreme Court and to fix their Compensation."

Made the special order for Wednesday, February 20th, at 12 o'clock M.

Senate Bill No. 134, "An Act to provide for the Recording of certain Papers affecting the Titles of Claims to Real Property."

Made special order for Thursday, February 21st, at 12 o'clock M.

Mr. Sumner, by leave, introduced the following resolution:

Resolved, That the Committee on Ways and Means be authorized to communicate by telegraph with the State Treasurer at San Francisco, with regard to the Loan Bill, and the possibilities or probabilities of raising money thereon.

Adopted.

At 1:5 P.M., on motion of Mr. Sumner, the Senate took a recess until 3:30 P.M.

IN SENATE.

The Senate met at 3:30 P.M., President in the chair.

Roll called.

Quorum present.

MESSAGES FROM THE ASSEMBLY.

The following Messages were received from the Assembly:

ASSEMBLY CHAMBER, CARSON CITY, }
February 18th, 1867. }

To the Honorable the Senate:

I am instructed to return to your honorable body Senate Bill No. 89, "An Act to enable a Defendant to testify as a Witness in Criminal Prosecutions," which has this day passed the House, notwithstanding the Governor's objections. Ayes, 37; nays, 1.

Respectfully,

A. WHITFORD,
Clerk.

ASSEMBLY CHAMBER, CARSON CITY, }
February 18th, 1867. }

To the Honorable the Senate:

I am instructed to return to your honorable body Senate Substitute Bill No. 102, entitled "An Act to Transfer certain Moneys in the State Treasury to the County School Funds,' the House having refused to receive the same in its present shape, it not being properly engrossed.

Respectfully,

A. WHITFORD,
Clerk.

Mr. Stevenson, by leave without previous notice, introduced Senate Bill No. 156, "An Act to amend an Act entitled 'An Act to Incorporate the town of Gold Hill,' approved March 7th, 1865."

Read first time; rules suspended; read second time by title, and ordered engrossed.

Substitute Senate Bill No. 102, " An Act to transfer certain Moneys in the State Treasury to the County School Funds."

Ordered to be reëngrossed.

Mr. Grey, by leave, introduced the following resolution :

Resolved, That 240 copies of Substitute Senate Bill No. 130 be ordered printed, and that the resolution ordering the printing of the original bill be rescinded, provided the Secretary has not yet given the copy thereof to the State Printer.

Adopted.

Mr. Meder rose to a question of privilege on the part of the Hon. C. M. Brosnan, relative to an article appearing in a former issue of the *Gold Hill News*.

Mr. Hutchins rose to a question of privilege, explanatory of remarks made on a former occasion.

Mr. Sumner rose to a question of privilege, claiming that the question to which Mr. Meder rose was entirely unprecedented, asserting that the report of Senator Hutchins' remarks complained of originally appeared in the *Territorial Enterprise*, and declaring that the statement of the same was true.

Mr. Mason moved that the apology of the Hon. C. M. Brosnan be accepted. Carried.

The following communication was received from the Rev. A. F. White, late Superintendent of Public Instruction :

CARSON CITY, February 18th, 1867.

To the Senate of the State of Nevada:

I am informed that a remark contained in my last report, found on page 41, under the head " Proposed Amendments to the School Law," has been misunderstood by members of the Legislature, and construed as reflecting upon the Surveyor General. The remark is : " From the fact that the Surveyor General resides in Virginia City, it has been difficult to have full meetings of this Board at any time." The "difficulty" mentioned refers wholly to the distance, and the expense necessarily incurred in visiting Carson to attend meetings of the Board. There was no design whatever to imply that the Surveyor General was ever wanting in interest or willingness to perform faithfully and fully every duty as a member of the State Board of Education ; and hence, at the close of the paragraph in which the remark occurs, I recommended that he be retained as a member of the Board.

I have the honor to be,
Yours most obediently,
A. F. WHITE.

Assembly Concurrent Resolution No. 57, in relation to joint convention for the election of Commissioner.

Read and adopted.

At 4:10 P.M., on motion of Mr. Hutchins, the Senate adjourned.

JAMES S. SLINGERLAND,
President.

Attest—B. C. BROWN,
Secretary.

IN SENATE—FORTY-FOURTH DAY.

CARSON CITY, February 19th, 1867.

The Senate met pursuant to adjournment.
President in the chair.
Roll called.
Present—Messrs. Doron, Eastman, Edwards, Geller, Grey, Haines, Hastings, Hutchins, Linn, Meder, Monroe, Nelson, Proctor, Stevenson, Sumner, Terry, and Welty—17.
Absent—Mr. Nelson—1.
Prayer by the Chaplain.
The Journal of the Forty-third day was read and approved.
On motion, Mr. Mason was granted leave of absence for one day.
A Message was received from the Governor, and laid temporarily on the table.

REPORTS OF COMMITTEES.

Mr. Monroe, Chairman of Committee on Claims, submitted the following report:

Your Committee on Claims, to which was referred Senate Bill No. 96, entitled "An Act to make Compensation to the Hon. John Cradlebaugh, United States District Judge, the same as that of the late United States District Judges of the Territory of Nevada," would respectfully report that this claim, asking for the same compensation as above, required and has received the careful consideration of your Committee.

We find that said Cradlebaugh, in 1859, was one of the Associate Justices of the Supreme Court of the Territory of Utah, and was at that time located at Salt Lake City, and dispensing justice in a manner not satisfactory to the *Mormon population* of that portion of the Territory.

The Legislature of the Territory, at the session of 1858–9, established a district composed of the counties of Humboldt, St. Mary's, and Carson, which district substantially covered the territory which is now the State of Nevada, and assigned him to officiate in said district, which he did from August 1st, 1859, until March 15th, 1861, and had exclusive jurisdiction over all criminal and civil cases.

We find that the amount of business before his Court was extensive, and which required the holding of Court 181 days in 1860, some testimony going to show that he transacted more business than has ever been done by any other Court during the same time either in the State or Territory; that all the expenses of living and doing business in that day were much higher than since, and that the compensation paid by the Federal Government to its officials was totally inadequate to defray the necessary expenses of their positions.

We find that the Territory of Nevada paid to Justices Turner, Mott, Jones, North, Lock, all appointees of the Federal Government, the sum of $4,200 per annum as salary, aside from what they were then receiving from the Federal Government, as shown by an Act passed December 19th, 1862. In addition to this, certain fees arising in the District Court were paid to the Judges of the same, in accordance with a law passed November 9th, 1861. Also, that all Federal officers, including the Governor, and all officers appointed by and under said Cradlebaugh, have been paid by the Territory, in addition to what they received from the said Federal Government.

We find that the Territorial Legislature of Nevada audited and ordered paid to certain officers, acting under the laws of Utah Territory and before the Territory of Nevada was formed. Among them are the following cases:

October 31st, 1864. To John L. Blackburn, as Deputy United States Marshal of the Territory of Utah and Sheriff of Carson County, the sum of $11,631$\frac{25}{100}$.

November 7th, 1861. To A. James, Clerk of District Court, $620.

November 29th, 1861. To P. H. Clayton, for services and fees in Criminal cases, $669.

December 29th, 1862. To Wellington Stewart, for fees, etc., as Selectman and Justice of the Peace in Carson County, ——.

This case is one of equity, and not based upon statutory law, as we are unable to find any Act passed by the Legislature of either the State or Territory of Nevada, which assumed the indebtedness of that or any portion of Utah Territory out of which grew the Territory and State of Nevada; but we do find that former Legislatures, at a time when the cases were fresh before them, have passed upon, allowed, and ordered paid many if not all that have brought claims before them for services rendered in that portion of Utah which became Nevada; and we cannot see, as a matter of equity, why the State of Nevada is not as much bound to respect claims arising in Utah Territory, where the benefits derived from such services are the legitimate heritage of the people of the State of Nevada, as though they did arise under the government of our own State.

The precedents are numerous and to the point, in this, that several former Legislatures have by their Acts for relief, which they have passed from time to time, to give compensation for services performed of a similar character to the claim before us, is that it partakes of the color of law, aside from the equity. This case comes before us without any of the usual objections that are attached to old claims. No examination has ever been held, and reports or legislation thereon that would go to show that there had been doubts about the justice or equity of the claims, and the modesty of the Hon. Judge is the only reason we can see why he has not applied before for relief, while those who have been paid for similar services have all left the State and are no longer identified with our welfare or interests, while he has always been a resident (except when absent on business connected with the organization of the Territory of Nevada, and as our delegate in Congress, and also while serving in the Federal Army during a portion of the time of the late rebellion) and tax payer, and is intimately acquainted [connected] with all our interests; and inasmuch as former Legislatures have seen fit to compensate others that were here only temporarily, it would seem like injustice to not at least equally compensate one of her own citizens, who has performed a large amount of valuable and important service, and which by testimony is shown to be greater than by any other Court since. We would say, without intending any flattery, that the Hon. John Cradlebaugh exercised the duties of his office with marked ability and integrity, dispensing the law and justice in such a manner that it was a *terror to evil doers*, and gave universal satisfaction to all law-abiding citizens of the Territory; and as some proof of this, the Legislature of the Territory of Nevada, November 21st, 1861, passed a Memorial to Congress, a portion of which reads as follows:

"Your memorialists further represent that the labor to be performed by said official was of great importance and required almost the entire time and attention of the Judge, and that he was faithful and diligent in the discharge of the duties of the office. Your memorialists are advised that no payment of salary has been made since the year 1859." (The pay spoken of, he received in 1863.)

We are, therefore, of the opinion, from the fact of the service performed, and expenses incurred, the value of such services to the citizens of the State at large, and the equity of the claim, together with the precedents quoted touching cases of this kind; we recommend the passage of Substitute Bill, which is herewith submitted.

WM. G. MONROE, Chairman;
C. H. EASTMAN,
T. D. EDWARDS,
JOHN NELSON.

Mr. Sumner, from Committee on Ways and Means, to which was referred Senate Bill No. 150, "An Act to amend an Act entitled 'An Act authorizing a State Loan and levying a Tax to provide Means for the Payment thereof," approved Feb. 6th, 1867, reported that they had had the same under consideration, and report the same back without recommendation, and present the following telegraphic dispatches which they had received:

SAN FRANCISCO, Feb. 18th, 1867.

To Senate Committee on Ways and Means:

The bankers have answered the dispatch you sent me. But the principal reason we can't do better, is that money is worth fifteen and more, except on first class city mortgage and such securities.

E. RHOADES.

SAN FRANCISCO, Feb. 18th, 1867.

To Senate Committee on Ways and Means, Carson:

Mr. Rhoades has shown us your dispatch. Utterly impossible. Cannot exchange or sell at twelve (12). At fifteen (15) per cent. can arrange for a portion of the two hundred thousand (200,000) dollars bonds, we advancing the balance. Outside of the Pacific Insurance Co. and ourselves, cannot sell bonds at fifteen (15) per cent., but we will cheerfully aid and do all we can.

D. O. MILLS,
W. C. RALSTON,
JOHN PARROTT,
F. LIVINGSTON.

Mr. Stevenson asked leave to make a minority report February 20th, on the claim of John Cradlebaugh.

Granted.

Mr. Hastings, reported that the Standing Committee on Engrossment had carefully compared the following entitled bills with the originals, and found the same correctly engrossed, viz:

Senate Bill No. 131, "An Act to prohibit the Carrying of Concealed Weapons."

Also, Substitute Senate Bill No. 102, "An Act to transfer certain Moneys in the State Treasury to the County School Funds;" and herewith report the same back to the Senate.

Mr. Eastman, from Standing Committee on Corporations, to which was referred the bill entitled "An Act to amend an Act relating to Sheriffs, approved November 28th, 1861," report that they had had the same under consideration, had come to a favorable conclusion thereon, had directed their chairman to report the same to the Senate without amendments, and to recommend its passage.

Mr. Proctor, from the Standing Committee on Counties and County Boundaries, to which was referred Assembly Bill No. 13, entitled "An Act amendatory and supplementary of and supplemental to an Act entitled 'An Act to create the County of Lincoln, and provide for its Organization,' approved February 26th, 1866," reported that they had had the same under consideration, and recommend that it be amended, by striking out in Sec. 4, the fifth, sixth, seventh and eighth lines, and insert the following :

"Said county shall constitute the ――――― Judicial District, and a Judge thereof shall be appointed by the Governor, who shall hold his office until the next general election, and until his successor is elected and qualified. Said District Judge shall receive ―――――― dollars, payable out of the general fund of the County."

Also, amend by striking out Section 5.

When so amended, they recommend that the bill do pass.

Mr. Linn, Chairman of Standing Committee on Enrollment, reported that Senate Bill No. 14, entitled "An Act for the Relief of S. L. Baker," had been carefully compared with the engrossed bill as passed by the two Houses, found correctly enrolled, and had this day been delivered to the Governor for his approval.

Messrs. Proctor and Sumner presented the following minority report from Committee on Judiciary :

Mr. President :

The undersigned disagreeing with the majority of the Judiciary Committee in their report concerning Assembly Bill No. 71, entitled "An Act to repeal all Acts or parts of Acts so far as they conflict with the provisions of an Act of Congress entitled 'An Act to protect all Persons in the United States in their Civil Rights, and furnish the means for their vindication,' passed April 9th, 1866," begs leave to suggest in general terms the following objections to the bill:

1st. That the general terms employed leave it in doubt and uncertainty as to which of the laws of the State are repealed ; and the result may be that the laws will be by judicial construction declared repealed, which the present Legislature did not design to annul, and for the repeal of which a constitutional vote could not possibly be obtained.

The undersigned deem it unwise to amend and set aside entire codes relating to specific subjects in such sweeping terms, and think that a repealing clause should never be inserted in a law except for the purpose of annulling laws in direct conflict with the provisions of the law of which the repealing clause is a part.

2d. The effect of this bill, if it become a law, is to render persons competent to sit as jurors, and to testify in civil cases, who cannot become, under our Constitution, voters ; while the undersigned feel confident that bills rendering such persons competent jurors and witnesses in all cases, could not receive the assent of the Legislature, or meet the approbation of the people of the State.

3d. The Civil Rights Bill passed by Congress, has been declared unconstitutional by the President of the United States ; and late decisions of the Supreme Court of the United States indicate very clearly that that great tribunal and safeguard to the liberties of the people will concur with the Chief Executive of the nation.

If, then, that bill should be declared unconstitutional by all the Courts of the country, including our own, the result would still be that our laws, repealed by the bill under consideration, would remain dead ; and we would be placed in the anomalous condition of having abrogated important laws to prevent a supposed conflict with that which proves not to be a law.

4th. The passage of this bill is unnecessary, because if the Act of Congress, known as the Civil Rights Bill, be constitutional, all laws, both National and State, which are in conflict with it, cease to be laws, and become inoperative until a repeal of said Act, as though never enacted. It is, therefore, in the opinion of the Committee, better to allow our laws intended to be repealed, to stand as heretofore, and to be suspended or revived as the Congress may by its constitutional legislation determine.

Your Committee, for the reasons given, and many more that might be urged, recommend that the bill do not pass.

Mr. Meder, from Special Committee, to which was referred Senate Bill No. 122, entitled "An Act to further prescribe Rules and Regulations for the Execution of the Trusts arising under the Act of Congress, approved May 23d, 1844, entitled 'An Act for the Relief of Citizens of Towns upon Lands of the United States under certain circumstances,'" reports that they have had the same under consideration, substituted a new bill, and recommend the passage of the substitute.

Mr. Terry, from the Select Committee consisting of Lander County delegation, to which was referred the bill entitled "An Act amendatory of and supplementary to an Act entitled an Act to amend an Act entitled an Act amendatory of and supplementary to an Act of the Legislative Assembly of the Territory of Nevada entitled 'An Act to Incorporate the City of Austin,' approved Feb. 20th, A.D. 1864, approved March 8th, 1865, approved February 27th, 1866," report that they have had the same under consideration, come to a favorable conclusion thereon, and directed their chairman to report the same to the Senate without amendments, and recommend its passage.

The following Message was received from the Governor:

EXECUTIVE DEPARTMENT, CARSON CITY, }
February 19th, 1867. }

To the Hon. Senate of Nevada:

I have this day approved Senate Bill No. 40, (by substitute) "An Act to repeal an Act of the Legislative Assembly of the Territory of Nevada, entitled 'An Act authorizing the Private Secretary of the Governor to demand and receive certain Fees,' approved Nov. 29th, 1861; also, to repeal an Act of the Legislature of the State of Nevada, entitled 'An Act in relation to the Collection of certain Fees heretofore collected by the Governor's Private Secretary,' approved Feb. 17th, 1866."

Also, Senate Bill No. 69, (by substitute) "An Act supplementary to an Act entitled 'An Act to create a Board of County Commissioners in the several Counties of this State, and to define their Duties and Powers,' approved March 8th, 1865."

H. G. BLASDEL,
Governor.

INTRODUCTION OF BILLS.

Substitute Senate Bill No. 122, reported from Special Committee consisting of Ormsby and Washoe County delegations, "An Act to further prescribe Rules and Regulations for the Execution of the Trusts arising under the Act of Congress approved March [May] 23d, 1844, entitled 'An Act for the Relief of Citizens of Towns upon Lands of the United States under certain circumstances."

Read first time; rules suspended; read second time by title.

Substitute Senate Bill No. 96, reported from the Committee on Claims, " To make Compensation to the Hon. John Cradlebaugh, late United States District Judge, the same as that of the late United State District Judges of the Territory of Nevada."

Read first time; rules suspended; read second time by title.

GENERAL FILE.

Senate Bill No. 131, "An Act to prohibit the Carrying of Concealed Weapons." Read third time by sections.

The yeas and nays were called on the final passage of the bill, and recorded as follows:

YEAS—Messrs. Eastman, Grey, Haines, Hastings, Hutchins, Linn, Meder, Nelson, Stevenson, Sumner, Terry, and Welty—12.

NAYS—Messrs. Doron, Edwards, Geller, Monroe, Proctor—5.

So the bill passed.

Mr. Hutchins in the chair.

Senate Bill No. 150, "An Act to amend an Act entitled 'An Act authorizing a State Loan, and levying a Tax to provide means for the payment thereof,' approved Feb. 6th, 1867."

Bill considered engrossed.

Read third time by sections.

The yeas and nays were called on the final passage of the bill, and recorded as follows:

YEAS—Messrs. Doron, Eastman, Edwards, Geller, Grey, Hastings, Hutchins, Linn, Meder, Monroe, Stevenson, Sumner—12.

NAYS—Messrs. Haines, Nelson, Proctor, Terry, and Welty—5.

So the bill passed.

A Message was received from the Assembly, and laid temporarily on the table.

Senate Bill No. 149, "An Act amendatory of and supplementary to an Act entitled an Act to amend an Act entitled an Act amendatory of and supplementary to an Act of the Legislative Assembly of the Territory of Nevada entitled 'An Act to Incorporate the City of Austin,' approved Feb. 20th, 1864, approved March 8th, 1865, approved February 27th, 1866."

Ordered engrossed.

At 1 o'clock P.M., on motion of Mr. Sumner, the Senate took a recess until 2 o'clock.

IN SENATE.

The Senate met at 2 P.M., Mr. Sumner, President *pro tem.*, in the chair.

Roll called.

Quorum present.

On motion of Mr. Welty, the Senate went into Committee of the Whole for the consideration of the General File, Mr. Sumner in the chair.

The Committee rose, and submitted the following report:

Mr. President:

The Senate, in Committee of the Whole, have had under consideration Senate Bill No. 140, "An Act to amend an Act to provide for Organizing and Disciplining the Militia of this State, approved March 4th, 1865," which they report back with amendments, and recommend it be ordered engrossed.

Also, Assembly Bill No. 71, " An Act to repeal all Acts, or parts of Acts, so far as they conflict with an Act of Congress entitled 'An Act to protect all Persons in the United States in their Civil Rights, and furnish the means of their

19

Vindication,' passed April 9th, 1866," which they report back, and recommend that the bill be recommitted to the Judiciary Committee.

Also Assembly Bill No. 60, " An Act to amend an Act entitled ' An Act relating to Sheriffs,' approved November 28th, 1861," which they report back, and recommend the bill do pass.

Also Assembly Bill No. 13, " An Act amendatory of and supplemental to an Act to create the County of Lincoln, and provide for its organization, approved February 26th, 1866," which they report back, and ask leave to sit again.

A Message was received from the Assembly, and laid temporarily on the table.

GENERAL FILE.

Senate Bill No. 140, " An Act to amend an Act to provide for Organizing and Disciplining the Militia of this State, approved March 4th, 1865."

The amendments of the Committee of the Whole were adopted, and the bill ordered engrossed.

Assembly Bill No. 71, " An Act to repeal all Acts or parts of Acts so far as they conflict with an Act of Congress entitled ' An Act to protect all Persons in the United States in their Civil Rights, and furnish the means of their Vindication,' passed April 9th, 1866."

Recommitted to the Judiciary Committee.

Assembly Bill No. 60, " An Act to amend an Act entitled ' An Act in relation to Sheriffs,' approved November 28th, 1861."

Read third time by sections. The yeas and nays were called on the final passage of the bill, and recorded as follows:

YEAS—Messrs. Eastman, Edwards, Geller, Haines, Hastings, Hutchins, Linn, Mason, Monroe, Nelson, Proctor, Stevenson, Sumner, and Welty—14.

NAYS—Messrs. Doron, Grey, Meder, and Terry—4.

So the bill passed.

Assembly Bill No. 13, " An Act amendatory of and supplemental to ' An Act to create the County of Lincoln, and to provide for its organization,' approved February 26th, 1866."

Leave granted to sit again.

The following communication was received from the Secretary of State:

OFFICE OF SECRETARY OF STATE, }
Carson City, February 19th, 1867. }

To the Senate of Nevada:

GENTLEMEN—I have the honor to transmit herewith the claim of Messrs. Kinkead, Harrington & Co. against the State of Nevada for 556\frac{55}{100}$, the same having been examined and rejected by the State Board of Examiners, as not being a legitimate charge against the State.

Very respectfully,

C. N. NOTEWARE,
Secretary of the Board of Examiners.

Referred to Commitee on Claims.

At 4:15 P.M., on motion of Mr. Hutchins, the Senate adjourned.

JAMES S. SLINGERLAND,
President.

Attest—B. C. BROWN,
Secretary.

IN SENATE—FORTY-FIFTH DAY.

CARSON CITY, February 20th, 1867.

The Senate met pursuant to adjournment, President in the chair.

Roll called.

Present—Messrs. Doron, Eastman, Edwards, Geller, Grey, Haines, Hastings, Hutchins, Linn, Mason, Meder, Monroe, Nelson, Proctor, Stevenson, Sumner, Terry, and Welty—18.

Absent—0.

Prayer by the Chaplain.

The Journal of the Forty-fourth day was read and approved.

REPORTS OF COMMITTEES.

Mr. Linn, Chairman Committee on Enrollment, reported that Senate Bill No. 150, entitled "An Act to amend an Act entitled 'An Act authorizing a State Loan, and levying a Tax to provide means for the Payment thereof,' approved February 6th, 1867," had been carefully compared with the engrossed bill, as passed by the two Houses, found correctly enrolled, and that the same had this day been delivered to the Governor for his approval.

Mr. Hastings reported that the Standing Committee on Engrossment had carefully compared the following entitled bills with the originals, and found the same correctly engrossed, viz:

Senate Bill No. 149, "An Act amendatory of and supplementary to an Act entitled an Act to amend an Act of the Legislative Assembly of the Territory of Nevada, entitled 'An Act to Incorporate the City of Austin,' approved February 20th, A.D. 1864, approved March 8th, 1865, approved February 27th, 1866."

Also, Senate Bill No. 156, "An Act to amend an Act entitled 'An Act to Incorporate the Town of Gold Hill,' approved March 7th, 1865 ;" and herewith report the same back to the Senate.

Mr. Nelson, from Committee on State Library, reported that they had had under consideration Senate Bill No. 94, entitled "An Act to compensate J. F. Hatch for services in the State Library," that they had amended the same, and recommend its passage as amended.

Mr. Mason, from Standing Committee on Federal Relations, to whom was referred Assembly Concurrent Resolution No. 89, relating to a Weekly Mail, from Aurora to the Lower Crossing of the Truckee, reported that they had had the same under consideration, had come to a favorable conclusion thereon, and recommend their passage.

Mr. Stevenson, from the Standing Committee on Claims, to which was referred the claim of Hon. John Cradlebaugh, late Judge of Nevada Territory, submits the following as a minority report:

In the opinion of a minority of your Committee, there [are] many statements in the majority report heretofore submitted, and in the testimony before the Committee, on which such majority report is based, which tend to make a wrong impression.

The claimant says he went to Washington in December, 1859, on business connected with the Territory, and returned in March or April. What authority had he for going on business connected with the Territory? The records of that date show that John J. Musser was the only one sent by authority. In the opinion of a minority of your Committee, the fact of his neglecting the important judicial business of that time to go unauthorized to Washington, is an argument against the allowance by the State of his claim.

The minority of your Committee also differs from the majority on the statement that the claimant gave universal satisfaction. But although his unpopularity, of which every old resident is cognizant, should not argue against any just claim, yet, on the other hand, a statement that he gave "universal satisfaction" should be allowed no weight in his favor.

The claimant has not been unrewarded for his services. By virtue of an Act of Congress, the Judges of Utah Territory were allowed an annual salary of $2,500; and this amount the claimant received.

Nor should the fact of the payment by the Legislature of the claims of John Blackburn and others argue in favor of allowing every extravagant bill which may be presented for payment; more especially should such precedents be disregarded at this time, when the State is groaning under a load of debt; but in legislation, as in private affairs, we should be just before we are generous.

By reference to Sec. 7 of "An Act creating the Office and defining the Duties of Territorial Auditor," approved Nov. 29, 1861, it will be seen that the Territorial Legislature intended to put a stop to the endless presentation of claims; for it requires all claims against the Territory to be presented within two years after the same accrue, *and not afterwards*. And this provision acts as a bar to the payment of the demand of the claimant, and should outweigh any precedents heretofore established by the former payment of similar claims.

Believing that if this claim were allowed, there would be hundreds of others of equal merit presented to the Legislature of this State, the minority of your Committee recommend that it be disallowed, and that the bill relating thereto do not pass.

C. C. STEVENSON.

MOTIONS AND RESOLUTIONS.

Senate Concurrent Resolution No. 158, relating to printing the Report of the Surveyor General.

Read and adopted.

On motion, Assembly Memorial No. 18, to Congress, asking a reduction of Freight and Fare upon the Central Pacific Railroad of California, special order for 12 o'clock, was postponed until to-morrow, Feb. 21st, at 2 o'clock P.M.

On motion, Senate Bill No. 139, "An Act to increase the number of Justices of the Supreme Court, and to fix their Compensation," special order for 12 o'clock, was postponed until Monday, Feb. 25th, at 12 o'clock M.

On motion, the Code of Civil Procedure, which was special order for 12 o'clock M., was postponed until Thursday, Feb. 21st, at 2 P.M.

MESSAGES FROM THE ASSEMBLY.

ASSEMBLY CHAMBER, CARSON CITY,
February 19th, 1867.

To the Hon. the Senate :

I am instructed to inform your honorable body that the House on yesterday concurred in Senate amendments to Assembly Bill No. 20, "An Act to amend an Act entitled 'An Act in relation to the Distribution of the Reports of the Supreme Court of the State of Nevada,' approved March 4th, A.D. 1866."

I also transmit to your honorable body for your consideration, Assembly Bill No. 5, entitled "An Act to create three additional Commissioners to represent the State of Nevada at the World's Fair, to be held at Paris, France, in the year of our Lord 1867," which passed the House this day, notwithstanding the objections of the Governor.

YEAS—32.
NAYS—5.

Respectfully,

A. WHITFORD,
Clerk.

ASSEMBLY CHAMBER, CARSON CITY, }
February 19, 1867.

To the Honorable the Senate:

I am instructed to return to your honorable body, Senate Bill No. 113, "An Act to amend an Act entitled 'An Act to regulate Fees and Compensation for Official and other Services in the State of Nevada,' approved March 9th, 1865," the same having passed the House this day, amended as follows: At the end of section one, by adding the following words: " Provided that nothing in this Act shall be so construed as to require personal attendance in filing such statements, and such statements may be transmitted by mail, express, or otherwise directed to the Clerk of the Board of County Commissioners."

Also, Senate Bill No. 150, "An Act to amend an Act entitled 'An Act authorizing a State Loan, and levying a Tax to provide Means for the Payment thereof,' approved February 6th, 1867," the same having passed the House this day, without amendment.

Respectfully,

A. WHITFORD,
Clerk.

Senate Bill No. 113, "An Act to amend an Act entitled 'An Act to regulate Fees and Compensation for Official and other Services in the State of Nevada,' approved March 9th, 1865."

The yeas and nays were called on the question of concurring in the Assembly amendments to bill and recorded as follows:

YEAS—Messrs. Eastman, Edwards, Geller, Haines, Hastings, Linn, Mason, Meder, Nelson, Proctor, Stevenson, Sumner, Terry, and Welty—14.
NAYS—0.

So the amendments were concurred in.

Assembly Bill No. 5, entitled "An Act to create three additional Commissioners to represent the State of Nevada at the World's Fair, to be held in Paris, France, A.D. 1867."

The question being: Shall the bill pass notwithstanding the objections of the Governor?

The yeas and nays were called on motion of Mr. Sumner.

The announcement of the vote was postponed until to-morrow, at 12 o'clock M.

GENERAL FILE.

Senate Bill No. 149, "An Act amendatory of and supplementary to an Act entitled an Act to amend an Act entitled an Act amendatory and supplemental to an Act of the Legislative Assembly of the Territory of Nevada, entitled 'An Act to Incorporate the City of Austin,' approved February 20, 1864, approved March 8th, 1865, approved February 20, 1866."

Read third time by sections.

The yeas and nays were called on the final passage of the bill, and recorded as follows:

YEAS—Messrs. Doron, Eastman, Geller, Haines, Hastings, Linn, Mason, Meder, Monroe, Nelson, Proctor, Stevenson, Sumner, Terry, and Welty—15.

NAYS—0.

So the bill passed.

Senate Bill No. 156, "An Act to amend an Act entitled 'An Act to Incorporate the Town of Gold Hill,' approved March 7th, 1865."

Read third time by sections.

The yeas and nays were called on the final passage of the bill, and recorded as follows:

YEAS—Messrs. Doron, Eastman, Edwards, Geller, Haines, Hastings, Hutchins, Linn, Mason, Meder, Monroe, Nelson, Proctor, Stevenson, Sumner, Terry, and Welty—17.

NAYS—0.

So the bill passed.

Senate Bill No. 94, "An Act to compensate J. F. Hatch for Services in the State Library."

The question was on the adoption of the amendments as made by the Committee on State Library.

The yeas and nays were called for by Messrs. Welty, Terry, and Hastings, and recorded as follows:

YEAS—Messrs. Doron, Edwards, Haines, Hastings, Hutchins, Mason, Meder, Nelson, Proctor, Stevenson, Terry, and Welty—12.

NAYS—Messrs. Eastman, Geller, Linn, Monroe, and Sumner—5.

So the amendments were concurred in.

On motion of Mr. Monroe, the Senate went into Committee of the Whole for the consideration of Senate Bill No. 94.

President in the chair.

The Committee rose, and submitted the following report:

Mr. President:

The Senate, in Committee of the Whole, have had under consideration Senate Bill No. 94, "An Act to compensate J. F. Hatch for Services in the State Library." which they report back, and recommend to strike out the words, "one hundred," and insert the words "one hundred and fifty."

Senate Bill No. 94, "An Act to compensate J. F. Hatch for Services in the State Library."

The amendments of the Committee of the Whole were adopted.

The yeas and nays were called for by Messrs. Meder, Welty, and Stevenson, on the reëngrossment of the bill, and recorded as follows:

YEAS—Messrs. Doron, Eastman, Edwards, Geller, Grey, Hastings, Hutchins, Linn, Mason, Monroe, Proctor, Sumner, and Terry—13.

NAYS—Messrs. Haines, Meder, Stevenson, and Welty—4.

So the bill was ordered reëngrossed.

Assembly Concurrent Resolution No. 39, relating to a Weekly Mail from Aurora to the lower crossing of the Truckee.

Read; the yeas and nays were called on the passage of the resolution, and recorded as follows:

YEAS—Messrs. Doron, Eastman, Geller, Haines, Hastings, Hutchins, Linn, Mason, Meder, Monroe, Nelson, Proctor, Stevenson, Sumner, Terry, and Welty —16.

NAYS—0.

So the resolution passed.

On motion, the Senate went into Committee of the Whole, for the consideration of the General File, President *pro tem.* in the chair.

The Committee rose, and submitted the following report:

Mr. President:

The Senate in Committee of the Whole have had under consideration, Senate Bill No. 96, "An Act to make Compensation to Hon. John Cradlebaugh, late United States District Judge, the same as that ot the United States District Judge of the Territory of Nevada," which they report back, and recommend that the substitute be adopted, and ordered engrossed.

Senate Bill No. 96, "An Act to make Compensation to Hon. John Cradlebaugh, late United States District Judge, the same as that of the late District Judge of the Territory of Nevada."

The substitute was adopted; the question being on ordering the bill engrossed, the yeas and nays were called for by Messrs. Hastings, Edwards, and Hutchins, and recorded as follows:

YEAS—Messrs. Doron, Eastman, Edwards, Geller, Grey, Hutchins, Linn, Mason, Monroe, Nelson, Proctor, Sumner, and Terry—13.

NAYS—Messrs. Hastings, Meder, Stevenson, and Welty—4.

So the bill was ordered engrossed.

At 2 o'clock P.M., on motion of Mr. Hastings, the Senate adjourned.

CHARLES A. SUMNER,
President [*pro tem.*]

Attest—B. C. BROWN,
Secretary.

IN SENATE—FORTY-SIXTH DAY.

CARSON CITY, February 21st, 1867.

The Senate met pursuant to adjournment, Mr. Sumner, President *pro tem.*, in the chair.

Roll called.

Present—Messrs. Doron, Eastman, Edwards, Geller, Grey, Haines, Hastings, Linn, Mason, Meder, Monroe, Stevenson, Sumner, Terry, Welty, and Nelson—16.

Absent—Messrs. Hutchins and Proctor—2.

Prayer by the Chaplain.
The Journal of the Forty-fifth day was read and approved.
On motion, Mr. Proctor was granted leave of absence for one day.

REPORTS OF COMMITTEES.

Mr. Hastings reported that the Standing Committee on Engrossment had carefully compared the following entitled bills with the originals, and found them correctly engrossed, viz:

Substitute Senate Bill No. 96, " An Act to make Compensation to the Hon. John Cradlebaugh, late United States District Judge, the same as that of the late United States District Judges of the Territory of Nevada."

Also Senate Bill No. 140, "An Act to amend an Act to provide for Organizing and Disciplining the Militia of this State,' approved March 4th, 1865."

Also, as correctly reëngrossed, Senate Bill No. 94, " An Act to compensate J. F. Hatch for Services in the State Library ;" and herewith reports the same back to the Senate.

Mr. Welty, from Judiciary Committee, to which was referred Assembly Bill No. 71, entitled " An Act to repeal all Acts, or parts of Acts, so far as they conflict with the Act of Congress, entitled 'An Act to protect all Persons in the United States in their Civil Rights, and furnish means of their vindication,' " reported that they had had the same under consideration, and a majority of the Committee had come to a favorable conclusion on the subject matter thereof; had directed their chairman to report to the Senate a substitute for the same, and to recommend its passage.

Mr. Linn, Chairman Committee on Enrollment, reported that Senate Bill No. 113, entitled " An Act to regulate Fees and Compensation for Official and other services in the State of Nevada," approved March 9th, 1865, had been carefully compared with the engrossed bill, as passed by the two Houses, found correctly enrolled, and will this day be delivered to the Governor for his approval.

Mr. Edwards submitted the following report:

Mr. President:

Your Committee of Conference appointed to meet a like Committee on the part of the Assembly, in relation to the differences between the two Houses on Senate Bill No. 31, report that they have met said Committee, have failed to adjust said differences, and have agreed to recommend the appointment of a Committee of Free Conference ; all of which is most respectfully submitted.

T. D. EDWARDS.

Senate Bill No. 31, " An Act concerning the Office of Public Administrator." On motion a Committee of Free Conference was appointed, consisting of Messrs. Edwards, Mason and Doron.

INTRODUCTION OF BILLS.

Senate Bill No. 146, (substitute for Assembly Bill No. 71) " An Act to repeal section 13 of the Act of the Legislative Assembly of the Territory of Nevada entitled ' An Act concerning Crimes and Punishments,' approved November 26th, 1861," and to amend section 342 of an Act of the Legislative Assembly aforesaid, approved November 29th, 1861, entitled " An Act to regulate Proceedings in the Courts of Justice of the Territory of Nevada."

Read first time ; rules suspended ; read second time by title, and referred to Committee of the Whole, and ordered printed.

GENERAL FILE.

Substitute Senate Bill No. 96, "An Act to make Compensation to the Hon. John Cradlebaugh, late United States District Judge, the same as that of the late United States District Judges of the Territory of Nevada."

On motion that further consideration of the bill be postponed until Monday, February 25th, the yeas and nays were called for by Messrs. Hastings, Meder and Stevenson, and recorded as follows:

YEAS—Messrs. Doron, Eastman, Edwards, Geller, Haines, Mason, Monroe, Sumner—8.

NAYS—Messrs. Grey, Hastings, Meder, Stevenson, Terry, and Welty—6.

So the consideration of the bill was postponed.

Senate Bill No. 140, "An Act to provide for Organizing and Disciplining the Militia of this State," approved March 4th, 1865.

Read third time by sections ; the yeas and nays were called on the final passage of the bill, and recorded as follows:

YEAS—Messrs. Eastman, Edwards, Geller, Grey, Haines, Hastings, Linn, Mason, Meder, Stevenson, Sumner, Terry, and Welty—14.

NAYS—Messrs. Doron and Monroe—2.

So the bill passed.

Senate Bill No. 94, "An Act to compensate J. F. Hatch for Services in the State Library."

Read third time by sections ; the yeas and nays were called on the passage of the bill, and recorded as follows:

YEAS—Messrs. Doron, Eastman, Edwards, Geller, Grey, Hastings, Linn, Mason, Monroe, Stevenson, Sumner, Terry, and Welty—13.

NAYS—Messrs. Haines and Meder—2.

So the bill passed.

A Message was received from the Assembly, and temporarily laid on the table.

Senate Bill No. 142, "An Act amendatory of an Act entitled ' An Act to provide for the Maintenance and Supervision of Public Schools,' approved March 20th, 1865."

Referred to Committee of the Whole.

On motion of Mr. Hastings, the Senate went into Committee of the Whole for the consideration of the General File.

President in the chair.

The Committee rose, and submitted the following report:

Mr. President:

The Senate, in Committee of the Whole, have had under consideration Substitute Senate Bill No. 122, "An Act to further prescribe rules and regulations for the execution of the Trusts arising under the Act of Congress approved May 23d, 1844, entitled ' An Act for the relief of Citizens of Towns upon Lands of the United States, under certain circumstances,' " which they report back, and recommend the bill to be ordered engrossed.

Also Senate Bill No. 151, "An Act to amend an Act entitled ' An Act to

20

regulate Proceedings in Criminal Cases in the Courts of Justice in the (Territory) State of Nevada, and making further provisions relating thereto,'" which they report back, and ask leave to sit again.

The hour having arrived for the announcement of the vote taken yesterday on the question: Shall Assembly Bill No. 5, entitled "An Act to create three additional Commissioners to represent the State of Nevada at the World's Fair, to be held at Paris, France, A.D. 1867," pass, notwithstanding the objections of the Governor? the vote was recorded as follows:

YEAS—Messrs. Doron, Edwards, Geller, Grey, Hastings, Hutchins, Linn, Mason, Monroe, Proctor, Stevenson, Sumner, Terry, and Welty—14.
NAYS—Messrs. Eastman, Haines, Meder, and Nelson—4.

So the bill passed.
Mr. Doron gave notice that on to-morrow he would move a reconsideration of the vote.
The President ruled the motion out of order, on the ground that according to the Constitution the bill was now a law.
Senate Concurrent Resolution, in relation to appointing a Joint Committee of Examination.
Read and adopted.
At 12 : 20 [P.]M., on motion of Mr. Edwards, the Senate took a recess until 2 o'clock P.M.

IN SENATE.

The Senate met at 2 P.M., Mr. Sumner, President *pro tem.*, in the chair.
Roll called.
Quorum present.
Senate Bill No. 134, "An Act to provide for the Recording of certain Papers affecting the Titles or Claims to Real Property."
The bill being the special order for 12 o'clock, was, on motion, placed on the General File.
Special order for 2 o'clock, Assembly Memorial No. 18, "Asking a Reduction of Freight and Fare upon the Central Pacific Railroad of California," was, on motion of Mr. Sumner, recommitted to a Committee of one, with instructions to amend the first preamble, making it read as follows:

Whereas, The Central Pacific Railroad of California, a Corporation aided and endowed under the laws of the United States to run eastward from the navigable waters of the Pacific Ocean, and whose road is being almost wholly built at the expense of the Federal Government, have seen fit to impose a tariff on passengers equivalent to ten cents per mile in coin—a rate exorbitant, and three-fold greater than ever known in the history of railways, except upon this Coast; and a tax upon freight corresponding in proportion.

The Committee reported the resolution amended as directed.
The report was adopted, and the resolution amended in accordance therewith.
A Message was received from the Governor, and laid temporarily upon the table.
A Message was received from the Hon. J. Neely Johnson, Civil Code Commissioner, and laid temporarily on the table.

At 4:10 P.M., on motion of Mr. Proctor, the Senate adjourned until Saturday, February 23d, at 11 o'clock A.M.

CHARLES A. SUMNER,
President [*pro tem.*]

Attest—B. C. BROWN,
Secretary.

IN SENATE—FORTY-EIGHTH DAY.

CARSON CITY, February 23d, 1867.

The Senate met pursuant to adjournment, Mr. Sumner, President *pro tem.*, in the chair.

Roll called.

Present—Messrs. Doron, Eastman, Edwards, Geller, Grey, Haines, Hastings, Hutchins, Linn, Mason, Meder, Monroe, Nelson, Proctor, Stevenson, Sumner, Terry, and Welty—18.

Absent—0.

The Journal of the Forty-sixth day was read, and amended so as to show that prior to the announcement of the vote on Assembly Bill No. 5, Mr. Doron moved a new roll call.

The Chair ruled the motion out of order; and after correction, approved.

REPORTS OF COMMITTEES.

Mr. Monroe, Chairman of Committee on Claims, submitted the following report:

Your Committee on Claims, to whom was referred, February 1st, the claim of S. H. Marlette, (Surveyor General) who seeks to obtain the sum of $712, for rent of office, porterage, printing, postage, express charge, copying, and other contingent expenses connected with the office, from December 1st, 1864, to May 1st, 1866; and have since had presented a further bill of items of same character, amounting to $205, which brings the account down to January 1st, 1867, and which makes the relief asked for, $917—

Would respectfully report as follows:

We find that the said Surveyor General submitted his account to the State Board of Examiners, and that they refused to approve of said account, except upon items amounting to 45\frac{75}{100}$. The following is the language of a portion of the record of said Board, in relation to this claim:

"And upon said examination, the Board do consider that the said account be approved for 45\frac{75}{100}$, being amount of proper contingent expenses, since January 1st, 1866. Rent deemed improper charge, because there is no authority of law for allowing the Surveyor General an office; porterage and printing errata deemed improper charges. All expenses incurred in 1864 and 1865 are rejected on the ground that the annual report of the Surveyor for the year 1865 (page 28) shows, that up to the close of that year, the Surveyor General's office had been running on its own responsibility, and paying its own expenses, for post office and express charges, stationery, fuel, rent, etc."

We find that there is no law compelling the State to furnish an office for the Surveyor General, or pay the contingent expenses connected with the same; but we do find that, by an Act approved March 10th, 1865, the Governor, Secretary of State, Supreme Judges, Clerk of the Supreme Court, State Treasurer, and Attorney General were allowed offices ; and that in some cases, former Legislatures have ordered the State to pay for offices other than above.

We find on a close examination of the items, that those for porterage, amounting to $107, should not be allowed, and that of $90, for eighteen days' assistance in copying and compiling statistics, we could not report favorably upon, only under the circumstances of the case, requiring that his report be made out by a certain day in accordance with law ; and the delay of the county surveyors to send in their reports made it necessary to employ such assistance. The charges for rent we deem very reasonable, being one-fourth of the amount which he paid for an office to transact both his own and the business connected with State. The balance being for contingent expenses, we can see no reason or precedent why it should not be allowed.

We find that the duties of the office are much greater than we had supposed, requiring about three months' labor to make out the annual report required by law ; and here we are happy to state that the reports of the Surveyor General are very elaborate and able, reflecting credit upon him as an officer, and imparting valuable information to the citizens at large, both of this and other States.

In view of all the contingent expenses having been paid by him in coin (should he not be reimbursed) the salary of $1,000 in currency is a very small compensation for the duties enjoined, services performed, and expenses incurred ; and with all due respect to the State Board of Examiners, we cannot see how they could interpret from the quotation taken from the Surveyor General's Report of 1865, that the office itself has reimbursed the officer, while, on the contrary, he says the office "has been running on its own responsibility, and paying its own expenses." It seems plain enough that he has individually paid all these expenses. From the equity of the claim, and believing that the Surveyor General should be entitled to a reasonable rent for an office and the necessary expenses of the same, do recommend that a bill herewith submitted appropriating $810, do pass.

All of which is respectfully submitted.

Senate Bill No. 160, "An Act to provide for the Payment of the Contingent Expenses of the Surveyor General's Office from December, 1864, to December, 1866, inclusive." Reported from Committee on Claims.

Read first time ; rules suspended ; read second time by title, and placed on General File.

Mr. Linn, Chairman Committee on Enrollment, reported that Senate Bill No. 141, entitled "An Act to provide for the Payment of James Cochran for certain Services rendered and Expenses incurred in arresting and conveying W. S. Broadwater, a refugee from justice, from Trinity County, California, to this State," had been carefully compared with the engrossed bill, as passed by the two Houses, found correctly enrolled, and that the same had this day been delivered to the Governor for his approval.

MESSAGE FROM THE GOVERNOR.

The following Message was received from the Governor:

EXECUTIVE DEPARTMENT, }
Carson City, February 21st, 1867. }

To the Hon. the Senate of Nevada:

I hereby return to your honorable body, without approval, Senate Bill No. 150, entitled "An Act to amend an Act entitled 'An Act authorizing a State Loan, and levying a Tax to provide Means for the Payment thereof,' approved Feb. 6th, 1867."

The rate of interest proposed by this bill is greater than the State can pay on so large a sum of money. If the amount asked cannot be obtained under the original Act, at 12 per cent. per annum, would it not be better to pass another repealing it, and providing for a loan of a sufficient amount only to pay the Bonds due under Act of January 19th, 1866, and for immediate wants, the Bonds to run, say four years; and then provide for territorial and floating indebtedness by Bonds, to run, say eight or ten years?

But in no event can the State pay seventy-five thousand ($75,000) dollars per annum interest, and five hundred thousand ($500,000) dollars, principal, in five years.

I, therefore, return the bill for your future action.

H. G. BLASDEL,
Governor.

On motion, the vote whereby Senate Bill No. 150, entitled "An Act to amend an Act entitled 'An Act authorizing a State Loan, and levying a Tax to provide Means for the Payment thereof,' approved February 6th, 1867," was passed, was reconsidered.

The question being, "Shall the bill pass, notwithstanding the objections of the Governor?" the yeas and nays were called, and recorded as follows:

YEAS—Messrs. Doron, Eastman, Edwards, Geller, Grey, Hastings, Hutchins, Linn, Mason, Meder, Monroe, Nelson, Proctor, Stevenson, and Sumner—15.

NAYS—Messrs. Haines, Terry, and Welty—3.

So the bill passed.

MESSAGE FROM THE ASSEMBLY.

A Message was received from the Assembly.

At 1:5 P.M., the Senate, on motion of Mr. Mason, took a recess until two o'clock.

IN SENATE.

The Senate met at 2 o'clock P.M., Mr. Sumner, President *pro tem.*, in the chair.

Roll called.

Quorum present.

MESSAGE FROM THE GOVERNOR.

The following Message was received from the Governor:

EXECUTIVE DEPARTMENT, CARSON CITY, }
February 21st, 1867. }

To the Honorable the Senate of Nevada:

I have this day approved Senate Bill No. 14, "An Act for the Relief of S. L. Baker, late Probate Judge of Nye County."

H. G. BLASDEL,
Governor.

MOTIONS AND RESOLUTIONS.

Mr. Edwards moved that Assembly Bill No. 38, "An Act authorizing the Issuance and Exchange of certain State Bonds, levying a Tax to provide means for their Payment, and providing for the surrender of Bonds now outstanding, and to repeal all Laws in conflict therewith," be taken from the table.

Carried.

On motion of Mr. Edwards, the bill was indefinitely postponed.

MESSAGES FROM THE ASSEMBLY.

The following Messages were received from the Assembly :

ASSEMBLY CHAMBER, CARSON CITY, }
February 20th, 1867.

To the Hon. the Senate :

I am instructed to transmit to your honorable body, for your consideration, the following Assembly Bills, viz :

No. 86, " An Act to provide for the Official Publication of Laws and Resolutions, and other public documents," which passed the House on yesterday. Yeas, 22 ; nays, 15.

No. 97, " An Act to amend an Act entitled ' An Act for the Relief of Insolvent Debtors and Protection of Creditors,' " which passed the House this day. Yeas, 25 ; nays, 3.

No. 89, " An Act to amend an Act authorizing Rufus Walton and Westley Lambert to complete and maintain a Toll Road," approved December 19th, 1862, which passed the House this day. Yeas, 31 ; nays, 3.

I also return to your honorable body Senate Bill No. 141, "An Act to provide for the payment of James Cochran, for certain services rendered and expenses incurred in arresting and conveying one W. S. Broadwater, a refugee from justice, from Trinity County, California, to this State," the same having passed the House this day without amendment. Yeas, 30 ; nays, 5.

I am also instructed to inform you that the House has this day concurred in Senate amendments to Assembly Bill No. 43, "An Act to provide for properly taking Care of the Indigent Insane of the State of Nevada, and to create a Fund for that purpose," as per recommendation of Conference Committee.

Also, that the House have appointed, as a Committee of Free Conference on Senate Bill No. 31, " Relating to Public Administrators," consisting of Messrs. St. Clair, Tennant, and Wingate.

All of which is respectfully submitted.

A. WHITFORD,
Clerk.

ASSEMBLY CHAMBER, CARSON CITY, }
February 21st, 1867.

To the Hon. the Senate :

I am instructed to transmit to your honorable body for your consideration, Assembly Concurrent Resolution No. 42, relating to adjournment, the same having passed the Assembly this day unanimously.

I also return to you Senate Concurrent Resolution No. 158, relating to printing the Report of the Surveyor General, the same having passed the House this day.

Respectfully,

A. WHITFORD,
Clerk.

On motion, Mr. Doron was excused from the Committee of Free Conference on Assembly amendments to Senate Bill No. 31, "An Act relating to Public Administrators."

The Chair appointed Mr. Haines to fill the vacancy.

The following Message was received from the Assembly :

ASSEMBLY CHAMBER, CARSON CITY,
February 21st, 1867.

To the Honorable the Senate:

I am instructed to transmit to your honorable body for your consideration, the following Assembly Bills, which passed the House on yesterday, viz:

No. 84, "An Act providing for the Removal of County Seats, and the Permanent Location of the same."

No. 88, "An Act to amend Chapter 113, of the Statutes of 1866, entitled 'An Act to Consolidate and Pay certain Indebtedness of the County of Ormsby, approved March 12th, 1866."

Also, Assembly Bill No. 80, "An Act to amend an Act entitled 'An Act to provide Revenue for the Support of the Government of the State of Nevada,' approved March 9th, 1865," the same having passed the House this day.

I also return to you the following Senate Bills and Resolution which passed the House this day without amendments, viz:

No. 131, "An Act to prohibit the Carrying of Concealed Weapons."

Substitute Senate Bill No. 103, "An Act to transfer certain Moneys in the State Treasury to the County School Fund."

Senate Concurrent Resolution, No. 159, "In relation to appointing a Joint Committee of Examination."

Respectfully,
A. WHITFORD,
Clerk.

Assembly Bill No. 86, "An Act to provide for the Official Publication of Laws and Resolutions, and other Public Documents."

Read first time ; rules suspended: read second time by title, and referred to Committee on State Affairs.

Assembly Bill No. 97, "An Act to amend an Act entitled 'An Act for the Relief of Insolvent Debtors, and Protection of Creditors,' approved March 10th, 1865."

Read first time ; rules suspended ; read second time by title, and referred to Committee on Judiciary.

Assembly Bill No. 89, "An Act to amend an Act authorizing Rufus Walton and Westley Lambert to complete and maintain a Toll Road, approved December 19th, 1862."

Read first time ; rules suspended ; read second time by title, and referred to Committee on Corporations.

Assembly Concurrent Resolution, No. 42, "Relating to Adjournment."

Read and laid on the table.

Assembly Bill No. 84, "An Act providing for the Removal of County Seats, and the Permanent Location of the same."

Read first time ; rules suspended ; read second time by title, and referred to Committee on Counties and County Boundaries.

Assembly Bill No. 80, "An Act to amend an Act entitled 'An Act to provide Revenue for the Support of the Government of the State of Nevada,' approved March 9th, 1865."

Read first time ; rules suspended ; read second time by title, and referred to Committee on Ways and Means.

INTRODUCTION OF BILLS.

Mr. Haines, by leave without previous notice, introduced Senate Bill No. 167, "An Act to amend an Act of the Legislature of the Territory of Nevada, entitled ' An Act concerning Conveyances,' approved November 5th, 1861."

Read first time; rules suspended; read second time by title, and referred to Committee on Judiciary, and ordered printed.

Mr. Linn, by leave without previous notice, introduced Senate Bill No. 168, " An Act relative to Transcribing and Indexing certain Records in Humboldt County."

Read first time; rules suspended; read second time by title, and placed on the General File.

Mr. Welty, by leave without previous notice, introduced Senate Bill No. 169, " An Act to amend an Act, entitled an 'Act to provide for Reporting the Decisions of the Supreme Court of the State of Nevada,' approved March 14th, 1865."

Read first time; rules suspended; read second time by title, and referred to Committee on State Affairs.

Mr. Welty, by leave without previous notice, introduced Senate Bill No. 170, " An Act to amend an Act entitled ' An Act concerning the Office of Secretary of State,' approved February 14th, 1865.

Read first time; rules suspended; read second time by title, and referred to Committee on State Affairs.

Mr. Monroe, by leave without previous notice, introduced Senate Bill No. 171, "An Act to amend the Boundaries of Churchill County."

Read first time; rules suspended; read second time by title, and referred to the Committee on Counties and County Boundaries.

Mr. Edwards, by leave without previous notice, introduced Senate Bill No. 173, " An Act to amend an Act entitled ' An Act to regulate Fees and Compensation for Official and other Services in the State of Nevada,' approved March 9th, 1865."

Read first time; rules suspended; read second time by title, and referred to Committee on State Affairs.

Mr. Eastman, by leave without previous notice, introduced Senate Bill No. 172, " An Act supplementary to an Act entitled ' An Act to provide Revenue for the Support of the Government of the State of Nevada,' approved March 9th, 1865, and other Acts amendatory of and supplementary thereto."

Read first time; rules suspended; read second time by title, and referred to Committee on Ways and Means.

A Message was received from the Governor.

On motion of Mr. Welty, the Senate went into Committee of the Whole, for the consideration of the bills referred to Committee of the Whole and on General File, President in the chair.

The Committee rose, and submitted the following report:

The Senate, in Committee of the Whole, have had under consideration Senate Bill No. 151, " An Act to amend an Act entitled ' An Act to regulate Proceedings in Criminal Cases in the Courts of Justice in the (Territory) State of Nevada, and making further provisions in relation thereto," which they report back with amendments, and recommend the bill be engrossed as amended.

Also, Senate Bill No. 142, amendatory of an Act entitled ' An Act to provide for the Maintenance and Supervision of Public Schools,' approved March 20th, 1865," which they report back with amendments, and recommend the bill be ordered engrossed as amended.

Also, Assembly Bill No. 13, " An Act amendatory of and supplemental to ' An Act to create the County of Lincoln and provide for its Organization,' approved

February 26th, 1866," which they report back, and recommend the bill do not pass.

Senate Bill No. 151, "An Act to amend an Act entitled 'An Act to regulate Proceedings in Criminal Cases in the Courts of Justice in the (Territory) State of Nevada, and making further provisions relating thereto.' "

Amendments of the Committee of the Whole adopted, and the bill ordered engrossed.

Assembly Bill No. 13, "An Act amendatory of and supplemental to 'An Act to create the County of Lincoln, and provide for its Organization,' approved February 26th, 1866."

Placed at the foot of the General File.

Assembly Memorial No. 18, asking a reduction of Freight and Fare upon the Central Pacific Railroad of California.

Placed at the foot of the General File.

Senate Bill No. 142, amendatory of "An Act entitled 'An Act to provide for the Maintenance and Supervision of Public Schools,' approved March 20th, 1865."

The amendments of the Committee of the Whole were adopted, and the bill ordered engrossed.

Senate Bill No. 122, "An Act to further prescribe rules and regulations for the execution of the Trusts arising under the Act of Congress approved May 23d, 1844, entitled 'An Act for the Relief of the Citizens of Towns upon Lands of the United States under certain circumstances.' "

Ordered engrossed.

At 4:15 P.M., on motion of Mr. Hastings, the Senate adjourned until Monday, February 25th, at 11 o'clock A.M.

CHARLES A. SUMNER,
President [pro tem.]

Attest—B. C. BROWN,
Secretary.

IN SENATE—FIFTIETH DAY.

CARSON CITY, February 25th, 1867.

The Senate met pursuant to adjournment, Mr. Sumner, President pro tem., in the chair.

Roll called.

Present—Messrs. Doron, Eastman, Edwards, Geller, Grey, Haines, Hastings, Hutchins, Linn, Mason, Meder, Monroe, Nelson, Proctor, Stevenson, Sumner, Terry, and Welty—18.

Absent—0.

Prayer by the Chaplain.

The Journal of the Forty-eighth day was read and approved.

The Chaplain was, on motion, granted leave of absence for Saturday, February 23d.

A Message was received from the Assembly.

·21

REPORTS OF COMMITTEES.

Mr. Linn, Chairman Committee on Enrollment, reported that Senate Bill No. 131, entitled " An Act to prohibit the Carrying of Concealed Weapons;" Substitute Senate Bill No. 102, " An Act to transfer certain Moneys in the State Treasury to the County School Funds," had been carefully compared with the engrossed bills as passed by the two Houses, found correctly enrolled, and that the same had this day been delivered to the Governor for his approval.

Mr. Hastings reported that the Standing Committee on Engrossment had carefully compared the following entitled bill with the original, and found the same correctly engrossed, viz :

Senate Bill No. 142, entitled " An Act amendatory of ' An Act to provide for the Maintenance and Supervision of Public Schools,' approved March 20th, 1865,'" and herewith reports the same back to the Senate.

Mr. Proctor reported that the Committee on Counties and County Boundaries had had under consideration the Senate Bill No. 101, entitled " An Act to amend the Boundaries of Churchill County ;" had directed their chairman to report a substitute bill.

Also, Assembly Bill No. 84, entitled " An Act to provide for the removal of County Seats and the Permanent Location of the same," and had directed their chairman to report the same back with amendments, and to recommend its passage as amended.

Mr. Doron, from the Standing Committee on State Affairs, to which was referred Senate Bill No. 170, entitled " An Act to amend an Act entitled ' An Act concerning the Office of Secretary of State,' approved February 14th, 1865," reported that they had had the same under consideration, had come to a favorable conclusion thereon, and directed their chairman to report the same to the Senate without amendments, and recommend its passage.

MESSAGE FROM THE GOVERNOR.

The following Message was received from the Governor :

EXECUTIVE DEPARTMENT, CARSON CITY, }
February 23d, 1867.

To the Hon. Senate of Nevada :

I have this day approved Senate Bill No. 113, " An Act to amend an Act entitled ' An Act to regulate Fees and Compensation for Official and other Services in the State of Nevada,' approved March 9th, 1865."

H. G. BLASDEL,
Governor.

The following communication was received from Hon. J. Neely Johnson, Civil Practice Commissioner:

CARSON CITY, February 21st, 1867.

To the Honorable Senate of Nevada :

In pursuance of the duties devolved on me by the Act of March 1st, 1866, appointing a Commissioner to prepare and report to the Legislature at its present session, a Civil Practice Act, I herewith transmit the additional and concluding portions of this work, which, with the report heretofore submitted, embraces pages 772 and sections 1,614.

Respectfully,

J. NEELY JOHNSON.

MOTIONS AND RESOLUTIONS.

Mr. Proctor submitted the following resolution:

Resolved, That no new bills shall be introduced into the Senate after Thursday the 28th day of February, except by unanimous consent.

Adopted.

MESSAGE FROM THE ASSEMBLY.

The following Message was received from the Assembly:

ASSEMBLY CHAMBER, CARSON CITY, }
February 23d, 1867. }

To the Hon. the Senate:

I am instructed to transmit to your honorable body for your consideration, the following Assembly Bills, which passed the House this day, viz:

No. 96, "An Act for the Incorporation of Religious, Charitable, Literary, Scientific and other Associations."

No. 98, "An Act to amend an Act entitled ' An Act relating to Elections; the manner of conducting and contesting the same; election returns and canvassing the same; fraud upon the ballot box; destroying or attempting to destroy the ballot box; illegal, or attempted illegal voting and misconduct at elections,' approved March 9th, 1866."

No. 50, "An Act to restrict Gaming."

No. 86, "An Act to provide for the Payment of the Indebtedness of Esmeralda County."

No. 113, [112] "An Act to amend an Act in relation to Public Highways, approved March 9th, 1866."

Substitute Assembly Bill No. 101, "An Act entitled ' An Act in relation to Highways.'"

I also return to you Senate Bill No. 35, "An Act to amend an Act entitled ' An Act concerning Crimes and Punishments;'" the same having failed to pass the House this day. Yeas, 13; Nays, 14.

Respectfully,

A. WHITFORD,
Clerk.

Assembly Bill No. 96, "An Act for the Incorporation of Religious, Charitable, Literary, Scientific and other Associations."

Read first time; rules suspended; read second time by title, and referred to Committee on Corporations.

Assembly Bill No. 98, "An Act to amend an Act entitled ' An Act relating to Elections; the manner of conducting and contesting the same; election returns, and canvassing the same; fraud upon the ballot box; destroying or attempting to destroy the ballot box; illegal or attempted illegal voting, and misconduct at elections.'"

Read first time; rules suspended; read second time by title, and referred to Committee on Ways and Means.

Assembly Bill No. 50, "An Act to restrict Gaming."

Read first time; rules suspended; read second time by title, and referred to Committee on Ways and Means.

Assembly Bill No. 36, "An Act to provide for the Payment of the Indebtedness of Esmeralda County."

Read first time; rules suspended; read second time by title, and referred to Esmeralda County delegation.

Assembly Bill No. 112, "An Act to amend an Act in relation to Highways, approved March 9th, 1866."

Read first time; rules suspended; read second time by title; rules further suspended; read third time by sections.

The yeas and nays were called on the final passage of the bill, and recorded as follows:

YEAS—Messrs. Doron, Eastman, Edwards, Geller, Grey, Haines, Hastings, Hutchins, Linn, Mason, Meder, Monroe, Nelson, Proctor, Stevenson, Sumner, Terry, and Welty—18.

NAYS—0.

So the bill passed.

Substitute Assembly Bill No. 101, "An Act entitled 'An Act in relation to Public Highways.'"

Read first time; rules suspended; read second time by title, and referred to Committee on Corporations.

NOTICES OF BILLS.

Mr. Geller gave notice that he would at an early day introduce a bill entitled " An Act to prohibit Members of the Senate and Assembly from dealing in State Scrip issued during their term of office."

INTRODUCTION OF BILLS.

Mr. Terry, by leave without previous notice, introduced Senate Bill No. 174, "An Act to amend an Act entitled 'An Act to provide Revenue for the Support of the Government of the State of Nevada,' approved March 9th, 1865."

Read first time; rules suspended; read second time by title, and referred to Committee on Ways and Means.

Mr. Monroe, by leave without previous notice, introduced Senate Bill No. 175, "An Act concerning the Location and Possession of Wood Lands and Mill Sites."

Read first time; rules suspended; read second time by title, and referred to Committee on Public Lands.

Mr. Welty by leave without previous notice, introduced Senate Bill and Memorial No. 176, "An Act for the Relief of Registry Agents."

Read first time; rules suspended; read second time by title, and referred to the Committee on Counties and County Boundaries.

Substitute Senate Bill No. 171, "An Act to amend an Act entitled ' An Act to create Counties and establish the Boundaries thereof,' approved Nov. 23d, 1861," reported from Committee on Counties and County Boundaries.

Read first time; rules suspended; read second time by title, and referred to the Committee of the Whole.

President in the chair.

GENERAL FILE.

Senate Bill No. 142, "An Act amendatory of an Act to provide for the Maintenance and Supervision of Public Schools, approved March 20th, 1865."

Mr. Linn moved that the bill be referred to a Committee of one, with instruction to strike out from section 21 the following words: "When five heads of families sending pupils to the school shall object."

Mr. Sumner moved to amend the motion by referring the bill back to the Committee on Education, with instructions to amend section 21 by inserting after the word "same" the words "and the Board of Trustees of any district shall establish separate schools when there are fifteen persons in said district, Negroes, Mongolians, or Indians, who desire to attend such separate schools."

A division of the question was had.

The yeas and nays were called for by Messrs. Sumner, Hastings, and Grey, on Mr. Linn's amendment, and recorded as follows:

YEAS—Messrs. Doron, Edwards, Geller, Linn, Monroe, Nelson, Proctor, and Sumner—8.

NAYS—Messrs. Eastman, Grey, Haines, Hastings, Hutchins, Mason, Meder, Stevenson, Terry, and Welty—10.

So the motion was lost.

Mr. Sumner's motion was carried, and the bill was so referred.

A Message was received from the Assembly.

At 2 o'clock P.M., on motion of Mr. Hutchins, the Senate took a recess until 3 o'clock P.M.

IN SENATE.

The Senate convened at 3 o'clock, President in the chair.

Roll called. Quorum present.

A Message was received from the Assembly.

Mr. Grey submitted the following report:

Mr. President:

Your Committee on Education, to which was referred Senate Bill No. 142, beg leave to report the same amended, as per instructions.

Adopted.

The bill was ordered reëngrossed.

The Committee on Ways and Means reported Assembly Bill No. 50, "An Act to restrict Gaming," and recommend its passage when amended, as per suggestion below:

Amend section two by striking out "$1,000," and inserting "$3,000;" and by striking out "three months," and inserting "one year."

Amend the proviso to section two so as to read: "provided, that the license imposed by this section shall only be required in counties which, at the General Election in 1866, polled a vote of two thousand and upwards; and, further provided, that an annual license of $300 shall be imposed in all other counties for each five hundred votes, or fraction thereof, cast therein at the election aforesaid."

Amend section three, so as to read: "All moneys received for licenses under the provisions of this Act shall be paid, one-half into the State, and one-half into the County Treasury, for general State and County purposes."

On motion of Mr. Doron, the Senate went into Committee of the Whole for the consideration of the General File, President in the chair.

Mr. Hutchins in the chair.

The Committee rose, and submitted the following report:

Mr. President:

The Senate, in Committee of the Whole, have had under consideration Substitute Senate Bill No. 130, " An Act for the Organization of a Board of Education in Counties that polled 3,000 votes or more at the General Election in the State of Nevada, November, A.D. 1866, or that may hereafter at any General Election cast that number of votes or more, and amendatory of, and supplemental to 'An Act to provide for the Maintenance and Support of Public Schools,' approved March 20th, 1865 ;" on which they report progress, and ask leave to sit again.

Report adopted.
At 5:15 P.M., on motion of Mr. Grey, Senate adjourned.

CHARLES A. SUMNER,
President [*pro tem.*]

Attest—B. C. BROWN,
Secretary.

IN SENATE—FIFTY-FIRST DAY.

CARSON CITY, February 26th, 1867.

The Senate met pursuant to adjournment, Mr. Sumner, President *pro tem.*, in the chair.
Roll called.
Present—Messrs. Doron, Eastman, Edwards, Geller, Grey, Haines, Hastings, Hutchins, Linn, Mason, Meder, Monroe, Nelson, Proctor, Stevenson, Sumner, Terry, and Welty—18.
Absent—0.
Prayer by the Chaplain.
The Journal of the Fiftieth day was read and approved.

REPORTS OF COMMITTEES.

Mr. Linn, Chairman Committee on Enrollment, reported that Senate Concurrent Resolution No. 158, " In relation to printing Surveyor General's Report," had been carefully compared with the engrossed resolution as passed by the two Houses, found correctly enrolled, and that the same had been deposited with the Secretary of State.
Mr. Hastings reported that the Standing Committee on Engrossment had carefully compared the following entitled bills with the originals, and found the same correctly engrossed, viz:
Substitute Senate Bill No. 122, " An Act to further prescribe Rules and Regulations for the execution of the Trusts arising under the Act of Congress, approved May 23, 1844, entitled ' An Act for the Relief of Citizens of Towns upon Lands of the United States, under certain circumstances."
Also, Senate Bill No. 142, " An Act amendatory of an Act to provide for the Maintenance and Supervision of Public Schools,' approved March 20th, 1865," as correctly reëngrossed ; and herewith report the same back to the Senate.

Mr. Eastman, from the Standing Committee on Corporations, to which was referred the bill entitled "An Act in relation to Public Highways," reported that they had had the same under consideration, had come to a favorable conclusion thereon, had directed their chairman to report the same to the Senate without amendments, and recommend its passage.

Also, "An Act to amend an Act authorizing Rufus Walton and Westley Lambert to complete and maintain a Toll Road, approved December 19th, 1862," had had the same under consideration, had come to a favorable conclusion thereon, had directed their chairman to report the same to the Senate without amendments, and recommend its passage.

Mr. Proctor, from the Standing Committee on Counties and County Boundaries, to which was referred the bill entitled "An Act for the Relief of Registry Agents," reported that they had had the same under consideration, had come to an unfavorable conclusion thereon, had directed their chairman to report the same to the Senate without amendments, and recommend it be indefinitely postponed.

The Committee on State Affairs, to which was referred Senate Bill No. 178, entitled "An Act to regulate Fees and Compensation for Official and other Services in the State of Nevada, approved March 9, 1865," reported the bill back, and recommend its reference to the Committee of the Whole.

Mr. Sumner, Chairman of Committee on Ways and Means, submitted the following report:

Mr. President:

The Committee on Ways and Means, to whom was referred Senate Bill No. 132, "An Act concerning Crimes against the Revenue Laws of the State, and for the Punishment thereof," have had the same under consideration, and respectfully beg leave to report the same back, and recommend its indefinite postponement.

They also report back Senate Bill No. 172, "An Act supplementary to an Act entitled 'An Act to provide Revenue for the Support of the Government of the State of Nevada,' approved March 9th, 1865, and other Acts amendatory thereof," and recommend its passage.

They also report back Senate Bill No. 174, "An Act to amend entitled 'An Act to provide Revenue for the Support of the Government of the State of Nevada,' approved March 9th, 1865," and recommend its passage.

They also report back Assembly Bill No. 80, "An Act to amend an Act entitled 'An Act to provide Revenue for the Support of the Government of the State of Nevada,' approved March 9th, 1865," and recommend its passage.

They also report back Assembly Bill No. 57, "An Act to amend an Act entitled 'An Act to provide Revenue for the Support of the Government of the State of Nevada,' approved March 9th, 1865," and recommend that it be referred to the Committee of the Whole.

A majority of the Committee report back Senate Bill No. 108, "An Act to repeal an Act entitled 'An Act in regard to the Currency,' approved [March] 3d, 1866," with the following amendment, and recommend its passage as so amended:

Strike out the word "is," in the first section, and insert "and an Act entitled 'An Act in relation to Payment of Salaries and other Claims against the State,' approved February 27th, 1866," etc.

The minority of the Committee on Ways and Means submitted the following report:

The undersigned members of the Committee of Ways and Means, to whom was referred Senate Bill No. 108, entitled "An Act in regard to Currency, approved March 3d, 1866," ask leave to make a minority report. The bill providing in effect for the payment of all State and County officers, members of the Legislature and attachés, in coin.

We believe that in view of the fact that all the revenues of the State are paid in currency; that the system has been universally adopted; that the laws of the State recognize the system as in accordance therewith; and that even if we should now pass a law requiring the payment of taxes in coin, that we see no good reason for believing that such a law can be enforced; that a material increase in the amount of taxation must necessarily be made in order to meet the requirements of the bill; and furthermore, that the amounts now paid in currency to the various officers throughout the State is ample compensation for the amount of service performed, and that the State is not likely to suffer any detriment through the resignation of any of its servants in consequence of receiving their pay in currency. Therefore, we deem it unwise and inexpedient that this bill should become a law, and recommend that it do not pass.

C. H. EASTMAN,
D. L. HASTINGS.

Mr. Welty, from the Committee on Judiciary, reported that they had had under consideration Assembly Bill No. 97, entitled "An Act to amend an Act entitled 'An Act for the Relief of Insolvent Debtors and Protection of Creditors,' approved March 10th, 1865," had directed their chairman to report favorably thereon, and to recommend its passage.

Also, the various bills proposing amendments to Civil Proceedings, etc., in the Courts of Justice of this State, and had drawn a substitute for the same, and had directed their chairman to report favorably thereon, and to recommend the passage of the substitute.

Mr. Doron, from the Esmeralda County delegation, to which was referred Assembly Bill No. 36, entitled "An Act to provide for the Payment of the Indebtedness of Esmeralda County," reported that they had had the same under consideration, had come to a favorable conclusion thereon, and directed their chairman to report the same to the Senate without amendments, and to recommend its passage.

The Committee on Free Conference submitted the following report:

Mr. President:

Your Committee on Free Conference, to whom was referred Senate Bill No. 31, "An Act concerning the Office of Public Administrator," have had the same under consideration, and have instructed their chairman to report adherence to the Senate amendments, and the Assembly recede from their amendments.

Respectfully submitted.

T. D. EDWARDS, Chairman;
B. S. MASON,
J. W. HAINES,
Senate Committee.

JAMES A. St. CLAIR,
A. M. WINGATE,
THOMAS J. TENNANT,
Assembly Committee.

The Select Committee to which was referred Assembly Bill No. 88, entitled "An Act to amend Chapter 113 of the Statutes of 1866, entitled 'An Act to Consolidate and Pay certain Indebtedness of the County of Ormsby,' approved March 12th, 1866," reported that they had had the same under consideration, come to a favorable conclusion thereon, and recommend its passage.

MOTIONS AND RESOLUTIONS.

Mr. Edwards submitted the following resolution:

Resolved, That the Committee on Ways and Means be, and they are hereby instructed, to at once take steps to bring an agreed case before the Supreme Court, which shall decide the constitutionality of the Property Tax as at present levied; and the State Controller is hereby authorized and required to draw his warrant in favor of the Chairman of said Committee for such amount, not exceeding $100, as he shall certify to him as the expense of bringing such agreed case, payable out of the Contingent Fund of the Senate.

Mr. Hutchins moved to amend by striking out the words "with the proceeds of the mines exempted."

Amendment adopted.

The yeas and nays were called for on the adoption of the resolution as amended, and recorded as follows:

YEAS—Messrs. Doron, Eastman, Edwards, Geller, Haines, Hutchins, Linn, Mason, Meder, Monroe, Sumner, Terry, and Welty—13.

NAYS—Messrs. Hastings, Nelson, Proctor, and Stevenson—4.

So the resolution passed.

MESSAGES FROM THE ASSEMBLY.

The following Messages were received from the Assembly:

ASSEMBLY CHAMBER, CARSON CITY, }
February 25th, 1867. }

To the Honorable the Senate:

I am instructed to transmit to your honorable body, for your consideration, the following Assembly Bills, which passed the House this day, viz:

No. 121, "An Act to amend an Act entitled 'An Act concerning Crimes and Punishments,' approved November 26th, 1861."

No. 122, "An Act entitled 'An Act authorizing the County Commissioners of the several Counties in this State to appoint additional Justices of the Peace.'"

No. 106, "An Act in relation to the Redemption of Property sold for Taxes."

No. 92, "An Act to amend an Act entitled 'An Act to create a Board of County Commissioners in the several Counties of this State, and to define their Powers and Duties,' approved March 8th, 1865."

No. 110, "An Act to amend an Act entitled 'An Act relating to Marriage and Divorce.'"

I also return to you Senate Bill No. 149, "An Act amendatory of and supplementary to an Act entitled an Act to amend an Act entitled an Act amendatory of and supplementary to an Act of the Legislative Assembly of the Territory of Nevada, entitled 'An Act to Incorporate the City of Austin,' [approved Feb. 20th, A.D. 1864] approved March 8th, 1865, approved February 27th, 1866."

All of which is respectfully submitted.

A. WHITFORD,
Clerk.

ASSEMBLY CHAMBER, CARSON CITY, }
February 25th, 1867.

To the Hon. the Senate:

I am instructed to return to your honorable body Senate Bill No. 150, entitled "An Act to amend an Act entitled 'An Act authorizing a State Loan, and levying a Tax to provide means for the Payment thereof,' approved Feb. 6th, 1867," the same having passed the House this day, notwithstanding the objections of the Governor.

YEAS—29.

NAYS—8.

Respectfully,

A. WHITFORD,
Clerk.

ASSEMBLY CHAMBER, CARSON CITY, }
February 26th, 1867.

To the Hon. the Senate:

I am instructed to transmit to your honorable body, for your consideration, Assembly Joint Resolution No. 44, relating to Mail facilities from White Rock *via* Ellsworth, Cloverdale, Indian Springs, and Hot Creek, to Pahranagat, Nye County, which passed the Assembly this day.

Respectfully,

A. WHITFORD,
Clerk.

Assembly Bill No. 121, "An Act to amend an Act entitled 'An Act concerning Crimes and Punishments,' approved Nov. 26th, 1861."

Read first time; rules suspended; read second time by title, and referred to Judiciary Committee.

Assembly Bill No. 122, "An Act entitled 'An Act authorizing the County Commissioners of the several Counties of this State to appoint additional Justices of the Peace."

Read first time; rules suspended; read second time by title, and referred to Committee on State Affairs.

Assembly Bill No. 106, "An Act in relation to the Redemption of Property sold for Taxes."

Read first time; rules suspended; read second time by title, and referred to Committee on Ways and Means.

Assembly Bill No. 92, "An Act to amend an Act entitled ' An Act to create a Board of County Commissioners in the several Counties of this State, and to define their Powers and Duties,' approved March 8th, 1865."

Read first time; rules suspended; read second time by title, and referred to Committee on Counties and County Boundaries.

Assembly Bill No. 110, "An Act to amend an Act entitled ' An Act relating to Marriage and Divorce.'"

Read first time; rules suspended; read second time by title, and referred to Committee on Public Morals.

Assembly Joint Memorial No. 44, relating to Mail facilities from White Rock *via* Ellsworth, Cloverdale, Indian Springs, Belmont and Hot Creek, to Pahranagat, Nye County.

Read first time; rules suspended; read second time by title, and referred to Committee on Federal Relations.

Assembly Bill No. 27, "An Act to amend an Act entitled ' An Act concerning District Attorneys,' approved March 11th, 1865, approved February 26th, 1866."

Mr. Proctor moved that the Secretary be instructed to request of the Assembly the announcement of their Committee of Conference.

INTRODUCTION OF BILLS.

Substitute Senate Bill No. 4, " An Act making further provisions to regulate Proceedings in Civil Cases, and in Civil and Criminal Cases when the Venue is brought in question in the Courts of Justice in this State."

Reported from the Committee on Judiciary.

Read first time; rules suspended; read second time by title, and referred to Committee of the Whole.

GENERAL FILE.

Substitute Senate Bill No. 122, " An Act to further prescribe rules and regulations for the execution of the Trusts arising under the Act of Congress, approved May 23d, 1844, entitled ' An Act for the Relief of Citizens of Towns upon Lands of the United States under certain circumstances.' "

Read third time by sections.

The yeas and nays were called upon the final passage of the bill, and recorded as follows:

YEAS—Messrs. Doron, Eastman, Geller, Haines, Hastings, Hutchins, Linn, Mason, Meder, Monroe, Nelson, Proctor, Stevenson, and Terry—14.

NAYS—0.

So the bill passed.

Senate Bill No. 142, " An Act amendatory of an Act to provide for the Maintenance and Supervision of Public Schools, approved March 20th, 1865."

Read third time by sections.

On motion of Mr. Welty a call of the Senate was ordered.

Roll called.

Present—Messrs. Doron, Eastman, Edwards, Geller, Haines, Hastings, Linn, Mason, Meder, Monroe, Nelson, Proctor, Stevenson, Sumner, Terry, and Welty—17.

Absent—Mr. Grey.

On motion of Mr. Sumner, the Senate took a recess until 2 o'clock P.M., under the call.

IN SENATE.

Senate met at 2 P. M., President *pro tem.* in the chair.

Mr. Grey appearing, was, on motion, excused for absence.

Roll called. Quorum present.

On motion of Mr. Mason a call of the Senate was ordered.

Roll called. Mr. Hutchins absent.

Mr. Hutchins appearing, was, on motion, excused for absence.

On motion, further proceedings under the call were dispensed with.

Mr. Doron moved that the bill be recommitted to a Committee of one with special instructions to strike out in section twenty-one all after the words " as follows," and substitute therefor:

" Section Fifty: Negroes, Mongolians and Indians shall not be admitted into the Public Schools, but the Board of Trustees may establish a separate school for their education, and use the Public School Funds for the support of the same; provided, that the Board shall establish such separate schools when requested so to do by, or in behalf of ten pupils in any district, of the races above mentioned."

The yeas and nays were called for by Messrs. Welty, Grey and Mason on the passage of the motion, and recorded as follows:

Yeas—Messrs. Doron, Edwards, Geller, Hastings, Hutchins, Linn, Monroe, Nelson, Proctor, Sumner, and Terry—11.
Nays—Messrs. Eastman, Grey, Haines, Mason, Meder, Stevenson, and Welty—7.

So the motion was carried.
The Chair appointed Mr. Terry as such committee.
The Committee reported the bill back amended as instructed.
Report adopted.
Bill considered engrossed.
The yeas and nays were called on its final passage, and recorded as follows:

Yeas—Messrs. Doron, Eastman, Edwards, Geller, Grey, Hastings, Hutchins, Linn, Mason, Meder, Monroe, Nelson, Proctor, Stevenson, Sumner, Terry, Welty—17.
Nays—Mr. Haines—1.

So the bill passed.
Assembly Bill No. 84, "An Act providing for the removal of County Seats, and the Permanent Location of the same."
Rules suspended; read third time by sections. The yeas and nays were called on the final passage of the bill, and recorded as follows:

Yeas—Messrs. Eastman, Edwards, Geller, Grey, Haines, Hastings, Hutchins, Monroe, Nelson, Proctor, Sumner, Terry, and Welty—13.
Nays—Messrs. Doron, Linn, Mason, Meder, and Stevenson—5.

So the bill passed.
Mr. Hutchins gave notice that on to-morrow he would move a reconsideration of the vote by which the resolution of Mr. Edwards, in relation to the opinion of the Supreme Court on the Revenue Bill, was adopted.
On motion of Mr. Grey, the Senate went into Committee of the Whole for the consideration of unfinished business on General File, President in the chair.
The Committee rose, and submitted the following report:

Mr. President:
The Senate, in Committee of the Whole, have had under further consideration Substitute Senate Bill No. 130, "An Act for the Organization of a Board of Education in Counties that polled three thousand votes or more at the general election in the State of Nevada, in November, A.D. 1866, or that may hereafter at any general election cast that number of votes or more, and amendatory of and supplemental to an Act to provide for the maintenance and support of Public Schools, approved March 20th, 1865," which they report back with amendments, and recommend the bill be ordered engrossed as amended.
Also Substitute Senate Bill No. 171, "An Act to amend an Act entitled 'An Act to create Counties and establish the Boundaries thereof,' approved Nov. 25th,

1861" which they report back, and recommend the bill be ordered engrossed.

Also, Senate Bill No. 146, (Substitute for Assembly Bill No. 71) "An Act to repeal section 13 of the Act of the Legislative Assembly of the Territory of Nevada, entitled 'An Act concerning Crimes and Punishments, approved Nov. 26th, 1861,' and to amend section 342 of an Act of the Legislative Assembly aforesaid, approved Nov. 29th, 1861, entitled 'An Act to regulate Proceedings in the Courts of Justice of the Territory of Nevada,'" which they report back, and recommend the bill be indefinitely postponed.

Mr. Doron in the chair.

Senate Bill No. 130, " An Act for the organization of the Board of Education in Counties that polled three thousand votes or more at the general election in the State of Nevada, in November, A.D. 1866, or that may hereafter at any general election cast that number of votes or more ; and amendatory of and supplemental to an Act to provide for the maintenance and support of Public Schools, approved March 20th, 1865." The amendments of the Committee of the Whole were adopted, and the bill ordered engrossed.

Senate Bill No. 171, "An Act to amend an Act entitled ' An Act to create Counties and establish their Boundaries,' approved Nov. 25th, 1861." Ordered engrossed.

Senate Bill No. 146, (Substitute for Assembly Bill No. 71) "An Act to repeal section 13 of the Act of the Legislative Assembly of the Territory of Nevada, entitled 'An Act concerning Crimes and Punishments,' approved Nov. 26th, 1861 ; and to amend Section 242 of an Act of the Legislative Assembly aforesaid, approved Nov. 29th, 1861, entitled 'An Act to regulate Proceedings in Courts of Justice of the Territory of Nevada.'"

The yeas and nays were called for by Messrs. Meder, Haines, and Mason, on the indefinite postponement of the bill, and recorded as follows :

YEAS—Messrs. Doron, Geller, Grey, Hastings, Hutchins, Monroe, Proctor, Stevenson, and Sumner—9.

NAYS—Messrs. Eastman, Edwards, Haines, Linn, Mason, Meder, Nelson, and Terry—8.

So the bill was indefinitely postponed.

At 4 : 40 P.M., on motion of Mr. Sumner, the Senate adjourned.

CHARLES A. SUMNER,
President.

Attest—B. C. BROWN,
Secretary.

IN SENATE—FIFTY-SECOND DAY.

CARSON CITY, February 27th, 1867.

The Senate met pursuant to adjournment, President in the chair.

Roll called.

Present—Messrs. Doron, Eastman, Edwards, Geller, Grey, Haines, Hastings, Hutchins, Linn, Mason, Meder, Monroe, Nelson, Proctor, Stevenson, Sumner, and Terry—17.

Absent—Mr. Welty—1.

Prayer by the Chaplain.

The Journal of the Fifty-first day was read and approved.
Mr. Welty was granted indefinite leave of absence.

REPORTS OF COMMITTEES.

Mr. Monroe, Chairman of the Committee on Claims, reported as follows:

Your Committee have had presented through the State Board of Examiners, and have had under consideration, the claim of Kinkead, Harrington & Co., who seek to obtain $581 $\frac{55}{100}$ for certain pieces of scrip, or warrants, issued out of the County Court of Carson County, Utah Territory, and which was refused by said Board of Examiners on the ground of its "not being a proper charge against the State of Nevada." Have also had presented, in addition to above, a bill for a carpet to furnish the room of the Clerk of the Supreme Court of the Territory of Nevada, dated February 14th, 1862, for the sum of $109 $\frac{25}{100}$, amounting in the aggregate to $690 $\frac{80}{100}$.

We find that the scrip is of the same character as that presented by John S. Childs, (in a former case) and the same reasons that governed us then in regard to this kind of a claim being binding, either in law or equity, upon the State of Nevada, remains the same now, having had no new light shed or proofs shown by which we would be justified in coming to a different conclusion. The County Court of Carson County has been called "self-styled" by a former Legislature, in a legal enactment, and no authority of law has been shown by which that Court had the right to issue such scrip, or warrants, and no law ever authorized the Territory of Nevada to assume the indebtedness of any portion of Utah Territory; and we find that, by an Act passed by the Legislature of the Territory of Nevada, approved March 29th, 1861, all claims arising against the Territory should be presented to the Territorial Auditor, "to be audited, settled, and allowed, within two years after such claim shall accrue, and not afterwards."

We are of the opinion that parties having old claims against Carson County, or the Territory of Nevada, and having had two years by statutory law from the time they accrued to present and have them allowed or disallowed, and failing to do so, have lost all right to now come in and demand or ask of this Legislature to pay for their negligence in not attending to their own interests; and for these and other reasons given in the Childs case, (which was similar so far as the scrip was concerned) we recommend that the claim based upon the scrip, amounting to $581 $\frac{55}{100}$, be not allowed.

We find that the State of Nevada did assume the indebtedness of the Territory of Nevada, and that said Territory did receive a valuable consideration from Kinkead, Harrington & Co., in the matter of a carpet, of the value of $109 $\frac{25}{100}$, to furnish a room of one of the Territorial officers, and it was consequently a legitimate claim against the Territory; and notwithstanding it has been cut off by Statute of Limitation, your Committee think they can see some equity in that portion of the claim, and should a bill be introduced covering that amount, would recommend its passage.

Mr. Hastings reported that the Standing Committee on Engrossment had carefully compared the following bills with the originals, and found the same correctly engrossed, viz:
Senate Bill No. 151, "An Act to amend an Act entitled 'An Act to regulate Proceedings in Criminal Cases in the Courts of Justice in the (Territory) State of Nevada, and making further provisions relating thereto.'"
Also, Substitute Senate Bill No. 171, "An Act to amend an Act entitled 'An Act to create Counties, and establish the Boundaries thereof, approved November 25th, 1861;'" and herewith report the same back to the Senate.

Mr. Eastman, from Standing Committee on Corporations, to which was referred Assembly Bill No. 96, entitled "An Act for the incorporation of Religious, Charitable, Literary, Scientific, and other Associations," reported that they had had the same under consideration; had come to a favorable conclusion thereon; had directed their chairman to report the same to the Senate, without amendments, and to recommend its passage.

Mr. Linn, Chairman Committee on Enrollment, reported that Senate Concurrent Resolution No. 159, in relation to appointing a Joint Committee of Examination, had been carefully compared with the engrossed resolution, as passed by the two Houses, found correctly enrolled, and that the same had this day been deposited with the Secretary of State.

Mr. Doron, from the Standing Committee on State Affairs, to which was referred Senate Bill No. 169, entitled "An Act to amend an Act entitled an 'Act to provide for Reporting the Decisions of the Supreme Court of the State of Nevada,' approved March 14th, 1865," reported that they had had the same under consideration; had come to an unfavorable conclusion thereon; had directed their chairman to report the same to the Senate, together with a substitute therefor, and recommend the adoption of the substitute.

Mr. Mason, from the Standing Committee on Federal Relations, to which was referred Assembly Joint Resolution No. 44, "Relating to Mail Facilities from White Rock House *via* Ellsworth, Cloverdale, Indian Spring, Belmont, Hot Creek, to Pahranagat," reported that they had had the same under consideration, and recommend an amendment as follows: where the word "weekly" occurs, strike it out, and insert "tri-weekly," and recommend its passage as amended.

Mr. Doron, from the Standing Committee on State Affairs, to which was referred Assembly Bill No. 122, entitled "An Act authorizing the County Commissioners of the several Counties in this State to appoint additional Justices of the Peace," reported that they had had the same under consideration, and had directed their chairman to report the same to the Senate without recommendation.

Mr. Sumner, from the Standing Committee on Ways and Means, to which was referred Senate Substitute Bill No. 45, entitled "An Act appropriating Moneys for the Benefit of the Orphan Asylum at Virginia City," reported that they had had the same under consideration, had adopted a substitute by vote of a majority, and had directed their chairman to report the same to the Senate, and to recommend its passage.

On motion of Mr. Hastings, the rules were suspended, and the bill read first time; second time by title, and referred to Committee of the Whole.

On motion of Mr. Sumner, the Senate went into Committee of the Whole for the consideration of Substitute Senate Bill No. 45, the President in the chair.

The Committee rose, and submitted the following report:

Mr. President:

The Committee of the Whole have had under consideration Substitute Senate Bill No. 45, "An Act to provide for fostering and supporting the 'Nevada Orphan Asylum,' a duly incorporated benevolent institution, located at Virginia City," which they report back, and recommend the bill be considered engrossed, and placed upon its third reading and final passage.

A Message was received from the Assembly.
A Message was received from the Governor.

The report of the Committee of the Whole was adopted; the bill considered engrossed; rules further suspended.

Read third time by sections.

At 1:25 P.M., on motion of Mr. Meder, the Senate took a recess until 2:30 P.M.

IN SENATE.

The Senate met at 2:30 P.M.

President in the chair.

Roll called.

Quorum present.

Mr. Proctor in the chair.

On motion of Mr. Hastings, a call of the Senate was ordered.

Roll called.

Absent—Messrs. Edwards, Nelson, Monroe, and Mason.

Messrs. Edwards, Nelson, Monroe, and Mason appearing, were, on motion, excused.

On motion of Mr. Hutchins, further proceedings under the call were dispensed with.

A Message was received from the Assembly.

The bill was read third time by sections.

The yeas and nays were called on its final passage, and recorded as follows:

YEAS—Messrs. Doron, Edwards, Geller, Grey, Hastings, Hutchins, Linn, Monroe, Nelson, Proctor, Stevenson, Sumner, and Terry—18.

NAYS—Messrs. Eastman, Haines, Mason, and Meder—4.

So the bill passed.

Mr. Mason presented the following protest:

Mr. President:

I hereby enter my solemn protest against the bill, as a violation of the Constitution, and an attempt to connect Church and State.

B. S. MASON.

Mr. Linn, by leave, offered the following resolution:

Resolved, That hereafter no Senator shall be allowed to speak but once upon any question, nor more than five minutes at a time.

Adopted.

On motion of Mr. Hutchins, Assembly Bill No. 50, "An Act to restrict Gaming," was now taken up.

On motion of Mr. Hutchins, the Senate went into Committee of the Whole for the consideration of Assembly Bill No. 50.

President in the chair.

The Committee rose, and submitted the following report:

Mr. President:

The Senate in Committee of the Whole have had under consideration Assembly Bill No. 50, "An Act to restrict Gaming," which they report back with amendments, and recommend the same do pass as amended.

GENERAL FILE.

Assembly Bill No. 50, "An Act to restrict Gaming."
The amendments of the Committee of the Whole were adopted.
Read third time by sections.
The yeas and nays were called on the final passage of the bill, and recorded as follows:

YEAS—Messrs. Edwards, Geller, Grey, Hastings, Hutchins, Linn, Meder, Monroe, Nelson, Proctor, Stevenson, and Sumner—12.
NAYS—Messrs. Doron, Eastman, Haines, Mason, and Terry—5.

So the bill passed.
At 5:5 P.M., on motion of Mr. Doron, the Senate adjourned until 7:30 P.M.

IN SENATE.

The Senate met at 7:30 P.M., Mr. Sumner, President *pro tem.*, in the chair.
Roll called.
Quorum present.

MESSAGE FROM THE GOVERNOR.

The following Message was received from the Governor:

EXECUTIVE DEPARTMENT, CARSON CITY,
February 27th, 1867.

To the Honorable the Senate of Nevada:
I have this day approved the following Senate Bills, to wit:
No. 141, "An Act to provide for the Payment of James Cochran, for certain services rendered and expenses incurred in arresting and conveying one W. S. Broadwater, a refugee from justice, from Trinity County, California, to this State."
No. 131, "An Act to prohibit the Carrying of Concealed Weapons."
No. 102, "An Act to transfer certain Moneys in the State Treasury to the County School Funds."

H. G. BLASDEL,
Governor.

INTRODUCTION OF BILLS.

Mr. Geller, by leave without previous notice, introduced Senate Bill No. 189, "An Act to provide for Payment to Kinkead and Harrington, for Goods furnished the late Supreme Court of the Territory of Nevada."
Read first time; rules suspended; read second time by title, and referred to Committee on Claims.
Substitute Senate Bill No. 169, (reported from Committee on State Affairs) "An Act to provide for the Publication of the Decisions of the Supreme Court of the State of Nevada."
Read first time; rules suspended; read second time by title, and referred to Committee on Judiciary.
Mr. Hutchins moved that the vote by which the resolution of Mr. Edwards,

23

in relation to the opinion of the Supreme Court on the Revenue Bill, be now reconsidered.

Lost.

GENERAL FILE.

Senate Bill No. 151, "An Act to amend an Act entitled ' An Act to regulate Proceedings in Criminal Cases in the Courts of Justice in the (Territory) State of Nevada,' and making further provisions relating thereto."

Read third time by sections.

The yeas and nays were called on the final passage of the bill, and recorded as follows:

YEAS—Messrs. Doron, Eastman, Geller, Grey, Haines, Hastings, Linn, Mason, Meder, Monroe, Proctor, Stevenson, Sumner, and Terry—14.

NAYS—0.

So the bill passed.

Senate Bill No. 134, "An Act to provide for the Recording of certain Papers affecting the Titles or Claims to Real Property."

Indefinitely postponed.

Senate Bill No. 174, " An Act to amend an Act entitled ' An Act to provide Revenue for the Support of the Government of the State of Nevada,' approved March 9th, 1865."

Ordered engrossed.

Senate Bill No. 168, " An Act relative to Transcribing and Indexing certain Records in Humboldt County."

Rules suspended; read third time by sections.

The yeas and nays were called on the final passage of the bill, and recorded as follows:

YEAS—Messrs. Doron, Eastman, Geller, Grey, Haines, Hastings, Linn, Mason, Meder, Monroe, Proctor, Stevenson, Sumner, and Terry—14.

NAYS—0.

So the bill passed.

Senate Bill No. 170, " An Act to amend an Act entitled 'An Act concerning the [office of] Secretary of State,' approved February 14th, 1865."

Ordered engrossed.

Assembly Bill No. 13, " An Act amendatory of and supplementary to ' An Act to create the County of Lincoln and provide for its Organization,' approved February 26th, 1866."

Placed at the foot of the file.

Mr. Doron in the chair.

Substitute Senate Bill No. 171, " An Act to amend an Act entitled ' An Act to create Counties and establish the Boundaries thereof,' approved November 25th, 1861."

Placed at the foot of the file.

Substitute Assembly Bill No. 101, an Act entitled " An Act in relation to Public Highways."

Read third time by sections. The yeas and nays were called on the final passage of the bill, and recorded as follows:

YEAS—Messrs. Doron, Eastman, Geller, Grey, Haines, Hastings, Linn, Mason, Meder, Monroe, Proctor, Stevenson, Sumner, and Terry—13.

NAYS—0.

So the bill passed.

Assembly Bill No. 89, "An Act to amend an Act authorizing Rufus Walton and Westley Lambert to complete and maintain a Toll-road, approved December 19th, 1862."

Read third time by sections.

The yeas and nays were called on the final passage of the bill, and recorded as follows:

YEAS—Messrs. Eastman, Haines, Mason, Meder, Proctor, Stevenson, Sumner, and Terry—8.

NAYS—Messrs. Doron, Geller, Grey, and Linn—4.

So the bill was lost.

Mr. Meder moved a reconsideration of the vote just cast.

Carried.

The yeas and nays were then called on the passage of the bill, and recorded as follows:

YEAS—Messrs. Doron, Eastman, Geller, Haines, Hastings, Linn, Mason, Meder, Monroe, Proctor, Stevenson, Sumner, and Terry—13.

NAYS—Mr. Grey—1.

So the bill passed.

Senate Bill No. 172, "An Act supplementary to an Act entitled 'An Act to provide Revenue for the Support of the Government of the State of Nevada,' approved March 9th, 1865, and other Acts amendatory of and supplementary thereto."

Ordered engrossed.

Senate Bill No. 176, "An Act to amend an Act entitled 'An Act concerning the Office of Secretary of State,' approved February 14th, 1865."

Indefinitely postponed.

Senate Bill No. 132, "An Act concerning Crimes against the Revenue Laws of this State, and for the Punishment thereof."

Indefinitely postponed.

Senate Bill No. 174, "An Act to amend an Act entitled 'An Act to provide Revenue for the Support of the Government of the State of Nevada,' approved March 9th, 1865."

Ordered engrossed.

Assembly Bill No. 80, "An Act to amend an Act entitled 'An Act to provide Revenue for the Support of the Government of the State of Nevada,' approved March 19th, 1865."

Read third time by sections.

The yeas and nays were called on the final passage of the bill, and recorded as follows:

YEAS—Messrs. Doron, Eastman, Geller, Grey, Haines, Hastings, Linn, Mason, Meder, Monroe, Proctor, Stevenson, Sumner, and Terry—14.

NAYS—0.

So the bill passed.

Assembly Bill No. 57, "An Act to amend an Act entitled 'An Act to provide Revenue for the Support of the Government of the State of Nevada,' approved March 9th, 1865."

Made the special order for Monday, March 4th, at 12 o'clock M.

Senate Bill No. 108, "An Act to repeal an Act in regard to Currency, approved March 3d, 1866."

Placed at the foot of the General File.

Senate Bill No. 173, "An Act to amend an Act entitled 'An Act to regulate Fees and Compensation for Official and other Services,' approved March 9th, 1865."

Referred to Committee of the Whole.

Assembly Bill No. 97, "An Act to amend an Act entitled 'An Act for the Relief of Insolvent Debtors, and Protection of Creditors,' approved March 10th, 1865."

Read third time by sections.

Mr. Sumner moved to recommit to a Committee of one with instructions to amend: In section 1, line 11, insert after the word "published" "nearest to the county seat," and strike out " To be designated by said Judge."

Carried.

The Chair appointed Mr. Sumner.

The Committee reported bill amended as instructed.

Report accepted.

The yeas and nays were called on the final passage of the bill, and recorded as follows:

YEAS—Messrs. Doron, Eastman, Geller, Grey, Hastings, Linn, Meder, Monroe, Proctor, Stevenson, Sumner, and Terry—12.

NAYS—0.

So the bill passed.

Assembly Bill No. 36, "An Act to provide for the Payment of the Indebtedness of Esmeralda County."

Read third time by sections.

The yeas and nays were called on the final passage of the bill, and recorded as follows:

YEAS—Messrs. Doron, Eastman, Geller, Grey, Haines, Hastings, Linn, Mason, Meder, Monroe, Proctor, Stevenson, Sumner, and Terry—14.

NAYS—0.

So the bill passed.

Assembly Bill No. 88, "An Act to amend Chapter 113 of the Statutes of 1866, entitled 'An Act to Consolidate and Pay certain Indebtedness of the County of Ormsby,' approved March 12th, 1866."

Read third time by sections. The yeas and nays were called on the final passage of the bill, and recorded as follows:

YEAS—Messrs. Doron, Eastman, Edwards, Geller, Grey, Haines, Hastings, Linn, Mason, Meder, Monroe, Proctor, Stevenson, Sumner, and Terry—15.

NAYS—0.

So the bill passed.

Assembly Joint Resolution No. 44, "Relating to Mail Facilities from White Rock House via Ellsworth, Cloverdale, Indian Springs, Belmont, and Hot Creek, to Pahranagat, Nye County."

The amendments of the Committee adopted.

The yeas and nays were called on the passage of the resolution, and recorded as follows:

YEAS—Messrs. Doron, Eastman, Edwards, Geller, Grey, Haines, Hastings, Linn, Mason, Meder, Monroe, Proctor, Stevenson, Sumner, and Terry—15.
NAYS—0.

So the resolution passed.
Assembly Bill No. 122, "An Act entitled 'An Act authorizing the County Commissioners of the several Counties in this State to appoint additional Justices of the Peace.'"
Referred to Committee of the Whole.
Assembly Bill No. 96, "An Act for the Incorporation of Religious, Charitable, Literary, Scientific, and other Associations."
Read third time by sections. The yeas and nays were called on the final passage of the bill, and recorded as follows:

YEAS—Messrs. Doron, Eastman, Edwards, Grey, Haines, Hastings, Linn, Mason, Meder, Monroe, Stevenson, Proctor, Sumner, and Terry—14.
NAYS—0.

So the bill passed.
The following communication was received from the Secretary of State:

OFFICE OF SECRETARY OF STATE, }
Carson City, February 27th, 1867. }

To the Senate of Nevada:

GENTLEMEN—I have the honor to transmit herewith the claim of Storey County, Nevada, against the State, for the support and care of certain Indigent Insane Persons, the same having been examined and disapproved by the Board of Examiners. I also inclose all the papers in the case, including notice of appeal, and a statement of the reasons for which this claim was disapproved.
By order of the Board,
C. N. NOTEWARE,
Secretary.

Referred to Storey County delegation.
At 9:50 P.M., on motion of Mr. Hastings, the Senate adjourned.

CHARLES A. SUMNER,
President.

Attest—B. C. BROWN,
Secretary.

———

IN SENATE—FIFTY-THIRD DAY.

CARSON CITY, February 28th, 1867.

The Senate met pursuant to adjournment, Mr. Sumner, President *pro tem.*, in the chair.
Roll called.
Present—Messrs. Doron, Eastman, Edwards, Geller, Grey, Haines, Hutchins, Linn, Mason, Meder, Monroe, Nelson, Proctor, Stevenson, Sumner, and Terry—16.
Absent—Mr. Hastings—1.

Prayer by the Chaplain.

The Journal of the Fifty-second day was read and approved.

Mr. Hastings was, on motion, granted leave of absence until Monday, March 4th, 1867.

Messages were received from the Assembly.

REPORTS OF COMMITTEES.

Mr. Linn, Chairman of the Committee on Enrollment, reported that Senate Bill No. 149, entitled "An Act to amend an Act entitled an Act amendatory of and supplementary to an Act of the Legislative Assembly of the Territory of Nevada, entitled 'An Act to Incorporate the City of Austin,' approved February 20th, 1864, approved March 8th, 1865, approved February 27th, 1866," had been carefully compared with the engrossed bill as passed by the two Houses, found correctly enrolled, and that the same had this day been delivered to the Governor for his approval.

Mr. Edwards, from the Standing Committee on Public Lands, to which was referred Senate Bill No. 175, entitled "An Act concerning the Location and Possession of Wood Lands and Mill Sites," reported that they had had the same under consideration; had come to a favorable conclusion thereon; had directed their chairman to report the same to the Senate, without amendments, and recommend its passage.

Mr. Nelson, from Standing Committee on State Library, to which was referred Senate Bill No. 130, entitled "An Act authorizing the Secretary of State to employ a Clerk in the State Library, and Adjutant [General's] Office," reported that they had had the same under consideration; had come to an unfavorable conclusion thereon, and had directed their chairman to report the same back, without recommendation.

MOTIONS AND RESOLUTIONS.

On motion of Mr. Monroe, Substitute Senate Bill No. 171, "An Act to amend an Act entitled 'An Act to create Counties and to establish the Boundaries thereof,' approved November 25th, 1861," was now taken up; rules suspended; bill read third time by sections.

Mr. Proctor in the chair.

Mr. Monroe was, on motion, granted leave to withdraw the bill.

MESSAGES FROM THE ASSEMBLY.

The following Messages were received from the Assembly:

ASSEMBLY CHAMBER, CARSON CITY, }
February 27th, 1867. }

To the Honorable the Senate:

I am instructed to transmit to your honorable body the following Assembly Bills, which passed the House on yesterday:

No. 62, "An Act to protect the Elections of Voluntary Political Associations, and to punish Frauds thereon."

No. 78, "An Act to amend an Act entitled 'An Act to Incorporate the City of Virginia, provide for the government thereof, and repeal all other laws in relation thereto,' approved March 4th, 1865."

Respectfully,

A. WHITFORD,
Clerk.

ASSEMBLY CHAMBER, CARSON CITY,
February 26th, 1867.

To the Honorable the Senate:

I am instructed to inform your honorable body, that Messrs. Julien, May-hugh, and Welch, were appointed as a Conference Committee on Assembly Bill No. 27, "An Act to amend an Act entitled ' An Act concerning District Attorneys,' approved March 11th, 1865, approved February 26th, 1866."

Respectfully,

A. WHITFORD,
Clerk.

ASSEMBLY CHAMBER, CARSON CITY,
February 27th, 1867.

To the Honorable the Senate:

I am instructed to transmit to your honorable body, for your consideration, the inclosed Resolution, which passed the House this day.

Respectfully,

A. WHITFORD,
Clerk.

Resolved, That it is the deliberate sense of this House, that Assembly Bill No. 78, entitled "An Act to amend an Act entitled ' An Act to Incorporate the City of Virginia, to provide for the government thereof, and to repeal all other laws in relation thereto,' approved March 4th, 1865," which passed this House on yesterday, should have been so amended that the Chief Engineer of the Fire Department should receive a salary not to exceed one hundred and fifty dollars per month, instead of one hundred dollars as now provided in the bill, and also that the Secretary of the Fire Department should receive seventy-five dollars instead of fifty dollars per month, as now therein provided; and we most respectfully recommend to the Honorable Senate that they adopt the amendments herein suggested and recommended, and the Clerk is hereby instructed to forthwith transmit this resolution to the Senate.

Message and resolution laid on the table.

ASSEMBLY CHAMBER, CARSON CITY,
February 27th, 1867.

To the Hon. the Senate:

I am instructed to transmit to your honorable body for your consideration, Assembly Bill No. 126, entitled "An Act authorizing the County of Lyon to Fund the Outstanding Indebtedness against the General Fund of said County, to pay the Interest therefor, and for the gradual Liquidation of the same," which passed the House this day.

Also, Assembly Concurrent Resolution No. 45, instructing our Representatives to oppose the passage of a certain bill in Congress, entitled "An Act to allow the cutting of Timber in Alpine County, California," the same having passed the House this day unanimously.

Respectfully,

A. WHITFORD,
Clerk.

Assembly Bill No. 62, "An Act to protect the Elections of Voluntary Political Associations, and to punish Frauds thereon."

Read first time; rules suspended; read second time by title, and referred to Committee on Elections.

Assembly Bill No. 78, "An Act to amend an Act entitled 'An Act to Incorporate the City of Virginia, provide for the government thereof, and repeal all other laws in relation thereto,' approved March 4th, 1865."

Read first time; rules suspended; read second time by title, and referred to the Storey County delegation.

Assembly Bill No. 126, entitled "An Act authorizing the County of Lyon to Fund the Outstanding Indebtedness against the General Fund of said County, to pay the Interest thereon, and for the gradual Liquidation of the same."

Read first time; rules suspended; read second time by title.

On motion of Mr. Sumner, rules further suspended.

Read third time by sections.

The yeas and nays were called on the final passage of the bill, and recorded as follows:

YEAS—Messrs. Doron, Eastman, Geller, Haines, Hutchins, Linn, Mason, Meder, Monroe, Nelson, Proctor, Stevenson, Sumner, and Terry—14.

NAYS—0.

So the bill passed.

Assembly Concurrent Resolution No. 45, instructing our Representatives to oppose the passage of a certain bill in Congress, entitled "An Act to allow the cutting of Timber in Alpine County, California."

Read first time; rules suspended; read second time by title; rules further suspended; read third time.

The yeas and nays were called on the final passage of the resolution, and recorded as follows:

YEAS—Messrs. Doron, Eastman, Edwards, Geller, Grey, Haines, Hutchins, Linn, Mason, Monroe, Nelson, Proctor, Stevenson, Sumner, and Terry—16.

NAYS—0.

So the resolution passed.

On motion of Mr. Monroe, Senate Bill No. 96, "An Act to make Compensation to Hon. John Cradlebaugh, late United States District Judge, the same as that of the late United States District Judges of the Territory of Nevada," was now taken up and placed on its final passage.

Read third time by sections.

The yeas and nays were called on the final passage of the bill, and recorded as follows:

YEAS—Messrs. Eastman, Edwards, Geller, Hutchins, Linn, Mason, Monroe, Nelson, Proctor, and Sumner—10.

NAYS—Messrs. Doron, Grey, Haines, Meder, Stevenson, and Terry—6.

So the bill passed.

At 1:5 P.M., on motion of Mr. Mason, the Senate took a recess until 2:30 P.M.

IN SENATE.

The Senate met at 2:30 P.M.

President *pro tem.* in the chair.

Roll called.

Quorum present.

Senate Bill No. 108, " An Act to repeal an Act entitled ' An Act in regard to Currency,' approved March 3d, 1866."

Made special order for Friday, March 1st, at 2 P.M.

Senate Bill No. 138, " An Act authorizing the Secretary of State to employ a Clerk in the State Library and Adjutant General's Office."

On motion of Mr. Procter, a call of the Senate was ordered.

Roll called.

Absent—Messrs. Eastman, Monroe, Hutchins, Grey, Edwards, Stevenson, and Nelson.

Messrs. Nelson, Stevenson, Eastman, and Monroe appearing, were, on motion, excused.

On motion of Mr. Terry, further proceedings under the call were dispensed with.

The bill was made special order for Tuesday, March 5th, at 2 o'clock P.M.

Senate Bill No. 175, " An Act concerning the Location of Wood Lands and Mill Sites."

Ordered engrossed.

At 3:45 P.M., on motion of Mr. Doron, the Senate took a recess until 7 o'clock P.M.

IN SENATE.

The Senate met at 7 o'clock P.M., President *pro tem.* in the chair.

Roll called.

Quorum present.

Senate Bill No. 194, (introduced by leave by Printing Committee) " An Act to provide for certain Public Printing for the State of Nevada."

Read first time ; rules suspended ; read second time by title, and referred to Committee of the Whole.

A Message was received from the Assembly.

On motion of Mr. Hutchins, the Senate went into Committee of the Whole for consideration of such bills as have been referred to Committee of the Whole.

Mr. Hutchins in the chair.

The Committee rose, and submitted the following report :

Mr. President :

The Senate, in Committee of the Whole, have had under consideration Assembly Bill No. 122, " An Act entitled ' An Act authorizing the County Commissioners of the several Counties in this State to appoint additional Justices of the Peace,' " which they report back, and recommend the bill do pass.

Also, Senate Bill No. 173, " An Act to amend an Act entitled ' An Act to regulate Fees and Compensation for Official and other Services in the State of Nevada,' approved March 9th, 1865," which they report back, and recommend the bill be indefinitely postponed.

Also, Substitute Senate Bill No. 4, " An Act making further provisions to regulate Proceedings in Civil Cases, and in Civil and Criminal Cases where the Venue is brought in question, in the Courts of Justice in this State," which they report back, and recommend the bill do not pass.

Also, Senate Bill No. 194, " An Act to provide for certain Public Printing for the State of Nevada," on which they report progress, and ask leave to sit again.

GENERAL FILE.

Mr. Doron in the chair.

Assembly Bill No. 122, "An Act entitled 'An Act authorizing the County Commissioners of the several Counties in this State to appoint additional Justices of the Peace.'"

Read third time by sections.

The yeas and nays were called on the final passage of the bill, and recorded as follows:

YEAS—Messrs. Doron, Eastman, Edwards, Geller, Haines, Hutchins, Linn, Mason, Meder, Monroe, Nelson, Proctor, Sumner, and Terry—14.

NAYS—0.

So the bill passed.

Senate Bill No. 173, "An Act to amend an Act entitled 'An Act to regulate Fees and Compensation for Official and other Services in the State of Nevada,' approved March 9th, 1865."

Indefinitely postponed.

Substitute Senate Bill No. 4, "An Act making further provisions to regulate Proceedings in Civil Cases, and in Civil and Criminal Cases where the Venue is brought in question, in the Courts of Justice in this State."

Indefinitely postponed.

Senate Bill No. 194, "An Act to provide for certain Public Printing for the State of Nevada."

Leave was granted for the Committee of the Whole to sit again.

Mr. Edwards, by leave without previous notice, introduced Senate Bill No. 195, "An Act to amend an Act concerning District Attorneys, approved March 11th, 1865."

Read first time; rules suspended; read second time by title, and referred to the Committee on Judiciary.

Also, Senate Bill No. 196, "An Act to regulate the Sale of Lands selected by the State of Nevada in lieu of the sixteenth and thirty-sixth sections."

Read first time; rules suspended; read second time by title, and referred to Committee on Public Lands.

Also, Senate Bill No. 107, "An Act amendatory of an Act entitled 'An Act in relation to the Payment of Salaries and other Claims against the State,' approved February 27th, 1866."

Read first time; rules suspended; read second time by title, and referred to the Committee on Ways and Means.

At 8:15 P.M., on motion of Mr. Sumner, the Senate adjourned until to-morrow, at 10 o'clock A.M.

CHARLES A. SUMNER,
President.

Attest—B. C. BROWN,
Secretary.

IN SENATE—FIFTY-FOURTH DAY.

CARSON CITY, March 1st, 1867.

The Senate met pursuant to adjournment, Mr. Sumner, President *pro tem.*, in the chair.

Roll called.

Present—Messrs. Doron, Eastman, Edwards, Geller, Grey, Haines, Hutchings, Linn, Mason, Meder, Monroe, Nelson, Proctor, Stevenson, Sumner, and Terry—16.

Absent—None.

Prayer by the Chaplain.

The Journal of the Fifty-third day was read and approved.

REPORTS OF COMMITTEES.

Mr. Stevenson, Chairman of Committee on Mines and Mining, to which were referred the following entitled bills, to wit:

Assembly Bill No. 47, entitled "An Act to prescribe the number of Hours which shall constitute a Legal Day's Labor in certain cases;"

Senate Bill No. 133, "An Act entitled 'An Act to provide for establishing and maintaining a Mining School, and create the office of State Mineralogist,' approved March 9th, 1866," reported that they had had the same under consideration, and directed their chairman to report the same back to the Senate, with the recommendation that they be considered in Committee of the Whole.

Mr. Edwards, from the Standing Committee on Public Lands, to which was referred Senate Bill No. 196, entitled "An Act to regulate the Sale of Lands selected by the State of Nevada, in lieu of the 16th and 36th sections," reported that they had had the same under consideration; had come to a favorable conclusion thereon; had directed their chairman to report the same to the Senate, without amendments, and to recommend its passage.

Mr. Monroe, Chairman of the Committee on Claims, to which was referred Senate Bill No. 189, entitled "An Act to provide for Payment to Kinkead & Harrington for Goods furnished the late Supreme Court of the Territory of Nevada," reported that they had had the same under consideration; had directed their chairman to return the same to the Senate, and to recommend it do pass, on the ground of the equity of the claim.

The Committee on Public Morals, to which was referred Assembly Bill No. 110, entitled "An Act to amend an Act relating to Marriage and Divorce," reported that they had had the same under consideration; had come to a favorable conclusion thereon, and recommend it do pass.

Mr. Meder reported that the Standing Committee on Engrossment had carefully compared the following entitled bills with the originals, and found the same correctly engrossed, viz:

Substitute Senate Bill No. 130, "An Act for the Organization of a Board of Education in Counties that polled three thousand votes or more at the general election in the State of Nevada, A.D. 1866, or that may hereafter cast that number of votes or more, and amendatory of and supplemental to an Act to provide for the maintenance and support of Public Schools, approved March 20th, 1865."

Also, Senate Bill No. 160, "An Act to provide for the Payment of the Contingent Expenses of the Surveyor General's Office from December, 1864, to December, 1866, inclusive;" and herewith reports the same back to the Senate.

MESSAGE FROM THE ASSEMBLY.

The following Message was received from the Assembly:

ASSEMBLY CHAMBER, CARSON CITY, }
February 28th, 1867.

To the Hon. the Senate :

I am instructed to transmit to your honorable body, for your consideration, the following Assembly Bills, which passed the House this day, viz :

No. 127, "An Act to amend sections 72 and 74 of an Act entitled 'An Act relating to Officers, their qualifications, times of election, terms of office, official duties, resignations, removals, vacancies in office and the mode of supplying the same, misconduct in office, and to enforce official duty,' approved March 9th, 1866."

No. 116, "An Act to amend an Act entitled 'An Act to incorporate the Grand Lodge of Independent Order of Odd Fellows and Grand Lodge of Free and Accepted Masons and their subordinate Lodges in this State.'"

No. 111, "An Act to amend an Act entitled 'An Act to re-district the State of Nevada into Judicial Districts, and to fix the Salaries of Judges and the Terms of Court therein,' approved Feb. 27th, 1866."

I am also instructed to inform your honorable body that the House have this day concurred in Senate Amendments to Assembly Concurrent Resolution No. 44, relating to Mail facilities from White Rock House *via* Ellsworth, Cloverdale, Indian Springs, Belmont, and Hot Creek, to Pahranagat, Nye County.

I also return to you Senate Bill No. 94, "An Act to compensate J. F. Hatch for Services in the State Library," the same having passed the House this day, without amendment.

Respectfully,

A. WHITFORD,
Clerk.

Assembly Bill No. 127, "An Act to amend sections 72 and 74 of an Act entitled 'An Act relating to Officers, their qualifications, times of election, terms of office, official duties, resignations, removals, vacancies in office and the mode of supplying the same, misconduct in office, and to enforce official duty,' approved March 9th, 1866."

Read first time ; rules suspended ; read second time by title, and referred to Committee on State Affairs.

Assembly Bill No. 116, " An Act to amend an Act entitled 'An Act to incorporate the Grand Lodge of Free and Accepted Masons, the Grand Lodge of Odd Fellows, and their subordinate Lodges in this State.'"

Read first time ; rules suspended ; read second time by title, and referred to Committee on Incorporations.

Assembly Bill No. 10, "An Act to amend an Act entitled 'An Act to re-district the State of Nevada into Judicial Districts, and to fix the Salaries of Judges, and the Terms of Court therein,' approved Feb. 27th, 1866."

Read first time ; rules suspended ; read second time by title, and referred to Committee on Judiciary.

GENERAL FILE,

Senate Bill No. 160, " An Act to provide for the Payment of the Contingent Expenses of the Surveyor General's Office, from December, 1864, to December, 1866, inclusive."

Read third time by sections.

The yeas and nays were called on the final passage of the bill, and recorded as follows :

YEAS—Messrs. Doron, Eastman, Edwards, Geller, Grey, Linn, Mason, Meder, Stevenson, Sumner, and Terry—11.

Nays—0.

So the bill passed.

Senate Bill No. 196, "An Act to regulate the Sale of Lands selected by the State of Nevada in lieu of the sixteenth and thirty-sixth Sections."

Ordered engrossed.

Assembly Bill No. 110, "An Act to amend an Act entitled 'An Act relating to Marriage and Divorce.'"

Read third time by sections.

The yeas and nays were called on the final passage of the bill, and recorded as follows:

Yeas—Messrs. Doron, Eastman, Haines, Linn, Mason, Meder, Stevenson, and Terry—8.

Nays—Messrs. Geller, Grey, Monroe, and Sumner—4.

So the bill did not pass.

Senate Bill No. 189, "An Act to provide for Payment to Kinkead and Harrington for Goods furnished the late Supreme Court of the Territory of Nevada."

Ordered engrossed.

On motion of Mr. Monroe, the Senate went into Committee of the Whole for the consideration of the General File.

President in the chair.

The Committee rose, and submitted the following report:

Mr. President:

The Senate, in Committee of the Whole, have had under consideration Assembly Bill No. 47, "An Act to prescribe the Number of Hours which constitute a Legal Day's Labor in certain cases," which they report back, and recommend the bill be indefinitely postponed.

Also, Senate Bill No. 133, "An Act to repeal an Act to provide for Establishing and Maintaining a Mining School, and to create the office of State Mineralogist," which they report back, and recommend the bill be ordered engrossed.

Assembly Bill No. 7, "An Act to prescribe the Number of Hours which shall constitute a Legal Day's Labor in certain cases."

Indefinitely postponed.

Senate Bill No. 188, "An Act to provide for Payment to Kinkead and Harrington, for Goods furnished the late Supreme Court of the Territory of Nevada."

Ordered engrossed.

Mr. Hutchins, by leave, introduced the following resolution:

Resolved, That the Committee on Supplies and Expenditures are hereby requested to examine the accounts for stationery furnished the Senate, and report thereon at their earliest convenience.

Adopted.

UNFINISHED BUSINESS.

Assembly Bill No. 13, "An Act amendatory of and supplemental to 'An Act to create the County of Lincoln, and provide for its organization,' approved Feb. 26th, 1866."

Indefinitely postponed.

On motion of Mr. Sumner, Substitute Senate Bill No. 130, "An Act for the Organization of a Board of Education in Counties that polled three thousand votes or more at the General Election in the State of Nevada, A.D. 1866, or that may hereafter at any general election cast that number of votes, or more, and amendatory of and supplementary to 'An Act to provide for the Maintenance and Support of Public Schools,' approved March 20th, 1865," was now taken up.

Read third time by sections.

The yeas and nays were called on the final passage of the bill, and recorded as follows :

YEAS—Messrs. Eastman, Edwards, Geller, Haines, Linn, Mason, Meder, Monroe, Proctor, Sumner, and Terry—11.

NAYS—Messrs. Doron, Grey, Hutchins, Nelson, and Stevenson—5.

So the bill passed.

Mr. Proctor, by leave, submitted the following report:

The Judiciary Committee, to which was referred Senate Substitute Bill No. 169, "An Act to provide for the Publication of the Decisions of the Supreme Court of the State of Nevada," reported that they had had the same under consideration ; had come to a favorable conclusion thereon; report the same back to the Senate, and recommend its passage, with the following amendments : Fill up first blank in section six by inserting "fifteen cents ;" second blank in same section by inserting " one thousand;" also, amend section seven by striking out, in third line, " Chief Justice," and insert "Reporter ;" also, fill blank in section ten, by inserting " two thousand."

Also, Assembly Bill No. 121, "An Act to amend an Act entitled 'An Act concerning Crimes and Punishments,' approved November 26th, 1861," which they had had under consideration ; had come to an unfavorable conclusion thereon; report the same to the Senate, and recommend it do not pass.

Also, Senate Bill No. 195, "An Act to amend an Act concerning District Attorneys, approved March 11th, 1865," which they recommend be indefinitely postponed.

Also, Senate Bill No. 69, "An Act to amend an Act of the Legislature of the Territory of Nevada, entitled 'An Act concerning Conveyances,' approved Nov. 5th, 1861," which they report back to the Senate, and recommend its passage.

Mr. Linn, Chairman Committee on Enrollment, reported that Senate Bill No. 94, entitled " An Act to compensate J. F. Hatch for Services in the State Library," had been carefully compared with the engrossed bill, as passed by the two Houses, found correctly enrolled, and that the same will be delivered to the Governor for his approval.

Assembly Bill No. 121, "An Act to amend an Act entitled ' An Act concerning Crimes and Punishments,' approved November 26th, 1861."

Indefinitely postponed.

Senate Bill No. 195, " An Act to amend an Act concerning District Attorneys, approved March 11th, 1865."

Indefinitely postponed.

Substitute Senate Bill No. 167, " An Act to amend an Act of the Legislature of the Territory of Nevada, entitled ' An Act concerning Conveyances,' approved November 5th, 1861."

Ordered engrossed.

On motion of Mr. Hutchins, the Senate went into Committee of the Whole, for the consideration of Substitute Senate Bill No. 169, President in the chair.

The Committee rose, and submitted the following report :

Mr. President :

The Senate, in Committee of the Whole, have had under consideration Substitute Senate Bill No. 169, " An Act to provide for the Publication of the Decisions of the Supreme Court of the State of Nevada," which they report back, and recommend the amendments of the Judiciary Committee be adopted, and the bill ordered engrossed as amended.

Substitute Senate Bill No. 169, " An Act to provide for the Publication of the Decisions of the Supreme Court of the State of Nevada."
Ordered engrossed as amended.
The Chair appointed Messrs. Meder, Geller and Mason as a Committee of Conference on Assembly Bill No. 27, " An Act relating to District Attorneys."
At 12:35 P.M., on motion of Mr. Hutchins, the Senate took a recess until 3 o'clock P.M.

IN SENATE.

The Senate met at 3 o'clock P.M., President *pro tem.* in the chair.
Mr. Doron in the chair.

SPECIAL ORDER.

Senate Bill No. 108, " An Act to repeal an Act entitled ' An Act in regard to Currency,' approved March 3d, 1866."
Made special order for Saturday, March 2d, at 2 o'clock.
Mr. Terry gave notice that he would, on to-morrow, move a reconsideration of the vote whereby Substitute Senate Bill No. 130, " An Act for the organization of the Board of Education in Counties that polled three thousand votes or more at the General Election in the State of Nevada, in November, 1866, etc.," was passed.
On motion of Mr. Meder, the Senate went into Committee of the Whole for the consideration of Senate Bill No. 194, President in the chair.
The Committee rose, and submitted the following report :

Mr. President :

The Senate, in Committee of the Whole, have had under consideration Senate Bill No. 194, " An Act to provide for certain Public Printing for the State of Nevada," which they report back as amended, and recommend the bill be ordered engrossed as amended.

Senate Bill No. 194, " An Act to provide for certain Public Printing for the State of Nevada."
Amendments of Committee of the Whole adopted, and the bill ordered engrossed.
Mr. Proctor, (by leave) from Standing Committee on Counties and County Boundaries, to which was referred Assembly Bill No. 192, entitled " An Act to amend an Act to create a Board of County Commissioners in the several Counties of this State, and define their Powers and Duties, approved March 8th, 1865," reported that they had had the same under consideration, had come to an unfavorable conclusion thereon, had directed their chairman to report the same to the Senate without amendments, and recommend it do not pass.
Assembly Bill No. 92, " An Act to amend an Act to create a Board of County Commissioners in the several Counties of this State, and define their Powers and Duties, approved March 8th, 1865."

Indefinitely postponed.

Mr. Haines, (by leave) submitted the following resolution :

Resolved, That the Secretary be instructed to request of the Assembly the return of Assembly Bill No. 110, "An Act to amend an Act entitled ' An Act relating to Marriage and Divorce.' "

Adopted.

Mr. Proctor, (by leave) from the Judiciary Committee, to which was referred Assembly Bill No. 44, entitled " An Act amendatory of and supplementary to an Act defining the time of commencing Civil Actions, approved November 21st, 1861, and to repeal Acts amendatory of said Acts," reported that they had had the same under consideration, had come to a favorable conclusion thereon, had directed their chairman to report the same to the Senate without amendments, and recommend its passage.

On motion of Mr. Proctor, Assembly Bill No. 44, " An Act amendatory of and supplementary to an Act defining the time of commencing Civil Actions, approved November 21st, 1861, and to repeal Acts amendatory of said Acts," was now taken up.

Mr. Hutchins moved that the word " one " be stricken out, and the word " two " inserted in section 8 wherever it appears.

Carried.

Read third time by sections; the yeas and nays were called on the final passage of the bill, and recorded as follows:

YEAS—Messrs. Doron, Eastman, Geller, Haines, Hutchins, Linn, Mason, Meder, Monroe, Nelson, Proctor, Stevenson, and Terry—13.

NAYS—0.

So the bill passed.

At 3:30 P.M., on motion of Mr. Haines, the Senate took a recess until 6:30 P.M.

The Senate met at 6:30 P.M., Mr. Doron in the chair.

Roll called.

No quorum present.

On motion of Mr. Proctor, the Senate took a recess until 8 o'clock P.M.

The Senate met at 8 P.M., Mr. Doron in the chair.

Roll called.

Quorum present.

On motion of Mr. Sumner, the Senate adjourned until to-morrow at 11 o'clock A.M.

CHARLES A. SUMNER,
President.

Attest—B. C. BROWN,
Secretary.

IN SENATE—FIFTY-FIFTH DAY.

CARSON CITY, March 2d, 1867.

The Senate met pursuant to adjournment, Mr. Sumner, President *pro tem.*, in the chair.

Roll called.

Present—Messrs. Doron, Eastman, Edwards, Geller, Grey, Haines, Hutchins, Linn, Mason, Meder, Monroe, Proctor, Stevenson, Sumner, and Terry —15.

Absent—Mr. Nelson—1.

Prayer by the Chaplain.

The Journal of the Fifty-fourth day was read and approved.

A Message was received from the Assembly.

The special order set for 11 o'clock was postponed until the regular order of business of the day was gone through with.

REPORTS OF COMMITTEES.

Mr. Proctor, from the Committee on Judiciary, to which was referred Assembly Bill No. 111, entitled "An Act to amend an Act entitled 'An Act to redistrict the State of Nevada into Judicial Districts, and to fix the Salary and Terms of Court therein,' approved February 29th, 1866," reported that they had had the same under consideration ; had come to an unfavorable conclusion thereon, and had directed their chairman to report the same to the Senate without amendments, and recommend it be indefinitely postponed.

Also, Assembly Bill No. 15, entitled "an Act to amend An Act entitled 'An Act to regulate Proceedings in Civil Cases in Courts of Justice of the Territory of Nevada,' approved November 29th, 1861," which they had had under consideration ; had come to a favorable conclusion thereon, had directed their chairman to report the same to the Senate without amendments, and to recommend its passage.

Mr. Proctor, from Nye County delegation, to which was referred Assembly Bill No. 79, entitled "An Act for the Relief of A. Raney, Sheriff of Nye County," reported that they had had the same under consideration ; had come to a favorable conclusion thereon, had directed their chairman to report the same to the Senate without amendments, and to recommend its passage.

Mr. Grey, from the Standing Committee on Elections, to which was referred Senate Bill No. 54, entitled "An Act to amend an Act entitled 'An Act to provide for the Registration of the names of Electors, and for the ascertainment by proper proofs who shall be entitled to the right of Suffrage,' approved February 24th, 1866," reported that they had had the same under consideration ; had come to an unfavorable conclusion thereon, and directed their chairman to report the same back to the Senate without amendments, and to recommend it be indefinitely postponed.

Mr. Doron, from Committee on State Affairs, submitted the following report :

Mr. President :

A majority of your Standing Committee on State Affairs, to which was referred Assembly Bill No. 86, entitled "An Act to provide for the Official Publication of the Laws, Resolutions and other Documents," report that they have had the same under consideration ; have come to an unfavorable conclusion thereon, and herewith report the same back to the Senate, with the recommendation that the same do not pass.

LEWIS DORON,.
B. H. MEDER,.

Mr. Monroe, from same Committee, asked leave to make a minority report on Assembly Bill No. 86.

Granted.

Mr. Meder reported that the Standing Committee on Engrossment had

25

carefully compared the following entitled bills with the originals, and found the same correctly engrossed, viz:

Senate Bill No. 174, "An Act to amend an Act entitled 'An Act to provide Revenue for the Support of the Government of the State of Nevada,' approved March 9th, 1865."

Also, Senate Bill No. 172, "An Act supplementary to an Act entitled 'An Act to provide Revenue for the Support of the Government for the State of Nevada,' approved March 9th, 1865, and other Acts amendatory of and supplementary thereto."

Also, Senate Bill No. 170, "An Act to amend an Act entitled 'An Act concerning the Office of Secretary of State,' approved February 14, 1865;" and herewith report the same back to the Senate.

MESSAGE FROM THE ASSEMBLY.

The following Message was received from the Assembly:

ASSEMBLY CHAMBER, CARSON CITY, }
March 1st, 1867. }

To the Honorable the Senate:

I am instructed to return to your honorable body Senate Bill No. 142, "An Act amendatory of an Act to provide for the Maintenance and Supervision of Public Schools, approved March 20th, 1865," the same having passed the House this day, amended as follows:

In section 21, line 6, after the word "same," the words " provided that the Board shall establish such separate Schools when requested so to do by or in behalf of ten pupils in any district, of the races above named."

Respectfully,

A. WHITFORD,
Clerk.

On motion of Mr. Hutchins, the Secretary was instructed to return the Message to the Assembly, requesting them to indorse an interpretation thereof on the back of the same.

INTRODUCTION OF BILLS.

Mr. Sumner, by leave without previous notice, introduced Senate Bill No. 201, "An Act to provide for the Liquidation of certain Claims against the City of Virginia."

Read first time; rules suspended; read second time by title, and referred to Mr. Grey, of Storey County delegation.

GENERAL FILE.

Senate Bill No. 172, "An Act supplementary to an Act entitled 'An Act to provide Revenue for the Support of the Government for the State of Nevada,' approved March 9th, 1865, and other Acts amendatory of and supplementary thereto."

Read third time by sections. The yeas and nays were called on the final passage of the bill, and recorded as follows:

YEAS—Messrs. Doron, Eastman, Geller, Haines, Hutchins, Linn, Meder, Monroe, Proctor, Stevenson, Sumner, and Terry—12.
NAYS—0.

So the bill passed.
Senate Bill No. 174, " An Act to amend an Act entitled ' An Act to provide Revenue for the Support of the Government of the State of Nevada,' approved March 9th, 1865," was made the special order for Tuesday, March 5th, at 12 o'clock M.
A Message was received from the Assembly.
Senate Bill No. 170, " An Act to amend an Act entitled ' An Act concerning the Office of Secretary of State,' approved February 14th, 1867," [1865].
Read third time by sections. The yeas and nays were called on the final passage of the bill, and recorded as follows:

YEAS—Messrs. Doron, Eastman, Edwards, Geller, Grey, Haines, Hutchins, Linn, Mason, Meder, Nelson, Proctor, Stevenson, Sumner, and Terry—15.
NAYS—0.

So the bill passed.
Assembly Bill No. 111, " An Act to amend an Act entitled 'An Act to redistrict the State of Nevada into Judicial Districts, and to fix the Salaries of Judges, and the Terms of Courts therein,' approved February 27th, 1866."
Indefinitely postponed.
Assembly Bill No. 15, " An Act to amend an Act entitled ' An Act to regulate Proceedings in Civil Cases in the Courts of Justice of the Territory of Nevada,' approved November 29th, 1861."
Read third time by sections. The yeas and nays were called on the final passage of the bill, and recorded as follows:

YEAS—Messrs. Doron, Eastman, Edwards, Geller, Haines, Hutchins, Linn, Mason, Meder, Monroe, Nelson, and Proctor—12.
NAYS—Messrs. Grey, Stevenson, Sumner, and Terry—4.

So the bill passed.
Mr. Monroe, from Committee on State Affairs, by leave, submitted the following minority report:

Assembly Bill No. 86, " An Act to provide for the Official Publication of Laws, Resolutions, and other Public Documents," and which gives the printing of the same to the *Daily Trespass*, a newspaper published in Virginia City, and which bill was referred to the Committee on State Affairs, of which I am a member: I desire to make a minority report.
Having a few days since favored a bill giving the printing to one of the three papers in Storey County, to be let to the lowest bidder, it might now be considered that my action in supporting this is inconsistent. I at that time stated that I would be willing to name one of the three, and for the reason that the publication should be made in some paper that had a general circulation.
It has been the general custom, by all legislative bodies, to designate the particular [paper] that shall publish the laws and Acts passed by themselves, and other printing necessary to be done and under their control, the wisdom of which has not been questioned; and precedent so well established as this must have good foundation, and reasons to sustain such action. It is necessary that this kind of work should be well and accurately done, and should it be left to the

competition of the several papers of the State, to be bid for, and the lowest bidder be awarded the same, then, in my opinion, the work would be let at so low a figure that, as a natural consequence, it would be inaccurately and imperfectly performed, and thereby be of little or no value to the State, leading, as it would, to conflict of decisions between those rendered by our Courts made up from the laws as published, and those to be published in book form. To my mind it is a well settled fact, that work not sufficiently remunerated is seldom, if ever, properly done. This bill contemplates only a fair and reasonable compensation for the importance of the services demanded and expenses incurred, and I have no disposition to so legislate that the State may make money by the losses of an individual or individuals. The *Trespass* has quite a general circulation in all parts of the State, will do the work well, and thereby fully carry out the intentions of this Act; and I believe the State has the same right as an individual to foster any enterprise that is calculated to advance the public good in the dissemination of valuable information; and as no one in this day will dispute the fact, that the *Press* is one of the great *vehicles* that distribute knowledge throughout our country, making us a people more advanced in general information than any other; and as the *Territorial Enterprise* has from time to time said it wants no patronage from the State of Nevada, but is fixed upon a firm foundation, and above asking anything from the State in any manner or shape, which shows conclusively to my mind that there is no danger of the people being deprived of the *light* shed abroad by that *sheet;* and besides the many *complimentary* epithets it has constantly applied to this Legislature, both Senate and Assembly, calling us anything but honest or intelligent men, I am willing, as a member of this Senate, to grant their *prayer*, to wit: "that they do not want any of the patronage at the disposal of this Legislature."

The *Daily Trespass* has not shown so conclusively that its foundation rests upon so firm a base that it cannot be moved, and in order that it may receive the little assistance the State is bound to give to some paper, and the little time left of this session to be informed of the fate of the former bill or to introduce and pass a new bill designating any other paper, I respectfully recommend that Assembly Bill No. 86 do pass.

W. G. MONROE.

Senate Bill No. 54, "An Act to amend an Act entitled 'An Act to provide for the Registration of the Names of Electors, and for the ascertainment by proper proof who shall be entitled to the Right of Suffrage,' approved Feb. 24th, 1866."

Indefinitely postponed.

Assembly Bill No. 79, "An Act for the Relief of A. Ramirez, Sheriff of Nye County."

Read third time by sections.

The yeas and nays were called on the final passage of the bill, and recorded as follows:

YEAS—Messrs. Doron, Eastman, Edwards, Geller, Haines, Hutchins, Linn, Mason, Meder, Monroe, Nelson, Proctor, Stevenson, Sumner, and Terry—15.

NAYS—Mr. Grey—1.

So the bill passed.

Assembly Bill No. 86, "An Act to provide for the Official Publication of Laws and Resolutions, and other Public Documents."

Read third time by sections.

The yeas and nays were called on the final passage of the bill, and recorded as follows:

YEAS—Messrs. Grey, Hutchins, Mason, Monroe, Proctor, and Stevenson—6.
NAYS—Messrs. Doron, Eastman, Edwards, Geller, Haines, Linn, Meder, Nelson, Sumner, and Terry—10.

So the bill did not pass.
Mr. Sumner gave notice that on Monday, March 4th, he would move a reconsideration of the vote whereby Assembly Bill No. 86, above mentioned, was defeated.

The following Message was received from the Assembly:

ASSEMBLY CHAMBER, CARSON CITY, ⎱
————, 186 . ⎰

To the Hon. the Senate:
I return to your honorable body, as per request, Assembly Bill No. 110, "An Act in Relation to Marriage and Divorce," for your further consideration.
Respectfully,

A. WHITFORD,
Clerk.

Pursuant to notice, Mr. Haines moved a reconsideration of the vote whereby Assembly Bill No. 110, "An Act to amend an Act entitled 'An Act relating to Marriage and Divorce," was lost on Friday, March 1st.
The motion to reconsider was carried.
A Message was received from the Assembly.
On motion of Mr. Haines, Assembly Bill No. 110, "An Act to amend an Act entitled 'An Act relating to Marriage and Divorce,'" was now taken up.
The yeas and nays were called on the final passage of the bill, and recorded as follows:

YEAS—Messrs. Doron, Eastman, Edwards, Geller, Haines, Hutchins, Linn, Mason, Meder, Nelson, and Terry—11.
NAYS—Messrs. Grey, Monroe, Proctor, Stevenson, and Sumner—5.

So the bill passed.
Pursuant to notice, Mr. Terry moved that the vote whereby Substitute Senate Bill No. 130, "An Act for the Organization of a Board of Education, etc.," was passed, be now reconsidered.
Mr. Proctor in the chair.
The yeas and nays were called on the question by Messrs. Sumner, Mason, and Eastman, which resulted as follows:

YEAS—Messrs. Eastman, Grey, Hutchins, Linn, Meder, Monroe, Nelson, Stevenson, and Terry—9.
NAYS—Messrs. Doron, Edwards, Geller, Grey, Mason, Proctor, and Sumner—7.

So the vote was reconsidered.
Mr. Doron moved that the vote by which the bill was ordered to a third reading be reconsidered.
Carried.
Mr. Doron moved that the bill be referred to Messrs. Stevenson, Grey, and Nelson, of Storey County delegation.
Carried.

Mr. Hutchins, by leave without previous notice, introduced Senate Bill No. 202, "An Act to provide Stationery for the use of the Senate and Assembly of the State of Nevada."

Read first time; rules suspended; read second time by title, and referred to Committee on Supplies and Expenditures.

Mr. Meder, by leave, introduced a bill entitled "An Act to impose certain Duties on the Supreme Court."

Read for information.

Mr. Grey moved the bill be rejected.

The yeas and nays were called for on the question by Messrs. Sumner, Grey and Hutchins, and recorded as follows:

YEAS—Messrs. Geller, Grey, Haines, Mason, Monroe, Nelson, Proctor, Stevenson, Sumner, and Terry—10.

NAYS—Messrs. Doron, Eastman, Edwards, Hutchins, Linn, and Meder—6.

So the bill was rejected.

Mr. Doron, by leave, introduced Senate Concurrent Resolution No. 204, "Relative to certain claims for Mail Service between .Genoa, Carson County, Utah Territory, aud Monoville, Mono County, California."

Read first time; rules suspended; read second time by title; rules further suspended; read third time.

The yeas and nays were called on the final passage of the resolution, and recorded as follows:

YEAS—Messrs. Doron, Eastman, Geller, Grey, Haines, Hutchins, Mason, Meder, Monroe, Nelson, Proctor, Stevenson, Sumner, and Terry—14.

NAYS—0.

So the resolution passed.

At 2:15 P.M., on motion of Mr. Hutchins, the Senate took a recess until 3 o'clock P.M.

IN SENATE.

The Senate met at 3 P.M., Mr. Doron in the chair.
Roll called.
No quorum present.
On motion of Mr. Hutchins, the Senate took a recess until 7:30 P.M.

IN SENATE.

The Senate met at 7:30 P.M.
Mr. Doron in the chair.
Roll called.
Quorum present.

Mr. Terry, by leave, from the Standing Committee on Supplies and Expenditures, to which was referred Senate Bill No. 202, entitled "An Act to provide Stationery for the use of the Senate and Assembly of the State of Nevada," reported that they had had the same under consideration, had come to a favorable conclusion thereon, and directed their chairman to report the same to the Senate without amendments, and recommend it be considered in Committee of the Whole.

Mr. Linn, Chairman of Committee on Enrollment, reported that Substitute Senate Bill No. 45, "An Act to provide for Fostering and Supporting the 'Nevada Orphan Asylum,' a duly incorporated benevolent institution located at Virginia City," had been carefully compared with the engrossed bill, as passed by the two Houses, found correctly enrolled, and that the same had this day been delivered to the Governor for his approval.

Mr. Grey, by leave, from Special Committee from Storey County, to which was referred Senate Bill No. 201, entitled "An Act to provide for the Liquidation and Payment of certain Claims against the City of Virginia," reported that they had had the same under consideration; had come to a favorable conclusion thereon, and directed their chairman to report the same to the Senate without amendments, and recommend its passage.

On motion of Mr. Hutchins, the Senate went into Committee of the Whole, for the consideration of Senate Bill No. 202.

President in the chair.

The Committee rose, and submitted the following report:

Mr. President:

The Senate, in Committee of the Whole, have had under consideration Senate Bill No. 202, "An Act to provide Stationery for the use of the Senate and Assembly of the State of Nevada," which they report back, and recommend that the bill be ordered engrossed.

A Message was received from the Assembly.

Senate Bill No. 202, "An Act to provide Stationery for the use of the Senate and Assembly of the State of Nevada."

Ordered engrossed.

On motion of Mr. Sumner, Senate Bill No. 210, "An Act to provide for the Liquidation and Payment of certain Claims against the City of Virginia," was now taken up.

Rules suspended; read third time by sections. The yeas and nays were called on the final passage of the bill, and recorded as follows:

YEAS—Messrs. Doron, Eastman, Edwards, Geller, Grey, Haines, Hutchins, Linn, Mason, Meder, Monroe, Nelson, Proctor, Stevenson, Sumner, and Terry —16.

NAYS—0.

So the bill passed.

On motion of Mr. Proctor, the Senate went into Committee of the Whole for the consideration of Senate Bill No. 108, President in the chair.

The Committee rose, and submitted the following report:

Mr. President:

The Senate, in Committee of the Whole, have had under consideration Senate Bill No. 108, "An Act to repeal an Act entitled 'An Act in regard to Currency,' approved March 3d, 1866," which they report back, and ask leave to sit again on Monday, at 11 o'clock A.M.

A Message was received from the Governor.

Senate Bill No. 108, "An Act to repeal an Act entitled 'An Act in regard to Currency,' approved March 3d, 1867 [1866]."

Made special order for Monday, March 4th, at 11 o'clock A.M.

The following Message was received from the Assembly:

ASSEMBLY CHAMBER, CARSON CITY, }
March 2d, 1867. }

To the Hon. the Senate :

I am instructed to return to your honorable body, Substitute Senate Bill No. 45, the same having passed the House on yesterday without amendment; but was held in the House until to-day, under a motion to reconsider.

Respectfully,

A. WHITFORD,
Clerk.

Mr. Sumner moved that Senate Bill No. 142, "An Act amendatory of 'An Act to provide for the Maintenance and Supervision of Public Schools,' approved March 20th, 1865," be now taken up.

Carried.

The amendments of the Assembly were concurred in.

The following Messages were received from the Assembly:

ASSEMBLY CHAMBER, CARSON CITY, }
March 2d, 1867. }

To the Honorable the Senate:

I am instructed to inform your honorable body that the words "provided that the Board shall establish such separate schools when requested so to do by or in behalf of ten pupils, in any district, of the races above named," were stricken out of section 21, line 6, after the word "same," of Senate Bill No. 142, "An Act amendatory of 'An Act to provide for the Maintenance and Supervision of Public Schools,' approved March 20th, 1865."

A. WHITFORD,
Clerk.

ASSEMBLY CHAMBER, CARSON CITY, }
March 2d, 1867. }

To the Hon. the Senate :

I am instructed to transmit to your honorable body the following Assembly Bills for your consideration, the same having passed this House:

Assembly Bill No. 132, "An Act to amend section 86 of an Act to further amend an Act entitled 'An Act to provide Revenue for the Support of the Government of the State of Nevada.'"

Assembly Bill No. 133, "An Act for the Relief of Wallace Goodell, late County Treasurer of Churchill County."

Assembly Bill No. 59, "An Act to amend an Act entitled 'An Act to amend an Act to regulate proceedings in Civil Cases in the Courts of Justice of the Territory of Nevada,' approved November 29th, 1861, approved March 9th, 1865."

Assembly Bill No. 75, "An Act to amend section 52 of an Act entitled 'An Act to regulate the Settlement of the Estates of Deceased Persons,' approved November 29th, 1861."

Assembly Bill No. 109, "An Act to legalize the Publication of Summons in Suits for the Collection of Delinquent Taxes, in the several Counties in this State."

Substitute Assembly Bill No. 93, "An Act to amend an Act entitled 'An Act to amend an Act in relation to Wild Game and Fish,' approved November 21st, 1861, approved February 20th, 1864, approved March 1st, 1866."

I also transmit for your consideration Assembly Concurrent Resolution No. 47, relating to " Enrolled Bills."

All of which is respectfully submitted.

A. WHITFORD,
Clerk.

Assembly Bill No. 132, " An Act to amend section 86 of an Act to further amend an Act entitled "An Act to provide Revenue for the Support of the Government of the State of Nevada." Read first time; rules suspended; read second time by title, and referred to Committee on Ways and Means.

Assembly Bill No. 133, " An Act for the Relief of Wallace Goodell, late County Treasurer of Churchill County." Read first time; rules suspended; read second time by title, and referred to Churchill County delegation.

Assembly Bill No. 59, " An Act to amend an Act entitled ' An Act to amend an Act to regulate Proceedings in Civil Cases in the Courts of Justice of the Territory of Nevada,' approved November 29th, 1861, approved March 9th, 1865." Read first time; rules suspended; read second time by title, and referred to Committee on Judiciary.

Assembly Bill No. 75, " An Act to amend section 52 of an Act entitled ' An Act to regulate the Settlement of the Estates of Deceased Persons,' approved November 29th, 1861." Read first time; rules suspended; read second time by title, and referred to Committee on Judiciary.

Assembly Bill No. 109, " An Act to legalize the Publication of Summons in Suits for the Collection of Delinquent Taxes in the several Counties in this State." Read first time; rules suspended; read second time by title, and referred to Committee on Ways and Means.

Substitute Assembly Bill No. 93, " An Act to amend an Act entitled ' An Act to amend an Act in relation to Wild Game and Fish,' approved November 21st, 1861, approved February 20th, 1864, approved March 1st, 1866." Read first time'; rules suspended; read *third* time by title, and referred to Committee on State Affairs.

Assembly Resolution No. 47, relating to Enrolled Bills. Resolution adopted.

ASSEMBLY CHAMBER, CARSON CITY, }
March 2d, 1867. }

To the Hon. the Senate:

I am instructed to transmit to your honorable body, for your consideration, the following Assembly Bills, which passed the House this day, viz:

No. 77, " An Act providing for the Payment of certain Indebtedness due Geo. F. Jones from the City of Virginia."

No. 129, " An Act authorizing the construction of a Railroad from Virginia City to the Truckee River."

Also, Assembly Memorial to Congress, which passed the House this day.

I also return to your honorable body Senate Bill No. 172, " An Act supplementary to an Act entitled ' An Act to provide Revenue for the Support of the Government of the State of Nevada,' approved March 9th, 1865, and other Acts amendatory and supplementary thereof," the same having passed the House this day without amendment.

Also, Senate Bill No. 140, " An Act to amend an Act to provide for Organizing and Disciplining the Militia of this State, approved March 4th, 1865," the same having passed the House this day, amended as follows :

By striking out all of section 2 after the word "allow," in first line, second page, and insert the following : "for the care and custody thereof, and to defray the current expenses of military organizations therein, the sums, and in manner

26

as hereinafter in this section specified; that is to say: In any county wherein there shall be three companies organized, there shall be allowed and paid two thousand dollars; in any county wherein there shall be two companies, fifteen hundred dollars; and in any county wherein there shall be one company organized, one thousand dollars, annually; such sum so to be audited and allowed, quarter yearly, from the first day of January, A.D. 1867, on presentation of claims by the officers or Finance Committee of the several companies so organized; one-half of such allowance to be paid out of the funds in the County Treasury belonging to the State, and the other half out of the General Fund of the county, to be paid by the County Treasurer on presentation, by the proper officer of the company or companies entitled thereto, of the Auditor's certificate of such allowance having been made by the Board of County Commissioners. In counties wherein there are two or more companies so organized, such allowance to be equally divided among them; and the County Treasurer shall require from the officer or committee to whom he shall pay the State's proportion of such allowance, a receipt therefor, which shall be received by the State Treasurer as so much money, and be so allowed in the settlement by the County Treasurer with the Controller and Treasurer of State."

Also, at the end of section 3, by adding, " but any company so pre-uniformed shall, when they effect a change therein, conform to the requirements of this section."

I also return Senate Concurrent Resolution No. 203, relative to Claims for certain Mail Service, which passed the House this day unanimously.

Respectfully,

A. WHITFORD,
Clerk.

Senate Bill No. 140, "An Act to amend an Act to provide for Organizing and Disciplining the Militia of this State, approved March 4th, 1865."

The Assembly amendments were concurred in.

Assembly Bill No. 77, "An Act providing for the Payment of certain Indebtedness due Geo. F. Jones & Co., from the City of Virginia."

Read first time; rules suspended; read second time by title, and referred to the Storey County delegation.

Assembly Bill No. 129, "An Act authorizing the Construction of a Railroad from Virginia City to the Truckee River."

Read first time; rules suspended; read second time by title, and referred to the Washoe and Storey County delegations.

Assembly Memorial No. 48, relative to Claims of Wm. H. Brumfield and others during the year 1860.

Read first time; rules suspended; read second time by title, and referred to Committee on Military and Indian Affairs.

At 10 P.M., on motion of Mr. Meder, the Senate adjourned until Monday, March 4th, at 10 o'clock, A.M.

JAMES S. SLINGERLAND,
President.

Attest—B. C. BROWN,
Secretary.

IN SENATE—FIFTY-SEVENTH DAY.

CARSON CITY, March 4th, 1867.

The Senate met pursuant to adjournment, the President in the chair.

Roll called.

Present—Messrs. Doron, Eastman, Edwards, Geller, Grey, Haines, Hastings, Hutchins, Linn, Mason, Meder, Monroe, Nelson, Proctor, Stevenson, Sumner, Terry, and Welty—18.

Absent—0.

The Journal of the Fifty-fifth day was read and approved.

REPORTS OF COMMITTEES.

Mr. Hastings reported that the Standing Committee on Engrossment had carefully compared the following entitled bill with the original, and found the same correctly engrossed, viz:

Senate Bill No. 202, "An Act to provide Stationery for the use of the Senate and Assembly of the State of Nevada," and herewith report the same back to the Senate.

Mr. Meder, from Standing Committee on Engrossment, reported that the following entitled bills had been carefully compared with the originals, and found correctly engrossed, viz:

Substitute Senate Bill No. 169, "An Act to provide for the Publication of the Decisions of the Supreme Court of the State of Nevada."

Senate Bill No. 194, "An Act to provide for certain Public Printing for the State of Nevada."

Also, Senate Bill No. 133, "An Act to repeal an Act entitled 'An Act to provide for Establishing and Maintaining a Mining School, and create the Office of State Mineralogist,' approved March 9th, 1866."

Also, Senate Bill No. 175, "An Act concerning the Location and Possession of Wood Lands and Mill Sites."

Also, Senate Bill No. 189, "An Act to provide for Payment to Kinkead & Harrington, for Goods furnished the late Supreme Court of the Territory of Nevada."

Also, Senate Bill No. 167, "An Act to amend an Act of the Legislature of the Territory of Nevada, entitled 'An Act concerning Conveyances,' [approved] November 5th, 1861."

Also, Senate Bill No. 196, "An Act to regulate the Sale of Lands selected by the State of Nevada, in lieu of the sixteenth and thirty-sixth sections;" and herewith report the same back to the Senate.

Mr. Hutchins, from Committee on Military and Indian Affairs, reported that they had had under consideration Assembly Memorial No. 48, and report the same back to the Senate with the recommendation that it do pass.

Mr. Geller, from Standing Committee on State Prison, submitted the following report: (See Appendix.)

Mr. Eastman, from Standing Committee on Corporations, to which was referred Assembly Bill No. 116, entitled "An Act to amend an Act to Incorporate the Grand Lodge of Free and Accepted Masons, the Grand Lodge of Independent Order of Odd Fellows, and their Subordinate Lodges in this State," reported that they had had the same under consideration; had come to a favorable conclusion thereon; had directed their chairman to report the same to the Senate, with the following amendment, and to recommend its passage:

Amend section 1 by inserting in the fourth line, after the word "lodges," the following: "and the Grand Lodge of the Independent Order of Odd Fellows in the State of Nevada, and its Subordinate Lodges."

Mr. Doron, from the Standing Committee on State Affairs, to which was referred Assembly Bill No. 93, entitled "An Act to amend an Act entitled ' An Act in relation to Wild Game and Fish,' " reported that they had had the same under consideration ; had come to a favorable conclusion thereon ; had directed their chairman to report the same to the Senate, without amendments, and recommend its passage.

Also, Assembly Bill No. 127, entitled "An Act to amend sections 72 and 74 of an Act entitled 'An Act relating to Officers, their qualifications, times of election, terms of office, official duties, resignations, removals, vacancies in office and the mode of supplying the same, misconduct in office, and to enforce official duty,' approved March 9th, 1866," reported that they had had the same under consideration ; had come to an unfavorable conclusion ; had directed their chairman to report the same to the Senate, and to recommend it do not pass.

Mr. Sumner, Chairman of Standing Committee on Ways and Means, submitted the following report :

Mr. President :

Your Committee on Ways and Means report to the Senate the accompanying letter from State Treasurer Rhoades, dated San Francisco, February 19th, 1867, with the request that the same be read and spread upon the Journal:

SAN FRANCISCO, February 19th, 1867.

To Senate Committee on Ways and Means, Carson, Nevada :

GENTLEMEN—From your dispatch of yesterday, and the report in the *Enterprise* of the debate in the Senate last Friday, it is evident to me that misapprehension exists with regard to the proposed loan, and also with regard to the feasibility of obtaining money under the provisions of the bill as passed. I answered your dispatch ; but there are other considerations which cannot very well be embodied in a telegraphic message, and I will state as briefly as possible what I consider to be the actual condition of affairs here, and the conclusions which are forced upon me, and which will be shared by the additional Commissioner, were he appointed. There are *very few* parties here who will entertain any proposition for our Bonds—as Mr. Ralston very bluntly informed me : if reasons are required, they are these, viz : " We have no confidence in your Supreme Court since their decision in the Specific Contract case, through which decision many business men here have sustained large losses." They also, notwithstanding the improved condition and prospects of our mines, feel a sensitive want of confidence in their permanency sufficient to inspire great caution where time investments are concerned, they considering that the mining interest is all they have to depend on for security. Again : although money is regarded as " very easy" here, when applications are made for it, it is found that at the rate of ten or twelve per cent. per annum it can only be obtained on the very choicest class of city real estate securities, and then within certain street limits, or upon first class collaterals with a large margin. No money is obtainable at the leading banks at a rate under one and a quarter per cent. on discount paper. Donahoe, Kelly & Co. telegraphed to Eugene Kelly & Co., New York, and received an unfavorable reply. This was with regard to the Twelve-per-Cent. Bonds, and the reply intimated that they could not be placed there except at a considerable discount. Mr. D. tells me, however, that even at fifteen he can do nothing. The Occidental Insurance Co. wish the money for those they now hold.

Mr. Andrew McCreery (well known to you in connection with the Gould and

Curry) and other gentlemen here having large amounts of idle capital, cannot be induced to take the bonds, preferring ten per cent. city mortgages. Messrs. Ralston, Parrott, McLane, and others have done all they could, but the usual reply is: We don't wish to look to anything outside of this city or State. *Financially* [Finally] the State and city taxes here amounting to about 3.10 per cent. (the National tax nearly as much more), is considered a sufficient cause for making our bonds as "undesirable" for investment.

The Pacific Insurance Co. *will not* exchange at that rate, and any attempt to exchange bonds bearing twelve per cent. for our old bonds bearing eighteen would be regarded as repudiation. Mr. Proctor was mistaken (probably he has already discovered his error) in stating that the old Territorial Bonds bear twelve per cent. interest. They are eighteen per cent., and the holders will not probably surrender even for fifteen per cent. bonds. They say they regard the constitutional assumption of that debt as *superior* security to any legislative enactment.

Mr. Monroe also (if he is correctly reported) was mistaken in stating it as my opinion that money could be raised at twelve. I was simply willing to try the possibility of doing so, and you have the result. The palpable fact is, that our bonds are not in demand, and we cannot bring many arguments to prove that they should be when we consider that our revenue heretofore has been barely sufficient to meet our interest.

In great haste, very respectfully,

E. RHOADES,
State Treasurer.

The Storey County delegation submitted the following report:

Mr. President:

Your Committee, consisting of the Storey County delegation, to whom was referred Substitute Senate Bill No. 130, "An Act for the organization of a Board of Education in Counties that polled three thousand votes or more at the general election in the State of Nevada, November, A.D. 1866, or that may hereafter at any general election cast that number of votes or more, and amendatory of and supplemental to an Act to provide for the maintenance and support of Public Schools, approved March 20th, 1865," beg leave to report that they have had the same under consideration; have made the following amendments thereto, and recommend its passage.

In section three, strike out subdivisions three and five; and in subdivision ten, after the words "for such service," and before the words "and certify," insert "and in the aggregate not to exceed the sum of two hundred and fifty dollars in any one year."

In subdivision twelve of same section strike out all after the words "just obligations," and insert the following: "Not to exceed in the aggregate the sum of five thousand dollars, which shall be paid as provided in this subdivision."

In same section, fourteenth subdivision, after the words "sum of," and before the word "dollars," strike out "one hundred" and insert "fifty."

In section four strike out the ninth subdivision, and in subdivision eleven after the words "be credited" and before the words "and also," strike out "to the Building Fund" and insert "to the General School Fund."

In section six strike out all in the first subdivision after the words "as when teaching."

In subdivision six, after the words "for the General," and before the words "Fund whereupon," strike out "and the School Building" and insert "School."

Strike out the seventh subdivision, in the tenth subdivision, after the words "sum of," and before the word "dollars" strike out the words "two hundred" and insert "one hundred," also, same subdivision, after the words "suitable office" and before the words "as herein," strike out the word "furnished."

In section seven, in second subdivision, after the words "for the" strike out "General and School Building Funds," and insert "General School Fund."

In the third subdivision, after the words "salary of" and before the words "dollars payable" strike out "two hundred" and insert "one hundred;" also after the words "a room" and before the words "furnished as," strike out the word "suitably."

In section sixteen, after the words "education against" and before the words "unless there," strike out the words "either of the School Funds named herein" and insert "General School Fund."

In section seventeen strike out all before the words "all moneys collected;" also strike out the second subdivision.

MESSAGE FROM THE GOVERNOR.

The following Message was received from the Governor:

EXECUTIVE DEPARTMENT, CARSON CITY.

To the Hon. Senate of Nevada:

I have this day approved Senate Bill No. 149, "An Act amendatory of and supplementary to an Act entitled an Act to amend an Act amendatory of and supplementary to an Act of the Legislative Assembly of the Territory of Nevada, entitled 'An Act to Incorporate the City of Austin,' approved Feb. 20th, 1864, approved March 8th, 1865, approved February 27th, 1866."

Also Senate Bill No. 94, "An Act to compensate J. F. Hatch for Services in the State Library."

H. G. BLASDEL,
Governor.

MOTIONS AND RESOLUTIONS.

On motion of Mr. Proctor, 200 copies of the State Prison Report *were* ordered printed.

On motion of Mr. Meder, Substitute Senate Bill No. 169, "An Act to provide for the Publication of the Decisions of the Supreme Court of the State of Nevada," was now taken up.

On motion of Mr. Proctor, the bill was recommitted to Committee of the Whole.

On motion of Mr. Edwards the Senate went into Committee of the Whole for the consideration of Substitute Senate Bill No. 169. President in the chair.

The Committee rose, and submitted the following report:

Mr. President:

The Senate in Committee of the Whole have had under consideration Substitute Senate Bill No. 169, "An Act to provide for the Publication of the Decisions of the Supreme Court of the State of Nevada," which they report back and recommend the bill be ordered reëngrossed.

Substitute Senate Bill No. 169, "An Act to provide for the Publication of the Decisions of the Supreme Court of the State of Nevada." Amendments of the Committee of the Whole were adopted, and the bill ordered reëngrossed.

On motion of Mr. Hutchins, the Senate went into Committee, of the Whole for

the consideration of special order, Senate Bill No. 108. President in the chair.
The Committee rose, and submitted the following report :

Mr. President :
The Senate, in Committee of the Whole, have had under consideration Senate Bill 108, " An Act to repeal an Act entitled ' An Act in regard to Currency,' approved March 3d, 1866," which they report back, and recommend the bill be considered engrossed, and placed on its final passage.

Senate Bill No. 108, " An Act to repeal an Act entitled ' An Act in regard to Currency.' "
The report of the Committee of the Whole was adopted.
Read third time by sections.
The yeas and nays were called on its final passage, and recorded as follows :

YEAS—Messrs. Doron, Geller, Hutchins, Linn, Mason, Monroe, Proctor, Sumner, and Terry—9.
NAYS—Messrs. Eastman, Edwards, Grey, Haines, Meder, Nelson, Stevenson, and Welty—8.

So the bill did not pass.
On motion of Mr. Doron, the Senate went into Committee of the Whole for the consideration of Assembly Bill No. 57.
President in the chair.
The Committee rose, and submitted the following report :

Mr. President :
The Senate, in Committee of the Whole, have had under consideration Assembly Bill No. 57, " An Act to amend an Act entitled ' An Act to provide Revenue for the Support of the Government of the State of Nevada,' approved March 9th, 1865," which they report back with amendments, and recommend the bill pass as amended.

Assembly Bill No. 57, " An Act to amend an Act entitled ' An Act to provide Revenue for the Support of the Government of the State of Nevada,' approved March 9th, 1865."
Amendments of the Committee of the Whole were adopted.
Bill read third time by sections.
The yeas and nays were called on its final passage, and recorded as follows :

YEAS—Messrs. Doron, Eastman, Geller, Haines, Hastings, Hutchins, Linn, Mason, Meder, Monroe, Nelson, Proctor, Stevenson, Terry, and Welty—15.
NAYS—0.

So the bill passed.
At 1:20 P.M., on motion of Mr. Mason, the Senate took a recess until 2:30 P.M.

IN SENATE.

The Senate met at 2:30 P.M.
President in the chair.
Roll called. Quorum present.
Mr. Sumner moved that the resolution prohibiting the introduction of new bills, which was passed on a previous day, be rescinded.

Mr. Haines raised the point of order that to rescind the resolution required a two-third vote.

The Chair ruled the point of order not well taken.

Mr. Welty appealed from the decision of the Chair.

The yeas and nays were called for by Messrs. Hutchins, Terry, and Doron on the question, Shall the *Chair* be sustained? and recorded as follows:

YEAS—Messrs. Edwards, Geller, Grey, Hastings, Hutchins, Linn, Mason, Meder, Monroe, Nelson, Stevenson, Sumner, and Terry—14 [13].

NAYS—Messrs. Haines and Welty—2.

So the Chair was sustained.

The motion of Mr. Sumner was carried.

Mr. Hutchins moved that the Committee on Ways and Means have leave to introduce a bill.

The yeas and nays were called for on the question by Messrs. Hutchins, Sumner, and Terry, and recorded as follows:

YEAS—Messrs. Doron, Geller, Hastings, Hutchins, Linn, Mason, Proctor, Sumner, and Terry—10.

NAYS—Messrs. Edwards, Grey, Haines, Meder, Nelson, Stevenson, and Welty—7.

So the leave was granted.

Mr. Monroe, (by leave) from Special Committee of Churchill County delegation, to which was referred Assembly Bill No. 133, " An Act for the Relief of Wallace Goodell, late County Treasurer of Churchill County," reported that they had had the same under consideration, had come to a favorable conclusion thereon, and recommend its passage.

Mr. Hutchins, from Committee on Ways and Means, introduced Senate Bill No. 214, " An Act to establish the Financial Transactions of the State upon a Coin Basis."

Read first time; rules suspended; read second time by title.

Mr. Hutchins moved that the rules be further suspended, and the bill be considered engrossed, on which the yeas and nays were called by Messrs. Sumner, Hutchins and Mason, and recorded as follows:

YEAS—Messrs. Doron, Geller, Grey, Hastings, Hutchins, Linn, Mason, Monroe, Proctor, Stevenson, Sumner, and Terry—12.

NAYS—Messrs. Edwards, Haines, Meder, Nelson, and Welty—5.

So the rules were further suspended.

Mr. Hutchins moved the bill be now placed on its third reading and final passage.

The yeas and nays were called for by Messrs. Hutchins, Terry, and Doron, and recorded as follows:

YEAS—Messrs. Doron, Eastman, Geller, Grey, Hastings, Hutchins, Linn, Mason, Monroe, Proctor, Stevenson, Sumner, and Terry—12.

NAYS—Messrs. Edwards, Haines, Meder, Nelson, and Welty—5.

So the motion prevailed.

Senate Bill No. 214, " An Act to establish the Financial Transactions of the State upon a Coin Basis."

Read third time by sections.

The yeas and nays were called on the final passage of the bill, and recorded as follows:

YEAS—Messrs. Doron, Geller, Hastings, Hutchins, Linn, Monroe, Proctor, Sumner, and Terry—9.
NAYS—Messrs. Edwards, Grey, Haines, Meder, Nelson, and Stevenson—6.

So the bill passed.

SPECIAL ORDERS.

Senate Bill No. 139, "An Act to increase the number of Justices of the Supreme Court, and to fix their Compensation."
Mr. Sumner was granted leave until March 7th to make a minority report in connection with the bill.

GENERAL FILE.

Senate Bill No. 133, "An Act to repeal an Act entitled 'An Act to provide for Establishing and Maintaining a Mining School, and create the office of State Mineralogist,' approved March 9th, 1866."
Read third time by sections.
The yeas and nays were called on the final passage of the bill, and recorded as follows:

YEAS—Messrs. Doron, Edwards, Grey, Hastings, Hutchins, Mason, Meder, Monroe, Nelson, Proctor, Stevenson, Sumner, Terry, and Welty—14.
NAYS—0.

So the bill passed.
Senate Bill No. 167, "An Act to amend an Act of the Legislature of the Territory of Nevada, entitled 'An Act concerning Conveyances,' approved November 5th, 1865 [1861]."
Read third time by sections.
The yeas and nays were called on the final passage of the bill, and recorded as follows:

YEAS—Messrs. Doron, Edwards, Geller, Hastings, Linn, Mason, Meder, Monroe, Nelson, Proctor, Stevenson, Sumner, and Welty—13.
NAYS—0.

So the bill passed.
Senate Bill No. 196, "An Act to regulate the Sale of Lands selected by the State of Nevada in lieu of the sixteenth and thirty-sixth Sections."
Read third time by sections.
The yeas and nays were called on the final passage of the bill, and recorded as follows:

YEAS—Messrs. Eastman, Edwards, Geller, Grey, Hastings, Linn, Mason, Meder, Monroe, Nelson, Stevenson, Sumner, Terry, and Welty—14.
NAYS—Mr. Doron—1.

So the bill passed.
27

Senate Bill No. 175, "An Act concerning the Location and Wood Lands and Mill Sites."

Read third time by sections. The yeas and nays were call passage of the bill, and recorded as follows:

YEAS—Messrs. Doron, Edwards, Geller, Grey, Linn, M Nelson, Proctor, Stevenson, Terry, and Welty—12.

NAYS—Messrs. Hastings, Meder, and Sumner—3.

So the bill passed.

Senate Bill No. 189, "An Act to provide for Payment to Harrington for Goods furnished the late Supreme Court of the T vada."

Read third time by sections. The yeas and nays were called o sage of the bill, and recorded as follows:

YEAS—Messrs. Doron, Edwards, Geller, Hastings, Linn, Monroe, Nelson, Proctor, Stevenson, Sumner, Terry, and Welty

NAYS—Mr. Grey.

So the bill passed.

Senate Bill No. 202, "An Act to provide Stationery for t Senate and Assembly of the State of Nevada."

Read third time by sections. The yeas and nays were called o sage of the bill, and recorded as follows:

YEAS—Messrs. Doron, Eastman, Geller, Grey, Hastings, Meder, Monroe, Nelson, Proctor, Stevenson, Sumner, Terry,

NAYS—0.

So the bill passed.

Senate Bill No. 194, "An Act to provide for certain Public State of Nevada."

Read third time by sections. The yeas and nays were called o sage of the bill, and recorded as follows:

YEAS—Messrs. Doron, Eastman, Geller, Grey, Linn, Mason, Nelson, Proctor, Stevenson, Terry, and Welty—14.

NAYS—Mr. Sumner—1.

So the bill passed.

Mr. Hastings, by leave, reported that the Committee on En carefully compared the following entitled bill with the original, same correctly engrossed, viz:

Substitute Senate Bill No. 169, "An Act to provide for the the Decisions of the Supreme Court of the State of Nevada," report the same back to the Senate.

A Message was received from the Assembly.

Senate Bill No. 169, "An Act to provide for the Publication o of the Supreme Court of the State of Nevada."

Read third time by sections. The yeas and nays were called o sage of the bill, and recorded as follows:

YEAS—Messrs. Doron, Eastman, Geller, Hastings, Linn, Mason, Meder, Monroe, Nelson, Proctor, Stevenson, Terry, and Welty—13.
NAYS—0.

So the bill passed.
Assembly Memorial to Congress relative to the claim of W. H. Brumfield and others, during the war, —— A.D. 1860.
Read first time; rules suspended; read second time by title; rules further suspended; read third time by sections.
The yeas and nays were called on the final passage of the resolution, and recorded as follows:

YEAS—Messrs. Doron, Eastman, Geller, Hastings, Linn, Mason, Monroe, Nelson, Proctor, Stevenson, Sumner, Terry, and Welty—13.
Nays—0.

So the resolution passed.
Mr. Sumner, by leave, from the Committee on Ways and Means, to which was referred Assembly Bill No. 109, "An Act to Legalize the Publication of Summons in Suits for the Collection of Delinquent Taxes in the several Counties of the State," reported that they had had the same under consideration, had come to a favorable conclusion thereon, had directed their chairman to report the same to the Senate without amendments, and to recommend its passage.
Assembly Bill No. 116, "An Act to amend an Act entitled 'An Act to Incorporate the Grand Lodge of Free and Accepted Masons, the Grand Lodge of the Independent Order of Odd Fellows, and their Subordinate Lodges in this State."
Amendments of Committee on Corporations were adopted; the bill read third time by sections.
The yeas and nays were called on its final passage, and recorded as follows:

YEAS—Messrs. Doron, Eastman, Edwards, Geller, Grey, Hastings, Linn, Mason, Meder, Monroe, Nelson, Proctor, Stevenson, Terry, and Welty—15.
NAYS—0.

So the bill passed.
Assembly Bill No. 109, "An Act to Legalize the Publication of Summons in Suits for the Collection of Delinquent Taxes in the several Counties of this State."
Read third time by sections.
The yeas and nays were called on the final passage of the bill, and recorded as follows:

YEAS—Messrs. Doron, Eastman, Edwards, Geller, Grey, Hastings, Linn, Mason, Meder, Monroe, Nelson, Proctor, Stevenson, Terry, and Welty—15.
NAYS—0.

So the bill passed.
Assembly Bill No. 127, "An Act to amend sections 72 and 74 of an Act entitled 'An Act relating to Offices, [officers] their qualifications, times of election, terms of office, official duties, resignations, removals, vacancies in office, and the mode of supplying the same, misconduct in office, and to enforce official duty,' approved March 9th, 1866."
Indefinitely postponed.
Substitute Assembly Bill No. 93, "An Act to amend an Act entitled 'An

Act to amend an Act in relation to Wild Game and Fish,' approved November 21st, 1861, approved February 20th, 1864, approved March 1st, 1866."

Indefinitely postponed.

Substitute Senate Bill No. 130, " An Act for the organization of a Board of Education in Counties that polled three thousand votes at the General Election in the State of Nevada, A.D. 1866, or that may hereafter at any General Election cast that number of votes or more, and amendatory of and supplemental to an Act to provide for the Maintenance and Support of Public Schools, approved March 20th, 1865." Made special order for Tuesday, March 5th, at 11 : 30 A.M.

On motion of Mr. Welty, the Senate went into Committee of the Whole for consideration of Assembly Bill No. 133.

President in the chair.

The Committee rose, and submitted the following report :

Mr. President:

The Senate, in Committee of the Whole, have had under consideration Assembly Bill No. 133, " An Act for the Relief of Wallace Goodell, late County Treasurer of Churchill County," which they report back and recommend the bill do pass.

Assembly Bill No. 133, " An Act to repeal an Act entitled ' An Act to provide for Establishing and Maintaining a Mining School, and to create the office of State Mineralogist,' approved March 9th, 1866."

Read third time by sections.

The yeas and nays were called on the final passage of the bill, and recorded as follows :

YEAS—Messrs. Doron, Eastman, Geller, Grey, Hastings, Linn, Mason, Meder, Monroe, Nelson, Proctor, Stevenson, Terry, and Welty—14.

NAYS—0.

So the bill passed.

Mr. Grey, by leave, from Standing Committee on Elections, to which was referred Assembly Bill No. 62, entitled " An Act to protect the Elections of Voluntary Political Associations, and to punish Frauds thereon," reported that they had had the same under consideration, had come to an unfavorable conclusion thereon, and had directed their chairman to report the same to the Senate, with a recommendation that it be indefinitely postponed.

Also, Assembly Bill No. 98, entitled " An Act to amend an Act entitled ' An Act relating to Elections, the manner of conducting and contesting the same, Election Returns, and canvassing the same, Fraud upon the Ballot Box, destroying, or attempting to destroy the Ballot Box, Illegal, or attempted Illegal Voting and Misconduct at Elections,' approved March 9th, 1866," reported that they had come to an unfavorable conclusion thereon, and recommend the bill be indefinitely postponed.

MESSAGE FROM THE ASSEMBLY.

The following Message was received from the Assembly :

ASSEMBLY CHAMBER, CARSON CITY, }
March 4th, 1867. }

To the Hon. the Senate of the State of Nevada :

I have the honor to transmit to your honorable body for your consideration, Assembly Concurrent Resolution No. 40, relating to certain claims; also, Assembly Memorial and Joint Resolutions relating to hostile Indians within this State and adjoining Counties, the same having passed the House this day.

I am also instructed to return to your honorable body the following Senate Bills:

No. 97, "An Act defining the Duties of the Attorney General of the State of Nevada," the same having passed the House, amended as follows:

By striking out section eight, and substituting in lieu thereof the following: "The Attorney General shall receive as salary the sum of twenty-five hundred dollars per annum, payable quarterly; and he shall receive in the performance of his duty as Attorney General no other compensation whatever; and, except the necessary contingent expenses of the office, no claim against the State created in the office of the Attorney General, or in the performance of any duty by the Attorney General, shall be paid or allowed unless the same be first approved by the Board of Examiners, and afterwards presented to the Legislature, and a law enacted for the payment of the same."

No. 122, "An Act to further prescribe rules and regulations for the execution of the Trusts arising under the Act of Congress, approved May 23d, 1844, entitled 'An Act for the Relief of Citizens of Towns upon Lands of the United States, under certain circumstances,'" the same having passed the House this day, amended as follows:

Section one, line three, after the word "of" and before the word "act," the word "this" is stricken out and the word "the" inserted in lieu thereof. Also, all of section seven is stricken out, and the following substituted in lieu thereof:

"Section 7. By consent of the parties to such contested case, the Court may appoint one or more referees, as the parties may agree, to take the testimony in said case, and report a judgment thereon; provided, that no fees shall be allowed to such referees that will exceed in the aggregate the sum of fifteen dollars for such case."

Also, Senate Bill No. 123, "An Act amendatory of an Act entitled 'An Act relating to the Support of the Poor,' approved November 29th, 1861," the same having passed the House this day without amendment.

Mr. Welty (by leave) reported that the Committee on Judiciary had had under consideration Assembly Bill No. 75, entitled "An Act to amend an Act entitled 'An Act to regulate the Settlement of the Estates of Deceased Persons,' approved November 29th, 1861," had directed their chairman to report favorably thereon, and to recommend its passage.

Mr. Proctor gave notice that on to-morrow he would move a reconsideration of the vote whereby Substitute Assembly Bill No. 93, "An Act to amend an Act entitled 'An Act to amend an Act in relation to Wild Game and Fish,' approved November 21st, 1861, approved Feb. 20th, 1864, approved March 1st, 1866," was indefinitely postponed.

Assembly Concurrent Resolution No. 40, relating to certain claims.

Read first time; rules suspended; read second time by title, and referred to Committee on Federal Relations.

Assembly Memorial and Resolution No. 37, relating to hostile Indians within this State and adjoining Territories.

Read first time; rules suspended; read second time by title, and referred to Committee on Indian and Military Affairs.

Senate Bill No. 97, "An Act defining the Duties of the Attorney General of the State of Nevada."

Referred to Committee on Judiciary.

Substitute Senate Bill No. 122, "An Act to further prescribe rules and regulations for the Execution of the Trusts arising under the Act of Congress, approved May 23d, 1844, entitled 'An Act for the Relief of Citizens of Towns upon Lands of the United States under certain circumstances.'"

Referred to Washoe and Ormsby County delegations.

At 4:15 P.M., on motion of Mr. Hastings, the Senate adjourned.

JAMES S. SLINGERLAND,
President.

Attest—B. C. BROWN,
Secretary.

IN SENATE—FIFTY-EIGHTH DAY.

CARSON CITY, March 5th, 1867.

The Senate met pursuant to adjournment, President in the chair.

Roll called.

Present—Messrs. Doron, Eastman, Edwards, Geller, Grey, Haines, Hutchins, Linn, Mason, Meder, Monroe, Nelson, Proctor, Stevenson, Sumner, Terry, and Welty—18.

Absent—0.

Prayer by the Chaplain.

The Journal of the Fifty-seventh day was read and approved.

On motion, leave of absence was granted the Chaplain for yesterday.

A Message was received from the Assembly.

The following communication was received from the Secretary of State:

OFFICE OF SECRETARY OF STATE, }
Carson City, March 1st, 1867. }

To the Legislature of Nevada:

GENTLEMEN—I have the honor to report, that under the provisions of an Act concerning the office of Secretary of State, the following contracts for fuel, furniture, repairs of furniture and Capitol Building, have been made by me, for the use and benefit of your honorable body. I have also the honor to transmit herewith vouchers for the same as follows:

No. 1.	M. D. Junkins, repairs, etc.	$ 40 00
" 2.	John A. Lovejoy, wood	80 00
" 3.	W. A. Hawthorne, wood	60 00
" 4.	Cowing & Co., painting	65 00
" 5.	John Painter, porterage	16 00
" 6.	Amireaux & Bowie, mdse.	20 00
" 7.	John A. Fisk, whitening	7 50
No. 8.	E. B. Rail, ⅓ of bill rendered	27 77
	Total	$316 27

The above contracts were made and bills rendered upon a legal tender basis.

Respectfully,

C. N. NOTEWARE,
Secretary of State.

Referred to Committee on Supplies and Expenditures.

Mr. Proctor introduced a petition from residents of Pahranagat, which was received, read, and ordered on file.

Mr. Monroe rose to a question of privilege, in regard to the introduction by Mr. Haines of Senate Bill No. 96, entitled "An Act to make Compensation to the Hon. Cradlebaugh, late United States District Judge, the same as that of the late United States District Judges of the Territory of Nevada."

Mr. Grey rose to a question of privilege, relative to the report of his remarks in the "Territorial Enterprise" of March 3d, that he had applied to his colleague, Mr. Sumner, ungentlemanly epithets, which he asserted to be untrue.

SPECIAL ORDER.

Substitute Senate Bill No. 130, "An Act for the organization of a Board of Education in Counties that polled three thousand votes or more at the General Election in the State of Nevada, A.D. 1866, or that may hereafter, at any general election cast that number of votes or more, and amendatory of and supplemental to 'An Act to provide for the Maintenance and Supervision of Public Schools,' approved March 20th, 1865."

Made special order for 3 o'clock, this afternoon.

REPORTS OF COMMITTEES.

Mr. Linn, Chairman of Committee on Enrollment, reported that Senate Concurrent Resolution No. 203, "Relative to certain Mail Service between Genoa, Carson County, Utah Territory, Monoville and Aurora, in the County of Mono, State of California ;"

Senate Bill No. 172, "An Act supplementary to 'An Act to provide Revenue for the Support of the Government for the State of Nevada,' approved March 9th, 1865, and other Acts amendatory and supplementary thereof ;"

Senate Bill No. 140, "An Act to amend 'An Act to provide for Organizing and Disciplining the Militia of this State,' approved March 4th, 1865 ;" have been carefully compared with the originals, as passed by the two Houses, found correctly enrolled, and that the bills had this day been delivered to the Governor for his approval, and the resolution deposited with the Secretary of State.

Mr. Sumner, from the Committee on Ways and Means, to which was referred Senate Bill No. 97, entitled "An Act amendatory of an Act entitled 'An Act in relation to the Payment of Salaries and other claims against the State,'" reported that they had had the same under consideration ; had come to a favorable conclusion thereon ; had directed their chairman to report the same to the Senate without amendments, and recommend its passage.

Mr. Welty reported that the Committee on Judiciary had had under consideration Senate Bill No. 97, entitled "An Act defining the Duties of the Attorney General of the State of Nevada," and the Assembly amendments thereto ; had directed their chairman to report favorably on said amendments, and to recommend that the amendments be concurred in.

Mr. Hutchins, from Committee on Military and Indian Affairs, reported that they had had under consideration Assembly Memorial and Joint Resolution No. 37, and in view of the fact that the military operations of the United States Government, though incurring an expense of millions of dollars, for many years past, without accomplishing the desired peace ; herewith report the same back to the Senate, and recommend that it do pass.

Mr. Stevenson, Chairman of the Committee on Mines and Mining, to which was referred Senate Bill No. 51, "An Act in regard to assessment work upon Mining Claims," reported that they had had the same under consideration ; had directed their chairman to report the same back to the Senate with Substitute Bill, and to recommend the substitute do pass.

Mr. Grey, from majority of Storey County delegation, to which was referred Assembly Bill No. 78, entitled "An Act to amend an Act to Incorporate the City of Virginia, provide for the Government thereof, and repeal all other laws in relation thereto, approved March 4th, 1865," reported that they had had the same under consideration ; had come to a favorable conclusion thereon ; had directed their chairman to report the same to the Senate without amendments, and to recommend its passage.

Mr. Sumner, from minority of Storey County delegation, to which was referred Assembly Bill No. 78, entitled "An Act to amend an Act entitled 'An Act to Incorporate the City of Virginia,' " etc., reported that he has had the same under consideration ; had come to an unfavorable conclusion thereon ; reports the same to the Senate, and recommends its indefinite postponment.

Mr. Grey, from Select Committee of Storey County delegation, submitted the following :

Mr. President :

Your Committee, consisting of the Storey County delegation, to whom was referred Assembly Bill No. 77, "An Act providing for the payment of certain indebtedness due Geo. F. Jones & Co. from the City of Virginia," beg leave to report that they have had the same under consideration, have made the following amendment thereto, and recommend its passage, to wit:

Insert at the end of section 1, "and to pay all other holders of any and all warrants, orders, or other evidences of indebtedness for cash loaned the City of Virginia, the full amount due thereon, both principal and interest, at the time of such payment, and pay the same in order of the issuance thereof."

MOTIONS AND RESOLUTIONS.

Mr. Linn introduced the following resolution :

Resolved, That the Sergeant-at-Arms of the Senate be, and is hereby directed to draw his warrant on the Senate Contingent Fund, in favor of Joseph Cowing, for the sum of one hundred dollars, if paid in gold, or one hundred and thirty-three $\frac{33}{100}$, if paid in currency, the same being for rent of office for the Senate engrossing and enrolling clerks; also in favor of T. G. Smith for the sum of fifty dollars, currency, for rent of office for copying clerk.

Adopted.
Mr. Sumner introduced the following resolution :

Resolved, That the Clerk employed by the Storey delegation in the investigation into the financial affairs of Virginia City, under and by virtue of a resolution heretofore passed, be allowed pay for one week.

Adopted.
Mr. Grey introduced the following resolution :

Resolved, That the Sergeant-at-Arms be, and he is hereby instructed to draw his warrant in favor of D. C. Williams for the sum of forty dollars, for services rendered as Clerk to the Storey County delegation and Committee on Education.

Adopted.

MESSAGE FROM THE ASSEMBLY.

The following Message was received from the Assembly:

ASSEMBLY CHAMBER, CARSON CITY, }
March 4th, 1867. }

To the Hon. the Senate:

I am instructed to return to your honorable body Senate Bill No. 168, "An Act relative to Transcribing and Indexing certain Records in Humboldt County," the same having passed the House this day, without amendment.

Also, Senate Bill No. 143, "An Act for the Relief of John S. Childs," the same having passed this day without amendment.

Respectfully,

A. WHITFORD,
Clerk.

ITTRODUCTION OF BILLS.

Substitute Senate Bill (reported from the Committee on Mines and Mining) No. 51, "An Act to regulate the Recording of Mining Claims in the State of Nevada."

Read first time; rules suspended; read second time by title, and referred to Committee of the Whole.

Mr. Proctor, by leave without previous notice, introduced Senate Bill No. 217, "An Act amendatory of and supplementary to an Act entitled 'An Act to create the County of Lincoln and provide for its organization.'"

Read first time; rules suspended; read second time by title, and ordered engrossed.

MESSAGE FROM THE ASSEMBLY.

A Message was received from the Assembly.

SPECIAL ORDER.

Senate Bill No. 174, "An Act to amend an Act entitled 'An Act to provide Revenue for the Support of the Government of the State of Nevada,' approved March 9th, 1865."

Read third time by sections. The yeas and nays were called on the final passage of the bill, and recorded as follows:

YEAS—Messrs. Doron, Hastings, Hutchins, Mason, Meder, Sumner, and Terry—7.

NAYS—Messrs. Eastman, Edwards, Green, Grey, Haines, Monroe, Nelson, Proctor, Stevenson, *Sumner*, and Welty—10 [11].

So the bill did not pass.

Mr. Welty gave notice that on to-morrow he would move a reconsideration of the above vote.

Assembly Bill No. 62, "An Act to protect the Elections of Voluntary Political Associations, and to punish Frauds thereon."

Indefinitely postponed.

Assembly Bill No. 98, "An Act to amend an Act entitled 'An Act relating to Elections; the manner of conducting and contesting the same; election returns and canvassing the same; fraud upon the ballot-box; destroying or attempting to destroy the ballot-box; illegal or attempted illegal voting, and misconduct at elections,' approved March 9th, 1866.

Indefinitely postponed.

Assembly Bill No. 197, "An Act amendatory of an Act entitled 'An Act in relation to the Payment of Salaries and other claims against the State,' approved February 27th, 1866."

Rules suspended; bill considered engrossed.

Read third time by sections; the yeas and nays were called on the final passage thereof, and recorded as follows:

YEAS—Messrs. Eastman, Edwards, Geller, Grey, Hastings, Hutchins, Linn, Mason, Monroe, Proctor, Stevenson. Sumner, and Terry—13.

NAYS—Messrs. Doron, Meder, Nelson, Welty—4.

So the bill passed.

At 1 o'clock P.M., on motion of Mr. Grey, the Senate took a recess until 2 o'clock P.M.

IN SENATE.

The Senate met at 2 P.M. President in the chair.

Roll called.

Absent—Messrs. Doron, Edwards, Geller, Grey, Hastings, Mason, Nelson, and Stevenson.

On motion a call of the Senate was ordered. The absentees appearing, were, on motion, excused.

On motion of Mr. Welty, further proceedings under call of the Senate were dispensed with.

SPECIAL ORDER.

Senate Bill No. 138, "An Act authorizing the Secretary of State to employ a Clerk in the State Library and Adjutant General's Office."

Read third time by sections.

On motion of Mr. Meder the bill was amended by inserting "one hundred and fifty" in place of "two hundred," and ordered engrossed.

MESSAGE FROM THE ASSEMBLY.

A Message was received from the Assembly.

Mr. Terry, by leave, submitted the following report:

Mr. President:

Your Committee on Supplies and Expenditures beg leave to report that they have had the following bills under consideration and find them correct, and recommend that the Sergeant-at-Arms be authorized to draw his warrants in favor of the following-named persons for the amounts respectively named, to be paid out of the Contingent Fund of the Senate.

T. G. Smith (as per bill)...................................	$ 35 00
D. W. Welty, Judiciary Committee..........................	20 00
Mason, Huff & Co..	73 75
John H. Painter...	81 00
E. D. Sweeney	120 00
M. D. Judkins [Junkins].....................................	39 94
Amiraux & Bowie..	12 75
California State Telegraph Company..........................	84 65
M. M. Gaige (expenses to Virginia to obtain witnesses)..........	261 75
M. M. Gaige (stationery and papers to attachés)...............	886 49
E. B. Rail..	124 48
	$1,689 81

Bills for the same accompanying this report, and also the statement of the account of the Sergeant-at-Arms, are submitted.

Mr. Terry, by leave without previous notice, introduced Senate Bill No. 218, "An Act to transfer certain Moneys from the Legislative Fund to the Contingent Fund of the Senate."

Read first time; rules suspended; read second time by title; rules further suspended; considered engrossed.

Bill read third time by sections.

The yeas and nays were called on the final passage, and recorded [as] follows:

YEAS—Messrs. Doron, Eastman, Edwards, Geller, Grey, Hutchins, Linn, Mason, Meder, Monroe, Nelson, Proctor, Stevenson, Sumner, Terry, and Welty —16.

NAYS—0.

So the bill passed.

Assembly Bill No. 75, "An Act to amend section 52 of an Act entitled ' An Act to regulate the Settlement of the Estates of Deceased Persons,' approved November 29th, 1861."

Read third time by sections.

The yeas and nays were called on the final passage of the bill, and recorded as follows:

YEAS—Messrs. Doron, Eastman, Edwards, Geller, Hutchins, Linn, Mason, Monroe, Nelson, Proctor, Stevenson, Sumner, Terry, and Welty—14.

NAYS—0.

So the bill passed.

Mr. Meder submitted, by leave, the following resolution:

Resolved, That the Sergeant-at-Arms be, and is hereby authorized and directed to draw his warrants on the Senate Contingent Fund, to be paid in currency, in favor of the following persons:

Adopted—

T. G. Smith	$ 85 00
D. W. Welty	20 00
Mason, Huff & Co	73 75
John H. Painter	81 00
E. D. Sweeney	120 00
M. D. Judkins [Junkins]	39 94
Amiraux & Bowie	12 75
California State Telegraph Co.	34 65
M. M. Gaige	261 75
M. M. Gaige	886 49
E. B. Rail	124 48
	$1,689 81

Mr. Doron in the chair.

Senate Bill No. 97, "An Act defining the Duties of the Attorney General of the State of Nevada."

Assembly amendments concurred in.

Assembly Memorial No. 37, "Relating to hostile Indians within this State and adjoining Territories."

Read third time.

Mr. Mason moved that the memorial be indefinitely postponed; on which the yeas and nays were called for by Messrs. Grey, Hastings, and Proctor, and recorded as follows:

YEAS—Messrs. Doron, Eastman, Geller, Grey, Haines, Mason, Meder, Proctor, and Stevenson—9.

NAYS—Messrs. Hastings, Hutchins, Linn, Monroe, Nelson, Sumner, Terry, and Welty—8.

So the Memorial was indefinitely postponed.

Mr. Meder, by leave, reported that the Standing Committee on Engrossment had carefully compared the following entitled bill with the original, and found the same correctly engrossed, viz:

Senate Bill No. 217, entitled "An Act amendatory of and supplemental to an Act entitled 'An Act to create the County of Lincoln and provide for its Organization.'"

Mr. Hastings, by leave, reported that the Standing Committee on Engrossment had carefully compared the following entitled bill with the original, and found the same correctly engrossed, viz:

Senate Bill No. 138, "An Act authorizing the Secretary of State to employ a Clerk in the State Library and Adjutant General's Office;" and herewith report the same back to the Senate.

SPECIAL ORDER.

Substitute Senate Bill No. 130, "An Act for the Organization of a Board of Education in certain Counties," etc., was postponed for ten minutes.

On motion of Mr. Welty, Senate Bill No. 217, "An Act amendatory of and supplemental to an Act entitled 'An Act to create the County of Lincoln, and provide for its organization,'" was now taken up; rules suspended; read third time by sections. The yeas and nays were called on the final passage of the bill, and recorded as follows:

YEAS—Messrs. Doron, Eastman, Edwards, Geller, Haines, Hastings, Linn, Mason, Meder, Monroe, Nelson, Proctor, Stevenson, Sumner, and Welty—15.
NAYS—Messrs. Grey, Hutchins, and Terry—3.

So the bill passed.

Mr. Stevenson, by leave, submitted the following resolution:

Resolved, By the Senate, the Assembly concurring, that the Secretary of State be, and is hereby directed to distribute the Reports of the Surveyor General and State Mineralogist as follows: fifteen copies of each to each of the State officers, and to each Senator and Assemblyman; six copies of each to each of the attachés of the Senate and Assembly, and the balance shall be equally divided between the Secretary of State, the Surveyor General, and the State Mineralogist, for general distribution.

Adopted.

On motion, the rules were suspended, and Messages from the Assembly were taken up.

MESSAGE FROM THE ASSEMBLY.

The following Message was received from the Assembly:

ASSEMBLY CHAMBER, CARSON CITY, }
March 5th, 1867. }

To the Hon. the Senate:

I have the honor to transmit to your honorable body for your consideration, Substitute Assembly Bill No. 164, the same having passed the House this day: Yeas, 25; Nays, 10.

Respectfully,

A. WHITFORD,
Clerk.

Substitute Assembly Bill No. 164, "An Act for the organization of a Board of Education in Counties that polled three thousand votes or more, at the General Election in the State of Nevada, A.D. 1866," etc.

Read first time; rules suspended; read second time by title.

Mr. Sumner moved the bill be now considered; carried.

On motion of Mr. Grey, the Senate went into Committee of the Whole for the consideration of Substitute Assembly Bill No. 164, and Senate Bill No. 130. President in the chair.

The Committee rose, and submitted the following report:

Mr. President:

The Senate, in Committee of the Whole, have had under consideration Substitute Assembly Bill No. 164, "An Act for the Organization of the Board of Education in Counties that polled three thousand votes or more at the General Election, A.D. 1866," &c., which they report back, and recommend the bill do pass.

Also, Senate Bill No. 130, "An Act for the Organization of the Board of Education in Counties that polled three thousand votes," &c., which they report back, and recommend the bill be laid on the table.

Senate Bill No. 130, "An Act for the Organization of a Board of Education in Counties that polled three thousand votes or more at the General Election A.D. 1866," &c.

Laid upon the table.

Substitute Assembly Bill No. 164, "An Act for the Organization of a Board of Education in Counties that polled three thousand votes or more at the General Election A.D. 1866, or that may hereafter," &c.

Read third time by sections.

The yeas and nays were called on the final passage of the bill, and recorded as follows:

YEAS—Messrs. Eastman, Edwards, Geller, Haines, Hastings, Linn, Mason, Meder, Monroe, Proctor, Sumner, and Terry—12.

NAYS—Messrs. Doron, Nelson, Stevenson, and Welty—4.

So the bill passed.

Mr. Nelson rose to a question of privilege in relation to remarks made in debate concerning Speaker Ferguson.

Mr. Haines gave notice that on to-morrow he would move a reconsideration of the vote whereby Assembly Memorial No. 37, relating to hostile Indians in this State and adjoining Territories, was indefinitely postponed.

At 5:30, on motion of Mr. Doron, the Senate took a recess until 7:30 P.M.

The Senate met at 7:30 P.M., Mr. Doron in the chair.

MESSAGES FROM THE ASSEMBLY.

The following Messages were received from the Assembly:

ASSEMBLY CHAMBER, CARSON CITY,
March 5th, 1867.

To the Honorable the Senate:

I have the honor to transmit to your honorable body the following Assembly Bills, for your consideration, the same having passed the House:

No. 145, "An Act for the Relief of William M. Gillespie, late City Clerk of Virginia."

No. 150, "An Act to amend an Act defining the Duties of State Treasurer, approved Feb. 2d, 1866."

No. 158, "An Act for the Relief of Storey County."

No. 160, "An Act making Appropriation to pay Rent of Adjutant General's Office for the year 1866."

No. 163, "An Act concerning the Fees of Justices of the Peace."

Also, Assembly Memorial and Concurrent Resolution No. 51, in reference to the Indian Reservation on the Truckee River.

I also return Senate Bill No. 170, which passed the House this day without amendment.

Substitute Senate Bill No. 96, which passed the House this day without amendment.

Senate Bill No. 11, which was this day indefinitely postponed.

Respectfully,

A. WHITFORD,
Clerk.

ASSEMBLY CHAMBER, CARSON CITY, }
March 5th, 1867.

To the Hon. the Senate :

I have the honor to transmit to your honorable body the following Assembly Bills, which have passed the House :

No. 107, " An Act to enforce the Payment of two per cent. of the gross proceeds of all Toll Roads and Bridges, as provided by law, to the General School Fund of this State."

No. 149, " An Act to amend an Act entitled ' An Act to provide for the Construction and Maintenance of Toll Roads and Bridges in the State of Nevada," approved March 8th, 1865."

No. 136, "An Act to create a Board of Commissioners to examine and report upon the amount of just claims existing for property destroyed and for losses sustained by Indian Depredations, in Lander County, in this State, in the years 1864, 1865, and 1866."

Respectfully,

A. WHITFORD,
Clerk.

Assembly Bill No. 145, "An Act for the Relief of W. M. Gillespie, late City Clerk of Virginia."

Read first time ; rules suspended ; read second time by title, and referred to Storey County delegation.

Assembly Bill No. 150, " An Act to amend an Act defining the Duties of State Treasurer, approved February 2d, 1866."

Read first time ; rules suspended ; read second time by title.

On motion of Mr. Proctor, the bill was now considered.

Rules suspended. Bill read third time by sections.

The yeas and nays were called on the final passage of the bill, and recorded as follows :

YEAS—Messrs. Doron, Eastman, Geller, Grey, Hastings, Hutchins, Linn, Mason, Meder, Monroe, Proctor, Stevenson, Sumner, Terry, and Welty—15.
NAYS—0.

So the bill passed.

Assembly Bill No. 158, " An Act for the Relief of Storey County."

Read first time ; rules suspended ; read second time by title, and referred to Storey County delegation.

Assembly Bill No. 160, " An Act making Appropriation to pay the Rent of Adjutant General's Office for the year 1866."

Read first time ; rules suspended; read second time by title, and referred to Committee on Claims.

Substitute Assembly Bill No. 163, " An Act concerning the Fees of Justice of the Peace."

Read first time ; rules suspended; read second time by title, and referred to Committee on Judiciary.

Assembly Memorial and Concurrent Resolution No. 51, in reference to the Indian Reservation on the Truckee River.

Read first time ; rules suspended ; read second time by title, and referred to Committee on Federal Relations.

Assembly Bill No. 107, " An Act to enforce the Payment of two per cent. of the gross proceeds of all Toll Roads and Bridges, as provided by law, to the General School Fund of this State."

Read first time; rules suspended; read second time by title, and referred to Committee on Counties and County Boundaries.

Assembly Bill No. 149, "An Act to amend an Act entitled 'An Act to provide for the construction and maintenance of Toll Roads and Bridges in the State of Nevada,' approved March 8th, 1865."

Read first time; rules suspended; read second time by title, and referred to Committee on Corporations.

Assembly Bill No. 136, "An Act to create a Board of Commissioners to examine and report upon the amount of just claims existing for property destroyed, and for losses sustained by Indian Depredations in Lander County, in this State, in the years 1864, 1865 and 1866."

Read first time; rules suspended; read second time by title, and referred to Lander County delegation.

MESSAGE FROM THE ASSEMBLY.

The following Message was received from the Assembly:

ASSEMBLY CHAMBER, CARSON CITY,
March 5th, 1867.

To the Hon. the Senate:

I am instructed to transmit to your honorable body for your consideration, the following Resolutions, which passed the House this day, viz:

Concurrent Resolution No. 52, relative to giving Mr. W. K. Parkinson, State Controller, leave of absence.

No. 46, authorizing the Governor to submit the question of calling a Constitutional Convention to the people of this State, at the next general election.

Also, Assembly Memorial No. 50, "Memorializing Congress to repeal certain Neutrality Laws," which passed the House this day.

Respectfully,

A. WHITFORD,
Clerk.

Assembly Concurrent Resolution No. 52, "Relating to giving Mr. Parkinson, State Controller, six months' absence."

Read and adopted.

Assembly Memorial and Resolution No. 50, "Relating to the Enforcement of the Monroe Doctrine, and Repeal of certain Neutrality Laws."

Read first time; rules suspended; read second time by title, and referred to Committee on Federal Relations.

Assembly Concurrent Resolution No. 46, "Authorizing the Governor to submit the question of calling a Constitutional Convention to the People of this State, at the next General Election."

Read and referred to special Committee on Constitution, to report to-morrow morning.

GENERAL FILE.

Senate Bill No. 138, "An Act authorizing the Secretary of State to employ a Clerk in the State Library and Adjutant's General's Office."

Read third time by sections.

The yeas and nays were called on the final passage of the bill, and recorded as follows:

YEAS—Messrs. Doron, Eastman, Edwards, Geller, Grey, Hastings, Hutchins, Linn, Mason, Meder, Monroe, Nelson, Proctor, Stevenson, Sumner, Terry, and Welty—17.

NAYS—0.

So the bill passed.

Assembly Bill No. 77, "An Act providing for the Payment of certain Indebtedness due Geo. F. Jones & Co. from the City of Virginia."

Made special order for 12 o'clock to-morrow.

Assembly Bill No. 78, "An Act to amend an Act entitled 'An Act to Incorporate the City of Virginia, provide for the Government thereof, and repeal all other laws in relation thereto,' approved March 4th, 1865."

Indefinitely postponed.

On motion of Mr. Proctor, the Senate went into Committee of the Whole for the consideration of Substitute Senate Bill No. 51. President in the chair.

The Committee rose, and submitted the following report:

Mr. President:

The Senate in Committee of the Whole have had under consideration Substitute Senate Bill No. 51, "An Act to *register* [regulate] the Recording and Possession of Mining Claims in the State of Nevada," which they report back, and recommend the bill be ordered engrossed.

A Message was received from the Assembly.

Substitute Senate Bill No. 51, "An Act to regulate the Recording and Possession of Mining Claims in the State of Nevada."

Rules suspended; bill considered engrossed.

Read third time by sections.

The yeas and nays were called on its final passage, and recorded as follows:

YEAS—Messrs. Doron, Eastman, Geller, Grey, Haines, Hastings, Hutchins, Linn, Mason, Meder, Nelson, Proctor, Stevenson, Sumner, Terry, and Welty—16.

NAYS—0.

So the bill passed.

Mr. Sumner, by leave, introduced the following resolution:

Resolved, That J. Neely Johnson, Civil Practice Act Commissioner, be and he is hereby authorized and requested to file with the Secretary of State a copy of the Civil Code of Procedure submitted by him to the Senate, with such noted amendments to the printed text as may be required for conformity with the original copy.

Mr. Linn, Chairman of Committee on Enrollment, reported that Senate Bill No. 218, entitled "An Act to transfer certain Moneys from the Legislative Fund to the Contingent Fund of the Senate," had been carefully compared with the engrossed bill, as passed by the two Houses, found correctly enrolled, and that the same had this day been delivered to the Governor for his approval.

Mr. Welty, by leave, reported that the Committee on Judiciary had had under consideration the Assembly Bill No. 59, entitled "An Act to amend an Act to regulate Proceedings in Civil Cases, approved March 9, 1865," had amended the same, and had directed their chairman to report favorably thereon, and

29

recommend the passage of the bill as amended. Amend by striking out all of section 2, on 2d page, after line 7th, and insert the following:

After service of the summons, the defendant may in person, or by attorney, demand a copy of the complaint. The demand shall be in writing, and shall designate the place where the copy may be served, and the time for answering after such demand is made shall not run against the defendant until the copy is furnished.

MESSAGE FROM THE ASSEMBLY.

CARSON CITY, March 5th, 1867.

The following Message was received from the Assembly:

To the Honorable the Senate:

I am instructed to return to your honorable body the following Senate Bills, which passed the House this day, amended, viz:

No. 160, " An Act to provide for the Payment of the Contingent Expenses of the Surveyor General's Office, from December, 1864, to December, 1866, inclusive, the same having been amended as follows: In sec. 1, line 4, after the figures " 810," the words "in gold coin," were stricken out.

Senate Bill No. 151, "An Act to amend an Act entitled ' An Act to regulate Proceedings in Criminal Cases in the Courts of Justice in the (Territory) State of Nevada, and making further provisions relating thereto,' " the same having been amended as follows: At the end of sec. 3, the following is added: And such testimony so reduced according to the provisions of this section, shall be filed by the examining magistrate with the Clerk of the District Court of the county, and in case such prisoner be subsequently examined upon a writ of *habeas corpus*, such testimony shall be considered as given before such Judge or Court."

I also transmit to you for your consideration, Assembly Resolution No. 54, relating to Errors in Enrolling, the same having passed the House this day, unanimously.

Also, Assembly Conjoint Resolution No. 53, relating to Ireland, the same having passed the House this day unanimously.

Respectfully,

A. WHITFORD,
Clerk.

Senate Bill No. 160, "An Act to provide for the Payment of the Contingent Expenses of the Surveyor General's Office from December, 1864, to December, 1866, inclusive."

On motion of Mr. Haines, a Committee of Conference was appointed on the above bill, consisting of Messrs. Haines, Monroe, and Welty.

Senate Bill No. 151, "An Act to amend an Act entitled 'An Act to regulate Proceedings in Criminal Cases in the Courts of Justice in the (Territory) State of Nevada,' and making further provisions relating thereto."

Assembly amendments concurred in.

Assembly Resolution No. 54, " Relating to Errors in Enrolling."

Indefinitely postponed.

Assembly Conjoint Resolution No. 53, in relation to Ireland.

Read and referred to Committee on Federal Relations.

Mr. Edwards, by leave without previous notice, introduced Senate Bill No. 235, "An Act to amend an Act entitled 'An Act to provide for the Government of the State Prison of Nevada,' approved March 4th, 1865."

Read first time; rules suspended; read second time by title, and referred to Committee on State Prison, with instructions to report to-morrow morning.

At 9 o'clock P.M., on motion of Mr. Hastings, the Senate adjourned.

JAMES S. SLINGERLAND,
President.

Attest—B. C. BROWN,
Secretary.

IN SENATE—FIFTY-NINTH DAY.

CARSON CITY, March 6th, 1867.

The Senate met pursuant to adjournment, President in the chair.

Roll called.

Present—Messrs. Doron, Eastman, Edwards, Geller, Grey, Haines, Hastings, Hutchins, Linn, Mason, Meder, Monroe, Nelson, Proctor, Stevenson, Sumner, Terry, and Welty—18.

Absent—0.

Prayer by the Chaplain.

The Journal of the Fifty-eighth day was read and approved.

REPORTS OF COMMITTEES.

Mr. Geller reported that the Committee on State Prison had had under consideration Senate Bill No. 235, entitled "An Act to provide for the Government of the State Prison of the State of Nevada, approved March 4th, 1865," had come to a favorable conclusion thereon, had directed their chairman to report the same to the Senate, and recommend its passage.

Mr. Proctor, from the Standing Committee on Counties and County Boundaries, to which was referred Assembly Bill No. 107, entitled "An Act to enforce the Payment of two per cent. of the gross proceeds of all Toll Roads and Bridges, as provided by law, to the General School Fund of this State," reported that they had had the same under consideration; had come to a favorable conclusion thereon; had directed their chairman to report the same to the Senate without amendments, and to recommend its passage.

The Storey County delegation, to which was referred Assembly Bill No. 145, entitled "An Act for the Relief of W. M. Gillespie, late City Clerk of Virginia City," reported that they had had the same under consideration; had come to an unfavorable conclusion thereon, and report the same to the Senate without amendments, and recommend its indefinite postponement.

Mr. Welty reported that the Judiciary Committee had had under consideration Assembly Bill No. 173, entitled "An Act concerning the Fees of the Justices of the Peace," had amended the same, and a majority of the Committee had directed their chairman to report favorably thereon, and to recommend its passage as amended.

Amend by striking out the last four lines and inserting the following:

For each motion, exception, rule, order, default, dismissal, discontinuance, or nonsuit, and for filing each paper required to be filed, twenty-five cents.

The Lander County delegation, to which was referred Assembly Bill No. 136, entitled "An Act to create a Board of Commissioners to examine and report upon the amount of just claims existing for property destroyed, and for losses sustained by Indian Depredations in Lander County, in this State, in the years 1864, 1865, 1866," reported that they had examined said bill, and recommend its passage.

MOTIONS AND RESOLUTIONS.

Mr. Grey submitted the following resolution :

Resolved, That the Chairmen of the Committees of the Senate be allowed to certify to the number of days that the Clerks of their Committees have been employed, and instruct the Sergeant-at-Arms to draw his warrants for the same.

Adopted.

Mr. Edwards submitted the following resolution :

Resolved, That the Clerk of the following Committees : " Claims, Education, Public Lands, Federal Relations, Public Morals, Agriculture and Manufactures," be allowed per diem from the commencement of the session.

Adopted.

Mr. Hutchins submitted the following resolutions :

Resolved, That the State Controller be, and he is hereby authorized and required to draw his warrant in favor of M. M. Gaige, Sergeant-at-Arms of the Senate, for the amount in the Senate Contingent Fund.

Resolved, That the said Sergeant-at-Arms is hereby directed to deposit the amount of said warrant in the banking house of Wells, Fargo & Co., in this city, to be drawn out upon scrip issued by resolutions of this Senate on said Contingent Fund ; and any moneys remaining after all of said scrip shall have been paid, shall, upon order of the Controller, be returned to the treasury, to the credit of the General Fund.

Adopted.

MESSAGE FROM THE ASSEMBLY.

A Message was received from the Assembly.

Mr. Welty moved, that the vote whereby Senate Bill No. 104, " An Act to amend an Act entitled 'An Act to provide Revenue for the Support of the Government of the State of Nevada,' approved March 9th, 1865," was lost on yesterday, be now reconsidered.

Carried.

Senate Bill No. 104, " An Act to amend an Act entitled "An Act to provide Revenue for the Support of the Government of the State of Nevada."

The yeas and nays were called on the final passage of the bill, and recorded as follows :

YEAS—Messrs. Doron, Eastman, Linn, Mason, Meder, Sumner, Terry, and Welty—8.

NAYS—Messrs. Edwards, Geller, Grey, Haines, Hastings, Hutchins, Monroe, Nelson, Proctor, Stevenson—10.

So the bill did not pass.

Assembly Bill No. 77, "An Act to provide for the Payment of certain Indebtedness due George F. Jones & Co., by the City of Virginia."

Amen!ments of the Special Committee adopted.

Bill read third time by sections.

The yeas and nays were called on its final passage, and recorded as follows:

YEAS—Messrs. Doron, Edwards, Grey, Haines, Hastings, Mason, Monroe, Nelson, Proctor, Stevenson, Sumner, and Terry—12.

NAYS—Messrs. Eastman, Geller, Linn, and Welty—4.

So the bill passed.

Mr. Sumner gave notice, that on to-morrow he would move a reconsideration of the above vote.

On motion of Mr. Proctor, the title of the bill was amended, by striking out the words "George F. Jones & Co." and inserting the words "certain parties."

On motion of Mr. Edwards, Senate Bill No. 235, "An Act to amend an Act entitled 'An Act to provide for the Government of the State Prison of the State of Nevada,' approved March 4th, 1865," was read third time by sections.

The yeas and nays were called on the final passage of the bill, and recorded as follows:

YEAS—Messrs. Doron, Edwards, Geller, Haines, Hastings, Hutchins, Linn, Mason, Meder, Monroe, Nelson, Proctor, Stevenson, Sumner, Terry, and Welty—16.

NAYS—0.

So the bill passed.

Mr. Hastings, by leave without previous notice, introduced Senate Bill No. 236, "An Act to amend an Act entitled 'An Act to supply the Town of Dayton with Water.'"

Read first time; rules suspended; read second time by title; rules further suspended; considered engrossed.

Read third time by sections.

The yeas and nays were called on the final passage of the bill, and recorded as follows:

YEAS—Messrs. Doron, Edwards, Geller, Hastings, Hutchins, Linn, Mason, Meder, Monroe, Proctor, Stevenson, Sumner, Terry, and Welty—14.

NAYS—0.

So the bill passed.

Mr. Mason, by leave without previous notice, introduced Senate Bill No. 237, in relation to enrolling Laws, Resolutions, and other documents.

Read first time; rules suspended; read second time by title; rules further suspended; considered engrossed.

Read third time by sections.

The yeas and nays were called on the final passage of the bill, and recorded as follows:

YEAS—Messrs. Doron, Edwards, Geller, Haines, Hastings, Linn, Mason, Meder, Monroe, Proctor, Stevenson, Sumner, Terry, and Welty—14.
NAYS—0.

So the bill passed.

Mr. Proctor called the attention of the Senate to Rule 54, and asked that the notice of reconsideration by Mr. Sumner be stricken from the minutes.

The Chair rules Mr. Proctor's point of order well taken.

Mr. Sumner moved that Rule 54 be suspended; and that he have leave to give notice of his reconsideration of the vote whereby Assembly Bill No. 77 was this day passed.

Rules suspended and leave granted.

Mr. Sumner again gave notice that on to-morrow he would move a reconsideration of the vote whereby Assembly Bill No. 77 was this day passed.

At 1:20 P.M., on motion of Mr. Meder, the Senate took a recess until 2 [:30] o'clock P.M.

IN SENATE.

The Senate met at 2:30 P.M.

Mr. Doron in the chair.

Roll called.

Quorum present.

Mr. Linn, Chairman of Committee on Enrollment, reported that Senate Bill No. 123, entitled "An Act relating to the Support of the Poor, approved Nov. 29th, 1861 ;" Senate Bill No. 142, "An Act amendatory of an Act to provide for the Maintenance and Supervision of Public Schools. approved March 20th, 1865;" Senate Bill No. 143, "An Act for the Relief of John S. Childs," had been carefully compared with the engrossed bills, as passed by the two Houses, found correctly enrolled, and that the same had this day been delivered to the Governor for his approval.

Also, Senate Bill No. 168, entitled "An Act relative to Transcribing and Indexing certain Records in Humboldt County." had been carefully compared with the engrossed bill as passed by the two Houses, found correctly enrolled, and that the same had this day been delivered to the Governor for his approval.

On motion of Mr. Sumner, the delegations of Lyon and Esmeralda Counties were added to the Storey County delegation for the consideration of Senate Bill No. 158.

MESSAGE FROM THE ASSEMBLY.

The following Message was received from the Assembly:

ASSEMBLY CHAMBER, CARSON CITY, }
March 6th, 1867.

To the Honorable the Senate:

I am instructed to return to your honorable body Senate Bill No. 217, " An Act amendatory of and supplementary to an Act entitled ' An Act to create the County of Lincoln and provide for its organization,"' the same having passed the House this day without amendment.

Respectfully,

A. WHITFORD,
Clerk.

Mr. Monroe, (by leave) from the Committee on Claims, to which was referred Assembly Bill No. 160, entitled "An Act making Appropriation to pay Rent of Adjutant General's Office for the year 1866," reported that they had had the same under consideration ; had come to a favorable conclusion thereon ; had directed their chairman to report the same to the Senate without amendments, and o recommend its passage.

Mr. Hutchins (by leave) submitted the following resolution :

Resolved, That the Sergeant-at-Arms of the Senate be, and hereby is required to draw his warrant on the Legislative Fund in favor of J. S. Crosman. for two days' services as President of the Senate, and mileage, to the amount of $17.60.

Adopted.

Messrs. Haines, Monroe, and Welty (by leave) submitted the following report :

Mr. President :

Your Committee of Conference on Senate Bill No. 160, entitled " An Act to provide for the payment of the Contingent Expenses of the Surveyor General's Office, from December, 1864, to December, 1866, inclusive," beg leave to report, that the Assembly Committee have agreed to recommend that the Assembly do recede from its amendments, and they recommend that the Senate adhere to its refusal to concur in said amendments.

GENERAL FILE.

Assembly Bill No. 107, " An Act to enforce the Payment of two per cent. of the gross proceeds of all Toll Roads and Bridges, as provided by law, to the General School Fund of the State."

Read third time by sections.

The yeas and nays were called on the final passage of the bill, and recorded as follows :

YEAS—Messrs. Doron, Eastman, Edwards, Geller, Hutchins, Linn, Meder, Proctor, Stevenson, Sumner, and Terry—11.

NAYS—0.

So the bill passed.

A Message was received from the Assembly.

Substitute Assembly Bill No. 163, " An Act concerning the Fees of Justices of the Peace."

The amendments of the Committee on Judiciary were adopted.

Bill read third time by sections.

The yeas and nays were called on the final passage thereof, and recorded as follows :

YEAS—Messrs. Edwards, Geller, Haines, Hastings, Linn, Meder, Nelson, Stevenson, Sumner, and Welty—10.

NAYS—Messrs. Doron, Eastman, Hutchins, Monroe, Proctor, and Terry—6.

So the bill passed.

MESSAGE FROM THE ASSEMBLY.

The following Message was received from the Assembly :

ASSEMBLY CHAMBER, CARSON CITY, }
March 6th, 1867. }

To the Honorable the Senate:

I am instructed to request your honorable body to return to the Assembly Senate Bill No. 11, entitled "An Act to amend 'An Act to provide Revenue for the Support of the Government of the State of Nevada, and the acts amendatory thereof,'" for further action.

Respectfully,

A. WHITFORD,
Clerk.

Senate Bill No. 11, entitled "An Act to amend 'An Act to provide Revenue for the Support of the Government of the State of Nevada,' and the Acts amendatory thereof."

The request of the Assembly was complied with.

Assembly Bill No. 136, "An Act to create a Board of Commissioners to examine and report upon the amount of just claims existing for property destroyed and the losses sustained by Indian Depredations in Lander County in this State, in the year [s] 1864, 1865 and 1866."

Read third time by sections.

The yeas and nays were called on the final passage of the bill, and recorded as follows:

YEAS—Messrs. Doron, Eastman, Geller, Haines, Hastings, Hutchins, Linn, Mason, Meder, Proctor, Stevenson, Sumner, Terry, and Welty—14.
NAYS—Mr. Nelson—1.

So the bill passed.

Assembly Bill No. 145, "An Act for the Relief of W. M. Gillespie, late City Clerk of Virginia."

Made special order for 8 o'clock P.M.

Assembly Bill No. 160, "An Act making Appropriation to pay Rent of Adjutant General's Office for the year 1866."

Read third time by sections. The yeas and nays were called on the final passage of the bill, and recorded as follows:

YEAS—Messrs. Doron, Eastman, Edwards, Geller, Hutchins, Linn, Mason, Meder, Monroe, Proctor, Stevenson, Sumner, Terry, and Welty—14.
NAYS—Mr. Nelson—1.

So the bill passed.

MESSAGE FROM THE ASSEMBLY.

A Message was received from the Assembly:

ASSEMBLY CHAMBER, CARSON CITY, }
March 6th, 1867. }

To the Honorable the Senate:

I am instructed to transmit to your honorable body, for your consideration, Assembly Substitute to Senate Substitute Bill No. 50, "An Act entitled 'An Act to provide for the Selection and Sale of Lands granted by the United States to the State of Nevada,'" the same having passed the House on yesterday.

Respectfully,

A. WHITFORD,
Clerk.

Assembly Substitute to Senate Substitute Bill No. 50, "An Act entitled 'An Act to provide for the Selection and Sale of Lands granted by the United States to the State of Nevada.'"

Read first time; rules suspended; read second time by title, and referred to Committee of the Whole.

On motion of Mr. Hastings, the Senate went into Committee of the Whole for consideration of Assembly Substitute to Substitute Senate Bill No. 50.

President in the chair.

The Committee rose, and submitted the following report:

[*Mr. President:*]

The Senate, in Committee of the Whole, have had under consideration Assembly Substitute for Substitute Senate Bill No. 50, "An Act entitled 'An Act to provide for the Selection and Sale of Lands granted by the United States to the State of Nevada,'" which they report back, and recommend the bill do pass.

A Message was received from the Assembly.

Assembly Substitute to Substitute Senate Bill No. 50, "An Act entitled 'An Act to provide for the Selection and Sale of Lands granted by the United States to the State of Nevada."

Mr. Welty, by leave, submitted the following resolution:

Resolved, That the Sergeant-at-Arms of the Senate be, and he is hereby directed to deliver to J. Neely Johnson, one copy of the printed Civil Code of Procedure as reported by him to the Senate.

Adopted.

Mr. Sumner, by leave, introduced the following resolution:

Resolved, That the Sergeant-at-Arms be directed to make the warrant drawn for one week's pay to the Clerk of the Storey County delegation, payable out of the Senate Contingent Fund.

Adopted.

On motion, Mr. Hutchins was granted leave of absence for the evening session.

At 4:30 P.M., on motion of Mr. Proctor, the Senate took a recess until 7 o'clock P.M.

IN SENATE.

The Senate met at 7 o'clock P.M.

President in the chair.

Roll called.

Quorum present.

Mr. Sumner, from Committee on Ways and Means, (by leave) submitted the following report:

Mr. President:

The Committee on Ways and Means, to which was referred Assembly Bill No. 87, "An Act to appropriate Moneys to defray the Civil Expenses of the State Government up to the close of the fourth fiscal year," beg leave to report the same back with accompanying substitute, the passage of which they recommend.

30

On motion of Mr. Hastings, the Senate went into Committee of the Whole for the consideration of Substitute Assembly Bill No. 87, and Substitute Assembly Bill No. 50. President in the chair.

The Committee rose, and submitted the following report:

Mr. President;

The Senate, in Committee of the Whole, have had under consideration Substitute for Assembly Bill No. 87, "An Act making Appropriations for the Support of the Civil Government of the State of Nevada for the third and fourth fiscal years," which they report back, and recommend the bill do pass.

Also, Assembly Substitute for Substitute Senate Bill No. 50, "An Act entitled 'An Act to provide for the Selection and Sale of Public Lands granted by the United States to the State of Nevada,'" which they report back, and recommend the bill do not pass.

Substitute Assembly Bill No. 87, "An Act making Appropriations for the Support of the Civil Government of the State of Nevada for the third and fourth fiscal years."

Rules suspended; considered engrossed.

Read third time by sections.

The yeas and nays were called on the final passage of the bill, and recorded as follows:

YEAS—Messrs. Doron, Eastman, Edwards, Geller, Grey, Haines, Hastings, Linn, Mason, Meder, Monroe, Nelson, Proctor, Sumner, Terry, and Welty—16.
NAYS—0.

So the bill passed.

Substitute Assembly Bill for Substitute Senate Bill No. 50, "An Act entitled 'An Act to provide for the Selection and Sale of Lands granted by the United States to the State of Nevada.'"

Read third time by sections.

The yeas and nays were called on the final passage of the bill, and recorded as follows:

YEAS—Messrs. Doron, Eastman, Haines, Hastings, Linn, Meder, Nelson, Proctor, Stevenson, Terry, and Welty—10.
NAYS—Messrs. Edwards, Geller, Grey, Hutchins, Mason, Monroe, Proctor, and Sumner—8.

So the bill passed.

On motion of Mr. Sumner, Assembly Bill No. 145, "An Act for the Relief of W. M. Gillespie, late City Clerk of Virginia," was now taken up.

Mr. Sumner moved to amend by striking out all after the words "the last eight months of the year 1866," and insert "provided, that from the amount of said warrant as calculated as aforesaid, there shall be deducted the sum of ($125) one hundred and twenty-five dollars in currency."

Carried.

Read third time by sections.

The yeas and nays were called on the final passage of the bill, and recorded as follows:

YEAS—Messrs. Doron, Eastman, Geller, Grey, Hastings, Hutchins, Linn,

Mason, Meder, Monroe, Nelson, Proctor, Stevenson, Sumner, Terry, and Welty —16.

NAYS—0.

So the bill passed as amended.

MESSAGES FROM THE ASSEMBLY.

The following Messages were received from the Assembly:

ASSEMBLY CHAMBER, CARSON CITY,
March 6th, 1867.

To the Hon. the Senate of the State of Nevada:

I have the honor to inform your hon. body that the House have this day appointed as a Conference Committee on Senate Bill No. 160, as to the differences between the two Houses, consisting of Messrs. St. Clair, Prince and Huse.

Respectfully,

A. WHITFORD,
Clerk.

ASSEMBLY CHAMBER, CARSON CITY,
March 6th, 1867.

To the Hon. the Senate:

I am instructed to inform your hon. body that the House have concurred in Senate amendments to Assembly Bill No. 27, relating to District Attorneys, as per report of Conference Committee. Also, that the House have receded from their amendments to Senate Bill No. 160, relating to Surveyor General, as per report of Conference Committee.

Respectfully,

A. WHITFORD,
Clerk.

ASSEMBLY CHAMBER, CARSON CITY,
March 6th, 1867.

To the Honorable the Senate:

I am instructed to transmit to your honorable body for your consideration, the following Assembly Bills, which passed the House this day, viz:

No. 168, "An Act to amend an Act entitled an Act to amend section one of an Act passed by the Legislative Assembly of the Territory of Nevada, entitled 'An Act to provide for the appointment of Notaries, and defining their duties,' approved February 9th, 1864, approved March 20th, 1865, approved February 9th, 1866."

No. 142, "An Act to create the office of State Inspector of Boilers and Engineers."

Substitute Assembly Bill No. 117, "An Act amendatory *to* an Act entitled 'An Act to regulate the Settlement of Estates of Deceased Persons.'"

I also return to your hon. body Senate Bill No. 197, which passed the House this da .

Also, Senate Concurrent Resolution No. 232, relating to distribution of reports, which was concurred in this day.

Respectfully,

A. WHITFORD,
Clerk.

Assembly Bill No. 168, "An Act to amend an Act entitled an Act to amend section one of an Act to amend an Act passed by the Legislative Assembly of the Territory of Nevada, entitled 'An Act to provide for the appointment of Notaries, and defining their duties,' approved February 9th, 1864, approved March 20th, 1865, approved February 9th, 1866."

Read first time; rules suspended; read second time by title; rules further suspended; read third time by sections.

The yeas and nays were called on the final passage of the bill, and recorded as follows:

YEAS—Messrs. Doron, Eastman, Geller, Haines, Hastings, Hutchins, Meder, Monroe, Nelson, Proctor, Stevenson, Sumner, Terry, and Welty—14.
NAYS—0.

So the bill passed.

Assembly Bill No. 142, "An Act to create the office of State Inspector of Boilers and Engineers."

Read first time; rules suspended; read second time by title, and referred to Committee on State Affairs.

MESSAGES FROM THE ASSEMBLY.

ASSEMBLY CHAMBER, CARSON CITY,
March 6th, 1867.

To the Hon. the Senate:

I am instructed to transmit to your honorable body for your consideration, Assembly Bill No. 185, "An Act to authorize the Board of County Commissioners of Lander County to audit certain claims."

Assembly Bill No. 186, "An Act to create a Secret Service Fund."

I also return to your honorable body Senate Bill No. 175, which was indefinitely postponed.

I also return Senate Bill No. 214, "An Act to establish the Financial Transactions of the State upon a Coin Basis," the same having been indefinitely postponed.

Respectfully,
A. WHITFORD,
Clerk.

ASSEMBLY CHAMBER, CARSON CITY,
March 6th, 1867.

To the Hon. the Senate:

I am instructed to transmit to your honorable body the following Assembly Bills, for your consideration, which passed the House this day:

No. 181, "An Act for the Relief of certain parties herein named."

No. 146, "An Act to amend section 58 of 'An Act to provide Revenue for the Support of the Government of the State of Nevada.'"

I also return to your honorable body Senate Bill No. 235, which passed the House this day.

Respectfully,
A. WHITFORD,
Clerk.

ASSEMBLY CHAMBER, CARSON CITY,
March 6th, 1867.

To the Hon. the Senate:

I am instructed to return to your honorable body, Senate Bill No. 236,

"An Act to amend an Act entitled 'An Act to supply the town of Dayton, in Lyon County, with Water, and to protect the town against fire, and to define the Boundaries thereof,' approved July [Feb.] 20th, 1864."

Also, Senate Bill No. 167, "An Act to amend an Act of the Legislature of the Territory of Nevada, entitled 'An Act concerning Conveyances,' approved Nov. 5th, 1861."

Respectfully,

A. WHITFORD,
Clerk.

Substitute Senate Bill No. 117, "An Act amendatory of an Act entitled 'An Act to regulate the Settlement of Estates of Deceased Persons.'"

Read first time; rules suspended; read second time by title, and referred to the Committee on Judiciary.

Assembly Bill No. 185, "An Act to authorize the Board of County Commissioners of Lander County to audit certain claims."

Read first time; rules suspended; read second time by title; rules further suspended; read third time by sections.

The yeas and nays were called on the final passage of the bill, and recorded as follows:

YEAS—Messrs. Doron, Eastman, Geller, Haines, Hastings, Hutchins, Meder, Nelson, Proctor, Stevenson, Sumner, Terry, and Welty—13.

NAYS—Messrs. Edwards and Monroe—2.

So the bill passed.

Assembly Bill No. 186, "An Act to create a Secret Service Fund."

Read first time, and laid on the table.

Assembly Bill No. 181, "An Act for the Relief of certain parties named."

Read first time; rules suspended; read second time by title, and referred to Committee on Claims.

Assembly Bill No. 146, "An Act to amend section 58 of an Act to provide Revenue for the Support of the Government of the State of Nevada."

Read first time; rules suspended; read second time by title; rules further suspended; read third time by sections.

The yeas and nays were called on the final passage of the bill, and recorded as follows:

YEAS—Messrs. Doron, Eastman, Edwards, Geller, Haines, Hastings, Hutchins, Linn, Meder, Monroe, Nelson, Proctor, Stevenson, Sumner, Terry, and Welty—16.

NAYS—0.

So the bill passed.

Mr. Meder, from Select Committee, submitted the following report:

The Select Committee of Ormsby and Washoe County delegations, to which was referred Senate Substitute Bill No. 122, "An Act to further prescribe rules and regulations for the execution of certain Trusts under the Act of Congress," report the bill back, and recommend the adoption of the Assembly amendments.

Substitute Senate Bill No. 122, "An Act to further prescribe rules and regulations for the execution of the Trusts arising under the Act of Congress, approved May 25th, [23d] 1844, entitled 'An Act for the Relief of citizens of Towns upon Lands of the United States, under certain circumstances.'"

Assembly amendment to bill concurred in, and placed on the General File.

Mr. Edwards presented the following protest:

SENATE CHAMBER, March 6th, 1867.

I hereby enter my protest against the passage of Assembly Substitute for Substitute Senate Bill No. 50, "An Act to provide for the selection and sale of Lands granted by the United States to the State of Nevada."

T. D. EDWARDS.

At 8:30 P.M., on motion of Mr. Terry, the Senate adjourned.

JAMES S. SLINGERLAND,
President.

Attest—B. C. BROWN,
Secretary.

———

IN SENATE—SIXTIETH DAY.

CARSON CITY, March 7th, 1867.

The Senate met pursuant to adjournment, President in the chair.

Roll called.

Present—Messrs. Doron, Eastman, Edwards, Geller, Grey, Haines, Hastings, Hutchins, Linn, Mason, Meder, Monroe, Nelson, Proctor, Stevenson, Sumner, Terry, and Welty—18.

Absent—0.

Prayer by the Chaplain.

The Journal of the Fifty-ninth day was read and approved.

Mr. Linn, by leave, submitted the following resolutions:

Resolved, That the Sergeant-at-Arms be, and is hereby required to draw his warrant on the Contingent Fund of the Senate, in favor of the President *pro tem.,* C. A. Sumner, in the sum of $60; and also in favor of the temporary President, Lewis Doron, in the sum of $60, as extra compensation for services in presiding over the Senate, and discharging other duties connected with the presidency.

Adopted.

Resolved, That the Sergeant-at-Arms be, and he is hereby authorized and directed to draw his warrant on the Senate Contingent Fund in favor of Richard R. Parkinson, for extra services as Journal Clerk of the Senate, for the sum of one hundred and fifty dollars.

Adopted.

Mr. Meder, by leave, submitted the following resolution:

Resolved, That the Sergeant-at-Arms be authorized and directed to draw his warrant in favor of Andrew Whitford for the sum of $100, payable out of the

Senate Contingent Fund, for services as Clerk of Railroad Committee, Session of 1864–5, as per resolves of March 20th, 1867, [1866] and that the resolution of February 15th, 1867, be rescinded.

Adopted.

Mr. Linn, by leave, submitted the following resolution:

Resolved, That C. C. Wallace be allowed $120 additional pay; and that the Sergeant-at-Arms be, and is hereby authorized to draw his warrant upon the Senate Contingent Fund for the same.

The yeas and nays were called on the adoption of the resolution, and recorded as follows:

YEAS—Messrs. Grey, Linn, Mason, Proctor, Sumner, Terry, and Welty—7.

NAYS—Messrs. Doron, Eastman, Edwards, Geller, Haines, Hutchins, Meder, Monroe, Nelson, and Stevenson—10.

So the resolution was not adopted.

Mr. Mason, by leave, submitted the following resolution:

Resolved, That the thanks of the Senate be hereby tendered to the attachés of the Senate for the able, efficient, and courteous discharge of their several duties.

Adopted unanimously.

REPORTS OF COMMITTEES.

Mr. Terry presented several bills from Secretary of State, which were referred to Committee on Supplies and Expenditures.

Mr. Mason reported that the Committee on Federal Relations had had under consideration Assembly Memorial and Concurrent Resolution in reference to the Indian Reservation on the Truckee River; had come to a favorable conclusion thereon; had directed the chairman to report the same back, and to recommend its passage.

Also, Memorial and Resolution to Congress relating to the enforcement of the "Monroe Doctrine" and repeal of certain Neutrality Laws, had come to a favorable conclusion thereon; had directed their chairman to report the same back, and to recommend its passage.

Also, Assembly Concurrent Resolutions No. 40, relating to certain Claims, had come to a favorable conclusion thereon; had directed their chairman to report the same back, and to recommend its passage.

Mr. Sumner, from the Storey and Lyon County delegation, to whom was referred Assembly Bill No. 158, entitled "An Act for the Relief of Storey County," reported that they had had the same under consideration; had directed the undersigned to report a substitute to the Senate, and to recommend its passage: Charles A. Sumner, Storey County; D. L. Hastings, Lyon County; and B. J. Mason, Esmeralda County.

Senate Substitute Bill No. 227, for Assembly Bill No. 158, "An Act to create a State Board of Commissioners for the purpose of ascertaining and reporting the number of Indigent Insane from other counties in this State, which have been taken care of by the County of Storey during the years 1860, 1861, 1862, 1863, 1864, 1865, and 1866, and the expenses incurred and paid by Storey County for such hospital care," was now taken up.

Read first time; rules suspended; read second time by title; rules further suspended; considered engrossed; read third time by sections.

The yeas and nays were called on the final passage of the bill, and recorded as follows:

YEAS—Messrs. Doron, Eastman, Edwards, Geller, Grey, Haines, Hastings, Hutchins, Mason, Monroe, Proctor, Sumner, and Welty—13.

NAYS—Mr. Stevenson—1.

So the bill passed.

Mr. Mason, by leave without previous notice, introduced Senate Bill No. 247, "An Act to prevent the Exercise of Improper Influence pending the Passage of Acts of the Legislature."

Read first time; rules suspended; read second time by title; rules further suspended; bill considered engrossed; read third time by sections.

The yeas and nays were called on its final passage, and recorded as follows:

YEAS—Messrs. Doron, Grey, Haines, Linn, Mason, Meder, Nelson, Stevenson, Terry, and Welty—10.

NAYS—Messrs. Edwards, Hastings, Hutchins, Monroe, Proctor, and Sumner—6.

So the bill passed.

Mr. Proctor moved to amend the title as follows: "An Act to enhance the Veto power."

The yeas and nays were called on the motion, and recorded as follows:

YEAS—Messrs. Edwards, Hastings, Hutchins, Monroe, Proctor, and Sumner—6.

NAYS—Messrs. Doron, Grey, Haines, Mason, Meder, Nelson, Stevenson, Terry, and Welty—9.

So the motion was lost.

REPORTS OF COMMITTEES.

Mr. Monroe, from Committee on Claims, to which was referred Assembly Bill No. 181, entitled "An Act for the Relief of certain parties herein named," reported that they had had the same under consideration, had come to a favorable conclusion thereon, had directed their chairman to report the same to the Senate without amendments, and to recommend its passage.

Mr. Terry, from Committee on Supplies and Expenditures, submitted the following report:

Mr. President:

Your Committee, to whom was referred the following bills, beg leave to report that they have carefully examined them, and recommend that warrants be drawn for the respective amounts.

Mr. Grey, from Select Committee on "Constitutional Amendments," to which was referred Senate Concurrent Resolution No. 55, proposing certain amendments to the Constitution of the State, reported as follows:

Amend section proposing to amend section one of Article fifteen, by adding the following words:

" Provided no such Act shall be passed prior to the year 1788."
And your Committee, with said amendment, recommend the adoption of the resolution.

MOTIONS AND RESOLUTIONS.

Senate Concurrent Resolution No. 249, relating to Adjournment of the Legislature.
Read and passed.
Assembly Memorial and Concurrent Resolution No. 51, in reference to the Indian Reservation on the Truckee River.
Rules suspended; read third time by sections. The yeas and nays were called on the final passage of the resolution, and recorded as follows:

YEAS—Messrs. Eastman, Edwards, Geller, Grey, Haines, Hastings, Mason, Meder, Monroe, Nelson, Proctor, Stevenson, Sumner, Terry, and Welty—15.

So the resolution passed.
The Committee on Claims introduced the following resolution:

Resolved, That the Sergeant-at-Arms be, and is hereby required to draw his warrants for the following amounts, on the Contingent Fund, in favor of the within named persons:

M. D. Judkins [Junkins].....................................$40 00
John A. Lovejoy... 80 00
John A. Fisk... 7 50
Amiraux & Bowie... 20 00
John Painter.. 16 00
Cowing & Co... 65 00
W. A. Hawthorne... 60 00
E. B. Rail 27 87

Total..$316 37

Adopted.

REPORTS OF COMMITTEES.

Mr. Grey, (by leave) from Special Committee on Constitutional Amendments, to which was referred Concurrent Resolution No. 46, authorizing the Governor to submit the question of calling a Constitutional Convention to the people of this State at the next General Election, reported that they had had the same under consideration, and recommend it be indefinitely postponed.
Mr. Eastman, (by leave) from the Select Committee of the Washoe and Storey County delegations, to which was referred the bill entitled " An Act authorizing the Construction of a Railroad from Virginia City to the Truckee River," reported that they had had the same under consideration, and there being considerable diversity of opinion concerning the merits of the bill, had directed that the same be reported back to the Senate, and recommend it be referred to Committee of the Whole.
Mr. Eastman, (by leave) from Standing Committee on Corporations, to which was referred Assembly Bill No. 149, " An Act to amend an Act entitled ' An Act to provide for the Construction of Toll Roads and Bridges in the State,' approved March 8th, 1865," reported that they had had the same under con-

sideration; had come to an unfavorable conclusion thereon; had directed their chairman to report the same to the Senate without amendments, and to recommend that it do not pass.

ASSEMBLY CHAMBER, CARSON CITY,
March 6th, 1867.

To the Hon. the Senate:

I am instructed to transmit to your honorable body for your consideration, Assembly Bill No. 159, "An Act to pay the Lander Guard." I also return to you Senate Bill No. 189, "An Act to provide for Payment to Kinkead & Harrington, for Goods furnished the late Supreme Court of the Territory of Nevada;" also Substitute Senate Bill No. 169, "An Act to provide for the Publication of the Decisions of the Supreme Court of the State of Nevada;" both of which have passed the House.

Respectfully,
A. WHITFORD,
Clerk.

To the Hon. the Senate:

I am instructed to transmit to your honorable body for your consideration, Assembly Bill No. 189, the same having passed the House yesterday.

I also return to your honorable body, Senate Bill No. 194, the same having been indefinitely postponed.

I also return Senate Bill No. 169, "An Act to provide for the Publication of Decisions of Supreme Court," the same having passed the House yesterday.

I am also requested to inform your honorable body, that the House has concurred in Senate amendments to Assembly Bill No. 163, "An Act concerning the Fees of Justices of the Peace."

A. WHITFORD,
Clerk.

To the Hon. the Senate:

I am instructed to transmit to your honorable body, for your consideration, Assembly Bill No. 131, "An Act to amend an Act entitled 'An Act creating County Recorders, and defining their Duties,'" which passed the House this day.

Also, Assembly Bill No. 161, [171] "An Act to amend an Act entitled 'An Act to create a Board of County Commissioners in the several counties of this State, and to define their Powers and Duties,' approved March 8th, 1865," the same having passed the House this day.

Also, Substitute Assembly Bill No. 147, "An Act in relation to the Fees of Jurors, and to repeal an Act entitled 'An Act concerning the Compensation of Jurors in the District Courts of this State,' approved March 22d, 1865," which passed the House this day.

I also return to your honorable body, Senate Bill No. 237, which passed the House this day.

Also, Senate Bill No. 133, which passed the House this day.

Also, Senate Bill No. 138, which passed the House this day.

I also return to your honorable body, Senate Bill No. 156, which was this day considered in the House, and was indefinitely postponed.

I also inform your honorable body that the House concurred in Senate amendments to Assembly Bill No. 145, "An Act for the Relief of W. M. Gillespie."

I also transmit for your consideration, Assembly Resolution No. 56, relating to Joint Committee to wait on the Governor.

A. WHITFORD,
Clerk.

To the Hon. the Senate:

I am instructed to transmit to your honorable body for your consideration, Substitute to Assembly Bill No. 190, " An Act to provide for the Election of a Board of Regents, and to define their Duties," which passed the House this day.

Respectfully,

A. WHITFORD,
Clerk.

Assembly Bill No. 169, " An Act to appoint a Commissioner to take Testimony in certain Cases."

Read first time ; rules suspended ; read second time by title, and referred to Committee on Judiciary.

Assembly Bill No. 159, " An Act to pay the Lander Guard."

Read first time ; rules suspended ; read second time by title, and referred to the Lander County delegation.

Assembly Bill No. 131, " An Act to amend an Act entitled ' An Act creating County Recorders, and defining their Duties.' "

Read first time ; rules suspended ; read second time by title, and referred to Committee on Counties and County Boundaries.

Assembly Bill No. 171, " An Act to amend an Act entitled 'An Act to create a Board of County Commissioners in the several counties of this State, and to define their Powers and Duties,' approved March 8th, 1865."

Read first time ; rules suspended ; read second time by title ; rules further suspended ; read third time by sections.

The yeas and nays were called on the final passage of the bill, and recorded as follows :

YEAS—Messrs. Geller, Mason, Monroe, Proctor, Terry, and Welty—6.

NAYS—Messrs. Doron, Eastman, Haines, Hastings, Hutchins, Linn, Meder, Nelson, Stevenson, and Sumner—10.

So the bill did not pass.

Substitute Assembly Bill No. 147, " An Act in relation to the Fees of Jurors, and to repeal an Act entitled ' An Act concerning the Compensation of Jurors in the District Courts of this State.' "

Read first time ; rules suspended ; read second time by title, and indefinitely postponed.

Mr. Linn, Chairman from Committee on Enrollment, reported that Senate Concurrent Resolution No. 282, relating to the Distribution of Reports, had been carefully compared with the engrossed resolution as passed by the two Houses, found correctly enrolled, and that the same had this day been deposited with the Secretary of State.

Mr. Linn reported that Substitute Senate Bill No. 96, entitled "An Act to make Compensation to the Hon. John Cradlebaugh, late United States District Judge, the same as that of the late United States District Judges of the Territory of Nevada."

Senate Bill No. 97, "An Act defining the Duties of the Attorney General of the State of Nevada."

Senate Bill No. 170, "An Act to amend an Act entitled 'An Act concerning the Office of Secretary of State,' approved March 14th, 1865."

Senate Bill No. 217, "An Act amendatory of and supplemental to an Act entitled 'An Act to create the County of Lincoln, and provide for its organization.'"

Senate Bill No. 236, "An Act to amend an Act entitled 'An Act to supply the Town of Dayton, in Lyon County, with Water, and to protect the Town against Fire, and to define the Boundaries thereof,' approved February 20th, 1864."

Senate Bill No. 167, "An Act to amend an Act of the Legislature of the Territory of Nevada, entitled 'An Act concerning Conveyances,' approved November 5th, 1861."

Senate Bill No. 160, "An Act to provide for the payment of the contingent expenses of the Surveyor General's Office, from December, 1864, to December 1866, inclusive."

Senate Bill No. 197, "An Act amendatory of an Act entitled 'An Act in relation to the Payment of Salaries and other Claims against the State,' approved February 27th, 1866."

Senate Bill No. 235, "An Act to amend an Act entitled 'An Act to provide for the Government of the State Prison of the State of Nevada,' approved March 4th, 1865."

Substitute Senate Bill No. 169, "An Act to provide for the Publication of the Decisions of the Supreme Court of the State of Nevada;" had been carefully compared with the engrossed bills, as passed by the two Houses, found correctly enrolled, and that the same had this day been delivered to the Governor for his approval.

Assembly Joint Resolution No. 56, relating to Joint Committee to wait on the Governor. Read and adopted. The chair appointed Messrs. Eastman and Terry.

Substitute to Assembly Bill No. 190, "An Act to provide for the election of a Board of Regents, and to define their duties." Read first time; rules suspended; read second time by title, and referred to Committee on Education.

MESSAGE FROM THE ASSEMBLY.

The following Message was received from the Assembly:

ASSEMBLY CHAMBER, CARSON CITY, }
March 7th, 1867. }

To the Hon. the Senate:

I am instructed to inform your honorable body that the House refuse to concur in Senate amendments to Assembly Substitute to Substitute Senate Bill No. 50, "An Act entitled an Act to provide for the Selection and Sale of Lands granted by the United States to the State of Nevada."

Respectfully,

A. WHITFORD,
Clerk.

Mr. Meder moved that the Senate recede from its amendments.
On motion of Mr. Edwards, a call of the Senate was ordered.
Roll called.
Absent—Mr. Mason.
At 1:30 P.M., on motion of Mr. Meder, the Senate took a recess until 2:30 P.M.

IN SENATE.

The Senate met at 2:30 P.M.

President in the chair.

Roll called.

Absent—Mr. Mason. Mr. Mason appearing, was, on motion, excused.

On motion, further proceedings under the call were dispensed with.

The Chair ruled that the question before the Senate was: Will the Senate recede from their amendments to Assembly Substitute to Substitute Senate Bill No. 50.

On motion of Mr. Welty, a call of the Senate was ordered.

Roll called.

Absent—Mr. Linn.

On motion of Mr. Doron, further proceedings under a call were dispensed with.

Mr. Proctor appealed from the decision of the Chair in relation to the question pending before the Senate. On the question: Shall the decision of the Chair be sustained? the yeas and nays were called for by Messrs. Proctor, Edwards and Hastings, and recorded as follows:

YEAS—Messrs. Eastman, Haines, Hastings, Meder, Nelson, Stevenson, Terry, and Welty—8.

NAYS—Messrs. Doron, Edwards, Geller, Grey, Hutchins, Mason, Monroe, Proctor, and Sumner—9.

So the decision of the Chair was not sustained.

Mr. Hutchins, by leave without previous notice, introduced Senate Bill No. 259, "An Act to amend an Act entitled 'An Act to prevent Gaming.'"

Read first time; rules suspended; read second time by title; rules further suspended; bill considered engrossed; read third time by sections. The yeas and nays were called on its final passage, and recorded as follows:

YEAS—Messrs. Doron, Eastman, Edwards, Geller, Grey, Haines, Hastings, Hutchins, Mason, Meder, Monroe, Nelson, Proctor, Stevenson, Sumner, Terry, and Welty—17.

NAYS—0.

So the bill passed.

Mr. Meder, by leave without previous notice, introduced Senate Bill No. 260, "An Act authorizing the State Board of Examiners to audit and allow claims against the Legislative Fund of the first Biennial Session of the Legislature, to be paid out of the General Fund."

Read first time; rules suspended; read second time by title; rules further suspended; the bill considered engrossed; read third time by sections.

The yeas and nays were called on the final passage of the bill, and recorded as follows:

YEAS—Messrs. Eastman, Edwards, Haines, Hastings, Hutchins, Mason, Meder, Monroe, Proctor, Stevenson, Sumner, Terry, and Welty—13.

NAYS—Messrs. Doron, Geller, and Nelson—3.

So the bill passed.

Mr. Grey moved that the vote whereby Assembly Bill No. 77, "An Act providing for the payment of certain Indebtedness due certain parties from the City of Virginia," was on yesterday carried, be now reconsidered.

The yeas and nays were called on the question by Messrs. Haines, Hastings, and Mason, and recorded as follows:

YEAS—Messrs. Eastman, Edwards, Geller, Sumner, and Welty—5.
NAYS—Messrs. Doron, Grey, Haines, Hutchins, Mason, Meder, Monroe, Nelson, Proctor, Stevenson, and Terry—12.

So the Senate refused to reconsider.

MESSAGES FROM THE ASSEMBLY.

The following Messages were received from the Assembly:

ASSEMBLY CHAMBER, CARSON CITY, }
March 7th, 1867. }

To the Honorable the Senate:

I am instructed to transmit to your honorable body for your consideration, Substitute Assembly Bill No. 30, "An Act to regulate the Location and Abandonment of Mines and Mining Claims in the State of Nevada," which passed the House this day.

Respectfully,

A. WHITFORD,
Clerk.

To the Honorable the Senate:

I am instructed to transmit to your honorable body, for your consideration, Assembly Bill No. 137, "An Act to amend an Act entitled 'An Act to provide Revenue for the Support of the Government of the State of Nevada,' approved March 9th, 1865," which passed the House this day.

I also return to your honorable body, Senate Bill No. 201, which passed the House this day.

I also transmit to your honorable body, for your consideration, Assembly Bill No. 161, "An Act in relation to Jurisdictions within this State," which passed the House this day.

Respectfully,

A. WHITFORD,
Clerk.

To the Honorable the Senate:

I am instructed to inform your honorable body that the House have appointed a Conference Committee on Assembly Substitute to Senate Bill No. 50, consisting of Messrs. Jones, Browne, and Bence.

A. WHITFORD,
Clerk.

To the Hon. the Senate:

I have the honor to transmit to your honorable body, Assembly Bill No. 194, "An Act for the Relief of A. Whitford," which passed the House this day. Yeas, 29; nays, 0.

A. WHITFORD,
Clerk.

Substitute Assembly Bill No. 30, "An Act to regulate the Location and Abandonment of Mines and Mining Claims in the State of Nevada."

Read first time; rules suspended; read second time by title, and referred to Committee on Mines and Mining.

On motion of Mr. Haines, a Committee of Conference, consisting of Messrs. Haines, Proctor, and Welty, was appointed by the Chair to confer with a like Committee from the Assembly on amendments to Substitute Assembly Bill No. 50.

The Lander County delegation, to which was referred Assembly Bill No. 159, "An Act to pay the Lander Guard," reported favorably, and recommended the passage thereof.

Mr. Welty (by leave) reported that the Committee on Judiciary had had under consideration Assembly Bill No. 117, entitled "An Act amending an Act to regulate the Settlement of the Estates of Deceased Persons," had directed their chairman to report favorably, and recommend its passage.

Mr. Mason (by leave) reported that the Committee on Federal Relations had had under consideration Assembly Conjoint Resolution in relation to Ireland, and report the same back without recommendation.

Assembly Joint Resolution No. 53, " In relation to Ireland."

Mr. Hutchins moved that the resolution be laid on the table.

The yeas and nays were called on the motion, and recorded as follows:

YEAS—Messrs. Doron, Haines, Hastings, Hutchins, Meder, Monroe, Proctor, and Stevenson—8.

NAYS—Messrs. Eastman, Geller, Mason, Sumner, Terry, and Welty—6.

So the resolution was laid on the table.

Assembly Bill No. 194, " An Act for the Relief of A. Whitford."

Read first time; rules suspended; read second time by title; rules further suspended; considered engrossed; read third time by sections.

The yeas and nays were called on the final passage of the bill, and recorded as follows:

YEAS—Messrs. Doron, Eastman, Edwards, Geller, Haines, Hastings, Hutchins, Mason, Meder, Monroe, Nelson, Proctor, Stevenson, Sumner, Terry, and Welty—16.

NAYS—0.

So the bill passed.

On motion of Mr. Meder, the resolution of Mr. Meder, passed this morning, in relation to paying money to A. Whitford, was rescinded.

Assembly Bill No. 161, " An Act in relation to Injunction within this State."

Read first time; rules suspended; read second time by title, and referred to Judiciary Committee.

Mr. Welty (by leave) without previous notice introduced Senate Bill No. 264, " An Act to regulate the Presentation and Auditing of Demands against Counties."

Read first time; rules suspended; read second time by title; rules further suspended; read third time by sections.

The yeas and nays were called on the final passage of the bill, and recorded as follows:

YEAS—Messrs. Doron, Haines, Mason, Meder, Monroe, Nelson, Proctor, Stevenson, Terry, and Welty—10.

NAYS—Messrs. Eastman, Edwards, Geller, Hastings, Hutchins, and Sumner —6.

So the bill passed.

Mr. Sumner presented the following protest:

The undersigned, Senator from Storey County, respectfully protests against the action of the Senate in passing Assembly Bill No. 77, "An Act to pay certain Claims against the City of Virginia"; because the bill named will result, according to the calculation of the present Mayor, John Piper, of that city, which was submitted to the Senate by the undersigned and not denied or questioned by any Senator, in a positive loss to the City of Virginia of not less than $70,000 : besides working rank injustice to creditors of said city, whose claims are not provided for in the bill.

CHARLES A. SUMNER.

Ordered spread on the Journal.

On motion, Mr. Linn was granted leave of absence for the rest of the day.

·Mr. Grey, (by leave) from Standing Committee on Education, to which was referred Assembly Bill No. 190, entitled " An Act to provide for the Election of a Board of Regents, and to define their duties," reported that they had had the same under consideration ; had come to a favorable conclusion thereon ; had directed their chairman to report the same to the Senate without amendments, and to recommend its passage.

Assembly Bill No. 187, " An Act to amend an Act entitled ' An Act to provide Revenue for the Support of the Government of the State of Nevada,' approved March 9th, 1865."

Read first time ; rules suspended; read second time by title, and referred to Committee on Ways and Means.

Mr. Linn, Chairman of Committee on Enrollment, reported that Senate Bill No.   entitled " An Act to regulate Proceedings in Criminal Cases in the Courts of Justice in the State of Nevada, and making further provisions relating thereto ;" also, Senate No. 189, " An Act to provide for the Payment of Kinkead and Harrington for Goods furnished the late Supreme Court of the Territory of Nevada," had been carefully compared with the engrossed bills as passed by the two Houses, found correctly enrolled, and that the same had this day been delivered [to the Governor] for his approval.

At 4 o'clock P.M., on motion of Mr. Monroe, the Senate took a recess until 7 o'clock P.M.

IN SENATE.

The Senate met at 7 o'clock P.M., President in the chair.

Roll called.

Quorum present.

Mr. Proctor, by leave without previous notice, introduced Senate Concurrent Resolution Bill No. 263, in relation to Fifteenth Rule.

Read, and adopted.

Mr. Meder, from Committee on State Affairs, to which was referred Assembly Bill No. 142, entitled " An Act to create the Office of State Inspector of Boilers and Engines," reported that they had had the same under consideration, had come to an unfavorable conclusion thereon, and recommend it do not pass.

To the Hon. the Senate :

Your Committee of Conference on the nonconcurrence of the Assembly to the amendment of the Senate to Assembly Substitute for Senate Substitute Bill No. 50, entitled " An Act to provide for the Selection and Sale of Lands granted by the United States to the State of Nevada," report that they recommend that the Senate do recede from its amendments.

HAINES,
WELTY.

Mr. Proctor made a minority report, recommending that the Senate do not concur.

Question on the adoption of the majority report.

Mr. Sumner raised point of order, that on the question the yeas and nays should be called, as the Senate could not recede from its amendments, except by vote of constitutional majority.

The Chair ruled the point of order not well taken.

Mr. Sumner appealed from the decision of the Court [Chair].

The yeas and nays were called on the question, by Messrs. Edwards, Doron, and Geller, and recorded as follows:

YEAS—Messrs. Doron, Eastman, Haines, Hastings, Linn, Meder, Nelson, Terry, and Welty—9.

NAYS—Messrs. Edwards, Geller, Grey, Hutchins, Mason, Monroe, Proctor, Sumner, and Terry—9.

So the decision of the Chair was not sustained.

Mr. Haines moved that the report of the Committee be adopted.

Mr. Hutchins moved, as a substitute, that the report lie upon the table.

The yeas and nays were called upon the question to lie upon the table, and recorded as follows:

YEAS—Messrs. Edwards, Geller, Grey, Hutchins, Mason, Monroe, Proctor, Stevenson, and Sumner—9.

NAYS—Messrs. Doron, Eastman, Haines, Hastings, Meder, Nelson, Terry, and Welty—8.

So the substitute motion was carried.

Mr. Sumner, from the Committee on Ways and Means, to which was referred Assembly Bill No. 137, "An Act to amend 'An Act to provide for the Support of the Government of the State of Nevada,' approved March 9th, 1865," reported the accompanying substitute, and recommend the passage thereof.

Mr. Hastings moved that Senate Bill No. 258, "An Act to provide Revenue for the Support of the Government of the State of Nevada," be now taken up. Carried.

Read first time; rules suspended; read second time by title; rules further suspended—considered engrossed—read third time by sections.

The yeas and nays were called on the final passage of the bill, and recorded as follows:

YEAS—Messrs. Doron, Eastman, Edwards, Geller, Grey, Hastings, Hutchins, Mason, Monroe, Proctor, Stevenson, Sumner, and Terry—12.

NAYS—Messrs. Haines, Meder, and Welty—3.

So the bill passed.

Mr. Doron moved that the report of Committee of Conference, in reference to Assembly Substitute to Senate Substitute Bill No. 50, (Land Bill) be now taken up.

Mr. Hastings moved to adjourn.

The President refused to entertain the motion, on the ground that Mr. Sumner having the floor, no motion was in order.

Mr. Haines appealed from the decision of the Chair.

The decision of the Chair was sustained.

Mr. Meder raised the point of order that Mr. Sumner was not speaking to the question, and moved that further discussion cease.

The Chair ruled the motion out of order.

Mr. Meder appealed from the decision of the Chair.

The decision of the Chair was not sustained.

The Chair declared further remarks by Mr. Sumner out of order, and he refusing to take his seat, was arrested by the Sergeant-at-Arms by order of the President.

Mr. Proctor raised point of order, that during the arrest of a member by order of the President, the Senate could transact no business.

Chair ruled the question out of order.

Mr. Proctor appealed from the decision of the Chair.

The decision of the Chair was sustained.

Mr. Sumner was released from arrest.

MESSAGE FROM THE ASSEMBLY.

The following Message was received from the Assembly:

To the Hon. the Senate:

I herewith return to your honorable body, Senate Bill "An Act to make Appropriations for the Support of the Civil Government of the State of Nevada for the third and fourth fiscal years," the same having passed the House this day without amendments.

A. WHITFORD,
Clerk.

Mr. Linn, Chairman of Committee on Enrollment, reported that Senate Substitute for Assembly Bill No. 87, "An Act making Appropriations for the Support of the Civil Government of the State of Nevada for the third and fourth fiscal years, had been carefully compared with the original, found correctly *engrossed*, [enrolled] and delivered to the Governor for his approval.

Also, Senate Bill No. 201, "An Act to provide for the Liquidation and Payment of Certain Claims against the City of Virginia."

Senate Bill No. 138, "An Act authorizing the Secretary of State to employ a Clerk in the State Library and Adjutant General's Office."

Senate Bill No. 133, "An Act to repeal an Act entitled 'An Act to provide for establishing and maintaining a Mining School, and create the office of State Mineralogist,' approved March 9th, 1866."

Substitute Senate Bill No. 122, "An Act to further prescribe Rules and Regulations for the execution of the Trusts arising under the Act of Congress, approved May 23d, 1844, entitled 'An Act for the Relief of Citizens of Towns upon Lands of the United States under certain circumstances.'"

Senate Bill No. 237, "An Act in relation to Enrolling Laws, Resolutions, and other documents;" had been carefully compared with the engrossed bills, as passed by the two Houses, found correctly enrolled, and that the same had this day been delivered to the Governor for his approval.

The following Messages were received from the Assembly.

ASSEMBLY CHAMBER, CARSON CITY,
March 7th, 1867.

To the Honorable the Senate:

I have the honor to return to your honorable body Senate Substitute to Assembly Bill No. 158, the same having passed the House this day.

I also inform your honorable body that the House has this day concurred in Senate amendments to Assembly Bill No. 77, " An Act providing for the Payment of certain Indebtedness due certain parties from the City of Virginia."

I also return to your honorable body, Senate Bill No. 261 ; also, Senate Bill 260, both of which passed the House this day.

Also, Senate Bill No. 259, which the House refused to pass.

Also, Senate Concurrent Resolution No. 263, which was unanimously concurred in by the House.

Also, Senate Concurrent Resolution No. 248, which was indefinitely postponed this day by the House.

I also transmit to your honorable body for your consideration, Assembly Resolution relating to Federal Relations, etc.

I also return to your honorable body, Senate Bill No. 258, which the House refused to pass.

Also, Substitute Senate Bill No. 51, " An Act to regulate the Recording and Possession of Mining Claims in the State of Nevada," the same having been indefinitely postponed.

Also, Senate Bill No. 11, " An Act to amend an Act entitled ' An Act to provide Revenue for the Support [of the Government] of the State of Nevada, and the Acts amendatory thereof," the same having been indefinitely postponed.

I also inform you that the House have concurred in Senate amendments to Assembly Bill No. 145, and that Messrs. Mayhugh, Strother, and Stampley have been appointed a Committee to act with a like Committee from your House to wait upon the Governor.

I also return Senate Bill No. 102, the same having passed the House without amendment.

Respectfully,

A. WHITFORD,
Clerk.

Mr. Linn, Chairman of Committee on Enrollment, reported that Senate Bill No. 202, "An Act to provide Stationery for the use of the Senate and Assembly of the State of Nevada ;"

Senate Bill No. 261, "An Act to regulate the Presentation and Auditing of Demands against Counties ;"

Senate Bill No. 260, "An Act authorizing the State Board of Examiners to audit and allow certain Claims against the Legislative Fund of the First Biennial Session of the Legislature, to be paid out of the General Fund ;" had been carefully compared with the engrossed bills as passed by the two Houses, found correctly enrolled, and had this day been delivered to the Governor for his approval.

Also Senate Concurrent Resolution No. 263, suspending Joint Rule 15 ; and had been deposited with the Secretary of State.

MESSAGE FROM THE ASSEMBLY.

The following Message was received from the Assembly :

ASSEMBLY CHAMBER, CARSON CITY, }
March 7th, 1867.

To the Hon. the Senate :

I transmit to your honorable body, Assembly Bill No. 96, "An Act to transfer certain Moneys from the Legislative Fund to the Contingent Fund of the Assembly."

I also return to your honorable body, Senate Bill No. 247, which was this day indefinitely postponed.

A. WHITFORD,
Clerk.

At 12 o'clock (midnight) by virtue of the Constitution, the President declared the Senate adjourned *sine die.*

JAMES S. SLINGERLAND,
President.

Attest—B. C. BROWN,
Secretary.

JOURNAL

OF THE

PROCEEDINGS OF THE SENATE,

SPECIAL SESSION,

1867.

NEVADA LEGISLATURE.---SENATE.

SPECIAL SESSION, 1867.

FIRST DAY.

CARSON CITY, March 15th, 1867.

Pursuant to a Proclamation issued by his Excellency, H. G. BLASDEL, Governor, of which the following is a copy:

"PROCLAMATION.

STATE OF NEVADA, EXECUTIVE DEPARTMENT, }
Carson City, March 12th, 1867.   }

Whereas, the Legislature of this State, which convened on the 7th day of January, A.D. 1867, adjourned without adopting such amendments to existing Revenue Laws, as will assure the payment of interest on the State Debt, and provide the means for defraying the necessary expenses of the State Government, which will be required before the next Regular Session of the Legislature; and whereas, the pledged faith of the State to its creditors, and a proper administration of Public Affairs imperatively demand that such Constitutional enactments be passed as will supply these wants;

Now, therefore, I, H. G. Blasdel, in pursuance of the authority vested in me as Governor of the State of Nevada, by the Constitution and laws thereof, do hereby direct and authorize the Senate and Assembly, constituting the Legislature of this State, to convene in Special Session, at Carson City, at 12 o'clock M., on Friday, the fifteenth day of March, A.D. 1867, for the purpose of considering and enacting needful amendments to "An Act to provide Revenue for the Support of the Government of the State of Nevada," approved March 9th, 1865, and the Acts amendatory thereof; and for the transaction of such other legislative business as the Governor of this State may call to the attention of said Legislature, while in said Special Session.

In witness whereof, I have hereunto set my hand, and caused to be affixed the Great Seal of the State of Nevada. Done at Carson City, this 12th day of March, 1867.

[L. S.]   HENRY G. BLASDEL.
Attest—C. N. NOTEWARE,
          Secretary of State:"

the Senate convened at 12 o'clock M., President in the chair.

The Proclamation was read.

Roll called by the Secretary, B. C. Brown.

Present—Messrs. Doron, Eastman, Edwards, Grey, Haines, Hastings, Hutchins, Linn, Mason, Meder, Monroe, Nelson, Proctor, Stevenson, Sumner, Terry, and Welty—16.

Absent—Messrs. Carpenter and Geller—2.

Mr. Hastings, by leave, offered the following resolution:

Resolved, By the Senate, the Assembly concurring, that the two Houses adjourn to meet on the thirty-first day of December, A.D. eighteen hundred and sixty-eight.

Mr. Welty raised the point of order that it was not competent for the Senate to transact any business until after organization.

The Chair ruled the point well taken.

Mr. Hutchins appealed from the decision of the Chair.

The yeas and nays were called for by Messrs. Meder, Hutchins, and Welty on the question, and recorded as follows:

YEAS—Messrs. Doron, Eastman, Edwards, Haines, Linn, Mason, Meder, Nelson, Stevenson, Terry, and Welty—11.

NAYS—Messrs. Grey, Hastings, Hutchins, Monroe, Proctor, and Sumner—6.

So the decision of the Chair was sustained.

Mr. Welty moved the Senate now proceed to organization.

Mr. Sumner raised the point of order that the Senate could not now organize, until a Message of the Governor was received.

The Chair ruled the point of order not well taken.

Mr. Monroe offered the following resolution as a substitute:

Resolved, That, in accordance with uniform and unvarying custom, the elective and appointed officers, and the Committees of the Senate of the Third Regular Session of the Nevada Legislature, be and they are hereby declared the duly chosen Senate officers and Committeemen of the present Special Session.

Resolved, That the Secretary be, and he is hereby directed to notify the Assembly of the organization of the Senate, and its readiness to proceed to the transaction of legislative business.

Mr. Hutchins moved to amend the substitute resolution by striking out the words "and Committeemen."

Carried.

The substitute resolution, as amended, was adopted.

Mr. Welty moved that a Committee of three be appointed to wait on the Governor, and inform [him] that the Senate is ready for business.

Carried.

The Chair appointed Messrs. Welty, Doron, and Mason.

Mr. Hastings offered the following resolution:

Resolved, By the Senate, the Assembly concurring, that the Legislature do now adjourn until December 31st, 1868.

The Chair ruled the resolution out of order.

At 1 o'clock, on motion of Mr. Edwards, the Senate took a recess until 3 o'clock P.M.

IN SENATE.

The Senate met at 3 o'clock P.M.

President in the chair.

Roll called.

Quorum present.

On motion of Mr. Edwards, the rules of the last session were adopted as the rules of this session.

Mr. Welty, from Special Committee appointed to wait on the Governor and inform him of the organization, reported that the Committee had performed the duty assigned them.

Mr. Mason, by leave, offered the following resolution:

Resolved, That no Senator be allowed to speak longer than ten minutes nor more than once on any question before the Senate, unless by unanimous consent; and such leave, when given, shall be considered withdrawn when any member objects.

The yeas and nays were called on the adoption of the resolution, by Messrs. Mason, Grey, and Edwards, and recorded as follows:

YEAS—Messrs. Doron, Eastman, Haines, Linn, Mason, Meder, Terry, and Welty—8.

NAYS—Messrs. Edwards, Grey, Hastings, Hutchins, Monroe, Nelson, Proctor, Stevenson, Sumner—9.

So the resolution was not adopted.

To the Hon. the Senate of Nevada:

John C. Medley, the Copying Clerk of the Senate, being absent, I hereby appoint J. R. Williamson to fill the vacancy; and I hereby confirm all other appointments made by me at the Third Session of the Senate.

Respectfully,
B. C. BROWN,
Secretary of the Senate.

The officers, elective and appointive, were duly sworn to oath of office.

The President announced his appointment of the following Standing Committees:

Judiciary—Messrs. Welty, Proctor, Sumner, Nelson, Hutchins.

Ways and Means—Messrs. Haines, Doron, Meder, Welty, Eastman.

Corporations—Messrs. Carpenter, Eastman, Haines, Stevenson, Monroe.

Supplies and Expenditures—Messrs. Terry, Geller, Linn.

Engrossment—Messrs. Hastings, Meder, Welty.

Enrollment—Messrs. Linn, Carpenter, Mason.

Mines and Mining—Messrs. Stevenson, Linn, Doron, Nelson, Terry.

Federal Relations—Messrs. Mason, Monroe, Edwards.

State Affairs—Messrs. Doron, Meder, Monroe.

Agriculture and Manufactures—Messrs. Haines, Eastman, Meder.

Education—Messrs. Grey, Edwards, Terry.

Public Printing—Messrs. Doron, Carpenter, Meder.

Counties and County Boundaries—Messrs. Proctor, Hutchins, Grey, Terry, Eastman.

State Prison—Messrs. Geller, Sumner, Proctor.
Militia and Indian Affairs—Messrs. Hutchins, Nelson, Carpenter.
State Library—Messrs. Nelson, Haines, Hastings.
Internal Improvements—Messrs. Eastman, Carpenter, Mason.
Public Lands—Messrs. Edwards, Doron, Grey.
Claims—Messrs. Monroe, Nelson, Edwards.
Public Morals—Messrs. Meder, Mason, Welty.
Mileage—Messrs. Linn, Mason, Hastings.

MESSAGE FROM THE GOVERNOR.

STATE OF NEVADA—EXECUTIVE DEPARTMENT, }
Carson City, March 15th, 1867. }

Gentlemen of the Senate and Assembly:

The late Legislature, after authorizing a State Loan of five hundred thousand dollars, to bear interest at fifteen per cent. per annum, payable semi-monthly, adjourned on the 7th instant without providing means for the payment of the principal or interest of the debt as created; without providing adequate means to defray the expenses of the State Government for the ensuing two years; indeed, without enacting any revenue law whatever, of a beneficial character. In view of existing facts, it must be apparent that, unless this omission be promptly supplied by the enactment of a just and comprehensive revenue law, the faith of the State must be broken, its honor and credit destroyed, and the administration of its government seriously embarrassed, if not entirely obstructed.

It is upon this "extraordinary occasion," and for the "purpose" of enacting a *Revenue Law*, I have convened you in "Special Session."

In enacting new or amending existing revenue laws, you will wisely keep prominently in view Article Ten (10) of the State Constitution. *Uniformity* and *equality* of assessment and taxation are not only indispensable to the validity of the law, but are imperatively demanded in justice to the people. If the tax levied be not uniform and equal, collection by process is impossible. If you force the property of one class of our citizens to contribute to the support of the State Government, and exempt, or but partially tax, the property of another, your legislation will become oppressive and obnoxious, and the State will derive, perhaps, no revenue from the measure. It is a universal maxim of political economy that the citizens of a State shall contribute equally, according to their means, to its support. I know no just cause exempting Nevada from this rule. Nor is there any good reason why one individual should be made to bear the burdens or pay the taxes justly due from another.

The absolute exemption of the mines (in value the most considerable interest in the State) from taxation renders the assessment levied upon the limited taxable property necessarily onerous. For this reason, and in order to relieve the people, every article of property, not exempt, should be made to contribute its just and equable proportion to the support of the State Government.

Under present laws, three-fourths only of the property designated in the Constitution as the "proceeds of the mines," after deducting twenty dollars per ton from the value thereof, is taxed for *State and County purposes* one dollar on each one hundred dollars' valuation, while all other property is taxed, at its full valuation, one dollar and twenty-five cents on each one hundred dollars' valuation, for State and Territorial purposes alone. I do not hesitate to say, that the taxes levied by this law are not uniform nor equal, and that their payment cannot be enforced by legal process.

Nor do I hesitate to express the opinion, that if the existing *Revenue Law* is not amended so as to conform to the requirement of Article Ten (10) of the Constitution, no property tax can, or will be collected for the current Fiscal Year.

In view of these considerations, I earnestly hope that some measure of taxation, just to the people, and equal and uniform in its operation throughout the State, will be devised, by the instrumentality of which the necessary means may be realized to enable the State to promptly meet the existing liabilities, and current expenses, for the next two years.

H. G. BLASDEL,
Governor.

On motion of Mr. Hutchins, two hundred and forty copies of the above Message were ordered printed.

On motion of Mr. Sumner, the Message was referred to Committee of the Whole for Saturday, March 16th, at 12 o'clock m.

At 4:35 p.m., on motion of Mr. Monroe, the Senate adjourned.

JAMES S. SLINGERLAND,
President.

Attest—B. C. BROWN,
Secretary.

IN SENATE, SPECIAL SESSION—SECOND DAY.

CARSON CITY, March 16th, 1867.

The Senate met pursuant to adjournment.

President in the chair.

Roll called.

Present—Messrs. Doron, Eastman, Geller, Grey, Haines, Hastings, Hutchins, Linn, Mason, Meder, Monroe, Nelson, Proctor, Stevenson, Sumner, Terry, Welty, and Edwards—18.

Absent—Mr. Carpenter—1.

Prayer by the Chaplain.

The Journal of the First day was read and approved.

The following communication was received:

To the Hon. the Senate :

C. C. Wallace, the Assistant Sergeant-at-Arms, being absent, I hereby appoint M. N. Haynie to fill the vacancy.

Respectfully,
M. M. GAIGE,
Sergeant-at-Arms, Senate.

Carson City, March 15th, 1867.

Mr. Linn, Chairman of Committee on Mileage, submitted the following report:

To the Hon. the President of the Senate :

The Committee on Mileage, having had the same under consideration, beg leave to submit this report, with the accompanying table, showing the distance traveled by the several members of the Senate from their respective places of residence, in coming to and returning from the Capital of the State, together with the amount due to each member, in accordance with the provision of the seventeenth article, third section and ninth clause of the Constitution, which provides for the payment of mileage of members of the Legislature:

	Miles.	Amount.
Mr. Doron	220	$ 88 00
Mr. Eastman	50	20 00
Mr. Edwards	..	....
Mr. Geller	50	20 00
Mr. Grey	30	12 00
Mr. Haines	34	13 60
Mr. Hastings	30	12 00
Mr. Hutchins	320	128 00
Mr. Linn	300	120 00
Mr. Mason	220	88 00
Mr. Meder	..	.....
Mr. Monroe	340	136 00
Mr. Nelson	30	12 00
Mr. Proctor	460	184 00
Mr. Stevenson	30	12 00
Mr. Sumner	30	12 00
Mr. Terry	400	160 00
Mr. Welty	400	160 00
Mr. Slingerland	50	20 00

MOTIONS AND RESOLUTIONS.

Mr. Linn offered the following resolution:

Resolved, That F. F. Wright be, and he is hereby elected Official Reporter of the Senate, and that he shall receive a per diem of ten dollars.

Adopted.

Mr. Haines offered the following resolution:

Resolved, That the Sergeant-at-Arms be, and he is hereby authorized to procure such stationery as may be necessary for the use of Senators and attachés of the Senate.

Lost.

MESSAGE FROM THE ASSEMBLY.

The following Message was received from the Assembly:

ASSEMBLY CHAMBER, CARSON CITY, }
March 15th, 1867. }

To the Hon. the Senate:

I am instructed to inform your honorable body that the Assembly is fully organized, as follows: Speaker, R. D. Ferguson; Speaker *pro tem.*, T. V. Julien; Chief Clerk, A. Whitford; Assistant Clerk, W. Darling; Sergeant-at-Arms, Wm. Woodhurst; Assistant Sergeant-at-Arms, John E. Isaacs; Minute Clerk, T. S. Davenport; Journal Clerk, R. P. Dayton; Engrossing Clerk, R. L. Thomas; Chaplain, Rev. A. F. White.

Also, that the House has appointed a Committee of three, consisting of Messrs. Mayhugh, Strother, and Walton, to act with a like Committee from your honorable body, when appointed, to wait on the Governor, and inform him that the two Houses are fully organized, and ready to receive any communication that he may have to make.

Respectfully,

A. WHITFORD,
Clerk.

NOTICE OF BILLS.

Mr. Monroe gave verbal notice that, on Tuesday, March 19th, he would introduce a bill entitled "An Act for the Collection of Revenue, to provide adequate means to defray the expenses of the State Government, and to provide means for the payment of interest and principal of five hundred thousand dollar bonds."

INTRODUCTION OF BILLS.

Mr. Edwards, by leave without previous notice, introduced Senate Bill No. 1, "An Act to amend an Act entitled 'An Act to provide Revenue for the Support of the Government of the State of Nevada,' approved March 9th, 1865, as amended by an Act entitled 'An Act to amend an Act entitled an Act to provide Revenue for the Support of the Government of the State of Nevada,' approved March 9th, 1865, approved Feb. 24th, 1866."

Mr. Proctor moved the bill be indefinitely postponed.

Mr. Edwards moved, as a substitute, that the bill be referred to the Committee on Ways and Means.

The yeas and nays were called for on the question by Messrs. Grey, Doron, and Edwards, and recorded as follows:

YEAS—Messrs. Doron, Eastman, Edwards, Haines, Linn, Mason, Meder, Nelson, Stevenson, Terry, and Welty—11.

NAYS—Messrs. Geller, Grey, Hastings, Hutchins, Monroe, Proctor, and Sumner—7.

So the bill was referred to the Committee on Ways and Means.

At 11:35 A.M., on motion of Mr. Mason, the Senate adjourned.

JAMES S. SLINGERLAND,
President.

Attest—B. C. BROWN,
Secretary.

IN SENATE, SPECIAL SESSION—FOURTH DAY.

CARSON CITY, March 18th, 1867.

The Senate met pursuant to adjournment, President in the chair.

Roll called.

Present—Messrs. Doron, Eastman, Edwards, Geller, Grey, Haines, Hastings, Hutchins, Linn, Mason, Meder, Monroe, Proctor, Stevenson, Sumner, Terry, and Welty—17.

Absent—Messrs. Carpenter and Nelson—2.

Prayer by the Chaplain.

The Journal of the Second day was read and approved.

Mr. Doron moved the Senate take a recess until 3 o'clock P.M.

The yeas and nays were called on the question by Messrs. Hastings, Monroe and Mason, and recorded as follows:

YEAS—Messrs. Doron, Eastman, Edwards, Haines, Linn, Mason, Meder, Terry, and Welty—9.

NAYS—Messrs. Geller, Grey, Hastings, Hutchins, Monroe, Proctor, Stevenson, and Sumner—8.

So the Senate took a recess until 3 o'clock P.M.

IN SENATE.

The Senate met at 3 o'clock P.M.

President in the chair.

Roll called.

Quorum present.

Mr. Monroe (by leave) offered the following resolution:

Resolved, That the Sergeant-at-Arms of the Senate be, and he is hereby authorized to provide the members and attachés of the Senate with stationery, postage, and newspapers.

Mr. Mason offered the following as a substitute:

Resolved, That the Sergeant-at-Arms be ordered to draw his warrant for the amount of $25 for each member and attaché of the Senate, for the purpose of purchasing the requisite stationery for the Special Session.

The substitute was adopted.

MESSAGE FROM THE GOVERNOR.

The following Message was received from the Governor:

EXECUTIVE DEPARTMENT, CARSON CITY, }
March 18th, 1867. }

Gentlemen of the Senate and Assembly:

By reference to sections eight and nine of the "Enabling Act," (page 37, Statutes of 1864–5) you will see that, unless an Act be passed during your Special Session on the subject of the selection, location, and sale of the public lands granted to this State by the United States, forty entire sections (or 25,600 acres) will be wholly lost to the State. Nor is this all the material loss the State would sustain if such measure fail of consummation. Before the convening of the Legislature again, in regular session, much of the first-class agricultural lands would be disposed of under the laws of Congress, so that the State could never get them; whereas, if you pass an Act to meet the emergency, you may save much to the State, and hasten the settlement of those lands by desirable population, and greatly increase the amount and value of taxable property.

I call this matter of legislation to your attention, that you may take such action in the premises, and pass such Act, as will subserve the interests of the State.

H. G. BLASDEL,
Governor.

The Message was referred to the Committee on Public Lands.

Mr. Hutchins moved that the Senate do now go into Committee of the Whole for the consideration of the Governor's first Message concerning Revenue.

The yeas and nays were called on the question by Messrs. Geller, Sumner, and Grey, and recorded as follows:

YEAS—Messrs. Geller, Grey, Hastings, Hutchins, Monroe, Proctor, and Sumner—7.

NAYS—Messrs. Doron, Eastman, Edwards, Haines, Linn, Mason, Meder, Stevenson, Terry, and Welty—11.

So the motion was lost.

On motion of Mr. Proctor, the Committee on Ways and Means were instructed to report on to-morrow, March 19th, at the convening of the Senate.

Ou motion of Mr. Doron, the Assembly Messages were now taken up.

The following Message was received from the Assembly:

ASSEMBLY CHAMBER, CARSON CITY,
March 18th, 1867.

To the Honorable the Senate:

I am instructed to transmit to your honorable body, for your consideration, Assembly Bill No. 1, entitled "An Act to amend an Act entitled 'An Act to provide Revenue for the Support of the Government of the State of Nevada,' approved March 9th, 1865, as amended by an Act entitled 'An Act to provide Revenue for the Support of the Government of the State of Nevada,' approved March 9th, 1865, approved February 24th, 1866," the same having passed the House this day. Yeas, 26; nays, 11.

Also, Assembly Bill No. 2, entitled "An Act to create certain Funds," the same having passed the House this day. Yeas, 24; nays, 2.

Respectfully,
A. WHITFORD,
Clerk.

Assembly Bill No. 1, "An Act to amend an Act entitled 'An Act to provide Revenue for the Support of the Government of the State of Nevada,' approved March 9th, 1865, as amended by an Act entitled 'An Act to amend an Act entitled an Act to provide Revenue for the Support of the Government of the State of Nevada,' approved March 9th, 1865, approved Feb. 24th, 1866."

Read first time.

Mr. Sumner moved that the bill be rejected.

Mr. Edwards moved, as a substitute, that the bill be referred to Committee on Ways and Means.

Mr. Sumner rose to a point of order, that the motion to reject can be the only motion entertained.

The Chair ruled the point of order well taken.

The yeas and nays were called on the question by Messrs. Linn, Mason, and Welty, and recorded as follows:

YEAS—Messrs. Geller, Grey, Hastings, Hutchins, Monroe, Proctor, Stevenson, and Sumner—8.

NAYS—Messrs. Doron, Eastman, Edwards, Haines, Linn, Mason, Meder, Nelson, Terry, and Welty—10.

So the Senate refused to reject the bill.
At 4 o'clock P.M., on motion of Mr. Mason, the Senate adjourned.

JAMES S. SLINGERLAND,
President.

Attest—B. C. BROWN,
Secretary.

IN SENATE, SPECIAL SESSION—FIFTH DAY.

CARSON CITY, March 19th, 1867.

The Senate met pursuant to adjournment, President in the chair.
Roll called.
Present—Messrs. Doron, Eastman, Edwards, Geller, Grey, Haines, Hastings, Hutchins, Linn, Mason, Meder, Monroe, Nelson, Proctor, Stevenson, Sumner, Terry, and Welty—18.
Absent—Mr. Carpenter—1.
Prayer by the Chaplain.
The Journal of the Fourth day was read and approved.

REPORTS OF COMMITTEES.

Mr. Haines, from Committee on Ways and Means, to which was referred Assembly Bill No. 1, entitled "An Act to amend an Act entitled ' An Act to provide Revenue for the Support of the Government of the State of Nevada,' approved March 9th, 1865, and the Acts amendatory thereof," reported that they had had the same under consideration; had come to a favorable conclusion thereon; had directed their chairman to report the same to the Senate with amendments, and to recommend its passage, as amended.
Amend original bill, as follows:
Strike out "1" in first section, and insert in lieu thereof, the section herewith presented.
Also, insert as section "2" the section herewith reported and presented.
Also, strike out "section 2" of original bill, and insert in lieu thereof, the section herewith reported and presented.
Also, amend section 3 of original bill, as follows:
After the third clause, being these words: "The assessed value per Ton," add the following: "provided that ores, quartz or minerals containing gold or silver, or either, which yield less per ton than is by this Act directed, for expenses of working the same, shall not be assessed or included in the assessment roll, but shall be included in the statement furnished to the Assessor."
Also, amend section 4 of original bill, by striking out as the number of the section proposed to be amended "117," and inserting "118."
Also, add as section No. —, as an amendment to section 117 of said Act, the section herewith reported and presented.
Also amend section 5 of original bill, as follows:
On the 14th line of section, after the word "Act," insert as follows: "and

including therein the time employed in making the assessment for both State and County purposes."

Also, in same section, after the words "Eight dollars per day," insert the following: "which shall be in full for all services in making the assessment for both State and County purposes, and which shall be paid as in this Statute provided."

Also, in same section, strike out "two" as the per centum of compensation to Assessors, and insert "three."

Section 1. An annual ad valorem tax of one hundred cents upon each one hundred dollars' value of taxable property is hereby levied and directed to be collected and paid for State purposes upon the assessed value of all taxable property in this State, including the proceeds of mines and the proceeds of mining claims, except such property as is by this Act exempted from taxation. Seventy cents of said tax on all property other than proceeds of mines and mining claims is and shall be held to be the same as that levied under the provisions of an Act to amend an Act, entitled "An Act authorizing a State Loan and levying a tax to provide means for the payment thereof, approved February 6th, A.D. 1867;" and the money coming into the State Treasury from said tax, to the extent of seventy cents on all property except proceeds of mines and mining claims, shall be [applied] exclusively to the payment of the principal and interest of the bonds provided to be issued by the last mentioned Act. Twenty-five cents of the one hundred cents, other than the tax of [on] the proceeds of the mines and mining claims, is hereby appropriated to the payment of Territorial indebtedness, funded under the provisions of an Act entitled "An Act to provide for carrying out in part the provisions of Section 7, Article 17, of the Constitution of the State of Nevada, approved February 14th, 1865," which shall be applied exclusively to the extinguishment of such funded debt. Five cents of the one hundred cents by this Act levied on the proceeds of mines and mining claims is hereby set apart for the support and maintenance of a State University and Common Schools; and ninety-five cents of the one hundred cents levied on the proceeds of mines and mining claims is hereby set apart for general revenue purposes.

Sec. 2. Section two of said Act is hereby amended, so as to read as follows:

Sec. 2. The Boards of County Commissioners of each county shall, prior to the first Monday of April of each year, cause to be prepared suitable and well-bound books for the use of the Assessor, in which the County Assessor shall enter his Tax List and Assessment Roll as hereinafter provided, and in which list and assessment roll shall be assessed and included all taxes levied by authority of law for county purposes. Said books shall contain suitable printed heads, and be ruled to conform with the form of the Assessment Roll as provided by this Act.

Section ninety-nine of said Act is hereby so amended as to read as follows:

Section 99. All ores and minerals shall be assessed for purposes of taxation for State and County purposes, at their value, when severed from the mine and deposited on the surface; and to determine the value of ores containing gold and silver, or either, the Assessor shall deduct from the gross yield of such ores when the same are worked by the common process without washing, the sum of eighteen dollars per ton; and when worked by the Freiburg, or roasting process, or by smelting process, the sum of forty dollars per ton.

Section 117 of said Act is hereby amended, so as to read as follows:

Section 117. The revenue arising from the tax of one hundred cents on the valuation of the proceeds of mines and mining claims as fixed in this statute shall be paid into the County Treasury for the use and benefit of the State, to be appropriated as in this Act provided, and by the County Treasurer shall be

34

paid over to the State Treasurer, as he is directed and required by law to pay over other moneys belonging to the State.

On motion of Mr. Proctor, 240 copies of the bill with amendments were ordered printed.

Mr. Geller gave notice that he would at some future time introduce a bill to create a Secret Service Fund for the use and benefit of the Governor, said fund not to exceed one hundred thousand dollars a year during his term of office of four years.

Assembly Bill No. 1, " An Act to amend an Act entitled ' An Act to provide Revenue for the Support of the Government of the State of Nevada, approved March 9th, 1866, as amended by an Act entitled an Act to provide Revenue for the Support of the Government of the State of Nevada, appoved March 9th, 1865,' approved February 24th, 1866."
Read second time.
Mr. Hastings moved that the bill be indefinitely postponed.
Mr. Edwards moved the bill be referred to Committee on Ways and Means.
Mr. Sumner moved the bill be referred to Committee of the Whole.
The yeas and nays were called for on the question, by Messrs. Doron, Grey, and Sumner, and recorded as follows:

YEAS—Messrs. Geller, Grey, Hastings, Hutchins, Monroe, Proctor, Stevenson—8.
NAYS—Messrs. Doron, Eastman, Haines, Linn, Mason, Meder, Nelson, Terry, Welty, and Edwards—10.

So the Senate refused to refer the bill to Committee of the Whole.
The yeas and nays were called for by Messrs. Hastings, Grey, and Edwards, on the question of referring the bill to Committee on Ways and Means, and recorded as follows:

YEAS—Messrs. Doron, Eastman, Edwards, Haines, Linn, Mason, Meder, Nelson, Stevenson, Terry, and Welty—11.
NAYS—Messrs. Geller, Grey, Hastings, Hutchins, Monroe, Proctor, and Sumner—7.

So the bill was referred to Committee on Ways and Means.

Mr. Monroe introduced Senate Bill No. 3, " An Act to amend an Act entitled ' An Act to provide Revenue for the Support of the Government of the State of Nevada, approved March 9th, 1865, as amended by an Act entitled an Act to amend an Act entitled an Act to provide Revenue for the Support of the Government of the State of Nevada, approved March 9th, 1865,' approved February 24th, 1866."
On motion of Mr. Welty, the bill was read at length ; rules suspended ; read

second time by title, and on motion of Mr. Proctor, was referred to a Special Committee of three, appointed by the Senate.

The Senate appointed Messrs. Monroe, Proctor, and Grey.

The bill was ordered printed.

Mr. Linn, by leave without previous notice, introduced Senate Bill No. 4, "An Act to amend an Act entitled 'An Act to provide Revenue for the Support of the Government of the State of Nevada,' approved March 9th, 1865, and other Acts amendatory thereof."

Read first time; rules suspended; read second time by title, and referred to Committee on Ways and Means.

Mr. Welty, by leave without previous notice, introduced Senate Bill No. 5.

Mr. Proctor raised the point of order that the bill referred [to] service of summons, and not directly to collection of revenue.

The Chair ruled that the bill, being amendatory of the Revenue Bill, its introduction was in order.

Mr. Edwards appealed from the decision of the Chair.

The decision of the Chair was sustained.

Mr. Welty, by leave, withdrew the bill.

Mr. Sumner, by leave, introduced the following protest:

The undersigned respectfully protest against any action on the part of the Senate, at this session, on bills proposing to amend Revenue Law in accordance with the convening Proclamation and the recent Revenue Message of the Governor; as they hold and declare that the statements of the Governor in his Proclamation and Message in regard to additional taxation, assumed by him to be needed, are incorrect and unwarranted in every respect; there being, in the opinion of the undersigned, no just cause whatever for the calling of the present session.

> CHARLES A. SUMNER,
> F. M. PROCTOR,
> FRED. HUTCHINS,
> D. L. HASTINGS,
> S. GELLER.

At 12:15 P.M., on motion of Mr. Doron, the Senate took a recess until 3:30 P.M.

IN SENATE.

The Senate met at 3:30 P.M.

President in the chair.

Roll called. Quorum present.

UNFINISHED BUSINESS.

Assembly Bill No. 2, "An Act to create certain Funds."

Read first time; rules suspended; read second time by title, and referred to Committee on State Affairs.

Mr. Haines (by leave) reported that the Committee on Ways and Means had had under consideration Senate Bill No. 4, entitled "An Act to amend an Act entitled 'An Act to provide Revenue for the Support of the Government of the State of Nevada, approved March 9th, 1865,' and other Acts amendatory thereof," and had directed their chairman to report the same back, with a recommendation that it do pass.

Mr. Sumner moved that the Senate now take up the Governor's Message.

The yeas and nays were called for on the question by Messrs. Welty, Hutchins, and Sumner, and recorded as follows:

YEAS—Messrs. Edwards, Geller, Grey, Hastings, Hutchins, Monroe, Proctor and Sumner—8.

NAYS—Messrs. Doron, Eastman, Haines, Linn, Mason, Meder, Nelson, Stevenson, Terry, and Welty—10.

So the Senate refused to take up the Message.

At 3:40 P.M., on motion of Mr. Mason, the Senate adjourned.

JAMES S. SLINGERLAND,
President.

Attest—B. C. BROWN,
Secretary.

———

IN SENATE, SPECIAL SESSION—SIXTH DAY.

CARSON CITY, March 20th, 1867.

The Senate met pursuant to adjournment, President in the chair.

Roll called.

Present—Messrs. Doron, Eastman, Edwards, Geller, Grey, Haines, Hastings, Hutchins, Linn, Mason, Meder, Monroe, Nelson, Proctor, Stevenson, Sumner, Terry, and Welty—18.

Absent—Mr. Carpenter—1.

Prayer by the Chaplain.

The Journal of the Fifth day was read and approved.

The President appointed Aaron Campton as Messenger of the Senate, to fill the vacancy caused by the resignation of John Craddock.

MOTIONS AND RESOLUTIONS.

Mr. Hastings, by leave, offered the following resolution:

Resolved, That the Sergeant-at-Arms be, and hereby is directed to draw his warrant on the Senate Contingent Fund, in favor of Fred. Hutchins, for the sum of fifty-six dollars.

Adopted.

On motion of Mr. Welty, the Senate went into Committee of the Whole. President in the chair, for the consideration of Senate Bill No. 1, together with the amendments.

The Committee rose, and submitted the following report:

Mr. President:

The Senate, in Committee of the Whole, had had under consideration Senate Bill No. 1, "An Act to amend an Act entitled 'An Act to provide Revenue for the Support of the Government of the State of Nevada,' approved March

9th, 1865, as amended by an Act entitled 'An Act to provide Revenue for the Support of the Government of the State of Nevada, approved March 9th, 1865, approved February 24th, 1866," which they report back, and ask leave to sit again at 2 o'clock P.M.

Report of the Committee adopted.

At 12:30 P.M., on motion of Mr. Hutchins, the Senate took a recess until 2 o'clock P.M.

IN SENATE.

The Senate met at 2 P.M., President in the chair.

Roll called. Quorum present.

Mr. Monroe, from Special Committee, (by leave) reported that they had had under consideration Senate Bill No. 3, which was referred to them; had directed their chairman to report the same back, and to recommend its passage.

On motion of Mr. Welty, the Senate went into Committee of the Whole, President in the chair, for the consideration of Senate Bill No. 1.

The Committee rose, and submitted the following report:

Mr. President :

The Senate, in Committee of the Whole, have had under consideration Senate Bill No. 1, "An Act to amend an Act entitled 'An Act to provide Revenue for the Support of the Government of the State of Nevada,' etc., etc.," on which they report progress, and ask leave to sit again on to-morrow at 11 o'clock A.M.

Leave granted.

At 4:45 P.M., on motion of Mr. Welty, the Senate adjourned until to-morrow at 10 A.M.

CHARLES A. SUMNER,
President pro tem.

Attest—B. C. BROWN,
        Secretary.

IN SENATE, SPECIAL SESSION—SEVENTH DAY.

CARSON CITY, March 21st, 1867.

The Senate met pursuant to adjournment, President in the chair.

Roll called.

Present—Messrs. Doron, Eastman, Edwards, Geller, Grey, Haines, Hastings, Hutchins, Linn, Mason, Meder, Monroe, Nelson, Proctor, Stevenson, Sumner, Terry, and Welty—18.

Absent—Mr. Carpenter—1.

The Journal of the Sixth day was read and approved.

Mr. Hutchins in the chair.

REPORTS OF COMMITTEES.

Mr. Monroe, from minority of Committee on State Affairs, to which was referred Assembly Bill No. 2, entitled "An Act to create certain Funds," reported that he had the same under consideration, reported favorably, and recommended its passage.

MOTIONS AND RESOLUTIONS.

Mr. Sumner introduced Senate Concurrent Resolution No. 6, relating to Ireland.

Read, and referred to Committee on Federal Relations.

INTRODUCTION OF BILLS.

Mr. Mason, (by leave) without previous notice, introduced Senate Bill No. 7, "An Act to provide for the selection and sale of Lands granted by the United States to this State."

Read first time; rules suspended; read second time by title, and referred to Committee on Public Lands, and the usual number of copies were ordered printed.

NOTICES.

Mr. Welty gave notice that he would, at an early day, introduce a bill to provide for levying, assessing and collecting Revenue for County purposes.

GENERAL FILE.

Senate Bill No. 4, "An Act to amend an Act entitled 'An Act to provide for the Support of the Government of the State of Nevada, approved March 9th, 1865,' and other Acts amendatory thereof."

Referred to Committee of the Whole.

Senate Bill No. 3, "An Act to amend an Act entitled 'An Act to provide for the Support of the Government of the State of Nevada, approved March 9th, 1865," as amended by an Act entitled "An Act to amend an Act entitled 'An Act to provide Revenue for the Support of the Government of the State of Nevada,' approved March 9th, 1865,' approved February 24th, 1866."

Referred to Committee of the Whole.

On motion of Mr. Doron, the Senate went into Committee of the Whole for consideration of special order at 12 o'clock, Senate Bill No. 1, relating to Revenue. The President in the chair.

The Committee rose, and submitted the following report:

Mr. President:

The Senate, in Committee of the Whole, have had under consideration Senate Bill No. 1, "An Act to amend an Act entitled 'An Act to provide Revenue for the Support of the Government of the State of Nevada,' approved March 9th, 1865, as amended by an Act entitled an Act to amend an Act entitled 'An Act to provide Revenue for the Support of the Government of the State of Nevada,' approved March 9th, 1865, approved February 14th, 1866," on which they report progress, and ask leave to sit again, at 2 o'clock P.M.

Leave was granted.

At 12:40 P.M., on motion of Mr. Grey, the Senate took a recess until 2 o'clock P.M.

IN SENATE.

The Senate met at 2 P.M., the President in the chair.

Roll called. No quorum being present, on motion of Mr. Doron, a call of the Senate was ordered.

Absent—Messrs. Eastman, Geller, Grey, Hastings, Proctor, and Haines.

The absentees appearing, were, on motion, excused.

On motion of Mr. Hutchins, further proceedings under the call were dispensed with.

Mr. Doron, from the Standing Committee on State Affairs, to which was referred Assembly Bill No. 2, entitled "An Act to create certain Funds," reported that they had had the same under consideration, had come to a favorable conclusion thereon, had directed their chairman to report the same back to the Senate, and to recommend its passage.

On motion of Mr. Hutchins, the Senate went into Committee of the Whole for consideration of Senate Bill No. 1. President in the chair.

The Committee rose, and submitted the following report:

Mr. President:

The Senate, in Committee of the Whole, have had under consideration Senate Bill No. 1, "An Act to amend an Act entitled 'An Act to provide Revenue for the Support of the Government of the State of Nevada,' approved March 9th, 1865," as amended by an Act entitled "An Act to amend an Act entitled 'An Act to provide Revenue for the Support of the Government of the State of Nevada,' approved March 9th, 1865, approved February 24th, 1866," on which they report progress, and ask leave to sit again on to-morrow at 11 o'clock A.M.

Leave granted.

The following communication was received from the Secretary of State:

OFFICE OF SECRETARY OF STATE, }
Carson City, March 21st, 1867. }

To the Legislature of Nevada, Senate Chamber:

GENTLEMEN—In accordance with the provisions of section thirty-five of Article four of the Constitution of this State, I have the honor to transmit herewith the following Senate bills, together with the Governor's Messages relating thereto. Said bills originated in the Senate at the Third Session of the Nevada Legislature, passed both Houses, and were presented to the Governor at such session, but the return thereof by the Governor was prevented by the final adjournment of the Legislature.

Bills Nos. 260, 218, 236, 2 [202] and 96, were filed in my office, together with the objections of the Governor, on the 18th of March, 1867, and Bill No. 133, with objections, was filed March 19th, 1867.

Very respectfully,

C. N. NOTEWARE.

Mr. Welty rose to a point of order, that it is not competent for the Senate to receive said Messages and accompanying bills, the same not being included in the business placed before the Special Session under Proclamation of the Governor.

The decision on point of order was reserved until to-morrow.

At 4:15 P.M., on motion of Mr. Grey, the Senate adjourned.

JAMES S. SLINGERLAND,
President.

Attest—B. C. BROWN,
Secretary.

IN SENATE, SPECIAL SESSION—EIGHTH DAY.

CARSON CITY, March 22d, 1867.

The Senate met pursuant to adjournment, President in the chair.

Roll called.

Present—Messrs. Doron, Eastman, Edwards, Geller, Grey, Haines, Hastings, Hutchins, Linn, Mason, Meder, Monroe, Nelson, Proctor, Stevenson, Sumner, Terry, and Welty—18.

Absent—Mr. Carpenter—1.

Prayer by the Chaplain.

The Journal of the Seventh day was read, and amended to show that after Mr. Welty raised the point of order of yesterday, Mr. Doron raised the point of order that Mr. Welty's parliamentary objection was too late, the communication having already been received by the Senate.

Mr. Hutchins rose to a question of privilege, in relation to a quotation from the Reese River *Reveille*, in the *Daily Trespass* of March 21st, 1867.

REPORTS OF COMMITTEES.

Mr. Edwards, from Committee on Public Lands, reported that they had had under consideration Senate Bill No. 7, " An Act to provide for the selection and sale of Lands granted by the United States to this State," had come to a favorable conclusion thereon, and had directed their chairman to report the same back, with a recommendation that it be referred to Committee of the Whole.

MOTIONS AND RESOLUTIONS.

Mr. Stevenson offered the following resolution:

Resolved, That the Attorney General be, and he is hereby requested to furnish to the Senate his opinion as to the authority of the Senate to act in Special Session on vetoes or bills which have been passed at the General Session of the Legislature (3d session) and were vetoed by the Governor and returned by him to the Secretary of State, said bills not having been delivered to the Governor more than five days prior to the adjournment of the session, and their subject matter not being embraced in any special Message or statement by the Governor as business for which the Special Session was convened, and not specially called to the attention of the Legislature since the convening of the Legislature in Special Session.

Mr. Monroe rose to a point of order, that Mr. Haines was not discussing the resolution, but giving the opinion of the Attorney General.

The Chair ruled the point of order well taken.

Mr. Proctor moved to lay the resolution on the table.

The yeas and nays were called for on the question by Messrs. Proctor, Doron, and Meder, and recorded as follows:

YEAS—Messrs. Edwards, Geller, Grey, Hastings, Hutchins, Monroe, Proctor, and Sumner—8.

NAYS—Messrs. Doron, Eastman, Haines, Linn, Mason, Meder, Nelson, Stevenson, Terry, and Welty—10.

So the Senate refused to lay the resolution [on] the table. •
Mr. Proctor in the chair.
Mr. Sumner moved to strike out all after the words "3d session."
Carried.
The yeas and nays were called for by Messrs. Hutchins, Grey, and Monroe, on the adoption of the resolution as amended; but no vote was had, as
Mr. Stevenson (by leave) withdrew the resolution.

MESSAGE FROM THE ASSEMBLY.

The following Message was received from the Assembly:

ASSEMBLY CHAMBER, CARSON CITY, }
March 21st, 1867. }

To the Honorable the Senate:

I am instructed to transmit to your honorable body for your consideration, Assembly Bill No. 126, entitled "An Act authorizing the County of Lyon to Fund the Outstanding Indebtedness against the General Fund of said county, to pay the Interest thereon, and for gradual Liquidation of the same," together with the veto Message of the Governor, the same having passed the Assembly this day, notwithstanding the objections of the Governor, by the following vote: Yeas, 33; Nays, 11.

Respectfully,

A. WHITFORD,
Clerk.

Mr. Hutchins moved that the bill and accompanying Message be now taken up.
Mr. Welty rose to a point of order, that it was not competent for the Senate to receive said Message and accompanying bills, the same not being included in the business placed before the Special Session under Proclamation of the Governor.
Mr. Sumner rose to a point of order, that the objection of Mr. Welty could not be considered and entertained as a point of order.
At 1 o'clock, on motion of Mr. Welty, the Senate took a recess until 2 o'clock P.M.

IN SENATE.

The Senate met at 2 P.M.
President in the chair.
Roll called.
Quorum present.
On motion of Mr. Sumner, a call of the Senate was ordered.
Absent—Messrs. Edwards, Hutchins, Mason, Nelson, Stevenson, Welty.
On motion of Mr. Hastings, the name of Mr. Carpenter was ordered to be omitted. i
The absentees appearing, were, on motion, excused.
On motion of Mr. Hutchins, further proceedings under the call were dispensed with.
On motion of Mr. Hastings, the bill and all matters thereto pertaining, was made the special order for Monday, March 25th, at 12 o'clock M.
On motion of Mr. Hutchins, the communication of the Secretary of State was taken up.
Mr. Doron moved that the Secretary of the Senate be instructed to return to

the Secretary of State his communication and the accompanying bills, with the explanation that the Senate refuses to consider them.

Mr. Proctor rose to a point of order, that there was already a point of order pending before the Senate.

Mr. Welty (by leave) withdrew his point of order raised on yesterday.

Mr. Hutchins in the chair.

The yeas and nays were called on the adoption of Mr. Doron's resolution, by Messrs. Proctor, Sumner, and Welty, and recorded as follows:

YEAS—Messrs. Doron, Eastman, Haines, Meder, Nelson, Stevenson, and Welty—7.

NAYS—Messrs. Edwards, Geller, Grey, Hastings, Hutchins, Linn, Mason, Monroe, Proctor, Sumner, and Terry—11.

So the resolution was not adopted.

At 4:20 P.M., on motion of Mr. Proctor, the Senate adjourned.

JAMES S. SLINGERLAND,
President.

Attest—B. C. BROWN,
Secretary.

IN SENATE, SPECIAL SESSION—NINTH DAY.

CARSON CITY, March 23d, 1867.

The Senate met pursuant to adjournment, President in the chair.

Roll called.

Present—Messrs. Doron, Eastman, Edwards, Geller, Grey, Haines, Hastings, Hutchins, Linn, Mason, Meder, Monroe, Nelson, Proctor, Stevenson, Sumner, Terry, and Welty—18.

Absent—0.

Prayer by the Chaplain.

The Journal of the Eighth day was read and approved.

On motion of Mr. Hastings, indefinite leave of absence was granted to Mr. Carpenter.

MOTIONS AND RESOLUTIONS.

Mr. Linn offered the following resolution:

Resolved, That the Sergeant-at-Arms be directed to draw his warrant on the Senate Contingent Fund, from the first day of the Special Session, for the per diem of the Official Reporter.

Adopted.

The following Message was received from the Assembly:

ASSEMBLY CHAMBER, CARSON CITY, }
March 22d, 1867. }

To the Hon. the Senate:

I am instructed to transmit to your honorable body, for your consideration, Assembly Joint Resolution No. 4, relating to the Enforcement of the Monroe Doctrine and Repeal of certain Neutrality Laws, the same having passed the House this day. Yeas, 31; nays, 0.

Respectfully,

A. WHITFORD,
Clerk.

Assembly Joint Resolution No. 4, "In relation to the Enforcement of the Monroe Doctrine."

Read first time; rules suspended; read second time by title.

Referred to the Committee on Federal Relations.

INTRODUCTION OF BILLS.

Mr. Welty introduced Senate Bill No. 9, "An Act supplementary to an Act entitled ' An Act to provide Revenue for the Support of the Government *of the Government* of the State of Nevada,' approved March 9th, 1866, [1865] and the Acts amendatory thereof, and to provide for Levying and Collecting Revenue for County purposes, and further prescribing the powers and duties of the Board of County Commissioners of the several Counties of this State relative thereto."

Read first time.

Mr. Proctor moved that the bill be rejected.

The yeas and nays were called for by Messrs. Hutchins, Proctor, and Sumner on the question, and recorded as follows:

YEAS—Messrs. Hastings, Hutchins, Monroe, Proctor, and Sumner—5.

NAYS—Messrs. Doron, Eastman, Edwards, Geller, Grey, Haines, Linn, Meder, Nelson, Stevenson, Terry, and Welty—12.

So the Senate refused to reject the bill.

Mr. Monroe rose to a question of privilege in relation to language used towards him by Mr. Meder, in debate.

On motion of Mr. Hutchins, the Senate went into Committee of the Whole for the consideration of Assembly Bill No. 2. President in the chair.

The Committee rose, and submitted the following report:

Mr. President:

The Senate, in Committee of the Whole, have had under consideration Assembly Bill No. 2, "An Act to create certain Funds," which they report back, and recommend the bill do pass as amended.

The amendments of the Committee of the Whole were adopted.

GENERAL FILE.

Assembly Bill No. 2, "An Act to create certain Funds."

Read third time by sections.

The yeas and nays were called on the final passage of the bill, and recorded as follows:

YEAS—Messrs. Doron, Eastman, Edwards, Geller, Grey, Haines, Hastings, Hutchins, Linn, Mason, Meder, Monroe, Nelson, Proctor, Sumner, Terry, and Welty—17.

NAYS—Mr. Stevenson—1.

So the bill passed.

Mr. Sumner moved that when the Senate adjourn, it do so until Monday, March 25th, at 12 o'clock M.

Carried.

On motion of Mr. Edwards, the Senate went into Committee of the Whole for the consideration of Senate Bill No. 1.

President in the chair.

The Committee rose, and submitted the following report:

Mr. President:

The Senate, in Committee of the Whole, have had under consideration Senate Bill No. 1, "An Act to amend an Act entitled 'An Act to provide Revenue for the Support of the Government of the State of Nevada,' approved March 9th, 1865, as amended by an Act entitled 'An Act to amend an Act to provide Revenue for the Support of the Government of the State of Nevada,' approved March 9th, 1865, approved Feb. 24th, 1866," on which they report progress, and ask leave to sit again at 3 o'clock P.M.

The report of the Committee was adopted.

Mr. Doron (by leave) offered the following resolution:

Resolved, That the amounts allowed by Resolution of the Senate of March 18th, 1867, for the purchase of stationery, be ordered paid out of the Senate Contingent Fund.

Adopted.

Mr. Sumner moved the Senate do now adjourn.

The yeas and nays were called for by Messrs. Terry, Sumner, and Grey on the question, and recorded as follows:

YEAS—Messrs. Geller, Grey, Hastings, Hutchins, Monroe, Proctor, and Sumner—7.

NAYS—Messrs. Doron, Eastman, Edwards, Haines, Linn, Mason, Meder, Nelson, Stevenson, Terry, and Welty—11.

So the Senate refused to adjourn.

At 1 : 45 P.M., on motion of Mr. Welty, the Senate took a recess until 3 o'clock P.M.

IN SENATE.

The Senate met at 3 P.M., President in the chair.

Roll called. Quorum present.

On motion of Mr. Linn, the Senate went into Committee of the Whole for the consideration of Senate Bill No. 1. President in the chair.

The Committee rose, and submitted the following report:

Mr. President:

The Senate, in Committee of the Whole, have had under consideration Senate Bill No. 1, "An Act to amend an Act entitled 'An Act to provide Revenue for the Support of the Government of the State of Nevada,' approved March 9th, 1865, etc.," which they report back with various amendments, and recommend the bill be ordered engrossed as amended.

The amendments recommended by the Committee were adopted.

Senate Bill No. 1, "An Act to amend an Act entitled 'An Act to provide Revenue for the Support of the Government of the State of Nevada,' approved March 9th, 1865, etc."

Mr. Welty moved the bill be ordered engrossed.

The yeas and nays were called for on the question by Messrs. Welty, Hutchins, and Proctor, and recorded as follows:

YEAS—Messrs. Doron, Eastman, Edwards, Haines, Linn, Mason, Meder, Stevenson, Terry, and Welty—10.

NAYS—Messrs. Geller, Hastings, Hutchins, Monroe, and Proctor—5.

So the bill was ordered engrossed.

At 5 P.M., on motion of Mr. Hastings, the Senate adjourned.

JAMES S. SLINGERLAND,
President.

Attest—B. C. BROWN,
Secretary.

––––––

IN SENATE, SPECIAL SESSION—ELEVENTH DAY.

CARSON CITY, March 25th, 1867.

The Senate met pursuant to adjournment, President in the chair.

Roll called.

Present—Messrs. Doron, Eastman, Edwards, Geller, Grey, Haines, Hastings, Hutchins, Linn, Mason, Meder, Monroe, Nelson, Proctor, Stevenson, Sumner, Terry, and Welty—18.

Absent—0.

Prayer by the Chaplain.

The Journal of the Ninth day was read and approved.

SPECIAL ORDER.

Assembly Bill No. 126, entitled "An Act authorizing the County of Lyon to Fund the outstanding Indebtedness against the General Fund of said County, to pay the interest, and for further liquidation of the same."

Mr. Hastings presented a Petition from residents of Lyon County, representing $1,200,000 taxable property, against passage of said bill.

The petition was referred to the Committee on Counties and County Boundaries.

On motion of Mr. Hastings, the bill was made the special order for Thursday, March 28th, at 12 o'clock.

REPORTS OF COMMITTEES.

Mr. Welty reported that the Standing Committee on Engrossment had carefully compared the following entitled bill with the original, and found the same correctly engrossed, viz:

Senate Bill No. 1, "An Act to amend an Act entitled 'An Act to provide Revenue for the Support of the Government of the State of Nevada,' approved March 9th, 1865," as amended by an Act entitled "An Act to amend an Act entitled 'An Act to provide Revenue for the Support of the Government of the State of Nevada,' approved March 9th, 1865, approved Feb. 24th, 1866," and herewith report the same back to the Senate.

MESSAGES FROM THE ASSEMBLY.

The following Messages were received from the Assembly:

ASSEMBLY CHAMBER, CARSON CITY, }
March 23d, 1867.

To the Hon. the Senate:

I am instructed to inform your honorable body that the House has this day concurred in the amendments of the Senate to Assembly Bill No. 2, entitled " An Act to create certain Funds."

Respectfully,

A. WHITFORD,
Clerk.

ASSEMBLY CHAMBER, CARSON CITY, }
March 22d, 1867.

To the Hon. the Senate:

I am instructed to transmit to your honorable body for your consideration. Assembly Bill No. 164, entitled " An Act for the organization of a Board of Education in Counties that polled three thousand votes or more at the general election in November, A.D. 1866, or that may thereafter at any general election cast that number of votes or more, and amendatory of and supplemental to 'An Act to provide for the Maintenance and Support of Public Schools,' approved March 20th, 1865," the same having passed at the Third Session of the Legislature of the State of Nevada, and returned to the Secretary of State without the approval of the Governor; the Secretary of State having laid the same before the House, for further action, and the House this day passed the bill notwithstanding the objections of the Governor: Yeas, 29; Nays, 4.

Respectfully,

A. WHITFORD,
Clerk.

SECOND READING OF BILLS.

Senate Bill No. 9, " An Act supplementary to an Act entitled 'An Act to provide Revenue for the Support of the Government of the State of Nevada, approved March 9th, 1865,' and the Acts amendatory thereof, and providing for Levying and Collecting Revenue for County Purposes, and further prescribing the Powers and Duties of the Board of County Commissioners of the several Counties of this State relative thereto."

Read second time by title, and referred to Committee on Ways and Means.

GENERAL FILE.

Senate Bill No. 1, "An Act to amend an Act entitled 'An Act to provide Revenue for the Support of the Government of the State of Nevada, approved March 9th, 1865,' as amended by an Act entitled an Act to amend an Act entitled 'An Act to provide Revenue for the Support of the Government of the State of Nevada,' aproved March 9th, 1865, approved February 24th, 1866."

On motion of Mr. Welty, the bill was referred to a Committee of one, with instructions to insert the words "section one."

The Chair appointed Mr. Welty.

The Committee reported the bill amended as directed.

The report was adopted.

The bill was read third time by sections.

Mr. Doron in the chair.

Mr. Proctor moved that the bill be referred to a Select Committee of three, to ascertain if the bill be correctly engrossed.

Lost.

Mr. Proctor in the chair.

Mr. Sumner moved that the bill be made the special order for Wednesday, March 27th, at 12 o'clock M.

The yeas and nays were called for on the question, by Messrs. Doron, Welty, and Hutchins, and recorded as follows:

YEAS—Messrs. Geller, Grey, Hastings, Hutchins, Monroe, Nelson, Proctor, and Sumner—8.

NAYS—Messrs. Doron, Eastman, Edwards, Linn, Mason, Meder, Stevenson, Terry, and Welty—10.

So the Senate refused to defer the bill.

Mr. Doron moved the previous question.

The yeas and nays were called for by Messrs. Welty, Haines, and Linn, and recorded as follows:

YEAS—Messrs. Doron, Eastman, Edwards, Haines, Linn, Mason, Meder, Nelson, Stevenson, Terry, and Welty—11.

NAYS—Messrs. Geller, Grey, Hastings, Hutchins, Monroe, Proctor, and Sumner—7.

So the previous question was ordered.

The yeas and nays were called on the final passage of the bill, and recorded as follows:

YEAS—Messrs. Doron, Eastman, Edwards, Haines, Hutchins, Linn, Mason, Meder, Nelson, Stevenson, Sumner, Terry, and Welty—13.

NAYS—Messrs. Geller, Grey, Hastings, Monroe, and Proctor—5.

So the bill passed.

Mr. Hutchins gave notice, that on to-morrow he would move a reconsideration of the vote whereby the bill passed.

Mr. Sumner gave notice that on to-morrow he would move a reconsideration of the vote whereby the bill passed.

On motion of Mr. Welty, the title of the bill was amended so as to strike out all after the figures first appearing—1865—and insert the words "and other Acts amendatory thereof."

On motion of Mr. Welty, Senate Bill No. 4 was now taken up, "An Act to amend an Act entitled 'An Act to provide Revenue for the Support of the Government of the State of Nevada,' approved March 9th, 1865, and other Acts amendatory thereof."

On motion of Mr. Welty, the vote whereby the bill was referred to Committee of the Whole was now reconsidered.

Mr. Hutchins moved to adjourn.

The yeas and nays were called for on the question, by Messrs. Sumner, Doron, and Haines, and recorded as follows:

YEAS—Messrs. Geller, Grey, Hastings, Hutchins, Monroe, Proctor, Sumner, and Terry—8.

NAYS—Messrs. Doron, Eastman, Edwards, Haines, Linn, Mason, Meder, Nelson, Stevenson, and Welty—10.

So the Senate refused to adjourn.

Mr. Welty moved the bill be ordered engrossed.

The yeas and nays were called for on the question, by Messrs. Grey, Welty, and Terry, and recorded as follows:

YEAS—Messrs. Doron, Eastman, Haines, Hastings, Linn, Mason, Meder, Nelson, Terry, and Welty—10.

NAYS—Messrs. Edwards, Geller, Grey, Hutchins, Monroe, Proctor, Stevenson, and Sumner—8.

So the bill was ordered engrossed.

At 4:30 P.M., on motion of Mr. Monroe, the Senate adjourned.

JAMES S. SLINGERLAND,
President.

Attest—B. C. BROWN,
Secretary.

IN SENATE, SPECIAL SESSION—TWELFTH DAY.

CARSON CITY, March 26th, 1867.

The Senate met pursuant to adjournment, President in the chair.

Roll called.

Present—Messrs. Doron, Eastman, Edwards, Geller, Grey, Haines, Hastings, Hutchins, Linn, Mason, Meder, Monroe, Nelson, Proctor, Stevenson, Sumner, Terry, and Welty—18.

Absent—0.

Prayer by the Chaplain.

The Journal of the Eleventh day was read and approved.

REPORTS OF COMMITTEES.

Mr. Mason, from Standing Committee on Federal Relations, to which was referred Assembly Joint Resolution No. 4, relating to the Enforcement of the Monroe Doctrine and Repeal of certain Neutrality Laws, reported that they had had the same under consideration, had come to a favorable conclusion thereon, and recommend its passage.

Also, Senate Memorial and Joint Resolution No. 6, concerning Ireland, had come to a favorable conclusion thereon, and recommend its passage.

Mr. Hastings reported that the Standing Committee on Engrossment had carefully compared the following entitled bill with the original, and found the same correctly engrossed, viz:

Senate Bill No. 4, "An Act to amend an Act entitled 'An Act to provide Revenue for the Support of the Government of the State of Nevada,' approved March 9th, 1865, and other Acts amendatory thereof," and herewith report the same back to the Senate.

MOTIONS AND RESOLUTIONS.

Mr. Edwards moved that the reconsideration of the vote had on yesterday, on Senate Bill No. 1, be now taken up.

Mr. Edwards moved the previous question.

Mr. Hutchins raised the point of order, that Mr. Edwards not having given notice to reconsider, could not make the motion.

The Chair ruled the point of order well taken.

Mr. Edwards appealed from the decision of the Chair.

On the question: Shall the decision of the Chair be sustained? the yeas and nays were called for by Messrs. Doron, Proctor, and Hutchins, and recorded as follows:

YEAS—Messrs. Geller, Hastings, Hutchins, Monroe, Proctor, and Sumner—6.

NAYS—Messrs. Doron, Eastman, Edwards, Grey, Haines, Linn, Mason, Meder, Nelson, Stevenson, Terry, and Welty—12.

So the decision of the Chair was not sustained.

On the motion of Mr. Edwards, in relation to the previous question, the yeas and nays were called for by Messrs. Sumner, Proctor, and Hastings, and recorded as follows:

YEAS—Messrs. Doron, Eastman, Edwards, Haines, Mason, Meder, Stevenson, Terry, and Welty—10.

NAYS—Messrs. Geller, Grey, Hastings, Hutchins, Monroe, Nelson, Proctor, and Sumner—8.

So the previous question was ordered.

On the question: Shall the vote whereby Senate Bill No. 1 was passed on yesterday be now reconsidered? the yeas and nays were called for by Messrs. Sumner, Proctor, and Geller, and recorded as follows:

YEAS—Messrs. Geller, Grey, Hastings, Hutchins, Monroe, Nelson, Proctor, and Sumner—8.

NAYS—Messrs. Doron, Eastman, Edwards, Haines, Linn, Mason, Meder, Stevenson, Terry, and Welty—10.

So the Senate refused to reconsider the vote.

Messrs. Hutchins and Sumner requested leave to have the record of yesterday changed, to show that they voted against Senate Bill No. 1.

Granted.

The following protest was received:

The undersigned protest against the passage of Senate Bill No. 1, for the following reasons:

Because it is exceedingly impolitic to change the present Revenue Laws so as to increase the burden of taxation on our mining interests, even if additional State income were required.

Because there is no necessity for changing the present Revenue Laws so as to increase the present amount of taxation; the State income, under existing levies, being fully adequate to meet the interest on the State debt, and the current expenses of the State Government.

Senate Chamber, Carson City, Nevada, March 26th, 1867.

> O. H. GREY,
> CHARLES A. SUMNER,
> F. M. PROCTOR,
> FRED. HUTCHINS,
> S. GELLER,
> D. L. HASTINGS.

Mr. Meder moved that the protest be rejected.

The yeas and nays were called for on the question, by Messrs. Sumner, Doron, and Meder, and recorded as follows:

YEAS—Messrs. Doron, Eastman, Haines, Linn, Mason, Meder, Stevenson, and Welty—8.

NAYS—Messrs. Edwards, Geller, Grey, Hastings, Hutchins, Monroe, Nelson, Proctor, Sumner, and Terry—10.

So the Senate refused to reject the protest.

Mr. Welty rose to a question of privilege, in relation to language used some days since, in which he is quoted as saying, " that he would rather be successful than right."

Mr. Doron in the chair.

Mr. Proctor charged that Mr. Welty, by his own admission, had ordered Senate Bill No. 1 to be engrossed differently from what it passed the Senate.

Mr. Welty demanded a committee of investigation on the charge.

The Chair appointed Messrs. Edwards, Mason, and Grey.

Mr. Sumner presented a remonstrance of the citizens of Virginia City, Storey County, protesting against the passage of Assembly Bill No. 77, " An Act providing for the Payment of certain Indebtedness due certain parties from the City of Virginia."

MESSAGE FROM THE ASSEMBLY.

The following Message was received from the Assembly:

> ASSEMBLY CHAMBER, CARSON CITY,
> March 26th, 1867.

To the Hon. the Senate:

I am instructed to transmit to your hon. body for your consideration, Assembly Bill No. 5, entitled "An Act supplementary to an Act entitled 'An Act to provide Revenue for the Support of the Government of the State of Nevada,' approved March 9th, 1865, and providing for Levying and Collecting Revenue for County purposes, and further prescribing the powers and duties of the Board of County Commissioners of the several counties of this State relative thereto," the same having passed the House on yesterday. Yeas, 24; Nays, 3.

Respectfully,

A. WHITFORD,
Clerk.

Assembly Bill No. 5, "An Act supplementary to an Act entitled 'An Act to provide Revenue for the Support of the Government of the State of Nevada,' March 9th, 1865, and providing for Levying and Collecting Revenue for County purposes, and further prescribing the powers and duties of the Board of County Commissioners of the several counties of this State relative thereto."

Read first time; rules suspended; read second time by title, and referred to Committee on Ways and Means.

Mr. Hastings moved to adjourn.

Mr. Haines moved, as a substitute motion, that the Senate take a recess until 3:30 P.M.

The yeas and nays were called for on the question by Messrs. Sumner, Meder, and Haines, and recorded as follows:

YEAS—Messrs. Doron, Eastman, Edwards, Haines, Linn, Meder, Stevenson, Terry, and Welty—9.

NAYS—Messrs. Geller, Grey, Hastings, Hutchins, Mason, Monroe, Nelson, Proctor, and Sumner—9.

The President declared the motion lost.

At 1:20 P.M., on motion of Mr. Hastings, the Senate adjourned.

JAMES S. SLINGERLAND,
President.

Attest—B. C. BROWN,
Secretary.

IN SENATE, SPECIAL SESSION—THIRTEENTH DAY.

CARSON CITY, March 27th, 1867.

The Senate met pursuant to adjournment, President in the chair.

Roll called.

Present—Messrs. Doron, Eastman, Edwards, Geller, Grey, Haines, Hastings, Hutchins, Linn, Mason, Meder, Monroe, Nelson, Proctor, Stevenson, Sumner, Terry, and Welty—18.

Absent—0.

Prayer by the Chaplain.

The Journal of the Twelfth day was read and approved.

PRESENTATION OF PETITIONS.

Mr. Sumner presented a remonstrance from the citizens of Storey County, represented in mass meeting, against the passage of Senate Bill No. 1.

REPORTS OF COMMITTEES.

Mr. Haines, Chairman of Committee on Ways and Means, reported that they had had under consideration Assembly Bill No. 5, had come to a favorable conclusion thereon, had agreed upon certain amendments thereto, and recommend the passage thereof as proposed to be amended.

Amendments: On line 15 of section 1 strike out "twenty-five" and insert "fifty."

Also, on nineteenth line, or last line but one of section, strike out "fifty" and insert "twenty-five."

Also, section 5, strike out on first line the word "the" between "of" and "Mines."

Also, section 7, after the words "for County purposes," insert "except License taxes."

Also, strike out the words "one hundred" preceding the word "cents" and insert "seventy-five."

The Special Committee, to which was referred the charge of Mr. Proctor against Mr. Welty, to wit: having ordered Senate Bill No. 1 to be engrossed different from the way in which it was ordered to engrossment on yesterday by the Senate, reported that they had had the matter under consideration, and from the testimony adduced by Messrs. Welty and Meder, had come to the conclusion that Mr. Welty only performed the duty required of him as a member of the Standing Committee on Engrossment; that he could not have acted otherwise; and that the charge having no foundation in fact, they recommend it be dismissed by the Senate.

MOTIONS AND RESOLUTIONS.

Senate Joint Resolution No. 11, "Relating to Claims of the State of Nevada against the Government of the United States."

Read first time; rules suspended; read second time by title, and referred to Committee on Federal Relations.

Mr. Doron offered the following resolution:

Resolved, That the Sergeant-at-Arms be directed to issue his warrant to the Official Reporter, for the same amount as to other attachés of the Senate, for stationery.

Adopted.

GENERAL FILE.

Senate Bill No. 4, "An Act to amend an Act entitled 'An Act to provide Revenue for the Support of the Government of the State of Nevada,' approved March 9th, 1865, and other Acts amendatory thereof."

Mr. Linn was, on motion, granted leave to withdraw the bill.

Senate Bill No. 7, "An Act to provide for the Selection and Sale of Lands granted by the United States to the State of Nevada."

Referred to Committee of the Whole.

Assembly Joint Resolution No. 4, relating to the enforcement of the Monroe Doctrine and repeal of certain Neutrality Laws.

Read third time.

The yeas and nays were called on the final passage of the bill, and recorded as follows:

YEAS—Messrs. Doron, Eastman, Edwards, Geller, Grey, Haines, Hastings, Hutchins, Mason, Meder, Monroe, Nelson, Proctor, Stevenson, Sumner, Terry, and Welty—17.

NAYS—0.

So the resolution passed.

Mr. Hastings (by leave) gave notice that on to-morrow he would introduce a land bill.

Senate Memorial and Joint Resolution concerning Ireland ordered engrossed.

On motion of Mr. Welty, the Senate went into Committee of the Whole for consideration of Assembly Bill No. 5.

President in the chair.

The Committee rose, and submitted the following report:

Mr. President:

The Senate in Committee of the Whole have had under consideration Assembly Bill No. 5, " An Act supplementary to an Act to provide Revenue for the Support of the Government of the State of Nevada, approved March 9th, 1865, and providing for Levying and Collecting Revenue for County purposes, and further prescribing the Powers and Duties of the Board of County Commissioners of the several Counties of this State relative thereto."

On which they report progress, and ask leave to sit again at 3 o'clock P.M.

Leave granted.

On motion of Mr. Welty, the report of the Committee was adopted.

At 1 : 30 P.M., on motion of Mr. Welty, the Senate took a recess until 3 o'clock P.M.

IN SENATE.

The Senate met at 3 o'clock P.M.

President in the chair.

Roll called.

Quorum present.

Mr. Hastings (by leave) reported that the Standing Committee on Engrossment had carefully compared the following entitled Joint Resolution with the original, and found the same correctly engrossed, viz : " Senate Memorial and Joint Resolution No. 6, concerning Ireland," and herewith report the same back to the Senate.

On motion of Mr. Hastings, Senate Memorial and Joint Resolution No. 6 was now taken up.

Senate Memorial and Joint Resolution No. 6, relative to Ireland.

Read third time.

The yeas and nays were called on the final passage of the resolution, and recorded as follows:

YEAS—Messrs. Doron, Eastman, Edwards, Geller, Haines, Hasting, Hutchins, Linn, Mason, Meder, Nelson, Stevenson, Sumner, Terry, and Welty—15.

NAYS—0.

So the resolution passed.

On motion of Mr. Stevenson, the Senate went into Committee of the Whole for the further consideration of Assembly Bill No. 5.

President in the chair.

The Committee rose, and submitted the following report:

Mr. President:

The Senate in Committee of the Whole have had under consideration Assembly Bill No. 5, " An Act supplementary to an Act entitled 'An Act to provide Revenue for the Support of the Government of the State of Nevada,' 'etc.," which they report back, with amendments, and recommend the bill do pass as amended.

The report of the Committee was adopted.

Assembly Bill No. 5, "An Act supplementary to an Act entitled 'An Act to provide Revenue for the Support of the Government of the State of Nevada,' approved March 9th, 1867, [1865] etc."

Read third time by sections. The yeas and nays were called on the final passage of the bill, and recorded as follows:

YEAS—Messrs. Doron, Eastman, Edwards, Haines, Linn, Mason, Meder, Nelson, Stevenson, Sumner, Terry, and Welty—12.

NAYS—Messrs. Geller, Hastings, Hutchins, and Monroe—4.

So the bill passed.

Mr. Sumner gave notice that on to-morrow he would move a reconsideration of the vote whereby Assembly Bill No. 5 was passed.

MESSAGES FROM THE ASSEMBLY.

The following Messages were received from the Assembly:

ASSEMBLY CHAMBER, CARSON CITY, }
March 26th, 1867. }

To the Honorable the Senate:

I am instructed to transmit to your honorable body for your consideration, Assembly Bill No. 5, [3] entitled " An Act to provide for the Selection and Sale of Lands granted by the United States to the State of Nevada," the same having passed the House on yesterday. Yeas, 28; nays, 2.

Respectfully,

A. WHITFORD,
Clerk.

ASSEMBLY CHAMBER, CARSON CITY, }
March 27th, 1867. }

To the Hon. the Senate:

I am instructed to transmit to your honorable body for your consideration, the following Assembly Resolutions, viz:

No. 7, relative to Reconstruction Measures;

Preamble and Resolutions No. 8, relating to Lands granted to the State of Nevada by the United States;

No. 9, relating to Jeff. Davis; all of which have passed the House.

Respectfully,

A. WHITFORD,
Clerk.

To the Hon. the Senate:

I am instructed to transmit to your honorable body for your consideration, Assembly Bill No. 77, entitled "An Act providing for the Payment of certain Indebtedness due certain parties from the City of Virginia," which passed the Third Session of the Legislature, and returned to the Secretary of State with the Governor's objections, and placed before the Assembly by the Secretary of State, the same having passed the Assembly notwithstanding the objections of the Governor.

Respectfully,

A. WHITFORD,
Clerk.

Assembly Bill No. 3, "An Act to provide for the Selection and Sale of Lands granted by the United States to the State of Nevada."

Read first time; rules suspended; read second time by title, and referred to Committee of the Whole.

Assembly Joint Resolution No. 7, relative to Reconstruction Measures.

Read first time; rules suspended; read second time by title, and referred to Committee on Federal Relations.

Assembly Preamble and Resolution No. 8, relating to Lands granted to the State of Nevada by the United States.

Read first time; rules suspended; read second time by title, and referred to Committee on Public Lands.

Assembly Concurrent Resolution No. 9, relating to Jeff. Davis.

Read first time.

Mr. Hutchins moved the resolution be indefinitely postponed.

Mr. Sumner moved, as a substitute, to refer the resolution to the Committee on Federal Relations.

Carried.

Assembly Bill No. 77, "An Act providing for the Payment of certain Indebtedness due certain parties from the City of Virginia."

Mr. Doron moved that the bills and veto Messages, with the exception of the Lyon County Funding Bill, be made the special order for Friday, March 29th, 1867, at 12 o'clock.

Carried.

On motion of Mr. Monroe, the Senate went into Committee of the Whole for consideration of Senate Bill No. 3.

Mr. Doron in the chair.

The Committee rose, and submitted the following report:

Mr. President:

The Senate in Committee of the Whole have had under consideration Senate Bill No. 3, "An Act to amend an Act entitled 'An Act to provide Revenue for the Support of the Government of the State of Nevada,' approved March 9th, 1865," as amended by "An Act entitled 'An Act to amend an Act to provide Revenue for the Support of the Government of the State of Nevada,' approved March 9th, [1865] approved Feb. 24th, 1866," which they report back, and recommend the bill be indefinitely postponed.

Senate Bill No. 3, "An Act to amend an Act entitled 'An Act to provide Revenue for the Support of the Government of the State of Nevada," etc.

Mr. Meder moved that the report of the Committee be adopted.

The yeas and nays were called for on the question by Messrs. Sumner, Mason, and Grey, and recorded as follows:

YEAS—Messrs. Doron, Eastman, Edwards, Haines, Linn, Mason, Meder, Terry, and Welty—9.
NAYS—Messrs. Geller, Hastings, Monroe, Stevenson, and Sumner—5.

So the bill was indefinitely postponed.
At 4:20 P.M., on motion of Mr. Monroe, the Senate adjourned.

JAMES S. SLINGERLAND,
President.

Attest—B. C. BROWN,
  Secretary.

IN SENATE, SPECIAL SESSION—FOURTEENTH DAY.

CARSON CITY, March 28th, 1867.

The Senate met pursuant to adjournment.
President in the chair.
Roll called.
Present—Messrs. Doron, Eastman, Geller, Grey, Haines, Hastings, Hutchins, Linn, Mason, Meder, Proctor, Stevenson, and Sumner—13.
Absent—Messrs. Edwards, Monroe, Nelson, Terry, and Welty—5.
On motion of Mr. Proctor, a call of the Senate was ordered.
Absent—Messrs. Edwards, Monroe, Terry, and Welty.
Messrs. Terry, Monroe and Welty appearing, were excused on paying a fine of one dollar each.
On motion of Mr. Doron, further proceedings under the call were dispensed with.
On motion of Mr. Doron, Mr. Edwards was granted leave of absence for one day.
Prayer by the Chaplain.
The Journal of the Thirteenth day was read and approved.

REPORTS OF COMMITTEES.

Mr. Mason, from Standing Committee on Federal Relations, to which was referred Joint Resolution in regard to Claims of the State of Nevada against the Government of the United States, reported that they had had the same under consideration, had directed their chairman to report the same to the Senate, and recommend its passage.

MOTIONS AND RESOLUTIONS.

Mr. Sumner, in accordance with the notice given yesterday, moved that the vote whereby Assembly Bill No. 5 was passed, be now reconsidered.
The yeas and nays were called for on the question, by Messrs. Welty, Meder, and Terry, and recorded as follows:

YEAS—Messrs. Geller, Grey, Hastings, Hutchins, Monroe, Proctor, and Sumner—7.
NAYS—Messrs. Doron, Eastman, Haines, Linn, Mason, Meder, Nelson, Stevenson, Terry, and Welty—10.

So the Senate refused to reconsider.

MESSAGES FROM THE ASSEMBLY.

The following Message was received from the Assembly:

ASSEMBLY CHAMBER, CARSON CITY,}
March 28th, 1867.

To the Honorable the Senate:

I am instructed to request your honorable body to return to the Assembly, Concurrent Resolution No. 9, relating to Jefferson Davis, for their further consideration.

Respectfully,

A. WHITFORD,
Clerk.

On motion of Mr. Doron, the Committee on Federal Relations were requested to report back Assembly Concurrent Resolution No. 9.

Mr. Mason, from Committee on Federal Relations, reported that they had had under consideration Assembly Concurrent Resolution No. 9, concerning Jeff. Davis, and reported the same back, without recommendation.

On motion of Mr. Doron, the Secretary was instructed to return said resolution to the Assembly, in accordance with their request.

INTRODUCTION OF BILLS.

Mr. Hastings introduced Senate Bill No. 16, "An Act to provide for the Selection and Sale of Lands granted by the United States to *this* [the] State of Nevada."

Read first time; rules suspended; read second time by title, and referred to Committee of the Whole, and the usual number ordered printed.

SPECIAL ORDER.

Assembly Bill No. 126, "An Act authorizing the County of Lyons to Fund the outstanding Indebtedness against the General Fund of said County, to pay the interest thereon, and for the gradual liquidation of the same."

Mr. Proctor rose to a point of order, that the Senate could not act on the bill, inasmuch as the Message was directed to the Secretary of State, instead of the House where the bill originated.

The Chair ruled the point of order not well taken.

Mr. Proctor appealed from the decision of the Chair.

The yeas and nays were called on the question, by Messrs. Welty, Terry, and Proctor, and recorded as follows:

YEAS—Messrs. Doron, Haines, Hastings, Linn, Mason, Meder, Monroe, Nelson, Stevenson, Terry, and Welty—11.

NAYS—Messrs. Geller, Proctor, and Sumner—3.

So the decision of the Chair was sustained.

Mr. Welty raised the point of order, that the question before the Senate was the reconsideration of the vote whereby the bill passed, would require a majority vote.

The Chair ruled the point of order not well taken.

On the question : "Shall the bill pass, notwithstanding the objections of the Governor ?" the yeas and nays were called, and recorded as follows:

YEAS—Messrs. Geller and Proctor—2.
NAYS—Messrs. Doron, Grey, Haines, Hastings, Linn, Mason, Meder, Monroe, Nelson, Stevenson, Sumner, Terry, and Welty—13.

So the bill did not pass.
Mr. Nelson rose to a question of privilege, in relation to a publication in the "Territorial Enterprise" of March 28th, 1867.
At 12 : 50 P.M., on motion of Mr. Stevenson, the Senate took a recess until 2 o'clock P.M.

IN SENATE.

The Senate met at 2 P.M., President in the chair.
Roll called.
Quorum present.
Senate Joint Resolution No. 11, "In regard to Claims of the State of Nevada against the United States."
Read third time; the yeas and nays were called on the final passage of the bill, and recorded as follows:

YEAS—Messrs. Doron, Eastman, Geller, Haines, Hastings, Linn, Mason, Meder, Nelson, Proctor, Stevenson, and Terry—12.
NAYS—0.

So the resolution passed.
Mr. Mason, by leave, introduced Senate Joint Resolution No. 17, "Requesting Congressional and Executive action in regard to affairs in Utah Territory."
Read first time; rules suspended; read second time by title; referred to Committee of the Whole, and made the special order for to-morrow at 11 A.M.
On motion of Mr. Terry, a call of the Senate was ordered.
Absent—Messrs. Grey, Hutchins, Monroe, Sumner, and Welty.
On motion, Mr. Sumner was granted leave of absence for the day.
On motion of Mr. Mason, further proceedings under the call were dispensed with.
On motion of Mr. Linn, the Assembly Messages were now taken up.

MESSAGE FROM THE ASSEMBLY.

The following Message was received from the Assembly :

ASSEMBLY CHAMBER, CARSON CITY, ⎱
March 28th, 1867. ⎰

To the Hon. the Senate :
I am directed to inform your honorable body that the House this day concurred in the third and fourth amendments of the Senate to Assembly Bill No. 5 ; and refused to concur in first, second, and fifth amendments, and respectfully ask that your honorable body do recede therefrom.
Respectfully,
A. WHITFORD,
Clerk.

Mr. Doron moved that the Senate adhere to its amendments on Assembly Bill No. 5, not concurred in by the Senate.

Mr. Proctor moved as a substitute, that the Senate recede from its amendments to Assembly Bill No. 5.

Mr. Geller raised the point of order, that on the question the yeas and nays should be called, and that a constitutional majority is required to recede from its amendments.

The Chair ruled the point of order not well taken.

The question on Mr. Proctor's substitute motion, "That the Senate recede from its amendments to Assembly Bill."

Lost.

Question on Mr. Doron's motion, "That the Senate adhere to its amendments to Assembly Bill No. 5?"

Carried.

On motion of Mr. Haines, a Committee of Conference on Assembly Bill No. 5, consisting of three, was appointed by the Chair, viz: Messrs. Haines, Stevenson, and Nelson.

At 3:5 P.M., on motion of Mr. Proctor, the Senate adjourned.

JAMES S. SLINGERLAND,
President.

Attest—JOHN R. EARDLEY,
Assistant Secretary.

IN SENATE, SPECIAL SESSION—FIFTEENTH DAY.

CARSON CITY, March 29th, 1867.

The Senate met pursuant to adjournment, President in the chair.

Roll called.

Present—Messrs. Doron, Eastman, Geller, Grey, Haines, Hastings, Hutchins, Linn, Mason, Meder, Monroe, Nelson, Proctor, Stevenson, Terry, and Welty —16.

Absent—Messrs. Edwards and Sumner—2.

Prayer by the Chaplain.

The Journal of the Fourteenth day was read and approved.

On motion of Mr. Grey, Mr. Sumner was granted leave of absence for one day.

On motion of Mr. Hastings, leave of absence was granted to Mr. Edwards for one day.

On motion of Mr. Haines, indefinite leave of absence was granted to Mr. B. C. Brown, Secretary of the Senate.

On motion of Mr. Proctor, the Senate went into Committee of the Whole for the consideration of Senate Joint Resolution No. 17.

President in the chair.

The Committee rose, and submitted the following report:

Mr. President:

The Senate, in Committee of the Whole, have had under consideration Senate Joint Resolution No. 17, requesting Congressional and Executive action in regard to affairs in Utah Territory, which they report back, and recommend the resolution do pass.

Senate Joint Resolution No. 17, requesting Congressional and Executive action in regard to Utah Territory.
On motion, the recommendation of the Committee of the Whole was adopted.
Read third time.
Mr. Hutchins raised the point of order, that the Governor had not called the attention of the Legislature to the subject.
The Chair ruled the point of order not well taken.
The yeas and nays were called on the final passage of the resolution, and recorded as follows:

YEAS—Messrs. Doron, Haines, Hastings, Linn, Mason, Meder, Monroe, Nelson, Terry, and Welty—10.
NAYS—Messrs. Eastman, Geller, Grey, Hutchins, Proctor, and Stevenson—6.

So the resolution passed.
Mr. Grey presented a petition from citizens of Storey County, praying for the passage of "An Act for the Payment of certain Indebtedness of the City of Virginia," over the Governor's veto.

MOTIONS AND RESOLUTIONS.

Mr. Hutchins introduced Senate Concurrent Resolution No. 18, in relation to adjournment of Special Session.
Mr. Hutchins was granted leave to withdraw the resolution.
On motion of Mr. Haines, Assembly Messages were now taken up.

MESSAGE FROM THE ASSEMBLY.

The following Message was received from the Assembly:

ASSEMBLY CHAMBER, CARSON CITY, }
March 29th, 1867. }

To the Honorable the Senate:
I am directed to return to your honorable body Senate Bill No. 1, entitled "An Act to amend an Act entitled 'An Act to provide Revenue for the Support of the Government of the State of Nevada,' approved March 9th, 1865, and other Acts amendatory thereof," the same having passed the House on yesterday, without amendment. Yeas, 32; nays, 4.
Respectfully,
A. WHITFORD,
Clerk.

Mr. Monroe offered the following resolution:

Resolved, That a committee of three be appointed to consider the propriety of buying a State Capitol, to save the expense of renting.

Adopted.
The Chair appointed Messrs. Monroe, Geller, and Meder.

SPECIAL ORDER.

The bills and veto Messages of the Governor from the last session.

Mr. Eastman moved, that the bills and veto Messages be indefinitely postponed.

Mr. Hutchins raised the point of order, that such a motion could not be entertained at this time, the only question being: Shall the bills pass, notwithstanding the veto of the Governor?

The Chair ruled the point of order well taken.

On motion of Mr. Proctor, the bills and veto Messages of the Governor were now taken up.

Assembly Bill No. 77, "An Act providing for the Payment of certain Indebtedness due certain parties from the City of Virginia."

On the question: Shall the bill pass, notwithstanding the objection of the Governor? the yeas and nays were called, and recorded as follows:

YEAS—Messrs. Geller, Grey, Hastings, Hutchins, Linn, Mason, Meder, Monroe, Nelson, Proctor, Stevenson, Terry, and Welty—13.

NAYS—Messrs. Doron, Eastman, and Haines—3.

So the bill passed.

Assembly Bill No. 164, "An Act entitled 'An Act for the organization of a Board of Education in Counties that polled three thousand votes or more at the General Election in the State of Nevada, in November, A.D. 1866, or that may hereafter at any General Election cast that number of votes or more, and amendatory of and supplemental to an Act to provide for the Maintenance and Support of Public Schools,' approved March 20th, 1865."

On motion of Mr. Proctor, the bill was made the special order for to-morrow, at 12 o'clock M.

EXECUTIVE DEPARTMENT, CARSON CITY, }
March 18th, 1867. }

To the Hon. C. N. Noteware, Secretary of State, State of Nevada:

I herewith deposit with you Senate Bill No. 96, entitled "An Act making the Compensation of the Hon. John Cradlebaugh, late United States District Judge, the same as was paid to each of the late Judges of the Territory of Nevada," without approval.

By Act of March 2d, 1861, Congress fixed the salaries of the United States Judges of Nevada at eighteen hundred dollars per annum. By Act of December 19th, 1862, the Legislative Assembly of the Territory of Nevada increased their salaries four thousand two hundred dollars, so that from the United States and the Territory, the Territorial Judges received in all a salary of six thousand dollars each. This bill proposes that the State of Nevada shall now pay the Hon. John Cradlebaugh, for services rendered as United States Judge of Utah, a sum per annum equal to the difference ($3,500) between the amount ($2,500) paid him by the United States and the salary ($6,000) paid to each of the Judges of Nevada Territory.

During the years 1859, 1860, and a portion of 1861, the Hon. John Cradlebaugh held commission as a Federal Judge, within and for the Territory of Utah. At the date of his appointment and commission by Act of Congress then in force, his salary was fixed at $2,500 per annum. He therefore took the office and entered upon the discharge of its duties, with full knowledge of the compensation to be received. He agreed to serve the United States and the people of Utah Territory for the salary fixed by law—at his option continued to hold the office, and actually received the compensation fixed and agreed upon. ($2,500) per annum, may or may not have been an adequate compensation for the services rendered; but from the voluntary acceptance of the office by the incumbent, and his voluntary continuance in office at that salary, it would seem to have been considered adequate at the time. But whether the compensation received was adequate or not, it must be apparent that the Hon. John Cradlebaugh has no claim, legal or equitable, against the State of Nevada, for increased compensation as United States Judge of Utah.

The Act of March 2d, 1861, organizing Nevada Territory, determined the jurisdiction of the Hon. John Cradlebaugh, as a Federal Judge, over or within the new organization. He was at no time a Judge of Nevada Territory. He rendered no service; he has no legal claim against the State. His demand is not a debt or liability of the Territory of Nevada lawfully incurred, and was not therefore assumed or agreed to be paid by the State in virtue of Section 7, of Article 17, of the State Constitution.

It is true in the division of Utah into Judicial Districts, it was his fortune to be assigned to Carson County, out of which the present State of Nevada was carved; but Carson County did not agree to pay him additional compensation, nor did the Territory of Utah agree to pay additional compensation for the services rendered; and if the Territory had so agreed, it would have become a legitimate claim against Utah, and not against the State of Nevada.

The bill proposes that the State of Nevada shall pay the Hon. John Cradlebaugh ($3,500) per annum increased compensation, for services rendered the United States as a Federal Judge at a time prior to the existence of Nevada Territory. In my opinion the demand is neither just nor legal. In my opinion the financial condition of the State will not warrant such donations of money, no matter how worthy the donee.

Nor is the sum proposed to be given the most forcible argument against the bill. The precedent it proposes to establish is by far more dangerous and hurtful than the amount donated. The officers of Utah Territory were not less the officers of Carson County than of other Counties within that Territorial jurisdiction. Their services were rendered not less to the people of Carson County than to the people of other Counties in that Territory. If relief may be granted to the Hon. John Cradlebaugh, why may not it be granted equally to other officers whose compensation was less than that subsequently paid by the Territory of Nevada to her officers? Why, with still greater propriety, may not the United States officers for the Territory of Nevada, one and all, demand increased compensation for services rendered as such officers, upon the theory, notoriously true, that for the first years of the Territorial existence their salaries provided by law were insufficient? Why, especially, may not the Judges first appointed, after the organization of the Territory, at a salary of $1,800 per annum, demand relief at the rate of $4,200 per annum for the period intervening between their appointment and December 19th, 1862? And how, if the precedent be once established, can we reasonably or justly deny the relief?

In consideration of these objections, much as I may personally desire to reward a worthy and faithful officer, I cannot approve the bill. You will dispose of it as directed by Section 35, of Article 4, of the Constitution.

H. G. BLASDEL,
Governor.

Question: Shall the bill pass, notwithstanding the objections of the Governor?

Mr. Haines raised the point of order, that Mr. Hutchins was not speaking to the question before the Senate.

The Chair ruled the point of order well taken.

Mr. Hastings raised the point of order, that Mr. Welty was passing a eulogy upon the Governor, and not discussing the veto question.

The Chair ruled the point of order well taken.

The yeas and nays were called on the passage of the bill, and recorded as follows:

YEAS—Messrs. Geller, Grey, Hastings, Hutchins, Linn, Mason, Monroe—7.

NAYS—Messrs. Doron, Eastman, Haines, Meder, Nelson, Proctor, Stevenson, Terry, and Welty—8 [9].

So the bill did not pass.

Mr. Proctor gave notice that on to-morrow he would move a reconsideration of the vote whereby the above bill was lost.

Mr. Mason (by leave) offered the following resolution:

Resolved, That the State Controller be, and he is hereby authorized and required to draw his warrant in favor of M. M. Gaige, Sergeant-at-Arms of the Senate, for the amount in the Senate Contingent Fund for the Special Session. That the said Sergeant-at-Arms is hereby directed to deposit the amount of said warrant in the banking house of Wells, Fargo & Co., in this city, to be drawn out upon scrip issued by resolution of this Senate on said Contingent Fund, and any moneys remaining after all of said scrip shall have been paid, shall, upon order of the State Controller, be returned to the Treasury to the credit of the General Fund.

Adopted.

On motion of Mr. Stevenson, Assembly Messages were now taken up.

MESSAGE FROM THE ASSEMBLY.

The following Message was received from the Assembly:

ASSEMBLY CHAMBER, CARSON CITY, }
March 29th, 1867. }

To the Hon. the Senate:

I am directed to return to your hon. body Senate Memorial and Joint Resolution No. 6, concerning Ireland, the same having passed the House: Yeas, 30; Nays, 1. I also return Senate Concurrent Resolution No. 11, in regard to claims of the State of Nevada against the Government of the United States, the same having passed the House this day.

I am also instructed to inform your hon. body that the House has appointed Messrs. Munckton, Wheeler and Strother, as a Committee of Conference, to act with a like committee from your hon. body upon Assembly Bill No. 5.

Respectfully,

A. WHITFORD,
Clerk.

At 2:40 P.M., on motion of Mr. Welty, the Senate took a recess until 3 o'clock P.M.

IN SENATE.

The Senate met at 3 o'clock, P.M., President in the chair.

Roll called.

No quorum present.

On motion of Mr. Linn, a call of the Senate was ordered.

Absent—Messrs. Doron, Eastman, Haines, Hastings, Hutchins, and Proctor. The above named gentlemen appearing, were, on motion, fined one dollar each.

On motion of Mr. Hutchins, further proceedings under call of the Senate were dispensed with.

EXECUTIVE DEPARTMENT, CARSON CITY,
March 18th, 1867.

To Hon. C. N. Noteware, Secretary of State, State of Nevada:

I herewith deposit with you Senate Bill No. 236, entitled " An Act to amend an Act entitled ' An Act to supply the town of Dayton in Lyon County with Water, and to protect the town against Fire, and to define the Boundaries thereof,' approved February 20th, 1864," without approval.

On the day above stated, the Act this bill would amend granted to Alfred James and others, under the Territorial Government, the exclusive right to supply Dayton with water during the then ensuing ten years, upon condition that they were to commence in one year, and so far complete in two the laying of pipes that a certain portion of said town could be supplied with water. This condition has not been fulfilled, and the franchise has therefore reverted to the State. The State cannot grant it again by special Act. (See Section 1 of Article eight and Section twenty-one of Article four of the Constitution.)

Because of these objections I cannot approve the bill. This bill was presented to me on the 7th day of March, 1867. You will dispose of it as directed by the thirty-fifth section of Article 4 of the Constitution.

H. G. BLASDEL,
Governor.

On the question : Shall the bill pass, notwithstanding the objections of the Governor ?

The yeas and nays were called, and recorded as follows :

YEAS—Messrs. Geller, Grey, Hastings, Hutchins, Linn, Mason, Monroe, Proctor, Stevenson, and Terry—10.

NAYS—Messrs. Doron, Eastman, Haines, Meder, Nelson, and Welty—6.

So the bill did not pass.

STATE OF NEVADA, EXECUTIVE DEPARTMENT,
Carson City, March 18th, 1867.

To the Hon. C. N. Noteware, Secretary of State, State of Nevada :

I herewith deposit with you Senate Bill No. 260, entitled "An Act authorizing the State Board of Examiners to audit and allow Claims against the Legislative Fund of the First Biennial Session of the Legislature, to be paid out of the General Fund," without approval.

Sec. 2 of this bill provides in terms that the Board of Examiners shall regard as just demands all amounts which the Senate and Assembly have, by resolution, ordered paid out of their respective " Contingent Funds," remaining unpaid at the close of the late session, thus depriving the Board of Examiners of any discretion in the premises, and expressly legalizing all demands, whether just or not, which may have received the approval, by resolution merely, of either branch of the Legislature.

The unfairness of this is apparent upon its face. Its purpose cannot be mistaken. Its object and effect would compel the payment of "extra pay," voted to attachés, in direct violation of the Constitution.

I cannot sanction a measure which would *compel* the application of the public money to purposes expressly prohibited by the fundamental law.

Because of these objections, I cannot approve this bill.

You will dispose of it as directed by Section thirty-five of Article four of the Constitution.

H. G. BLASDEL,
Governor.

On the question : Shall the bill pass, notwithstanding the objections of the Governor? the yeas and nays were called, and recorded as follows :

YEAS—Messrs. Geller, Grey, Hastings, Hutchins, Monroe, and Proctor—6.
NAYS—Messrs. Doron, Eastman, Haines, Meder, Nelson, Stevenson, Terry, and Welty—8.

So the bill did not pass.

Mr. Monroe moved that the bills and veto Messages be laid upon the table.

Mr. Proctor moved as a substitute, that the reading of the veto Messages be dispensed with.

The Chair ruled the motions out of order.

Mr. Proctor appealed from the decision of the Chair.

The decision of the Chair was sustained.

STATE OF NEVADA, EXECUTIVE DEPARTMENT,
Carson City, March 18th, 1867.

To the Hon. O. N. Noteware, Secretary of State, State of Nevada :

I herewith deposit with you Senate Bill No. 218, entitled "An Act to transfer certain Moneys from the Legislative Fund to the Contingent Fund of the Senate," without approval.

This bill was presented to me on the fifth day of March, 1867.

If this bill were to become a *law*, the sum therein named would, chiefly, if not altogether, be paid to liquidate claims of the attachés for extra pay not allowed by law. See Section 28th of Article 4 of the Constitution. For this reason I cannot approve the bill.

You will dispose of it as directed by Section 35th of Article 4 of the Constitution.

H. G. BLASDEL,
Governor.

On the question : Shall the bill pass, notwithstanding the objections of the Governor? the yeas and nays were called, and recorded as follows :

YEAS—Messrs. Geller, Grey, Hastings, Hutchins, Monroe, and Proctor—6.
NAYS—Messrs. Doron, Eastman, Haines, Mason, Meder, Nelson, Stevenson, Terry, and Welty—9.

So the bill did not pass.

STATE OF NEVADA, EXECUTIVE DEPARTMENT,
Carson City, March 19th, 1867.

To the Hon. O. N. Noteware, Secretary of State, State of Nevada :

I herewith deposit with you Senate Bill No. 133, entitled "An Act to repeal an Act entitled 'An Act to provide for establishing and maintaining a Mining School, and create the Office of State Mineralogist,' approved March 9th, 1866," without approval.

This bill was presented to me on the 7th day of March, 1867.

The Constitution, Section four of Article eleven, requires the Legislature to provide for the establishment of a " State University," "which shall embrace Departments for Agriculture, Mechanic Arts, and Mining." Also the eighth section of the same Article seems to contemplate, if not positively require, the early establishment of said Mining Department. If this bill were approved, the last named and very important [object] must be thereby postponed at least two years more, and the State lose all benefits to arise from the researches and reports of a State Mineralogist. This, I think, would be detrimental to the public good.

Because of these objections I withhold my approval.

You will dispose of the bill as Constitutionally required.

H. G. BLASDEL,
Governor.

On the question: Shall the bill pass, notwithstanding the objections of the Governor ? the yeas and nays were called, and recorded as follows:

YEAS—Messrs. Doron, Geller, Grey, Hastings, Hutchins, Linn, Monroe, Proctor, Stevenson, and Terry—10.

NAYS—Messrs. Eastman, Haines, Mason, Meder, Nelson, and Welty—6.

So the bill did not pass.

STATE OF NEVADA, EXECUTIVE DEPARTMENT,
Carson City, March 18th, 1867.

To the Hon O. N. Noteware, Secretary of State, State of Nevada:

I herewith deposit with you Senate Bill No. 202, entitled "An Act to provide Stationery for the use of the Senate and Assembly of the State of Nevada," without approval.

This bill was presented to me on the 7th day of March, 1867.

1st. The Constitution, Section 33, Article 4, contemplates that members shall provide themselves with stationery, etc., and that the State shall pay to each member in lieu of stationery, etc., a sum not exceeding $60 *actually expended* for those purposes. This bill provides that members shall be furnished stationery by the State, without limit in quantity, and makes no provision that the amount furnished shall be deducted from the allowance made by the Constitution.

2d. This bill does not provide that the Sergeants-at-Arms of the respective Houses shall be responsible to the State for stationery furnished, nor that the Sergeant-at-Arms shall pay to the State or to any officer for the use of the State any money received from members for stationery.

Deeming this bill insufficiently guarded, and as not meeting the necessities of the case, I cannot approve it.

You will dispose of it as Constitutionally directed.

H. G. BLASDEL.

On the question: Shall the bill pass, notwithstanding the objections of the Governor ? the yeas and nays were called, and recorded as follows:

YEAS—Messrs. Geller, Hastings, Linn, Monroe, Proctor, Stevenson, and Terry—7.

NAYS—Messrs. Doron, Eastman, Grey, Haines, Mason, Meder, Nelson, and Welty—8.

So the bill did not pass.

Mr. Linn, Chairman of Committee on Enrollment, reported that Senate Memorial and Joint Resolution No. 6, and Senate Bill No. 1, entitled " An Act to amend an Act to provide Revenue for the Support of the Government of the State of Nevada, approved March 9th, 1865, and other Acts amendatory thereof," had been carefully compared with the Engrossed Resolution and Bill, as passed by the two Houses, and that the resolution had been deposited with the Secretary of State, and the bill delivered to the Governor for his approval.

Mr. Mason (by leave) introduced Senate Concurrent Resolution No. 18, providing for printing the Revenue Law.

Mr. Proctor moved to amend by inserting before the words " Revenue Law " the words " amendments to the."

Read and adopted as amended.

At 4:20 P.M., on motion of Mr. Proctor, the Senate took a recess until 7 o'clock P.M.

IN SENATE.

The Senate met at 7 P.M.
President in the chair.
Roll called.
Quorum present.
On motion of Mr. Proctor, a call of the Senate was ordered.
Absent—Messrs. Grey, Hastings, Hutchins, and Mason.
On motion of Mr. Meder, further proceedings under the call were dispensed with.

On motion of Mr. Meder, the charge preferred against Senator Welty, by Senator Proctor, was now taken up.

Ou motion of Mr. Meder, the report of special committee appointed to investigate said charge was adopted.

On motion of Mr. Haines, the Senate went into Committee of the Whole for consideration of the various Land Bills.

President in the chair.
The Committee rose, and submitted the following report:

Mr. President :

The Senate, in Committee of the Whole, have had under consideration Assembly Bill No. 3, " An Act to provide for the Selection and Sale of Lands granted by the United States to the State of Nevada," which they report back, and recommend the bill do pass as amended.

The report of the Committee of the Whole was adopted.

Assembly Bill No. 3, " An Act to provide for the Selection and Sale of Lands granted by the United States to the State of Nevada."

Read third time by sections.

The yeas and nays were called on the final passage of the bill, and recorded as follows:

YEAS—Messrs. Doron, Eastman, Geller, Haines, Hastings, Linn, Mason, Meder, Monroe, Nelson, Proctor, Stevenson, Terry, and Welty—14.

NAYS—Mr. Grey—1.

So the bill passed.

Mr. Hastings gave notice that on to-morrow he would move a reconsideration of the vote whereby Assembly Bill No. 3 passed.

At 8:25 P.M., on motion of Mr. Monroe, the Senate adjourned.

JAMES S. SLINGERLAND,
President.

Attest—JOHN R. EARDLEY,
Assistant Secretary.

IN SENATE, SPECIAL SESSION—SIXTEENTH DAY.

CARSON CITY, March 30th, 1867.

The Senate met pursuant to adjournment.

President in the chair.

Roll called.

Present—Messrs. Doron, Eastman, Edwards, Geller, Grey, Haines, Hastings, Hutchins, Linn, Mason, Meder, Monroe, Nelson, Proctor, Stevenson, and Welty —16.

Absent—Messrs. Sumner and Terry—2.

Prayer by the Chaplain.

The Journal of the Fifteenth day was read and approved.

REPORTS OF COMMITTEES.

Mr. Linn, Chairman of Committee on Enrollment, reported that they had carefully compared Senate Joint Resolution No. 11, in regard to claims of the State of Nevada against the Government of the United States, with the engrossed resolution, found the same correctly enrolled, and that it had this day been deposited with the Secretary of State.

Mr. Mason, from Standing Committee on Federal Relations, to which was referred Assembly Joint Resolution No. 7, relative to Reconstruction Measures, reported that they had had the same under consideration, report the same back to the Senate, and recommend its passage.

Mr. Haines submitted the following report:

Mr. President:

Your Committee of Conference, to which was referred Assembly Bill No. 5, "An Act entitled 'An Act to provide Revenue for the State of Nevada,'" have had the same under consideration, failed to agree, and recommend that a Committee of Conference be appointed.

Adopted.

The Chair appointed Messrs. Haines, Welty and Stevenson as such committee.

MOTIONS AND RESOLUTIONS.

Mr. Hastings moved that the vote whereby Assembly Bill No. 3 was on yesterday passed, be now reconsidered.

Mr. Grey was granted leave to have his vote on Assembly Bill No. 3, passed on yesterday, recorded in the negative.

The yeas and nays were called for on the question by Messrs. Hutchins, Welty, and Grey, and recorded as follows:

YEAS—Messrs. Hastings, Hutchins, Mason, and Stevenson—4.

NAYS—Messrs. Doron, Eastman, Edwards, Geller, Grey, Haines, Linn, Meder, Monroe, Nelson, Proctor, and Welty—12.

So the Senate refused to reconsider.

On motion, Mr. Hutchins was granted indefinite leave of absence.

Mr. Edwards, (by leave) from Committee on Public Lands, to which was referred Assembly Joint Resolution No. 8, relating to lands granted to the State of Nevada, reported that they had had the same under consideration, report the same back, and recommend its passage.

On motion of Mr. Welty, the resolution was now taken up.

Assembly Joint Resolution No. 8, relating to lands granted to the State of Nevada.

Read first time; rules suspended; read second time by title; rules further suspended; read third time.

The yeas and nays were called on the final passage of the resolution, and recorded as follows:

YEAS—Messrs. Doron, Eastman, Edwards, Geller, Grey, Haines, Hastings, Linn, Mason, Meder, Nelson, Proctor, Stevenson, and Welty—14.

NAYS—0.

So the resolution passed.

GENERAL FILE.

Assembly Conjoint Resolution No. 7, relative to Reconstruction Measures.

Read third time.

The yeas and nays were called on the final passage of the resolution, and recorded as follows:

YEAS—Messrs. Doron, Eastman, Edwards, Haines, Hastings, Linn, Mason, Meder, Nelson, Stevenson, and Welty—11.

NAYS—Messrs. Geller, Monroe, and Proctor—3.

So the resolution passed.

SPECIAL ORDER.

Substitute Assembly Bill No. 164, "An Act for the organization of a Board of Education in Counties that polled three thousand votes or more at the General Election in the State of Nevada in November, A.D. 1866, or that may hereafter at any General Election cast that number of votes or more, and amendatory of and supplemental to an Act to provide for the Maintenance and Support of Public Schools, approved March 20th, 1865."

On the question : Shall the bill pass, notwithstanding the objections of the Governor? the yeas and nays were called, and recorded as follows:

YEAS—Messrs. Edwards, Geller, Hastings, Mason, Meder, Monroe, and Proctor—7.

NAYS—Messrs. Doron, Eastman, Grey, Haines, Nelson, Stevenson, and Welty—7.

So the bill did not pass.

On motion, Mr. Hastings was granted leave to withdraw the remonstrance of Citizens of Lyon County in relation to Lyon County Funding Bill.

At 12:15 P.M., on motion of Mr. Mason, the Senate took a recess until 3 o'clock P.M.

IN SENATE.

The Senate met at 3 o'clock P.M.
President in the chair.
Roll called.
Quorum present.
On the motion of Mr. Linn, the Senate took a recess until 4 o'clock P.M.

IN SENATE.

The Senate met at 4 P.M.
President in the chair.
Roll called.
Quorum present.

MESSAGE FROM THE ASSEMBLY.

The following Message was received from the Assembly :

ASSEMBLY CHAMBER, CARSON CITY, }
March 30th, 1867. }

To the Honorable the Senate :

I herewith transmit Assembly Bill No. 14, entitled "An Act to amend an Act to create certain Funds, approved March 28th, 1867," which passed the Assembly this day, for your approval.

Respectfully,

WILKIE DARLING,
Assistant Clerk.

Assembly Bill No. 14, "An Act to amend an Act entitled 'An Act to create certain Funds.'"

Read first time ; rules suspended ; read second time by title ; rules further suspended ; read third time by sections.

The yeas and nays were called on the final passage of the bill, and recorded as follows :

YEAS—Messrs. Doron, Eastman, Edwards, Geller, Grey, Hastings, Linn, Mason, Monroe, Proctor—10.

NAYS—Mr. Meder—1.

So the bill passed.

Mr. Monroe, from Special Committee, to which was referred the subject of the propriety of purchasing a suitable building or buildings for a capitol and other State purposes, reported that they had had the same under consideration, and find as follows : The present buildings used for the above purposes cost the State the sum of $6,650 per annum, or for the next six years the sum of $39,900, and that the accommodations are inadequate and unfit for the use of the State. The repairs on the rooms and charge for storage of the furniture of the Senate and Assembly Chambers cost about $1,000 per annum. Suitable buildings can be bought that will accommodate both branches of the Legislature and all the State officers, at a price that will save to the State, during the next six years, about $29,000. That Section 1, Article 15, of the State Constitution reads as follows: "The seat of Government shall be at Carson City, but no appropriation for the erection or purchase of capitol buildings shall be made during the next three years." The Committee believe that a bill could be drawn that would obviate this constitutional objection and secure the object desired, and that is, by leasing the same, and conferring the power to buy after the first of November next, when this clause in the Constitution ceases to be in force; and, should the Governor think best not to call the attention of the present session to the subject of a purchase of such buildings on constitutional grounds, then we would recommend that the buildings spoken of be leased, which would bring all the State offices conveniently together, and save the State a large amount in the reduction of rent.

Mr. Grey by leave, offered the following resolution:

Resolved, That H. H. Griswold be allowed per diem, during this session, as Clerk of Committee on Public Lands, and that the Sergeant-at-Arms be instructed to draw his warrant for the same.

Adopted.

On motion, a Committee was appointed to confer with the Governor upon the expediency of purchasing capitol buildings.

The Chair appointed Messrs. Edwards, Doron, and Mason.

Mr. Welty, by leave without previous notice, introduced Senate Bill No. 20, "An Act to amend an Act entitled an Act supplementary to an Act entitled 'An Act to provide Revenue for the Support of the Government of the State of Nevada,' approved March 9th, 1865, and providing for Levying and Collecting Revenue for County purposes, and further prescribing the Powers and Duties of the Board of County Commissioners of the several Counties of this State relative thereto."

Read first time; rules suspended; read second time by title, and placed on the General File.

At 4:45 P.M., on motion of Mr. Haines, the Senate adjourned.

JAMES S. SLINGERLAND,
President.

Attest—JOHN R. EARDLEY,
Assistant Secretary.

IN SENATE, SPECIAL SESSION—EIGHTEENTH DAY.

CARSON CITY, April 1st, 1867.

The Senate met pursuant to adjournment.

President in the chair.

Roll called.

Present—Messrs. Doron, Eastman, Geller, Haines, Linn, Mason, Monroe, Proctor, and Welty—9.

Absent—Messrs. Edwards, Grey, Meder, Nelson, Stevenson, and Hastings—6.
On motion of Mr. Proctor, a call of the Senate was ordered.
Absent—Messrs. Edwards, Grey, Hastings, Meder, Nelson, Stevenson, and Sumner.
Mr. Edwards appearing, was, on motion, excused, on paying a fine of one dollar.
On motion of Mr. Mason, Mr. Terry was granted indefinite leave of absence.
On motion of Mr. Proctor, Mr. Hastings was granted leave of absence for one day.
On motion of Mr. Monroe, leave of absence was granted to Mr. Sumner for one day.
On motion of Mr. Mason, further proceedings under the call of the House were dispensed with.
Prayer by the Chaplain.
The Journal of the Sixteenth day was read and approved, with certain corrections.

REPORTS OF COMMITTEES.

The Special Committee appointed to confer with his Excellency the Governor, upon the subject of purchasing capitol buildings, reported that they have conferred with his Excellency, and he states that he has addressed a written communication to the Senate, which will fully explain his views upon the subject.
Mr. Doron presented the following communication from his Excellency, Governor Blasdel, which on motion was ordered read:

EXECUTIVE DEPARTMENT, CARSON CITY, }
March 30th, 1867. }

GENTLEMEN—Your favor, calling upon me to lay before the Legislature, now in Special Session, the subject of legislation in regard to rents of State officials' offices, came to hand yesterday, and has been duly considered by me.
In reply, I have the honor to say, that your session being near its close; the business of the Special Session being yet unfinished; the State not in such financial condition as to justify any expenditures for the purchase or erection of Public Buildings; and there being a grave question as to the constitutionality of any appropriation you might make for either of those purposes, I deem it inexpedient to comply with your request.
I am, very respectfully,
Your obedient servant,
H. G. BLASDEL.
Hon. L. Doron, J. J. Linn, C. C. Stevenson, John Nelson, W. G. Monroe, and others of the Senate.

Mr. Haines, from Committee of Free Conference, submitted the following report:

Mr. President:

The undersigned, your Committee, having been named to meet a corresponding number on behalf of the House, and to confer in free conference upon matters of disagreement existing between the two Houses in relation to Assembly Bill No. 5, "An Act supplementary to an Act entitled 'An Act to provide Revenue for the Support of the Government of the State of Nevada,' approved March 9th, 1865, and providing for levying and collecting Revenue for County purposes, and further prescribing the powers and duties of the Board of County Commissioners of the several counties of this State relative thereto," beg leave respectfully to report the following proceedings and results of that conference:

On meeting for the discharge of their duties, the *House Committee* submitted to the Conference the following propositions, viz: First—To strike out all of the second proviso in *Section One* of said bill, and adopt in lieu thereof, in the first proviso to said section, a uniform basis of taxation of eighty-seven and a half cents upon each one hundred dollars' valuation of all taxable property, including proceeds of the mines. This modification was claimed by the Assembly Committee as being in accordance with the provisions of Article Ten of the Constitution. The proposition was opposed by the members of your Committee, and after much discussion, the Assembly Committee abandoned it.

Second—The Committee then from the House proposed to retain the basis of taxation as contemplated by the bill, but to so change the amendment proposed by the Senate, as to impose a rate of taxation of one hundred and thirty-eight cents on each one hundred dollars' valuation of all taxable property other than the proceeds of mines as contemplated in the first proviso to section one, and thirty-seven cents upon each one hundred dollars' valuation of the proceeds of mines. This proposition we could not agree to, and it was therefore abandoned.

Your Committee then insisted, in view of the impending difficulties and embarrassments to our State, which would inevitably grow out of a failure of agreement between the two Houses, upon this all-important question, that the House should concur in the Senate amendments. And your Committee are most happy in being able to report that the House Committee agreed to make a report in favor of the House concurring in Senate amendments, and if the Assembly indorse *such* report, and adopt the Senate amendments to the bill, no further action will be necessary on the part of the Senate.

All of which is most respectfully submitted.

J. W. HAINES,
D. W. WELTY.

MOTIONS AND RESOLUTIONS.

Mr. Linn submitted the following resolution:

Resolved, That the Sergeant-at-Arms be authorized and required to draw his warrant on the Senate Contingent Fund in favor of Mason, Huff & Co., for the sum of nine ($9) dollars; also, in favor of E. D. Sweeney, for the sum of forty ($40) dollars; also, in favor of M. D. *Judkins*, [Junkins] for the sum of five ($5) dollars; also, in favor of John H. Painter, for nine dollars and seventy-five cents ($9 75).

Adopted.

Mr. Mason introduced Senate Concurrent Resolution No. 21, in relation to Capitol Buildings.

Read and adopted.

On motion of Mr. Monroe, at 11:50 A.M. the Senate took a recess until 2 o'clock P.M.

IN SENATE.

The Senate met at 2 P.M., President in the chair.
Roll called.
No quorum present.
On motion of Mr. Linn, a call of the Senate was ordered.

39

Absent—Messrs. Doron, Edwards, Meder, and Proctor.

Messrs. Meder, Doron, and Edwards appearing, were, on motion, excused on paying a fine of one dollar each.

On motion of Mr. Linn, further proceedings under call of the Senate were dispensed with.

On motion of Mr. Doron, Assembly Messages were taken up.

MESSAGES FROM THE ASSEMBLY.

The following Messages were received from the Assembly:

ASSEMBLY CHAMBER, CARSON CITY, }
April 1st, 1867. }

To the Hon. the Senate:

I am instructed to inform your honorable body that the House have this day refused to adopt the report of the Conference Committee, upon the differences between the two Houses, in relation to Assembly Bill No. 5.

Respectfully,

A. WHITFORD,
Clerk.

ASSEMBLY CHAMBER, CARSON CITY, }
April 1st, 1867. }

To the Honorable the Senate:

I am instructed to inform your honorable body that the House concurred in Senate amendments to Assembly Bill No. 3, "An Act to provide for the Selection and Sale of Lands granted by the United States to the State of Nevada," on Saturday, March 30th, 1867.

I am also instructed to return to you Senate Concurrent Resolution No. 18, in relation to printing Revenue Law, the same having passed the Assembly on Saturday, March 30th, without amendments.

Respectfully,

A. WHITFORD,
Clerk.

GENERAL FILE.

Senate Bill No. 20, "An Act to amend an Act entitled ' An Act to provide Revenue for the Support of the Government of the State of Nevada,' approved March 9th, 1865, and providing for Levying and Collecting Revenue for County Purposes, and further prescribing the powers and duties of the Board of County Commissioners of the several Counties of this State relative thereto. "

On motion of Mr. Welty, the bill was passed over for one hour.

Mr. Meder moved that the Committee of Free Conference be now discharged.

The Chair ruled the motion out of order.

Mr. Edwards moved that the Senate do now reconsider the vote whereby the Senate refused to recede from their amendments to Assembly Bill No. 5.

Mr. Mason moved as a substitute, that a new Committee of Free Conference be appointed.

Carried.

The Chair appointed Messrs. Mason, Nelson, and Doron.

The Committee of Ways and Means, to which was referred Senate Bill No. 9, reported that they had had the same under consideration, and submitted the following amendments:

Amend section 1 as follows : Strike out of the first proviso of section, " one hundred and twenty-five cents," and insert in its stead the words "one hundred and fifty cents." Also, strike out all of section 2, and insert the following new section:

Sec. 2. The Board of County Commissioners of each county is hereby authorized and empowered annually, prior to the third Monday in April, unless otherwise provided by special Act, to levy and assess the amount of taxes that shall be levied for county purposes, designating the number of cents which shall on each one hundred dollars of taxable property be levied for each purpose, and shall add thereto the amount levied by law on each one hundred dollars of taxable property for State purposes ; *provided*, however, that when the Board of County Commissioners levy any tax they shall cause such levy to be entered on the records of their proceedings, and shall direct their clerk to deliver a certified copy thereof to the Auditor, Assessor, and Treasurer, each of whom shall file said copy in his office.. The Board of County Commissioners of each county shall apportion the revenues coming into the County Treasury, under the provisions of this Act, after deducting the four per cent. as hereinafter provided for the Treasury's Salary Fund, into such Funds as are now or hereafter may be provided by law ; *provided*, that the Board of County Commissioners are hereby authorized to set aside such portion of all the revenues of the county, to create a Redemption Fund for the payment of outstanding indebtedness, as is provided by any law now in force, or which may hereafter be passed. The Board of County Commissioners is hereby authorized and empowered, annually, to levy and collect such additional and special taxes as the statutes or laws of this State may authorize and require them to levy and collect.

Also, amend section 7 of bill as follows : Strike out " one hundred cents," and insert " seventy-five cents."

On motion of Mr. Doron, the Senate took a recess until until 7 : 30 P.M.

IN SENATE.

The Senate met at 7 : 30 P.M., President in the chair.

Roll called.

Quorum present.

Senate Bill No. 16, "An Act to provide for the Selection of Lands granted by the United States to the State of Nevada."

Laid upon the table.

Senate Bill No. 7, "An Act to provide for the Selection of Lands granted by the United States to the State of Nevada."

Laid upon the table.

Senate Bill No. 9, " An Act supplementary to an Act entitled ' An Act to provide Revenue for the Support of the Government of the State of Nevada,' approved March 9th, 1865, and the Acts amendatory thereof, and providing for levying and collecting Revenue for County purposes, and further prescribing the powers and duties of the Board of County Commissioners of the several Counties of this State relative thereto."

On motion of Mr. Doron, the bill was now taken up.

On motion of Mr. Doron, the bill was temporarily passed, in order to take up Assembly Message.

MESSAGE FROM THE ASSEMBLY.

The following Message was received from the Assembly:

ASSEMBLY CHAMBER, CARSON CITY,
April 1st, 1867.

To the Hon. the Senate:

I am directed to inform your honorable body, that the House has appointed as a Free Conference Committee on Assembly Bill No. 5, Mr. Speaker Ferguson, Messrs. Cary and Walton.

Respectfully,

A. WHITFORD,
Clerk.

On motion of Mr. Doron, the Senate took a recess until 8:16 P.M.

IN SENATE.

The Senate met at 8:16 P.M., Mr. Haines in the chair.
Roll called.
No quorum present.
At 8:20 P.M., on motion of Mr. Edwards, the Senate adjourned.

JAMES S. SLINGERLAND,
President.

Attest—JOHN R. EARDLEY,
Assistant Secretary.

IN SENATE, SPECIAL SESSION—NINETEENTH DAY.

CARSON CITY, April 2d, 1867.

Roll called.
Present—Messrs. Eastman, Geller, Grey, Hastings, Linn, Meder, Proctor, Stevenson, and Welty—8.
Absent—Messrs. Doron, Edwards, Haines, Mason, Monroe, and Nelson—6.
On motion of Mr. Proctor, a call of the Senate was ordered.
The absentees appearing, were, on motion, excused.
On motion of Mr. Proctor, further proceedings under the call were dispensed with.
Prayer by the Chaplain.
The Journal of the Eighteenth day was read and approved.

MOTIONS AND RESOLUTIONS.

Mr. Doron offered the following resolution:

Resolved, That the Sergeant-at-Arms be, and he is hereby required to draw his warrant on the Contingent Fund, in favor of W. E. Skeen, for one hundred dollars.

Adopted.

On motion of Mr. Welty, the Senate went into Committee of the Whole, for the consideration of Senate Bill No. 9. President in the chair.

The Committee rose, and submitted the following report:

Mr. President:

The Senate, in Committee of the Whole, have had under consideration Senate Bill No. 9, "An Act supplementary to an Act entitled ' An Act to provide Revenue for the Support of the Government of the State of Nevada,' approved March 9th, 1865, and the Acts amendatory thereof, and providing for levying and collecting Revenue for County purposes, and further prescribing the powers and duties of the Board of County Commissioners of the several Counties of this State relative thereto," which they report back with amendments, and recommend the rules be suspended, the bill considered engrossed, and placed upon its third reading and final passage as amended.

The amendments of the Committee of the Whole were adopted.

Senate Bill No. 9, "An Act supplementary to an Act entitled "An Act to provide Revenue for the Support of the Government of the State of Nevada,' approved March 9th, 1865, etc., etc."

Read third time by sections.

On motion of Mr. Edwards, the rules were suspended, the bill considered engrossed, and placed on its final passage.

The yeas and nays were called on the final passage of the bill, and recorded as follows:

YEAS—Messrs. Doron, Eastman, Edwards, Haines, Linn, Mason, Meder, Nelson, Stevenson, and Welty—10.

NAYS—Messrs. Geller, Grey, Hastings, Monroe, and Proctor—5.

So the bill passed.

The following report was received from the Free Conference Committee:

Mr. President:

Your Second Committee of Free Conference having met with a like Committee of the other branch of the Legislative department, and having freely interchanged views in regard to Assembly Bill No. 5, concerning the revenue of the Counties of the State, beg leave to report:

That while five of the Joint Committee still maintain and adhere to the justice of the original proposition contained in the House Bill, which proposes to levy an assessment of fifty cents on each one hundred dollars' value of the proceeds of the mines, after deducting the eighteen (18) and forty (40) dollars for extracting the bullion therefrom; yet, feeling and knowing the impossibility of passing the same through the Senate, we have yielded to the other member of the Committee, and consent that all other property outside of the mines may be taxed in a ratio six times the amount, or one dollar and twenty-five cents on the one hundred dollars' value, while, from sheer necessity, we agree to adopt the Senate amendments, which levies only *twenty-five cents* for each one hundred dollars of the proceeds as above; and we recommend that the House reconsider its action had on yesterday, and adopt the report of the First Committee of Free Conference had between the two Houses upon the bill under consideration.

B. S. MASON,
Chairman Senate Committee.
R. D. FERGUSON,
Chairman House Committee.

On motion of Mr. Doron, the Sergeant-at-Arms was granted leave of absence for the balance of the day.

On motion of Mr. Grey, indefinite leave of absence was granted to Senator Sumner.

On motion of Mr. Welty, the Senate took a recess until 2 o'clock P.M.

IN SENATE.

The Senate met at 2 o'clock P.M.
President in the chair.
Roll called.
Quorum present.

Mr. Linn, Chairman of Committee on Enrollment, reported that Senate Concurrent Resolution No. 18, in relation to printing Revenue Laws, had been carefully compared with the original resolution as passed by the two Houses, found correctly enrolled, and that the same had this day been deposited with the Secretary of State.

On motion of Mr. Doron, the Senate took a recess until 2:30 P.M.

IN SENATE.

The Senate met at 2:30 P.M.
President in the chair.
Roll called.
Quorum present.

MESSAGE FROM THE ASSEMBLY.

The following Message was received from the Assembly:

ASSEMBLY CHAMBER, CARSON CITY, }
April 2d, 1867. }

To the Hon. the Senate:

I am directed to return to your honorable body Senate Bill No. 9, the same having passed the Assembly this day. Yeas, 23 ; Nays, 5.

Respectfully,

A. WHITFORD,
Clerk.

On motion of Mr. Doron, the Senate took a recess until 3:30 P.M.

IN SENATE.

The Senate met at 3:30 P.M.
President in the chair.
Roll called.
No quorum present.

On motion of Mr. Hastings, a call of the Senate was ordered.

The absentees appearing, were, on motion, excused.

On motion, further proceedings under the call of the Senate were dispensed with.

The following Message was received from the Assembly:

ASSEMBLY CHAMBER, CARSON CITY, }
April 2d, 1867. }

To the Hon. the Senate:

I am instructed to transmit to your honorable body, for your consideration, Assembly Concurrent Resolution No. 16, relative to adjournment *sine die*, which passed this House this day unanimously.

Respectfully,

A. WHITFORD,
Clerk.

Assembly Concurrent Resolution No. 16, relative to adjournment *sine die.* Read and adopted.

The following Message was received from the Governor:

EXECUTIVE DEPARTMENT, CARSON CITY, }
April 2d, 1867. }

To the Hon. Senate of Nevada:

I have this day approved Senate Bill No. 1, (Special Session) entitled " An Act to amend an Act entitled ' An Act to provide Revenue for the Support of the Government of the State of Nevada,' approved March 9th, 1865," as amended by an Act entitled "An Act to amend an Act entitled ' An Act to provide Revenue for the Support of the Government of the State of Nevada,' approved March 9th, 1865, approved February 24th, 1867 [1866]."

H. G. BLASDEL,
Governor.

Mr. Mason, from Standing Committee on Enrollment, reported that they had carefully compared the following entitled bill with the engrossed bill as passed by the two Houses, found correctly enrolled, viz:

Senate Bill No. 9, entitled " An Act supplementary to an Act entitled " An Act to provide Revenue for the Support of the Government of the State of Nevada,' approved March 9th, 1865, and the Acts amendatory thereof, and providing for Levying and Collecting Revenue for County purposes, and further prescribing the powers and duties of the Boards of County Commissioners of the several counties of this State relative thereto," and that the same had this day been handed to the Governor for his approval.

Senate Bill No. 20, " An Act to amend an Act, entitled ' An Act supplementary to an Act entitled an Act to provide Revenue for the Support of the Government of the State of Nevada,' approved March 9th, 1865, and to provide for Levying and Collecting Revenue for County purposes, and further prescribing the powers and duties of the Board of County Commissioners of the several counties of this State relative thereto."

Laid on the table.

Mr. Meder (by leave) introduced the following resolution :

Resolved, That the office of President *pro tem.* of the Senate be, and the same is hereby declared vacant, and that the Senate do now proceed to the election of a President *pro tem.* of the Senate.

The yeas and nays were called for on the adoption of the resolution, by Messrs. Proctor, Hastings and Geller, and recorded as follows :

YEAS—Messrs. Eastman, Haines, Linn, Mason, Meder, Nelson, and Welty —7.

NAYS—Messrs. Edwards, Geller, Hastings, Proctor, and Stevenson—5.

So the resolution passed.

Mr. Hastings raised the point of order, " that nothing less than a constitutional majority can pass a resolution of that nature."

The Chair ruled the point of order not well taken.

Mr. Monroe was granted leave to have his name recorded in the negative on the adoption of the resolution relative to President *pro tem.*

Mr. Meder moved that the Senate now proceed to the election of a President *pro tem.*

Mr. Welty raised the point of order, " that the resolution itself provided for immediately proceeding in an election."

The Chair ruled the point of order well taken.

Mr. Hastings moved that the resolution be rescinded.

The yeas and nays were called for on the question by Messrs. Grey, Proctor, and Hastings, and recorded as follows :

YEAS—Messrs. Edwards, Geller, Grey, Hastings, Monroe, Proctor, Nelson, and Stevenson—8.

NAYS—Messrs. Eastman, Haines, Linn, Mason, Meder, and Welty—6.

So the resolution was rescinded.

At 5 o'clock P.M., on motion of Mr. Hastings, the Senate adjourned until to-morrow at 10 o'clock A.M.

JAMES S. SLINGERLAND,
President.

Attest—JOHN R. EARDLEY,
      Assistant Secretary.

IN SENATE, SPECIAL SESSION—TWENTIETH DAY.

CARSON CITY, April 3d, 1867.

The Senate met pursuant to adjournment, President in the chair.

Roll called.

Present—Messrs. Doron, Eastman, Edwards, Geller, Grey, Haines, Hastings, Linn, Mason, Meder, Monroe, Nelson, Proctor, Stevenson, and Welty—15.

Absent—0.

On motion of Mr. Linn, the Chaplain was granted leave of absence for the day.

The Journal of the Nineteenth day was read and approved.

MESSAGES FROM THE ASSEMBLY.

The following Messages were received from the Assembly:

ASSEMBLY CHAMBER, CARSON CITY, }
April 3d, 1867. }

To the Hon. the Senate:

Herewith, I transmit for the concurrence of your honorable body, Assembly Concurrent Resolution No. 19, asking the Governor to return to the Assembly Assembly Bill No. 14, entitled "An Act to amend an Act creating certain Funds."

Respectfully,

A. WHITFORD,
Clerk

ASSEMBLY CHAMBER, CARSON CITY, }
April 3d, 1867. }

To the Hon. the Senate:

I am directed to transmit, for your consideration, Assembly Concurrent Resolution No. 20, relating to Adjournment.

Respectfully,

A. WHITFORD,
Clerk.

INTRODUCTION OF BILLS.

Mr. Welty, by leave without previous notice, introduced Senate Bill No. 23, "An Act providing for the Payment of the Contingent and other necessary Expenses of the Third General and the Special Session of the Legislature of the State of Nevada."

Read first time; rules suspended; read second time by title.

On motion of Mr. Hastings, the rules were further suspended; the bill considered engrossed, and placed upon its third reading and final passage.

Mr. Doron moved, as a substitute, that the bill be referred to Messrs. Doron, Meder, and Welty.

On motion, the bill was passed over for the consideration of other business.

Assembly Concurrent Resolution No. 19, relative to Assembly Bill No. 14.

Read and adopted.

Assembly Concurrent Resolution No. 20, relative to Adjournment.

Read and laid upon the table.

Mr. Doron, by leave without previous notice, introduced Senate Bill No. 24, "An Act to provide for the Payment of the Expenses of Copying the Journals of both Houses of the Legislature, and to create a Fund for the Payment of the same."

Read first time; rules suspended; read second time by title.

On motion of Mr. Doron, the rules were further suspended; the bill considered engrossed, and placed on its third reading and final passage.

Read third time by sections.

The yeas and nays were called on the final passage of the bill, and recorded as follows:

40

YEAS—Messrs. Doron, Edwards, Grey, Hastings, Mason, and Stevenson—7.
NAYS—Messrs. Eastman, Geller, Meder, Nelson, and Proctor—5.

So the bill did not pass.
Senate Bill No. 23 was now taken up.
The motion of Mr. Doron, to refer to a Committee of three, was carried.
On motion of Mr. Hastings, the Senate took a recess until 12 : 8 P.M.

IN SENATE.

The Senate met at 12 : 8 P.M.
President in the chair.
Roll called.
Quorum present.
Mr. Doron, Chairman of Committee to which was referred Senate Bill No. 23, "An Act providing for the Payment of the Contingent Expenses of the Third General and Special Session of the Legislature of the State of Nevada,' reported that they had had the same under consideration, report the bill back, and recommend its passage.
On motion of Mr. Doron, the rules were suspended; the bill considered engrossed, and placed on its third reading and final passage.
Read third time by sections.
The yeas and nays were called on the final passage of the bill, and recorded as follows:

YEAS—Messrs. Doron, Eastman, Edwards, Geller, Grey, Haines, Linn, Mason, Meder, Monroe, Nelson, Proctor, Stevenson, and Welty—12.

So the bill passed.
On motion of Mr. Edwards, the Senate took a recess until 12 : 35 P.M.

IN SENATE.

The Senate met at 12 : 35 P.M.
President in the chair.
Roll called.
Quorum present.

MESSAGES FROM THE GOVERNOR.

The following Messages were received from the Governor:

EXECUTIVE DEPARTMENT, CARSON CITY,
April 3d, 1867.

To the Hon. the Senate of Nevada :

I approved, on the 2d instant, Senate Bill No. 9, (passed during the Special Session) "An Act supplementary to an Act entitled 'An Act to provide Revenue for the Support of the Government of the State of Nevada,' approved March 9th, 1865, and Acts amendatory thereof, and providing for Levying and Collecting Revenue for County Purposes, and further prescribing the Powers and Duties of the Boards of County Commissioners of the several Counties of this State relative thereto."

H. G. BLASDEL,
Governor.

EXECUTIVE DEPARTMENT, CARSON CITY, }
April 3d, 1867. }

Gentlemen of the Senate and Assembly :

In pursuance of the authority vested in me by the Constitution, I respectfully call to your attention, as a matter necessary and proper to be considered by the Legislature at this Special Session, amendments to the Act of the Second Session, approved January 31st, 1866, entitled "An Act prescribing Rules and Regulations for the execution of the Trust arising under the Act of Congress, entitled 'An Act for the Relief of Citizens of Towns upon Lands of the United States, under certain circumstances, approved May 23d, 1844.' "

From information deemed reliable, Congress has amended the Act having relation to the procurement of titles to town lots in this State, which is above cited, in such manner as renders necessary corresponding amendments to our State law, whereby we may be enabled to secure the benefits of the Federal Act.

I therefore recommend to your consideration, such needed amendments to the Act first cited, page 54, Statutes 1866, as will fully secure the benefits of the amendatory Act of Congress, and such other Acts in relation to the same subject matter as may be passed hereafter by Federal authority.

I herewith transmit communications Nos. 1 and 2, from the Controller to myself, and call to your attention the respective matters of needed legislation in them specified, that you may act as you deem proper in the premises.

Respectfully submitted,

H. G. BLASDEL,
Governor.

STATE CONTROLLER'S OFFICE, }
Carson, Nevada, April 2d, 1867. }

To His Excellency H. G. Blasdel:

I beg leave to call your attention to the fact that the appropriation made by an Act of the Legislature of the State of Nevada, entitled "An Act to encourage Enlistments, and provide Bounties and Extra Pay for our Volunteer Soldiers called into the Service of the United States, passed March 11th, 1865," is exhausted, and that an additional appropriation, not exceeding ten thousand ($10,000) dollars, will be necessary to meet outstanding claims.

I lodge this information with you, that you may take such action in the matter as you may deem necessary.

Yours, respectfully,

W. K. PARKINSON,
State Controller.

To H. G. Blasdel, Governor of the State of Nevada:

SIR—Upon a careful examination of the appropriation bill passed by the Third Session of the Nevada Legislature, I find there will be a deficiency in the appropriation to defray the expenses of the State Government for the succeeding two years, in the sum of seven thousand eight hundred and fifty-two dollars, ($7,852) as follows :

For Rent of Office for Governor (no appropriation)	$1,440 00
Porter for Governor's Office (no appropriation)	480 00
For Secretary of State, Copying Journals, etc., Regular and Special Sessions	1,080 00
Porter, Capitol Building (deficiency)	1,500 00
" State Treasurer's Office, "	400 00
" Controller's " "	400 00

Rent of Attorney General's Office (no appropriation)	1,200	00
Attorney General's Contingent, "	150	00
Bailiff Supreme Court, "	800	00
Expense of procuring Title to Plaza at Carson from H. S. Wright, Trustee	100	00

The above items of expenditure are, in my opinion, necessary and indispensable, and unless appropriations are made therefor, must be increased at greatly advanced rates, perhaps at an additional expense to the State of two thousand dollars.

I therefore deem it my duty to call your attention to the matter, and would respectfully suggest that you call the attention of the Legislature, now in extra session, to these deficiencies in appropriation.

Yours, respectfully,

W. K. PARKINSON,
State Controller.

Carson, Nevada, April 3d, 1867.

Mr. Hastings moved, that Assembly Concurrent Resolution No. 20, be now taken from the table.

Carried.

Assembly Concurrent Resolution No. 20, relating to Adjournment *sine die.*

Read and adopted.

Mr. Doron moved, that so such of the Messages as referred to Public Lands, be referred to Committee on Public Lands, and so much as referred to Expenditures, be referred to the Committee on Ways and Means.

Carried.

On motion of Mr. Edwards, the Senate took a recess until 3 o'clock P.M.

IN SENATE.

The Senate met at 3 o'clock P.M.
President in the chair.
Roll called.
Quorum present.

MESSAGE FROM THE ASSEMBLY.

The following Message was received from the Assembly:

ASSEMBLY CHAMBER, CARSON CITY, }
April 3d, 1867. }

To the Hon. the Senate:

I am directed to return to your honorable body, Senate Bill No. 23, the same having passed the House this day. Yeas, 24; Nays, 1.

Respectfully,

A. WHITFORD,
Clerk.

Mr. Linn, Chairman of Standing Committee on Enrollment, reported that Senate Bill No. 23, "An Act providing for the Payment of the Contingent and other necessary expenses of the Third General and the Special Session of the Legislature of the State of Nevada," had been carefully compared with the original bill as passed by the two Houses, found correctly enrolled, and that the same had this day been delivered to the Governor for his approval.

The following Message was received from the Governor:

EXECUTIVE DEPARTMENT, CARSON CITY, $\}$
April 3d, 1867.

Gentlemen of the Senate and Assembly:

I respectfully call your attention to the fact that there is no law in this State prescribing the manner of qualification of Public Administrators, and prescribing their duties as such, and as Coroners.

I think you should pass a suitable Act upon this subject.

Respectfully submitted,

H. G. BLASDEL,
Governor.

Mr. Linn (by leave) submitted the following resolution:

Resolved, That the thanks of this Senate be, and are hereby tendered to John R. Eardley, Assistant Secretary; John P. Coolidge, Minute Clerk; R. R. Parkinson, Journal Clerk; and F. F. Wright, Official Reporter, for the able and satisfactory manner in which they have performed their several duties, and their strict attention to business.

Adopted.

Mr. Welty (by leave) without previous notice, introduced Senate Bill No. 27, "An Act supplemental to an Act entitled 'An Act making Appropriations for the Support of the Civil Government of the State of Nevada for the third and fourth fiscal years,' approved March 12th, 1867."

Read first time; rules suspended; read second time by title, and referred to Committee of the Whole.

On motion of Mr. Hastings, the Senate went into Committee of the Whole for the consideration of Senate Bill No. 27. President in the chair.

The Committee rose, and submitted the following report:

Mr. President:

The Senate, in Committee of the Whole, have had under consideration Senate Bill No. 27, "An Act supplemental to an Act entitled 'An Act making Appropriations for the Support of the Civil Government of the State of Nevada for the third and fourth fiscal years,' approved March 12th, 1867," which they report back with amendments, and recommend the bill be considered engrossed, and placed upon its final passage.

The amendments of the Committee of the Whole were adopted.

Senate Bill No. 27, "An Act supplemental to an Act entitled 'An Act making Appropriations for the Support of the Civil Government of the State of Nevada for the third and fourth fiscal years,' approved March 12th, 1867."

Read third time by sections.

The rules further suspended; bill considered engrossed.

The yeas and nays were called on its final passage, and recorded as follows:

YEAS—Messrs. Doron, Eastman, Edwards, Haines, Hastings, Linn, Mason, Meder, Monroe, and Welty—10.

NAYS—Mr. Geller—1.

So the bill passed.

Mr. Mason (by leave) introduced Senate Bill No. 28, "An Act concerning the office of Public Administrator and the Estates of Deceased Persons."

Read first time; rules suspended; read second time by title; rules further suspended; bill considered engrossed.

Read third time by sections.

The yeas and nays were called on the final passage of the bill, and recorded as follows:

YEAS—Messrs. Doron, Eastman, Edwards, Geller, Haines, Hastings, Linn, Mason, Meder, Monroe, and Welty—11.

NAYS—0.

So the bill passed.

Mr. Hastings (by leave) offered the following:

Resolved, That the thanks of this Senate are due, and are hereby tendered to the Hon. James S. Slingerland for the able and impartial manner in which he has discharged the duties of presiding officer of this Senate during the present session of the Legislature.

Unanimously adopted.

Mr. Haines (by leave) offered the following:

Resolved, That the thanks of this Senate are due, and are hereby tendered to M. M. Gaige for the efficient manner in which he has discharged the duties of the office of Sergeant-at-Arms of this body.

Adopted.

On motion of Mr. Monroe, the Senate took a recess until 6 o'clock P.M.

IN SENATE.

The Senate met at 6 P.M.

President in the chair.

Roll called.

Quorum present.

On motion of Mr. Doron, a call of the Senate was ordered.

Absent—Messrs. Edwards, Grey, Hastings, Proctor, and Welty.

The absentees appearing, were, on motion, excused.

On motion, further proceedings under the call were dispensed with.

MESSAGES FROM THE ASSEMBLY.

The following Messages were received from the Assembly:

ASSEMBLY CHAMBER, CARSON CITY, }
April 3d, 1867. }

To the Honorable the Senate:

I herewith transmit to your honorable body, Assembly Bill No. 23, which passed the House this day. Yeas, 22; Nays, 4.

Also, Senate Bill No. 21, which passed the House this day. Yeas, 27; Nays, 0.

Respectfully,

A. WHITFORD,
Clerk.

To the Honorable the Senate:

I am instructed to return to your honorable body Senate Bill No. 28, the same having passed the House this day.

Also, Senate Bill No. 27, the same having passed this House this day.

Respectfully,

A. WHITFORD,
Clerk.

Assembly Bill No. 23, making appropriations for the Support of the Civil Government of the State of Nevada for the third and fourth fiscal years, and for supplying the deficiency of appropriations for the payment of Bounties and extra pay for our Volunteer Soldiers called into service of the United States.

Read and laid upon the table.

Assembly Bill No. 21, "An Act amendatory of and supplementary to an Act entitled 'An Act prescribing Rules and Regulations for the Execution of the Trust arising under the Act of Congress entitled 'An Act for the relief of Citizens of Towns upon Lands of the United States under certain circumstances, approved May 23d, 1844,' approved January 31st, 1866.'"

Read first time; rules suspended; read second time by title; rules further suspended; considered engrossed; read third time by *title* [sections]. The yeas and nays were called on the final passage of the bill, and recorded as follows:

YEAS—Messrs. Doron, Eastman, Edwards, Geller, Haines, Mason, Meder, Monroe, Nelson, Stevenson, and Welty—11.

NAYS—0.

So the bill passed.

Mr. Linn, Chairman of Committee on Enrollment, reported that Senate Bill No. 27 had been carefully compared with the original bill as passed by the two Houses, found correctly enrolled, and that the same had this day been delivered to the Governor for his approval.

On motion of Mr. Welty, the Chair appointed Messrs Welty, Geller, and Nelson a Committee to wait on his Excellency, Governor Blasdel, and inform him that the hour for adjournment *sine die* is fixed at 8 o'clock P.M., and to inquire of him if he has any further Messages to communicate to this body.

On motion of Mr. Monroe, the Senate took a recess until 7:15 P.M.

IN SENATE.

The Senate met at 7:15 P.M., President in the chair.

Roll called.

Quorum present.

Mr. Welty, from Committee appointed to wait on the Governor, reported that they had performed the duty assigned them, and that his Excellency had informed the Committee that he had no further communications to make.

On motion, Mr. Hastings was granted leave to have his vote recorded in the affirmative on the passage of Assembly Bill No. 21.

Mr. Linn, Chairman of Committee on Enrollment, reported that Senate Bill No. 28, concerning the Office of Public Administrator and the Estates of Deceased Persons, had been carefully compared with the original bill as passed by the two Houses, found correctly enrolled, and that the same had this day been delivered to the Governor for his approval.

Mr. Nelson, by leave, offered the following:

Resolved, That the Sergeant-at-Arms be, and he is hereby directed to draw his warrant in favor of D. C. Williams for seven days' services as Clerk of the Committee on Education.

Adopted.

The Journal of the Twentieth day was read and approved.

At 8 o'clock P.M., in pursuance of Concurrent Resolution passed by both branches of the Legislature, the President declared the Senate adjourned *sie die.*

JAMES S. SLINGERLAND,
President.

Attest—JOHN R. EARDLEY,
Assistant Secretary.

REPORT OF COMMITTEE

ON

WAYS AND MEANS,

OF THE

RECEIPTS AND EXPENDITURES

FOR THE

THIRD, FOURTH AND FIFTH FISCAL YEARS.

41

REPORT.

Mr. President :

The Committee on Ways and Means respectfully beg leave to report, in connection with the Loan Bill, the following estimates of the receipts and expenditures of the State for the third, fourth, and fifth fiscal years :

RECEIPTS.

Third Fiscal Year :

Property Tax at 95c	$152,000
Stamp Tax	18,000
Poll Tax	15,000
Capitation Tax	10,000
Mining Tax	15,000
Miscellaneous	5,000
Bonds Sold	300,000
Total	**$515,000**

Fourth Fiscal Year :

Property Tax, at $1.20	$240,000
Stamp Tax	20,000
Poll Tax	20,000
Capitation Tax	20,000
Mining Tax	20,000
Miscellaneous	5,000
Total	**$325,000**

Fifth Fiscal Year:

Property Tax at $1.20	$288,000
Stamp Tax	20,000
Poll Tax	15,000
Capitation Tax	20,000
Mining Tax	20,000
Miscellaneous	5,000
Total	$368,000

Total for Third, Fourth, and Fifth Fiscal Years $1,208,000

EXPENDITURES.

Third Fiscal Year	$420,000
Fourth Fiscal Year	170,000
Fifth Fiscal Year (including Redemption Bonds)	520,000
Total	$1,110,000

The above estimates do not include the principal and interest on outstanding Territorial Bonds, Soldiers' Bounty Warrants, or the School Funds, they being or to be provided for by special taxes. The estimates are based, so far as receipts are concerned, upon the present laws in relation to revenue; and none of the various propositions mooted—such as a tax upon bullion or crude amalgam, a tax upon Mongolians, thousands of whom will soon be brought within the State by the Central Pacific Railroad Company, and moneys to be derived from the sale of lands—are taken into the account.

In computing the property tax, the assessable wealth of the State is placed at $16,000,000 for the third fiscal year, $20,000,000 for the fourth, and $24,000,000 for the fifth. It is believed that the rapid progress of the Pacific Railroad, which will doubtless entirely cross our State before the expiration of the fifth fiscal year, will increase the taxable property far more than is estimated.

The stamp tax varies but little from year to year, and is estimated at the same figure for each year.

The poll tax is estimated $5,000 higher for the fourth fiscal year, when a general election will be held. Experience has shown that the collection of this tax under the Registry Law, in years when general elections are held, produces much more satisfactory results than attained in other years by the Assessors.

The capitation tax, it is thought, will increase, as estimated, as the advance of the railroad renders travel more easy and convenient.

It is also believed that the mining tax would increase somewhat, even if the provisions of the present Revenue Law in relation thereto remain in force. The yield of the Comstock has considerably increased the past six months, and there are fair prospects that it will continue to improve. The Counties of Lander and Nye also promise a much greater yield in the future.

In the calculations in regard to the probable expenditures, the amount of the outstanding bonds of 1866 — $140,000 — and of unpaid Controller's warrants—$60,000—is included in the estimate for the third fiscal year. For the fourth fiscal year the sum of $50,000 is deducted—there being no Session of the Legislature. For the fifth fiscal year the same amount is retained. In the estimate no calculation is made for the interest ceased by bonds being redeemed.

but the figures include an annual interest of $45,000 for the three years. Without doubt a large part of the bonds will be retired within that time ; and to the extent of the interest thereon the estimates of expenditures will be too large.

It may be proper to remark here, that the estimates throughout are made on a purely coin basis.

It will be seen that, even at the low estimates of receipts and the high ones for expenditure here presented, the State will, at the expiration of three years from date, not only be free from debt, save territorial obligations and Soldiers' Bounty claims, but have in the General Fund the handsome sum of $98,000.

Very respectfully,

CHARLES A. SUMNER,
FRED. HUTCHINS,
F. M. PROCTOR,
D. L. HASTINGS,
C. H. EASTMAN,
Committee of Ways and Means.

REPORT OF JOINT COMMITTEE

OF THE

SENATE AND ASSEMBLY,

ON

STATE PRISON.

REPORT.

The Joint Committee, composed of the Committee on State Prison, from the Senate, and State Institutions, from the Assembly, who were directed by concurrent resolution to visit and make a thorough examination relative to the condition of the State Prison, and the manner in which the affairs of the same are conducted, beg leave to submit the following report:

SANITARY CONDITION.

Your Committee are gratified in being able to report the Prison in a satisfactory sanitary condition. There is no sickness among the prisoners at the present time, nor has any prevailed to any great extent during the past year.

The Prison is kept in a cleanly and wholesome condition; the inmates are comfortably and warmly clothed, and the food furnished them is of an excellent quality.

Your Committee would suggest that some improvement should be made in the matter of ventilation, by providing grated doors for the cells already constructed and now in use, and for those about to be constructed.

While all other arrangements with regard to the sanitary condition of the prisoners are as perfect as could be desired, it is certainly to be hoped that this one, which would perhaps conduce more than all others to their health and comfort, should not be neglected. The arrangements are not yet completed which were designed to supply the Prison with water for bathing purposes. There was not sufficient money to carry out the original plan, and your Committee recommend that the work be completed as soon as possible, as a sanitary measure. The supply of water is abundant, and only a small outlay is necessary to complete the plans heretofore projected.

BUILDING.

During the past year a new building, twenty-two (22) by seventy-six (76) feet, has been completed in the rear of the main prison building. It is substantially constructed, well lighted and ventilated, and properly secured against the escape of prisoners. It is divided into two apartments by a wall thirty (30) feet from the east end, and is intended as a kitchen, and the other portion for a prisoners' dining room. We would recommend that an addition be erected on the west end of this building, of the same width and forty-one (41) feet in length, which would extend it to the end of the Territorial addition (now in use as a dining and cell room). This would afford room for thirty-two (32) new cells, in case the necessity for the same should arise.

42

NEW CELLS.

Your Committee would also recommend the erection of sixteen (16) new cells as soon as practicable. Eight (8) of them should be located in the Territorial addition, opposite those already erected, and the other eight (8) in the proposed new building, against the south wall of the Territorial addition. By this arrangement none of the cells thus constructed would be connected with the outer walls, there being a passage-way for the guard entirely around them, which would add greatly to the security of the Prison. The rock for eight (8) new cells is now quarried and dressed. We would advise that no further improvements be made within the walls of the old buildings, the outer walls of which are very weak and insecure, requiring extra vigilance to prevent the escape of prisoners.

REPAIRS NEEDED.

The east end of the main building, lower floor, now used as an officers' dining room, offices, store room and Warden's quarters, is scarcely habitable, and needs lathing and plastering throughout; nearly all the plastering, which was done at an early day, has crumbled and fallen; some of the partitions are of adobe brick, and others, which are simply posts and studs, canvased, are rotting with age and damp. These partitions should be made permanent in order to support the upper story of the building, the weight of which is now almost entirely supported by the outside walls. The east (end) wall is badly cracked, and the State will be saved expense in rebuilding the same if the necessary improvement is soon made.

We would also recommend that, as soon as it can be done consistently, the barn be removed and rebuilt, as it now stands in such a position, apart from the main building, as to require extra vigilance on the part of the officers to keep the prisoners in view, working in that part of the yard. Workshops should be built as soon as possible, and we would suggest that when plans for the same are finally determined on, the stable should be made part of the same building, as by this arrangement the guards can be more advantageously placed while on duty.

WALL.

Your Committee would recommend that a substantial wall, to surround the Prison, be commenced at an early day. Such an improvement is much needed, and while contributing to the security of the Prison, it would also lessen the expense now incurred for police force.

Your Committee would urge in favor of pushing forward these improvements: the State has no contracts at the present time from which any revenue can be derived from the labor of prisoners, and they will consequently remain, in a measure, unemployed, unless employed on these works. The additional expense that would be incurred by the State in completing these improvements, would be slight in comparison to the benefits that would arise from them. All that would be required in addition to the labor of the prisoners, would be the purchase of lime and sand, and the employment of one or two mechanics to supervise the work.

It is certainly to be regretted that the Prison is so located that the labor of the prisoners affords no material revenue to the State, and it is only by improvements upon the Prison itself, that such labor can be made of any benefit.

Your Committee would suggest that some arrangement should be made with those superintending the construction of the United States Branch Mint, to furnish rock for that institution.

TOOLS REQUIRED.

Your Committee find that many additions are needed to the supply of tools used in the various branches of business now being carried on, viz : quarrymen, stone-cutters, carpenter, blacksmith, and shoemaker.

MATERIAL, ETC.

All the shoes and uniform clothing required, are manufactured by the prisoners. The material for the uniform is bought directly from the manufacturer, and it would be a considerable saving to the State if other material used in the several departments of labor, were bought in San Francisco.

DISCIPLINE.

Your Committee found the Prison in an excellent state of discipline, and have no suggestions to make in regard to the same.

APPROPRIATION.

In order to carry out the proposed improvements, and furnish the Warden with sufficient funds to purchase supplies at all times for cash, your Committee would recommend a liberal appropriation to the State Prison Fund, for the next two years. A balance of $3,488.98, reported by the late Warden as remaining in the State Prison Fund at the end of the fiscal year 1866, reverted on or about the first day of January, 1867, to the General Fund. Your Committee are of the opinion that an appropriation of $70,000 should be made for the ensuing two years.

OFFICERS.

We find that the number of officers and guards employed by J. S. Slingerland (the present Warden) are necessary for the care and safety of the prisoners under his charge, while the same force would effectually guard and control a greater number.

As the Prison is situated, with its imperfect securities for the prevention of escapes, constant vigilance is required on the part of all of the officers connected with the Prison.

We also submit a full and complete inventory, as near as the same could be obtained, of all the material, supplies, etc., remaining on hand on the 8th day of January, 1867.

SOLOMON GELLER, Chairman,
F. M. PROCTOR,
CHARLES A. SUMNER,
Senate Committee.

GEO. H. DANA, Chairman,
J. L. SWANEY,
O. K. STAMPLEY,
Assembly Committee.

INVENTORY.

INVENTORY

INVENTORY

OF FURNITURE, FIXTURES, CROCKERY, DINING ROOM, KITCHEN, AND TABLE WARE, ON HAND ON THE EIGHTH DAY OF JANUARY, 1867.

KITCHEN AND DINING ROOM.

1 stove, 3 large pans, 3 small pans, 6 baking pans, 3 dippers, 2 steamers, 2 large spoons, 1 meat fork, 3 ladles, 2 slicers, 2 frying pans, 4 sauce pans, 3 coffee pots, 1 tea kettle, 2 boilers, 9 pans, 6 small pans, 2 sieves, 2 small milk pans, 2 tin cups, 1 clock, 12 knives, 12 forks, 24 dinner plates, 24 breakfast plates, 24 cups, 24 saucers, 3 milk pitchers, 12 soup plates, 12 bowls, 12 side dishes, 6 table dishes, 6 tumblers, 1 castor, 2 salt cellars, 1 small tea pot, 18 tea spoons, 12 table spoons, 2 mince knives, 1 coffee mill, 1 looking glass, 1 steel.

OFFICE.

1 bed and bedding, 2 maps, 1 book case and books, 1 desk and lamps, 1 dozen large files, 1 half dozen tacks, 1 dozen lamp chimneys, 4 chairs, prison keys and duplicates, stationery—small supply, 1 stove and pipe.

CELL ROOM.

8 double cells—bedding complete for fourteen prisoners, 8 cell lamps, 2 dining and 1 side table, 8 benches, 1 locker, 1 glass, 1 stove and pipe, tin cups, plates, pans, knives and forks for 22 prisoners, towels for same, 1 force pump and fifty feet of hose, 4 wash basins, 1 set stocks.

GUARD ROOM.

Bed and bedding for 2 guards, bed and bedding for 7 prisoners, 4 cell lamps for prisoners, 1 stove and pipe, 2 lamps, 1 table, 1 desk, 2 lounges, 1 clock, 1 medicine chest, 4 chairs, 1 set shelves for books, 1 large lamp reflector, 1 wash stand and sink, towels, looking glass, combs, etc., for guards.

ARMORY ROOM.

1 ammunition chest, 1 double-barrel shot gun, 1 Sharp's pistol, 1 gun bored for rifle and shot, 7 muskets, 1 Sharp's carbine, 2 Henry rifles, 2 revolvers, 2 pair handcuffs, 200 musket cartridges, 100 Henry rifle cartridges.

NEW ADDITION.

One large force pump and pipe. Part of this room partitioned off for tailor and shoe shop.

MISCELLANEOUS.

Five bales of hay, ten hogs, wheelbarrows, derrick, with necessary rigging complete, one U. S. flag, stable and garden tools, one thousand feet dressed stone. stone for eight cells, gas and lead pipe for tank, three extra lengths gas pipe, 1 sleigh, 1 horse and wagon and harness, 1 cow, 1 pump in lower yard, 1 pump in garden.

TAILOR AND SHOE SHOP.

1 bolt of 40 yards uniform cloth for pants, 1 kit shoemaker's tools—incomplete, one stove and pipe.

CLOTHING ROOM.

3 dozen uniform shirts, 7 dozen undershirts, 1-2 dozen drawers, 7 pair socks.

STORE ROOM AND CELLAR.

1 meat safe, 2 tons potatoes, and small amounts of provisions, which are bought from time to time as required.

Stone-cutters' and quarrying tools need many additions.

Blacksmiths and carpenters have tools sufficient for ordinary work. A small amount of iron on hand; enough charcoal for six weeks or two months, but little of it fit for use.

Wash-room and kitchen stores are almost useless. 2 wash-boards, 2 wash-tubs, clothes-pins, 50 feet hose, 8 flat-irons, 2 boxes starch, 1 small box store and pipe.

LARGE HALL.

1 carpenter's bench, 1 keg white lead, 100 lbs. nails, 1 chest for storing powder, 1 double bed and bedding, 1 single bed and bedding.

INDEX.

48

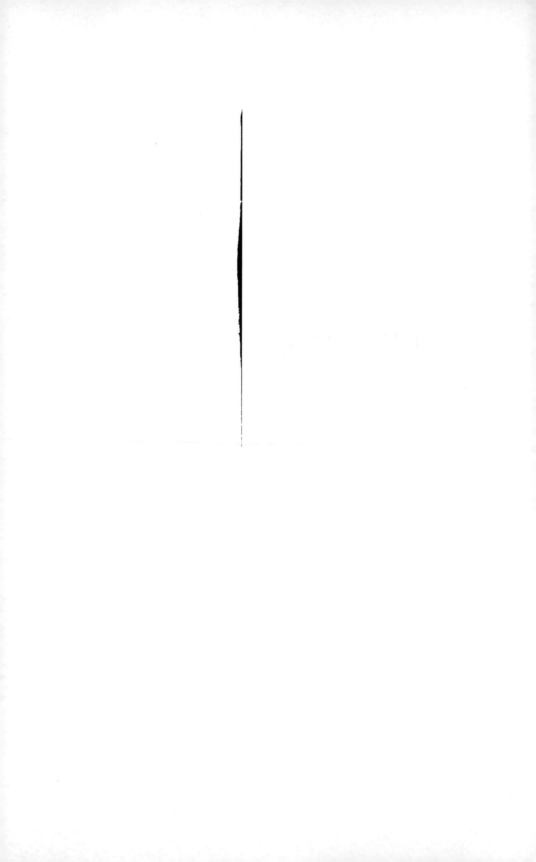

GENERAL INDEX.

A

AGRICULTURE AND MANUFACTURES. Committee appointed on, 18, 257.

B

BARCLAY, FURMAN. Appointed Page, 13.
BLASDEL, H. G. Oath of office administered to, 12.
BROWN, B. C. Elected Secretary, 6.

C

CARPENTER, C. Answered to name, 5.
    Motions by, 38.
    Appointed on Committees, 9, 16, 18, 22, 257, 258.
    Reports by, 53.
    Introduced bills, 24, 37.
COOLIDGE, J. P. Appointed Minute Clerk, 7.
CUTTER, WILLIAM M. Nominated for Secretary, 6.
COMMUNICATIONS. From the Governor, 18, 59, 63.
    From the Secretary of State, 21, 49, 80, 130, 146, 181, 214, 271.
    From the Hon. J. Neely Johnson, 96, 100, 162.
    From the Hon. A. F. White, 139.
    From the Hon. E. Rhoades, 142, 204.
    From the Hon. D. O. Mills and others, 142.
    From the Hon. W. K. Parkinson, 315.
CORPORATIONS. Committee appointed on, 16, 257.
    Report from, 53, 103, 118, 142, 167, 175, 203.
COUNTIES AND COUNTY BOUNDARIES. Committee appointed on, 18, 257.
    Reports of, 23, 49, 102, 114, 118, 127, 133, 162, 167, 191, 227.
CLAIMS. Committee appointed on, 22, 258.
    Reports of, 93, 113, 114, 122, 140, 147, 155, 174, 187, 231, 240.
CRADDOCK, JOHN. Appointed Messenger, 13.

D

DORON, LEWIS. Answer to name, 5.
    Motions by, 12, 18, 44, 49, 74, 99, 101, 110, 120, 165, 171, 177, 185, 197, 222, 245,
        249, 262, 263, 267, 270, 273, 287, 288, 289, 306, 307, 308, 310, 313, 314, 316,
        318.
    Resolutions by, 54, 55, 101, 124, 276, 284, 308.
    Appointed on Committees, 9, 13, 16, 18, 22, 109, 257, 258, 303, 306.
    Reports by, 23, 39, 49, 54, 57, 61, 78, 97, 118, 161, 168, 175, 193, 204, 271, 314.

Notice of bills, 23, 25, 34, 71, 90.
Introduced bills, 28, 34, 76, 111, 160.
HASTINGS, D. L. Answer to name, 5.
    Motions by, 11, 13, 22, 27, 36, 66, 105, 119, 130, 151, 153, 161, 175, 176, 181, 214, 227, 233, 249, 266, 273, 274, 277, 278, 283, 285, 310, 312, 313, 314, 316, 317, 319.
    Resolutions by, 19, 45, 88, 256, 268, 318.
    Appointed on Committees, 8, 16, 18, 22, 41, 257, 258.
    Reports by, 27, 29, 39, 42, 48, 53, 57, 60, 65, 74, 83, 87, 88, 90, 92.
    Notice of bills, 285.
    Introduced bills, 51, 229, 289.
HAYNIE, M. N. Appointed Assistant Sergeant-at-Arms, 259.
HUTCHINS, FRED. Answer to name, 5.
    Motions by, 5, 9, 18, 20, 35, 45, 52, 59, 62, 68, 74, 79, 92, 94, 119, 120, 130, 139, 176, 177, 185, 190, 191, 192, 194, 199, 206, 208, 249, 256, 259, 263, 268, 271, 273, 275, 280, 287, 296.
    Resolutions by, 8, 10, 28, 41, 50, 58, 68, 228, 231.
    Appointed on Committees, 8, 16, 18, 22, 41, 64, 71, 257, 258.
    Reports by, 9, 23, 25, 29, 54, 97, 128, 203, 215' 247.
    Notice of bills, 25.
    Introduced bills, 43, 119, 130, 189, 197, 208, 245.

I

INTERNAL IMPROVEMENTS. Committee appointed on, 22, 258.

J

JUDICIARY. Committee appointed on, 16, 18, 257.
    Reports of, 28, 42, 48, 67, 89, 108, 114, 122, 133, 134, 143, 152, 168, 190, 192, 193, 215, 225, 227.
JOINT CONVENTION. Inauguration, 12.
    Joint Convention to elect United States Senator to succeed James W. Nye, 32, 35.

L

LINN, J. J. Answer to name, 5.
    Motions by, 124, 165, 216, 248, 276, 290, 296, 302, 305, 306, 313.
    Resolutions by, 21, 176, 238, 239, 260, 274, 305, 317.
    Appointed on Committees, 13, 16, 18, 124, 257, 258.
    Reports by, 17, 28, 33, 41, 48, 57, 60, 67, 75, 78, 89, 94, 100, 107, 115, 117, 143, 147, 152, 162, 166, 175, 182, 190, 199, 215, 225, 230, 243, 248, 250, 251, 259, 300, 310, 316, 319.
    Notice of bills, 10, 37.
    Introduced bills, 79, 86, 111, 160, 267.

M

MASON, B. S. Answer to name, 5.
    Motions by, 68, 73, 106, 139, 157, 171, 184, 207, 220, 261, 264, 268, 290, 302, 304, 306.
    Resolutions by, 239, 257, 262, 295, 299, 305.
    Appointed on Committees, 13, 16, 18, 22, 64, 109, 137, 191, 257, 258, 303, 306.
    Reports by, 42, 48, 53, 61, 64, 79, 100, 147, 168, 175, 239, 247, 281, 288, 289, 300, 309, 311.
    Notice of bills, 25, 30, 34, 57.
    Introduced bills, 43, 51, 229, 240, 270, 318.
    Protest by, 176.
MEDER, B. H. Answer to name, 5.
    Motions by, 47, 50, 78, 91, 125, 176, 179, 191, 202, 206, 218, 244, 247, 282, 299, 306, 312.
    Resolutions by, 123, 128, 219, 238, 312.
    Appointed on Committees, 16, 18, 191, 257, 258.
    Reports by, 78, 89, 97, 134, 143, 187, 193, 203, 220, 248.
    Notice of bills, 40.

W

WELTY, D. W. Answer to name, 5.
    Motions by, 10, 12, 69, 71, 73, 76, 81, 96, 99, 106, 116, 125, 137, 145, 160, 171, 212, 218, 220, 228, 245, 256, 266, 268, 269, 276, 277, 279, 280, 285, 295, 301, 306, 309, 310, 319.
    Resolutions by, 7, 18, 19, 21, 25, 69, 110, 118, 233, 305.
    Appointed on Committees, 8, 16, 18, 41, 257, 258, 279.
    Reports by, 11, 28, 42, 48, 67, 75, 88, 103, 114, 122, 152, 168, 213, 215, 225, 227, 247, 249, 257, 278, 319.
    Notice of bills, 8, 15, 23, 30, 34, 42, 43, 51, 270.
    Introduced bills, 15, 19, 21, 24, 28, 30, 34, 43, 58, 76, 79, 86, 90, 111, 119, 132, 133, 160, 164, 247, 266, 275, 303, 313, 317.
WAYS AND MEANS. Committee appointed on, 16, 257.
    Reports of, 23, 36, 38, 39, 54, 74, 142, 165, 167, 175, 211, 215, 233, 249, 264, 267, 284, 306.
WALLACE, C. C. Appointed Assistant Sergeant-at-Arms, 7.
WALTERS, D. P. Appointed Journal Clerk, 7.
WILLIAMSON, J. R. Elected Enrolling Clerk, 6.
    Appointed Copying Clerk, 257.
WILLIAMS, WILLIAM H. Nominated for Engrossing Clerk, 7.
WILLIAMS, THOMAS H. Nominated for United States Senator, 26.
WINTERS, JOHN B. Nominated for United States Senator, 26.
WRIGHT, F. F. Elected Official Reporter, 260.

Y

YEAS AND NAYS. 10, 18, 20, 22, 30, 31, 38, 40, 44, 47, 50, 52, 55, 56, 57, 58, 60, 61, 62, 65, 68, 69, 72, 73, 74, 77, 79, 80, 81, 82, 86, 87, 90, 92, 95, 96, 99, 101, 104, 105, 106, 109, 112, 117, 120, 121, 124, 125, 126, 127, 128, 131, 132, 133, 135, 137, 145, 146, 149, 150, 151, 153, 154, 157, 164, 165, 169, 171, 172, 173, 176, 177, 178, 179, 180, 181, 184, 185, 186, 188, 189, 190, 192, 193, 195, 196, 197, 198, 199, 207, 208, 209, 210, 211, 212, 217, 218, 219, 220, 221, 222, 225, 228, 229, 230, 231, 232, 234, 236, 237, 239, 240, 241, 243, 245, 246, 247, 249, 256, 257, 261, 262, 263, 266, 268, 272, 275, 276, 277, 279, 280, 281, 282, 283, 286, 288, 289, 290, 292, 293, 295, 296, 297, 298, 299, 301, 302, 309, 312, 314, 317, 318, 319.

44

INDEX TO SENATE BILLS.

THIRD SESSION.

SENATE BILLS.

SENATE BILLS.

SENATE BILLS.

SENATE BILLS.

SPECIAL SESSION.

SENATE CONCURRENT AND JOINT RESOLUTIONS.

SENATE RESOLUTIONS.

INDEX TO ASSEMBLY BILLS.

THIRD SESSION.

ASSEMBLY BILLS.

ASSEMBLY BILLS.

ASSEMBLY BILLS.

ASSEMBLY BILLS.

SPECIAL SESSION.

ASSEMBLY BILLS.

ASSEMBLY CONCURRENT RESOLUTIONS.

ASSEMBLY RESOLUTIONS.

TITLE.	Pages.
Relative to reconstruction measures.	286, 287, 300, 301
Relative to lands granted by the United States to the State of Nevada.	286, 287, 301
Relative to Jefferson Davis.	286, 287, 289
Relative to return of Assembly Bill No. 14.	313

APPENDIX

TO

SENATE PROCEEDINGS.

SECOND INAUGURAL ADDRESS

OF

HON. H. G. BLASDEL,

GOVERNOR OF THE STATE OF NEVADA,

DELIVERED JANUARY 8TH, 1867,

BEFORE THE SENATE AND ASSEMBLY, IN JOINT CONVENTION.

SECOND INAUGURAL ADDRESS.

DELIVERED JANUARY 8TH, 1867.

FELLOW CITIZENS:

Upon again taking the official oath as your Executive, and entering upon the duties of that responsible office for the next four years, it is becoming that I return my grateful acknowledgments to a confiding constituency, and assure them that, in the future as in the past, my earnest efforts shall be to do my whole duty. When first inaugurated, Nevada had been a member of the Federal Union but one month. Many then doubted our ability to maintain separate State organization, and sincerely questioned the wisdom and policy of the step. Happily, I may now congratulate the people upon the disappearance of these doubts, upon the certain and permanent success of the State, and upon the great progress made in the discovery and development of our mineral and other resources.

The visionary schemes of speculation which distempered and well nigh ruined the legitimate business of the people, have given place to more healthy and permanent existence ; and now every department of labor and all branches of industry are conducted with system, economy, and profit. The blind reliance upon fortune or chance, which at first characterized so many of our citizens— the delusion that the possession of an undeveloped mining claim was, in itself, a certain guarantee of exhaustless wealth—have given place to the consciousness that development will alone insure results. And now, stimulated by the certain knowledge of the permanence and value of our mines, honest labor and determined effort are everywhere seen.

Mining has become systematized, science and invention are brought to the aid of labor, and a business once considered speculative and hazardous has become legitimate and safe. In the past year much larger quantities of the precious metals were taken from our older mines than that preceding. The developments made in the new districts are more than satisfactory. In some localities, where twelve months ago minerals were not supposed to exist in sufficient quantities to be worthy of attention, mines of great value have been discovered, and from some of them large amounts of bullion have been received. We may reasonably expect during the ensuing year new and more valuable discoveries, greater developments, and increased products. Our mines, though permanent, extensive, and rich, are not our only source of wealth. Our agricultural lands are productive, and gradually being occupied, improved, and cultivated. The time is not far distant when we may confidently expect them to yield an abundance for home demands.

To render all our natural resources fully available, railroad communication is indispensable. It is encouraging, indeed, to know that this necessity is being supplied by the rapid approach of the Central Pacific from the west and the Union Pacific from the east. The energy and perseverance displayed by the former company in pushing forward their work, is highly commendable. I am credibly informed—and congratulate you thereupon—that it is their intention to complete their road to a point some twenty miles within our borders during the coming summer, thus affording us cheap and speedy transportation to and from tide water.

What has already been accomplished by the Union Pacific Railroad Company has materially shortened the time necessary for communication between us and the East; and from the energy displayed by both, I doubt not that within three years we will communicate with the Atlantic by this mode. When this great work shall have been completed, new and more profitable fields of industry and enterprise will be opened; the tide of material prosperity, in all its departments, will pour in upon us; immigration, now retarded by the present expensive and tedious means of transit, will be vastly increased, multiplying the number of our farmers, mechanics, laborers, and all classes of citizens so essential to the development of the country.

Then will society become more permanent and elevated—our people be, and feel that they are, surrounded by the associations, comforts, and ties of home.

I congratulate you upon the increased morality of the State, and the advanced condition of our system of public instruction. The higher standard of morals attained; the rapid advancement of our youth in all the departments of useful knowledge; the disappearance of many of the vices prevalent during the first years of our history; the impartial enforcement and prompt execution of the laws by those in authority; and the cheerful and almost universal obedience rendered by the citizen, form a pleasing contrast with the past, and afford us matter of just pride and special congratulation. Continued fidelity upon the part of those filling the places of public trust, continued obedience upon the part of the people, and united effort upon the part of both, cannot fail to promote the happiness and insure the general prosperity of all.

Since the admission of Nevada into the Union, great events have passed to the pages of our nation's history, the most momentous of which is its triumph over armed rebellion in its efforts to destroy the Government and subvert its authority. Peace has been measurably restored throughout our borders—actual war having ceased. The instruments of warfare have been exchanged for implements of husbandry. A pleasing hope of lasting tranquillity has lighted again thousands of firesides, lately stricken and made desolate by sanguinary strife; and notwithstanding the severity of the ordeal through which we have passed, the final triumph of Republican institutions is sure, and the name AMERICAN encircled by a brighter halo of glory than ever before.

But it is a source of intense mortification to every patriot that such a wide difference of opinion and policy existed between the Executive and Legislative branches of the General Government when the country was just emerging from the throes of war, when questions were pending more vital to the nation than at any previous period, and when the peculiar exigencies of the times demand unity of purpose, the exercise of the soundest judgment, and the adoption of the wisest policy statesmen could devise.

Could they thus widely differ upon questions involving the reconstruction and the future destiny of the Union, unless one or the other was intent upon the sacrifice of some fundamental principle, indispensable to the security of the Government? In this connection, I can but justify and commend the action and the policy of the late Congress, while I regretfully disapprove that of the President.

The former, prompted by a spirit of fidelity to principle and patriotic devotion to the whole country, earnestly endeavored to reunite it upon terms just and equitable to all.

The latter, seeming to forget that Congress were the immediate representatives of the people, having the right to devise and adopt measures other than such as he might originate or personally approve, vainly endeavored to thwart the will of the people by the immediate restoration of treason to power, without the exaction of sufficient guarantees for the future safety of the Republic.

But Congress with firmness maintained its legitimate prerogative, carried out its policy to the extent of its authority, and the results of the recent elections show that the people—the final arbiters between them—have decided against the theories of the President, and ratified the views of Congress. Thus have they evinced their wisdom, given proof of their fidelity and patriotism, and furnished the world with yet another assurance of man's capacity for self-government and of the permanency and worth of Republican Institutions. I have faith in the Congress of the people. I believe they will complete the work so nobly begun. I believe they will reconstruct these dissevered States upon a broader and more permanent foundation, re-unite the people by ties of closer intimacy and more enduring friendship, and restore the Union with more than its former dignity and splendor upon principles of Universal Liberty, Justice, and Humanity.

For these blessed hopes and reassuring prospects, let us be ever grateful to Him " in whose hands nations are as men."

APPENDIX

TO

SENATE PROCEEDINGS.

SECOND INAUGURAL ADDRESS

OF

HON. H. G. BLASDEL,

GOVERNOR OF THE STATE OF NEVADA,

DELIVERED JANUARY 8TH, 1867,

BEFORE THE SENATE AND ASSEMBLY, IN JOINT CONVENTION.

those lately in rebellion to their forfeited lives and estates and clothe them again with all the rights, privileges and dignity of American citizens.

Can a victorious nation, jealous of its honor and vigilant of its liberty, exact less? Can conquered rebels reasonably expect more? Rome hurled her traitors from the Tarpeian Rock, and all other civilized governments punish treason with death.

Shall America commit to the keeping of her criminal enemies, without qualification and without guarantees, the Government they so madly made war to destroy and the liberties they so wickedly attempted to subvert? I heartily approve the proposed Amendment. I believe its adoption by the requisite number of States will effect the perfect restoration of the Union and complete an equitable readjustment of our national difficulties. I believe it is just to the Southern people themselves and necessary to their moral, social and material advancement; that through it the obstacles that have retarded their progress in the past will be swept away. I believe it will remove that prejudice, allay that hatred which was the great source of our national ills, and induce that comity and friendship always indispensable to the public prosperity and peace. I believe it will place the national life beyond the hazard of another rebellion, and, by securing the great results of the war, perpetuate republican institutions. I believe it will give to humanity a new impulse, and surround liberty with new barriers alike impregnable to anarchy and despotism. I transmit the proposed Amendment to you with the confident belief that your patriotism, fidelity and zeal for the public welfare will prompt your immediate action, and with the earnest hope that the wisdom, justice and necessity of the measure will command your unqualified approval.

FINANCE AND STATE DEBT.

The Treasurer and Controller have not yet submitted their annual reports; it is impossible, therefore, to give an exact detailed statement of the finances of the State. The State debt, exclusive of Territorial liabilities assumed, approximates $278,000 in coin. Of this amount there will be due, February 1st, 1867, $218,000, and of floating debt, $60,000. The balance in the Treasury, January 1st, 1866, was $51,000. The total receipts during the last fiscal year, from all sources, were $425,000. The total disbursements were $320,000. The balance on hand, in all the different funds, is about $156,000, mostly in currency. As the Legislature will not again convene until January, 1869, it will be necessary to make appropriations to defray the expenses of the State Government for two years. To meet these expenses, provide for the payment of outstanding indebtedness and place the affairs of the State upon a permanent cash basis. I recommend the negotiation of a loan of $300,000. This amount, with accruing revenues, will, in my opinion, entirely relieve our financial embarrassment and leave us with ample means in the treasury to meet current expenses. I would recommend the issuance of ten per cent. bonds, to run ten years, and the appropriation of a sufficient amount of the first revenue arising from the property tax to pay the interest thereon semi-annually and create a sinking fund which will extinguish the principal within ten years. In addition to the debt strictly that of the State, there are outstanding liabilities, incurred by the late Territory of Nevada and assumed by the State, which are not fully provided for. I recommend the passage of a law providing for their payment.

PUBLIC LANDS.

Through the generosity of the General Government, this State is the donee of the following lands:

First—The sixteenth and thirty-sixth sections of each township.

Second—Five hundred thousand acres, under Act of Congress, 1841.

Third—Thirty thousand acres for each Senator and Representative of the State in Congress, under Act of Congress, July 2, 1862.

Fourth—Twenty sections under section 8 and twenty sections under section 9 of the Enabling Act of March 21, 1864.

Fifth—Seventy-two entire sections, under Act of July 4, 1866.

These donations, exclusive of the sixteenth and thirty-sixth sections, amount to 661,680 acres. Of the sixteenth and thirty-sixth sections there are over 8,000,000 acres. These gifts were made for the following specified purposes, named in the above order:

The first for educational purposes, and is so applied by the Constitution. The second for internal improvements, applied by the Constitution to university and educational purposes, which application was sanctioned by Congress July 4th, 1866. The third (90,000 acres) for teaching "agriculture and the mechanic arts," applied by the Constitution to university and education; and Congress, July 4, 1866, gave permission for it to be used for the additional purpose of teaching the theory and practice of mining. The fourth for public buildings at the State Capitol, for legislative and judicial and State Prison purposes equally, is applied by the Constitution to university and education, subject to Congressional sanction not yet given. The fifth, for university purposes exclusively. In disposing of the proceeds of the sales of these lands, the Legislature can place so much as it chooses arising from the sales of the first and second donations in each, the University Fund and the Public School Fund; must place all from the third and fifth in the University Fund, and those from the fourth equally in a "Legislative and Judicial Public Building Fund" and a "State Prison Building Fund" (or if otherwise appropriated, it must be subject to the approval of Congress).

In addition to the above, Congress has provided that this State shall receive five per cent. of all the moneys realized from sales, by the United States, of public lands lying within our limits after the admission of Nevada into the Union, to be applied to "making and improving public roads and constructing ditches or canals, to effect a general system of irrigation of the agricultural lands of the State, as the Legislature shall direct."

In view of the fact that the State is already provided with Prison buildings, and has no means on hand with which to construct legislative and judicial buildings, would it not be well to provide that the proceeds of the sale of all the lands granted for those purposes, as well as the five per cent. upon lands sold by the United States, be placed in a "Legislative and Judicial Building Fund," and to obtain, if possible, the sanction thereof by Congress? If done, these moneys can be temporarily invested in State or national securities.

An Act of 1864–5, amended in 1866, provides for the sale in part of the sixteenth and thirty-sixth sections. Some 2,127 acres have been sold, at the price fixed by law, which, in my opinion, is too high. It is not fair to presume that any considerable portion of those lands will be sold by the State at two and a half dollars per acre, when the United States is selling at one and a quarter.

The amendatory Act of 1866 renders the law ambiguous and defective. There are other Acts which provide for the *location* only of the forty sections and the 500,000 acres above stated. No action has yet been taken under them. It would be well to repeal all former legislation upon this subject, and, carefully preserving all rights acquired under it, pass one general law embodying plain and full provisions for the sale of all the above enumerated lands, and the application of the various proceeds as indicated; the issuance and sale of floating land warrants to be located upon them before or after official survey should be provided for. In order to prevent complicity, secure the interests of the State in the best possible manner, and expedite the location and sale of all the lands belonging to the State, it would be well to establish a State "General Land Office," and create the offices of "General Agent" and "Locating Commissioner." It should be made the duty of the Locating Commissioner to ascertain, as speedily as possible, all instances in which the 16th and 36th sections have been disposed of by the General Government, and locate other lands in lieu thereof, as permitted, that we may not lose them entirely. Also, to locate all the different donations as fast as surveyed by the United States Surveyor General, report them to the General Agent, and he by proper legal proceedings obtain the patent of the United States therefor. In this particular the State would lose much by delay. In enacting these provisions, especially in relation to location and sale, it would be necessary to observe closely the privileges given and the restrictions made by " An Act concerning certain Lands granted to the State of Nevada," approved July 4, 1866. Also, the 7th, 8th, and 9th sections of the Enabling Act. These locations may be made as a whole without reference to the donations severally, but if so made, the proceeds of sales, as fast as paid into the Treasury, should be apportioned to the several funds above designated, ratably in proportion to the whole.

The manner of issuing, selling, locating, and making proper proof and record of locating floating land warrants, should be carefully specified; also, when, where, from whom and under what requirements patents may be obtained. Failure to provide for the early location and prompt sale of these State lands can but result in great injury; on the other hand, if judiciously disposed of, the general prosperity of the State will thereby be greatly advanced.

STATE OFFICERS.

The duties of all the State officers have not been defined by law. Some of them are discharging their duties by virtue of the Constitution only, or by virtue of that and incidental provisions of statutes. It is evidently perplexing to them to be guided only by the general permissions and restrictions of the fundamental law. Among the legislation needed under this head may be instanced that contemplated by the 13th and 14th sections of the 5th Article of the Constitution.

STATE MINERALOGIST.

Herewith I transmit the Annual Report of the State Mineralogist, made as required by law to the " Board of Regents of the State University." I recommend that the salary of this officer be fixed at a definite sum, and made payable as those of other State officers, from the fact that the moneys now or to be placed in the " University Fund " are by the Constitution otherwise applied.

APPORTIONMENT OF SENATORS AND ASSEMBLYMEN.

Under existing laws the Legislature is composed of fifty-seven members. nineteen of them Senators and thirty-eight Assemblymen, apportioned among the several counties as follows: Storey County, 4 Senators and 12 Assemblymen; Douglas County, 1 Senator and 2 Assemblymen; Esmeralda County, 2 Senators and 4 Assemblymen; Humboldt County, 2 Senators and 3 Assemblymen; Lander County, 2 Senators and 4 Assemblymen; Lyon County, 2 Senators and 3 Assemblymen; Churchill County, 1 Senator and 2 Assemblymen; Nye County, 1 Senator and 2 Assemblymen; Ormsby County, 2 Senators and 3 Assemblymen; Washoe and Roop Counties, 2 Senators and 3 Assemblymen.

In my opinion it would be prudent and just to re-apportion the representation in both branches, basing the new apportionment principally upon present population; thus giving to each county, as near as may be, its equal and fair voice in determining the policy and prescribing the laws of the State. It would be wise to reduce the aggregate representation in the Legislature. Twelve Senators and twenty-five Assemblymen would, in my judgment, constitute a body sufficiently numerous to protect the general interests of the people at large as well as the local interests of the several communities.

LOSSES BY INDIANS.

During the last session an Act was passed by which a Commission was created to ascertain the losses sustained by citizens of Humboldt County by Indian depredations during the years 1864, 1865 and 1866, and report thereon to the Governor. The Commission have faithfully performed their duty, and submitted their report, which I herewith transmit, and recommend that you forward the report and accompanying proofs to and memorialize Congress, asking an appropriation for the payment of the claims and expenses incident to the Commission.

ELECTION LAW.

The 31st section of this Act, page 216, Statutes of 1866, provides, in effect, that if any two or more candidates for a State office shall receive an equal, and the highest, number of votes cast for the same office, the Governor shall issue a proclamation, ordering a new election therefor. That provision is in contravention of Section 4, Article V, of the Constitution, which requires that in such cases "The Legislature, by joint ballot of two branches, shall elect one of said persons to fill said office." The law should be made to conform to the Constitution. It should be further amended so as to provide a mode by which, in all proper cases, the offices of Senators and Assemblymen may be officially declared vacant, and writs of election thereupon be issued to fill them.

EASTERN AND SOUTHERN BOUNDARIES.

By Act of Congress, approved May 5, 1866, there was added to this State on the east all the territory lying between the 37th and 38th degrees of longitude, west from Washington, extending from the 37th to the 42d degree of north latitude, embracing 18,000 square miles, or 11,530,000 acres. This grant was anticipated and provided for in the formation and adoption of the State Constitution, and, therefore, no further action is required. A further addition "commencing on the 37th degree of north latitude at the 37th degree of longitude, west from Washington, and running thence south on said degree of longitude to he middle of the river Colorado of the West; thence down the middle of said river to the eastern boundary of the State of California; thence northwesterly, along said boundary of California, to the 37th degree of north latitude; and hence east, along said degree of latitude, to the point of beginning," was contingently made to become effectual upon the acceptance of the State, through its Legislature. This grant, connecting us as it does with the navigable waters of the Colorado River, and embracing extensive and valuable agricultural and mineral lands, is of great importance to the State, and should be promptly accepted. Looking alone to the Act of Congress, it would seem that all the action necessary on the part of the State, for a full and final acceptance of this last named cession, would be that of the Legislature in the form of an Act or joint resolution. But the establishment of boundary lines by the Constitution would seem to leave the Legislature without present authority to bind the State in the premises. In order that no misapprehension may arise from a failure to comply with the Act, I suggest the propriety of immediate legislative acceptance as therein contemplated. And in order to legally and fully extend the jurisdiction of the State over the ceded territory, I suggest the propriety of proposing and submitting to the people, for their ratification, an amendment to the Constitution conforming our southern boundary to the lines designated in the grant.

GAMING.

The only law against gaming is that on pages 169 and 170, Statutes of 1864-5. The second section appropriates fines collected under it to purposes not permitted by Section 3, Article XI, of the Constitution, which devotes "all fines collected under the penal laws of the State" to educational purposes. The law should be conformed to the Constitution, and, if possible, made more effectual in the detection and punishment of the crime. Gaming is an intolerable and inexcusable vice. It saps the very foundation of morality, breeds contempt for honest industry, and totally disqualifies its victims for the discharge of the ordinary duties of life. Every energy of the State should be invoked to suppress it.

CARE OF THE INSANE.

In my last Annual Message it was recommended that provision be made for the care of the insane. A Fund should be created for this purpose, to be drawn upon, and the State never without such means, when needed, until provided with an Asylum, and permanent arrangements for the safe keeping, support and proper medical treatment for those thus unfortunate. I hope this important subject will receive, as it merits, your prompt and favorable action.

EDUCATION.

It is truly gratifying that so thorough a system of education has been inaugurated throughout the State; that in all places where a sufficient number of pupils are found, Free Schools are in successful operation; that the average attendance thereon is commendably large, and this great cause in such an advanced and prosperous condition. For detailed information and valuable suggestions as to needed legislation upon this subject, I refer you to the accompanying Annual Report of our late worthy Superintendent of Public Instruction, and to the Eleventh Article of the Constitution.

STATE LIBRARY.

The number of volumes added to the State Library during the last year is 1,432, of which 1,828 are law, and 104 are miscellaneous—making a total now of 4,721 volumes; of law, 2,209, and of miscellaneous works, 2,512. The rapidity with which this Library has been accumulated—the number, value and importance of the volumes it contains, reflect great credit upon the State. With continued fostering care, it will soon be an object of great pride.

PARDONS.

Jim, (an Indian boy) on the 2d of January, 1866, was, by the Recorder's Court at Virginia City, convicted of petit larceny, and sentenced to imprisonment in the Storey County Jail for four months. He was pardoned on the 8th of February, 1866, on the recommendation of the City Recorder, before whom tried, and the attorney who prosecuted the case, for reasons of good behavior, paltry character of the offense, and sufficient punishment.

H. F. Swazey, on the 8th of December, 1863, was convicted by the First Judicial District Court, Washoe County, N. T., of manslaughter, and sentenced to three years in the Territorial Prison. He was pardoned, and restored to citizenship on the 9th of March, 1866, at the request of many good citizens, amongst them all the Senators and all the Assemblymen (except one) of the second session of the Legislature, and because he had been imprisoned sufficiently long, as the Board of Pardons were convinced, to fully answer the demands of public justice.

Antonio Martinez, on the 29th of January, 1866, was convicted of petit larceny by the Recorder's Court of Virginia City, and sentenced to six months in the Storey County Jail. He was pardoned on the 22d day of June, 1866, on recommendation of said City Recorder and many good citizens of said county, for reasons of good conduct and sufficiency of punishment.

John Egbert, on the 28th of September, 1865, was convicted of grand larceny by the Second Judicial District Court, and sentenced to one year in the State Prison. He was pardoned and restored to citizenship on the 15th of March, 1866, on recommendation of the prosecuting witness, the District Attorney, who prosecuted, the Judge who sentenced him, and many others, for reasons of good conduct and doubt of guilt.

J. F. Hewitt, on the 19th of January, 1866, was convicted of forgery by the First Judicial District Court, and sentenced to one year in the State Prison. He was pardoned and restored to citizenship September 15th, 1866, on recommendation of many good citizens, because of mitigating circumstances, first offense, advanced age, dependent family, and good conduct in prison.

Jesse Bonds, on the 20th of March, 1865, was convicted of murder in the second degree, by the Seventh Judicial District Court, and sentenced to ten years in the State Prison. He was pardoned and restored to citizenship October 13th, 1866, on the recommendation of many good citizens of Lander County, on grounds of previous good character, excellent deportment in prison, and sufficient punishment.

F. W. Ames, on the 19th of January, 1866, was convicted of forgery by the Seventh Judicial District Court, and sentenced to one year in the State Prison. He was pardoned and restored to citizenship November 23d, 1866, because of good conduct and term about expired.

Charles Moreau, on the 25th of January, 1866, was convicted of grand larceny by the Seventh Judicial District Court, and sentenced to eighteen months in the State Prison. He was pardoned and restored to citizenship November 26th, 1866, because of infirmity, good conduct, and sufficiency of punishment.

Henry Charles Kettles, on the 2d of December, 1865, was convicted of arson in the second degree, by the Second Judicial District Court, and sentenced to five years in the State Prison. He was pardoned and restored to citizenship December 29th, 1866, because of committing offense at instigation of another, whose conviction and punishment he was the means of procuring by his confession and evidence.

J. McGahan, on the 27th of June, 1866, was convicted of " an assault with a deadly weapon with intent to inflict great bodily injury upon another person," by the First Judicial District Court, and sentenced to two years in the State Prison. He was pardoned and restored to citizenship December 31st, 1866, because strongly recommended by many, among them the Judge before whom tried, and eleven of the trial jury, and for good conduct.

Frank Woods, on the 8th of July, 1864, was convicted of grand larceny by the Third Judicial District Court of Nevada Territory, and sentenced to five years in the Territorial Prison. He was pardoned January 2d, 1867, because of severity of sentence, first offense, and sufficiency of punishment.

REMISSION.

On the 6th of October, 1862, A. W. Nightingill, in Humboldt County, N. T., became a surety on the bail bond of one Robert Ferris, held to answer the charge of murder. Said Ferris did not appear as required, and his bail was forfeited. This forfeiture as to said Nightingill, was remitted September 26th, 1866, upon recommendation of the County Commissioners of Humboldt County, it appearing satisfactory that the homicide committed by said Ferris was in self-defense.

MISCELLANEOUS SUGGESTIONS.

The charge made by the State for each commission issued to a Commissioner of Deeds is fifteen dollars; this is more than is charged by any other State, and should be reduced.

The choice at the last general election of a Public Administrator (to be ex-officio Coroner) in each county, was provided. This was in accordance with the requirements of the Constitution. The people choose such officers, but when and how to qualify, their duties, and the manner of discharging them, are not provided. A general law should be passed at the earliest practicable time upon this subject.

Section 3, Article XI, of the Constitution, pledges all fines collected under penal laws to educational purposes. A law should be enacted carrying out this provision.

I recommend the repeal of an Act of the Territorial Legislative Assembly, approved December 9th, 1862, limiting to six months the time of commencing civil actions upon judgments, contracts, obligations or liabilities for the payment of money or damages obtained, made, or executed out of the State. The period fixed by this Act is too short, and the discrimination against non-resident creditors is odious and unjust. In repealing it, all acquired rights should be carefully preserved.

I also recommend the amendment of the existing Attachment Law, by extending its provisions to non-resident creditors.

These measures, as they exist, while radically unjust, present also a serious barrier to the obtaining that credit abroad so indispensable to our business prosperity, and the repeal and amendment suggested will, in my opinion, if adopted, promote the general interests of the people.

Provision should be made by law for the disposal of persons convicted of murder, whose punishment may be commuted from death to imprisonment.

CONCLUSION.

I have thus briefly called your attention to those measures of legislation which I deem most important. In conclusion, permit me to express the hope that your labors may be pleasant, and characterized throughout by prudence, economy, and wisdom; that all branches of the Government may act with harmony, unity, and fidelity of purpose, so indispensable to the adoption of wise and just laws, and the promotion of the public welfare.

H. G. BLASDEL.

ANNUAL REPORT

OF

CONTROLLER OF THE STATE OF NEVADA,

FOR 1866.

ANNUAL REPORT

OF

THE CONTROLLER

OF THE

STATE OF NEVADA,

FOR THE

SECOND FISCAL YEAR, ENDING DECEMBER 31, 1866.

A. W. NIGHTINGILL,
STATE CONTROLLER.

———————

CARSON CITY:
JOSEPH E. ECKLEY, STATE PRINTER.
1867.

STATE CONTROLLER'S REPORT.

OFFICE OF STATE CONTROLLER,
CARSON, Nevada, Jan. 25, 1867.

HON. H. G. BLASDEL,
Governor of State of Nevada:

SIR—I herewith submit the Annual Report of the transactions of this office, commencing January 1, 1866, and ending December 31, 1866, inclusive, being the second fiscal year. A detailed statement of receipts and expenditures, and all transactions of this office, are arranged under the following headings:

A—Statement of the Receipts by counties and from all sources of revenue for the second fiscal year, ending December 31, 1866.

B—Statement showing the apportionment to the different funds.

C—Statement showing the balances in the State Treasury, December 31, 1866, belonging to the different funds.

D—Statement showing the total expenditures from January 1, 1866, to December 31, 1866, inclusive.

E—Statement showing the amount of warrants drawn against the different funds.

F—Statement showing the transactions of the different funds.

G—Statement showing the amount of State indebtedness, December 31, 1866.

H—Statement showing the amount collected for the State, the amount of expenses allowed, and the net amount paid into the State Treasury.

I—Statement showing the assessment roll of 1864–5, 1865, 1866, and the delinquent tax of 1866.

K—Estimate of receipts for the fiscal years 1867 and 1868.

L—Estimate of expenditures for the fiscal years 1867 and 1868.

M—Statement of the warrants paid by the State Treasurer during the fiscal year 1866.

N—Statement showing the amount of receipts into the State Treasury in coin and currency.

The receipts have not come up to the estimates made by this office in the last Report: not, however, from the inefficiency of the Revenue Law, but principally from the depreciation in value of the assessable property of the State. For the present fiscal year the prospects are more cheering. Under the Acts of Congress, passed last winter, having reference to public lands donated to the State, a large amount of valuable agricultural domain can be surveyed and sold, adding greatly to the revenue.

The Pacific Railroad now being graded within our limits, will probably before the next Report is made cross the State, vastly increasing the value of property in its vicinage, besides constituting in itself a very considerable source of taxation.

It may reasonably be hoped, in view of the many circumstances which will conspire in the immediate future to augment and render permanent the sources of revenue, that the end of the fourth, or, at farthest, the fifth fiscal year will find the State comparatively, if not wholly, free from debt, and the Treasury in a flourishing condition.

CAPITATION TAX.

The amount derived from the tax on passengers, under the amendment made to the Revenue Law last winter, has not realized the expectations formed. Total receipts from this source have but little exceeded $6,000—a sum so much smaller than was anticipated as to raise some doubts as to the law being faithfully complied with. If this tax is fully collected during the coming year, the aggregate amount should be largely increased, as the facilities for convenient and easy transportation afforded by the fast approaching railroads will induce more frequent and general travel.

POLL TAX.

In regard to the Poll Tax, I would earnestly recommend the passage of a law of a character sufficiently stringent to fully secure the large revenue which may and should be derived from the thousands of Mongolians soon to become inhabitants of the State as laborers on the Pacific Railroad. From this source an annual income of not less than $40,000 can be obtained, if a proper bill is framed. But, inasmuch as Chinese thus employed are engaged in California, and their wages paid to agents in San Francisco, it will require the utmost care to draft a bill in such a manner as to secure from them this tax. As this is about the only revenue which can be derived from this class of population, I commend this matter to the Legislature, trusting that, in their wisdom, they may devise some scheme which will successfully accomplish the desired result.

MINES.

The revenue from the proceeds of mines has fallen very far short of even the low estimate made at the commencement of the first fiscal year. The law appears ample to enforce collections, and the fault is solely in the rate imposed. During the past year the tax upon the proceeds of mines yielded the State Treasury the paltry sum of but little over $10,000 ; that being the entire revenue derived from a bullion product exceeding $16,000,000 in assay value. The Revenue law should, in my judgment, be so amended as to include bullion and crude amalgam, with other assessable property ; repealing the present tax upon the proceeds of the mines and levying thereon the State rate of taxation, and providing a penalty for its shipment from the State without being first stamped as having paid the amount assessed. There can be no valid reason why an individual owning one thousand dollars' worth of bullion should not pay to the State the same tax as the individual who owns one thousand dollars' worth of any other property. And in view of the fact that the mines are almost wholly the property of foreign capitalists and non-residents, who, while draining the State of its metallic wealth, render scarcely any equivalent therefor, it would seem but simple justice that they should bear their equal share of the burdens of the State. Besides, it is asserted by many of our ablest and most eminent jurists that the property tax, as at present assessed, is directly in violation of the organic law of the State, for the reason that it is not levied upon bullion as well as all other species of property; Section 1, Article 10 of the Constitution, prescribing that "the Legislature shall provide by law for a uniform and equal rate of taxation." Should the State rate be levied upon the proceeds of the mines, a revenue would be derived nearly sufficient to defray the current expenses of the State Government. By including them in the assessment roll, the rate of taxation could with safety be reduced from one and one-quarter per cent. to òne per cent.; as it would more than double the taxable property of the State. By such a course the finances of the State would at once be placed on a healthy foundation, the burdens of the people greatly lightened, and the intent of the Constitution carried out. To this matter, of so vast importance to the State and its individual citizens, I call the especial attention of the Legislature.

STAMP TAX.

The proceeds of the Stamp Tax have been about the same as for 1865; but being collected for the past year in currency, the amount falls considerably short of that received for that preceding, and below the estimate in my last report. The receipts would undoubtedly have been much larger had the law been strictly complied with. While being satisfied that many parties have evaded the provisions of the law, I have had no opportunity to ascertain to a certainty who the offenders were, and consequently have been unable to enforce the statute. No fault can be found with the law itself, which is sufficiently clear and explicit; but it is a matter of great difficulty to obtain the proof of its violation, necessary to a conviction and the imposition of the penalties provided.

COIN AND CURRENCY.

By the terms of an Act passed at the last session of the Legislature, it was provided that after the first day of April, 1866, all taxes should be collected, and all salaries and other demands against the State paid in legal tender notes of the United States, excepting only the public printing. At the time it was thought this course, although not required by the decision of the Supreme Court annulling the Specific Contract Act, would inure to the benefit of the State by inducing the adoption of United States currency as the currency of general circulation, causing a rapid influx of capital from the East. The result of the experiment, however, has proved that this supposition was entirely fallacious, and plainly shown that the citizens of the State are too strongly prejudiced in favor of coin as a circulating medium to look with any degree of favor upon any measure tending to replace specie with paper. And whilst the result sought to be obtained has utterly failed of accomplishment, the effect upon the finances of the State has been most disastrous. In most instances property has been assessed at the same valuation in paper dollars that it would have been in metallic dollars; and in consequence the State has lost in revenue the exact difference between the market worth of the two. The total receipts from the property tax of 1866 fall about $80,000 short of the receipts from the same source for 1865, and being collected in 1866 in currency instead of in coin, as was the case in 1865, they do not in reality amount to but little more than half the sum obtained during the former year. It cannot be contended that the value of the taxable property of the State depreciated fifty per cent. in the twelvemonth between the two assessments; but the fault must be attributed to the suicidal transition from coin to currency; while the receipts have been lessened, the expenses of carrying on the government have been largely increased from the same cause. Whenever articles have been purchased for the use of the various departments, the price has invariably been raised by the vendors to a figure in currency equivalent to the charge made in coin to private buyers. Inasmuch as no advantage has been derived by either the State or any of its citizens from the workings of the Act referred to, but on the contrary, great detriment, it would seem but wisdom to return as speedily as possible to the system under which all the transactions of the government were conducted upon a coin basis. Believing that a large majority of the people would sanction such a course, as in accordance with the dictates of sound public policy, I call your attention and that of the Legislature to the matter, that the change may be made should your judgment and theirs coincide with my own.

Your most obedient servant,
A. W. NIGHTINGILL,
State Controller.

[A]—Statement Showing the Receipts in the State Treasury from all Sources of Revenue during the Second Fiscal Year, Commencing January 1st, 1866, and Ending December 31st, 1866.

COUNTIES.	Prop'y Tax, 1863-4.	Property Tax, 1864-5.	Property Tax, 1865.	Property Tax, 1866.	Poll Tax.	Proceeds of Mines, 1866.	Assessm't Dues on Mines, 1866.	Property Tax on Mines, 1863-4.	Pomsc'y Titles, 1866.	Estates of Deceased Persons, 1866.	Fines from Justices' Courts, 1866.	State Passenger Tax, 1866.	Insur'nce Licenses, 1866.	Total.
Storey	$357 43	$1,061 92	$6,023 22	$52,193 82	$6,897 61	$8,886 27		$2,299 48				$5,131 44	$293 28	$83,144 47
Washoe	19 30	129 14	3,367 71	15,938 30	2,692 80		$81 60				$106 00			22,334 85
Ormsby	16 70	98 20	604 02	15,721 34	1,638 00		24 00				41 00	694 45		18,837 71
Douglas	21 50	10 92	1,150 86	5,850 19	806 40					$98 00		129 65		8,067 52
Lyon	17 20	154 45	2,225 22	14,720 73	1,859 40		20 00				374 75			19,371 75
Lander		63 92	1,807 78	19,723 17	3,635 20	1,440 13	362 00		$36 90	164 37	569 25	477 47		28,300 19
Esmeralda		593 93	1,497 83	3,623 19	714 80	30 24	6 00							6,465 99
Humboldt	45 94	284 19	1,493 86	2,046 82	671 40	20 40								4,562 61
Churchill		52 46	651 49	3,027 09	483 40						55 00			4,268 44
Nye			206 57	2,077 19	1,056 60		384 00		7 20					3,731 56
Total	$478 07	$2,449 13	$19,028 56	$134,921 84	$20,454 61	$10,377 04	$877 60	$2,299 48	$44 10	$262 37	$1,166 00	$6,433 01	$293 28	$199,085 09

2

MISCELLANEOUS.

Total amount of receipts from counties, brought down	$199,085	09
Fees of State Controller's office	5	00
Fees of Secretary of State's office	1,466	00
From the Clerk of the Supreme Court, for Attorneys' Licenses	100	00
From the Clerk of the Supreme Court, for Docket Tax	610	00
From State Bond Commissioners, Sale of State Bonds	200,000	00
From Two per cent. Tax on gross receipts of Toll Roads and Bridges	2,596	58
From sale of State School Lands	1,392	00
From Warden of the State Prison	2,061	00
From per centage due from State Sealer of Weights and Measures	342	45
From J. S. Mayhugh, overpaid as Member of the Assembly, first session	56	00
From State Treasurer, sale of State Stamps	17,810	60
Total	$425,524	72
Balance on hand, January 1st, 1866	51,009	54
Grand total of receipts, December 31st, 1866	$476,534	26
Total amount of receipts brought down	$476,534	26
Balance of unexpended Appropriation for Assembly Contingent Fund of 1866, returned by H. P. Burnham, Sergeant-at-Arms	61	00
Grand total amount apportioned during the fiscal year 1866	$476,595	26

B.

STATEMENT SHOWING THE APPORTIONMENT TO THE DIF-
FERENT FUNDS OF THE TOTAL RECEIPTS FOR THE
FISCAL YEAR ENDING DECEMBER 31st, 1866.

General Fund	$273,250 59
State School Fund	17,382 92
General School Fund	14,269 62
State Interest and Sinking Fund	105,872 51
Territorial Interest and Sinking Fund	59,448 58
State Library Fund	1,851 49
Soldiers' Fund	1,447 44
Judicial Salary Fund	610 00
State Prison Fund	2,062 91
Mining School Fund	899 20
Total	$476,595 26

C.

STATEMENT SHOWING THE BALANCE ON HAND IN THE
STATE TREASURY, DECEMBER 31st, 1866, BELONGING
TO THE FOLLOWING FUNDS:

General Fund	$2,320 32
State School Fund	21,201 70
General School Fund	6,119 04
Soldiers' Fund	1,743 76
Library Fund	559 52
Prison Fund	4,628 73
State Interest and Sinking Fund, 1866	75,561 63
Territorial Interest and Sinking Fund, 1865	29,515 75
Mining School Fund	407 89
Total	$142,058 34

D.

TOTAL EXPENDITURES FOR THE FISCAL YEAR COMMENC-
ING JANUARY 1st, 1866, AND ENDING DECEMBER 31st,
1866.

For Judicial Department.................................	$22,927 64
For Legislative Department	53,337 53
For Executive Department..............................	7,616 90
For current expenses...................................	41,920 94
For support of State Prison........................	31,547 02
For expenses of State Library...........................	1,829 86
For support of Common Schools.........................	7,960 95
For Military purposes	40,411 26
For relief purposes	100 00
For redemption of Territorial Bonds	35,000 00
For redemption of State Bonds..........................	79,972 62
For interest on Territorial Bonds	25,250 00
For interest on State Bonds on Territorial indebtedness, 1865...	9,960 21
For interest on State Bonds, 1866	27,367 63
For State Printing.....................................	18,683 66
For publishing decisions of Supreme Court.................	1,977 80
For publishing laws of second session....................	314 08
For Commissioner (J. Neely Johnson) for revising Civil Practice Act	2,500 00
For testing validity of State Capitation Tax, to Geo. A. Nourse.	500 00
For expenses of State Stamps	684 75
For pay of State Mineralogist	2,205 16
For miscellaneous expenses.......	2,693 26
For State Bond Commissioner's expenses	5,975 22
Total	$420,736 49

E.

STATEMENT SHOWING THE AMOUNT OF WARRANTS DRAWN AND AGAINST WHAT FUND, DURING THE FISCAL YEAR 1866.

General Fund..	$74,241 41
Current Expense Fund.................................	68,930 14
General School Fund	7,960 95
State Interest and Sinking Fund......................	87,367 68
Territorial Interest and Sinking Fund................	29,932 83
State Library Fund	1,829 86
Soldiers' Fund	40,411 26
State Prison Fund	31,547 02
Judicial Salary Fund.................................	21,000 00
Legislative Fund	45,137 58
Senate Contingent Fund	4,196 90
Assembly Contingent Fund............................	4,000 00
Mining School Fund	2,205 16
Supreme Court Decision Fund.........................	1,977 80
Total	$420,788 49

F.

STATEMENT SHOWING THE TRANSACTIONS OF THE DIFFERENT FUNDS.

GENERAL SCHOOL FUND.		
Cr.		
By balance in Fund, January 1, 1866..........		$7,093 08
By amount received from General Fund for premium on gold...........................		6 87
By State School Tax.......................		6,980 04
Dr.		
To warrants drawn for January and July apportionment to counties, 1866....................	$7,960 95	
To balance..................................	6,119 04	
	$14,079 99	$14,079 99
By balance in Fund		$6,119 04

STATEMENT SHOWING THE TRANSACTIONS

STATE SCHOOL FUND.
Cr.

By balance January 1st, 1866...................	$11,943 47
By sale of State School Lands................	1,392 00
By receipts from two per cent. tax upon gross receipts of Toll-Roads and Bridges.............	2,596 58
By premium on gold on hand April 1st, 1866, sold to General Fund........................	8,342 02
By premium on gold subsequently received and sold to General Fund........................	476 76
By receipts from County Treasurers...........	1,971 65
Total.................................	$21,722 48

JUDICIAL SALARY FUND.
Cr.

By amount transferred from General Fund......		$20,299 27
By premium on gold sold to General Fund......		90 73
By amount received from Clerk of Supreme Court on account of Docket Tax.................		610 00
Dr.		
To warrants drawn against the Fund..........	$21,000 00	
	$21,000 00	$21,000 00

STATE PRISON FUND.
Cr.

By balance in Fund January 1st, 1866.........	$ 1 91	
By amount of appropriation 1865..............	5,000 00	
By amount of appropriation February 27th, 1866.	25,000 00	
By amount of appropriation March 1st, 1866.....	8,000 00	
By amount received from J. S. Crosman, Warden, being receipts for labor, etc., for the year 1866..	2,061 00	$40,062 91
Dr.		
To Warrants issued........................	$31,547 02	
To premium paid to the General Fund for gold to pay Gold Warrants......................	2,698 24	
Amount unexpended........................	5,817 65	
	$40,062 91	$40,062 91

OF THE DIFFERENT FUNDS—Continued.

SOLDIERS' FUND.

Cr.

By balance on hand in Fund January 1st, 1866...	$471 64	
By amount received from General Fund for premium on gold.............................	296 32	
By amount received from County Treasurer......	975 80	
		$1,743 76

Dr.

To balance unpaid Warrants issued in 1865......	$32,412 12	
To Warrants issued in 1866...................	40,411 26	
Balance................................		$71,079 62
	$72,823 38	$72,823 38
To balance...............................		$71,079 62

STATE LIBRARY FUND.

Cr.

By amount of balance on hand January 1, 1866..		$262 99
Amount of receipts from all sources during 1866..		1,571 00
Amount transferred from General Fund.........		462 00
Premium on gold sold to General Fund.........		203 09

Dr.

Amount of warrants issued	$1,829 86	
Premium on gold from General Fund	135 05	
Balance unexpended........................	534 17	
	$2,499 08	$2,499 08
By balance		$534 17

STATEMENT SHOWING THE TRANSACTIONS

LEGISLATIVE FUND.

Cr.

By amount of appropriation....................		$60,000 00

Dr.

To amount transferred to the Senate Contingent Fund....................................	$4,200 00	
To amount transferred to the Assembly Contingent Fund....................................	4,000 00	
To amount of Warrants issued	45,137 53	
To amount unexpended.......................	6,662 47	
	$60,000 00	$60,000 00

SENATE CONTINGENT FUND.

Cr.

By amount transferred from the Legislative Fund.		$4,200 00

Dr.

To amount Warrants issued	$4,196 90	
To amount unexpended.......................	3 10	
	$4,200 00	$4,200 00

ASSEMBLY CONTINGENT FUND.

Cr.

By amount transferred from the Legislative Fund.		$4,000 00

Dr.

To amount Warrants issued...................	$4,000 00	
	$4,000 00	$4,000 00

ABSTRACT OF THE LEGISLATIVE FUND.

Pay of Members of the Senate................	$ 8,704 00
Pay of Members of the Assembly..............	17,392 00
Pay of Attachés of the Senate.................	6,747 00
Pay of Attachés of the Assembly	8,446 52
Mileage of Senators	954 40
Mileage of Assemblymen	1,961 60
Contingent expenses of the Senate.............	4,200 00
Contingent expenses of the Assembly...........	4,000 00
Miscellaneous legislative expenses for articles purchased in 1865...........................	932 01
Total.........................	$53,337 53

OF THE DIFFERENT FUNDS—Continued.

TERRITORIAL INTEREST AND SINKING FUND.

"For Territorial Interest and Sinking Fund, 1865, for State Bonds issued under Acts of February 14th and March 10th, 1865."

Cr.

By balance on hand January 1st, 1866	$28,741 19	
Receipts from County Treasurers	30,707 39	
		$59,448 58

Dr.

To redemption of Bonds	$19,972 62	
To Interest due January 1st, 1866	5,214 48	
To Interest due July 1st, 1866	4,745 73	
Balance	29,515 75	
	$59,448 58	$59,448 58
Balance		$29,515 75

STATE INTEREST AND SINKING FUND, 1865.

Cr.

By balance on hand January 1st, 1866	$ 1,808 13
By transfer from the General Fund	64,705 28
By amount from Treasurer of Washoe County	1,526 59
Total	$68,040 00

Dr.

To amount of the balance of principal and interest paid	$68,040 00	$68,040 00

STATE INTEREST AND SINKING FUND, 1866.

Cr.

By amount of receipts from County Treasurers	$102,037 79

Dr.

To interest August, 1866	$19,327 63	
To premium on gold bought of the General Fund	7,148 53	
Balance	75,561 63	
	$102,037 79	$102,037 79
Balance		$75,561 63

3

CURRENT EXPENSES.

JUDICIAL DEPARTMENT.

Salaries of Justices of the Supreme Court.......		$21,000 00
Pay of Bailiff and Porter.....................	$800 00	
Stationery....................................	246 50	
Repairs and fixtures..........................	782 90	
Sundries.....................................	98 24	
		1,927 64
Total..................................		$22,927 64

EXECUTIVE DEPARTMENT.

Salary of Governor.........................		$4,000 00
Salary of Governor's Private Secretary.........		2,400 00
Contingent expenses of the office—		
Rent of Office.	$794 00	
Stationery................................	95 80	
Express franks........	52 50	
Sundries, fuel, lights, etc...................	274 60	
		1,216 90
Total.......................		$7,616 90

SECRETARY OF STATE'S OFFICE.

Salary of Secretary........................		$3,600 00
Salary of Deputy Secretary of State..........		2,900 00
Contingent expenses of the office—		
Clerical services.......................	$1,765 70	
Furniture	876 78	
Postage and express charges	591 32	
Pay of Porter.............................	479 00	
Lights and fuel............................	108 06	
Stationery................................	316 13	
Sundries..................................	195 94	
		4,832 93
Total....................		$10,832 93

CURRENT EXPENSES—Continued.

STATE CONTROLLER'S OFFICE.

Salary of State Controller......................		$3,600 00
Salary of Deputy State Controller.............		3,000 00
Contingent expenses of the office—		
Lights and fuel.............................	$178 75	
Stationery.................................	38 63	
Pay of Porter..............................	330 00	
Rent of office..............................	712 50	
Furniture and repairs.......................	92 92	
Postage and express charges	145 89	
Sundries...................................	57 68	
		1,556 37
Total................................		$8,156 37

STATE TREASURER'S OFFICE.

Salary of State Treasurer		$3,600 00
Salary of Clerk in Treasurer's Office		2,300 00
Contingent expenses of the office—		
Rent of office..............................	$712 50	
Lights and fuel	178 75	
Pay of porter	330 00	
Stationery	47 50	
Express and postage envelopes	78 00	
Telegrams	10 00	
Furniture..................................	28 50	
Sundries	232 50	
		1,617 75
Total		$7,517 75

ATTORNEY GENERAL'S OFFICE.

Salary of Attorney General..................		$2,500 00
Contingent expenses of the office—		
Stationery	$105 13	
Rent of office..............................	600 00	
Lights and fuel.............................	10 00	
Sundries	104 75	
		819 88
Total		$3,319 88

CURRENT EXPENSES—Continued.

ADJUTANT GENERAL'S OFFICE.

Salary of Adjutant General		$2,000 00
Contingent expenses of the office—		
Rent of office	$60 00	
Stationery and postage	58 70	
Light and fuel	24 81	
Sundries	9 50	
		153 01
Total		$2,153 01

SUPERINTENDENT OF PUBLIC INSTRUCTION.

Salary of Superintendent of Public Instruction		$2,000 00
Contingent expenses of the office—		
Traveling expenses, stationery, etc	$221 18	
		221 18
Total		$2,221 18

SURVEYOR GENERAL'S OFFICE.

Salary of Surveyor General		$1,000 00
Sundries	$45 75	
		45 75
Total		$1,045 75

STATE PRINTING.

Pay of State Printer		$17,399 06
Pay of Expert on State Printing		552 00
Paid for sundry extra printing		732 60
Total		$18,683 66

CURRENT EXPENSES—Continued.

Secretary and Assistant Secretary of the Senate, turning over the books and property of the Senate......................	$ 50 00
Chief Clerk and Assistant Clerk of the Assembly, turning over the books and property of the Assembly..............	50 00
Lockhart and Gregg, taking evidence in contested land cases....	32 40
California State Telegraph Company, telegraphing resolutions on National Bank Fund to Washington..................	86 88
S. D. King, drawing and making abstract of Prison Ground....	20 50
California State Telegraph Company, telegraphing resolutions on Mines	83 78
Ormsby County, chairs and desks for Capitol Building.........	495 20
W. T. Lockhart, fees for selection of school lands.............	368 00
D. S. Gregg, fees for selection of school lands...........	368 00
H. B. Pomeroy, fees as County Clerk in case of Geo. Kirk	59 50
H. B. Pomeroy, fees as County Clerk in case of Geo. Kirk	28 50
J. A. Fiske, repairs on State Library......................	15 00
Amount paid for exchange on moneys paid State on orders of State Controller and Treasurer from County Treasurers..	52 25
J. G. Fox, record book for Board of Regents..........	10 00
Wells, Fargo & Co., freight on statutes sent to County Clerks..	14 80
E. B. Rail, material for repairs of State Library	31 75
J. H. Cowing & Co., painting at Capitol Building.............	150 00
Alfred Helm, Clerk of Supreme Court, fees in case *ex parte* T. G. Smith..	17 70
Pay of Porter for Capitol Building	474 00
Total	$2,693 26

RECAPITULATION.

CURRENT EXPENSES FOR THE YEAR 1866.	
Executive Department..	$7,616 90
Secretary of State's Office...................................	10,882 98
State Controller's Office.....................................	8,156 87
State Treasurer's Office......................................	7,517 75
Attorney General's Office	8,319 88
Superintendent of Public Instruction........................	2,221 18
Adjutant General's Office	2,153 01
Surveyor General's Office	1,045 75
State Printing	18,688 66
Contingent expenses of the Supreme Court...................	1,927 64
Miscellaneous current expenses.............................	2,693 26
Total...	$66,168 83

GENERAL FUND.

Cr.

By balance on hand		$473 18
By receipts from sale of State Bonds, Jan. 19, 1866.		200,000 00
By receipts from County Treasurers		54,507 41
By receipts from State Treasurer for sale of State Stamps		17,810 60
By amount returned from Legislative Fund		6,662 47
By amount paid by Jno. S. Mayhugh, overdrawn, as Member of the Assembly, First Session		56 00
By amount unexpended of the Assembly Contingent Fund, Second Session		61 00
By amount received from State Sealer of Weights and Measures		342 45
By amount received for premium on gold sold to other funds		9,871 42
By outstanding Warrants against the General and Current Expense Funds		62,480 92
Balance		137 70

Dr.

To amount of unpaid Warrants of 1865	$10,177 60	
To amount transferred to State Interest and Sinking Fund	64,705 28	
To amount transferred to State Prison Fund, 1865	5,000 00	
To amount transferred to Legislative Fund, 1866.	60,000 00	
To amount transferred to State Library Fund, Act of March 1st, 1866	462 00	
To amount transferred to Judicial Salary Fund	20,299 27	
To amount transferred to State Prison Fund, 1866	25,000 00	
To amount transferred to Supreme Court Decision Fund	1,977 80	
To amount paid for premium on gold bought of other Funds	4,280 74	
To amount paid for relief of Jno. F. Stone, School Land Warrant Act of March 3d, 1866	100 00	
To amount paid to State Bond Commissioner for negotiating short loan, Act of Jan. 19th, 1866..	975 22	
To amount paid State Bond Commissioner for negotiating long loan, Act of Feb. 26th, 1866....	5,000 00	
To amount paid for exchange on coin received from County Treasurers	54 25	
To amount paid for publishing Debates of Constitutional Convention	4,177 19	
To amount paid J. Neely Johnson, Commissioner for revising Civil Practice Act	2,500 00	
To amount paid Attorney General for testing the validity of State Capitation Tax	500 00	
To amount paid for expense of State Stamps	684 75	
Amount carried forward	$205,894 10	$352,403 10

GENERAL FUND—Continued.

Amount brought forward...........	$205,894 10	$352,403 10
To amount paid for discount on sales of currency..	17,328 86	
To principal of Territorial Bonds of 1864, due February 1st, 1866........................	25,000 00	
To interest on principal of Territorial Bonds of 1864, due February 1st, 1866...............	18,500 00	
To interest on principal of Territorial Bonds of 1864, due August 1st, 1866.....	11,250 00	
To principal of Territorial Bonds of 1862, due February 1st, 1866.......	10,000 00	
To interest on principal of Territorial Bonds of 1862, due February 1st, 1866...............	. 500 00	
To total amount transferred to the Current Expense Fund	68,930 14	
	$352,403 10	$352,403 10
Balance.....................	$137 70	

MISCELLANEOUS ACCOUNTS.

RELIEF PURPOSES. **Cr.**		
By amount of appropriation for the relief of J. F. Stone, Act approved March 3, 1866..........		$100 00
Dr.		
To amount of warrant issued to J. F. Stone	$100 00	
	$100 00	$100 00

STATE BOND COMMISSIONER—SHORT LOAN. **Cr.**		
By appropriation for expenses in making short loan in San Francisco, Act approved January 19, 1866 ....\....		$2,000 00
Dr.		
To warrants issued for amount of expenses incurred in making short loan.......................	$975 22	
Amount unexpended.........................	1,024 78	
	$2,000 00	$2,000 00
By balance		$1,024 78

STATE BOND COMMISSIONER—LONG LOAN. **Cr.**		
By appropriation for expenses in making long loan in New York, Act approved Feb. 26, 1866....		$5,000 00
Dr.		
To warrant issued.........................	$5,000 00	
	$5,000 00	$5,000 00

[The Commissioner reports to this office as unexpended of the above amount, $2,456 02, which amount reverted to the General Fund, January 1st, 1867, but does not appear in this report as being a portion of the General Fund.]

4

MISCELLANEOUS ACCOUNTS—Continued.

SUPREME COURT DECISION FUND.		
Cr.		
By amount of appropriation, Act approved February 28, 1866		$2,500 00
Dr.		
To amount of warrants issued.................	$1,977 80	
To amount unexpended	522 20	
	$2,500 00	$2,500 00
PUBLISHING LAWS, SECOND SESSION.		
Cr.		
By amount of appropriation, Act approved March 1, 1866............................		$1,000 00
Dr.		
To amount of warrants issued.................	$314 08	
To amount unexpended	685 92	
	$1,000 00	$1,000 00

MISCELLANEOUS ACCOUNTS—Continued.

EXPENSE OF PRINTING DEBATES OF CONSTITU-		
TIONAL CONVENTION.		
Cr.		
By amount of appropriation, Act approved February 21, 1865		$10,000 00
Dr.		
To amount expended during the year 1865	$3,225 12	
Amount unexpended........................	6,774 88	
	$10,000 00	$10,000 00
Cr.		
By balance on hand January 1, 1866...........		$6,774 88
Dr.		
To amount expended during the year 1866:		
Amount paid F. Eastman for composition	$457 40	
Amount paid A. J. Marsh, reporter	500 00	
Amount paid F. Eastman for composition ..:..	473 54	
Amount paid F. Eastman for composition	479 60	
Amount paid A. J. Marsh, reporter.......... .	600 00	
Amount paid F. Eastman for composition	481 65	
Amount paid A. J. Marsh, reporter...........	1,185 00	
Amount unexpended.......................	2,597 69	
	$6,774 88	$6,774 88
By balance		$2,597 69
J. NEELY JOHNSON, COMMISSIONER FOR REVISING		
THE CIVIL PRACTICE ACT.		
Cr.		
By amount of appropriation, Act approved March 1, 1866................................		$3,000 00
Dr.		
To amount of warrants issued................	$2,500 00	
Balance due J. Neely Johnson and payable Feb. 1, 1867...................	500 00	
Total	$3,000 00	$3,000 00

·MISCELLANEOUS ACCOUNTS—Continued.

GEO. A. NOURSE, TESTING THE VALIDITY OF THE STATE CAPITATION TAX.

Cr.
By amount of appropriation, Act approved March 1, 1866 ..... | $500 00

Dr.
To amount of warrant issued .... | $500 00

EXPENSE OF STATE STAMPS.

Cr.
By amount of appropriation, Act approved March 9, 1865 .... | | $3,000 00

Dr.
To amount expended during the year 1865 ...... | $1,950 00 |
Amount unexpended .... | .1,050 00 |

| | $3,000 00 | $3,000 00 |

Cr.
·By balance on hand, January 1, 1866 .... | | $1,050 00

Dr.
To amount expended during the year 1866 ...... | 684 75 |
Amount unexpended .... | 365 25 |

| | $1,050 00 | $1,050 00 |

Cr.
By balance on hand in fund, December, 31, 1866.. | | $365 25

G.

STATEMENT SHOWING THE AMOUNT OF STATE INDEBTEDNESS, DECEMBER 31, 1866.

Territorial bonds, Acts of February 16th and 20th, 1864, payable as follows :	
February 1, 1867	$35,000 00
February 1, 1868	40,000 00
February 1, 1869	50,000 00
Accrued interest on the above to date, January 1, 1867	9,375 00
State bonds for Territorial indebtedness, issued under Act of February 14, 1865	96,156 00
Passed due coupons on above bonds not presented for payment	83 79
Interest on above bonds to date, January 1, 1867	4,795 08
State bonds, Act of January 19, 1866, due February 1, 1867	200,000 00
Interest on above to date, February 1, 1867	15,000 00
Unpaid warrants on General Fund, payable in gold	24,918 55
Unpaid warrants on General Fund, payable in currency, $37,560 37 ; estimated in gold	28,170 28
Unpaid warrants on Prison Fund, payable in gold	830 87
Unpaid warrants on Prison Fund, payable in currency, $10,315 46 ; estimated in gold at	7,736 60
Unpaid warrants on Soldiers' Fund, payable in gold	68,507 88
Unpaid warrants on Soldiers' Fund, payable in currency, $4,787 14 ; estimated in gold at	3,590 36
Unpaid warrants on Mining School Fund, payable in currency, $1,338 50 ; estimated in gold at	1,003 88
Total	$585,168 29

H.

STATEMENT SHOWING AMOUNT DUE STATE AS PER COUNTY AUDITOR'S REPORT, AND EXPENSES ALLOWED AND AMOUNT PAID STATE TREASURER.

COUNTIES.	Amount Due State.	Expense.	Amount Paid the State Treasurer.
Storey..............	$88,510 11	$5,365 64	$83,144 47
Lander..............	32,844 41	4,544 22	28,300 19
*Lyon..............	21,074 69	1,617 74	19,456 95
*Washoe.......:....	25,031 95	2,258 52	22,778 43
Ormsby.............	20,635 10	1,797 39	18,837 71
Humboldt	5,639 25	1,076 64	4,562 61
Esmeralda	7,594 72	1,128 73	6,465 99
Nye	5,200 72	1,469 16	3,781 56
Douglas	9,687 39	1,619 87	8,067 52
Churchill...........	5,835 75	1,567 31	4,268 44
Totals..........	$222,054 09	$22,445 22	$199,608 87

* The difference between this statement and that of the statement of revenue is caused by $520 78 being paid by toll roads and bridges to County Treasurer of Lyon and Washoe Counties—the above amount being deducted from grand receipts and credited to account of toll-roads and bridges.

I.

ASSESSMENT ROLL OF 1864–5.

COUNTIES.	Valuation.	State.	Military.
Storey	$15,406,869 68	$46,191 49	$30,794 32
Lander.............	2,722,528 38	8,167 58	5,445 05
Lyon	2,847,663 00	8,542 98	5,695 33
Washoe............	2,810,000 00	8,432 40	5,621 60
Ormsby............	2,088,657 00	6,265 97	4,177 31
Humboldt	792,746 00	2,378 23·	1,585 49
Esmeralda	1,518,010 80	4,554 03	3,036 02
Churchill..	370,902 00	1,112 71	741 80
Nye	95,128 67	285 38	190 25
*Douglas...........	1,174,631 45	3,523 90	....
Totals..........	$29,826,636 98	$89,454 67	$57,287 17

* There was no military tax levied in Douglas County in 1864 and 1865.

ASSESSMENT ROLL OF 1865.

COUNTIES.	Valuation.	State, 95 Cents.	Total, $1 25.
Storey..............	$6,924,482 79	$65,782 60	$86,556 05
Lander..............	2,154,994 00	20,472 94	26,937 42
Lyon	2,581,765 00	24,526 75	32,272 04
Washoe.............	2,254,461 00	21,417 38	28,180 76
Ormsby.............	1,995,792 00	18,960 03	24,947 40
Humboldt	385,460 00	3,661 87	4,818 25
Esmeralda.	845,498 30	8,032 24	10,568 73
Churchill...........	335,767 87	3,189 79	4,197 09
Nye	190,205 50	1,806 94	2,377 55
Douglas............	1,029,849 30	9,783 57	12,873 12
Totals.........	$18,698,275 76	$177,634 11	$233,728 41

ASSESSMENT ROLL OF 1866.

COUNTIES.	Valuation.	State, 95 Cents.	School, 5 Cents.	Territorial Interest and Sink'g Fund, 25c.	Total, $1 25.
Storey........	$6,343,353 20	$60,261 85	$3,171 68	$15,858 88	$79,291 91
Lander........	3,049,108 00	28,966 53	1,524 55	7,622 77	38,113 85
Lyon	1,727,090 00	12,469 59	656 29	3,281 47	21,588 62
Washoe........	1,785,862 20	16,965 69	892 93	4,464 65	22,323 27
Ormsby........	1,670,151 00	15,866 43	835 07	4,175 38	20,876 88
Douglas........	721,494 32	6,852 20	362 75	1,803 73	9,018 68
Humboldt........	551,970 00	5,453 46	287 02	1,485 12	7,175 60
Esmeralda........	840,012 07	7,980 12	420 00	2,100 03	10,500 15
Churchill........	419,174 87	3,982 16	209 59	1,047 94	5,239 69
Nye........	541,999 20	5,148 99	271 00	1,354 99	6,774 98
Totals........	$17,650,214 86	$168,947 02	$8,630 88	$43,144 46	$220,903 63

5

DELINQUENT TAXES—1866.

Storey	$11,164 14
Lander	13,976 12
Lyon	4,689 72
Washoe	3,739 03
Ormsby	3,738 43
Douglas	1,580 94
Humboldt	3,763 98
Esmeralda	6,190 11
Churchill	1,891 87
Nye	2,398 48
Total	$53,132 82

K.

ESTIMATE OF RECEIPTS FOR THE FISCAL YEARS 1867 & 1868.

From delinquent taxes of 1866	$20,000 00
From property tax of 1867 and 1868	300,000 00
From taxes on proceeds of mines for 1867 and 1868	40,000 00
From poll tax of 1867 and 1868	40,000 00
From sale of State stamps 1867 and 1868	40,000 00
From State passenger tax 1867 and 1868	20,000 00
From miscellaneous sources	10,000 00
From sale of new bonds	300,000 00
	$770,000 00
Add amount on hand (estimated)	60,000 00
Total	$830,000 00

L.

ESTIMATE OF EXPENDITURES FOR THE FISCAL YEARS
1867 AND 1868.

For Legislative Department.............................	$50,000 00
For current expenses...................................	90,000 00
For Judicial Department........................	42,000 00
For State Prison	50,000 00
For miscellaneous purposes...	10,000 00
For State bonds due February 1, 1867.....................	200.000 00
For interest on State bonds due February 1, 1867............	18,000 00
For interest on $300,000 new State loan for two years.........	90,000 00
For interest on $225,000 new State bonds for funding the Territorial bonds of 1864, and the indebtedness against the Soldiers' Fund, estimated at 10 per cent. per annum for two years..	45,000 00
Unpaid warrants.......................................	60,000 00
Total	$655,000 00
Estimated excess of receipts above the expenditures for the third and fourth fiscal years, available on the 31st day of December, 1868, for the redemption of the anticipated new State loan of $300,000...................................	$175,000 00

M.

MEMORANDUM SHOWING THE AMOUNT OF WARRANTS PAID, AND UPON WHAT FUNDS, DURING THE FISCAL YEAR ENDING DECEMBER 31st, 1866.

Legislative Fund.	$45,137 53
Senate Contingent Fund.................................	4,196 90
Assembly Contingent Fund..............................	4,000 00
State Interest and Sinking Fund.........................	87,367 63
Territorial Interest and Sinking Fund.....................	29,932 83
Judicial Salary Fund...................................	21,000 00
State Library Fund...	1,822 01
General School Fund....................................	8,157 45
State Prison Fund......................................	24,735 94
General Fund..	81,310 01
Current Expense Fund..................................	9,561 32
Supreme Court Decision Fund...........................	1,977 80
Mining School Fund....................................	466 66
Total	$319,666 08

N.

STATEMENT SHOWING AMOUNTS OF RECEIPTS FOR THE YEAR IN GOLD AND CURRENCY, AND THE APPORTIONMENT OF THE DIFFERENT FUNDS.

FUNDS.	Coin.	Currency.	Total.
General Fund..............	$208,375 33	$64,402 13	$272,777 46
State School Fund..........	1,963 38	3,476 07	5,439 45
General School Fund........	566 29	6,413 75	6,980 04
State Interest and Sinking Fund	2,001 67	101,562 71	103,564 38
Territorial Int. and Sink'g Fund	2,386 92	28,320 47	30,707 39
Judicial Salary Fund........	370 00	240 00	610 00
State Library Fund	520 00	1,051 00	1,571 00
Soldiers' Fund	492 32	483 48	975 80
State Prison Fund	....	2,061 00	2,061 00
Mining School Fund........	....	899 20	899 20
Totals................	$216,675 91	$208,909 81	$425,585 72

ANNUAL REPORT

OF THE

STATE TREASURER

OF THE

STATE OF NEVADA,

FOR THE YEAR 1866.

CARSON CITY:
JOSEPH E. ECKLEY, STATE PRINTER.
1867.

REPORT.

TREASURER'S OFFICE, STATE OF NEVADA,
CARSON, January 1st, 1867.

Hon. H. G. Blasdel,

Governor of Nevada—

SIR—I herewith transmit my Report of the transactions in this office for the fiscal year ending December 31st, 1866.

All of the funded obligations of the State, including those of the Territory of Nevada assumed, which became due during the year, were promptly paid as presented; but there is a considerable indebtedness in the form of warrants, as will be noticed by reference to Statement H.

Warrants on the General and Current Expense Funds have been paid only to the first of April, and those on the Prison Fund to the first of November, while the large amount on the Soldiers' Fund remains as before, unprovided for.

The tabular statements appended are as follows:

A. Total Receipts.
B. Total Disbursements.
C. Recapitulation and Statement of Balances.
D. Currency and Gold Accounts.
E. Total Transactions in each Fund.
F. Sales of Stamps in Detail.
G. Statement of Funded Territorial Debt.
H. Exhibit of the Whole State Debt.

The one-year gold bonds for $200,000, authorized by the Act of January 19th, 1866, bearing interest at the rate of eighteen per cent. per annum, were sold in San Francisco at par. They will be due on the first of February ensuing.

The ten years' loan authorized by the Act of February 26th, 1866, has not been negotiated. Bonds could not then, and cannot now, be sold in San Francisco at the rate required by the provisions of that bill. The action of the Legislature in passing it was undoubtedly based upon the well-founded opinion current in financial circles throughout the country, that during the year 1866, the premium on gold would decline to a rate which would have admitted of the negotiation of our gold bonds in the New York money market, on terms advantageous to the State.

This opinion still prevailed when I arrived there on the first of May, the premium then being twenty-seven per cent.; and negotiations for the sale of the bonds were progressing favorably, when, almost without warning, the news of the financial crisis in Europe came upon the money market, and the premium on gold rapidly advanced to such a rate as rendered success out of the question.

To explain this result, it is necessary to add that although the provisions of the law required the bonds to be sold for gold, negotiations were conducted on the basis of a currency price; and it can be readily understood that the price for which the bonds could, and can be sold, viz: about 105 in currency for gold bonds bearing interest at the rate of seven or eight per cent. per annum, required that the premium on gold should recede to about twenty-three per cent. in order that the currency proceeds, reckoning a currency dollar at eighty-one cents, could be converted into coin, and the bonds bring, as required by the provisions of the bill, at least eighty-five cents in gold.

Under the circumstances, I could do nothing; but being advised by leading financiers that a favorable change might be expected by July, I waited until then; and was reluctantly compelled, after making arrangements for the sale of the bonds in the event of an improvement in the market, to return without accomplishing the desired object.

Of course nothing has since been done, as the premium on gold having only recently receded from forty per cent. and upwards, still remains at too high a rate.

In making provision for our present indebtedness, I presume there will be no difference of opinion—taking into consideration the fact that nearly all of it is payable in coin—as to the inexpediency of issuing any but gold bonds.

The notably improved condition of the State from what it was one year ago, and the increasing evidences of permanent prosperity, have inspired a confidence which will probably make practicable, in the San Francisco market, whatever negotiations for money the Legislature may deem expedient to authorize.

Although a large amount of money may be derived from the sale of lands donated to the State by Congress for educational purposes, which can be invested in State securities, it would probably be better not to consider this, except incidentally, in connection with the provisions for the State debt: as any anticipated benefit from this source, can be readily realized at any time by the purchase of State bonds, or, if they are not in the market, Government bonds can always be easily obtained for the investment of School Fund moneys.

I would, therefore, suggest that bonds be issued for State purposes to the full extent authorized by the Constitution, and that the money derived from their sale be used only for State purposes; leaving the outstanding Territorial and Soldiers' Fund indebtedness to be provided for by the issuance and sale of other bonds.

Supposing the time for these bonds to run to be ten years, and estimating the annual property valuation of the State during that time at twenty million dollars in gold—certainly not too high an estimate—a tax of sixty cents on each one hundred dollars of valuation would provide an ample fund for the payment of the principal and interest of the largest amount of bonds it would be necessary to issue—say $600,000—even in case they should be sold at as great a discount as twenty per cent.

With some well devised plan, having in view the consolidation of our entire debt, we can probably soon succeed in placing our finances in a better condition than they have hitherto been.

Very respectfully,
Your obedient servant,
E. RHOADES,
State Treasurer.

A.

TOTAL RECEIPTS INTO THE TREASURY FROM JANUARY 1, 1866, TO DECEMBER 31, 1866.

1866.	
Jan. 1.—Balance in Treasury	$51,009 54
From Treasurer of Storey County......	83,144 47
From Treasurer of Esmeralda County ..	6,465 99
From Treasurer of Churchill County ...	4,268 44
From Treasurer of Nye County	3,731 56
From Treasurer of Humboldt County...	4,562 61
From Treasurer of Lander County	28,300 19
From Treasurer of Washoe County	22,770 43
From Treasurer of Douglas County	8,067 52
From Treasurer of Lyon County	19,456 95
From Treasurer of Ormsby County	18,837 71
From sales of Bonds, Act of Jan. 19, 1866	200,000 00
From sales of Revenue Stamps, net...	17,810 60
From sales of School Land Warrants ..	1,392 00
From two per cent. tax on gross receipts of Toll Roads and Bridges........	2,075 80
From State Sealer of Weights and Measures	842 45
From Warden of State Prison	2,061 00
Balance of unexpended appropriation returned by Sergeant-at-Arms of Assembly	61 00
Overpayment to Hon. J. S. Mayhugh in 1865, returned	56 00
Fees from Secretary of State.........	1,456 00
Fees from State Controller...........	5 00
Docket fees, Supreme Court	610 00
Attorneys' Licenses	100 00
	$476,595 26

B.

For account of Legislative Department	$54,911 70
For account of Executive Department..........	9,377 21
For account of Judicial Department	21,331 25
State Printing	8,825 34
Support of Prison..........................	24,785 94
State Library................................	1,822 01
Apportionment to Counties of School Money.....	8,157 45
Publishing Debates of Constitutional Convention..	5,121 51
Publishing Decisions of Supreme Court	1,977 80
Expense of State Revenue Stamps.............	684 75
Telegraphing Legislative Resolutions to Washington	170 66
Expended by Bond Commissioner, under Act February 26, 1866	254 98
Discount on Currency sales	17,328 86
Balance of principal of State Bonds, Act January 4, 1865, due January 10, 1866...........	60,000 00
Interest due on same........................	8,040 00
Redemption of Territorial Funded Debt Bonds, Act February 14, 1865.................	19,972 62
Interest on same, due January 1, 1866	5,214 48
Interest on same, due July 1, 1866	4,745 73
Principal of Territorial Bonds of 1864, due February 1, 1866	25,000 00
Interest on same, due February 1, 1866.........	13,500 00
Interest on same, due August 1, 1866	11,250 00
Principal of Territorial Bonds of 1862, due February 1, 1866.......................	10,000 00
Interest on same, due February 1, 1866.........	500 00
Interest on State Bonds, Act January 19, 1866 ...	19,327 63
	$334,536 92

C.

Total receipts		$476,595 26
Total disbursements		334,536 92
Balance in Treasury...................		$142,058 34
Apportioned:		
General Fund.............................	$2,320 32	
State School Fund (irreducible)	21,201 70	
General School Fund (for distribution).........	6,119 04	
Soldiers' Fund............................	1,743 76	
Library Fund	559 52	
Prison Fund	4,628 73	
State Interest and Sinking Fund (1866)	75,571 63	
Territorial Interest and Sinking Fund (1865)	29,515 75	
Mining School Fund........................	407 89	
		$142,058 34

D.

	Dr.		
1866.			
Jan. 1.—Balance on hand	$1,116 00		
Receipts for 1866	207,351 02		
	Cr.		
Warrants paid, 1866..................		$30,209 93	
Converted into gold..................		64,831 96	
Balance		113,425 13	
	$208,467 02	$208,467 02	
1866.			
Dec. 31.—Balance on hand	$113,425 13		

	Dr.		
1866.			
Jan. 1.—Balance on hand....................	$49,893 54		
Receipts from Revenue, including sales of Bonds........................	218,234 70		
Receipts from currency sales	47,503 10		
	Cr.		
Warrants paid in 1866		$286,998 13	
Balance		28,633 21	
	$315,631 34	$315,631 34	
1866.			
Dec. 31.—Balance on hand	$28,633 21		

NOTE.—The average price obtained for currency from November 13, 1866, when the first sale was made, up to date, is a little over 73¼ cents.

E.

STATEMENT OF TRANSACTIONS IN EACH FUND, FROM JANUARY 1, 1866, TO DECEMBER 31, 1866.

GENERAL FUND.

1866. Dr.

Jan. 1.—Balance on hand	$473 13	
Receipts from sales of Bonds, Act January 19, 1866	200,000 00	
Receipts from County Treasurers	54,507 41	
Receipts from Stamp sales	17,810 60	
Returned from Legislative Fund	6,662 47	
Returned from Senate Contingent Fund	3 10	
Received from Hon. J. S. Mayhugh	56 00	
Received from Serg.-at-Arms of Assembly	61 00	
Received from State Sealer of Weights and Measures	342 45	
Received for premium on gold sold to other funds	9,871 42	

Cr.

Transfer to State Interest and Sinking Fund, 1865		$64,705 28
Transfer to Prison Fund for 1865		5,000 00
Transfer to Legislative Fund		60,000 00
Transfer to Library Fund		462 00
Transfer to Judicial Salary Fund		20,299 27
Premium paid to other Funds for balance of gold in them on April 1, 1866, and for subsequent receipts into those funds		4,280 74
Transfer to Prison Fund, 1866		25,000 00
Warrants paid		107,719 97
Balance		2,320 32
	$289,787 58	$289,787 58

1866.
Dec. 31.—Balance on hand ... $2,320 32

SOLDIERS' FUND.

1866. Dr.

Jan. 1.—Balance on hand	$471 64
Received from General Fund for premium on gold	296 32
Received from County Treasurers	975 80
1866. Dec. 31.—Balance on hand	$1,743 76

GENERAL SCHOOL FUND.

1866. **Dr.**		
Jan. 1.—Balance on hand.....................	$7,289 58	
Received from General Fund for premium on gold........................	6 87	
Received from County Treasurers	6,980 04	
1866. **Cr.**		
Apportionment to Counties...........		$8,157 45
Balance on hand		6,119 04
	$14,276 49	$14,276 49

NOTE.—The above balance is subject to the January, 1867, apportionment.

JUDICIAL SALARY FUND.

Dr.		
Transfers from General Fund	$20,299 27	
Premium on gold sold to General Fund..	90 73	
Received from Docket Tax...........	610 00	
Cr.		
Warrants paid		$21,000 00
	$21,000 00	$21,000 00

LIBRARY FUND.

1866. **Dr.**		
Jan. 1.—Balance on hand	$280 49	
Transfer from General Fund	462 00	
Premium on gold sold to General Fund.	68 04	
Fees from State Controller...........	5 00	
Attorneys' Licenses.................	100 00	
Fees from Secretary of State..........	1,466 00	
Cr.		
Warrants paid		$1,822 01
Balance		559 52
	$2,381 58	$2,381 53
1866.		
Dec. 31.—Balance on hand	$559 52	

LEGISLATIVE FUND.
Dr.

Transfer from General Fund	$60,000 00	
Cr.		
Transfer to Senate Contingent Fund....		$4,200 00
Transfer to Assembly Contingent Fund..		4,000 00
Warrants paid		45,137 53
Returned to General Fund...........		6,662 47
	$60,000 00	$60,000 00

ASSEMBLY CONTINGENT FUND.
Dr.

Transfer from Legislative Fund........	$4,000 00	
Cr.		
Warrants paid		$4,000 00
	$4,000 00	$4,000 00

SENATE CONTINGENT FUND.
1866.
Dr.

Transfer from Legislative Fund........	$4,200 00	
Cr.		
Warrants paid		$4,196 90
Returned to General Fund...........		3 10
	$4,200 00	$4,200 00

PRISON FUND.
Dr.

1866.

Jan. 1.—Balance on hand	$1 91	
Transfers from General Fund..........	30,000 00	
Received from Warden of Prison	2,061 00	
Cr.		
Warrants paid		$24,785 94
Premium paid to General Fund for gold to pay gold warrants............		2,698 24
Balance		4,628 73
	$32,062 91	$32,062 91
1866.		
Dec. 31.—Balance on hand	$4,628 73	

MINING SCHOOL FUND.
Dr.

Receipts from County Treasurers.......	$899 20	

Cr.

By warrants paid....................		$466 66
Premium paid General Fund for gold...		24 65
Balance		407 89
	$899 20	$899 20

1866.
Dec. 31.—Balance on hand $407 89

TERRITORIAL INTEREST AND SINKING FUND, 1865 (FOR STATE BONDS ISSUED UNDER ACTS OF FEBRUARY 14 AND MARCH 10, 1865).

1866. **Dr.**

Jan. 1.—Balance on hand....................	$28,741 19	
Receipts from County Treasurers	30,707 39	

Cr.

Paid for $23,390 of Bonds surrendered..	$19,972 62	
Interest due Jan. 1, 1866	5,214 48	
Interest due July 1, 1866.............	4,745 73	
Balance..........................	29,515 75	
	$59,448 58	$59,448 58

1866.
Balance $29,515 75

STATE SCHOOL FUND.
1866. **Dr.**

Jan. 1.—Balance on hand....................	$11,943 47
Sales of Land Warrants	1,392 00
Receipts from Toll Roads and Bridges...	2,075 80
Premium on gold on hand April 1, 1866, sold to General Fund.......	3,342 02
Premium on gold subsequently received and sold to General Fund	476 76
Receipts on County Treasurers' settlements	1,971 65
Dec. 31.—Balance on hand	$21,201 70

STATE INTEREST AND SINKING FUND, 1865.
Dr.

1866.
Jan. 1.—Balance on hand.................... ..	$1,808 13	
Transfer from General Fund	64,705 28	
From Treasurer of Washoe County.....	1,526 59	

Cr.
Balance of principal and interest paid..........		$68,040 00
	$68,040 00	$68,040 00

STATE INTEREST AND SINKING FUND, 1866.
Dr.

Receipts from County Treasurers.......	$102,037 79	

Cr.
By August, 1866, interest		$19,327 63
By premium on gold bought of General Fund		7,148 53
Balance		75,561 63
	$102,037 79	$102,037 79

1866.
Dec. 31.—Balance on hand	$75,561 63	

F.

STATEMENT OF STATE STAMP SALES FOR THE YEAR 1866.

Sales in Storey County........................		$7,912 83
Sales in Esmeralda County		697 42
Sales in Churchill County		281 41
Sales in Nye County........,.................		584 64
Sales in Humboldt County.....................		894 10
Sales in Lander County :......................		7,163 79
Sales in Washoe County		656 13
Sales in Douglas County......................		68 23
Sales in Ormsby County		815 73
Sales in State Treasurer's office...............		614 86
		$19,689 14
Commissions allowed purchasers	$1,814 49	
County Treasurers' per centage................	537 10	
Exchange on remittances	26 95	1,878 54
Net Revenue for 1866		$17,810 60

NOTE.—The amount sold in Lyon County is about $500, but the report has not yet been received.

G.

ABSTRACT OF PROCEEDINGS

Under the Act entitled "An Act to provide for carrying out in part the provisions of Section Seven, Article Seventeen, of the Constitution of the State of Nevada," approved February 14, 1865; also under "An Act supplementary to and amendatory of the same," approved March 10, 1865.

1866.	
Jan. 1.—Amount of Bonds outstanding	$116,042 00
Issued in 1866	3,504 00
	$119,546 00
Feb. 7.—Surrendered and canceled.............	23,390 00
Dec. 31.—Balance outstanding	$96,156 00

NOTE.—The Bonds canceled February 7, 1866 ($23,390) were surrendered at rates varying from seventy-five to ninety per cent., amounting to $19,972.62.

The amount on hand in the Interest and Sinking Fund after reserving sufficient to pay the July, 1867, interest, is, estimated in gold, about $16,000, which will be advertised for another surrender of these bonds, in accordance with the provisions of the law.

H.

EXHIBIT OF STATE INDEBTEDNESS, DECEMBER 31, 1866.

Territorial Bonds, Acts of February 16 and February 20, 1864, due, viz:		
February 1, 1867	$35,000	00
February 1, 1868	40,000	00
February 1, 1869	50,000	00
Accrued interest to date on above Bonds for Territorial indebtedness	9,375	00
Act February 14, 1865	96,156	00
Interest coupons on above not presented for payment	83	79
Interest on above bonds, due January 1, 1867	4,795	08
State Bonds, Act January 19, 1866, due February 1, 1867	200,000	00
Interest on above, accrued to date	15,000	00
Warrants on General Fund, payable in gold	24,918	55
Payable in currency, $37,560 87, estimated in gold	28,170	23
Warrants on Prison Fund, payable in gold	830	87
Payable in currency, $10,315 46, estimated in gold	7,736	60
Warrants on Mining School Fund, payable in currency, $1,338 50, estimated in gold	1,003	88
Warrants on Soldiers' Fund, payable in gold	68,507	88
Payable in currency, $4,787 14, estimated in gold	3,590	36
	$585,168	29

Cr.

By amount on hand available to meet the above, estimated in gold	89,791	86
Total State debt over and above available assets (gold)	$495,376	43

NOTE.—The Bonds issued under the Act of February 14, 1865, ($96,156) are amply provided for by a special tax. This amount will soon be reduced to less than $80,000, which, deducted from the net State debt, leaves $415,000 to be provided for.

FIRST BIENNIAL REPORT

OF THE

Superintendent of Public Instruction

OF THE

STATE OF NEVADA,

• FOR THE

SCHOOL YEAR ENDING AUGUST 31, 1866.

———————

CARSON CITY:

JOSEPH E. ECKLEY, STATE PRINTER.

1867.

COMMUNICATION.

CARSON CITY, NOV. 24TH, 1866.

To His Excellency
    HENRY G. BLASDEL,
        Governor of Nevada:

In obedience to the requirements of the law, I have the honor to submit to you the Second Annual Report of the Superintendent of Public Instruction of the State of Nevada, for the School Year ending August 31, 1866.

Very respectfully,
        Your obedient servant,
                A. F. WHITE,
             Superintendent of Public Instruction.

REPORT.

To form a correct estimate of the progress and present condition of the Public Schools of the State of Nevada, it is necessary to consider the returns of the past year, and compare them in the aggregate with those of the preceding year.

STATISTICS FROM THE RETURNS OF SCHOOL CENSUS MARSHALS, 1865–6.

	1865.	1866.
Number of boys between six and eighteen years of age Increase....17	1,289	1,306
Number of girls between six and eighteen years of age Decrease....59	1,312	1,258
Total number of white children between six and eighteen years of age................... Decrease....32	2,591	2,559
Number of white children under six years of age... Decrease....287	1,913	1,626
Number of white children between eighteen and twenty-one years of age .... Increase....4	152	156
Number of white children under twenty-one born in Nevada..................... Increase....143	989	1,132
Number of children between four and six years of age Decrease....102	538	436
Number of children between four and six years of age, attending public schools .... Decrease....101	284	183

6

	1865.	1866.
Total number of children reported as attending public schools.............................. Increase....164	1,848	1,512
Total number of children reported as attending private schools.............................. Decrease....162	725	563
Number of children between six and eighteen years of age, not attending any school .... Increase....29	626	655
Number of Indian children .... Increase....57	121	178
Number of Mongolian children	24	24
Number of negro children .... Decrease....2	23	21
Number of deaf and dumb, irrespective of age..... Decrease....1	1	0
Number of blind, irrespective of age............ Decrease....1	1	0

STATISTICS FROM RETURNS OF TEACHERS AND TRUSTEES, 1865–6.

	1865.	1866.
Whole number of boys enrolled on Public School Register .... Increase....152	1054	1206
Whole number of girls enrolled on Public School Register .... Increase... 35	940	975
Total number of pupils enrolled on Public School Register .... Increase....187	1,994	2,181

	1865.	1866.
Average number belonging............ Increase....81	999	1,080
Average daily attendance........... Increase....58	886	944
Per centage of average daily attendance on the average number belonging............. Decrease....2	.82	.80
Total number of days' attendance, taken from School Register............. Increase....65,574	96,910	162,484
Total number of days' absence, taken from the School Register............. Increase....3,843	19,135	22,978
Number of times tardy, taken from School Register. Increase....4,402	4,682	9,084
Number attending school between four and six years of age............. Decrease....68	298	230
Number of calendar months during which school was maintained............. Decrease....16¾	165	148½
Average number of months during which schools were maintained............. Increase.....8	7.4	8.2
Number of classes in schools............. Decrease....160	273	113
Number of pupils studying History of the United States............. Increase....295	112	307
Number of pupils studying Physiology and Hygiene. Increase....139	281	420

MISCELLANEOUS STATISTICS, 1865–6.

	1865.	1866.
Number of primary schools .... Decrease 7	20	13
Number of intermediate schools.............. Decrease 2	7	5
Number of unclassified schools............... Increase 12	3	15
Number of grammar schools..................	3	3
Total number of schools .... Increase 13	23	36
Number of districts which have made reports according to law .... Decrease 8	18	10
Number of districts using the entire State series of text books .... Increase 16	1	17
Number of districts which have voted a district tax..	0	0
Total number of school districts	23	23
Number of school houses built of brick	2	2
Number of school houses built of stone .... Increase 1	1	2
Number of school houses built of wood .... Increase 10	12	22
Number of school houses built of adobe........... Increase 2	0	2
Number of school houses rented................ Decrease 3	9	6
Number of school houses which disgrace the State.. Decrease 2	8	6
Number of new school houses erected .... Decrease 4	6	·2

	1865.	1866.
Number of schools maintained only three months... Increase....1	0	1
Number of schools maintained more than three and less than six months .... Increase....1	4	5
Number of schools maintained more than six and less than nine months...................... Increase....5	8	13
Number of schools maintained nine months and over.	21	21
Number of schools for colored children............ Increase....1	0	1
Number attending such school .... Increase....29	0	29
Number of public schools maintained without rate bills	31	31
Number of male teachers employed during the year. Increase....4	14	18
Number of female teachers employed during the year Increase....5	23	28
Total number of teachers .... Increase....9	37	46
Number of teachers who have taught the same school two years and over .... Increase....1	1	2
Number of teachers who have made returns according to law .... Increase....4	31	35
Number of teachers who have not made returns according to law .... Increase....5	6	11
Number of teachers who attended County Teachers' Institute .... Increase....21	0	21

	1865.	1866.
Number of teachers allowed pay for time in attendance on County Institutes................ Increase....21	0	12
Number of teachers who subscribe for an educational journal............................... Decrease....11	26	15
Number of volumes in public school libraries....... Increase....99	184	283
Number of school visits made by County Superintendents .... Increase....220	115	335
Number of school visits made by Trustees......... Increase....256	127	383
Number of school visits made by other persons ..... Increase....387	632	1,019
Number of first grade certificates issued by County Boards of Examiners .... Decrease....12	26	14
Number of second grade certificates issued by County Boards of Examiners .... Increase....3	21	24
Number of temporary certificates issued by County Boards of Examiners .... Decrease....4	5	1
Number of applicants rejected by County Boards of Examiners .... Decrease....8	13	

FINANCIAL STATISTICS, FROM THE REPORTS OF COUNTY SUPERINTENDENTS.

Receipts.

	1865.	1866.
Balance on hand at beginning of school year... Increase....$7,742 62	$7,559 72	$15,302 34
Amount of School Fund received from the State Increase....$3,878 56	4,769 01	8,647 57
Amount received from County taxes.......... Decrease ..$25,486 34	52,035 16	26,548 82
Amount received from city taxes	—	—
Amount received from district taxes.........	—	—
Amount received from miscellaneous sources ... Increase $809 25	501 75	1,311 00
Amount received from rate bills............. Increase $504 00	105 00	609 00
Total receipts .... Decrease ..$12,551 91	$64,970 64	$52,418 73

Expenditures.

	1865.	1866.
Amount paid for teachers' salaries .... Decrease ..$10,182 79	$38,843 30	$28,660 51
Amount paid for sites, buildings, repairs, etc... Decrease......493 20	9,862 56	9,369 36
Amount paid for school libraries............. Decrease.....$148 50	175 00	26 50
Amount paid for school apparatus .... Decrease.....$294 40	472 00	177 60
Amount paid for rent, fuel, and contingent expenses........................ Decrease ...$1,730 22	6,379 72	4,649 50
Total expenditures .... Decrease ...$7,849 11	$50,732 58	$42,883 47
Balance..........................	$15,068 43	$9,535 26

12

MISCELLANEOUS FINANCIAL STATISTICS.

	1865.	1866.
Valuation of school houses, furniture, and lots.. Increase $863 50	$34,733 50	$35,617 00
Valuation of school libraries................ Increase $39 00	150 00	189 00
Valuation of school apparatus............... Decrease.....$177 00	852 00	675 00
Average monthly wages paid male teachers.. Increase $23 52	89 76	113 28
Average monthly wages paid female teachers... Increase $10 17	82 20	92 37
Average monthly wages paid all teachers...... Increase $15 34	87 48	102 82
Amount paid for salaries of County Superintendents	3,150 00	3,150 00
Average annual salary of County Superintendents	450 00	450 00

REVIEW OF STATISTICS.

It should be borne in mind, in considering the results comprised in these tables, that they cover a period of great financial depression. The spirit of speculation, so wild and ungovernable under Territorial rule, was followed, as it nearly always is, with embarrassment and disaster. Families who had taken up their abode, and who began to feel a particular interest in the cause of education, suddenly found themselves unsettled, and compelled to seek a residence elsewhere. The stream of population which, at an early day, turned so strongly towards this silver land, was checked or diverted into other channels. Property depreciated in value, and the means necessary to completely organize and efficiently sustain the Public Schools were wanting. It is to be hoped that the crisis is past. The sober thought, chastened judgment, determined purpose and patient industry everywhere manifested, indicate the adoption of a sounder policy, the existence of a more healthy state of business, a better condition of society, and the return of a more permanent prosperity.

How the system of Public Schools, but partially inaugurated, withstood the trial to which it was thus early subjected, is apparent from the returns exhibited.

The reports of the School Census Marshals show only a decrease of thirty-two in the whole number of white children between six and eighteen years of age, while there is a small increase in the number between eighteen and twenty-one. Of those under six there is a decrease of two hundred and eighty-seven, which is partly compensated by an increase of one hundred and forty-three of those under twenty-one born in Nevada. The number of children between four and six years of age who attended public school, has fallen off almost one-half. This diminution is not to be regretted. Children at so tender an age should not be closely confined to the school room, nor should their mental capacities be subjected to severe discipline : judicious parental instruction, the power of well regulated home influences, the force of good example, wise counsel, and free exercise in the open air, are far more important.

The number of children reported as attending private schools is five hundred and sixty-three—one hundred and sixty-two less than were reported last year, while the number enrolled on the School Registers is two thousand one hundred and eighty-one—one hundred and eighty-seven more than were enrolled last year. This fact clearly indicates the growing attachment of the people to the public schools. It shows an increasing confidence in the efficiency of these institutions, and a willingness to sustain them.

The number of children between six and eighteen years of age who do not attend any school, has not materially increased. There are but twenty-nine more than were reported last year. It is to be hoped that every obstacle which may have deprived these children of the advantages of instruction, whether existing in parental indifference or a want of proper facilities, will be speedily removed.

In examining the statistics from the reports of teachers and trustees, it is found that there has been a gain in every point essential to real growth and prosperity. This year there is an increase in the number of pupils enrolled on the Registers; the average number belonging to the schools; the average daily attendance; the number studying the advanced branches; the number of schools maintained; the number using the entire State series of text books; and in the number maintained more than six months. Evidence of progress is also apparent in the increased number of good substantial school houses, the convenient manner in which they are furnished, and the fact that comparatively few changes have been made in teachers, two of whom are reported to have taught the same schools for two years or more.

A public school for colored children, the first and only one in the State, was organized and maintained for nearly six months. It had an average attendance of twenty-nine pupils.

These statistics certainly present no very discouraging features. The first school law was enacted in October, 1861. The first attempt to organize public schools under its provisions was made during the year 1862.

The following tables exhibit the comparative growth and development of the system.

15

STATISTICS FROM THE REPORTS OF CENSUS MARSHALS, 1862–3–4.

Number of white children between four and twenty-one years of age in 1862		1,134
Number of white children between four and twenty-one years of age in 1863		2,425
Increase	1,291	
Number of white children between four and twenty-one years of age in 1864......................		3,657
Increase over 1863	1,232	
Number of white children under four years of age in 1862 Not given		
Number of white children under four years of age in 1863 Not given		
Number of white children under four years of age in 1864		523
Number of white children born in Nevada reported in 1862 Not given		
Number of white children born in Nevada reported in 1863 Not given		
Number of white children born in Nevada reported in 1864		235
Number of deaf and dumb reported in 1862—not given		
Number of deaf and dumb reported in 1863—not given		
Number of deaf and dumb reported in 1864..........		2
Number of Indian children reported in 1862—not given..		
Number of Indian children reported in 1863—not given..		
Number of Indian children reported in 1864..........		225
Number of negro children reported in 1862—not given...		
Number of negro children reported in 1863—not given...		
Number of negro children reported in 1864............		12

16

STATISTICS FROM THE REPORTS OF TEACHERS AND TRUSTEES, 1862–3–4.

Number of boys enrolled on School Register in 1862—not given		
Number of boys enrolled on School Register in 1863—not given		
Number of boys enrolled on School Register in 1864....		777
Number of girls enrolled on School Register in 1862—not given		
Number of girls enrolled on School Register in 1863—not given		
Number of girls enrolled on School Register in 1864		747
Total number of pupils enrolled on School Register in 1862 Not given		
Total number of pupils enrolled on School Register in 1863 Not given		
Total number of pupils enrolled on School Register in 1864		1,524
Number of pupils belonging, as reported in 1862		200
Number of pupils belonging, as reported in 1863 .... Increase	455	655
Number of pupils belonging, as reported in 1864 .... Increase	632	1,287
Average daily attendance in 1862—not given..........		
Average daily attendance in 1863—not given..........		
Average daily attendance in 1864		940
Number of calendar months during which school was maintained in 1862—not given		
Number of calendar months during which school was maintained in 1863—not given		
Number of calendar months during which school was maintained in 1864............................		265

MISCELLANEOUS STATISTICS, 1862-3-4.

Number of primary schools in 1862.................		5
Number of primary schools in 1863.................		11
Increase	6	
Number of primary schools in 1864.................		31
Increase	25	
Number of intermediate schools in 1862—not given.....		
Number of intermediate schools in 1863		2
Number of intermediate schools in 1864		6
Increase	4	
Number of grammar schools in 1862—not given........		
Number of grammar schools in 1863.................		1
Number of grammar schools in 1864............		1
Total number of schools in 1862		5
Total number of schools in 1863		14
Increase	9	
Total number of schools in 1864		87
Increase	23	
Number of school districts reported in 1862		10
Number of school districts reported in 1863		12
Increase	2	
Number of school districts reported in 1864		84
Increase	22	
Number of school houses reported in 1862		8
Number of school houses reported in 1863		6
Increase	8	
Number of school houses reported in 1864		8
Increase	2	

FINANCIAL STATISTICS, 1862-3-4.

Amount of the Territorial school fund in 1862..	—	—
Amount of the Territorial school fund in 1863..		$4,803 65
Amount of the Territorial school fund in 1864.. Increase	$4,453 46	9,257 11
Amount of private contributions for school purposes in 1863		1,944 73
Amount of private contributions for school purposes in 1863—probably .... Increase	37 88	1,982 61
Amount of private contributions for school purposes in 1864 .... Increase	3,272 26	5,254 87
Amount of county and city school taxes in 1862	—	—
Amount of county and city school taxes in 1863		3,965 61
Amount of county and city school taxes in 1864 Increase	43,506 96	47,472 57
Total amount of school fund derived from all sources in 1862		1,944 73
Total amount of school fund derived from all sources in 1863 .... Increase	8,807 14	10,751 87
Total amount of school fund derived from all sources in 1864................		61,984 55
Total amount of Territorial school fund		74,681 15

By a careful consideration of these statistics, it will be seen that during the years 1863 and 1864 there was a rapid increase of pupils, and a great advancement of all the material interests of the public schools. The little fountain that had been opened amid the deserts, had suddenly been swollen, and become quite a stream. At first there were willing hands to contribute to its wants, until the public resources became sufficient to sustain it. When the State was organized, it had a practical working system of education, which had established school districts in every county—had erected and furnished seventeen good substantial school houses, some of them made of brick, and some of them of stone—it had in successful operation thirty-seven different schools, under the direction of competent teachers, rapidly supplying the mental wants of three thousand six hundred and fifty-seven children. It had enrolled on its school registers, one thousand five hundred and twenty-four pupils—had made liberal provisions for an irreducible fund for educational purposes, and had rendered that fund and other resources productive to the amount of seventy-four thousand six hundred and eighty-one dollars. It had also provided for the proper gradation of the Public Schools, and had wisely foreshadowed departments for the "benefit of Agriculture, the Mechanic Arts and Mining, which should constitute the nucleus of a future university."

As we have seen from the statistics of 1865–66, this system possessed sufficient vitality not only to live through the period of financial depression which embarrassed the State for the last two years, but it has gained a surer hold in the hearts of the people—grown in usefulness, and developed in its resources.

The following table is an exhibit of the salary of the State Superintendent, amounts annually expended in visiting schools, office expenses, cost of printing, &c., from 1862 to the close of the year 1866 inclusive:

Salary of Superintendent ten months in 1862..	$1,000 00	
Traveling expenses	100 00	
Total in 1862		$1,100 00
Salary of Superintendent twelve months in 1863	1,223 30	
Traveling expenses	381 75	
Total in 1863		1,605 05
Salary of Superintendent in 1864	1,396 75	
Traveling expenses :....................	470 25	
Total in 1864		1,867 00
Salary of Superintendent in 1865..........	2,000 00	
Traveling expenses, stationery, postage, and expressage	250 50	
Total in 1865		2,250 50
Salary of Superintendent in 1866...........	2,000 00	
Traveling expenses, stationery, postage, and expressage	221 18	
Total in 1866		2,221 18
Total expenditure for the purposes named.		9,043 73
For printing blank forms for school officers in 1865	258 50	
Express charges on blank forms	20 00	
Total for printing and expressage.......		278 50
Total for all purposes		$9,322 23

The salary and traveling expenses charged in eighteen hundred and
sixty-two were for Rev. W. G. Blakeley, who was the acting Superintendent
of Public Instruction until about the close of that year. The blank forms
printed in eighteen hundred and sixty-five, included full sets for all the
school officers and teachers. There is a supply remaining sufficient, at
least, for the next two or three years. There have been no expenditures
for office rent, fuel, lights, or clerk hire. At all times and under all circumstances, the strictest economy has been studied and practiced, consistent
with the demands and interests of the school.

PUBLIC SCHOOL PROPERTY.

The total valuation of the property belonging to the Public Schools in
this State is reported at thirty-five thousand six hundred and seventeen
dollars. Last year, it was thirty-four thousand seven hundred and fifty-three
dollars and fifty cents. The increase is eight hundred and sixty-three
dollars and fifty cents—not very large—but it is gratifying to know that,
amid the general downward tendency of property, the schools have suffered
so little.

In the valuation of school apparatus, there has been a slight decrease.
Last year, it was eight hundred and fifty-two dollars. This year, it is only
six hundred and seventy-five—less than it was last year by one hundred
and seventy-seven dollars.

The valuation of the Public School libraries has not materially changed.
In eighteen hundred and sixty-five, it was estimated at one hundred and fifty
dollars; this year, at one hundred and eighty-nine dollars—a gain of thirty-
nine dollars.

THE AVERAGE LENGTH OF SCHOOLS.

In this State four school weeks are regarded as a month. The following
table, compiled by Hon. John Swett, Superintendent of Public Instruction
in California, and published in his "First Biennial Report," page 41, shows
how the schools of Nevada compared with those of other and older States in
eighteen hundred and sixty-five.

STATES.	Average length in months.
Massachusetts	7.8
Nevada	7.4
California	7.86
New York	7.86
Illinois	6.5
Ohio	6.28
Vermont	6.0
Pennsylvania	5.8
Wisconsin	5.5
Maine	5.7
Kansas	4.0
Kentucky	4.3
New Hampshire	5.7
Indiana	4.3

The returns make eight months and more than twenty-three one-hundredths as the average length of the schools in this State for the year 1866, being an increase over the year 1865 of more than eighty-three one-hundredths of a month. It is probable that, in this respect, Nevada will now head the list of States.

FREE SCHOOLS.

Not a district in the State voted a district tax to raise school funds, and thirty-one schools were maintained without rate bills. It is confidently expected that in a short time the opportunities of a thorough practical education will be offered as freely as the mountain air, to every child.

TEACHERS' WAGES.

There has been an increase in the average monthly wages of teachers over the year 1865 of fifteen dollars and thirty-four cents. In California, the average monthly wages of male teachers, in 1865, was seventy-four dollars. In Nevada, in 1866, it is one hundred and thirteen dollars and twenty-eight cents, thirty-nine dollars and twenty-eight cents more than in California. The average monthly wages of female teachers in California, in 1865, was sixty-two dollars. In Nevada, in 1866, it is ninety-two dollars and thirty-seven cents, or thirty dollars and thirty-seven cents more than in California.

Board in California is estimated at an average of twenty-five dollars per month. In Nevada, it is estimated at thirty-five dollars. This leaves a salary in California for male teachers, of forty-nine dollars; for females, of thirty-seven dollars, and is paid in coin. In Nevada, it leaves a salary for male teachers, of seventy-eight dollars and twenty-eight cents; for female teachers, of fifty-seven dollars and thirty-seven cents, and is paid in currency *at gold value.* In fact, there is no other State where teachers are so well paid, especially females.

The public schools which offer such remunerative inducements, should command the best talent in the country. It is certainly no small encouragement for persons whose opportunities, qualifications and tastes are favorable, to adopt teaching as a profession. Ability, experience and genuine worth will be appreciated, and faithful labor rewarded. By this liberality, Nevada asks that the standard of excellence for the instructors of her youth be elevated; that teachers by the manifestation of the highest type of manhood and womanhood command respect, and merit the lasting gratitude and love of those committed to their charge.

FEMALE TEACHERS.

One distinguishing element of power in the public schools of this State is the preponderance of female talent and influence. Twenty-eight of the forty-six teachers employed during the school year which has just closed, were females. In the course of nature, children, during their infancy, are necessarily committed to the fostering care of mothers. Habituated thus to be directed and governed by women, the transition to the school room where she presides is easy and natural. Here she fulfills one of the great objects of her earthly mission. Her active sympathies, her clear perceptions, her delicate sense of right, her gentleness, purity, soundness of judgment and refined tastes, enable her to win and retain the confidence of childhood, to restrain its waywardness, to awake and direct its aspirations for that which is good and noble with peculiar success. She knows more of human nature in its early history and manifestations than man. Its secret springs and latent powers have not escaped her observation. Their development has fixed her attention, engaged her thoughts, and opened to her a most pleasing and deeply interesting study. She loves children, and hence female teachers of thorough qualifications excel in a correct knowledge of the capabilities of their pupils, and the best methods of instruction. They are the best acquainted with their intellectual, moral and physical wants, and are the accurate judges of character. They have more tenderness, more patience, and more congeniality than men, and easily and naturally become the most acceptable and efficient instructors of the young.

A doubt has been expressed by some as to the ability of female teachers to discipline a school, especially in a country so new, where children young in years are often old in vice—where there is but little judicious home government, parental restraint or example. This doubt disappears before the experience of the last four years. The first schools organized and established were taught by females. They came with the first tide of immigration after the discovery of the mines, and began the work of instruction before Nevada had a name or a Territorial existence. At that early day, society was in its most chaotic state. The civil law was the arm of might; and the tribunal from the decisions of which there was no appeal, was the revolver and the bowie knife. It was a period of the wildest excitement, and of the most desperate adventures, affecting all classes, all ages and all conditions. Yet amid these scenes of confusion, the schools lived, flourished, and accomplished good. If the discipline was not of that high character attained since, and observed in older communities, it was, nevertheless, sufficient to answer the purposes of instruction, and the pupils of these schools are said to have made commendable improvement. From that early day to the present time, female teachers have been identified with the progress of the cause of education, and many of the most orderly and best conducted schools now in operation, are governed, disciplined and instructed by capable, accomplished female teachers. The pupils are of both sexes, among the most advanced classes, and of all ages.

It is not maintained that it is best to place the public schools wholly under the care and direction of female teachers. Judgment must be exercised in all cases. It is only intended that where the way is open, where the circumstances are favorable, and where there are thoroughly qualified, intelligent, faithful female teachers, their claims to preference should be carefully considered by both parents and trustees. They must not be ignored and denied a field of usefulness to which experience has proven they are peculiarly adapted, and in which God designed they should reap an abundant harvest.

REPORTS.

Some improvement has been made by the County Superintendents, in preparing the statistical part of their annual reports. Too great care cannot

23

be given, to have every number correct and correctly entered. All the returns of the School Officers, compiled by the County Superintendents, should be made ready for publication before leaving their hands. Mistakes will occur, and experience has shown that errors will multiply in copying, and in printing; but every officer should discharge his duty faithfully, and not leave, as has often been done, a mass of statistical matter and of facts in a state of confusion, to be arranged by some one higher in authority.

While statistical tables furnish the clearest evidence of the progress and true condition of the Public Schools, still there are many facts, circumstances, results, and suggestions, not to be expressed by figures. The moral power of a school, in a given district or county, the intellectual development of pupils, their attainments in scholarship, the excellencies or particular defects of the law, the efficiency of its administration, the peculiar wants of a people, the standard of public opinion, and many other matters of interest —must be expressed in words. Hence, written statements accompanying the statistics are essential. Heretofore, something of this kind has been attempted, and, whenever prepared with any considerable care, has been published. Usually, abstracts have been made, as nearly as possible, in the words of the authors. This year, only one brief, *written* report has been received. In every other instance, the blank forms, furnished from this office, were filled and returned without comment.

The Treasurers of Lander, Lyon, Ormsby, and Washoe Counties, have made reports, as required by section fifteen, division fourth, of the School Law. The Treasurers of Douglas, Esmeralda, Humboldt, Storey, Churchill, Nye, and Roop Counties, have not reported. The important statistical information, in regard to the County School Fund, which can only be derived from these returns, faithfully prepared, has not been received. Any compilation of the reports made, would not only be unsatisfactory but useless, and has, therefore, been omitted.

The returns of the Census Marshals have been received, from twenty-three districts; but the teachers and trustees of only eighteen districts have made reports, and several of these are very deficient.

COUNTY BOARDS OF EXAMINERS.

As the School Law now is, the authority to decide on the qualifications, and grant certificates to applicants wishing to teach, is committed to County Boards of Examiners, consisting of " three competent persons, appointed by the Superintendent of Public Instruction." These appointments were primarily made, in almost every instance, on the recommendation and petition of prominent citizens in the respective Counties. Some of these Boards have been faithful and earnest in the discharge of their duties. They placed the standard of qualification much higher than it had ever been before; and, consequently, the Schools in these Counties have risen, proportionably, in character and efficiency.

Other Boards, without a just appreciation of the need of thoroughness and ability in the school-room have granted certificates, if not to incompetent persons, at least to those who are deficient in many qualifications necessary to insure success. This action works a hardship upon the schools. The Trustees are prohibited from employing persons to teach, who do not hold a certificate of qualification from the Board of Examiners in the county within which their district is located. They must, therefore, engage only such persons as hold certificates from the Boards mentioned, whatever their deficiencies may be. It is not designed to condemn the system, but the indifferent mode of complying with the spirit and intent of the law. There is no subject of such vital importance to the Public Schools as the qualification and ability of the teachers, and there is no point which should be more carefully guarded. As the County Boards of Examiners are only authorized to grant certificates of qualification " of the first grade for teaching unclassified, grammar and high schools, which shall be good for two years," and " certificates of the second grade for teaching primary schools, which shall be good for one year," it seems necessary to complete the system ; that the State Board of Education be empowered to examine applicants and to grant certificates of all grades, especially for the higher departments, which shall be valid for a period of two or more years, and render the holder eligible to a position in the schools of any district in the State as the law may provide.

The State Board of Education should also be authorized to grant life diplomas to applicants who have held certificates of the first grade granted by the Board, who have taught successfully in this State for two years or more, and who pass a satisfactory examination in such studies as the Board may determine and the Legislature may require.

This arrangement, it is hoped, would obviate the difficulty arising from the inefficiency of the County Boards of Examiners. It would also encourage teachers to study and to become proficient in their profession. The repeated thorough examinations and the test of experience required would be a sure guarantee against the commitment of the grammar and high schools to the care and direction of incompetent and unqualified teachers. The liberal salaries now paid for instruction, and the actual wants of the schools, seem to demand the adoption of some such system without delay.

SCHOOL TRUSTEES.

The principle intended to be established by the law providing for the election of district trustees " for the term of one, two and three years respectively," is productive of the greatest good, and, under proper regulations, should be maintained. When the law was approved, the twentieth of March, one thousand eight hundred and sixty-five, the time positively fixed for the first election and for deciding the " terms by lot " had passed nearly two weeks. The County Superintendents filled the vacancies by appointment, but there was no authority to decide " the terms," and the law specifically states that each succeeding year thereafter (1865) " one trustee shall be elected for the full term of three years." In some districts difficulties arose from this complication, which, for a time, greatly embarrassed the interests of the schools. By amendment of the law, no further trouble need be apprehended, and the benefits arising from always retaining in office two trustees of experience, will be secured.

SCHOOL VISITS.

The number of school visits made by School Trustees in 1865 was one hundred and twenty-seven. This year it was three hundred and eighty-three, an increase of two hundred and fifty-six. Last year the number of school visits made by other persons was six hundred and thirty-two. This year it was one thousand and nineteen, an increase of three hundred and eighty-seven. This is certainly a gratifying result, and augurs good for the future. It is evidence of a growing public interest in the schools of the State, and of an increasing faithfulness on the part of the officers most nearly associated with them. If parents, guardians, and citizens generally would spend more time in the school-room, it would have a most salutary effect. It would greatly stimulate the efforts of both teachers and pupils. None perceive more readily than children when others are interested in their intellectual growth. They know, intuitively, when a parent is moved with sympathy with them in their mental conflicts. Words of encouragement are well, but the frequent presence, in the school-room, of those whom they love, and whom they delight to please, is of the greatest moment. It attaches importance to the child's mental efforts and to its studies, and makes it feel that the school is a place of privilege, and that it is favored by being there, where the scroll of knowledge is enrolled—where the elements of its nature are expanded—its latent energies developed, and its character moulded after the most perfect type of true manliness. Such visits are of the utmost importance to teachers. They greatly need the hearty sympathy and efficient co-operation of parents and guardians. Often overworked, frequently tried by the waywardness and thoughtlessness of their pupils, worn by protracted confinement to the school-room, perplexed by many questions pertaining to the physical, moral and intellectual welfare of those committed to their trust, and, in many instances, far away from former counselors, an approving smile, a word of encouragement, a kindly visit from a patron of the school, greatly lessens their burden of care. It does much to awaken their sympathies and give them a feeling of personal identity with their pupils. In addition to all this, it aids the teacher in the work of discipline, impresses and sustains his authority, fosters respect for his instructions and character, and places him in his true position in the school, and in the community, as an honorable and invaluable assistant to parents in the education of their children. The obligation to educate a family rests primarily upon its united head, and cannot be neglected with impunity, or transferred to others. The work begins as soon as the child is born, and changes in manner only as the infant passes into childhood, and from childhood into manhood. To the son, the father is, and of right must be, the pattern of all that is great and excellent in human nature. To the daughter, the mother is the embodiment of the perfections of womanhood ; hence, the lessons of the fireside are always the most enduring. This home-teaching is ever the most effectual, and is cherished with the most hallowed associations of life. Teachers are only to supply the want of opportunities, and the deficiencies in parental instruction. They are *aids*, not principals in the work of education. By the association of the members of different households in the school-room, they assist many families at the same time. But it is not intended to exclude the parents, or that their efforts in behalf of the complete development of all that is susceptible of improvement in their children shall cease ; and yet, how often it is, that they seem to lose all sense of any further responsibility ? Months and years go by, and they have not visited the school, and, in many instances, are scarcely able to recognize the teacher to whose instructions they have committed their families. Is this right ? Is it just? The merchant places his goods in the hands of a faithful salesman, but he goes every day to see how his business prospers. The householder in the parable planted a vineyard and let it out to husbandmen and went into a far country, but he sent his servants to look after his vineyard, and receive of its fruits. In business transactions men are usually punctual and careful, but often in the education of their children they are culpably negligent. The Great Father above watcheth over the sparrows, and careth for them. Are not these little ones of our households "of more value than many sparrows?"

Let parents, let guardians and citizens generally, realize that their presence is often needed in the school-room ; that the moral and intellectual welfare of the children assembled there requires it, and that the obligations they owe to the rising generation demand it.

STATE TEACHERS' INSTITUTES.

Should the suggestions made in this Report meet with the approval of the Legislature, and should the School Law be amended as hereinafter recommended, it will be the duty of the State Board of Education to hold an annual meeting for the purpose of examining applicants for State Certificates and Life Diplomas. A State Teachers' Institute might be held at the same time with but a small additional expense, which the State Board of Education might determine. Such an Institute would be productive of the greatest good. It would be an occasion for the assembling of the best talent in the State, and ought to be accompanied with lectures, addresses, and essays, and a full and free discussion of the provisions of the School Law, and of all subjects pertaining to the interests of the Public Schools, and of the cause of education generally.

EDUCATIONAL JOURNAL.

Two years ago, the "California Teacher" was introduced into the Public Schools of this State. In eighteen hundred and sixty-five, it was supplied to twenty-six teachers. This year, for some cause not stated in the reports, it has been furnished to only fifteen teachers. It is made the duty of each County Superintendent (Sec. 18, Division 8 of the law) "to subscribe annually for a sufficient number of copies * * * to furnish each school officer and teacher in his county with a copy of the same, and one copy to be filed with the records of the district."

The "Teacher" was offered to the schools of this State on the most liberal terms, and is, and has been a faithful, earnest, and able advocate of every judicious improvement in the manner of conducting schools, and in the system upon which they should be established. It has invited candid and thorough discussions upon a wide range of topics, embracing all that was calculated to encourage parents and guardians to embrace every opportunity for the mental and moral improvement of the children under their charge. It has done much to sustain teachers, trustees, and school officers in the faithful discharge of their duties. It is the only journal on the Pacific Coast devoted exclusively to " educational purposes," and wherever it has been read has awakened interest, quickened effort, and hastened the fulfillment of noble purposes. Our teachers and trustees cannot do without it, and the County Superintendents do them and the schools a great wrong when they neglect to subscribe for it as the law directs.

AGRICULTURAL COLLEGE.

The Legislature, during its session in 1865, passed " An Act to establish an Agricultural and Mechanical College in Washoe County in this State." This law created a Board of Regents, consisting of the Governor, Secretary of State, and Superintendent of Public Instruction, who were " authorized and required to appoint five suitable persons as Commissioners, three of whom shall be residents of said county, to select a location for the College aforesaid."

The Board of Regents fulfilled the duty assigned them in the appointment of Gen. J. L. Slingerland, Hon. Charles Lambert, and Capt. H. A. Cheever, of Washoe County; Hon. John A. Collins, of Storey County, and C. L. Anderson, M.D., of Ormsby County, as the Commissioners required.

These Commissioners have made no report to the present time, and it is presumed have made no progress towards establishing the contemplated College. In this connection, I submit to the candid consideration of the friends of education in this State, the following able exposition of this whole subject pertaining to Agricultural Colleges, by the Hon. Isaac Newton, Commissioner of the National Agricultural Department.

He says: This Department has received various letters asking its views relative to the best system of instruction for the Agricultural Colleges to be established under the Act of Congress of July 2d, 1862, donating public lands to the several States and Territories to provide Colleges for the benefit of agricultural and mechanic arts. As Congress had in view the establishment of, at least, one College in each of the States and Territories, and as the experience of the United States in such institutions has not been either extensive or successful, it is highly necessary that public sentiment should be awakened, that by enlightened action, success may be obtained. This public sentiment cannot be acted on in this matter, more speedily than through this Department, and hence it now complies with the request in these letters; not expecting to control public sentiment, but simply to aid in its development, and to be the means of uniting its action.

But there are other reasons why the Department must ever be deeply interested in the successful establishment of these colleges; some of them are the following :

1. The Department needs much the aid it would derive from these colleges. They will have experimental gardens and farms, skillful professors to properly conduct experiments, to carefully note them, and to properly report them. Hence, when the Department imports new seeds and plants, it can, through their aid, at once determine their adaptability to this country, and the climate, soil, and cultivation proper to each. The distribution of

seeds, cuttings, etc., could then be made on a most economical basis, because they would be distributed only where they could be advantageously grown. Seeds, when thus tested, could be grown by these institutions, and thus a large sum of money sent abroad would be distributed at home.

2. From these colleges would be received reports of the experiments made, and these would be placed before the farming public through the reports of the Department; and thus, with the seeds and cuttings distributed, would be communicated the mode of cultivation adapted to each.

3. A great object with this Department must be to systematize the agriculture of the United States; and how can this be so well done over a country so extensive and of such diversified latitudes and products, as by the aid of local institutions, under the direction of high intelligence, and aided by the special agencies which will be found in them?

4. To render most practicable and useful such systematized farming, the aid of institutions having local influence will be essential, as instructors of leading farmers, and to obtain such State legislation as may, from time to time, become necessary to a more speedy advancement.

These reasons, without stating others, are sufficient to show how deep an interest this Department must ever take in the proper establishment of these industrial colleges.

In considering such establishment, the first inquiry to be made is: *What course of instruction should be adopted by them?*

There are no settled opinions in answer to this question to be found in the United States. So far as they have been expressed in the course of study in our few agricultural schools, and in the writings of those who have sought to mould public opinion, the instruction proposed has contemplated a preparation for the farm only. The languages have generally been regarded as useless, and the course of mathematical studies has been too limited. In this, we think, lies the failure of our agricultural colleges. Such limitation may be adapted to European affairs, where the son seeks to continue in the father's occupation; but here, the farmer's son is no more destined to agricultural pursuits than the son of a professional man. Here the merchant longs to be released from the distracting cares of commercial pursuits, and the opulent manufacturer from the danger of changing markets: both anxiously desire the rest and enjoyment found in the country life. And with them in this wish, is the professional man and the politician. And it is a natural desire: it is a part of man's nature, as it was in conformity with it that God placed our first parents in the Garden of Eden, and that the homes of illustrious Americans have become a part of their fame, as Mount Vernon, Monticello, Ashland, and Mansfield. And this desire would be a hundred fold strengthened if early education fitted all for an intelligent pursuit of agriculture, as well as other occupations of civilized life. A system of education, to be successful, must be in conformity to the tastes and pursuits of a people. The time is not yet come in the United States when the son will inherit the father's occupation; nor is it desirable that it ever should be. The eminent success of Americans in all the pursuits of life; the intellectual and physical energy they have displayed in them, the facility with which this intellect takes hold of the most diverse pursuits, all point to a condition so different, both mentally and socially, from the countries of Europe, that its agricultural schools furnish but an imperfect basis upon which to rear our own. We must mark out a path for ourselves. Congress, in the act referred to, seems to have been governed by this American condition of things. Its provisions are broad and liberal. It recites that in the colleges to be established "the leading object shall be, without excluding other scientific and classical studies, and including military tactics, to teach such branches of learning as are related to agriculture and the mechanic arts in such manner as the Legislatures of the States may respectively prescribe, in order to promote the liberal and practical education of the industrial classes in the several pursuits and professions of life."

It will be seen from this, that these Colleges are not to be agricultural only. The education of mechanic, manufacturer, merchant, and miner, is demanded as well as the tiller of the soil. *All* the industrial classes are to be fitted for an intelligent career in the several pursuits of life. Anything less broad would not have been equal justice to all. It requires, too, military instruction, that the citizen may be qualified for duties, the discharge of which is now demanded of so many ; and it does not exclude " other scientific and classical studies."

The American youth have a broad career before them. Neither the farm nor the workshop, nor a subdivided labor in either, is to be the bound of their emulation or labor. The son of the farmer must be permitted to obey the promptings within him, and, like Mr. Webster, to hang the scythe on the tree ; or, like Mr. Clay, to ride to the highest political stations, as well as on the horse's back to mill. Like Washington, he should be fitted for the chain and the compass, or the camp, or political rule, or the management of a landed estate.

It may be answered, in the senseless aphorism, that a " Jack-of-all-trades is master of none." The career of Henry Ward Beecher furnishes a reply. He lately told us, when in England, that he was bellringer in his first church. When at Indianapolis, he published an agricultural paper ; and, during the past summer, the Journal of that city, alluding to the admiration of strangers for the beauty of its gardens and yards, ornamented with flowers and evergreens and shrubs, gave all the credit to Mr. Beecher's teachings when there. He left in the West, " the Beecher rhubarb," a seedling variety, originated by him, not inferior to any other ; and he reformed the butter market of that city. And he did these things whilst he was the first of its preachers. His political speeches, in England, exhibit his power in another field.

Another case, showing the superiority of a general education of the faculties of the mind over the disciplining of a few only, is seen in an eminent American manufacturer and inventor. In exhibiting, in England, one of his inventions, he had the work mostly done there, but made slow progress in completing it. Writing home, he said, that in English shops, the workmen are trained to such subdivisions of labor, that one of them can do the work of only one part of an engine ; that one part must be done before another workman can do his part ; that few of them can superintend the entire work of an engine ; whilst in his own manufactory here, most of his workmen were competent to do this. And to this subdivision he attributes the want of inventive talent in England.

Apart, then, from pre-eminent ability, we see that both in education and labor, a development of mental power is promoted by a general discipline of all the faculties of the mind; and that instruction, dwarfed to a particular pursuit, results in a dwarfed mind itself. The powers of the mind, like those of the body, achieve most when their fully developed strength is centered, for the time, on the accomplishment of a certain object. If our greatest minds have found this developed strength in liberal studies, lesser minds must be governed by the same law of progress. Confine their faculties to a narrow routine of study, and whilst a few facilities may be partially strengthened, others remain undeveloped.

In the agriculture of England and of the Continent, we see the influence of limited instruction. A plowman continues to be a plowman; and a worker in the vineyard occupies the place filled by his grandfather's grandfather. Whatever of progress we find in England and Scotland, is to be attributed to a higher and broader development of mind. Turn to France, and in the following description of the agriculture of the South, we see the results of subdivided instruction. One of our most intelligent Consuls thus writes:

"I received the request from the agricultural department to furnish its statistics. I know not what to do. I who have always so loved agricultural and horticultural pursuits, would certainly be expected to do much in this line. But when I look around I find absolutely nothing in all France to interest our country in that line. So far is France behind us in all labor saving machinery, in everything relating to agriculture, or the mechanic arts even, that I know it is the wrong place to seek light. Many things are unearthed in Pompeii and Herculaneum that are much in advance of everything in France. The ploughs are of the style of the ancient Egyptians—a forked tree. The carts and wagons of the farm are four times the size of our own; awkward and clumsy affairs. You might worship and not break the second commandment, for they are the likeness of nothing on earth. The peasants drive in a single log to market, as in Ireland, and everything else is in the same piddling, picayune style. Is this the style to be imitated by our own large-minded, great-souled, enlightened, freeborn Americans! Not by my aid or consent.

"This district, and the whole south of France, from here to Nice, on the Italian border, is a land mostly of grapes; the eastern half of olives, also: a poor, miserable character of farming, which we should leave, I think, after looking over the whole ground, to the small-minded, small farmers of Europe. Or when we do go at grape-raising, as we will largely in California, let us go at it in our own grand style, as we raise hogs, corn, wheat, etc. etc.; no piddling or scratching like this."

Here we have graphically described the difference between the enlarged American agricultural mind, and the dwarfed European agricultural mind. Our agriculture presented a scope that demanded thought; it was vast in itself, and by its own greatness, raised up the farmers of our own country to the higher standard we find in the foregoing contrast. But as population becomes more dense, there will be a tendency to European division of labor, and its narrow views. This must be counteracted by liberal education. Grand as have been the achievements of American agriculture, it has been aided by a natural richness of the soil, which must be replaced and sustained by the riches of science.

But the American farmer and artisan have not yet achieved their greatest elevation, either in their occupations or in their positions as American citizens. Look into the army, and at the civil officers. A stranger to our institutions might readily suppose that the profession of law constituted a privileged class in this country, and that no one outside of its ranks could hold a civil or military position. Is this just to the industrial classes? Or is it safe to the government? The mission of these classes is not one of toil merely, but of equal position as citizens. The skillful artisan, the comprehensive farmer, the far-reaching merchant, the enterprising manufacturer, should be competent, when occasion demands, to be an officer in the army, or statesman at home, or minister abroad.

Our agricultural colleges have heretofore failed, because they aimed to educate for the pursuit of agriculture only. The sons of our farmers are not less ambitious of distinction than others; and an education that regards them as farmers only, cannot meet their approbation. The purpose of education is to teach men to observe and think: these are alike essential to all pursuits, and in these operations of the mind, all the faculties are called in requisition. A skillful and correct use of their power is the boon of instruction. Their general development is first to be accomplished, and subsequently this developed power is to be applied to particular pursuits. A course of instruction regarded merely as information is not less necessary to one pursuit than another; for a mere farmer or mechanic is not less to be discountenanced than a mere lawyer. General science and knowledge is as essential, and is as becoming to the one as to the other. All pursuits, then, may have a common course of instruction.

From these general remarks, rendered necessary by prevailing erroneous opinions respecting the instruction suitable to the industrial classes, we return to the question asked, that it may now be answered specifically—*What course of instruction should be adopted in our Industrial Colleges?*

1. *Languages.*—Besides the considerations just advanced, a knowledge of the English language to express his thoughts, either in writing or speaking, clearly, forcibly and elegantly, is as important to one engaged in an industrial pursuit as in a professional. In early years, as twelve to sixteen, a youth cannot make more progress in learning it than by a study of the Latin language. It is a language that has added much to our own. Its study familiarizes the pupil with English words and their meaning, and their use to express ideas both correctly and elegantly. The study of the Latin grammar instructs him in the English grammar. And the knowledge of Latin is absolutely essential if he would better understand and more readily remember the numerous words derived from this language used in works on the natural sciences.

The German language is used so extensively in the business transactions of many parts of the United States, that opportunity to acquire it should be given in these colleges. It need not, however, be made an essential part of the regular course of studies.

2. *The Mathematics.*—The study of the mechanical laws is directly connected with the mechanical and manufacturing arts. So far as mathematics is essential to their understanding, to disciplining the mind, and a thorough knowledge of natural sciences, it should be made a part of the course of study.

3. Of the other branches of study we cannot do better than adopt the

following, transmitted to the Department by Richard Owen, a brother of Robert Dale Owen, and of the late David Dale Owen—a name familiar to every intelligent citizen on account of his eminent attainments in science, and his practical application of them in geological and mineralogical surveys. Mr. Richard Owen is now a Professor in the State University of Indiana, at Bloomington, and is not less thorough in his scientific acquirements. He has received a military education, also; and, until recently, commanded a division of the Indiana troops.

A course of study, although briefly laid down, by one who is as practical as learned, cannot but receive the careful consideration of all. Mr. Owen, in his letter, says:

"I hasten now to furnish, as you request, an outline of the plan of study which I think might be advantageously adopted, throwing out other hints which can receive consideration, provided the means are sufficient and the public mind prepared.

"Finding the great advantage of addressing all instruction, as far as practicable, to the eye, (in addition to that given through the medium of the ear) I would recommend a Museum, (besides the lecture room, each having its own appropriate specimens and diagrams) to contain—

"1. All the most important minerals, arranged according to Dana's Text-book.

"2. The necessary rocks and fossils to illustrate pretty thoroughly each geological period.

"3. Suite of plants, arranged according to the natural orders.

"4. Specimens of all the most important seed vessels (chiefly fruits) and seeds, (grains, grapes, &c.)

"5. A zoölogical department, exhibiting the most important animals, from the sponge and polyp, up through the star-fishes and sea-eggs, worms, crustaceans and insects, (particularly those injurious to agriculture) mollusks, fishes, reptiles, birds and mammals, (including the skeletons of all domestic animals) to end with man.

"6. Numerous charts, exhibiting streams of time, chemical tables, geological sections, maps of physical geography, giving meteorology, distribution of plants, animals, rain, &c.

"7. A good set of philosophical instruments, to illustrate the department of natural philosophy and land surveying, such as the air pump, electrical machine, mechanical powers, rain-gauge, barometers, thermometers, hygrometers, hydrometers, microscope, sextant with horizon, &c.

"8. Models of machinery, as grist-mills, saw-mills, paper-mills, cotton machinery and the like. Also, improved agricultural implements of every description, and models of barns, bridges, grain-houses, &c.

"[N. B.—This museum should be open to the agricultural and normal institutions.]"

INSTRUCTION.

1st. For *physical* development, gymnastics, agricultural operations, in suitable weather, at least for a part of the classes, (the others taking the succeeding day) as plowing, digging, mowing, sowing, &c.

2d. For *moral* culture, religious instruction, moral philosophy, music, (especially vocal, in parts) social gatherings, reunions, at least for some classes, each week, when they should meet the professors and their families, having some object to bring them together, such as microscopic examinations, or the magic lantern, music, or portfolios of engravings, &c., to examine.

3d. For *mental* improvement—supposing the elementary branches mastered—then drawing and surveying, geography, book-keeping, human anatomy, physiology and hygiene, comparative anatomy and physiology, vegetable physiology, chemistry, mineralogy and geology, botany and zoölogy, lectures on gardening, pruning, fruit raising, wine making, &c., agricultural chemistry, embracing lectures on manures, improving wornout lands, drainage, &c., and lectures on stock raising and farriery.

THE NORMAL SCHOOL.

In this, a great object should be, not so much to convey any particular information on subjects to be taught, as to discipline the would-be teachers in the best method of imparting instruction in any branch or department.

Instruction how to convey information to the youthful mind might be given on the following points :

1st. Lessons on things (objects surrounding us) of every day occurrence.

2d. Pestalozzi's system of arithmetic (mental).

3d. Writing on blackboard before using either slate or paper, to give freedom to the hand.

4th. The elements of drawing, and practice in estimating distances, areas, &c.

5th. Proper mode of teaching vocal music, with metronome, tuning forks, &c.

(These last three comprise improvement of the hand, eye and ear: consequently the development of three senses—the taste and sense of smell do not require much cultivation.)

6th. Making each would-be teacher lecture alternately on some of the subjects under discussion, so as to practice the imparting of instruction—the professor criticising, if necessary, his style, mode of handling the subject, &c.

N. B.—If female teachers are to be received and instructed, there should be a model kitchen for the instruction of young ladies in the proper mode of preparing wholesome food, such as household bread; and *knowing*, not guessing, when things are sufficiently cooked ; also, how to cook without the wasteful and unwholesome use of so much lard, and the advantage of boiling instead of frying constantly in grease, &c.

MODEL FARM.

Connected with the Agricultural College, there should be of course a model farm, and the best stock, implements, &c.; also, a model garden and greenhouse. Connected with the normal institution, there ought to be a model school house and appurtenances, and, as above suggested, a model kitchen.

MILITARY TRAINING.

Perhaps, by carrying out the West Point system of training, as far as consistent with study, work, &c., the necessity of a gymnasium might not be so great as in ordinary schools and colleges, where it ought always, undoubtedly, to be introduced, under proper instructions.

The above may seem to convey, to some extent, the plan which had been in my head for some, time, but which had never assumed quite a definite form, for want of knowing the exact circumstances under which such a plan could be worked out; and many details would, of course, depend upon that. For instance: Congress may, in the grant, perhaps, prescribe a certain course; the State, in accepting, may prescribe a course differing in many points. The community, in sending, may demand certain things; but the above may, perhaps, at least serve for a basis on which any one knowing the circumstances, can work out the superstructure.

AN EVIL AND ITS REMEDY.

This admirable course of study, thus briefly sketched by Professor Owen, needs no comment; it sufficiently recommends itself. But it demands what few of our collegiate institutions have, viz: a museum, apparatus, &c., which aid so greatly the acquisition of knowledge by presenting through the senses clear ideas to the mind.

Why our institutions are deficient in these, is obvious enough when we look at their too great number. The educational means of the community have been expended in building edifices, to the great detriment of thorough instruction, by the help of those agencies referred to by Mr. Owen. Each State has its dozen of colleges, and the apparatus, museum, library, &c., of all would be insufficient for one. *Are these Industrial Colleges to be virtually destroyed by a like waste of means?*

What are these means? The Act of Congress gives to each State a quantity of land equal to 30,000 acres for each Senator and Representative in Congress. A State that has unsold lands within its own borders, may locate this grant; but those that have not, are to receive land scrip, which cannot be located by the State, but only by the assignees of the State, at $1 25 per acre. When we reflect that the homestead law gives away the public lands to actual settlers, and that no large bodies of good public farming lands remain for entry, it is pretty clear that the fund from the grant to the older States will be slowly realized, and then only at a great sacrifice. The law ought to be so amended as to allow immediate location by all the States. *Must the industrial classes wait for this slow realization of the fund, before colleges, so important to them, can be established; and must they be limited to an inadequate course of instruction by reason of insufficiency of the funds?* No! Kansas has answered, and its admirable precedent should be followed by all other States like situated. No! Connecticut replies, bestowing its grant of lands upon Yale College. The one answers for the west, the other for the east. The new States of the west and southwest have had donations granted them by Congress for the establishment of universities or seminaries of learning. Among these, is Kansas; and wisely determining to consolidate and not dissipate its college funds, it has consolidated the grant for both, merging the first one into the second, thus saving the useless expense of building two edifices, when one is all-sufficient; in having two sets of professors when only one is required: and by this economy securing a museum, apparatus, library, &c., so necessary for the proper instruction of all occupations, whether professional or industrial.

Under like grants we have the following universities : Ohio, at Athens ; Indiana, at Bloomington ; Illinois, at Springfield ; Missouri, at Columbia ; Wisconsin, at Madison ; Iowa, at Iowa City ; Michigan, at Ann Arbor. Since these universities were established, many others have been founded in these and other States, mostly by religious denominations, in which is usually found such course of instruction as is adapted to professional pursuits ; but not to the industrial, for want of the museums, apparatus, library, model farm, &c., mentioned by Mr. Owen. Why retain these State Universities as competitors of the private colleges ? Why not render them efficient, economical, more truly State institutions, by consolidating the grants, and thus creating a college competent to the thorough education of all occupations ? The sound policy of such union is the more obvious, when it is remembered that the last act does not allow any of the fund created by it to be used in buildings. The former grants have provided these and a skeleton library and apparatus, with a fund competent only to sustain a faculty inadequate to such instruction as the wants of the age and our own condition demand. But all these would constitute a basis on which, as the funds from the recent grant were realized, colleges adapted to these wants could be built up. These views are now placed before the public, in compliance with the requests that have been made, and with the hope that they will lead others to express themselves.

The discussion here presented is so thorough, so condensed, and yet so wide in its range, that there is but little to add. It shows forcibly what an Agricultural College ought to be, and announces the only true policy in regard to the use of the university fund. No thought should be entertained of dissipating that fund by the establishment of a feeble, insufficient school, nominally for agricultural purposes, in Washoe county, and a mining school, equally as weak and unproductive of good results, in some other county. If testimony to the evils of scattering our educational resources in the establishment of many institutions were necessary, it is not wanting. One of the profoundest thinkers in Europe, Gustus Leibig, recently used the following language in regard to agricultural colleges. Addressing a distinguished American, Mr. Klippart, he said :

" You don't want much land—a few hundred acres is all-sufficient for all manner of experiments ; and you must allow me to repeat—you don't want to teach a specific system of model farming, for many reasons : *first*, not one student, perhaps, can get a farm precisely like your model farm ; he may not be able to get so much grass land, or so much upland, or he may be unable to have farm buildings precisely like the model ones. Then, what good does your model do, when nobody can copy it ? Now, when you get home, pray, do not misrepresent this idea. I want you to make experiments : not simply to show what can be done, but make experiments to show what can be done profitably, and what may be done by any intelligent farmer. Of course, you cannot expect to accomplish much for the present generation of farmers ; but these seeds you sow will be reaped by the next and future generations. In Ohio, you do not want to build a palace for an Agricultural School. In America, you spend too much money in putting up your educational buildings, and then starve your professors. I learn that you put up a very grand building in your city of Columbus, called the Starling Medical College; I have a picture of it. I am told it cost some seventy or seventy-five thousand dollars; and now you are starving the professors in it. You did the same in Cleveland and Cincinnati. Then I am told you built two Universities in Ohio; and now the professors can barely live on the salaries you pay. The consequence is, that these schools, colleges, or universities must run down. There is no place in the whole world where knowledge can make so much money, as in America; therefore, your best men will not become teachers or professors, simply because they can make more money out of something else; and they naturally apply their talent and ability where it pays the best. No man will engage in an educational course of life, for life, on a salary of twelve hundred or fifteen hundred dollars a year, when, by applying the same ability in some other pursuit, he can make four thousand or five thousand dollars a year. Hence, you have no first-class professors in America; but you have, instead, first-class business men, first-class mechanics and managers of large and colossal establishments."

Congress has been liberal in its grants of land; but the proceeds should be invested with the greatest care. The work of organizing and establishing a University, such as will meet the peculiar wants of the State, must necessarily be laborious and expensive, and will tax the energies of the best talent and finest executive ability. The departments should be kept together, while in their incipiency, in the same building. There should not be more than one library, one laboratory, one museum, one course of study, and one faculty. Make these sufficiently comprehensive to embrace all that is demanded, and there will be a hope of success.

MINING DEPARTMENT OF THE STATE UNIVERSITY.

The preceding discussion in regard to the Agricultural College, clearly indicates the policy which should be adopted in relation to a mining school. These are but different departments of the same institution, and should not be separated. They are so regarded by the Constitution of the State. Economy demands that they should be kept together; and the success and efficiency of the whole enterprise pertaining to the University, depend upon it. Section eighth, of the Constitution, provides "that all the proceeds of the public lands, donated by Act of Congress, approved July second, eighteen hundred and sixty-two, for a College, for the benefit of Agriculture, the Mechanic Arts, and including Military Tactics, shall be invested by the said Board of Regents, in a separate fund, to be appropriated, exclusively, to the benefit of the first-named departments of the University, as set forth in Section four above."

Section four, just named, reads: "The Legislature shall provide for the establishment of a State University, which shall embrace departments for Agriculture, Mechanic Arts, and Mining, to be controlled by a Board of Regents, whose duties shall be prescribed by law." Referring again to Section eight, it is made imperative that " the Board of Regents shall, from the interest accruing from the first funds which come under their control, immediately organize and maintain the said mining department, in such a manner as to make it the most effective and useful." It is apparent, then, that the mining department of the University should take precedence. It is one of "the departments first named" in Section four, and, as such, is especially provided for, by a direct and specific statement of the source from whence the fund is to be derived for its maintenance, followed by directions for its immediate organization. There are no such imperative requirements in the Constitution, in regard to the establishment of a College, for the "benefit of Agriculture, the Mechanic Arts, including Military Tactics." With this understanding of the Constitution, Congress enacted a law, approved July fourth, eighteen hundred and sixty-six, confirming this appropriation of the proceeds of the grant of lands mentioned.

In the act making this confirmation, the following language is used (Chap. CLXVI, Sec, 8, Statutes of Congress, 1865 and 1866) : "And the diversion of the proceeds of these lands in Nevada, from the teaching of agriculture and mechanic arts to that of the theory and practice of mining, is allowed and authorized without causing a forfeiture of said grant." With an unprecedented liberality, that body, in the same act above named, donated for University purposes, seventy-two entire sections of land, in addition to all its previous grants. This donation was made with the distinct understanding that, according to the Constitution of this State, the Mining department of the University would be the first established, and hence the proceeds of the land granted be appropriated to this purpose. Congress has thus manifested the deep interest felt by the nation in the organization and maintenance of an efficient mining school. By its action, it has designated our State as the appropriate seat of a University in which a principal department shall be devoted chiefly to the subject of mining, which is now more than ever engaging the attention of the leading intellects, both in this country and in Europe.

Art. 11, Sec. 3, of the Constitution of the State, provides a liberal, irreducible fund for educational purposes, the interest only of which may be used from year to year, and also " that such portions of said interest as may be necessary, may be apportioned for the support of the State University." From all these resources, the Mining department of the University might probably be organized at no distant day, under a system of careful economy and prudent management. The interests of the State demand it. With us, mining in all its departments is in its infancy, and must be, for a long time to come, under the most favorable circumstances. The errors that have been practiced, and the mistakes which have been made during the last four years, have impoverished the State, for the time, destroyed public confidence and driven capital into other fields, while the mineral resources of the country, probably unsurpassed, if not the richest in the world, have remained undeveloped, and comparatively unproductive. Such a department as that contemplated, however feeble it might be in the beginning, would be a powerful stimulant to effort. It would afford the means of progress, and give facilities for investigation. Nature is fixed and unalterable in its laws. It is truth, abiding and eternal, embodied. A treatise correctly stating the principles of geology, if prepared when the foundations of the world were laid, would be correct to-day. An accurate essay on metallurgy written when God commanded the dry land to appear, or when Tubal Cain became the "instructor of every artificer in brass and iron," would be true now. There may be new facts, but there are no new laws in the physical world. The province of science is discovery. Lyell, Mantell, Hitchcock, and Dana never created a crystal, or the smallest particle of gold that gilds the sands. Such men are but successful explorers, and demonstrate that Lord Bacon was correct when he affirmed that man was merely " the minister and interpreter of nature." Werner and Hutton did not originate the power of fire and of water in transforming the crust of the earth. These agencies wrought changes, kindled volcanoes, piled mountains, formed and destroyed islands, made continents, and convulsed both sea and land, before man was created. The sixty elemental substances of which the universe consisted in the beginning, are the same to-day that they ever were. The principles of their combinations, their chemical changes forming an opal, a diamond, a wall of granite, a vein for the gold or for the silver, or a mountain of iron, continue now, as they were at the commencement of time. But to discover them, to define them, to describe their laws and modes of operation, and to predict results—this is science; this is the field for mental conquest. We need to summon to our aid the wisdom and experience of the past, the discoveries of other lands, and the combined learning and genius of our own. This can only be successfully done in a well-endowed University, with an appropriate library, laboratory, cabinet, and an efficient faculty of thorough, practical men, devoted to the work for life.

With proper legislation, now, the way is open to commence this important enterprise—at least, to lay the foundation-stone of the first, and to the interests of the State the most important department. A delay of two years will be an irreparable loss, a self-inflicted injury, for which there is neither apology nor reason.

STATE NORMAL SCHOOL.

Nevada, it is hoped, will soon become of age, and be able to stand alone; to think, plan, and act for itself. Hitherto, the public schools have depended for teachers very much upon our older sister of the golden tiara. She has sent to us some worthy instructors, a few of whom have excelled; and we have drawn somewhat and profitably, too, upon the talent and enterprise of the Atlantic States. But, it is apparent we must soon provide for the mental discipline and proper training of our own teachers. We cannot expect to command the best scholars and the most competent minds in California. There is an increasing home demand with which it is impossible for us to compete. The additional amount of salary which we offer will not avail. Should it induce a few of the best qualified and most enterprising teachers to seek employment in our State, no general supply, adequate to our wants, could be expected, and the greater number of our schools would be compelled to engage second-rate talent. As a matter, then, of self-defense, we must have a State Normal School.

Such an institution, properly conducted, would secure a permanent supply of well qualified teachers, thoroughly identified with the interests of the schools and of the State. It would do more than anything else to introduce uniformity of government, to insure a high character of mental discipline, and to harmonize the various methods of imparting knowledge. It would vitalize the whole system of public instruction, and give dignity to the profession of teaching. It would command public confidence, and do much to destroy the prejudice against popular education. All the educational interests of the State demand the Normal School; and the intelligence and standard scholarship of the children and youth in every district, depend upon it in a great measure.

As a matter of economy, and as a guarantee of efficiency and success, this school ought to be associated intimately with the first organized department of the State University. The aid would be mutual. It is probable, that for several years to come, the same buildings and grounds might be used; and it is certain, that many of the lectures and experiments, and much of the instruction in the class-room, ought to be in common. It is not maintained that the same Board of Instruction throughout, would be sufficient for both schools, but only that an economical arrangement might be made for the mutual accommodation of pupils, where the studies prescribed were the same. This plan of concentrating all the higher departments of education into one institution, is consistent with the graded system of public schools already established. The preliminary school is the first step in the ladder. Then there is the intermediate department, the grammar school, and the high school. Shall we not complete the plan, and have the State Normal School, the Mining School, and, when the means justify it, the Agricultural College, the Medical, and other departments, until, by a sound and healthy growth, the State University is perfected in all its parts? Is not this the safest mode of progress?

If nothing more can be done in the course of the next year, let the State Mineralogist and the Superintendent of Public Instruction be required to deliver, at the State Capital, a course of lectures before such persons, miners, teachers, and others, as may choose to attend; each selecting for his subject such matters of interest as may appropriately appertain to the duties of his office, and which may constitute an introduction to the study of mining and metallurgy, and to the theory and practice of teaching. Perhaps the year following a class or two might be instructed for a time, and thus the nucleus of the Mining Department of the State University, and of a State Normal School, be formed at once. This would, at least, have the merit of an earnest purpose, and would lead to investigation, and arrest public attention.

SCHOOL LANDS.

The Constitution of the State, in Article eleven, Section three, sets apart generally for educational purposes " all the proceeds of lands that have been or may hereafter (from the time of the adoption of the Constitution in 1864) be granted or appropriated by the United States to this State." It then specifies: " the proceeds of the sixteenth and thirty-sixth sections in every township, granted by Act of Congress, March twenty-first, eighteen hundred and sixty-four, for the support of common schools." It also designates for the same purpose the proceeds of the grant of five hundred thousand acres of land, made under Act of Congress, September fourth, one thousand eight hundred and forty-one, for internal improvements. This division was approved and confirmed by Congress, July fourth, one thousand eight hundred and sixty-six. The proceeds derived from these and other sources, specified in the article and section above named, were to constitute an irreducible fund, to be invested in United States Bonds or in the Bonds of this State, and the interest only to be apportioned for the support of the public schools.

Article eleven, Section eight, of the Constitution, appropriates "all the proceeds of the public lands donated to the State by Act of Congress, approved July second, eighteen hundred and sixty-two, " to the organization and maintenance of a Mining Department of the State University." This land was originally a grant of thirty thousand acres for each senator and representative in Congress for an Agricultural College. The diversion of the proceeds of this land was allowed and authorized by Congress, July fourth, eighteen hundred and sixty-six, and, at the same time, an additional donation of "land equal in amount to seventy-two entire sections, was made for the establishment and maintenance of a university." This last grant remains to be accepted by act of the next Legislature of this State.

The whole amount of land thus appropriated for university purposes, the interest on the proceeds of which, by Article eleven, sections eight and four, of the Constitution, to be applied in "organizing and maintaining the Mining Department," is one hundred and thirty-six thousand and eighty acres.

The Constitution also provides in addition, (Art. 11, Sec. 3) "that such portions of said interest" (derived from the proceeds of the school lands and other sources mentioned) "as may be necessary, may be apportioned for the support of the State University."

There is but one other source whence a fund may be derived for the establishment of a mining school, but this is not from the proceeds of public lands. Section forty-four of an act concerning the location and possession of mining claims, approved February twenty-seventh, eighteen hundred and sixty-six, provides that, " all moneys paid to the District Recorder as assessment dues, * * * shall be set apart as a mining school fund." As yet, no funds have come under the control of the Board of Regents from this source.

Soon after the approval of the law (March 9th, 1866) creating the office of State Mineralogist, the Board of Regents, in the discharge of their duties, gave the appointment for that position to Prof. R. H. Stretch, who at once began the work of exploration, the collection of facts pertaining to the mineralogy of the country, the investigations of its peculiar geological formations; and has already gathered the nucleus of a State cabinet. He will, in due form, report the results of his labors and investigations. He has been greatly embarrassed in the discharge of his duties for the want of means to enable him to pursue successfully his most economical plans. To make this office available for good, a more liberal policy must be adopted.

Under the provisions of the law, approved March third, eighteen hundred and sixty-six, requiring the Superintendent of Public Instruction, in cases where portions of the " sixteenth and thirty-sixth sections have been entered under the provisions of the preëmption laws of the United States, to select from the public lands of the United States a like quantity of land so entered," selections have been made to the amount of eight hundred acres.

Under the requirements of section four of the law above named, twenty-eight thousand one hundred and twelve acres and twenty-three one-hundredths have been " reported " to the Surveyor General, and to the Board of State Land Commissioners.

PROPOSED AMENDMENTS TO THE SCHOOL LAW.

The law under which the present system of public schools is maintained, constitutes the Governor, the Superintendent of Public Instruction and the Surveyor General, a State Board of Education. The duties enjoined on this Board are : to have a seal ; to hold two sessions annually to devise plans for the better organization of the Public Schools, and for the improvement and management of the public school fund ; to invest the principal in United States Bonds, or in the bonds of this State ; to prescribe and cause to be adopted a uniform series of text books, and to prepare rules and regulations for the County Boards of Examiners. From the fact that the Surveyor General resides in Virginia City, it has been difficult to have full meetings of this Board at any time. The constantly pressing and multifarious duties devolving upon the Governor, in immediate connection with his office, necessarily occupy all his time, and severely tax his energies ; and now that Congress, during its last session, made such liberal grants of the public lands, from the proceeds of which it is confidently expected that the principal of the fund for educational purposes will, in a short time, be greatly increased, and thus proportionably increase the responsibility of the State Board of Education ; and furthermore, in view of the fact, that before the time fixed in the Constitution for the convening of the Legislature in 1869, a new series of text books will be required, to prepare which is a work within itself of great magnitude, and of the most vital importance to the schools ; it is, therefore, recommended that the school law be so amended that the Board of Education shall be made to consist of the Governor, the Superintendent of Public Instruction, the Surveyor General, the Secretary of State, and the State Mineralogist.

Also, that in addition to the duties already required of this Board, a clause be added to the law empowering the Board to examine applicants and to grant certificates of qualification to persons wishing to teach, of the first grade, which shall be valid for four years, for teaching grammar and high schools ; of the second grade, which shall be valid for two years, for teaching grammar and high schools ; and of the third grade, which shall be valid for two years, for teaching primary and ungraded schools ; and also that the State Board of Education be further empowered to grant life diplomas to applicants who propose to continue teaching as a profession in this State, and who have held a certificate of the first grade above named, and who have been successfully engaged in teaching for two years or more, and who sustain a satisfactory examination in such studies as the Board may determine and the Legislature may require. These certificates and diplomas to be sufficient evidence of qualification, and render the holder eligible to a corresponding position in any public school in the State. It should further be made the imperative duty of this Board, and of the County Boards of Examiners, to revoke any certificate or diploma upon convicting evidence of immoral or unprofessional conduct, such as profanity, intemperance, gambling, Sabbath breaking, cruelty, &c.

Every examination should be required to be conducted mainly in writing; and every applicant for a certificate of qualification, before examination should be required to pay a fee of one dollar towards a fund for the purchase of school libraries or apparatus.

The State Board of Education should be required to prepare a list of books suitable for public school libraries, from which it should be the duty of district Trustees to select in all cases before purchasing. Otherwise school libraries may, by injudicious selections, become sources of evil, if not positive immorality.

The State Board of Education, by and with the consent of the Board of Regents of the University, should be required at an early day to organize and maintain a State Normal School in connection with the Mining Department of the University. They should have power to provide and furnish rooms, examine and employ teachers, prescribe the course of study, the text books to be used, and to have the full supervision of the school. No persons should be admitted to the privileges of the school who are not willing to pursue ordinarily, or to be examined in the whole course of studies prescribed, and to pledge themselves to engage in teaching for a definite period in this State. The funds required for the support of this school, and necessary to defray the expenses of a State Teachers' Institute, should be set apart from the general school fund of the State, by the State Controller, the amount in each case being certified by the State Board of Education, and subject to be drawn from the treasury by the warrant of the Superintendent of Public Instruction.

The school law needs amending, so as to fix the terms of office of the Trustees in the various districts. See Sections 22, 23 and 18, division sixth.

The provision in Section 41, by which the State Board of Education is empowered to "remove, examine and fill vacancies," in County Boards of Examiners, is superfluous. The members of the County Boards act voluntarily by the appointment of the Superintendent of Public Instruction, and will not submit to examinations. The branches designated to be taught in the various grades of the schools are not stated with sufficient definiteness in Sec. 42. This section combines two subjects which should have been kept separate. The proviso at the end of the section should properly be inserted after the words "eighteen and sixty-five," and before the word "orthography."

There are other amendments apparent to the careful reader, necessary to make the law harmonious in all its parts and workings. It is hoped that the verbal inaccuracies will be corrected.

Laws "for establishing an Agricultural and Mechanical College in Washoe County, approved March 9th, 1865," and "for establishing and maintaining a Mining School, and create the office of State Mineralogist, approved March 9, 1866."

It is recommended that these laws be repealed, and that such parts of them as relate to the office and duties of the Board of Regents, and of the State Mineralogist, and the organization of a Mining department of the University, be compiled, carefully revised, and embodied in one Act.

In addition to the duties enjoined at present on the Board of Regents, they should have power to invest the University funds, and to control the interest for the immediate organization of the Mining department, and in connection with it, permit the State Board of Education to establish and conduct a State Normal School. It is not intended that these institutions should be united further than for mutual aid in their incipiency; and in all cases the funds of each should be kept separate, and under the control of the proper Board. There should also be a provision made for the election of a new Board of Regents in eighteen hundred and sixty-eight, as set forth in the Constitution, Art. 11, Sec. 7, of which the State Mineralogist should be a member and the Secretary. The law should definitely fix his salary, and provide for its payment, and also for the payment of his traveling and other expenses, in the same manner and from the same fund as the salaries and expenses are paid of the other State officers.

Laws providing "for the disposition of the sixteenth and thirty-sixth sections of the public lands, approved February 27th, 1865," and the "Act amendatory thereto, approved March 3, 1866."

Through the action of Congress, such liberal grants of public lands have been made to this State, that it seems necessary that the next Legislature should make provisions for a State Land Office, to which should attach all the rights, authorities, and powers necessary and usual in such cases. The office of State Land Commissioner should also be created, who should, among other duties, have the selection and location of all the lands thus granted to the State for various purposes mentioned in the Acts by which the grants were made. Therefore, it is respectfully recommended that the laws above named be repealed, and also that such parts of them as may be pertinent to an arrangement by which these lands may be brought into market on reasonable terms and at an early day, be carefully revised and condensed into one Act. The duties, responsibilities, and compensations of all the officers engaged in the disposition of these lands, should be clearly and fully defined and stated.

STATISTICAL TABLES.

Table number one attached to this report, shows the apportionment of the General School Fund for January and July of this year. Table number two includes the Financial Reports of the County Superintendents. Table number three includes the returns of the Census Marshals, Teachers, and District Trustees.

NATIONAL BUREAU OF EDUCATION.

In my last Annual Report the subject of a National Bureau of Education was discussed and urged upon the attention of the Legislature. The importance of such a department must be apparent. The annual expenditures of the United States for educational purposes is about $22,000,000 ; the number of pupils in the public schools is about 5,000,000. When efficient systems of public instruction shall be established in the Southern States, these expenditures will probably be doubled, and the number of school children greatly increased.

This Government has, by a bitter experience for the last five years, been taught the absolute necessity of popular education to its peace, prosperity, and perpetuity. If the character of a nation depends on the intelligence of its citizens, then, is it not time for legislative bodies to memorialize Congress upon this deeply important subject? Is it not time that statesmen should see that the growth, moral and mental education of children is of, at least, equal importance to the rearing and improvement of cattle and sheep—or to the cultivation of the different varieties of grasses and grains? If we *must* have a National Agricultural Bureau, is the necessity any less for a National Bureau of Education?

NATIONAL MONUMENT TO THE MEMORY OF ABRAHAM LINCOLN.

Attention was called to this subject in the Report of eighteen hundred and sixty-five. It was desired that the public schools of Nevada might make a voluntary offering towards the erection of a National monument in memory of our martyred President, Abraham Lincoln. The schools in California have contributed liberally, and the patriotism of the children of other States is manifested by the most generous offerings for this purpose; but, as yet, nothing has been done in this State. It is hoped that efficient measures will speedily be taken by County Superintendents, Teachers and Trustees, to awaken an interest, and to show that the Public Schools of Nevada are not wanting in patriotic zeal and in heartfelt gratitude to the defender and preserver of the nation in its hour of greatest peril.

CONCLUSION.

In closing this Report, it may not be improper to record an earnest hope that the system of public instruction which it little more than foreshadows, may be developed and established, until it is complete and harmonious in all its departments; and until in its efficient workings the benefits of a good, sound, practical education are freely extended, without money and without price, to every child and youth in the State.

A. F. WHITE,
Superintendent of Public Instruction.

TABLE NO. 1.

APPORTIONMENT OF THE GENERAL SCHOOL FUND FOR 1866.

COUNTIES.	JANUARY.	JULY.	JULY.	TOTALS.
	Coin.	Coin.	Currency.	
Douglass................	$676 32	$49 54	$33 21	$759 07
Esmeralda	256 34	18 78	12 58	287 70
Lander	651 76	47 74	32 00	731 50
Lyon	796 30	58 33	39 10	893 73
Ormsby	1,262 63	92 49	62 00	1,817 12
Storey	2,318 00	169 80	113 82	2,601 62
Washoe	1,131 73	82 90	55 58	1,270 21
Totals	$7,093 08	$519 58	$348 29	$7,960 95

Cr.

By cash received from County Taxes, from the apportionment of the County Superintendent.	By cash received from City Taxes.	By cash received from District Taxes.	By cash received from Miscellaneous Sources.	Amount received from Rate Bills and Subscription, as reported by School Trustees.	Total Credits.
$303 04	....	....	....	....	$517 16
554 08	....	....	....	....	877 65
339 68	....	....	....	....	1,117 11
277 02	....	....	....	....	444 25
1,473 82	....	....	....	....	2,956 17
918 62	....	....	75 00	....	1,274 97
25 82	....	....	....	....	542 72
1,413 75	....	....	....	....	1,795 56
1,054 21	....	....	196 00	....	1,534 64
251 59	....	....	....	....	309 40
119 82	....	....	....	....	147 32
2,839 37	....	....	196 00	....	3,786 92
1,413 42	....	....	....	....	2,234 80
2,755 42	....	....	200 00	479 00	4,025 14
4,168 84	....	....	200 00	479 00	6,259 44
2,133 62	....	....	....	....	3,225 05
553 93	....	....	840 00	....	2,024 28
141 45	....	....	....	....	331 84
2,829 00	....	....	840 00	....	5,581 17
11,207 94	....	....	....	....	25,984 70
364 30	....	....	....	....	579 05
408 91	....	....	....	130 00	772 69
684 00	....	....	....	....	1,215 32
267 65	....	....	....	....	625 91
178 44	....	....	....	....	332 16
550 17	....	....	....	....	788 21
386 60	....	....	....	....	1,372 32
245 34	....	....	....	....	846 98
3,085 41	....	....	....	130 00	6,032 64
26,548 82	....	....	1,311 00	609 00	52,418 73

Total number times tardy, taken from the School Register	Number attending School between 4 and 6 years of age	Number of calendar months during which School was maintained	Monthly salary, board included, paid the Teacher
....	..	....	....
780	5	9	$ 100
322	2	6	85
....	..	....	....
1102	7	15	185
2320	17	6½	125
....	4	3	60
82	22	9	100
78	24	11	100 [1]
21	7	9	100
181	53	29	300
1258	...	11	125 [1]
....	4	6¼	195
1258	4	17½	320
...	10	11	100
....	...	....	....
....	...	....	....
....	10	11	100
3098	115	10	100 [1]
264	...	10	90
....	4	6	125
327	7	9	120
85	4	6	85 [2]
....	...	....	....
229	1	8	80
220	3	8½	88
....	1	9	75
....	...	....	....
1125	20	56½	663
9084	230	148¼	$1853

ANNUAL REPORT

OF

THE WARDEN

OF THE

NEVADA STATE PRISON,

FOR THE FISCAL YEAR ENDING DEC. 31, 1866.

J. S. CROSMAN,
WARDEN.

CARSON CITY:
JOSEPH E. ECKLEY, STATE PRINTER.
1867.

OFFICERS OF THE PRISON.

Warden,

J. S. CROSMAN.

Assistant Warden,

W. D. MASON.

Lieutenant Guard,

N. E. JUDD.

Superintendent of Labor,

N. E. MURDOCK.

Gate Keeper,

THOS. HAINS.

Guards

H. THOMAS,	**WM. McGEE,**
A. LESSER,	**B. E. SCOTT.**

REPORT.

To the Honorable the Legislature of the State of Nevada:

GENTLEMEN—In accordance with the requirements of the law, I herewith submit this, my annual Report.

The management and government of Criminals is a subject requiring much thought and experience: not all who are so unfortunate as to get into the State Prison are so hardened in sin and crime as to be beyond the hope of reformation, and of restoration to their friends and to society as good citizens, being made wiser by the hard experience of the past. To the accomplishment of this object, as well as for their safe keeping, I have given much thought. I have endeavored to treat them kindly, and in such a manner as to lead them to think more of themselves, and to know that their punishment was intended for their reformation as well as for the protection of society, rather than that society was taking revenge on them; and the less hardened to feel that they yet have reason to hope for their former rights with all attendant blessings.

IMPROVEMENTS.

The improvements recommended in my former Report to the Legislature, have been in part carried out. The new building in the rear of the main Prison building is twenty-two by seventy-eight feet with two feet walls, well built, with as good mortar as the country affords. It has two skylights and four windows, all thoroughly grated with iron bars, one-half inch by two inches. The doors are four inches in thickness, well ironed with fastenings, so arranged that when locked they hang on the four heavy iron bars in such a manner as not to be easily tampered with. The building is divided by a wall thirty feet from the east end, making a large and airy kitchen, so situated as to connect with the officers' dining-room, through a double-grated door in the hall of the main building. The west end, forty-eight feet, is intended for a prisoners' dining-room; at present, a portion of it is temporarily partitioned off and used as a shoemaker and tailor shop, where the making and repairing for the prisoners is done. The roof is tinned, and has had two coats of oil paint upon it. The inner surfaces of the walls of both these rooms have been plastered. This new building is so arranged, that when an addition of the same width and forty-one feet long is put on the west end, in the rear of the present cell-room, connected therewith by a hall, there will be but one door between the kitchen and the dining-room, and but one door between the dining-room and the cell-room—which will be a material improvement on the present condition of the institution, as by this arrangement there will be a block of cells in the center of a building surrounded by a hall between them and the outer wall of the building.

WATER.

On the east end of this new building, next to the main building, I have built a water tank of masonry of sufficient capacity to hold fifty barrels of water, which is supported by masonry from the main bed-rock below. It is supplied with water by the use of a force pump located in the new dining-room, drawing water one hundred and twenty feet from the well sunk last season near the Warm Springs Hotel; then forced up perpendicularly about twenty feet, to the eaves of the main building; thence through a horizontal pipe to the tank. The distributing pipes are not yet all complete, one leading into the hall on the second floor of the main building, and one into the new kitchen—giving only two points for present use; but these we find a very great improvement on our former means of supplying water to the institution, viz: the barrel and wheel-barrow; and in case of fire, would give us a good supply of water ready at hand.

CELL-ROOM.

The walls of the cell-room were very loosely and imperfectly built; so much so that the wind came through in places, sufficiently so as to blow out a candle. It was from this room that five prisoners made their escape, last year, by digging through the wall. I have had the walls plastered, which I think adds materially to the security, by making a smooth surface, so that they cannot so easily cover their tracks as with a rough wall. It must also make the room materially warmer, requiring much less fuel.

WALL.

The wall of the southwest corner of the yard, adjoining, or in the rear of the Warm Springs Hotel, has been raised four (4) feet, which somewhat increases the security in that direction.

CHIMNEYS.

The chimneys in the old Prison Building have been a source of trouble from time to time since I have been here—at times refusing to draw entirely. In November, I built a large one from the second story through the center of the roof, which effectually answers the purpose.

YARD.

The yard in the rear of the building has been much improved this season, by being enlarged in blasting out the quarry, and making a good road from the lower yard. The front yard was sown in clover and alfalfa—the latter did well, the former was a failure.

The place where the hogs were kept, was in a bad condition. I have had a new pen built.

GARDEN.

Our garden this year was a moderate success, furnishing a good supply of vegetables, besides the satisfaction of looking at it while growing, appearing like an oasis in this sage brush desert.

QUARRY.

The quarry is in good condition for getting out rocks; the stone dressed this year, is about equal to the amount sold.

ARMORY.

The armory is well supplied with arms and ammunition; several additions have been made this year.

TOOLS, FIXTURES AND SUPPLIES.

I have been continually adding to the tools and fixtures about the place. The stonecutters and quarrymen are now well supplied with all that they need in their line. I bought a second-hand derrick for ninety dollars, ($90) and have expended about sixty dollars ($60) in repairing and improving it; we find it useful.

BLACKSMITH.

The blacksmith has a fair set of tools, with probably one hundred and fifty (150) bushels of coal, and four hundred pounds of iron.

CARPENTER.

In the carpenter shop there is also a fair set of tools for ordinary work, to which several additions have been made during the past year. There are probably fifteen hundred (1,500) feet of lumber on the place, besides the wheeling planks. There are now four (4) pumps in working order; two (2) single acting, and two (2) double acting, force pumps; one hundred feet of India rubber hose, with necessary couplings and pipe; also seventy-five feet of gas pipe, which will be needed to complete the water works; a good kit of shoemaker's tools, with considerable leather on hand; horse, wagon and harness, the two latter much the worse for wear; one good saddle; one cow; two tons of hay; ten hogs; six stoves and pipes; ten cords of wood; two and one-half tons of potatoes; with the usual amount of other supplies for the table on hand.

The officers' dining room (with the exception of chairs) is fully supplied with crockery and all other necessary fixtures.

The kitchen and washroom each have all the necessary conveniences that their names entitle them to. The kitchen stove is badly burned out, and will soon need replacing.

. The only addition made to the office fixtures during the year is that of a bookcase for the prison library, which is a convenient piece of furniture.

The guard room remains with the same amount of furniture as reported last year.

The cells, fourteen in number, are calculated to accommodate two prisoners each.

Each prisoner has a mattress, which has recently been filled with oat straw; a pulu pillow, with a slip, three pairs of blankets, and a towel.

PRISONERS' CLOTHING.

During the month of March I made an arrangement by which I obtained from the Mission Woolen Mills, at San Francisco, thirty-seven suits of striped gray and black woolen cloth, such as is worn at San Quentin, which makes a good warm suit, but bears a striking contrast to citizens' .clothing. It is our invariable rule, on the receipt of a prisoner, to have him take a bath, and put on an entire suit of State clothing, or uniform, do up his citizen's clothes in a bundle and put on a ticket, so that he can have them to wear when he is discharged. I also, in September, sent down and got four dozen more of the shirts or blouses (over three dozen of which are now on hand): so that now the prisoners are all warmly and comfortably clothed, with a good supply of good clothing and bedding on hand.

IMPROVEMENTS NEEDED.

There should be built, at an early day, a range in the new kitchen, as the cooking stove now in use, is failing; otherwise there will have to be another one bought.

Eight new cells, for which the rock is now dressed, should be built early in the spring, which would probably give sufficient cell capacity for another year.

I would recommend the building, as soon as 1868, of an addition to the prison, twenty-two by forty-one feet, connected with the present cell rooms in such a manner as to afford a space for a block of cells, (one-half in the present cell rooms) with a hall between them and the walls of the building.

Workshops are needed for the prisoners, and could probably be built next season without much extra expense.

The office and other rooms on the lower floor in the east end of the building, should be lathed and plastered.

A wall inclosing the yard is much needed, but it does not seem practicable to attempt to do much in that direction until we get out from under the one per cent. limit of our Constitution, (which expires next year) or have it amended in regard to the limitation of indebtedness to $300,000, or else have more taxable property in our State; as any attempt to push the building of an outer wall would be attended with heavy expense.

REVIEW OF PRISONERS.

I commenced the year with twenty-one (21) prisoners; during the year, sixteen (16) new ones have been received; five (5) discharged by expiration of sentence; and seven (7) pardoned and restored to citizenship, most of whom had, in connection with the commutation they had secured, nearly served out their time; one discharged on a writ of *habeas corpus*: leaving the present number twenty-four (24). For further information, reference will be had to the tabular statement hereunto attached.

REMARKS.

Continued observation and experience confirm my faith in the wisdom of that legislation which provides that the prisoner may commute five days per month of his sentence by good behavior and faithful labor. Most of the number have received the credit for each month in the year.

The system of government has been such that we have been able to maintain good order and discipline, and administer much less punishment this year than last, during which time no prisoners have escaped.

LIBRARY.

In my report of last year, I recommended that there be furnished, for the use of prisoners, a library, which was done by an act of the Legislature, transferring from the State Library "Harper's School Library," consisting of three hundred and two (302) volumes of well-selected miscellaneous reading.

From observations of the year, I am fully convinced of the wisdom and humanity of the act, as by it they are furnished with good, profitable reading, a privilege which most of them prize very highly: as while they are improving the mind, it aids them much in passing off many a dreary hour while in their cells, as each cell is furnished with a lamp until nine o'clock, P.M.

During the past season, previous to October, the Rev. Warren Nimms has regularly held religious services on the Sabbath in the prison, in which many of the prisoners have seemed to take a lively interest; to some, no doubt, it has only been a pleasant pastime—a change from the dull monotony of prison life; while others, apparently, have been led to make new resolves to lead a more moral and upright life. I feel that he is entitled to much credit for his untiring efforts to promote the moral and educational interests of the institution, and that it would be well to provide for the same in future.

SANITARY.

During the past year, the sanitary condition of the prison has been good. There have been a few cases of severe illness, which have readily yielded to the wise and skillful treatment of Dr. George Munckto, of Carson. I attribute, in a great degree, the good health thus enjoyed by the prisoners to the care and constant attention to the quality, preparation and variety of food prepared for their use.

MISCELLANEOUS.

Whereas, I was advised about the first of January, by L. G. Smith, Sheriff of Ormsby County, that one H. C. Kittles had been sentenced by the District Court of the Second Judicial District, to the State Prison;

And whereas said sheriff informed me that he would like to hire said Kittles, and that he would feed, clothe, and become his keeper, and be responsible for his safe keeping; and for the services of said Kittles he would pay the State the sum of ten dollars ($10) per month;

And whereas, upon consultation with the Board of State Prison Commissioners the whole matter was laid before and considered by them, upon which it was agreed and so ordered by them at their meeting on the first day of February, 1866, that I might accept the proposition of said Sheriff Smith, and consider him the keeper of said Kittles:

Hence, I have received the pay for said services, although the name of said H. C. Kittles does not appear on the records of the prison, he not having been formally delivered to me; and now as the said Kittles was, on this thirty-first day of December, pardoned by the proper authorities, the above statement will account for the fact that his name does not appear in the list of prisoners hereunto attached.

APPROPRIATIONS.

If we had an overflowing treasury, I would suggest that an appropriation be made to the prison fund for the year 1867 that would allow of pushing forward the improvements; but for reasons already given, and as there is a balance left over from this year of $3,483.98 to be continued in the fund, which with the sum of $1,180.91, earnings of the year that will probably be paid in during the first quarter, as hereafter shown, making a total of $4,664.89, which is now left to the credit of the fund, I would recommend that the sum of twenty-five thousand dollars ($25,000) be set apart to the Prison Fund, making a total for the fiscal year of twenty-nine thousand six hundred sixty-four and eighty-nine hundredths dollars, ($29,664.89) which is twenty-six hundred fourteen and thirty-nine hundredths dollars ($2,614.39) more than the institution has cost the State this year; and as there is no session of the Legislature next winter, I would recommend that the further sum of thirty-five thousand dollars ($35,000) be appropriated from the first moneys that may come into the treasury after the first day of January, 1868, as a Prison Fund for the fiscal year of 1868, as it is probable that by that time greater improvements will be needed.

FINANCE.

Prisoners must be fed, clothed, and guarded, and it would be great economy for the State if the financial affairs of the Prison could be placed on a cash basis, as the following facts and figures will show:

The sum of thirty-three thousand dollars ($33,000) was appropriated by the last Legislature as a Prison Fund, out of which was to be paid the sum of fifteen hundred and sixty-five dollars and fifty-two cents ($1,565.52) of indebtedness of last year; and the sum of nine hundred dollars ($900) was, by enactment, ordered paid out of the same for expenses incurred last year in looking up escapes, for which amounts warrants were issued.

The total expense of this year, for which warrants have been drawn, is twenty-nine thousand one hundred and eleven dollars and fifty cents ($29,111.50). If, from this amount, we take the sum of two thousand and sixty-one dollars ($2,061) which has been paid into the Prison Fund (for which I have the Comptroller's receipt) as receipts from all sources for the year, we find that to support the prison, with the improvements that have been made, has cost the State twenty-seven thousand and fifty dollars and fifty cents ($27,050.50) for the fiscal year 1866 ; we also find that there are three thousand four hundred and eighty-three dollars and ninety-eight cents, ($3,483.98) still in fund.

RECAPITULATION.

Legislative appropriation	$33,000 00	
Receipts from Prison	2,061 00	
Last year's indebtedness		$1,565 52
Ordered paid for looking for escapes of last year..		900 00
Total expense of this year		29,111 50
	$35,061 00	$31,577 02
	31,577 02	
Balance in Fund	$3,483 98	

For the expenses of January, February, and March, warrants were issued on a coin basis to the

Amount of	$5,660 50
And for the two amounts for 1865	2,465 52
Making total of coin warrants issued	$8,126 02

Now, if we take the amount of coin warrants issued for the first quarter ($5,660.50) from the twenty-seven thousand and fifty dollars and fifty cents ($27,050.50) which is the amount of cost to the State above the receipts of the prison, we have the sum of twenty-one thousand three hundred and ninety dollars ($21,890) of currency warrants, which, as I will hereafter show, have been mostly issued on the basis of three dollars for two, showing that the prison has cost the State seven thousand one hundred and thirty dollars ($7,130) more than it would have done if we had paid coin monthly, upon which basis the prison would have only cost the State nineteen thousand nine hundred and twenty dollars and fifty cents ($19,920.50).

It was ascertained, immediately after the adjournment of the Legislature, that there was not a dollar of cash to go into the Prison Fund, so that I have been greatly crippled in the way of financiering for the institution, as the first sack of flour bought in January has not yet been paid for. Then again, all indebtedness incurred since April 1st was to be on a currency basis. This would not have been so bad, had there been currency in the treasury with which to have paid every month ; but as there was none, and as there was much uncertainty as to when the treasury would be replenished, and as there was much fluctuation in the price of currency, it left us in a very unsatisfactory condition. But, owing to the confidence and faith in our Government and its officers on the part of Mason, Huff & Co., E. B. Rail, George Bence, and most of the others who had been supplying us, I have been able to get our supplies through the year by an addition of fifty per cent. to the coin prices. This arrangement, though it adds immensely to our current expenses, was the best that could be effected; and at the same time, I believe it was liberal on the part of our creditors, in view of the uncertainties as to time and the price of currency.

It also became necessary to increase the salaries of guards and other officers. At first, currency was worth about eighty (80) cents; guards who were getting sixty dollars ($60) per month on a coin basis, had their salaries increased to seventy-five dollars, ($75) with expectation of getting their pay in July. Very soon, currency went down to about seventy (70) cents, with a poor prospect of getting it during the year; then their salaries were raised to ninety dollars, ($90) and other officers in the same ratio. These prices and salaries were matters I could not fix without the approval of the Board of Commissioners. It was necessary to increase the salaries in order to retain the services of competent and responsible men, as I consider it inexpedient to change officers unless for good cause.

It would be very gratifying if I was able to show a much larger credit t the Prison Fund; but, situated as we are, building stone is about the only thing we have to depend upon for revenue; and as there has been comparatively no building done within hauling distance of the prison, our receipts are not what they would otherwise have been.

In August, I took a contract to furnish 100 cords of rubble stone, delivered on the Mint lot in Carson City at $16.50 per cord in currency, out of which I paid $10 for hauling as soon as received, leaving to the credit of the State $650 on the contract. After the same was completed, by agreement, I continued to deliver stone, and was to have the same price as the next contract was let for, which was $30 per cord; twenty-two (22) cords were thus delivered, on which there is now due $660. The hauling of the same has been fixed at $15 per cord, making $330, on which I have paid $46.50, leaving a balance of $283.50 to be paid to John Wagner as soon as received, as per agreement—leaving a balance to be placed to the credit of the State of $376.50, on account of rock furnished the U. S. Branch Mint at Carson.

Last year, I entered into a contract to furnish dressed and rubble stone for building a Methodist Church at Carson, a portion of which was furnished last year, the balance this year. Total charge for stone and work on the same, $1,534.50. $319.14 was paid last year, which was embraced in my former report. $410.95 has been paid this year, making a total of $730.09, most of which was paid in vegetables, hay and lumber. The balance, $804.41, now due, they say that they expect to pay within the next sixty or ninety days—making a total from the two sources of $1,180.91, of what I consider solvent debts, that will probably be paid during the next quarter.

I am fully aware of the fact that there are those on the outside who have had no experience in institutions like this, who will think our force of officers too large; yet I have thought best to act upon the principle that it is better to pay more for officers, and less for looking up escapes.

Therefore, in April, I divided the duties of the office of Lieutenant of the Guard and Superintendent of Labor, and have one man for each position, so that the latter could be constantly among the prisoners when at labor; and the latter part of the season I thought best to employ another man as a support for the front and to attend to the gate, so as to have the place so secured as to give the prisoners no reason to hope for success in getting up a general *émeute*, in which the lives of officers would be endangered.

Therefore I have two more men employed now than one year ago, and am satisfied that it is an improvement on my former policy.

We must not lose sight of the fact that this institution is in its infancy, and has not got the strong, high walls of older ones; therefore the greater vigilance and the stronger force is required.

In conclusion, allow me to say that the prisoners have been well fed, warmly clothed, comfortably lodged and well cared for when sick, and when in health kept steadily at work; and, from the experience of the past, I think I have avoided errors and mistakes into which, as a beginner, I may have fallen.

I hope my course has given satisfaction; but be that as it may, the intention to do right, and to do it in the best possible manner, has been my governing purpose.

The care and custody of such men as find their way into a State prison involves the necessity of strict discipline on the part of officers, and unceasing vigilance on the part of guards.

To the faithfulness of my officers and guards, and their strict attention to the rules and regulations of the prison, I am indebted in a great measure, for the fact that I am able to report that not a prisoner has escaped during the year.

J. S. CROSMAN,
Warden.

Office Nevada State Prison, December 31st, 1866.

TABLE.

Showing Cost of Material and Subsistence furnished State Prison,

FOR THE FISCAL YEAR COMMENCING JAN. 1st AND ENDING DEC. 81st, 1866.

1866. Months.	Table Supplies.	Clothing and Bedding.	Supplies.	Medical Attendance and Medicines.	Salaries.	TOTAL.
January	$488 00	$77 62	$146 14	$42 25	$595 00	$1,349 01
February	531 41	68 65	796 16	10 25	595 00	2,002 47
March	1,013 43	72 17	589 48	6 75	641 66	2,323 49
April	399 87	27 87	1,023 34	10 75	856 62	2,318 45
May	672 05	22 77	681 98	27 07	875 00	2,278 87
June	692 35	101 00	1,167 76	....	875 00	2,836 11
July	683 14	37 75	600 13	....	1,000 00	2,321 02
August	735 56	320 75	685 62	....	1,000 00	2,741 93
September	533 46	....	279 09	....	1,045 00	1,857 55
October	597 06	....	510 78	....	1,090 00	2,197 84
November	1,027 62	....	633 61	....	1,108 00	2,769 23
December	580 73	85 50	2,115 37	243 93	1,090 00	4,115 53
						$29,111 50

No..	Pardoned.	Discharged by order of Supreme Court.	Discharged by Expiration of Sentence.	Died.	
1..	....	....	....	....	....
2..	....	....	Aug. 20, 1866 ...	....	....
3..	March 9, 1866...	....	....	....	Board of Pardons.
4..	Oct. 13, 1866.....	....	....	....	Board of Pardons.
5..	....	....	May 19, 1866 ...	....	....
6..	....	....	....	....	....
7..	....	....	March 27, 1866..	....	....
8..	....	....	....	....	....
9..	....	....	....	....	....
10..	....	....	....	....	....
11..	....	....	....	....	....
12..	....	....	....	....	....
13..	....	....	....	....	....
14..	....	....	....	....	....
15..	....	Feb. 12, 1866 ...	....	....	....
16..	March 17, 1866..	....	....	....	Board of Pardons.
17..	....	....	Oct. 23, 1866....	....	Indian.
18..	....	....	Oct. 9, 1866.....	....	Indian.
19..	Sept. 15, 1866...	....	....	....	Board of Pardons.
20..	....	....	....	....	....
21..	....	....	....	....	....
22..	Nov. 24, 1866 ...	....	....	....	Board of Pardons.
23..	Nov. 24, 1866 ...	....	....	....	Board of Pardons.
24..	....	....	....	....	....
25..	....	....	....	....	....
26..	....	....	....	....	....
27..	....	....	....	....	....
28..	Dec. 31, 1866 ...	....	....	....	Board of Pardons.
29..	....	....	....	....	....
30..	....	....	....	....	....
31..	....	....	....	....	....
32..	....	....	....	....	....
33..	....	....	....	....	....
34..	....	....	....	....	....
35..	....	....	....	....	....
36..	....	....	....	....	....
37..	....	....	....	....	....

THIRD ANNUAL REPORT

OF THE

STATE LIBRARY.

THIRD ANNUAL REPORT

OF THE

BOARD OF DIRECTORS

OF THE

STATE LIBRARY,

FOR THE

STATE OF NEVADA.

CARSON CITY:
JOSEPH E. ECKLEY, STATE PRINTER.
1867.

REPORT.

To *His Excellency* HENRY G. BLASDEL,

       Governor of the State of Nevada:

SIR—In compliance with the requirements of the Statute creating the Board of Directors of the State Library, we have the honor to submit herewith a full report of the purchases and expenditures for the preceding year, on account of the State Library, and also the Report of the State Librarian.

No change has been made during the past year in the rules and regulations adopted by this Board for the government of the State Library.

We have purchased during the past year from Banks & Brothers, of New York, 392 volumes—mostly Law Reports—of which a list is given in the Report of the Librarian hereto annexed. These cost in New York the sum of sixteen hundred and ten dollars and fifty cents ($1,610 50). The premium paid for insurance to Sacramento was eighty-eight dollars and sixty cents, ($88 60) and the freight and charges from New York amounted to one hundred and thirty-four dollars and seventy-five cents ($134 75); making the whole cost of the 392 volumes delivered at the Library eighteen hundred and thirty-three dollars and fifty cents ($1,833 50) in greenbacks. To pay for these books we drew from the Library Fund, August 10, 1866, four hundred and forty dollars in coin, ($440) with which we purchased a coin draft on New York (deducting exchange) for four hundred and twenty-seven dollars and nineteen cents, ($427 19) and remitted it to Banks & Brothers as an advance payment. They sold it at current rates in New York and credited us with the proceeds, being six hundred and twenty dollars and fifty cents ($620 50) in greenbacks. Upon receipt of the books we drew eleven hundred dollars ($1,100) in greenbacks from the Library Fund, and remitted the same (less $5 50, commission of Post Master) by Post Office orders to Banks & Bros., thus paying the balance due them on books already purchased, and leaving a balance of fifteen dollars and ninety cents ($15 90) to credit of the State to apply on an order for some additional books sent with the remittance. The only other purchase of books made by the Board during the past year was of five volumes of law books bought of Isaac Atwater, costing the State twenty dollars ($20) in greenbacks.

The Library has received considerable accessions of books from other States and from Congress, during the past year, but they are scattering volumes of Statutes and Reports, for the most part of little real value to the State, except those sent from California. Sent to us, as they generally are, by Express, their cost delivered here (although a gift originally from the States sending them) is generally greater than if we should buy the same books in New York and have them sent us by slow freight across the Isthmus. The Report of the Librarian, hereto annexed, gives a schedule of the books so added to the Library

We append hereto a tabular statement of the disbursements made from the Library Fund during the year last past.

The last Legislature made no provision for a Clerk of the Secretary of State to take charge of the Library. The Secretary has found it necessary to employ a clerk for that purpose, as himself and his deputy cannot perform their official duties and attend upon the Library. Unless there is a Librarian constantly in attendance great inconvenience must ensue, and there is danger of frequent loss of books. We respectfully recommend an appropriation by the Legislature of a reasonable compensation to Joseph F. Hatch, who has had the care of the Library, under the Secretary, during the past year, and provision for clerk hire for the same purpose until the next session of the Legislature.

The State Library now contains a tolerable selection of law books. Still, it falls short of what a State Library should be in that respect. There are very many practicing lawyers in the country who have more extensive law libraries. But its great lack just now is, we think, in works of a political nature. We need very much a set of the "Congressional Globe" and "Niles' Register" from their commencement, and there is not a copy in the Library of the debates on the Federal Constitution, nor even of the Madison papers. The current receipts by fees, &c., under present laws, are no greater than should be expended for the purchase of law books, and we suggest the propriety of a small appropriation (say two thousand dollars) for the purchase of works of the class above referred to.

CARSON CITY, NEVADA, Jan. 7, 1867.

GEO. A. NOURSE,
Attorney General.
A. W. NIGHTINGILL,
Controller of State.

DISBURSEMENTS FROM LIBRARY FUND.

1866.			
June 15 ...	Paid I. Atwater for 5 vols. Law Books.		$20 00
August 10 .	Coin for draft sent Banks Bros.......	$440 00	
	Greenbacks for P.O. orders—Banks Bros	1,100 00	
	Freight and exchange paid on books by C. N. Noteware	134 75	
			1,674 75
	E. B. Rail, hardware................		27 75
January 16	Express charges and postage on books from other States............		242 15
			$1,964 75

LIBRARIAN'S REPORT.

NEVADA STATE LIBRARY,
Carson City, January 1st, 1867.

To the Directors of the Nevada State Library:

GENTLEMEN — In compliance with the requirements of an Act entitled "An Act in relation to the State Library," approved February 14th, 1865, I have the honor to transmit my Annual Report of the condition of the State Library.

The whole number of books now in the State Library is four thousand seven hundred and twenty-one, (4,721) of which two thousand two hundred and nine (2,209) are in the Law Department, and two thousand five hundred and twelve (2,512) are in the Miscellaneous Department. The Statutes of Nevada, and Journals of the Senate and Assembly, are included in this number.

Your attention has heretofore been called to the necessity of binding the State newspapers, the regular files of which are furnished to the Library by the publishers free of charge, and will, in the future, become a valuable acquisition to the Library, if they are properly preserved for reference. Large numbers of papers are now accumulating, but in their present form are almost useless. I would respectfully ask that an appropriation be made sufficient to bind these papers in substantial form.

I would respectfully call your attention to the necessity of an appropriation for the Library Contingent Fund. Almost all the exchange of Reports, Session Laws, and Legislative Documents are received by Express, and postage charges large, for which there is no appropriation provided.

The accumulation of books, during the past year, rendered the removal of the partition between the Library and the room occupied by the Justices of the Supreme Court necessary, and the shelf room, with this addition, is manifestly insufficient for the convenient and advantageous disposition of the books now belonging to the Library, and it will be difficult, even, to store the exchanges of the next year, without some additional room.

The almost constant use of the books in the Law Department demand the constant attendance of some competent person. For the past year I have employed J. F. Hatch, Esq., and would most respectfully recommend that an appropriation be made for the purpose of paying him therefor. Also that authority be given me to procure the services of some person to take charge of the Library, and to perform such other duties as may from time to time be required in the office of Secretary of State.

The following is a list of the books received from other States by exchange, and by individuals by donation.

I also furnish herewith a list of books bought of Banks & Bros., New York, and of Hon. J. Atwater.

All of which is most respectfully submitted.

C. N. NOTEWARE,
Secretary of State, and ex-officio State Librarian.

LIST OF BOOKS RECEIVED BY EXCHANGE AND DONATION.

DONOR.	TITLE.
Arizona.	Acts of Arizona, 1864.
Connecticut. " "	Adjutant General's Report, 1865. Statutes of Connecticut, 1866. Private Acts of Connecticut, 1865. Public Acts of Connecticut, 1865.
California. " "	California Reports, vols. 28 and 29 (2 copies each). California Laws of 1865–6 (2 copies). California Journals of Senate and Assembly (2 copies). California Appendix to Senate and Assembly Journals (6 copies). California State Library Catalogue.
Dakota. "	Laws of Dakota. Journals of Council and House, 1864–5 (2 copies).
Georgia.	Laws of Georgia, 1865–6.
Indiana. " "	Acts of General Assembly, 1865. Journals of Senate and House, 1865 (2 copies). Thirteenth Annual Report Superintendent Public Instruction, 1864. Annual Report State Auditor, 1864. Annual Report of Pardons, 1865. Message to the General Assembly, 1865. Message to the Special Session, 1865. Report of Allotment Commissioners, 1865. Eighteenth Annual Report of Trustees of Institute for the Blind, 1865. Indiana University, 1865. Southern Indiana State Prison, 1864–5. Common School Law, 1865. Report of Financial Secretary, 1864. Report of Superintendent and Trustees of Deaf and Dumb Institute, 1865. Report of State Treasurer, 1864. Report of State Debt and Sinking Fund, 1865. Catalogue of State Library, 1865.
Iowa. " "	Iowa Reports, volumes 17 and 18 (2 copies). Iowa Laws, 1866. Iowa Digest, vol. 2, 1866. Adjutant General's Report, 1864–5.
Illinois. " "	Senate and House Journals, 1863 (2 copies). Senate and House Journals, 1865 (2 copies). Reports to General Assembly, 1863. Reports to General Assembly, 1865. Illinois Reports, vols. 31, 32, 33.

LIST OF BOOKS—Continued.

DONOR.	TITLE.
Illinois.	Illinois Digest, vol. 3.
"	Illinois Laws of 1865.
"	Illinois Laws of 1864–5.
Kansas.	Kansas Reports, vol. 2.
Kentucky.	Journal of House, 1865–6.
Mississippi.	Mississippi Laws of 1865 (2 copies).
"	Mississippi Constitution (2 copies).
"	Debates of Constitutional Convention, 1864–5.
Maine.	Acts and Resolves of 1865, 1866 (2 copies).
"	Maine Reports, vols. 50 and 51.
Missouri.	Missouri Reports, vols. 35 and 36.
"	Compiled Statutes of Missouri, 1865 (3 copies).
Michigan.	Laws of Michigan, 1863–5.
"	Michigan Reports, vol. 12.
Maryland.	Statutes of 1865, 1866 (2 copies).
"	Maryland Digest.
North Carolina.	North Carolina Revised Code, 1865.
New Hampshire.	New Hampshire Reports, vol. 18.
"	Journals of House and Senate (2 copies).
"	Adjutant General's Report, 1866.
	Annual Report of School Commissioners, 1865.
Nebraska.	Revised Statutes of Nebraska Territory, 1866.
New Jersey.	Senate Journal, 1866.
"	Minutes of Assembly, 1866.
"	Legislative Documents, 1866.
Ohio.	Ohio State Reports, vol. 15.
Oregon.	General Laws of 1845–65.
Pennsylvania.	Pennsylvania State Reports, vols. 49, 50 (2 copies).
"	Laws of 1865.
Texas.	Texas Reports, vol. 24.
"	Texas Digest of Laws.
"	General Laws of 1860 (pamphlet). [phlet).
	General and Special Laws of 1861–5 (10 copies, pam-
	Report of Committee on Public Safety (pamphlet).
	Synopsis of Reports.

LIST OF BOOKS—Concluded.

DONOR.	TITLE.
Texas.	General and Special Laws of 1866 (pamphlet).
Tennessee.	Adjutant General's Report.
United States.	Catalogue of Additions made to Library of Congress.
"	Official Register.
"	Postal Laws and Regulations.
	Vol. 13 United States Statutes at Large.
	Catalogue of Authors, Library of Congress.
	Acts and Resolves of Congress.
	Smithsonian Report, 1865.
	Laws of 1865–6.
Vermont.	Auditor's Report, 1865.
"	Railroad Report, 1865.
"	School Report, 1865.
	Sixth Registration Report, 1865.
	Vermont Reports, vol. 34.
	Adjutant General's Report, 1865.
Wm. M. Cutter.	Pitman's Manual of Phonography.
"	Phonographic Magazine (3 copies).
"	Phonographic Psalmist.
	Phonographic Reporter (3 copies).
	Phonographic Manners.
	Phonographic Teacher.
	Phonographic Phrases.
	History of Short Hand.
	Classbook of Botany.
Hon. Jas. W. Nye.	Messages and Documents, Parts 1, 2, 3, 4—1865.
"	Army Register, 1865.
"	Smithsonian Report, 1865.
	Report of Post Master General, 1865.
	United States Coast Survey, 1863.
	Eighth Census, (Manufactories) 1860.
	Writings of James Madison, vols. 1, 2, 3, 4.
	Address on the Death of Hon. J. Foote.
	Address on the Life and Character of H. W. Davis.
	Bancroft's Address on Lincoln.
Hon. Wm. M. Stewart.	Messages and Documents, Parts 1, 2, 3, 4.
"	Commerce and Navigation, 1865.
"	Eighth Census, 1865.
U. E. Allen.	The Northern Whig, dated August 24, 1819.
"	The Kinderhook Herald, dated February 1, 1827.
John Vandewater.	Two copies of the Courier, dated January 1st, 1800.
"	One copy of the Californian, dated April 24th, 1847.
Hon. Wm. M. Hayden.	Copy of President Lincoln's Emancipation Proclamation.

LIST OF BOOKS BOUGHT BY DIRECTORS, OF MESSRS. BANKS & BROS., NEW YORK CITY.

No. Volumes.	TITLE.
8	Term Reports.
2	W. Blackstone.
3	H. Blackstone.
3	Saunders' Reports.
26	English Common Law Reports.
2	English Common Law Reports Index.
43	English Chancery Reports.
9	Kentucky Reports.
51	Maine Reports.
44	New Hampshire Reports.
36	Connecticut Reports.
35	Ohio Reports.
120	Pennsylvania Reports.
392	

BOOKS BOUGHT OF L ATWATER.

No. Volumes.	TITLE.
2	Jarman on Wills.
3	Stephens' Nisi Prius.
5	

REPORT

OF

Committee on Federal Relations

IN RELATION TO

JOINT MEMORIAL AND RESOLUTIONS ASKING GOVERNMENT AID IN THE CONSTRUCTION OF THE SUTRO TUNNEL.

CARSON CITY:
JOSEPH E. ECKLEY, STATE PRINTER.
1867.

REPORT.

The Committee on Federal Relations, to whom was referred " Joint Memorial and Resolutions, asking Government aid in the construction of the Sutro Tunnel," beg to report the same back, and recommend its passage.

Along with said Memorial, and as a part thereof, they likewise submit the following Report:

EXTENT OF THE MINING REGIONS.

The vast regions embracing portions of California, Nevada, Dakota, Nebraska, Colorado, New Mexico, Arizona, Utah, Washington, Oregon, Idaho and Montana, covering an area of one million of square miles, containing untold wealth in gold and silver mines, to-day command the attention of the American statesman.

GOLD MINING IN CALIFORNIA.

Mining for gold and silver is comparatively of recent date within this country. The discovery of gold in California gave the first active impulse to the search for precious metals. The immense "*placers*" of that region invited a numerous and adventurous population from all parts of the globe, and the facility with which the surface earth yielded its golden treasures, the implements required consisting only of a pick, a shovel and a rocker, within the reach of every one, soon swelled the amount of bullion produced to astounding figures, and worked a revolution in the financial condition of the entire world.

PLACER MINING NOT PERMANENT.

But the gold distributed in the alluvial deposits, attacked as it was by many thousands of miners, soon disappeared in the most favored localities. The enterprising mining population looked for more permanent deposits, and discovered them at some depth upon the bedrock, where ancient rivers had deposited the precious particles.

These also gave no promise of permanency; and the intelligent miner now turned his attention to the *fountain head, the true matrix of the precious metals, from whence the immense distribution had taken place, which covers the hill-sides and valleys—the quartz mines of the country.*

THE COMSTOCK LODE.

The discovery of the Comstock Lode, in the then Territory of Utah, on which are located the most productive mines at present wrought in the world, gave a new impulse to quartz mining.

This remarkable mineral deposit occurs in what is termed a true fissure vein, or a vein formed at a very remote period by some great volcanic convulsion, causing the crust of the earth to be rent in twain, thus creating an immense chasm or fissure, several hundred feet in width, and several miles in length.

CONTINUITY IN DEPTH.

This large fissure, which gradually filled up by ascending vapors and gases, carrying with them, in a volatile form, quartz, gold and silver, leaves no doubt to the scientific investigator, of its permanency; for the very theory of its formation, having been filled from unknown depth, compared with which the deepest mining works appear insignificant, proves it conclusively.

Independently of theory, however, practical experience has shown all over the world, that true fissure veins are continuous in depth; and not a single authenticated instance is recorded where one of them has failed. Notwithstanding, mining is looked upon as a hazardous undertaking; and no matter what theories demonstrate, or what experience in other countries teaches, capital is reluctantly invested in adventures of that kind.

As stated already, quartz lodes are the true source of the precious metals: to them must we look for the future supply, *and anything which tends to develop that interest, should be regarded by the legislators of the country as an all-important benefit to the nation.*

THE SUTRO TUNNEL.

What is required to thoroughly develop that interest, and to induce private capital hereafter to embark largely in mining pursuits, is a practical and positive demonstration of the continuity of the mineral lodes in depth; and no work will prove this proposition more thoroughly and satisfactorily than the proposed Sutro Tunnel. This tunnel, starting near the borders of Carson River, a distance of four miles, will cut the Comstock Lode at a depth of 2,000 feet; while if continued a short distance, it will reach a point under the summit of Mount Davidson at a depth of 3,500 feet. By means of the tunnel the mines can be worked at least 1,000 feet below its level, thus demonstrating the continuance of the Comstock Lode to a depth of 3,000 feet, a greater depth than has yet been reached in any mine in the world.

IMPORTANCE OF THE WORK.

The bearing this work will exercise upon the future of the mining interest in the United States, cannot be too highly appreciated. Capital will be invested in enterprises of the like character where no confidence exists now; millions of treasure will see the light which now lie buried deeply in the bowels of our mountain ranges. The immediate and direct results from this work will be the developments made on the Comstock Lode. This great lode was discovered in the year 1859, and has yielded thus far $64,000,000 in silver and gold—chiefly the former. The regular annual yield, now, is $16,000,000.

OTHER LODES.

If we compare this lode with other great mineral lodes, we find that none were ever worked in the old world of equal or approaching magnitude. The American continent has produced three similar mines—the great Potosi mine of Bolivia, which yielded $1,200,000,000, the Véta Madre, of Guanajuato, $800,000,000, and the Véta Grande, of Zacatecas, $650,000,000—the two last named being in Mexico. Competent geologists assert that the Comstock is a larger, more regular and permanent vein than either of the others mentioned. What can we expect to be its yield, with the proposed tunnel once finished, enabling the miner to explore the same to a depth of three thousand feet, with the modern improved appliances for mining, and the enterprise and energy of the American artisan to guide its operations?

FUTURE YIELD.

If we estimate its yield after the proposed tunnel is completed, at $30,000,000 per annum, *we will have, in thirty years, the enormous yield of* $900,000,000; and this may be be considered a moderate estimate. Without the projected tunnel, this vast and important property, which directly and indirectly gives employment to nearly or quite 100,000 people, will, after the lapse of a few years, have to be abandoned, for reasons which are at once apparent and conclusive.

DIFFICULTIES IN MINING.

The yield of these mines for the year ending December 31st, 1866, has been $16,000,000, which was procured at a cost to the mining companies of $15,500,000, leaving the paltry net profit of $500,000. This extraordinary result is due to various causes, prominent amongst which are, the difficulty of removing the water from the mines, want of ventilation, the increase of heat in going downwards, and the expense of transportation. These mines are situated on the side of a mountain, and are approached by perpendicular shafts, of which there are over forty. These have reached a depth of from 500 to 900 feet, and on each of them a steam engine is placed, which propels pumps, and at the same time hoists the ore and *débris*. The cost of fuel at Virginia City and Gold Hill, where these shafts are located, is sixteen dollars per cord, in gold; and the consumption of fuel is so great, that this item alone absorbs a large share of the yield, and that item of expenditure increases for every foot of descent. These engines are kept in motion day and night; for were they allowed to stop, the mine would fill with water.

INCREASE OF HEAT.

Another serious obstacle as depth increases, is the difficulty of keeping the mines supplied with a sufficiency of fresh air to furnish the oxygen required for respiration. The increase of heat, which amounts to one degree of Fahrenheit for every sixty feet in depth, prevents the miner from performing the same amount of work as if he were employed in a healthy atmosphere, and at a moderate temperature. The pecuniary loss from this source is very large, considering that 3,000 persons are employed at an average pay of three dollars and fifty cents in gold per day of eight working hours. This loss is estimated at twenty-five per cent.

EVIL EFFECT OF FOUL AIR.

But a consideration of a still graver character, is the evil effect a foul atmosphere exercises upon the health of the miner. Amadee Burat, an eminent French writer, says upon this subject:

"The circulation of fresh air is one of the most important in mining. This importance may be readily understood when we find that four-fifths of all workmen who perish in mines, are victims of foul air."

Scoffren, an English writer, makes use of the following language:

"The stagnant air acts on the organs of respiration, producing consumption and other allied diseases, which carry off the miner in the prime of life. As a class, they are robust and naturally less liable than even seamen to such diseases; but such are the pernicious effects of the impure air they breathe, that fifty-two per cent. die of consumption, in a country where the per centage amongst agricultural and other surface laborers amounts only to twenty per cent. in the worst localities." *The cause of humanity should provide a remedy, when an effectual one is within reach!*

Many other difficulties present themselves in deep mining, which increase in a fearful ratio as depth increases; and the profits, which have already dwindled down to a small amount, soon, thereafter, will be absorbed entirely, and then be exceeded by the cost of mining.

The fate of these mines, if no remedy is found, is therefore clearly foreshadowed.

NECESSITY OF A TUNNEL.

The only remedy, positive and sure in its operation, which presents itself is, the construction of a deep adit or tunnel. It will cut the mines at a depth of 2,000 feet, draining off the water to that depth by its natural flow, securing the best ventilation, cooling the atmosphere in the mine, furnishing facilities for transportation, and making it possible to dispense with all pumping and hoisting machinery: for the miner can enter the mines from below, work upwards, and the ore will fall by its own gravity, whilst a railroad in the Tunnel will transport the same at small cost to the adjacent valley.

Such are some of the considerations which present themselves, and which show *that the proposed work is a matter of vital importance, and one of absolute necessity to the State of Nevada.*

MINING COMPANIES.

The mining companies, which are mostly incorporated in California, and the stock owned to a large extent in San Francisco, are unfortunately mainly controlled by a class of men who speculate from day to day upon the varying fortunes of the mines, and only care to increase the momentary price of the shares. Their interest in the permanent yield is but small; and this cause, together with the present financial condition of most of the companies, give little hope of substantial aid from that source.

EUROPEAN MINES.

Whilst we are enriching the whole nation by the production of large amounts of bullion, we are ourselves growing poorer from day to day. In all European mining countries, the respective Governments, with an eye to the importance of the production of bullion, and to promote the general welfare of the population, have given substantial and liberal aid to similar undertakings—a number of which, on a much larger scale than the one here proposed, have been successfully carried out, and the future of their mines secured. A tunnel was lately finished in Hanover fourteen miles in length; one in Saxony is nearly completed eight miles in length; and another in Austria of equal length.

Your Committee now desire to call attention to the important bearing the increased production of bullion will exercise upon the financial condition of the country, and in the payment of the national debt.

DEPRECIATION IN VALUE OF MONEY.

The world's stock of coin in the year 1848 was, in round numbers, eighteen hundred millions of dollars; to this has been added to the present time, an equal amount, of which the United States have furnished, according to Secretary McCulloch's late Report, eleven hundred millions. Allowing two thousand millions as the natural increase of taxable property by the growth of the country, we still find that the same has doubled in the United States, within the period named. From seven thousand millions it has increased to sixteen thousand millions. This result is due, not to a direct depreciation of the precious metals, for that is regulated by the standard adopted by our Government, but by an increase in value of all property and commodities. Thus the same article that could have been bought eighteen years ago for one silver dollar, now requires two; or, in other words, two silver dollars at the present time only have the intrinsic value of what one then had.

DIFFERENCE BETWEEN THE PRECIOUS METALS AND OTHER COMMODITIES.

It must be borne in mind that there is a vast difference *between the production of gold and silver and all other commodities.* Most of the latter are articles of consumption; they are useful for a special purpose, in the application of which they are consumed, disappear, and cease to exist. The farmer who produces wheat to the value of $1,000, and the miner who digs out gold to that amount, may derive an equal profit from their different pursuits; and hence one stands on an equality with the other, so far as individual gain, or the interest of a particular locality is concerned: yet wheat is ground into flour, made into bread, and consumed, while the gold dug out by the miner finds its way into the channels of trade, is transferred from one nation to another, as the balance of trade may require, *and forms a permanent addition to the stock of the precious metals of the world.*

INCREASE IN QUANTITY OF THE PRECIOUS METALS.

At the time of the discovery of America, in 1492, the stock of the precious metals in Europe was estimated at $170,000,000. In the year 1600, it had increased to $650,000,000—a gain of nearly four fold.

That extraordinary addition to the precious metals in a little more than one hundred years, had a corresponding effect. Gold and silver became cheaper in the same ratio as their quantity had increased. It required four times the amount to buy any commodity—that is to say, all commodities increased in price four fold. The same increase in prices can be traced distinctly to the present day, as the stock of the precious metals gradually increased, while making due allowance for all other causes which would exercise a bearing in that direction, such as the increase of commerce, the growth of population, facilities for intercourse between different nations, etc., etc.

APPRECIATION IN VALUE OF PROPERTY.

The conclusion we arrive at, by carefully examining into this subject, which is clear and positive, is that the increase in quantity of the precious metals depreciates their value in precisely the same proportion as it appreciates the value of all kinds of property. Or, in other words, the per centage added to the stock of the precious metals in circulation, adds the same per centage to the money value of all property in the world.

Francis Bowen, the best American authority on political economy, expresses this view in the following words:

"The general principle is, that the value of money falls in precisely the same ratio in which its quantity is increased. If the whole money in circulation should be doubled, prices would be doubled; if it was only increased one-fourth, prices would rise one-fourth."

The same principle is laid down by John Stuart Mill, well known as the highest modern authority in England. He says:

"It is to be remarked that this ratio would be precisely that in which the quantity of money had been increased. If the whole money in circulation was doubled, prices would be doubled; if it was only increased one-fourth, prices would increase one-fourth."

INCREASE OF TAXABLE PROPERTY IN THE WORLD.

To illustrate the immense bearing this rise in prices exercises all over the world, we will assume the following figures:

Taking the taxable property of the whole civilized world at $200,000,000,000, the amount of money in existence at $3,600,000,000, the addition of $900,000,000 would depreciate the precious metals 25 per cent., and, in consequence, it would require $250,000,000,000 to purchase all the taxable property of the world. The addition of $900,000,000 in money, therefore, would have the effect of producing $50,000,000,000 in the increased value of property. Every addition of $100,000,000 has its corresponding influence on the increased value of all property; it adds over $5,000,000,000 to the property of the world. This increase of value may not be perceptible from year to year; the aggregate result however, after a number of years, is inevitable. Bowen refers to this as follows:

"There may be brief and violent fluctuations in the relative value of particular commodities, while the great movement is steadily going on which slowly enhances the value of all."

IT DOES NOT AFFECT INDIVIDUALS.

This increase in value, however, does not materially affect individuals: for when the cost of living increases, the rates of wages do, also; *but it acts as a stimulus to enterprise, and thus creates general prosperity.*

Hume, long ago, remarked that, "in every kingdom into which money begins to flow in greater abundance than formerly, everything takes a new face, labor and industry gain life, the merchant becomes more enterprising, the manufacturer more diligent and skillful, and even the farmer follows his plough with greater alacrity and attention. But when gold and silver are diminishing, the workman has not the same employment from the manufacturer and merchant, though he pays the same price for everything in the market; the farmer cannot dispose of his corn and cattle, though he must pay the same rent to his landlord. The poverty, beggary, and sloth that must ensue, are easily foreseen."

Even so cautious and conservative a writer as the distinguished English political economist, McCulloch, fully admits the truth of this view, though he adds the just qualification that the fall in money must proceed from natural causes.

William Jacob, in his valuable treatise on the precious metals, remarks:

" The world is very little really richer or poorer from the portion of metallic wealth that may be distributed over its surface: the whole mass of material wealth is neither diminished nor increased by any change in the relative weight of gold and silver to the usual measures of other commodities. The only benefit to the world in general, from the increase of those metals, is, that it acts as a stimulus to industry by that general rise of money prices which it exhibits to the view. It matters little to him who raises a bushel of wheat whether it is exchanged for a pennyweight or an ounce of silver, provided it will procure for him the same quantity of cloth, shoes, liquors, furniture, or other necessaries which may be desirable to him."

IT MATERIALLY AFFECTS A DEBT.

But when a debt already exists, being a fixed number of dollars, the decrease of value of each dollar reduces the debt in the same proportion. The immortal and much lamented LINCOLN thoroughly understood this question, when, in his annual message of 1862, he made use of the following language:

" The immense mineral resources of some of those Territories ought to be developed as rapidly as possible. Every step in that direction would have a tendency to improve the resources of the government and diminish the burdens of the people. *It is worthy of your serious consideration whether some extraordinary measures to promote that end cannot be adopted.*"

That wise and good man had carefully studied the effect which was then strongly felt in Europe, and which is alluded to by Alison, the English historian, as follows:

BENEFICIAL INFLUENCE IN GREAT BRITAIN.

" It will belong to a succeeding historian to narrate the wonderful spring which his country (England) made during the five years which followed 1852, under be influence of the gold discoveries in America and Australia. The annual supply of gold and silver for the use of the world was, by these discoveries, suddenly increased from an average of ten millions to thirty-five million pounds sterling. Most of all did Great Britain and Ireland experience the wonderful effects of this great addition to the circulating medium of the globe. Prices rapidly rose, wages advanced in a similar proportion, exports and imports enormously increased, while crime and misery rapidly diminished. Wheat rose from forty-five to sixty-five shillings, but the wages of labor of every kind advanced in nearly as great a proportion; they were found to be about 30 per cent. higher than they had been five years before. In Ireland, the change was still greater, and probably unequaled in so short a time in the annals of history. The effect of the immense addition to the currency of the world, to the industry of all nations, and in an especial manner of the British Isles, has been prodigious. It has raised our exports from £58,000,000 in 1851 to £97,000,000 in 1854, £95,000,000 in 1855, and £115,000,000 in 1856; and augmented our imports from £157,000,000 in the former to £172,000,000 in the latter year."

PROSPERITY OF THE UNITED STATES.

Thus, the influence of the increased metallic currency saved Great Britain from bankruptcy; and while its mysterious agency was working these wonders in Europe, it exercised a similar bearing in this country. Some years before the rebellion, this country had commenced to prosper; and when that deplorable event began, our resources were just beginning to expand under the beneficial influence of the increased metallic wealth. Had it not been for the constant and continuous flow from California, which increased the resources many fold, when they were most needed, the difficulties of providing the requisite means to carry on the war would have been so great that the disruption of the Union might have been the result. It has been the wonder and marvel of all Europe how the United States carried on that gigantic war for four years, kept one million of men in the field, contracted during that brief space of time a national debt of nearly $3,000,000,000, and came out in a more flourishing and prosperous condition than when engaged in it. The explanation of this wonderful phenomenon is simple—*the magic agency of gold wrought it.*

FINANCIAL CRISIS.

Since the war is ended, the immense increase in prices, which is particularly noticeable in the large cities of the East, where real estate, rents, wages, and everything else have assumed an apparently exorbitant value, has been mainly ascribed to an inflated paper currency, and an extensive financial crisis has been predicted as a necessary consequence. We have been expecting it for three years past, and it has not taken place yet, nor do we consider it probable that it will at all occur, so long as the increase of metallic wealth keeps pace with the expansion of trade. The credit system of the United States has been much curtailed since the war, and there has been no time in our history when the business community have been less in debt. How can a great financial crisis and panic occur when no overtrading on a credit basis has taken place, and not sufficient creditors exist to make their alarm the cause of such a commercial convulsion?

THE NATIONAL DEBT.

The issuance of a depreciated paper currency during the war has had the effect, as confidence became restored, and as its metallic value increased, of enriching the population at large who held that currency, enabling them to pay off their private debts, while the Government, issuing at one time as much as three paper dollars, which only had the value of one metallic dollar, became proportionally more in debt. The result, therefore, has been, that the individual debts of the American people have, to a large extent, been transferred to the Government, increasing the same to an enormous extent, and amounting to-day to $2,500,000,000. That debt is a burden on $16,000,000,000 of taxable property; if we increase the latter, we virtually reduce the former.

INCREASE OF TAXABLE PROPERTY IN THE UNITED STATES.

The amount of the precious metals at present in circulation throughout the world, amounts to $3,600,000,000. The proposed tunnel to the Comstock Lode will, within thirty years, add $900,000,000 to the same, or twenty-five per cent. It will consequently add twenty-five per cent. to the taxable property of the United States, equal to $4,000,000,000, which, at the rate of taxation of two per cent., will give an annual increase to the resources of this Government of $40,000,000 for each of the first thirty years, and $80,000,000 for each year thereafter.

INCREASE OF REVENUE.

The proposed work adds each year $30,000,000 to the stock of the precious metals, equal to the one hundred and twentieth part of the $3,600,000,000 in existence. It therefore adds the one hundred and twentieth part to the $16,000,000,000 of taxable property in the United States, equal to an annual increase of $133,333,333. That addition, made from year to year, gives the above stated result, as will be seen by the following table:

Increase of Taxable Property.			Increase of Revenue.
1st year...... $133,333,333	at two per cent.	=	$2,666,666
2d year...... 266,666,666	"	"	5,333,333
3d year...... 400,000,000	"	"	8,000,000
6th year 800,000,000	"	"	16,000,000
12th year...... 1,600,000,000	"	"	32,000,000
15th year...... 2,000,000,000	"	"	40,000,000
24th year...... 3,200,000,000	"	"	64,000,000
30th year 4,000,000,000	"	"	80,000,000

PAYMENT OF THE NATIONAL DEBT.

If this annual increase in revenue be set apart for the purpose, it will pay off the whole National debt in forty-six years.

When Francis Bowen wrote his "Principles of Political Economy," we had no National debt. In referring to that of Great Britain, he says:

"As the depreciation goes on, taxation may be extended *pari passu* without throwing any additional burden upon the community; and a sinking fund formed out of the surplus thus obtained, would pay off the National debt in less than one generation. Our National debt, it is true, is but small, and what little there is, will quickly be extinguished. But the debts of the individual States are large, amounting in the aggregate to over $200,000,000, a large portion of which is owned in Europe. It is, therefore, satisfactory to remember that as the monetary revolution will operate exclusively to the benefit of the indebted party, our own land will derive as much benefit from it, in proportion to our means, as any other country on earth."

SIR ROBERT PEEL.

The effect of the increase of bullion on taxable property and a National debt, has been long recognized by the financiers and statesmen of Great Britain, and was enunciated in the following language, held by Sir Robert Peel, in 1844:

"There is no contract, public or private, no engagement, National or individual, which is not affected by it. The enterprises of commerce, the profits of trade, the arrangements made in all domestic relations of society, the wages of labor, pecuniary transactions of the highest amount and the lowest, *the pay-*

ment of the National debt, the provision for the National expenditure, the command which the coin of the smallest denomination has over the necessities of life, are all affected by it."

M. CHEVALIER.

M. Chevalier, the well known French writer on Political Economy, in his treatise on "The Probable Fall in the Value of Gold," published in 1859, says: "Owing to the discovery of the new gold mines, a time will arrive when a change will come over the British Treasury as if some genii, an enemy of its creditors, had spirited away their dividend warrants, and substituted others of only half their value. Not that the number of pounds sterling, due to them as principal, and of which the interest is counted to them every six months, will be diminished—not that the quantity of gold contained in the pound sterling will be lessened; but the British Treasury will henceforth draw from the tax-payers each pound sterling, with as little difficulty to them as it previously took to pay a half sovereign."

IMPORTANCE OF THE QUESTION.

Your Committee, in presenting the above views on the importance of the proposed Tunnel as the means of furnishing a large addition to the stock of the precious metals of the world, has found it necessary to enter somewhat into details as to its bearing upon the future of the United States, and the payment of the National debt. This important question is but little understood; we have tried to throw as much light upon it, by giving quotations from eminent writers as the limited space of a report would allow, and hope the attention of our National Legislators will be drawn towards this subject.

NATIONAL AID.

The proposed tunnel to the Comstock Lode is, in our opinion, a work of such magnitude and vast national importance, that our Government, though it has always been reluctant to aid private enterprise, and was only induced to aid the Pacific Railroad as "*a war measure,*" will give such substantial aid to this enterprise, as will insure its being carried out upon the ground that it is eminently "*a peace measure.*"

B. S. MASON,
THEODORE D. EDWARDS,
WM. G. MONROE,
Committee on Federal Relations.

REPORT

OF THE

SURVEYOR GENERAL OF NEVADA

FOR 1866.

ANNUAL REPORT

OF THE

SURVEYOR GENERAL

OF THE

STATE OF NEVADA

FOR THE YEAR A.D. 1866.

CARSON CITY:
JOSEPH E. ECKLEY, STATE PRINTER.
1867.

SURVEYOR GENERAL'S OFFICE, }
Virginia, Storey County, Nevada, Feb. 11th, 1867. }

To His Excellency H. G. BLASDEL,
Governor of Nevada:

SIR—I herewith transmit, at the moment of its completion, my report for 1866.

A failure on the part of County Assessors and County Surveyors to comply with their duty in relation to this office, will account for many deficiencies in the report. The dilatory action of those who partially complied with the law, will account for much of the delay in sending in my report—some of theirs not having been received until January. An almost total neglect on the part of the Legislature to make provision for necessary expenses of this office (in the opinion of the Board of Examiners) will account for the rest of the delay, and for most other deficiencies.

I am very respectfully,
Your obedient servant,
S. H. MARLETTE,
Surveyor General.

CONTENTS.

viii CONTENTS.

REPORT.

Surveyor General's Office,
Virginia, Dec. 15th, 1866.

To His Excellency, H. G. BLASDEL,
Governor of Nevada:

SIR—In compliance with "An Act concerning the office of Surveyor General,"
I respectfully submit the following report:

GEOGRAPHICAL POSITION AND AREA OF THE STATE.

The State extends from about the 35th to the 42d degree of North latitude,
and from the 37th to the 43d degree of longitude West from Washington (114°
to 120° West from Greenwich).

In my former report, on the authority of the report of the Commissioner of
the General Land Office, the area of the State was given as 81,539 square
miles, or 52,184,960 acres. Congress, last session, cut off from Utah and added to
Nevada, a strip of land one degree of longitude in width, and five degrees of
latitude in length, containing 18,426$\frac{400}{1000}$ square miles, or 11,792,933 acres. An
irregular tract lying between the Colorado River on the east, California on the
west, and the parallel of 37° North latitude, was taken from Arizona, and given
to Nevada—equal, according to a statement of the *R. R. Reveille*, to 7,823,926
acres (12,224$\frac{884}{1000}$ square miles).

From the above data, the area of the State would be 112,190$\frac{342}{1000}$ square miles,
or 71,801,819 acres. The *R. R. Reveille* states the area to be 71,751,741 acres,
as copied in the *Gold Hill News*—less by 50,078 acres than the preceding estimate.

Assuming the water surface of the several lakes in the State to cover an area
of 1,690$\frac{342}{1000}$ square miles, or 1,081,819 acres, there will remain 110,500 square
miles, or 70,720,000 acres, as the land area of the State.

2

STATE LANDS.

The following is submitted as an approximate "estimate of the aggregate quantity of land belonging to the State:"

	Acres.
For support of Schools, the 16th and 36th sections...	3,928,889
For internal improvements..........................	500,000
For University, 2 townships..........................	46,080
For public buildings, 20 sections......................	12,800
For State prison, 20 sections.........................	12,800
For each Senator and Representative in Congress, 30,000 acres...	90,000
Total..................................	4,590,569

The Assessor of Humboldt County, in his last year's report, estimated the swamp and overflowed land of that county at about 158,000 acres, and as there is similar land in other portions of the State, it is probable that the State lands will equal 5,000,000 acres; all of which, together with five per cent. of the net proceeds of all sales of public lands made in the State by the General Government, having been donated to Nevada by the United States, and by the Constitution of the State having been devoted to the cause of education, it will be seen that the State has the material whence may be derived a School Fund of vast proportions.

SCHOOL LAND WARRANT LOCATIONS.

Under "An Act to provide for the disposition of the Sixteenth and Thirty-Sixth Sections of the Public Lands donated by the United States Government to the State of Nevada," approved February 27th, 1865, and under the amendment to said Act, approved March 3d, 1866, the following location has been made:*

Sept. 7th, 1866.—John P. Elliott, by his attorney, J. Neely Johnson, located No. 17, dated August 28th, 1866, for 40 acres, (issued to John P. Elliott) on the S.W. one-fourth of the N.W. one-fourth of Section 36, Township 15, [N.] Range 18 E., about one and one-half miles northwesterly from Spooner's Station, on King's Cañon Toll Road, Ormsby County.

---

* The fee for recording was paid by the locator directly to the State Treasurer, who sent receipt for same to this office.

LANDS DISPOSED OF BY CONTRACT, AS REPORTED BY THE STATE TREASURER TO THIS OFFICE.

Purchaser.	Date of Contract.	Date of Notice.	When Filed.	Acres.	Section.	Township.	Range.	Portion.
David Jones......	March 20, 1866..	March 21, 1866..	March 22, 1866.	120	16	12 N.	19 E.	N. ½ of S.W. ¼, and S.W. ¼ of S.W. ¼.
Warren Lockhart..	March 27, 1866..	March 27, 1866..	March 28, 1866.	280	16	19 N.	18 E.	N.W. ¼ and N. ½ of S.W. ¼, and S.E. ¼ of S.W. ¼.
John W. Averill...	Sept. 10, 1866...	Sept. 10, 1866...	Sept. 11, 1866...	160	18 17 20	14 N.	20 E.	S.E. ¼ of S.E. ¼, S.W. ¼ of S.W. ¼, W. ½ of N.W. ¼.
			Total........	560				

SUMMARY.

Located by School Land Warrant in 1866 .... 40 acres.
Disposed of by Contract in 1866 .... 560 "
Located by School Land Warrants in 1865........... 1,287 "
Total.... 1,887

The following "Report of Selections of Lands for School Purposes" was received at this office March 26th, 1866, and is presumed to have come from the Superintendent of Public Instruction:

No. 1. LAND OFFICE AT CARSON CITY, NEVADA.

SECTION OR PART.	Number of Section.	Number of Township.	Number of Range.	Quantity. Number of Acres.	Quantity. Number of ¼ Sections.
	16	12 N.	19 E.	640	4
	36	12 "	19 "	640	4
	16	12 "	20 "	640	4
	36	12 "	20 "	640	4
Lot I	16	13 "	18 "	$7\frac{88}{100}$	1
Lot II	16	13 "	18 "	$25\frac{15}{100}$	1
	36	13 "	18 "	640	4
	16	13 "	19 "	640	4
N. W. ¼	36	13 "	19 "	160	1
S. W. ¼	36	13 "	19 "	160	1
S. E. ¼	36	13 "	19 "	160	1
	36	14 "	18 "	640	4
	16	14 "	19 "	640	4
	36	14 "	19 "	640	4
W. ½ of N. E. ¼	16	15 "	20 "	80	1
N. ½ of N. W. ¼	16	15 "	20 "	80	1
	36	15 "	20 "	640	4
N. E. ¼	36	16 "	19 "	160	1
S. E. ¼	36	16 "	19 "	160	1
E. ½ of S. W. ¼	36	16 "	19 "	80	1
E. ½ of N. W. ¼	36	16 "	19 "	80	1
N. E. ¼	36	17 "	19 "	160	1
N. W. ¼	36	17 "	19 "	160	1
W. ½ of S. E. ¼	36	17 "	19 "	80	1
	36	18 "	19 "	640	4
N. E. ¼	16	18 "	20 "	160	1
E. ½ of S. E. ¼ and N. W. ¼ of S. E. ¼	16	18 "	20 "	120	1
N. W. ¼ of S. W. ¼	16	18 "	20 "	40	1
	36	18 "	20 "	640	4
N. W. frac. qr.	16	19 "	19 "	$157\frac{6}{100}$	1
S. W. " "	16	19 "	19 "	$146\frac{31}{100}$	1
S. E. " "	16	19 "	19 "	$154\frac{86}{100}$	1
W. ½	36	19 "	19 "	320	2
N. ½ of N. E. ¼ and S. W. ¼ of N. E. ¼	36	19 "	19 "	120	1
S. W. ¼ of S. W. ¼	36	19 "	19 "	40	1
E. ½ of S. E. ¼	16	19 "	20 "	80	1
Lot IV	16	19 "	20 "	$19\frac{17}{100}$	1
N. W. frac. qr.	16	19 "	20 "	122*	1

REPORT OF SELECTIONS OF LANDS FOR SCHOOL PURPOSES—CONTINUED.

SECTION OR PART.	Number of Section.	Number of Township.	Number of Range.	Quantity.	
				Number of Acres.	Number of ¼ Sections.
N. ½ of S. W. ¼ and S. W. ¼ of S. W. ¼	16	19 N	20 E	120	1
	36	19 "	20 "	640	4
	16	33 "	33 "	640	4
	36	33 "	33 "	640	4
	16	32 "	34 "	640	4
	36	32 "	34 "	640	4
	16	32 "	33 "	640	4
	36	32 "	33 "	640	4
	16	33 "	34 "	640	4
	36	33 "	34 "	640	4 *
	16	30 "	33 "	640	4
	36	30 "	33 "	640	4
	16	31 "	33 "	640	4
	36	31 "	33 "	640	4
	16	33 "	32 "	640	4
	36	33 "	32 "	640	4
	16	30 "	32 "	640	4
	36	30 "	32 "	640	4
	16	28 "	32 "	640	4
	36	28 "	32 "	640	4
	16	31 "	32 "	640	4
	36	31 "	32 "	640	4
	16	29 "	32 "	640	4
	36	29 "	32 "	640	4
	16	29 "	33 "	640	4
	36	29 "	33 "	640	4
	16	32 "	32 "	640	4
	36	32 "	32 "	640	¼

* There is a fraction here which I cannot decipher.—S. H. M.

The Plats for the Townships Nos. 12 N. R. 19 E., 12 N. R. 20 E., 13 N. R. 18 E., 13 N. R. 19 E., 14 N. R. 18 E., 14 N. R. 19 E., 15 N. R. 20 E., 16 N. R. 19 E., 17 N. R. 19 E., 18 N. R. 19 E., 19 N. R. 19 E., 19 N. R. 20 E., were received at this office on the 1st of March, 1864; and Township No. 32 N. R. 33 E. was received on the 30th of July, 1864; and Townships Nos. 33 N. R. 33 E., 32 N. R. 34 E., 33 N. R. 34 E., 30 N. R. 33 E., 31 N. R. 33 E., 33 N. R. 32 E., were received November 19th, 1864; and Nos. 30 N. R. 32 E., 28 N. R. 32 E., 31 N. R. 32 E., 29 N. R. 32 E., 29 N. R. 33 E., 32 N. R. 32 E., were received January 14, 1864.

(Signed)　　　　WARREN T. LOCKHART, Register.

(Signed)　　　D. L. GREGG, Receiver.

STATE OF NEVADA, }
March 16, 1866. }

I hereby apply, in behalf of the State of Nevada, for the tracts described in this list as being selected for said State for school purposes.

(Signed) A. F. WHITE,
Superintendent Public Instruction.

LAND OFFICE, CARSON CITY, NEVADA, }
March 16, 1866. }

I hereby certify that the foregoing list was filed in this office on the 16th day of March, 1866, and that the selections are correct, and that no valid conflicting right is known to exist.

(Signed) WARREN T. LOCKHART, Register.
(Signed) D. L. GREGG, Receiver.

————

The following list was received July 28th, 1866, and is presumed to have come from the Superintendent of Public Instruction:

LIST No. 1,

Exhibiting the tracts of Public Land situated in the district, of lands subject to sale at Carson City, Nevada, which have been selected in lieu of lands entered by pre-emption on the Sixteenth and Thirty-Sixth Sections, for the State of Nevada, under the Seventh Section of the Act of Congress, approved 21st March, 1864, entitled "An Act to enable the people of Nevada to form a Constitution and State Government, and for the admission of such State into the Union on an equality with the original States."

DESCRIPTION OF THE LAND SELECTED.				AREA OF TRACTS.	LAND IN LIEU OF.				
PARTS OF SECTIONS.	Section.	Township.	Range.	Acres.	PARTS OF SECTIONS.	Sections.	Township.	Range.	Acres.
E. ½ of S. E. ¼ and N.W. ¼ of N.W. ¼	19	14 N	20 E	120	N. ½ of N. E. ¼ and N. E. ¼ of S. E. ¼	16	15 N	20 E	120
W. ½ of S.W. ¼	20	14 N	20 E	80 }	S. W. ¼ of S. E. ¼ and S. E. ¼ of N. W. ¼	16	15 N	20 E	160
N. ½ of N. E. ¼	30	14 N	20 E	80 }					
				280					280

LAND OFFICE AT CARSON CITY.

I hereby certify that the foregoing list was filed in this office on the 21st day of July, 1866, and that the selections are correct, and that no valid conflicting right is known to exist.

(Signed)

WARREN T. LOCKHART,

Register.

STATE OF NEVADA, July 21st, 1866.

I hereby apply, in behalf of the State of Nevada, for the tracts described in this list as being selected for said State in lieu of lands entered on the 16th and 36th Sections.

(Signed)

A. F. WHITE,

Sup't Public Instruction of Nevada.

On the 10th instant I received " List No. 4 " similar to the preceding, (List No. 1) and presumed to have come from the Superintendent of Public Instruction, containing the information that the Superintendent of Public Instruction had applied on the 7th instant, on behalf of the State, for the southeast one-fourth of Section 14, Township 16 N. Range 21 E., containing 160 acres. Also for the southeast one-fourth of Section 34, Township 16 N. Range 19 E., for 160 acres, in lieu of lands entered by pre-emption on the 16th and 36th Sections, accompanied by the certificate of the Register and Receiver, that "no valid conflicting right is known to exist," bearing date December 7th, 1866.

Warrants have been presented for location upon lands selected in lieu of lands entered by pre-emption on the 16th and 36th Sections, but finding no provisions either in the original Act or the amendment concerning the sale of the 16th and 36th Sections for the sale of lands selected in lieu thereof, the warrants were retained, notice of application filed, but the recording of the same delayed, in order that the opinion of the Attorney General might be obtained as to the propriety of recording the desired locations.

The matter was immediately submitted to him, but his opinion has not yet been received (Dec. 18th, 1866).

In case the Statutes do not authorize the sale of such lands, immediate provision for such sale is recommended, at a price not much in excess of that established by the General Government.

STATE LAND OFFICE AND REGISTER.

The establishment of a State Land Office, of which the Surveyor General should be the Register, as in California, is recommended; which office should be located at Carson. It is believed that the State Board of Education should constitute a Board of Land Commissioners, to which should be intrusted the selection and supervision of all lands to which the State may be entitled, and that the Surveyor General should be authorized to obtain from the United States Surveyor General, and the Register and Receiver, such plats, maps and information as may, in the opinion of the Board, be requisite for a judicious selection of lands for the State, which plats and maps would furnish valuable material for the compilation of a map of the State.*

Should the foregoing suggestion not be adopted, it is recommended that measures be taken to abolish the office of Surveyor General.

IRRIGATION AND RECLAMATION OF LANDS.

In my former report attention was called to the fact that many millions of acres of land in this State now comparatively worthless would become valuable if irrigated, and that several hundred thousands of acres of swamp and overflowed land required drainage and protection from overflow.

Attention was also called to the fact that there is upon our western border one of the finest natural reservoirs in the world—Lake Tahoe—the waters of which might be brought in an extensive canal, (which might serve to float timber and wood to within a moderate distance from our mills and mines) to be used as a motive power and for the purposes of irrigation; and the opinion was expressed

---

* December 19th, 1866.—This day received Attorney General's opinion that the Statutes do not authorize the sale of lands other than the 16th and 36th sections. Should the foregoing suggestion be adopted it would be necessary to affix a salary to the State Register's office, which, with that of the Surveyor General, would justify the incumbent in devoting his whole time to the duties of those offices. His duties would then be the most laborious, and not the least responsible of any of the State Officers.

that were the facts laid before Congress a grant of these now useless lands might be obtained on condition of reclamation by irrigation.

This project may be regarded as one of the probabilities of the not very distant future; it may not, therefore, in this connection be improper to call attention to a project for the diversion of a portion of these waters from their natural channel, by which they are discharged into this State, (the Truckee River) for the benefit of California. There is a bill now before Congress for the authorization of this project, and if Congress has the right to authorize the same it certainly behooves Nevada to protest against the exercise of that right: for this State has, or will soon have use for every particle of water now possessed, or which can be obtained.

FOREST AND TIMBER TREES.

The great scarcity or entire absence of wood and timber in extensive portions of the State, and the fearful rapidity of their disappearance from portions where now abundant, would appear to suggest the necessity of making some provision for the encouragement of the cultivation of "Forests and Timber Trees." The great and beneficial effects upon the soil and climate resulting from an extensive cultivation of timber, it is believed, would alone repay the expenditure.

I call attention to the subject, in the hope that those much better informed than myself may be induced to propose a practicable scheme for the accomplishment of so desirable a result.

MAP OF THE STATE AND EASTERN BOUNDARY.

An accurate map of the State has become a necessity: in view of which fact I respectfully submit the following remarks, most of which were presented in my former report, and would also call attention to important suggestions upon this subject made by the State Mineralogist in his report.

The Act concerning the office of Surveyor General says: "When required by law, the Surveyor General shall make an accurate and complete survey, by astronomical observations and linear surveys of the boundaries of the State."

It will soon be necessary to have the southern portion, at least, of the eastern boundary of the State established; and I am of the opinion that provision should be made for this object by the present session of the Legislature. The expense would not be great, the determination of longitude having become an easy matter since the construction of the telegraph; but the whole boundary should be established at an early day; and I would recommend that Congress be requested to make immediate provision for this object.

The Act also provides that: "When required by law, he shall make an accurate map of the State, and shall survey and, when necessary, designate by plain visible marks or monuments, and shall describe on the map of the State, the boundary line of the several counties;" and, "When called upon by the County Commissioners, of any county," it requires him to run any county line, or portion of the same.

It has been made the duty of the County Surveyors to transmit, when called upon, to the Surveyor General, copies of field notes and plats of their official surveys. It has also been made the "duty of all railroad and toll companies to file in the office of the Surveyor General complete topographical maps of the roads, and the county through which their roads may run."

Scarcely any attention has been paid to the above requirements by County Surveyors, or railroad or toll road companies, which is to be regretted, for they are admirable provisions, so far as they go; but something further is necessary:

8

1st. It is recommended that a law be passed requiring the construction of an accurate map of the State.

2d. A penalty should be attached to the failure of County Surveyors to comply with their duties prescribed by law; but a fair compensation should be allowed for every duty imposed.

3d. The present law does not define the time at which topographical maps of railroads and toll roads shall be filed in this office, nor does it affix a penalty for non-compliance with this requirement.

It is therefore recommended that the law be so amended as to require topographical maps and profiles of all toll roads now in operation, also of all railroads and toll roads now surveyed, to be filed in this office within three months from the passage of this proposed amendment; also that railroad companies whose routes are not yet surveyed be required to file their maps and profiles within three months of the completion of the maps or profiles, or of the surveys; also that all toll road companies not now in operation be required to file the same within three months from the completion of maps and profiles, or surveys, and before they be entitled to collect toll. A severe penalty should be attached to a non-compliance with the law, sufficient to cover the expense of obtaining such maps and profiles.

The adoption of the above suggestions would secure valuable material for a correct map of the State.

The Surveyor General should be authorized to obtain copies of the United States township plats at an expense not to exceed   dollars each, to be used in compiling the State map, and in the selection of land belonging to the State.

This office ought to be furnished with a copy of maps and field notes of the State boundary surveys.

It is believed that in case a further survey of the State boundary, or surveys of county boundaries, should be deemed necessary, that such surveys should be made under the supervision of the Surveyor General; and such surveys should always be made with the view of obtaining all the data practicable for the State map, every line surveyed being used trigonometrically to determine the position of and to locate upon the map the topographical features of the adjoining county.

For the survey of county boundaries, an appropriation of eight thousand dollars ($8,000) is recommended. It is also recommended that in any county boundary survey, the counties interested be required to defray half the expense.

An appropriation of two thousand dollars ($2,000) is recommended, to defray the expense of employing a draughtsman in compiling the State map.

Any attempt at a geological survey of the State would be almost abortive, except so far as it might be based upon an accurate map, at least of those portions examined.

COUNTY ROADS.

For suggestions concerning county roads, reference is respectfully made to my former report, in which, it is believed, they have been presented at least one generation too early.

LIST OF REPORTS FROM COUNTY SURVEYORS AND ASSESSORS.

Valuable reports have been received from the following:

William A. Jackson, County Surveyor of Churchill County.
John Carroll, County Assessor of Churchill County.

Robert Lyon, County Assessor of Douglas County.
Charles O. Barker, County Assessor of Lander County.
H. H. Bence, County Assessor of Ormsby County.
Stephen Roberts, County Assessor of Nye County.

The reports of Mr. Bence and Mr. Lyon are valuable and interesting, particularly so, from being the first received from Ormsby and Douglas Counties.

I regret the necessity of transmitting a clipping from the Reese River *Reveille*, in which several errors in Mr. Barker's report are pointed out.

In view of the fact that in several counties the county commissioners have entirely failed to enforce a compliance with the law in regard to the collection and transmission of statistical reports by the county assessors and county surveyors, I would recommend that the law be so amended as to prevent the county commissioners auditing or paying any bills of the assessor or surveyor, unless accompanied by a certificate from the Surveyor General that the last-named officers have complied with the law defining their duties in relation to his office.

Should the above suggestion be acted upon, I am certain we will see a vast improvement in the next report over the last, or the assessing and surveying for the counties for the present year will be done for nothing.

STATISTICS.

The following summary, tabular list, and notes of mills crushing ore from the Comstock Lode in 1866, have been compiled with a great deal of labor and care, and although incomplete, and in some respects erroneous, yet I believe them to be approximately correct, and by far the most complete exhibit of the mills of Storey, Lyon, Ormsby, and Washoe Counties yet compiled, and, I believe, will be found valuable and interesting.

In compiling the tabular list, I have been greatly assisted by and have obtained a great deal of information from Mr. Buckman, Secretary of the Belcher Company, and I might say nearly the same concerning my professional partner, Geo. Hunt, C. E., who has at all times, when not necessarily otherwise engaged, willingly assisted in the collecting of statistics, and in copying, tabulating, etc. I have also used extensively in summary, table and notes, information furnished for my former report by D. A. Armstrong, Deputy Assessor of Lyon County, which was so erroneously printed as to be greatly depreciated in value; and last, but not least, I have availed myself of nearly all, if not the whole, information contained in a valuable article upon the "Quartz Mills about Virginia and Gold Hill Districts, Nevada," in the San Francisco *Mining and Scientific Press* of September 29th, 1866, from information furnished that journal by Mr. Thomas Starr. Much information has been obtained directly from parties owning or employed about the mills.

In all cases I have given the information deemed most reliable.

STOREY COUNTY.

The table contains a list of 33 mills, all steam, estimated to have cost $2,000,000, with an assessed value for 32 of $953,705, say, for the 33, $970,000, containing 607 stamps, with a crushing capacity of 846 tons per day, nearly 1.4 tons per stamp, consuming 180¼ cords of wood per day, average cost about $14 per cord; total, $2,527, or nearly $3 per ton, and about $4.15 per stamp.

24 mills pay the Virginia & Gold Hill Water Company $5,280 per month for

water, add water tax, $130 per month; total, $5,410, cost of water per month for 24 mills, which contain 899 stamps, with a crushing capacity of 562 tons, or 14,612 tons per month of 26 days. Cost per ton of ore worked for water, 37 cents, or 52 cents per stamp.

Aggregate distance of 33 mills from the mines about 48¼ miles; average distance about 1½ miles (for custom mills the distance is estimated, with one or two exceptions, from the Divide between Virginia and Gold Hill); and the average cost of hauling is about $1¼ per ton, ranging from 70 cents to $2.

846 tons per day for 26 days would equal

21,996 tons, at $3 for wood.................................	$65,988 00
*21,966 tons, at 37 cents for water...........................	8,127 42
21,966 tons, at $1¼ for hauling..............................	27,457 50

Total per month for wood, water, and hauling.............$101,572 92
or $4.62 per ton.

19 mills employ 263 men, the same proportion would give 457 men for 33 mills, or 1 man to 1.85 tons. 31 mills contain 27 tubs, 305 Knox pans, 91 Wheeler, 93 Hepburn, 9 Varney, 51 Wakelee, and 56 Phair pans, 101 settlers, 17 agitators, 2 concentrators, 1 small pan and settler, 4 breakers, 8 grinders, and 1 pan and settler for tailings.

LYON COUNTY.

Total mills, 27. Steam, 16; water, 8; steam and water, 3. Estimated cost of 15 steam, 7 water, 93 steam and water mills—$1,464,000.

The 27 mills contain 424 stamps, from which deduct 4 used for prospecting, and we have 420 stamps, with a crushing capacity of 641½ tons per day; from which deduct 1 mill with 10 stamps, capacity 7 tons, which has run but little during the year; also 1 mill with 15 stamps, capacity 25 tons, which has crushed but about 1,000 tons during the year of Comstock ore; and we have 25 mills with 395 stamps, with a capacity of 619½ tons per day, or 1.57 tons per stamp; using 100 cords of wood per day, costing about $10 per cord. Total, $1,000; equal to $1.61 per ton, or $2.53 per stamp.

The aggregate distance of 25 mills from the mines is about 135 miles; average distance 5.4 miles, and average cost for hauling about $2.75, ranging from $1.50 to $4.25.

25 mills employ 315 men, or 1 man for 1.97 tons.

619½ tons per day for 26 days equal 16,107 tons, add for Weston's† steam mill 93 tons per monthly average; total per month, 16,200 tons.

16,200 tons, at $2.75 per ton for hauling.....................	$44,550 00
16,200 tons, at $1.61 per ton for wood	26,082 00

Total per month for wood and hauling.................... $70,632 00
or $4.36 per ton.

25 mills contain: 76 tubs, 51 Knox pans, 61 Wheeler, 49 Hepburn, 24 Var-

---

* This is on the assumption that water costs the other 9 mills as much in proportion to the amount of ore worked, as it costs the 24 mills supplied by the water company.

† This mill has run mostly on Occidental rock during the year.

ney, 23 tubs and Wheeler pans, 12 seven-foot iron pans, 1 prospecting battery and pan, 16 flat seven-foot pans, 1 Excelsior, and 2 Wheeler and Randall pans, 64 settlers, 26 agitators, 3 breakers, 1 grinder, and 2 roasting furnaces.

In Weston's Mill there are 9 Wheeler pans, 6 flat-bottomed pans, 5 settlers, and 1 agitator.

ORMSBY COUNTY.

6 water, and 2 steam and water mills. Estimated cost, $825,000; with 170 stamps; crushing capacity 280 tons per day, or 1.65 tons per stamp; aggregate distance from mines, 80 miles; average distance, 10 miles; average cost for hauling, say $4 per ton; $11\frac{3}{4}$ cords of wood at, say $8 per cord, $94, or $33\frac{1}{3}$ cents per ton, or 55 cents per stamp.

280 tons per day for 26 days equal

6,780 tons at $4 for hauling..................................... $27,120
6,780 tons at $33\frac{1}{3}$ cents for wood............................... 2,260

Total per month for wood and hauling........................ $29,380
or $4.33 per ton.

Pans: 4 Knox, 37 Wheeler, 46 Hepburn, 9 Varney; settlers, 38; agitators, 13; breakers, 2; grinders, 3; also 1 prospecting battery and pan, 4 furnaces, and 10 barrels.

WASHOE COUNTY.

5 steam, and 4 steam and water mills; estimated cost, $794,000; containing 261 stamps; crushing capacity, 308 tons per day, or 1.18 tons per stamp, consuming about 82 cords of wood at, say $5 per cord; total, $410, or $1\frac{1}{3}$ per ton, or $1.57 per stamp.

Average distance of mills from mines, say 14 miles, and average cost of hauling $4.50 per ton.

308 tons per day for 26 days equal

8,008 tons, at $4.50 per ton for hauling...................... $36,036 00
8,008 tons, at $1\frac{1}{3}$ per ton for wood........................... 10,677 33

Total per month for wood and hauling.................... $46,713 33
or $5.83 per ton.

Pans: 48 Wheeler, 22 Varney, 16 "pans," 4 Wheeler and Randall pans; 33 settlers, 5 agitators, 5 breakers, 2 grinders, 17 furnaces, and 44 barrels.

In Storey County, the Granite Mill at Gold Hill is dismantled.* In Lyon County, the Apple, Bartolo, Lindauer, (or Sweet Apple) and Ophir (old) are dismantled. The Palmyra, at Como, has been removed to Owen's River Valley, and Phœnix No. 2 has been burnt. In Washoe County, the Washoe Valley Reduction Works were destroyed by fire on the evening of December 22d, 1866 —a great public as well as private loss.

---

* This mill is about starting again, February 7, 1867.

NOTES ON MILLS.

STOREY COUNTY.

BOWERS (1)—Paid this for 5 months only; has been idle 4 months; now running, with own water; (2) 5-foot pans.

CENTRAL (1)—To Virginia and Gold Hill Water Companies; also, pays $—— to Ophir Company.

(2)—Hepburn and Peterson's, working 500 tons per month wet; 4 furnaces and 6 barrels, working 170 tons dry.

CROWN POINT (1)—Just dismantled; engine used to drain mine.

CORNET (1)—Been idle for 7 months; just started again.

DOUGLAS (1)—10-inch cylinder, 30-inch stroke, 26 plain pans.

EMPIRE No. 1 (1)—Increasing stamps to 21; capacity to be 40 tons per day; to employ 16 men, 27 Wakelee pans.

EMPIRE No. 2 (1)—Concentrators and 2 stamps for breaking.

EMPIRE STATE (1)—4-foot pans.

GOLD HILL (1)—6-foot tubs.

HOOSIER STATE (1)—With steam chambers.

LAND's—(B) Throughout the table designates Blake's breakers.

MARIPOSA (1)—Also 1 prospecting stamp; (2) large.

MARYSVILLE (1)—30 5-foot plain pans.

PACIFIC (1)—Large.

PETALUMA (1)—Stamps being increased to 16, capacity to 26 tons per day, men to 11, wood to 5 cords, adding 8 improved Wheeler pans, 4 settlers and 1 agitator.

PIUTE (1)—8-foot settlers.

RHODE ISLAND (1)—18-inch cylinder; (2) 7-foot pans.

RIGBY's (1)—1 extra pan and settler for tailings, and 1 barrel.

ROGERS' (1)—Not running for 4 months.

SAPPHIRE (1)—Wheeler.

SIMCOOE (1)—Improved.

STEVENSON (1)—8¼-inch cylinder; (2) Howland's rotary battery; can crush 7 tons, and amalgamate 5 tons per day; (3) small.

SUCCOR (1)—24 Wakelee flat-bottomed pans.

SUMMIT (1)—Burnt and rebuilt in 1863; (2) small pan and settler.

LYON COUNTY.

BIRDSALL (1)—Mill, $110,000; Ditch, $40,000; total, $150,000.

CARPENTER (2)—Large-sized Wheeler.

DAYTON No. 1 (1)—4 of these for prospecting; (2) 8-foot settlers; (3) Knox.

DAYTON No. 2 (1)—2 roasting furnaces.

EASTERN SLOPE (1)—Large.

EUREKA (1)—Break 80 tons per day.

G. C. REDUCTION WORKS (1)—5-foot pans.

IMPERIAL ROCK PT. (1)—7-foot tubs and settlers ; (2) breaker, large size.

PHŒNIX No. 1 (1)—8 tubs and Wheeler pans.

PIONEER (1)—15 tubs and Wheeler pans.

SACRAMENTO (1)—12 7-foot iron pans.

SWANSEA (1)—6-foot tubs and 1 prospecting battery and pan.

TRENCH (1)—16 flat 7-foot pans, 1 Excelsior, and 2 Wheeler and Randall pans.

WESTON'S (Steam)—(1) Worked but about 1000 tons of Comstock ore this year ; hauling about $3 per ton.

WESTON'S (Water)—(1) 6 flat-bottomed pans ; has run but little this year for want of water.

ORMSBY COUNTY.

MERRIMAC (1)—Also, one prospecting battery and pan. (2) large.

MEXICAN (1)—4 furnaces and 10 barrels.

VIVIAN (1)—Hanscom's.

WASHOE COUNTY.

MANHATTAN (1)—16 pans.

OPHIR (1)—Working but 36 stamps—Freiberg process—9 furnaces.

REDUCTION WORKS—24 amalgamating barrels.

TEMELEC (1)—Large.

*WASHOE VALLEY (1)—Wheeler 12-feet breast. Full capacity about 300 horse-power.

REDUCTION WORKS—40 stamps used for Freiberg process, and 20 for wet ; 8 furnaces and 20 barrels for dry process, 4 Wheeler and Randall's pans for wet ; 4 more Varney pans to be introduced. (2) Blake's improved Saw.

---

* Burnt on the evening of December 22d, 1866.

TABLE OF MINES ON THE COMSTOCK LODE.

NOTES.

Sierra Nevada (1), original claim 3,000 ft.
Sides (2), 57 feet, claimed by the Gould & Curry Company.
Best and Belcher (3), claimed by the Gould & Curry Company.
Gould & Curry (4), 921 feet, undisputed; balance claimed by Best & Belcher and Sides Companies.
Bullion (5), approximate.
Apple & Bates (6), 607 feet, claimed by Imperial Company.
Imperial (7), 607 feet, claimed by Apple & Bates Company.
Overman (?), doubtful.
Baltimore American (?), doubtful.

* The "Ore Product of Mine" exhibits the number of tons reported to the Assessor as worked in the State and yielding over $20 per ton.

† The "Bullion Product of Mine" exhibits the proceeds from the "ore product of mine," mentioned above.

‡ By adding the proceeds from "Ore Sold," to the "Bullion Product of Mines," we obtain the "Total Yielding over $20 per Ton," and "Ore Sold," on which there is a tax of three-quarters of one per cent.

§ The "Total Yield of 1866" is taken from Hillyears & Co.'s Stock Circular; also Dividends and Assessments.

** The "Yield per foot of Claim," exhibits only that shown by the Assessor's books, viz: from ore worked in the State, yielding over $20 per ton, and from ore sold.

NOTE.—The yield per foot should be estimated from the entire yield of the mine; but as I have this from less than half of the mines, I have assumed the other as a basis of comparison. Much ore has been worked yielding less than $20 per ton, yet yielding a fair profit.

In many instances $15 ore will pay expenses.

For want of time and assistance, and in some cases from a disinclination on the part of owners of mines to have the facts made public, I am unable to present a full exhibit of our mines.

I have also omitted many interesting facts, where I had reason for supposing the same would be fully presented by the State Mineralogist.

4

DATA FURNISHED BY SUPERINTENDENTS OF MINES.

Below may be found some very valuable information concerning the Gould & Curry mine and mill, kindly furnished by Mr. Louis Janin, the Superintendent; also concerning the Savage mine and mills, by Mr. Chas. Bonner, Superintendent.

The admirable system of accounts of expenditure adopted in the Gould & Curry and Savage office, is worthy of all commendation, and it is to be hoped, will be adopted by other companies. By it, stockholders can learn where their money goes to; and all can learn what mining and milling cost, and can see in what direction, if any, they should look for greater economy. To Mr. C. C. Thomas, Superintendent of the Hale & Norcross Mine, I am under obligations for the following facts concerning that mine, which are particularly interesting, from the fact that until 1866, the mine has been yielding only assessments. As it has been, after years of unprofitable labor, demonstrated to be at least one of the best mines in the State, may we not expect that owners of other mines, thus far barren, may be encouraged to continue prospecting with a reasonable chance of ultimate success. To Mr. Peachey, Secretary of the Chollar-Potosi, I am under obligations for the information concerning that mine. Since the reception of the information furnished by the above named gentleman, I have not had time to compare it with the table, and to correct or make additions to the latter.

DETAIL COST OF RUNNING 1,252 FEET OF DRIFTS IN GOULD & CURRY MINE.

CONTRACTS.			COST OF MATERIALS.										
Feet.	Price per Foot.	Price paid for Excavation.	Timber.	Lumber.	Lagging.	Carpenter Work.	Carman.	Picks and Drills.	Powder and Fuse.	Candles.	Track Iron and Smith Work.	Extra Materials.	TOTAL.
298	$7 00	$2,086 00	$405 84	$182 40	$386 00	$180 00	$1,250 00	$84 00	....	$80 00	203 00	$150 00	$4,907 24
100	8 50												
50	7 00												
100	6 00												
5	10 00												
100	9 00												
77	9 00												
6	9 00	3,547 00	694 41	288 80	365 40	435 00	1,706 25	381 00	$74 00	188 00	148 00	84 00	7,861 86
155	11 00	1,705 00	374 60	70 68	130 20	155 00	530 00	160 50	67 50	48 00	53 50	25 00	8,819 95
71	8 00										91 20	25 00	116 20
190	10 00	2,468 00	784 77	118 56	370 20	380 00	840 00	176 00	....	72 00	89 20	25 00	5,223 73
100	13 00	1,430 00	120 84	91 20	56 00	50 00	325 50	84 00	27 00	32 00	....	....	2,216 54
1,252	$107 50	$11,236 00	$2,380 46	$751 64	$1,257 80	$1,160 00	$4,651 75	$885 50	$168 50	$320 00	$534 90	$309 00	$23,645 55

COST OF SINKING BONNER SHAFT, GOULD & CURRY MINE.

No. of Feet.	CONTRACT. Price.	Commenced.	Ended.	Amount paid per Contract.	Timber.	Lumber.	Cost of Framing.	Cost of placing Lumber.	Carmen.	Extra work, Repairs, etc.
	$	1864	1864	$	$	$	$	$	$	$
9¾	......	August	August	100 00	211 54	60 80	75 00	....	....	....
213	24 00	August 15 ..	October 17..	5,112 00	3,047 31	1,567 20	1,075 00	348 00	....	....
2⅞	......	November 20		81 25	133 19	67 26	75 00	....	....	45 00
			1865							
100⅞	32 50	December 20	February 25	8,266 25	1,354 90	767 60	500 00	325 00	770 00	775 50
		1865...								
100	37 50	February 27	April 17	8,750 00	1,354 90	767 60	500 00	250 00	875 00	825 00
200	35 00	July 1	October 5...	7,000 00	2,732 75	1,717 85	1,025 00	485 00	905 00	1,894 00
625½				19,309 50	8,834 59	4,948 31	3,250 00	1,408 00	2,550 00	3,539 50

TABLE—CONTINUED.

No. of Feet.	COST OF MATERIALS. Picks and Drills.	Powder and Fuse	Candles.	Sundries.	Cost of running Machinery, keeping Pumps in order, Pitman, etc.	TOTAL.	REMARKS.
	$	$	$	$	$	$	
9¾	20 00	....	15 00	....	....	482 34	The distance indicated is from the surface to the 4th station.
213	872 00	....	124 00	1,300 00	1,892 00	14,837 51	
2⅞	6 50	....	23 00	47 00	....	478 20	
100⅞	260 00	....	168 00	....	1,970 00	10,157 25	
100	278 00	....	168 00	....	1,250 00	10,018 50	
200	725 00	157 00	370 00	356 65	9,700 00	27,068 25	
625½	1,661 50	157 00	868 00	1,703 65	14,812 00	63,042 05	Average price per foot $100 78.

Estimated Cost of Framing Timbers by hand—Gould and Curry Mine.

1. Shaft timbers 12½ × 14, with spiling and wedges complete, per set.. $20 00
2. Large tunnel timbers 12½ × 13½, per set 1 50
3. Small tunnel timbers 8½ × 10½, per set 1 00

MINE TIMBERS.

	Large size (12½ × 18½).	Small Size (10½ × 12½).
Posts	60c.	46c.
Caps	40c.	37½c.
Girts	30c.	25c.
Sills (all kinds)	$1 50	$1 20 (all kinds).

Jobbing work and placing timbers not included.

Work done by Mine Blacksmiths during Eleven Months—Gould and Curry Mine.

Points sharpened	169,637
Picks laid with steel	2,266
Picks made	110
Drills made	143
Gads made	256
Picks and Sledges handled	2,181

Gould and Curry Mine.

Total number tons produced, 62,425—3d Class.
Cost of production, including materials......................$491,122 52

Cost per Ton.

Officials	$0 21
Prospecting and dead work	2 11
Extracting	3 10
Accessory	1 82
Improvements	0 62
	$7 86

Average yield per ton, $28 64.
Paid in dividends, $2 10 per foot, or $250,000.
Of the above 40,432 tons were worked at the Gould and Curry Mill, and 17,680 tons were worked at outside mills, at an average cost of $13 30.

Gould and Curry Mill.

	Tons.
Crushed	40,432
Amalgamated	36,001
Loss in slimes and moisture in ore	4,431
Assay per ton	$43 95
Yield "	33 02=75 per cent.

Bullion produced (Gold)........................ $363,803 92
   "   "   (Silver) 825,277 85

                                   $1,189,081 77

Labor $157,864 79
Materials 301,751 00
Hauling 36,389 13

                                   $496,004 92

COST PER TON IN DETAIL.

	Labor.	Wood.	Castings.	Sulphate of Copper.	Salt.	Quicksilver.	Sundries.	Total.
	$	$	$	$	$	$	$	$
Foreman, Watchmen and Laborers	0.71.33	......	......	......	......	......	......	0.71.33
Driving power.............	0.58.88	3.97.84	......	......	......	......	0.12.49	4.61.21
Breaking ore..........	0.41.32	......	......	......	......	......	0.03.33	0.44.65
Batteries.................	0.65.98	......	0.20.85	......	......	......	0.10.39	0.97.22
Amalgamating.............	0.76.81	0.04.65	0.59.36	0.43.50	0.27.06	0.86.59	0.10.96	3.08.96
Repairs	0.84.10	......	......	......	......	......	0.69.41	1.53.41
Hauling..................	......	......	......	......	......	......	0.90	0.90
	$	$	$	$	$	$	$	$
Totals...........	3.90.42	4.02.49	0.80.21	0.43.50	0.27.06	0.86.59	1.96.48	12.26.78

SAVAGE MINE,

For six months, beginning with July and ending with December, 1866 :

                                                Tons.   lbs.
Total amount of ore produced..........................30,250   1,810

Cost of Production—Per Ton.

For Officials.................................. $0 39
      Extracting Ore........................... 3 00
      Prospecting 0 65
      Accessory Work 1 64
      Improvements........................... 2 04
      Incidental Expenses 1 10

          Total Cost per ton..................$8 82

	Tons.	lbs.
Total amount of Ore reduced at the two mills belonging to the Savage Mining Company...	9,701	
Cost of Reduction per ton........\$12,04		
At Custom Mills...	16,997	1,160
Cost of Reduction per ton........\$14 92		
Total amount of Ore reduced at Custom Mills and at the mills belonging to the Savage Mining Company...........	26,698	1,160
Cost of Reduction per ton........\$13 87		
Amount of Bullion produced.............\$1,146,288 16		
Average yield of Ore per ton...........\$42 93		
Concentrated Tailings reduced	268	
Yield per ton \$27 21		

	Tons.	lbs.		
Total amount of Bullion produced from	26,698	1,160	Ore....	\$1,146,288 16
Total amount of Bullion produced from	268		Tailings	7,293 50
Total amount of Bullion				\$1,153,581 66

	Tons.	lbs.		
Total Cost of production of 30,250	1,810	Ore..	\$266,991 23	
Total Cost of reduction of 26,698	1,160	Ore..	370,413 25	
				\$637,404 48
				\$516,177 18
Amount of Dividends paid, \$360,000—or \$450 per share......				360,000 00
Excess of net profit over amount of dividends...				\$156,177 18

OFFICE HALE AND NORCROSS SILVER MINING CO.,
Virginia, Nevada, Jan. 30, 1867.

For six months, beginning with July and ending with December, 1866:

	Tons.	lbs.	
Total amount Ore reduced.....	16,836	280	
Yield in Bullion........			\$847,458 71
Average yield per ton.....			50 33
Cost of Reduction........			230,311 66
Average per ton of Cost of Reducing........			13 68
Dividends declared per foot.....			750 00

Amount paid out in dividends for Month of July........	\$30,000 00
" " " August	30,000 00
" " " September	40,000 00
" " October	40,000 00
" November.........	40,000 00
" December	120,000 00
	\$300,000 00

CHOLLAR–POTOSI MINE.

Abstract of operations at Chollar-Potosi Mine for the twelve months ending December 31st, 1866:

Tons of Ore worked............................... 35,582¾
Gross proceeds of Bullion $840,011 24
Gross average per ton............................ 23 60
Tons of Ore sold 2,078¾
                                                   ————
  Making total tons extracted for the year......... 37,661½

Lowest explorations made below Gould and Curry Bar line. ....878 feet
Length of Claim..1,434 "
Length of Claim, productive................................... 500 "

For the following estimate of the results of operations in "Tailings" in Six Mile Cañon, I am indebted to Mr. D. W. Balch, one of the County Commissioners, elected November, 1866. I have expected a similar document concerning Gold Cañon, but have been disappointed.

5

Names of Owners.	No. of feet.	Cost.	Yield for 1866.	Estimated yield for 1867.	Remarks.
Provost and Titus	850		$2,000	$6,000	Cost of sluices, about $1 per foot with blankets.
Ford and Dugan	1,200			7,000	
P. Ford	1,000		3,000	6,000	
Thomas Cassin	400			2,600	Quicksilver gained, about one pound to the ton.
W. Soverign	900			5,000	
John Vivian & Co.	450		1,000	1,200	
William Stanley	1,000			2,200	Wages of 26 men for one year, about $32,000.
Ira S. Parkes	900		800	2,000	
James Singleton	800		2,600	3,000	
Gould and Curry S. M. Co.	1,800		16,000	36,000	Cost of Washing 8,200 tons at $10 per ton, $82,000.
D. W. Balch	1,800		5,600	Taken out.	
John Sproston & Co.	1,800		5,000	28,000	
Dunn and Sproston	1,650		11,000	23,000	Cost of New Blankets and repairs for the coming year, $20,000.
John Hanford	800		6,000	5,000	
J. Nocens	1,000		8,000	6,800	
Andrew Elenholm	960		7,000	6,000	Net profit for year 1867, $30,000.
Irwin Beard	850		4,000	4,200	
Pat. Conners	2,000			10,000	
Stanley & Co.	2,000			10,000	
	22,160	$20,000	$72,000	$164,000	Yield of 8,200 tons of concentrated tailings.

GEN. S. H. MARLETTE:

The above is a rough estimate of the proceeds of sack and blanket washings for the year 1866-7. It is very difficult to procure reliable data in relation to the subject in the short period that I have to make this report; but I think that the above estimates are within $10,000 of the amounts taken out and to be taken out for the ensuing year. In Flowery there are two large reservoirs for the collection of tailings—one near the Gould and Curry Mill holding 100,000 tons, belonging to Janin & Bonner—working tests in the mill prove them to be worth from six to thirteen dollars per ton; the second one is situated at the mouth of the cañon near the Carson River, and will hold some 500,000 tons when finished. It belongs to Janin & Bonner. No tests in the mill have yet been made from it; but will work about the same as the other. As I do not receive the pay of County Assessor, please get Lloyd Frizell to pay me for the report, and oblige

Yours truly,   D. W. BALCH.

FLOWERY, December 15th, 1866.

In addition to the above, I would state that the Gould and Curry Silver Mining Company have built a mill of the capacity of ten tons per diem, expressly to work blanket washings. There are also on the same cañon three water mills, which find employment in the same manner.   D. W. B.

THE OCCIDENTAL MINE, ON LODE EAST OF THE COMSTOCK LODE.

[From the Mining and Scientific Press.]

EDITORS PRESS: As many of your readers are doubtless interested in the development of this State, and more particularly those mines in the immediate vicinity of the Comstock, a few remarks on a somewhat remarkable ledge running about two miles east and nearly parallel with this famous lode may not be altogether unacceptable. The lode in question commences northeast, exhibits well-defined croppings at its southern extremity at the Occidental Mine, situated about one and a half miles southeast of Virginia City, on the new Dayton road, and runs northerly nearly parallel with the Comstock as far as the Monte Christo Mine, a little to the north of the Gould and Curry Mill, a distance of between two and three miles. During the last three years it has been opened on and partially worked at various points with uniformly encouraging results— the most prominent mines being the Monte Christo, St. John, and Occidental; but it is only since the thorough development of the latter by the spirited and unaided exertions of Messrs. Weston & Co. that the great value of this deposit has begun to be appreciated by the public—a pretty general prejudice existing here against mines the matrix of whose vein matter is anything but quartz. The matrix of the lode in the Occidental is crystallized carbonate of lime at the southern extremity of the claim, (of 1,800 feet) terminating in white quartz at the northern end. This quartz continues northward through the St. George claim into the adjoining St. Patrick, where it begins to show evidences of carbonate of lime, which increases in quantity as we approach the next claim, the St. John, where it presents precisely the same crystalline appearance as we find in the southern part of the Occidental. This carbonate of lime continues with occasional streaks of quartz about a mile and a half farther north, till we reach the Monte Christo, and probably much farther.

The following analysis, made by me on the 2d of January, 1866, on a poor specimen of this ore, will give an idea of its mineralogical character:

Gold	0.0016
Silver	0.0250
Peroxyd of manganese	0.2500
Peroxyd of iron....	1.6370
Alumina	0.7750
Carbonate of lime	83.7240
Sulphur	0.0050
Chlorine	Traces.
Silica	13.2500
Loss	0.3324
Total	100.0000

The inference to be drawn from this is, that the silver exists chiefly in the form of sulphide, with a small proportion of chloride—the gold being, in the native condition, invisible, from the very fine state of division in which it is dis-·seminated through the mineralized portion of the ore. The general appearance of the ore is very similar to that of Copiapo, in Chile, (with which I am acquainted from a five years' residence as public assayer in that country) and from which most of the Chile silver is obtained. It was this remarkable similarity which induced me to advise my friend Mr. Weston to persevere in the development of his mine some nine months ago, when most of his Nevada friends were endeavoring to dissuade him from a further prosecution of the undertaking, assuring him that silver could not possibly be found in paying or lasting quantities in any other matrix but quartz. The result has proved the correctness of my views up to the present time, *i. e.*, within twelve months upwards of $180,000 worth of bullion has been taken out of this one mine, yielding at the mill an average of about twenty dollars per ton—the average value of the bullion being about $1.90 per ounce, *i. e.*, as near as possible the quality of that obtained from the Comstock ore. In all probability the average yield will be much larger next year, as the ore appears to increase in value as well as quantity as greater depth is reached. This is shown by the following assays, made within the last few weeks, on samples taken from the most recent workings:

Gold	$5 02	
Silver	50 27	
		$55 29 per ton.
Gold	$11 54	
Silver	78 54	
		$90 08 per ton.

Against those made in February last, viz:

Gold	$7 52	
Silver	26 70	
		$34 22 per ton.
Gold	$5 02	
Silver	25 12	
		$30 14 per ton.

The lode itself varies from eight to fourteen feet in thickness, and carries pay ore from one foot to two feet in width. This pay ore is distinguished from the barren portions of the vein by minute spots of black sulphide of silver, with arborescent black oxyde of manganese, which latter is beautifully developed on the milk white compact quartz at the northern extremity of the mine in the form of ferns, similar but more distinct to those found in the casing of some portions of the Comstock Lode. The lode dips to the east at an angle of about 48 deg., and has well defined walls of a hard schistose, like altered porphyry, the rock consisting of that formation, of a greenish gray color, and much harder than the bluish variety found in the Comstock. The result is, that although the mine has obtained a depth of three hundred and fifty feet, having been worked down from the croppings, no timbering has yet been required; and as the dip corresponds very closely with the slope of the mountain, the mine can be worked by means of short tunnels to a depth of over a thousand feet, thereby avoiding the very heavy expense of hoisting and pumping works. From the brilliant success which has attended the experiments of opening out the Occidental mine, it is to be hoped that other claims on this magnificent ledge, particularly the St. John and Monte Christo, will soon be put into vigorous operation, when we may expect this ledge will prove one of the richest and most enduring in the State, outside the Comstock.

W. T. RICKARD.

NOTES ON THE OCCIDENTAL MINE.

BY GEO. HUNT, C. E., DECEMBER, 1866.

From the croppings to the depth of one hundred feet (vertical) the vein had been worked out for about one hundred and fifty feet, with the exception of a few pillars, which are now being worked out. The "pay streak" is from two to fifteen feet in width; average width, five feet.

The above mentioned workings are from the middle tunnel to the surface. From this tunnel an incline has been sunk a distance of one hundred and seventy-five feet, to connect with lower tunnel in three hundred and five feet. Estimated length of lower tunnel to connection with incline, three hundred and fifty feet. Incline shows good ore throughout entire length.

PROCEEDS OF MINES IN LANDER COUNTY.

QUARTERLY RETURNS.

Following are the returns of bullion from producing mines in Lander County for the quarter ending thirtieth of September, as compiled from the books of C. O. Barker, County Assessor. It will be observed that in several instances ore was brought here from districts in Nye County for reduction, and they are marked thus: Philadelphia*, Danville† and Northumberland‡. The average yield per ton, as well as the production of the Savage mine, is lower than the preceding quarters, owing to the fact that they have been opening new levels in the direction of the deposits of richest ore, which they are now extracting, and which will augment the production and average value for the present quarter:

[From the " Reese River Reveille."]

NAME OF MINE.	Tons.	Lbs.	Average Per Ton.
Great Eastern	412	659	$176 82
Fortuna	23	....	85 71
North River	39	536	217 56
Troy	2	1,000	83 82
Diamond	1	402	132 57
Blind Ledge	2	1,965	128 64
Semanthe	2	774	276 97
Othello	5	1,135	86 35
Idora	16	1,237	212 62
Highbridge*	17	....	195 36
Eastern Oregon	1	....	86 46
Foster	26	1,212	48 47
La Plata	50	882	71 60
Chase & Zent	4	1,000	362 04
Canada	6	1,500	132 90
El Dorado	2	568	294 58
Magnolia	4	1,171	259 63
Washington	4	88	187 45
Vanderbilt†	2	1,670	145 46
Morgan & Muncey	17	684	107 75
Biana	17	563	180 40
Richey & Hussey‡	7	612	201 75
Detroit	14	1,800	116 18
Camargo	39	....	90 77
Timoke	28	253	167 92
Green & Oder*	1	600	178 43
Dover	2	450	161 64
Isabella	19	503	40 08
Harding & Dickman	1	1,233	87 19
Providential	79	1,000	39 04
Cortez Giant	227	....	65 07
Transylvania*	19	830	161 00
Folsom	5	1,019	166 00
Savage Consolidated No. 1	160	....	156 83
" " No. 2	230	....	74 06

The *Reveille* gives the following statistics of the produce of the mines in Lander County for the quarter ending December 31, 1866, as shown by the books of the Assessor :

NAME OF MINE.	Tons.	Lbs.	Average Per Ton.
Diana	148	1,909	$ 91 18
Amsterdam	1	250	168 75
Buel North Star	4	1,920	336 57
Camargo	12	973	116 57
Chase	4	1,438	405 10
Enterprise (White Pine Dist.)	1	....	111 53
East Oregon	4	779	187 65
Empire State	7	619	99 22
Ensign	1	667	66 25
Fortune Teller	4	416	177 28
Florida	18	1,900	255 60
Fenian Star	7	1,359	54 24
Fortuna	1	1,520	30 33
Farrel	8	1,453	71 12
Great Eastern	287	.....	217 94
Idora	22	1,695	220 42
J. R. Murphy	1	100	251 18
Joseph Cole	1	1,850	27 85
Jacob Bradley	1	....	116 80
Keystone	2	850	194 66
Kihock	1	....	197 27
Zaidee	1	728	100 61
Lodi	7	1,019	32 54
Livermore	8	500	157 79
Mount Tenabo Co. (Cortez)	...	.....	......
Morgan & Muncey	4	626	25 69
Magnolia	6	1,671	338 23
Metacom	26	....	100 99
Manhattan Co.	69	288	83 90
May & Davis	2	480	136 80
North River	18	1,924	56 03
Owens & Perkins	3	1,700	46 16
Providential	64	844	54 91
Pinney, Rev	6	600	51 73
Patten	2	824	200 43
Remington	6	1,500	49 63
Savage Consolidated	451	.....	103 25
Silver Queen	14	1,913	38 28
Surprise	1	.....	171 66
Semanthe	2	150	332 52
Timoke	79	1,138	148 41
Taylor & Passmore (Cortez)	5	982	160 43
Tunnehill (Eureka)	8	1,838	106 35
Victoria	4	1,176	91 20
Washington	12	67	479 52
Whitlatch Union	18	546	105 97
Zimmerman	5	1,278	71 75

The above table, says the *Reveille*, embraces forty-seven mines, which have yielded more or less bullion during the quarter, and, with few exceptions, the ore reduced is of a good grade, sufficiently so to admit its being worked here remuneratively. It will be observed, that a number of mines which were included in the previous quarters of the year do not appear in the present list, as well as that several mines appear for the first time. According to the Assessor's returns, there are in Lander County—and mainly in the Reese River District— fully seventy-five mines which have produced bullion during the past year. As we have remarked, the ore worked is very generally of a high grade, as the average yield per ton will show. A considerable number of the mines embraced in the quarterly lists were subjected only to testing operations, and the general results must be deemed very encouraging, and their excellent character argues well for the future of this district. In the case of the Savage Mine, the average yield of the ore is less than in several quarters preceding, but is still high, being $103.25 per ton. The yield of the Washington, Chase, Buel North Star, Great Eastern, Semanthe, Magnolia, Florida, Timoke, Idora, Metacom, Taylor & Passmore, etc., is grand, and as most of them are pretty well developed, they may be fairly classed henceforth among the producing and paying mines of the Reese River District.

REMARKS ON MILLING AND MINING OPERATIONS AT REESE RIVER.

In the Appendix may be found quite an interesting and elaborate, and, in my opinion, valuable article upon this subject, to which the attention of mining and mill men throughout the State is invited. It has been kindly furnished by Mr. C. A. Luckhart, mining engineer, by special request.

Mr. Luckhart has, at least, endeavored to direct us in the way in which our future prosperity evidently lies, viz: greater economy in our mining and milling operations, and improved processes for saving the precious metals.

THE SUTRO DRAIN TUNNEL.

The absolute necessity of providing drainage for the mines on the Comstock Lode, it is believed, will become more apparent with the development of each succeeding year. As this subject was somewhat extensively treated in my former report, it will now be dismissed with the remark that, as the great mining companies have now become convinced that they must do something to help themselves before others will assist them, and as several of them have already subscribed $100,000 each towards the project, and as others will probably do equally well, it is not improbable that the great project will be commenced before another year shall have been lost by delay.

THE VIRGINIA AND GOLD HILL WATER COMPANY.

This company was formed by the consolidation of the Virginia and Gold Hill Water Works, on the twelfth of May, 1863, and incorporated under the laws of the Territory of Nevada. Its capital stock is $1,000,000, in 10,000 shares of $100 each.

The following is a statement of the receipts and disbursements of these works from July, 1863, to February, 1866, inclusive:

Receipts in gold	$336,578 69
Disbursements in gold	163,549 39
Net profit	$173,029 30
Dividends paid in gold......................	166,250 00
Cash balance........................	$ 6,779 30

exhibiting a profit of over $200 per day.

About one-half was derived from mills and hoisting-works, the other half from Virginia and Gold Hill, for domestic use.

The following table exhibiting the receipts and disbursements may be of interest. It contains the proceeds for the latter half of February, 1866, which is included above. It shows that the mills and mines have paid over $79,000, and the citizens of Virginia and Gold Hill have paid over $54,000 during the year for water. Total, over $133,000; of which more than half, over $70,000, was profit.

REPORT OF THE RECEIPTS AND DISBURSEMENTS OF THE VIRGINIA AND GOLD HILL WATER COMPANY FOR THE YEAR ENDING JANUARY 8, 1867.

MONTHS.	From Mills and Mines.	F'm Virginia and Gold Hill.	From Sales of Real Estate.	Total.	MONTHS.	Salaries and Wages.	Construction Account.	Sundry Expenses.	Purchases.	Total.	Net Profits.
1866.					**1866.**						
February 13...	$5,746 84	$5,018 00	....	$10,764 84	February 13...	$1,465 00	$ 857 62	$1,750 91	....	$4,073 53	$6,691 31
March 13...	6,220 18	4,179 95	....	10,400 13	March 13...	1,405 00	582 00	1,272 15	....	3,259 15	7,140 98
April 10...	6,101 50	4,245 60	....	10,347 10	April 10...	1,565 00	490 68	1,468 98	....	3,524 66	6,822 44
May 8...	6,731 87	4,132 00	$2,000 00	12,863 87	May 8...	1,445 00	2,087 20	2,478 77	....	6,010 97	6,852 90
June 12...	6,919 84	4,911 75	....	11,831 09	June 12...	1,945 00	2,148 78	1,454 52	....	5,548 25	6,282 84
July 10...	6,449 41	4,215 25	....	10,664 66	July 10...	1,025 00	1,418 80	2,003 02	$1,000 00	5,441 82	5,222 84
August 14...	6,515 29	5,243 50	....	11,758 79	August 14...	1,525 00	1,200 14	3,082 68	....	5,807 82	5,950 97
September 11...	6,831 08	4,363 50	....	11,194 53	September 11...	1,530 00	1,508 63	5,615 19	....	8,653 82	2,540 71
October 9...	6,408 00	4,426 00	....	10,834 00	October 9...	1,115 00	764 42	1,660 69	1,020 00	4,560 11	6,278 89
November 13...	7,217 70	5,087 25	....	12,254 95	November 13...	1,265 00	2,201 64	2,077 58	....	5,544 22	6,710 73
December 11...	6,728 09	4,104 25	....	10,827 84	December 11...	1,315 00	1,044 86	2,528 89	....	4,887 75	5,939 59
1867.					**1867.**						
January 8.....	7,155 20	4,436 50	....	11,591 70	January 8.....	1,015 00	2,238 70	1,640 18	....	4,898 88	6,697 87
	$79,019 45	$54,818 55	$2,000 00	$135,838 00		$16,615 00	$16,587 99	$27,088 01	$2,020 00	$62,205 93	$73,127 07

Balance on hand January 9th, 1866............ 6,887 99

$79,465 06

Total amount of dividends paid.........$72,500 00
Balance on hand January 8th, 1867.........6,965 06

$79,465 06

O. G. FUNK, Secretary.

VIRGINIA, January 8th, 1867.

MECHANICAL INVENTIONS.

In the Appendix may be found a description of two inventions by citizens of Nevada:

1st. A new invention for laying railroad tracks: invented by W. D. Robertson, of Humboldt County,

2d. Grim's Concentrator and Settler: invented by A. K. Grim, of Virginia City.

CONTINGENT EXPENSES OF OFFICE.

APPEAL FROM DECISION OF BOARD OF EXAMINERS.

In my former report, complaint was made that "this office, for the past year," (1865) had "been running on its own responsibility, paying its own expenses for post office and express charges, fuel, rent, etc.," and a small appropriation as a contingent fund was asked for.

As a reason for the non-introduction of a bill to provide for such expenditure, I was informed by members of the Legislature that no specific appropriation for the Surveyor General's office was necessary, but that the Board of Examiners was authorized to audit and allow all claims for necessary contingent expenses. A bill was therefore made out against the State, and transmitted to the Board, April 2d, 1866, which elicited a call from the Board for a bill of items, verified by vouchers or affidavit, and on the twenty-eighth of that month the following bill of expenditures of $712 in coin, verified by my affidavit, and accompanied by the explanatory letter now appended to the bill, was transmitted to the Board:

VIRGINIA, April 28th, 1866.

State of Nevada

To S. H. MARLETTE,   Dr.

For rent of Surveyor General's office for December, 1864..$ 28 00		
" Wood for " " " " " " .. 5 00		
" Porterage, three weeks 3 00		
" Matting .... 23 75—$59 75		
" Rent of office, 1st quarter, 1865 .... 100 00		
" Wood for " " " " .... 21 50—121 50		
" Rent " " 2d " " 75 00		
" " " " 3d " " 62 50		
" " " " 4th " " 56 25		
" Wood " " " " " 34 12		
" Stationery 7 75		
" Envelopes 1 38		
" Postage-stamps 3 00		
" Porterage, fifty-two weeks 52 00		
" Mucilage .... 1 00—155 50		

Total, in coin............................. ......$474 25

Brought forward.................... .... $474 25

For rent of office 1st quarter, 1866 .... $56 25
" " for April, " 18 75
" Wood " *34 00
" Stationery .... * 2 75
" Postage-stamps .... * 2 00
" Mucilage .... * 1 00
" Freight on Reports.......................... * 3 00
" Distributing " .... * 8 00
" Porterage, seventeen weeks..................... 17 00
" Printing 2,500 copies "Errata," for Report.... ..... 10 00
" Amount paid E. B. Preston for assistance compiling
  statistics and copying Report, 18 days, at $5 per day. 90 00—237 75

Total, in coin...................................$712 00

VIRGINIA, Dec. 31st, 1866.

State of Nevada
To S. H. MARLETTE,   Dr.

For rent of Surveyor General's office for May & June, 1866.$ 87 50
" " " " July, " . 18 75
" " " " Aug. & Sept. " . 25 00
" " " " 4th quarter, " . 37 50
" Wood for 4th quarter, 1866, say................... 80 00
" Stationery................................... 6 50
" Porterage, 35 weeks 85 00
" Envelopes, stamps, ink, etc....................... 7 25
" One Record Book .... 7 50—205 00

Total, in coin, for twenty-five months..............$917 00

SURVEYOR GENERAL'S OFFICE, ⎫
Virginia, Nevada, April 28th, 1866. ⎭

Hon. C. N. Noteware,
Secretary of State and of State Board of Examiners:

DEAR SIR—In compliance with the requirements of the State Board of Examiners, as expressed in your favor of the 24th inst., I send, in duplicate, my account against the State, verified by my affidavit. * * *

Concerning rent, I will remark that at first I paid $150, then $125, then $100, and now the rent is $75 per month for the whole upper story of a fire-proof building, and what I require and occupy is worth about half the rent of the whole, which half I have divided equally between the State and myself. The expense of fuel I have divided equally between the State and myself, and with the porterage, I have done about the same. For oil, candles and matches, I have paid wholly myself. You will confer a favor by laying the above explanations before the Board.   Very respectfully,

S. H. MARLETTE.

P. S.—I omitted to State that the Surveyors, Assessors and others upon whom I relied for data for my Report were so dilatory [in furnishing their

Reports] that without assistance I could scarcely have been able to transmit mine until near the close of the session of the Legislature.   S. H. M.

A communication, of which the following is a copy, was received May 16th :

{ The Great Seal
of the
State of Nevada. }

OFFICE OF SECRETARY OF STATE,
Carson City, Nevada, May 14th, 1866. }

Hon. S. H. Marlette,
          Surveyor General, Virginia City, Nevada :

SIR—The following was the action on your bill by the Board of Examiners, April 30th, 1866, viz: Approved for $45.75, being amount of proper contingent expenses since January 1st, 1866. Rent deemed improper charge, because there is no authority of law for allowing the Surveyor General an office. Porterage and printing Errata deemed improper charges. All expenses incurred in 1864 and 1865 are rejected on the ground that the *Annual Report* of the Surveyor General for the year 1865 (page 28) shows that up to the close of that year the Surveyor General's office had been running on its own responsibility, and paying its own expenses for post office and express charges, stationery, fuel, rent, etc. You will find a warrant for the amount approved, at the Controller's office.   Respectfully,
          (Signed)   CHARLES MARTIN,
                                        Clerk of Board.

That the above is a remarkable document to issue from a Board consisting of the Governor, the Secretary of State, and the Attorney General of the State of Nevada, will, doubtless, be generally conceded; but, as your Excellency had been for some time absent from the capital at the time of its issuance, the glory of its authorship must be conceded wholly to the other members of the Board. At first view, it appears like a practical joke perpetrated at my expense, or like the quibble of a tricky lawyer employed by a dishonest debtor to defraud a creditor, but as the document bears the impression of the " Great Seal of the State of Nevada," it is doubtless genuine ; and as the Board was acting under a solemn oath to faithfully perform its duties, the supposition of a joke or a quibble must not be entertained, especially as the reason assigned by me for asking for an appropriation is ostentatiously paraded by the Board as a reason for rejecting my bill. viz : " That this office has been running on its own responsibility, paying its own expenses, etc. ;" in other words, that *I had paid the expenses*, which the Board ought to have known was the intended meaning, especially when followed by a bill of items, vouched for by affidavit. *Does not the foregoing document declare that the Board rejects my claim for expenses of this office because I had paid those expenses ?* Such a stultifying pretext for the rejection of a bill never should have been acknowledged by a Secretary of State and Attorney General. The bill for 1864 and 1865 amounts to $474.25 in coin; the bill for the first four months of 1866 is $237.75 in coin. Total, $712 in coin, all of which was rejected by the Board, except $45.75 of the latter bill, for the items designated thus, (*) for which I was offered a warrant worth about $20 in coin, which I declined to accept. The Board did allow six dollars for a record-book in 1865, the only sum received by the undersigned for contingent expenses of this office since its organization, over two years, to the close of 1866, and by the liberal action of the Board I might have received about $20 more, in coin, or $26 in all—a trifle more than one dollar per month. Has an equally rigid economy governed the Board in its action on the bills of other State officers? My bill for the last eight months of

1866 amounts to $205 in coin, of which the Board would, if presented to it, have rejected all but $51.25, for which it would probably have allowed a warrant worth about $25 in coin. To save time I therefore send this bill to be transmitted directly to the Legislature, to which I have appealed from the decision of the Board upon my former bill. It may not be improper to remark, in this connection, that when I assumed the duties of this office, the provision was that the salary should be paid in coin; but, by virtue of a decision of the Supreme Court, I understand it would have been paid, for the last three quarters of 1866, in greenbacks, had there been any greenbacks to pay with, but it has been paid in warrants, worth less than fifty per cent. in coin; and although I believe there are not more than two of the executive State offices which demand a greater amount of personal attention than does this, and although this is the poorest paid of all, yet as all are alike affected by the decision of the Court and the lack of funds in the treasury, I make no complaint, and, had a decent pretext been given for rejecting the bill of expense prior to 1866, merely a respectful appeal from the decision of the Board would have been presented. But when it was rejected under such a pretext, it appeared to me that intentional insult had been added to injury, and that a mild protest against the action of the Board would not be out of place.

The law requires my report to be transmitted to your Excellency on or before the fifteenth day of December; yet last year, and this, such reports as I could have transmitted at the specified time would have been comparatively worthless. Last year, though assisted somewhat by friends, I was compelled to have an assistant for eighteen days, for which I paid $90 in coin, in order to be able to transmit my report on the thirty-first of January. The Board deemed the $90 an "improper charge." It is now the eleventh of February, and I have been unable thus far to complete my report, although I have been greatly assisted by my partner, Mr. Hunt, and by Mr. Bruckman, and am also under obligations to Mr. Hetzel and Mr. Krutschnitt, the present Assessor of Storey County, and to Mr. Balch, of the Board of County Commissioners. No improper charges are made by these gentlemen. Last year's report was so full of errors, by fault of copying clerk or the compositor, as to be comparatively worthless. I paid $10 coin to the "Enterprise" for printing 2,500 copies of "errata," nearly 2,000 of which I sent to the Secretary of State. Some of these were used, but none were inserted in the appendix to the Journals. But the Board deemed the "charge" an "improper one." The Board allowed three dollars freight on reports from Carson, and three dollars for distributing the same in this city, but would not allow $10 for correcting an otherwise almost worthless document. Was the Board guided by law or by whim?

In conclusion, I would state that it has been my endeavor, under rather discouraging circumstances, to make this office useful to the State; and although I have fallen far below even my own expectations, and perhaps much more below those of others, yet I believe all intelligent men will concede it is no fault of mine. I therefore appeal to the Legislature, confidently expecting that justice will be done, and asking for nothing more.

I am, very respectfully,

Your obdt. servant,

S. H. MARLETTE,
Surveyor General.

APPENDIX

TO

SURVEYOR GENERAL'S REPORT.

CONTENTS OF APPENDIX.

7

CIRCULAR

TO

COUNTY SURVEYORS AND ASSESSORS.

CIRCULAR TO COUNTY SURVEYORS AND ASSESSORS.

SURVEYOR GENERAL'S OFFICE,
VIRGINIA, Nevada, January 28, 1866.

SIR: I respectfully call your attention to the duties of your office, in relation to that of the Surveyor-General.

From "An Act concerning the office of Surveyor-General," approved March 20th, 1865, I extract the following:

"SEC. 3. When required by law, he (the Surveyor-General) shall make an accurate Map of the State, and shall survey, and when necessary, designate by plain visible marks, or monuments, and shall describe on the map of the State, the boundary lines of the several counties, and incorporated cities and towns in the State; and when a boundary line of the State, or of any county, intersects with or passes in the immediate vicinity of any lake, stream, range of hills or mountains, or other conspicuous object on the surface of the earth, he shall, by the proper observation, determine the place of such intersection, or the distance and bearing from the said boundary line, of such point of such object as may be nearest to said boundary line, and will best serve as a distinguishing landmark. He shall also determine and describe on the map of the State, the length and course of every important stream and lake, and of every important range of hills or mountains, and the greatest elevation of [the] highest peak thereof, within the limits of any county. When called upon by the County Commissioners of any county, he shall run any boundary line, or portion of a line, between such county and an adjoining county."

(In case of application for surveys of county boundaries, from County Commissioners, the County Surveyor will be deputed to make the survey, unless th should be good reasons for a different appointment.)

"SEC. 5. The Surveyor-General shall be Chief Engineer and Commissioner of Internal Improvements. He shall deliver to the Governor, annually, on or before the fifteenth day of December, his report, which shall contain:

First—An accurate statement of the progress he may have made in the execution of the surveys enjoined on him by law, and in the preparation of the Map of the State.

Second—Plans and suggestions for the construction and improvement of roads, turnpikes, railroads, canals, and aqueducts; also, plans and suggestions for the preservation and increase of forests and timber trees; for the draining of marshes, prevention of overflows, and the irrigation of arable lands by means of reservoirs, canals, artesian wells, or otherwise.

Third—An estimate of the aggregate quantity of land belonging to the State, and the best information he may be able to obtain as to the characteristics of the same.

Fourth—An estimate of the aggregate quantity of all land used for or adapted to tillage and grazing within this State, and each county of the State; together with a description of the location in which the same may be situated.

Fifth—An estimate of the aggregate number of horses, cattle, sheep and swine within the State, and each county of the State.

Sixth—An estimate of the aggregate quantity of wheat, rye, maize, potatoes, grapes, and other agricultural productions of the preceding year.

Seventh—An estimate of the aggregate quantity of all mineral lands in the State, and the quantity and value of each mineral produced during the preceding year, together with a description of the locality in which such minerals may be found.

Eighth—All facts which may be within his personal knowledge, or which he may learn from reliable sources, and which may, in his opinion, be calculated to promote the full development of the resources of the State.

" Sec. 6. He shall address a circular letter to the County Surveyors and County Assessors, instructing them, and it is hereby made a part of their official duties, to use their utmost diligence in collecting information relative to each and every matter mentioned in section five of this Act, and to transmit to him quarterly, at the seat of government,* a report in writing, setting forth the results of their inquiries ; and it is hereby made the duty of the County Commissioners to refuse to audit or pay any bills for services of the County Surveyor or County Assessor, in case they shall have failed to comply with the requirements of this Act.

" It shall also be the duty of County Surveyors to transmit, when required, to the Surveyor-General, a copy of the field notes and plats of official surveys made by them, (except surveys of city or town lots) expressing the bearings from the true meridian, and noting the variations of the magnetic from the true meridian, and indicating plainly upon the plat at what point of any river, stream. or county line, or any line of the United States surveys, or any road, canal or railroad, may be touched or crossed; also indicating the position of any mountain or other prominent landmarks within or near the lines of the surveys.

" Sec. 7. It shall be the duty of all railroad and toll road companies to file. in the office of the Surveyor-General, complete topographical maps of the roads and the country through which their roads may run."

You are hereby instructed to " use your utmost diligence in collecting information in relation to each and every matter mentioned " specifically in the above extracts; also, all other facts which may be calculated to promote the full development of the resources of the State, or furnish data for a map of the State, and to transmit them, together with such suggestions and recommendations as you may be pleased to make, to this office.

Your attention is particularly directed to the following :

THE PRECIOUS AND OTHER METALS—MINERALS.

Gold, silver, copper, sulphur, lead, iron, etc.; coal, salt, lime, etc.

Where found ; in what conditions and quantities; to what extent worked: facilities for working—such as water power, wood, etc.; also, obstacles in the way, and cost of working; whether a source of profit—probabilities of becoming such ; modes of working ; defects of former or present modes, and suggested improvements.

* You will transmit your reports to this place, VIRGINIA.

Thickness and changes in thickness of lodes ("ledges") or strata, with their dip and changes of dip; also their "strike" or bearing, and changes of same; kind of rock constituting the walls; presence or absence of clay selvages; "horses"—size and position, and of what material.

Kind and amount of powder used in hoisting, hauling and crushing—with cost of each.

Inclines and shafts sunk, or tunnels run; size and length, and cost; kind of rock penetrated, and to what extent.

Amount of water found, and where; increase or diminution of same; cost of draining; suggestions for a general system of drainage of mines.

Observations upon the geology and mineralogy of mining districts, and sketches of the same.

Observations upon the mining laws of Mexico, showing what portions might be introduced into our legislative code.

Lists of fatal and serious accidents; mode of occurrence; suggestions for prevention.

Number of men and animals worked, and in what capacity; wages per day, and total.

Rock extracted; expense of extraction; where crushed; expense of crushing, and profit or loss.

Tons of rock taken out not worked, but which may be worked when the cost of working shall become less; estimated yield; also, amount of rock of similar character that might be taken out.

QUARTZ MILLS—STEAM OR WATER POWER.

Power of same; when erected; original cost; also, of improvements, additions or repairs, and when made.

Number of stamps; weight; fall.

Number of amalgamators; kind of ditto.

Tons crushed, and from what mines; dry or wet; fineness.

Tons amalgamated; yield per ton, and total.

Capacity for crushing and amalgamating.

Comparison of advantages of dry and wet crushing, and of different processes of amalgamating.

STEAM AND OTHER GRIST AND SAW MILLS.

When erected; original cost; expense of running, etc.

Kind and amount of grain ground; run of stone; amount of flour, meal, etc.

Kind, amount, cost, and value of lumber; cost of transportation, amount, cost and value of wood.

INTERNAL IMPROVEMENTS—METEOROLOGICAL TABLES OR OBSERVATIONS.

Canals, ditches, turnpikes, toll roads, toll bridges, railroads, completed or in process of construction, or contemplated; electro-magnetic telegraphs; all incorporated companies—their capital stock, value, expenditures, income, etc.

A complete list of all mining companies by whom work has been done, including "wildcat;" amounts expended, proceeds, etc.

County boundaries in dispute, or that should be run out during the year 1866.

Suggestions for the improvement of boundaries by substituting natural for artificial or arbitrary ones or otherwise, with a view to a better and more permanent subdivision of the State.

You will please transmit your last report for this year by the first of

November next, in order that I may avail myself of its contents in making my own, which must be transmitted to the Governor on or before the fifteenth of December.

Your report, and such others as you may obtain, if valuable, will accompany mine to the Governor, and may do much toward disseminating correct information concerning our young State.

I would suggest the furnishing of a copy of this Circular to all Superintendents of mines, and other men of intelligence, who will probably interest themselves in the matter, with the urgent request that they will coöperate with us in our efforts to obtain the materials for a complete statistical history of the State. Copies will be supplied on application.

Please acknowledge the receipt of this immediately, and oblige,

Very respectfully, yours, etc.,

S. H. MARLETTE,

Surveyor-General.

To_____Esq.

County Surveyor of_____County.

REPORTS

OF

COUNTY SURVEYORS AND COUNTY ASSESSORS.

8

CHURCHILL COUNTY.

To the Hon. S. H. Marlette,
       Surveyor General of the State of Nevada:

SIR—In compliance with the law we respectfully submit the following report:

Churchill County lies between the parallels of 39 and 40 degrees north latitude, and extends from Lander County on the east to Lyon County on the west, thus occupying the central portion of the State of Nevada. The western half, except along Carson and Old Rivers, and the upper and lower Sinks of the Carson, is a sandy and alkaline plain, surrounded on the northwest and south by low barren hills, and on the east by the silver range of mountains. The eastern portion of the county is quite mountainous, and contains three distinct ranges of mountains—Silver Hill, the western; Clan Alpine, the central; and Edwards Creek, or New Pass, the eastern range. These mountain ranges have the same general direction of about north 30 degrees east, by south 30 degrees west. Carson River enters the county from the west, in latitude about 39 degrees and 30 minutes north, from which point to Ragtown, a distance of about sixteen miles, its course is northeasterly. At Ragtown the river bears around to the southeast, which course it retains to Carson Lake, (or upper sink) a distance of nine miles. The river divides at St. Clair's Station, the main channel running into Carson Lake, thence through the outlet of the lake, and past Stillwater to the Lower Sink—a distance via the lake and river of about fifty miles. The other channel, called Old River, (and supposed in some former time to have been the main channel of the river) leaving the main channel at St. Clair's, runs in a northeasterly direction a distance of about thirty miles, when it also empties into the Lower Sink. This sink is a shallow lake of brackish water, and is about thirty miles long from east to west, by fifteen wide from north to south. In addition to the waters of the Carson it also receives the water from the outlet of the Humboldt Lake, and is therefore the common sink of both the Carson and Humboldt Rivers. Its elevation above the level of the sea is a little less than 4000 feet, being probably the lowest portion of the State of Nevada. Along the western and northern margin of Carson Lake (Upper Sink) there is a large body of tule and meadow land, and another extensive tract lies between Stillwater and the Lower Sink. These two tracts, embracing the principal meadow lands of the county, produced the present season about 2200 tons of hay. The principal arable lands of the county are located along the main Carson and Old Rivers. Much of the available land has already been taken up and improved. It yields in profusion all kinds of grain and vegetables common to this latitude. In a former report reference was made to the necessity existing of some method being devised to protect the farmers along Old River from the danger of overflow from the annual spring floods; and it was suggested that a bulkhead across Old River, near St. Clair's Station, would fulfill all the requirements of the case. The legislature at its last session passed an Act conferring the necessary authority for constructing the bulkhead. Under that authority a substantial bulkhead has been constructed by citizens of the county immediately interested, which, it is believed, will afford the necessary protection. As an immediate result a greatly increased quantity of land will be brought under cultivation, and a consequent increase of all kinds of farmers' produce.

The following is an estimate of the stock owned and of the products of the county the present season. Number of horses, 400; mules, 50; cattle, 600; hogs, 150. Number of tons of hay raised, 2,500; barley, 250; potatoes, 350, besides considerable quantities of wheat, corn, and all kinds of vegetables. The Overland Mail Road passes through the whole length of the county, entering the county about 33 miles east of Virginia, and leaving it at Mount Airy, a distance of about 120 miles. The California State and the United States Telegraph Companies each have a line passing through the county, of a united length of about 240 miles. There are four post offices in the county—St. Clair's Station, Stillwater, La Plata, and Clan Alpine, and each is supplied with a daily mail.

MINES AND MINING.

Since the report of last year little progress has been made towards the development of the mines of this county. In Desert District a five-stamp mill was completed and made a few runs with considerable success, but the mill was built on borrowed capital, drawing a heavy rate of interest; besides, the cost of wood being at the rate of $30 per cord—for these reasons the mill did not prove to be a paying investment, and passed into other hands, and the owners are waiting for the advance of the Pacific Railroad to supply them with fuel at a cheaper rate, or to ship their ore to some place where it can be worked cheaper. The ores of that district are rich in both gold and silver, but there is neither wood nor water within any convenient distance to the mines.

In Mountain Wells District are situated the mines of the Silver Wave Mining and Land Company; the Connecticut and Nevada Silver Mining Company; the Nevada Silver Mining Company; the Madison Silver Mining Company; the Wyoming Silver Mining Company, and the Monumental Silver Mining Company. The above companies are all incorporated in the east.

The Silver Wave Company have completed a ten-stamp mill with three furnaces. They have power to add ten additional stamps, and have made some progress in developing their mines. The management of their mines, unfortunately, was intrusted to inexperienced men, with the usual result. Large sums were expended in exploring near the surface, and of course neither the quality nor the worth of their mine has been ascertained. The company became embarrassed, and the works are at present at a standstill. This company own five ledges, only one of which has been worked. They also own the town site of La Plata, (the county seat) and a wood ranch adjoining their mines, of 1,500 acres.

The Connecticut and Nevada Company have also erected a ten-stamp steam mill, with sufficient power for ten additional stamps. No furnaces built yet. This company are prosecuting the work on their mines, their aim being to obtain ore in sufficient quantities to keep their mill going when they start up. They have already ascertained that the quality is satisfactory. This company own ten ledges in this district, and have been working on three of the number—the Satellite, Vermont, and the Washington. Some 2000 feet of shafts and tunnels have already been run. Their work at present is being expended on one ledge, with the view of getting to the water level. Rock from this ledge, near the surface, has worked from $30 to $135 per ton, and at a depth of 140 feet has assayed upwards of $1,600. This company own the town site of Averill and two wood ranches, containing over 2,000 acres.

The Nevada Silver Mining Company have continued their shaft on the Gray Eagle ledge to a depth of 100 feet, but have suspended work for a short time for want of funds. This company own four ledges and a wood ranch containing 465 acres.

The Monumental Company own three ledges, on one of which they have an incline sunk of 70 feet. This company is also waiting for funds.

The Madison Silver Mining Company have not commenced operations yet. This company owns three ledges.

The Wyoming Silver Mining Company is making arrangements to commence work. This Company owns four ledges.

The most prominent mines in this district outside of those belonging to the above named companies are the Sheba, Leviathan, Michigan, Mohawk, Lincoln, Red, White and Blue, Catharine Laura, Panillia, Laura Cluster, Anaconda, Eclipse, Cumberland, Everitt, Manhattan, Knickerbocker, Bancroft, Cousins, Ruby, Sherman, Cabin, Antelope, Jenny Lind, Warren, Fenton, Mathilde, Leah Francis, Menken, and New York. These and others have been worked by resident owners according to their means, some by tunnels of from ten to three hundred feet, and inclines and shafts of from ten to eighty feet. Many of these show large bodies of excellent mineral. The valuable minerals of this district, viz: gold and silver, are associated in many cases with copper, galena, iron, sulphur, arsenic, antimony, etc., rendering the roasting process absolutely necessary in nearly all cases. The country-rock of this region is highly metamorphosed, silicious, argillaceous, and calcareous sediments, among which are clay, slates, quartzites, gneiss, and blue argillaceous limestone, with intrusions of porphyry, granite, and trap. The vein matter is principally quartz, though in some instances combined with calcareous and manganese spars. There are two distinct systems of veins in this district, the oldest having a northwest and southeast bearing, and the more recent a northeast and southwest, the first mentioned being larger and containing more gold and less base metal as far as developed, and are attracting more attention of late. Silver Hill District, located northeast of Mountain Wells, and on the same range, has made little progress in developing its mineral resources during the past year. The advantages possessed by this district have been strangely overlooked. The number, size, and richness of the ledges; the facilities for working, such as wood and water, which are abundant; and its convenience to the great salt marsh, should certainly attract more attention and capital. A company is being formed in this county on the United States Series, (three ledges) who seem to have their eyes open to the advantages mentioned; and as $24,000 is to be spent in opening and prospecting the ledges prior to the erection of the "usual mill," we look for success to the undertaking. This district is rich in galena ores, and the abundance of nut pine wood in every part of the district will render their reduction easily accomplished. The country-rock is composed of granite, slates, argillaceous limestones, and porphyry, with their various modifications. There are also copper, iron, antimony, and zinc in this district. Alamo District is located east of Silver Hill, on the opposite range, and is also attracting considerable attention, having large, well defined ledges, which assay rich in both gold and silver. There are also copper, iron, and antimony lodes in this district, and it is abundantly supplied with wood and water. It is also convenient to the great salt marsh. In this district granite and slate predominate. Hiawatha and Augusta District are located, the former on the north and the latter on the east of Alamo, and are said to contain valuable mines rich in silver ores, with every facility to reduce them. All that is required is capital well applied to bring them into notice. New Pass District is located on the range opposite to Augusta due east, and is noted for its rich gold-bearing ledges. This district is well supplied with wood and water. Empire District is located at the head of Fair View Valley, south of the Mountain Wells District. Its ledges are gold bearing, but the district is nearly destitute of wood and water, as is the Sandspring District. The rock is also gold bearing. This district is located southwest from Mountain Wells, and is principally noted for its extensive salt bed. Clan Alpine District is located east of Mountain Wells, on the same range as Alamo, Hiawatha, and Augusta. The Silver Lode Mining Company have completed a splendid steam mill, ten stamps, which has made a successful run on rock from one of the company's ledges—the "McGregor"—on which they have an incline following the ledge down 200 feet. This ledge, not over twelve inches on the surface, has increased as they descend till it has attained a width of over twelve feet, and is well cased, showing every evidence of being a valuable and permanent ledge; and as the ore requires neither roasting nor chemicals in the working, it must prove a source of great profit to the owners. There are numerous ledges in this district, some of them extremely rich in silver, with no combinations of base metals. This district has an unfailing supply of wood of the best quality, and a fair supply of water.

OTHER MINERALS.

A former report mentions the extensive salt, sulphur, and soda deposits found in this county, to which may be added an excellent variety of limestone; also, fine clay, granite, sandstone, slate, and chalk for building purposes, and many other valuable minerals.

We remain, yours respectfully,
WM. A. JACKSON,
County Surveyor, Churchill County.
JOHN CARROLL,
County Assessor, Churchill County.

LA PLATA, October 22d, 1866.

DOUGLAS COUNTY.

GENOA, December 29th, 1866.

To the Hon. S. H. Marlette,
Surveyor General of the State of Nevada:

SIR—In compliance with the law, I hereby transmit to you my report as Assessor of Douglas County, for the present year. If not complete as desirable, and too late to be incorporated in your annual report, I rely for an excuse upon the fact that I am an invalid, and have been obliged to depend upon a deputy to perform most of the labor of assessing and collecting the desired statistical information. Your circular for the year 1866 has not reached me. Douglas County embraces an area of about 1,500 square miles, or 960,000 acres. Its surface is broken into mountains and valleys. The most extensive range of the former is a spur of the Sierras known as the East Summit, which (separates Lake and

Carson valleys) crosses its western border, while through its center an extensive spur of the Walker River range crosses, forming the eastern rim of Carson Valley. It also embraces portions of Lake, Walker, Mason's and nearly the whole of Carson Valley. These valleys comprise the entire arable portions of the county, with few exceptions, while the mountains and rolling hills afford bunch grass pasturage for herds of loose stock. Lake Valley, or that portion of it embraced within the county lines, lies on the western slope of the previously mentioned spur of the Sierras, and possesses few attractions beyond the beauties of its elevated scenery. The mountains slope abruptly to the shores of Lake Tahoe, and afford but little opportunity for cultivation. Some experiments have been tried, however, and considering the sandy nature of the soil, and its great altitude, (6,200 feet above the sea level) have proved a decided success. Oats, barley and wheat mature with a fair average yield, and all the hardier vegetables. Beets, rutabagas and potatoes grow to astonishing dimensions. A heavy growth of pine timber covers the valley and the slopes of the mountains, which, manufactured into lumber, finds its way into the markets of Virginia and Reese River. Carson Valley has an elevation of 5,500 feet, and skirts the eastern slope of the Sierras for about twenty-five miles. Its area is about 80,000 acres, one tenth of which lies within the boundary of California. Some 30,000 acres are under fence, cultivated principally to grass. Here, along the western side of the valley, and on either side of the Carson River, which, formed by the junction of the East and West forks, traverses its entire length, are found the luxuriant meadow lands that have supplied the markets of Nevada for the last six years with hay. So remunerative was this crop, that every available acre has been devoted to its production, the yield amounting to 15,000 tons for the year 1865, and scarcely less for the present. The prospective depreciation in price from excess of supply induced many farmers to attempt the cultivation of the cereals, and with splendid success, wherever water can be obtained to irrigate with. Early varieties of corn mature with a respectable yield. I am unable to give you anything like a reliable estimate per acre, as no one seems to have taken any pains to ascertain. The present low price of hay, and the vast quantities on hand, will have the effect of breaking up the exclusiveness of this crop. Grain will be cultivated extensively; more live stock will be raised, and dairies established. Heretofore some of the farmers have purchased Eastern butter for daily use, rather than maintain stock for its manufacture. The fact is, very little farming has been done. To raise sufficient vegetables for their own use, cut and gather their hay crop, seemed to be the whole end and aim of existence with the Carson Valley ranch men. Now that he has no market, necessity compels him to cultivate the soil, or devote his broad acres to pasturage. The change will be salutary in the end, for they will not be at the mercy of a fluctuating and ruinous market with their single crop.

Experiments on an extensive scale have been made for the past three years to cultivate the sage plains that lie along the eastern side of the valley, and between the forks of Carson River; but the difficulty of getting water in sufficient quantities to irrigate with, together with the cost of maintaining their supply against the mill companies below, who claim the right to use the water, has rendered these attempts, in most cases, disastrous failures. A light sandy soil, it requires an abundant supply of water, which is afforded by the east fork of Carson River; but the agents of the water monopolists patrol this stream whenever the supply begins to slacken, and shut off the water from the irrigating canals of the farmers—not unfrequently depriving them of a sufficient supply for stock, or even friendly use. Much litigation has grown out of this condition of affairs, but the mills have been sustained in their priority of right under the Common Law—no special statute existing for the protection of the settler, and the result is, thousands of acres of good arable land lie vacant and tenantless, because water cannot be obtained to irrigate them with; this, too, in the heart of one of the finest agricultural valleys in the State. A feeble attempt has been made on the part of our Senator to mitigate this evil, but it proved abortive; and how long the plodding farmer must continue to steal the water that raises his children's bread, or how long the agricultural interest of our young State must be held subservient to the *milling* interest, is a question for our Solons to answer. "You may grind quartz by steam, but you can't raise barley."

Genoa is the oldest town in the State—was settled by the Mormons in 1850. It is the county seat—the only town in the county; boasts a new court-house erected at an expense of $20,000, and is undoubtedly one of the best in the State; also a brick school-house, and about 150 souls. The transfer of the travel from the Placerville to the Dutch Flat route has had a Sunday afternoon effect upon it, which time will most likely render chronic.

Walker River Valley, like Carson Valley, is a grass and grain growing section. Distance from market renders the hay crop of little or no value beyond the local demand. An unusual quantity of barley was raised there this season, which will be increased each year until Walker Valley assumes its position as one of the leading grain growing sections of our State.

West Walker River courses the valley from one end to the other, affording unlimited facilities for irrigation, etc.

COUNTY BOUNDARY.

I desire to call your attention to the fact that the county lines are not established, and much dissatisfaction exists in consequence thereof. Parties who reside for miles on either side of the line claim their residence wherever it suits their individual purposes, and not unfrequently escape paying their taxes altogether.

MINES.

No paying mines exist in this county. The Sierra, located in the mountains near Genoa, was for several years thought to be one of the best prospective mines in the State. But after an expenditure of about $125,000, and five years' constant labor, work has been entirely suspended. The Mammoth ledge is still being run for, with fair prospect of success. Work has been vigorously prosecuted upon this ledge for about the same length of time, and perhaps an expenditure of $100,000. Another prospectively rich mine exists about two miles south from Genoa, known as the Fitch, or Hot Spring mine. Considerable amounts have been expended here for the control of the title, but very little work has been done towards developing it. One tunnel was driven in to a considerable distance, that demonstrated the fact that hell or hot water was very close by, and it was consequently abandoned.

MILLS.

2 steam saw mills .... } Not running.
4 water saw mills .... }
1 grist mill..2 run of stone.

AGRICULTURAL PRODUCTS, ETC.

Estimated quantity of acres in county............................960,000
Estimated quantity of acres grazing .:.........................200,000
Estimated quantity of acres tillable...........................100,000
Estimated quantity under cultivation............................ 7,000
Estimated quantity of meadow................................... 25,000
Estimated number of horses.....................................   800
Estimated number of cattle..................................... 1,800
Estimated number of swine......................................   400

    Tons of grain—
Wheat .... 70 ⎫
Barley ....350 ⎬   570
Oats ....150 ⎭
Potatoes, tons   400
Maize, tons   15

Wood, cords, 4000; value, $3 50 ....$14,000
Assessed value of land and improvements........................396,414
Personal property..325,080
                                                         ———
      Total....................................$721,494

FRUIT.

Strawberries and other fruits are being cultivated in limited quantities, but with marked success. The prevailing high winds are fatal to the peach, apple, &c., unless planted in some sheltered nook, but berries flourish luxuriantly, and yield equal to the average of New Jersey. It is estimated that strawberries will yield eighty bushels to the acre without extra attention. If so, Nevada may supply her own markets with these luxuries at no distant period.

                             ROB'T LYON,
                    Assessor, Douglas County, Nevada.

GENOA, Dec. 31, 1866.

ESMERALDA COUNTY.

                              AURORA, Sept. 26, 1866.
To Hon. S. H. Marlette,
      Surveyor General of Nevada:

DEAR SIR—In compliance with " An Act concerning the office of Surveyor eneral," I beg leave to submit the following report:
There has been no startling change during the year in this county, although me changes have taken place, most of them, I am happy to state, for the better. 'e have had one large fire, destroying a large portion of the business part of ɩ town of Aurora. Work upon the mines has been improving, and is being cɪducted in a manner which indicates work in earnest; and Esmeralda County ɹl no doubt continue to increase from now onward until she stands second to

9

none. The crops are about the same as last year: in fact, the report of last year will show nearly the present condition of this county; and from the present encouraging state of affairs I predict that the report of Esmeralda County from the Assessor of A.D. 1867 will contain an interesting account of many improvements.   Respectfully yours,
                                                        JAMES H. SMITH.

LANDER COUNTY.

AUSTIN, LANDER COUNTY, NEVADA, ⎰
                    November, 1866. ⎱

Hon. S. H. Marlette,
        Surveyor General of Nevada:

SIR—In compliance with law, and your circular, I hereby submit to you my annual Report of the property and resources of this county.

MINERAL RESOURCES AND MINING.

Most of the useful minerals are found in this county, but none of them are sought for much, excepting silver and gold. Salt is found and easily obtained from beds, and large quantities of it are used in the reduction of silver ore. It is delivered at the different mills and in Austin at about $45 per ton. The principal production of silver has been from the more developed mines in and about Austin. Lately many new, large and rich veins have been discovered and prospected in the eastern and southwestern part of the State, which show evidences of great and lasting wealth. The distance of Central and Eastern Nevada from the coast; the newness and undeveloped condition of the country, and consequent high cost of labor and supplies, and want of capital, has operated adversely to the interests of the miners, and caused many failures. As the country becomes more opened and cultivated, labor and materials lower in price, many mines which are now unproductive will be opened and made profitable, and occupation and means of good support thereby afforded for a large population. There are erected and in process of erection thirty-four steam hoisting works, varying in motive power from six to thirty horse power, and at an average cost of about $6,000 each. There are many other mines worked by horse whims and by hand. There are twenty-four mills for the reduction of silver ore, of which twenty-two are run by steam, and two by water power. They vary from five to twenty stamps each. The whole number of stamps is about two hundred and fifty. Dry-crushing and roasting is the general practice in the reduction of ores. About three-fourths of a ton of ore is crushed per stamp in twenty-four hours. It has been found necessary to roast all the ores to obtain a profitable return, which makes the cost of reduction much more than in the western portion of the State. The present cost of reduction at custom mills is $45 to $50 per ton. For the nine months ending 30th of September, 1866, there were reduced in this county, as per mining assessment roll, four thousand three hundred and sixty-four tons of ore, which produced $507,301, averaging in value $116.25 per ton. The deepest mining shaft, which is in the city of Austin, is upwards of five hundred feet in depth. There are several other shafts and inclines which reach three hundred feet and upwards. The best and most productive mines are those upon which deep shafts and inclines have been sunk. These are the Savage, Great Eastern, Diana, Yankee Blade, Whitlach, Union, Camargo, North River, Timoke, Cortez, and some others. Most of them produce ores which average in value $150 and upwards per ton.

BUILDING MATERIALS.

Lime is produced plentifully and cheaply. Good building stone is abundant. Good bricks are made easily in most parts of the county, and are sold at from $12 to $18 per thousand. Contrary to expectations, most of the lumber used in the erection of mills, hoisting works and building of other kinds has been obtained from our own mountains. Good timber scantling and boards of white pine are sold in this city at $100 per thousand feet. Some California and Carson lumber is used for finishing and particular work, which is sold for $125 to $175 per thousand feet.

WOOD.

The supply of wood continues to be abundant, and the price not exorbitant. Good wood is sold at the mills and in the city at $9 per cord.

STOCK.

There are in the county one thousand and eighty-five horses, two hundred and five mules, three thousand six hundred and fifty-seven horned cattle, one hundred and forty-two swine, one thousand five hundred and ninety sheep.

AGRICULTURE.

In consequence of frequent frosts, apparent barrenness of the land and absence of rains, it was thought by the first settlers that little of anything could be raised or cultivated; but from the large crops of grains and vegetables that have been successfully cultivated and gathered the past season, the doubts and fears of the inhabitants regarding agriculture have vanished, and they now feel satisfied that more than enough can be raised to supply our own wants, and for a much larger population. The products of the soil are now afforded at reasonable prices, and at much less than they can be brought from outside the county. The past season two thousand five hundred acres of grain, principally barley, together with some oats and wheat, have been raised. The yield averaged thirty bushels to the acre. Potatoes and vegetables of all the different kinds have been raised in large quantities. The crop of hay is large, and quantity cut unknown; the price is from $25 to $30 per ton. Barley is sold in the city at from five to six cents per pound. Potatoes are sold at from two to three cents per pound. The city of Austin, the county seat of Lander, has much improved in appearance and stability during the past year; several costly mills of brick have been erected in the city and vicinity, also numerous fine hoisting works. Two fine brick churches have been erected, one by the Methodist Episcopal Society, at a cost of about $40,000; the other by the Catholics, at a cost of about $30,000. A fine City Hall of brick, with lock-ups, has been put up by the city the past year; also several fine stores and dwellings of brick. There are two telegraphic lines running through the county, being the lines of the California State Telegraph Company and the Union Pacific Telegraph Company. The total number of miles of telegraph lines is about five hundred. The total assessed valuation of property in the county for the year 1866, is upwards of three millions of dollars.

Yours respectfully,   '   CHAS. O. BARKER,
County Assessor of Lander Co.

The *Reese River Reveille*, of December 1st, notices at length the report of the County Assessor of Lander Co. to Surveyor General, and points out some inaccuracies, as follows : The information conveyed in these official reports ought to be absolutely accurate. There are one or two errors in the report of our Assessor that are of sufficient importance to be corrected. It gives the number of quartz mills in the county at twenty-four, with about two hundred and fifty stamps. This is a careless, but serious misstatement. There are twenty mills in the county, with precisely two hundred and nineteen stamps. If the Assessor included in the number given the unfinished building of the New York and Lander Company, the Clifton " Mill," the Pioneer, at Big Creek, and the Coral and Aspinwall, at Amador, there would be twenty-four mills, with " about two hundred and fifty stamps ; " but they are not now mills for the reduction of quartz, any more than piles of brick and stone and iron and wood constitute such mills. The Pioneer, or Lippitts Mills, at Big Creek, was abandoned as an abortion shortly after it was built, and is now a total wreck. The New York and Lander (formerly the Pioneer) never has been a " mill " of any sort. The Coral and Aspinwall is a thunderbolt crusher—an exploded humbug—which absolutely cannot fitly crush potatoes, much less quartz ; while the little four-stamp mill at Clifton has been abandoned for nearly two years, and never successfully reduced anything but the hopes of the miner who carried his rock there, or the fortune of its owner or lessee. The incomplete structure of the New York and Lander Company may ultimately ripen into a quartz mill, but the others will certainly never again see the color of quartz. We have idle and inefficient mills enough in the country, without having abandoned abortions and myths foisted into the list of " mills " for the reduction of silver ore. In enumerating the " best and most productive mines," we should have found room for such old and well developed mines as the Oregon, North Star, and Metacom. While giving names, why did not the report specify them ? In the statement of the cost of the Catholic Church, which is given at $30,000, there is a considerable error, which we have been requested to correct. The whole cost of that edifice, when completed, will not exceed $9,000, in gold. We attribute these errors to carelessness and haste, which would seriously affect the reputation of a daily journal, and should not mar and lessen the value of an official report.

LYON COUNTY.

DAYTON, LYON COUNTY, NEVADA,
November 13th, 1866.

Hon. S. H. Marlette:

SIR—Our annual report is brief. The only addition to our reports of past year is the erection of a mill and furnace for working the tailings coming down Gold Cañon, for which a reservoir has been made, and about 200,000 tons saved. The mill at present is, unfortunately, closed by litigation. One mill has been destroyed by fire during the year. The rest appear to be doing a good business. The few farmers in the county appear satisfied with their crops, there being no material difference from last year's report. Our mines are undeveloped. Nut pine wood is the staple of the county. The Sutro Tunnel is expected soon to be under headway for the Comstock. We must apologize for the meagreness of this report, but it is difficult to make a lengthy one without the material.

Respectfully submitted,
JOHN DAY, Surveyor,
D. L. SMITH,
Assessor of Lyon County.

ORMSBY COUNTY.

. CARSON CITY, December 15, 1866.

To the Honorable S. H. Marlette,
Surveyor General of Nevada:

SIR—I herewith transmit to you my statistical report for the current year, containing such information as I have been able to obtain from reliable sources, and as taken from the Assessment Roll of this county, with some general observations tending to show the condition and resources of the county.

It has been almost a matter of impossibility for me to obtain a correct account of the agricultural and other products of the county, on account of the insufficiency of time allowed the Assessors for performing their official duties, and the inability or unwillingness of those engaged in agricultural and other pursuits to give true and exact statements of the condition and products of the enterprise in which they are engaged. Consequently, I have to compile from very incomplete and unreliable information, and make returns that will not convey much useful knowledge nor be of much interest to the State, aware of the fact that the aim proposed by the legislation demanding from the Assessors statistical reports is not attained.

AGRICULTURAL AND GRAZING LAND.

The estimate of the aggregate quantity of land in Ormsby County, used for or adapted to tillage and grazing, is 8,000 acres; being mostly confined to the valley in the vicinity of Carson City, and a few mountain ravines and meadows with some narrow bottoms on Carson River and along Clear Creek; of this amount of land about one-half is grazing and hay land, the remainder being adapted to the raising of grain and all kinds of vegetables natural to this latitude. The hills and sage-brush plains in this country, as in other portions of the State, furnish an excellent quality of bunch grass, upon which stock can feed and thrive well during summer and fall.

TIMBER LAND.

The timber land in Ormsby County comprises about 20,000 acres, situated on the west side of the county, commencing at the base of the mountain range about three miles west of Carson City, and extending west between the north and south boundary of the county to Lake Bigler. These lands contain a heavy growth of pine and fir timber, which is easy of access, and which will (on account of the limited quantity of timber land within our borders) be of vast future importance to the State. In addition to the above described lands, there are about 2,000 acres of piñon (pine timber) land situated in the southeastern corner of the county, bordering on Douglas and Lyon Counties. The timber upon the last mentioned land is of little use except for fuel, large quantities of which are being cut into cord wood and transported to market.

Although the amount of tillable land in this county is not large, the extensive water power afforded by the Carson River and numerous other streams coming down from the mountains, the heavy growth and excellent quality of the timber, and the facility with which it can be converted into lumber, compensate in a great measure for the want of farming lands, the wood, lumber and milling business forming the principal industrial feature of the county. The cord wood assessed in this county the present year amounts to 20,000 cords; of this amount about 14,000 cords are the product of this county. The remainder was floated down the Carson River from Alpine County, California. The estimated amount of lumber manufactured in the county during the present year is seven million feet, two million feet of which is from the timber lands of this county, the remainder is from Alpine County, California; the logs, like the wood, having been floated down the Carson River to Empire City, in this county, and manufactured into lumber and square timber at Messrs. Russell & Co.'s sawmill situated at that place.

AGRICULTURAL PRODUCTS, 1866.

Hay raised (tons) 200
Wheat " " 25
Oats " " 50
Barley " " 105
Potatoes " " (estimated) 250

The hay crop of the present year has not been as heavy as that of the preceding year, but cereals and all kinds of vegetables have yielded an excellent crop, the average yield of grain being about forty bushels to the acre.

LIVE STOCK.

	Number.
Horses owned	310
Mules "	119
Working oxen owned	448
Milch cows "	200
Other cattle "	50
Sheep "	250
Swine "	500

Animals slaughtered during year 1865 :

	Number.
Cattle exceeding three months old	1,205
Cattle under three months old	75
Sheep and lambs	2,077
Swine	171
Total	3,528

Animals slaughtered 1866, January to July inclusive—seven months :

	Number.
Cattle exceeding three months old	708
Cattle under three months old	54
Sheep and lambs	1,022
Swine	87
Total	1,871

The foregoing account of live stock is taken from the Assessment Roll of the present year; the cattle slaughtered, from returns made to the Federal Assessor. There is little or no stock raised in this county, most, if not all, of the cattle slaughtered having been driven to this market from California.

MINES AND MINERALS.

Mining in Ormsby County has not occupied the attention of the people to any great extent during the last two years, and at present there are no producing mines in this county, although quartz ledges are found in different parts of the county, all more or less impregnated with the precious metals. Near the base of the mountains, about three miles west of Carson City, is located the Athens Mine, the rock of which prospects very well in gold and silver. There has been some work done upon this mine, but it has not been sufficiently opened to determine its real character. There are other veins of quartz rock in the same vicinity, which, it is said, prospect well, but at present there is no work being done upon them. Should they prove to be permanent and paying ledges, their value will be enhanced by the extreme facility with which they can be worked and the ores reduced, owing to their proximity to wood and water power. In the foothills, near Cedar Creek, a number of ledges were located some time in the years 1861 and 1862, which, it is said, prospected well in both gold and silver, and extensive prospecting operations were set on foot. Many shafts were sunk, houses for the accommodation of workmen erected, and other expenses incurred, indicating a high degree of confidence in these ledges on the part of those opening them, but owing to the want of capital on the part of those who located them, work has been suspended, and most of them abandoned.

In Sullivan District, east of Carson River, a great number of ledges were located in the summer of 1860, but were subsequently abandoned. Lately, copper ore was discovered on the east side of Carson River, about six miles from Carson City, which, I have been informed, assays from forty to sixty per cent. of copper; but, as yet, there has been nothing done to indicate the extent of the ledge. There is also in the same vicinity a gold and silver bearing ledge, known as the "Wood Chopper Ledge," which prospects extremely well and is about twelve feet wide, but, like all others, remains undeveloped for want of capital.

It is confidently believed that there are many ledges in this county bearing gold, silver and copper that will pay when the cost of working them shall become less.

LIME.

There are extensive deposits of limestone at many points in the county—one about half a mile south of Carson City, and another on the east side of Carson ver.

BUILDING MATERIALS.

There is an abundance of building stone in this county, both sandstone and granite, unequaled for the excellence of the article and the facility with which it can be obtained. Suitable earths for making brick abound in many portions of the county.

QUARTZ MILLS.

There are eight quartz mills in this county, all of which, with the exception of two, the Sierra and Mexican mills, are in constant operation, reducing ores from the mines of Storey County—the former not having been in operation since March, 1865, and the latter having been mostly engaged in working over tailings which had accumulated in the reservoir.

THE FOLLOWING LIST

Embraces all the Quartz Mills in the County, showing the capacity of each, the number of Stamps, and the amount of
Ores worked by each during the years 1865–6:

10

TABULAR "LIST OF MILLS"

Name of Mill	Owner.	Location.	When built......	Estimated cost...	Assessed value...	Motive Power....	No. Horse Power.
Santiago ...	Santiago Company	Carson River, 4 miles below Empire.....	1861	....	$ 45,000	water	125
Vivian	P. Frothingham. ..	Carson River, 3¼ ml's below Empire.....	1861	$ 45,000	26,000	water & steam	65 45
Merrimac...	Merrimac Mill Co.	Carson River, 2 miles below Empire.....	1861	50,000	45,000	water	100
Brunswick..	Bank of California.	Carson River, 1¼ ml's below Empire.....	1863-4	50,000	25,050	water & steam	60
Yellow J'ckt	Yellow Jacket Co.	Carson River, ¼ mile below Empire.....	1864-5	200,000	135,000	water	....
Mexican....	* Mexican Mill Co.	Empire City........	1862	300,000	75,000	water	180
Carson	Bank of California	Three miles west of Carson City.......	1861	12,000	12,000	water	90
Sierra.......	Harrington&Beach	Three miles west of Carson City.......	1862	12,000	3,000	steam & water	25

* The tailings reworked by the Mexican Mill are not included in the amount of ores worked, they having been the products of ores worked prior to 1865, and are assessed as personal property. The manner of working them is by putting them through the pans without recrushing or grinding. I have no knowledge of the yield per ton, but am informed that they yield more profit to the mill than can be made by working rock.

IN ORMSBY COUNTY.

No. of Stamps	Weight of Stamps	Fall of Stamps	No. of Wheels	Kind of Wheel	Wood per cord	Tons per 24 hours	No. of Miles from Mines	Men employed	Hauling, per ton	No. of Tubs	No. of Pans	Kind of Pans	No. of Agitators	No. of Breakers	No. of Grinders	No. Tons worked during 1865	No. Tons worked in 9 months, 1866
		in.			$				$								
24	550	9	2	Central Dis.	7 50	40	10	15	4 50	..	18	Wheeler Hepburn & Coleman	..	1	1	6620.85	8037.23
16	650	12	1	Breast	7 50	30	10½	12	4 50	..	8	Wheeler	..	..	..	6549	5782
20	1000	12	1	Turbine	7 50	40	12	20	4 50	..	15 4	Wheeler Knox	..	..	..	9623.36	8974.35
8	1050	10	1	Central Dis.	7 50	20	12	12	4 50	..	1 9	Varney Varney	4	..	..	4544.18	4460.66
40	900	8	1	Turbine	7 50	80	12	36	4 50	..	30	Hepburn & Peterson	..	1	..	....	18795.31
44	900	9	1	Overshot	7 50	75	12		4 50	..	12	Hepburn	..	1	1	*2032 65	* 676.46
15	500	10	2	Overshot	5 00	20	18	8	5 50	3	5	Wheeler	..	..	..	1047	1376
8	500	8	1	Overshot	5 00	12	18	..	5 50	..	16 2	Knox Hepburn	..	..	..	344	....

Total of Tons of Ores worked........................ *30761.34 48102.01

* It will be seen by the statement of ores worked, that the number of tons worked during nine months of the year 1866, is greater than during the whole of the year 1865.

TOLL ROADS.

The Lake Bigler Road, owned by the Lake Bigler Road Company, commences at Carson City, runs up King's Cañon to its source, thence along the side of the mountain to the summit, thence to Lake Bigler, thence along the shore of Lake Bigler to Friday's Station. This road was built during the year 1863, at a cost of one hundred and twenty-five thousand dollars. Its length is twenty-one miles, ten miles of which are in this county, and the remainder in Douglas County. This road is kept in excellent condition, and the heaviest grade is eight feet to one hundred.

The Bedford and McDonald Road, now owned by the Devil's Gate Toll-road Company, commences at Carson City and runs along the foothills to the north of Empire City, to the Half-way House, a distance of six miles.

The Curry Road, leading from Carson City to Empire City, via the State Prison, a distance of four miles, is macadamized from Carson City to the State Prison with sandstone, which, though it slacks to a certain extent in extreme wet weather, still forms a tolerably firm bed, and is, in reality, a great improvement to the road.

In addition to these roads is the Walton Road, ten miles in length; the Washoe and Eagle Valley Road, one and one-half miles in length; the Marble Cañon Road, seven miles in length; and Craner & Co.'s Road, some twelve miles in length. The two latter roads are chiefly used as wood roads.

TELEGRAPH LINES.

We have about thirty miles of telegraph line in this county, belonging to the California State Telegraph Company, with an office in Carson City.

METEOROLOGICAL OBSERVATIONS.

From a record kept in Carson City eighteen months in 1864–5, by C. L. Anderson, M.D., I am permitted to make the following abstract:

Barometer.—Mean height of eighteen months 25.327

Thermometer.—Mean of eighteen months in 1864 and 1865:

Month	Temp			Mean
January	29 degrees	Fahrenheit		Mean of
February	28	"	"	Spring Months,
March	40	"	"	50 degrees.
April	52	"	"	Mean of
May	60	"	"	Summer Months,
June	60	"	"	67 degrees.
July	70	"	"	Mean of
August	71	"	"	Autumn Months,
September	60	"	"	48 degrees.
October	49	"	"	Mean of
November	36	"	"	Winter Months,
December	34	"	"	28 degrees.

Total mean . . . . 49 degrees.
Without frost in 1864 . . . . 75 consecutive days.
Without frost in 1865 . . . . 87 consecutive days.

Lowest temperature, February 20th, 1865—14 degrees below zero, at seven o'clock, A.M.

Highest temperature, July 24, 1864—94 degrees, at two o'clock, P.M.

ASSESSMENT OF PROPERTY—1866.

Value of real estate and improvements thereon $920,816
Value of personal property 740,335

Total value of property assessed... ....$1,661,151
Estimated value of property exempt from taxation under
the provisions of section four of the Revenue Law, not
including school lands or unoccupied lands belonging to
the United States............................ 100,000

Total...................................$1,761,151

In conclusion, I would suggest the propriety of furnishing the different County Assessors with elaborate printed blanks for the collection of statistics, to the end that uniformity in the returns may be observed throughout the State. All of which is respectfully submitted.

H. H. BENCE,
County Assessor of Ormsby County.

SUPPLEMENTARY REPORT.

CARSON CITY, January 3d, 1867.

Hon. S. H. Marlette:

SIR—Your interrogatories eliciting further statistical information in relation to the resources of Ormsby County are answered as follows, viz:

1. By a careful estimate made by competent judges, the amount of timber, lumber and wood contained in the 20,000 acres of timber land is, of lumber and timber:

Fifty "M" feet to the acre, 1,000,000 "M" ft.
Market price at Virginia City, $30 per "M," equal to.$30,000,000
Cost of cutting, hauling and manufacturing at mill, $12
per "M"....................$12,000,000
Cost of transportation, $14 per "M".... 14,000,000

Total cost delivered at Virginia City 26,000,000

Profit, $4 per "M"...........................$ 4,000,000

Of wood, it is estimated that there could be obtained from the tops, small trees, and trees not suitable for lumber or square timber, fifty cords of wood to the acre, making a total of 1,000,000 cords. The average price of wood at Carson City is $6.50 per cord, equal to.........................$6,500,000
Cost of cutting, $1.50 per cord,............................. 1,500,000
Cost of hauling to Carson City, $4 per cord,................... 4,000,000

Profit, $1 per cord $1,000,000

82

I would here remark that these lands have been surveyed by the United States Surveyor, and the plats deposited in the United States Land Office at Carson City. They are mostly embraced within the limits of Township Fifteen, north of Range Nineteen, east, according to the United States land surveys. It will be readily observed by reference to the foregoing estimate, that these lands are not only valuable at the present time, but must, on account of the limited amount of timber land within the borders of this State, as the State grows older, and the demand for wood, lumber and timber, becomes greater, as evidently will be the case, increase greatly in value.

It is confidently believed that it would be good policy on the part of this State, to cause to be selected as soon as possible a portion of the lands donated by Congress to this State, from among the unappropriated timber lands situated in the range of mountains along the western border of the State.

2. SAW MILLS.

Messrs. Russell & Co.'s saw mill is situated on the west bank of the Carson River, one quarter of a mile below Empire City. It was built in 1862, and has since been enlarged. The timber used is cut in Alpine County, California, a distance by the river of eighty miles, and driven down the stream to the mill. It takes about forty days to run a drive of logs to the mill. This mill is the best mill in the county, being a steam mill with ninety horse-power engine, and can cut 40,000 feet of lumber every twenty-four hours.

The cost of logs and transportation to the mill is eight dollars per " M " feet.

The cost of manufacturing into lumber, four dollars per " M," making the cost of lumber at the mill about twelve dollars per " M " feet.

The mill has advantages not possessed by any other saw mill in the county, its situation being some eight miles nearer market, and the cost of timber, delivered at the mill, not greater than that delivered at other mills.

There are four other saw mills in Ormsby County, two of which, the "Cayota" and "Clear Creek" mills, are situated on Clear Creek, about eight miles southwest of Carson City; the remaining two, the "Monitor" and "Ashes" mills, are situated on the timber land, about five miles west of Carson. Neither of the four last mentioned mills has been in operation much of the time during the last year, except the Monitor Mill, which has been engaged manufacturing lumber, but I have been unable to ascertain the exact amount of its operations.

3. The average yield of hay is one ton to the acre, that of potatoes three tons.

4. ANIMALS SLAUGHTERED DURING YEAR 1865.

Description.	No.	Cost.
Cattle exceeding three months old	1,205	$19,280 00
Cattle under three months old	75	225 00
Sheep and lambs	2,077	5,192 00
Swine	171	2,907 00
Total	3,528	$27,604 00

ANIMALS SLAUGHTERED IN 1866, JANUARY TO JULY INCLUSIVE, 7 MONTHS.

Description.	No.	Cost.
Cattle exceeding three months old......................	708	$21,240 00
Cattle under three months old.........................	54	270 00
Sheep and lambs.......................................	1,022	3,577 00
Swine......	87	1,827 00
Total.......................................	1,871	$26,914 00

5. Wood would cost (delivered at the mines situated west of Carson City) four dollars per cord, at those situated east of the Carson River, six dollars.

6. The cost of manufacturing lime is sixteen dollars per ton, that of brick, ten dollars per thousand.

7. Building stone costs at the quarries, situated two miles east of Carson City, one dollar and twenty-five cents per perch; cost of hauling to Carson City, one dollar and seventy-five cents—making the total cost at Carson City three dollars per perch.

I am, sir, very respectfully, your obedient servant,

H. H. BENCE,
County Assessor, Ormsby County.

NYE COUNTY.

To Hon. S. H. Marlette,
Surveyor General of Nevada:

DEAR SIR—I beg leave to submit the following report of the condition of our county :

FARMING AND GRAZING LAND.

The grazing land of Nye County embraces nearly one-half of its entire limits, but the tillable land consists of probably fifty thousand acres, about four thousand of which, in Monitor, Smoky, Reese River, and Pahranagat valleys, are settled, and produce excellent vegetables. The hay crop amounts to twelve hundred and fifty tons, and about one hundred tons of potatoes have been raised in the same vicinity, and one hundred tons of barley, thus dispelling the doubt that has heretofore existed concerning the successful raising of barley. We have fifteen hundred head of cattle, about five hundred head of the same being work oxen; about three hundred head of horses, one hundred head of mules, and about one hundred and fifty hogs.

QUARTZ MILLS.

There are eight mills in the county: one at Ione, cost about $50,000; one at San Antonio, ten stamps, cost $75,000; one at Pahranagat, five stamps, cost about

$30,000; one at Twin River, twenty stamps, been running since the middle of October, cost $200,000; one at Belmont, ten stamps, cost $30,000, been running since the middle of August; one at Silver Peak, ten stamps, cost $50,000; one at Red Mountain, three stamps, cost $4,000; Knickerbocker and Nevada, about three miles south of Ione, twenty stamps, cost $100,000, been running since June. The Atlantic and Pacific Company, six miles south of Ione, have most of the machinery on the ground for a twenty-stamp mill. There is also one mill in process of erection in Hot Creek District, at a cost of probably $50,000. The crushing power of the above mill is equal to about one thousand pounds of quartz in twenty-four hours, for each stamp. In the vicinity of Ione the ore requires roasting. In the more recently discovered districts, as Philadelphia and Hot Creek, the ore is being worked with much profit without roasting.

SAW MILLS.

There are six saw mills in the county, their capacity being about three thousand feet per diem. Lumber at the mills is worth from fifty to eighty dollars per thousand.

In regard to minerals, such as copper, galena, iron, etc., the same can be said as was set forth in my report of last year.

GENERAL REVIEW.

As was predicted, our most sanguine hopes as to the final mineral wealth and healthful prosperity of Nye County are fast being realized. The newly discovered mines in the eastern part of the county have added and bid fair to add vastly to its wealth and growing importance. Since my last report, the mining districts of Philadelphia and Hot Creek have been discovered, where there are mines being developed which thus far are unsurpassed by any in the State. The mines of Pahranagat are also rising in importance, and the vast amount of agricultural land lying in the vicinity of the mines greatly enhances their value.

Respectfully submitted,
STEPHEN ROBERTS,
Assessor of Nye County, Nevada.

Ione, November 14, 1866.

STOREY COUNTY.

S. H. Marlette,
  Surveyor General of Nevada:

DEAR SIR—In compliance with the duties of my office in connection with that of Surveyor General, I have to report as follows:

In regard to agricultural, horticultural, grazing or grass lands, I beg leave to refer you to my annual report of last year.

STATE AND COUNTY REVENUE.

The assessment roll of this county for the present fiscal year foots up in the aggregate $6,343,353.20. The levy being two and ninety-hundredths per cent., brings the amount of tax $183,957.24.

TAX FROM PROCEEDS OF MINES.

The tax derived from the proceeds of mines for the first three quarters of the fiscal year A.D. 1866, is $24,500.

PERSONAL PROPERTY TAX.

I have collected the present year of tax on personal property—having no realty connected therewith—in round numbers, $17,000. In regard to the defects of the Revenue Law in connection with the assessing and collecting of this tax, I beg leave to refer you to my report of last year.

POLL TAX.

The amount of revenue derived from this source in this county is $19,712. This law in connection with the registry law should be amended. Men who are maimed, cripples—those who are not able bodied—should be exempt from this tax, the legislature under our State Constitution having full power to do so. The imposing this tax on the above named classes of men is not in accordance with the spirit of our free institutions. Again: the law as it now exists, dividing the collection of this tax between the County Assessor and the Justices of the Peace of the respective counties, produces infinite confusion, and is the principal reason causing the delay of this report. The law gives the Assessor and Justices until the first day of November to make their final settlements with the County Auditor; so it is impossible for the Assessor to get the necessary statistics at an earlier date. The collection of this tax, together with the registration of voters, should be given entirely to the Assessor, as is the law in California, or should be given entirely to the Justices of the respective counties.

QUARTZ MILLS AND ARASTRAS.

In regard to quartz mills and arastras (their number, capacity, aggregate amount of horse power, etc.) I beg leave to refer to my report of last year, merely stating that considerable improvements have been made since that time in amalgamating pans, and in the saving of the precious metal.

11

Number of horses in the county, 450; mules, 400; milch cows, 275; swine. 850. For number of animals slaughtered I respectfully refer to my report last year.

MINES AND MINING.

During the past year great and permanent improvements in the nature of buildings, and of heavy and powerful machinery, have been placed on many of the principal mines in this county. The proofs and prospects of the richness and permanency of the mines were never so good as at the present time.
All of which is respectfully submitted.
                    LLOYD FIGELL,
                        Assessor of Storey County.
Virginia, December 8th, 1866.

REMARKS ON MILLING AND MINING OPERATIONS OF REESE RIVER.

We have no country on record in which both milling and mining operations have been taken up with such zeal, and where, considering all circumstances, such rapid progress has been made therein, as on the Pacific Coast, principally the States of Nevada and California. In the year 1850 the first attempt was made in the above named States to extract precious metals by anything but mechanical means—namely, washing. But since that time manifold have been the endeavors to improve on the beneficiation of gold and silver from their ores. In fact the manipulations of amalgamation for one, in particular, known in other older countries for so many centuries past, have never been so fully tried and experimented upon in so short a space of time, and with such success, as here. It is natural that this one, if not the most efficacious of all methods of extraction of precious metals, has so much more occupied the general attention, because the resources and circumstances of the country did not admit of any other. It is true operations were made easy by the richness and character of the ores which the country afforded, but metallurgical operations being comparatively a new thing, rich tailings occurred, and losses were sustained which gradually, more especially of late, have greatly diminished, but not to such an extent as to justify a disregard for further improvements thereon.

AMALGAMATION AS AN ONLY METHOD FOR US.

The most simple method of extraction, but at the same time subject to greater absolute, unavoidable losses in precious metals than any other, and for that reason almost abandoned in other countries where the general state of things admits of more completed methods: it has its own peculiarities, which, to insure success, have to be studied thoroughly, and followed in every point. In a great many cases, in both States, operations on a large scale have proven fatal to the purses of the operators, from the fact of having paid too little attention to these points. The mineral wealth of this country being so great, many mining districts affording such rich ores that the momentary natural success contented the miner and millman, they condescendingly left their probable successor to extract that which they did not think worth their attention at the time. But these rich ores are becoming more scarce; $1,000 to $6,000 Comstock ores, in bodies of 20 to 2,000 tons, are not a daily occurrence, and more and more attention must be paid to lower grade ores than there was formerly. The mines yielding rich ores and insuring lucrative operations are but very few indeed, whilst the number of those giving but poor ores yield by thousand fold the larger revenues, as for instance, according to Humboldt:

The Valentiana Mine (Mexico) produced £2,800,000 out of ores containing sixteen and three-quarter ounces gold and silver per ton, which would be equal to $16.93 per ton value.

The Potosi Mine (Mexico) produced £219,000,000 out of ores having a value of £2 18s. 0d. per ton.

The Pasco Mine (Mexico) produced £62,000,000 out of ores of a value of £3 13s. 0½d. per ton.

Bollardt gives the value of the ores coming from the desmontes (dead heaps) at the Valentiana Mine at £7 0s. 0d., giving a yield of £5 1s. 0d.

In Lima, now, eighteen mines yield annually 640,000 ounces of silver from ores varying from ninety to ninety-six ounces per cajon, (cajon has 5,000 pounds avoirdupois) which would be at the rate of $38.45 per ton.

The Mina Serro de Pasco, Peru, works ores four to five marks per cajon, (Peruvian cajon, three tons) which makes the ores worth $13.50 per ton, and yields annually $4,000,000.

All Freiberg yields annually $1,500,000 from its mines, the average ores of which cannot compete in richness with those from any of our fifth class mining districts. At the same time, it is true that the Saxony government has to defray the yearly occurring deficiency, varying from $15,000 to $100,000.

Mining operations, carried on so extensively in Europe, for instance in Hanover, Hungary, and Bohemia, produce, in comparison, much lower grade ores than the mines on this coast, and still nearly all of the former are very productive.

A branch of mining to which so little attention has been paid as yet, and which is, so to speak, almost unknown in this country, forms one of those mining operations, without the aid of which a great many of the above named mines, and hundreds not named, and many now prominent mining districts of the old world, would have had to be abandoned as worthless long ago, is that of concentrating or dressing the lower grade ores to such an extent as to fit them for amalgamation or smelting, as the case may be. Especially in the last few years, concentration of ores has arrived at a high state of perfection, and its results have been the cause of becoming an exclusive study to the mining engineer. As above said, in a great many of our mining districts we have large veins, which (if the expression is admittable) immortalized themselves through the massiveness and richness of their ores, and moreover, through their character, making mining and beneficiation so easy, and dressing dispensable. Only these districts have become generally known and appreciated, whilst others, and in comparison their number exceeds far that of the former, have not been thought worthy of exploration or the investment of capital, which would not have been the case had "dressing and concentration" of their ores been universally understood. Mining districts outside of California and Nevada, which yield but poor ores compared to those of these States, give in comparison, as above named, much larger revenues than our wealthiest mines have on the Pacific coast. In those cases where metals are obtained from ores by smelting, for instance, concentration is indispensable, because few metals occur massive enough, and free of gangue matter, (as iron ores) to justify a direct beneficiation; and still rarer are those ores, for example, some species of copper ores, (cigsfer schiefer) whose vein matrix is of such a character as to enable the metallurgist, with the addition of very little flux, to obtain good fusible slags.

Again, in other cases, (Washoe) concentration is dispensed with, *when you are by local circumstances compelled* to beneficiate gold and silver ores by amalgamation or other methods of extraction in a wet way. But if these ores should be of a character requiring washing, (as for instance Reese River ores) the cost of extraction is so high that lower grade ores cannot be worked profitably, and have to be laid aside as worthless. Again, in the working of very rich ores, the residue (tailings) obtained are to be compared with the above named low grade ores; and although it is known to every millman that this residue has a to-be-regarded value, nothing can be done with it, and it is an entire loss, if not dressed to such a grade that at least some of its metals can be obtained. That dressing or concentration with success is not adaptable to all classes of ores is not to be denied, but this waste affords a great many instances where it should by all means be adopted. Taking, for instance, the Reese River mining district as an example: Operations were commenced with great hopes for the future, the ores which some of the veins produced were exceedingly rich, and led to the investment of much capital; but such rich ores cannot be obtained in quantities sufficient to keep the already established extensive mills in continuous operation. The costs of milling here vary from $35 to $45, with a yield of 80 *to* 85 per cent. of their value in silver, (by fire assay) and ores of an absolute value of $40 to $50 per ton will scarcely cover milling expenses. Any one acquainted with this district knows that the greater bulk of ores taken from its mines is of a low grade, which has to be laid aside as worthless. The geology and topography of Reese River Mining District has been so often described in reports and pamphlets that it is useless to refer to that subject. It is universally known that the ores occur in small veins in granite, (and often irregular) having quartz as a vein matrix, and what there is of ore is of a very rich character, (see below, where the ores are classified) but often disseminated through the quartz in such a manner as to make but a poor average ore, which for want of easy mode of separation has often to be left standing in the mine, but oftener to be excavated to facilitate the stoppings of the vein. The veins are so irregular through their frequent dislocations that it is sometimes impossible to mine the ore pure—it *will* become mixed with the poorer ores, but what is still worse, with the granite, which latter is in such a high state of decomposition that a few hours' exposure to the atmosphere will make it crumble to a coarse sandy mass, and mix with the ore. Any one not conversant with this circumstance cannot credit the fact to what an enormous extent the ores diminish in value thereby; and this intermixing cannot always be prevented, even by using the greatest possible care in mining. From all these causes the cost of those ores which are extracted pure and fit for milling is considerable, and the afterwards absolutely necessary assorting by hand is an additional expense.

How much cheaper would it be to extract the whole ledge, regardless of assorting the ores in the mine, dispensing with that expensive care now requisite to separate the ores, and classify them by machinery afterwards? Much more ore could be taken out in this way than there is at present, and the cost of four or five fold the amount of tons would be but a trifle more, if any. It is strange that nothing has been done in this whole mining district to concentrate either ores or tailings—not even a common wash blanket is to be seen (and I have the honor to have been the first one who ever put the common Russian riffle in use here). In a great many places great wealth lies deposited in form of tailings and low grade ores, which have accumulated since the time when very rich ores were only amalgamated, in fact when only such would justify milling; and then the resources of the country at that period were so very limited that only a portion of the silver of these rich ores was extracted, especially in those days when roasting the ores had not been generally adopted. Even now some mills are beneficiating chloride ores, which contain a considerably quantity of sulphurets of silver, and which latter are an entire loss, if the ores are not roasted previous to amalgamating them. That from this mode of working, tailings of some value must exist, there can be no doubt.

The veins of Reese River yield two entirely different classes of ores. First group—as ores we have:

Pyrargyrite, specific gravity.. 5.8
Stephanite, or Melanglarz, specific gravity........................... 6.3
Polybasite, specific gravity... 6.1

With an accompanying vein matter, etc., of—
Quartz, specific gravity at highest.................................. 2.6
Calcspar, specific gravity.. 2.7
Manganspar, specific gravity.. 3.4

The calc, or limespar, occurs only subordinately, and is sometimes disseminated through the country-rock, lying in close proximity to the vein, and sticks often with great tenacity to the richest portions of the lode, and is therefore frequently obtained with the ores.

The ores from some of the most prominent mines, for example, the Oregon Mine, North Star, Great Eastern, Yankee Blade, etc., belong to the above first group.

Second group: These are the ores to which more attention should have been paid, as they form the larger bulk of all the second class ores, and have all *appearance and likelihood to continue to do so*. These ores set in universally below water level in all of the mines, and will probably fill, or rather compose, the entire vein in greater depths. Here we have:

Galena, specific gravity.. 7.5
Iron Pyrites, specific gravity...................................... 5.0
Copper Pyrites, specific gravity.................................... 4.2
Zincblende, specific gravity.. 4.1
Fahlor, (Fahlerz?) specific gravity................................. 4.5—5.1
(very rich in silver.)

Further, we have, but only subordinately, (more and more disappearing as the depth increases) pyrargyrite, stephanite, polybasite, but only in small spots, and many of the veins do not contain these ores at all. As accompanying gangue, we have here the same as in group number one, specific gravity not exceeding 2.9. Ores of this second group occur, for example, predominantly in Providential Mine, Stanger Mine. There exist, further, the ores near the surface—"chloride ores" (which brought Reese River at first into notice). They are not mentioned, as they, after amalgamation, (wet-crushing) give tailings which resemble in character the ores of the first group, above named. It will be seen what facilities for dressing these ores offer, taking in consideration that concentration depends upon the fact that when bodies of the *same form and size*, but of different density, (specific gravity) are forced by an equally divided uniform power through air or water, or inversely when water or air is driven against such bodies, then those bodies which possess the greatest density meet with the least resistance, and for this reason is separation made possible by proper machinery. The difference in specific gravity of the ores, and the barren substance (gangue) here, is so great, that even an imperfect observation of the above named rule, and only limited knowledge of the various mechanical manipulations employed in dressing ores, would, nevertheless, justify a surely successful trial, to illustrate and draw an approximate comparison.

Under the present method of mining in Reese River Mining District, one of the most prominent mines excavates and mines at an average:

Six tons of ore per day, at a cost of labor............$75 to $80 00
Machinery, etc.. 25 to 30 00

    Average...$105 00
Assorting by hand.. 15 00
And if the ores are worked to 83 per cent., (?) would cost: Milling,
    at $40 per ton, for five tons................................... 200 00

    Total cost..$320 00

By this method are obtained:
One and a half tons first class ore, average value..........$120 00 per ton:
    and three and a half tons second class ore, average value.. 75 00 per ton:
    and one ton, allowing value to be..................... 40 00 per ton.
    (valueless at present.)

As above stated, these five tons, obtained and beneficiated to 83 per cent. would give a yield of—total, $369.00; cost, $320.00. Net margin of gain $49.00, with a loss of $40.00, being in one ton waste. This calculation is made under favorable circumstances, the interest of requisite working capital not being included, as that varies so enormously in Reese River. Supposing the same mine is worked in such a manner as to excavate the entire lode from wall to wall, and obviate the laborious work of assorting twice, (once in the mine and once on the surface) do away with taking the ores out on cloths, (as is being done now) continuous filling and emptying of sacks—an incredible expense to any one not acquainted with Reese River mining operations—say, supposing these six tons of ore extracted with so much care could be easily increased to twenty tons per day by dispensing with all *now* requisite care, they would have an average value varying from $35.00 to $40.00 per ton, whilst the average of the above named six tons would not overreach $80.40 per ton.

Drawing the comparison that the six tons, at $80.40, would represent an absolute value of $483.00; the twenty tons, at $37.00, $740.00.

Allowing that the twenty tons can, at least, be dressed to $155.00 ore, with a natural occurring loss of twenty-five per cent. in dressing, reducing them to a bulk of three and one-half tons; allowing $25.00 per diem for extra mining expenses had in addition to the $105.00 had in extracting six tons only per day.

For amalgamating three and one-half tons........................ $ 84 00
    viz.: Amalgamating .... $ 6 00 per ton.
        Roasting .... 18 00 "

        Total............................. 24 00 "
And for crushing, preliminary to fit it for concentration, at the rate of
    $2.00 per ton for twenty tons, originally .... $ 40 00
And for concentration of twenty tons, and crushing before roasting,
    through sixty ☐ screens, of three and one-half tons: for the
    former, $4.00 per ton for twenty tons, and for the latter, $4.00
    per ton for three and one-half tons....................... 94 00

    Total cost of beneficiation, including concentration............ $348 00

The absolute value of twenty tons crude ore was................ $740 00
The occurring loss of twenty-five per cent. in dressing would be.... 185 00

Remaining absolute value of three and one-half tons of....... $555 00

Allowing eighty-three per cent. to be extracted by amalgamation there-
    from, would yield $460 00
Incurred entire costs, as above described...................... 348 00

Daily revenue $112 00

which, even allowing additional six per cent. for wear and tear of machinery
interest, etc., in addition to the ten per cent. already allowed in the above made
calculations, would still leave a better margin, working with dressing, as to mine
and mill, than is done and has been done heretofore.

The merits of concentration, under very unfavorable circumstances, with refractory material and the simplest of all machinery, can be seen daily all through
Washoe. Thousands of feet of plain-hearths fill all the ravines into which tailings are discharged, and are being worked profitably. [See Balch's estimate of
profits in Six-mile Cañon, on page 37, of this Report.—S. H. M.]

How much more profitable would concentration be if applied, for instance, in
Reese River. The requisite machinery for that purpose is all very simple, the
Reese River country affords every facility—plenty of clear water can be obtained,
and ores abundantly, and I allow myself to advance a few ideas regarding that
subject:

1. Assorting the ores in a rough manner would be requisite, according to their
richness and character, and their accompanying gangue-matter, which, in treating
Reese River ores, is not very laborious or expensive, as ores from one and the
same mine are generally very uniform and similar in character, and if a change
takes place the ores are very easily recognized.

2. Wet-crushing should universally be adopted. either through a battery,
crusher, or rollers. The crusher would be preferable, as the object is to obtain
the ores in a coarse powder—the finer pulp and slimes being subject to more
loss and costs in dressing than the coarser particles. If a battery is employed.
it should have sieves of not less than two ᵐᵐ holes, or from eight to twelve ☐
holes per inch. Such a battery could crush for stamp upwards of ten tons per
day: 500 pounds weight, sixty lift revolutions, thirteen-inch left.

3. Separation of the naturally obtained different sizes of " corn," which is the
most important point in dressing, and if neglected will cause failure, even if all
the other manipulations are carried out to perfection. There are a great variety
of machines in use for this purpose: the most feasible are rotary sieves. The
pulp coming from the battery, directly enters these sieves, (the more of them,
the easier the manipulations) with a stream of water, and all sands obtained under 1ᵐᵐ (or 25 ☐ holes to the inch) are better separated in funnel-shaped boxes,
such as are used universally in the European mines (Hartz, for instance). They
are machines constructed of wood, a square funnel 6 feet long, 2¾— 3 feet wide,
and 4 feet deep. The water, as a medium used here, enters at the bottom and
separates the sands (or "corn") in two or more different sizes, and allows the
slum or slimes with the very finest sands to run over.

4. The treatment of the different sizes of coarse or fine " corn," obtained in
different machines, are classified :

(1.) Sands obtained above 1ᵐᵐ diameter (or that which did not pass a 25 ☐
sieve) are most fully dressed on Jigger machines, (Setzmaschienen) such as are
in use in nearly all European mines. (For example, the third Thal Pockwerk
at Clausthal [Hartz, Europe] has 4 of these machines, and dresses 15 tons of

ore, requiring 330 cubic feet of water, and 1 horse power to drive them, assisted by 2 laborers.) The different sizes obtained by the rotary sieves, namely, above 1 $^{mm.}$ diameter, are worked all separately, but on the same machines.

(2.) Middlings, ranging from 1$^{mm.}$ diameter downwards, that class which was classified in two or more sizes in the funnel-shaped □ boxes, are best dressed on rotary continuous shaking tables, which require, according to size, from one-third to one-quarter horse power each, and will dress, if worked on uniform corn, according to the quality of the ore, from 4 to 15 tons in 24 hours. Their working capacity is greatly increased by paying attention to the separation of "corn" as above mentioned, each class is dressed separately, and the speed of the table regulated accordingly. The concentrator of Mr. Kustel would give, undoubtedly, excellent results with Reese River ores, as these ores are so much more easy to dress than Washoe ores as hardly to be compared.

(3.) The last and finest corn, slimes included, which run off from the sands above 1$^{mm.}$ diameter, is that portion of the ores which requires a little more attention than the coarser sands, especially where the difference in the specific gravity between the metal-bearing portion and the vein matter is not very great (as in Comstock ores). In Europe, these slimes, etc., are dressed on rotating sweep hearths, "Hunt's funnel hearth" being one of the best. The ores of Reese River could be just as well dressed on the common plain hearth, as it is now universally in use all over Washoe, thick, hairy blankets being greatly preferable to gunny sacks. All the manipulations and machinery described are very simple, and if once systematically constructed cannot fail to receive universal approbation. Reese River is by no means the only district in which we may look for success in concentrating ores. All the numerous copper and galena lodes now lying idle offer inducements enough to the enterprising capitalists, especially those districts which give us argentiferous galena ores of an assay value of $30 to $80 per ton : all of these are regarded as valueless, from the fact that, at the present, galena ores not containing at least 40 per cent. of lead, and not, at least, $100 per ton in silver, cannot possibly be profitably smelted, whilst by dressing, many of these ores could easily be brought to 60 per cent. in lead, with $200 in silver, occurring so abundantly, even allowing a loss of 35 to 40 per cent., the specific gravity of galena and quartz respectively (as generally accompanying vein matter) being 7.5 to 2.6.

C. A. LUCKHART,
Mining Engineer.

The Washoe *Eastern Slope* of December 8th says : "Some of our Eastern exchanges, in speaking of this State, say that 'it is a desert, capable only of producing sage brush.' The face of the country furnishes *prima facie* evidence of the truth of the statement, and experience has proved, and is yearly proving its entire falsity. Nevada has a very large breadth of most excellent farming land, that even under the present inefficient system of cultivation produces large crops of cereals. We attempted some time since to gather some statistics showing the productiveness of Washoe Valley, but have not succeeded to any considerable extent, simply because no one seemed to take any interest in the matter, and we could not spare the time necessary to visit each farm. The small number that we have seen report as follows : Richard Sides raised on his ranch the past season, fourteen tons of barley ; J. D. Champion raised this season, six tons of wheat and sixteen tons of oats ; G. N. Folsom raised seventy tons of barley and fifteen tons of oats ; Ross Lewers harvested on his farm, thirty tons of barley and fourteen tons of oats ; Mr. Musgrove harvested sixty tons of barley and sixty tons of oats ; John Marshall raised thirty tons of barley, one ton of wheat, and thirteen tons of oats ; William Sides harvested eleven tons

of barley, one ton of wheat, and twelve tons of oats; Mr. Simmons harvested
forty-five tons of barley and eleven tons of oats; and Mr. Norcross harvested
twenty tons of wheat—making an aggregate of four hundred and ninety tons of
grain produced by nine farmers in this valley, besides a very heavy root and
hay crop. Estimating the value of this grain, on the ranch, at twelve and a
half cents per pound, it amounts to the snug little sum of $22,050, an average
of $2,450 per ranch. In addition to this, it is fair to presume that the hay crop,
root crop, growth of stock, and pasturage, would pay as much more. Verily!
we cannot see that the farmers of Washoe Valley are likely to call on outside
barbarians for aid or sympathy, though they are compelled to draw their support
from the desert sage-brush wastes of Nevada."

A NEW TEXTILE.

[From the Philadelphia Gazette.]

" The last discovery which comes to us from Nevada, is agricultural rather
than mineral, but very important. It is a new textile, such as was eagerly
sought when the rebellion broke out, but unsuccessfully. The plant now discovered has its home in the Humboldt Valley, where it grows in great quantities,
and can of course be made to grow more thriftily by cultivation, whilst, if it
has the value ascribed to it, it will soon be removed to other fields, and propa-
gated among regular crops. The plant is said by the discoverers to be superior
to any textile now in use. Though styled hemp, it is so called on account of its
closer similarity to that than any other growth. It has a stronger and finer
fibre than the proper hemp, and a much longer staple. In proportion to the
wood, too, the fibre is much more abundant. It can be more easily separated
than flax or hemp, and can be stripped clean from the stalk without preparation.
Nevada lies between thirty-seven degs. and forty-two degs. north. This corresponds with the latitude of Northern California, of San Francisco, Salt Lake
City, Indianapolis, Columbus and Philadelphia. The Humboldt River, along
which the new hemp grows, runs from the mountains of that name westward,
through a mountainous country. If, therefore, experiment proves what is now
claimed for this textile, it can be prolonged in its cultivation from its original
habitat to our own doors, and will enhance the value of the hemp harvest in
those States where it is now an important feature."

MECHANICAL INVENTIONS.

A NEW INVENTION FOR LAYING RAILROAD TRACK.

We solicit the attention of our readers to the following communication from J.
S. Henning, civil engineer, in relation to an invention of W. D. Robertson, of
Star City, of a machine for laying railroad track. We have seen a fine drawing
of the machine by Mr. H., and from our knowledge of mechanics believe it to
be very simple and perfectly practical. Mr. Roots, County Surveyor, and an
experienced railroad engineer, has examined the plans, and is highly pleased

12

with it—thinks it practical and the very thing needed, and wonders from its simplicity that it has not been sooner discovered:

[From the Humboldt Register, Unionville, Nevada.]

STAR CITY, August 14, 1866.

EDITOR REGISTER: Humboldt is about to be made famous for being the birthplace of an invention, by W. D. Robertson, of a machine which, if successful, will prove second only to the steam engine—a machine for laying railroad track. A short description of it will doubtless be interesting to all who feel a desire to see the Central Pacific hurried to completion.

The machine is supplied in front with a movable scraper, to cut down or fill up irregularities of ground after hand grading. Immediately behind the scraper is a feed box, into which the ties are thrown, and by rods worked by cams or eccentrics are dropped at any given distance apart. This apparatus is similar to and as simple as the lever on a shot pouch for putting regular charges in a shot gun. Following the feed box, a battery of four stamps is arranged to drop at the same regular intervals that the rails are dropped; the stamps set the tie firmly in the ground, and retain it in position until revolving cutters, like those used in planing-machines, pass across and cut the tie to the grade to receive the rail. These cutters are adjustable, and may be made to cut the tie to any required depth. As soon as a sufficient number of the ties have been laid and cut, a rail with a chair properly placed, is lowered to the ties and driven back into the chair on the preceding rail. A very simple (though difficult to explain without drawings) apparatus follows, and sets the spike in each tie, and they are driven home by one or more stamps following, and each giving it a blow, but cannot fall so as to batter the head after it is driven. The ties and rails are supplied by hand cars on tracks on platform of main car, these cars running back on the cars of the supply train. The whole machinery is driven by gearing, belts, etc., from the wheels of the car; and the whole may be driven by a common locomotive moving the supply train, or by a small engine on the construction engine.

The whole machinery is arranged on true mechanical principles, and there is no more reason to doubt the accurate working of all the parts of it than there is to doubt the proportionate movements of the several hands of a watch. I had the honor of making the drawings for the Patent Office, and am thus familiar with its arrangements. It has been examined by several engineers and railroad men, and none doubt its final success.

Yours, &c.,

J. S. HENNING,
Civil Engineer.

P.S.—Since writing the above, Mr. R. has made some important improvements in the machine. They consist of an apparatus on rear of the construction car, for bending the rails for any given curve, and a little different arrangement of the machinery or gearing—making it more simple, lighter, and occupying less space than in the plans you have seen. I am now engaged in making a new drawing, and will send you a copy.

The machine is calculated to build road at the rate of one quarter of a mile per hour, and may be covered by tent or oil cloth, and accompanied by sleeping and cooking cars, so as to run night or day, or in any weather.

J. S. H.

GRIM'S CONCENTRATOR AND SETTLER.

This machine was invented by A. K. Grim, of Virginia, Nevada, in 1865. The inventor claims that this machine gathers the precious metals from the pulp after it has passed from the pans or grinders. It also re-collects the quicksilver in a pure state, and concentrates the sulphurets.

The machine is intended to follow the pans, and receive the pulp direct therefrom, thereby doing away entirely with the settlers, at present in use. The barrel, or hollow cylinder, is five feet in diameter, and eight feet in length. The lower half of the interior surface is lined with copper plate, with a groove at the bottom. There is a shaft running through the cylinder lengthwise, to which are attached two leather rubbers, which are intended to brighten the copper plates, and to rub the amalgam and quicksilver from the plates to the groove. The motion is reciprocal, and the cylinder moves one-sixteenth of a revolution each way *from the center*. The rubbers have the same kind of motion, but the reverse of that of the cylinder, and travel one-eighth of a revolution, thereby giving the rubbers a rubbing surface on the plates of one-half the circumference of the cylinder, or say eight feet square. The machine has about eighty motions per minute, and works a charge of one ton of pulp every two hours, and requires one horse-power to drive it. One man can attend to at least five machines. Each machine is capable of working twelve tons per day.

The inventor is constructing one at the Gould & Curry mill, which will be in successful operation in a short time.

If the inventor can demonstrate by actual working what he claims, this machine will be a most wonderful and useful invention. The saving of quicksilver will be enormous, as the loss per annum by present processes is estimated at more than $250,000 ; and the concentration of sulphurets, were the machine generally used, would dispense with the sluice and blanket washings now in operation in the ravines below our mills.

Several tests have been made with a model, which show that this invention will save eighty per cent. of what is being lost by present processes.

NEVADA STATE
MINERALOGIST'S REPORT
FOR 1866.

ANNUAL REPORT

OF THE

STATE MINERALOGIST

OF THE

STATE OF NEVADA

FOR 1866.

CARSON CITY:
JOSEPH E. ECKLEY, STATE PRINTER.
1867.

CONTENTS.

REPORT.

OFFICE OF THE STATE MINERALOGIST, }
Virginia, Dec. 15th, 1866. }

To the Hon. the Board of Regents of the State of Nevada:

GENTLEMEN—In compliance with an Act defining the duties of the State Mineralogist, I have the honor to present the following Report, which will be found to contain a large amount of valuable information relative to the mining interests of our State; much more, I believe, than has ever been put together in a collective form at any previous time. The Appendix will be found to contain, amongst other items:

First. An enumeration of nearly one hundred and fifty mining districts of the State, with such information relative to each as the limited means at my command have enabled me to procure.

Second. A catalogue of all the principal minerals hitherto discovered in Nevada, with the localities in which they have been noted.

Third. Analyses of ores and waters from various districts in the State.

Fourth. A table of quartz mills in the State: and,

Fifth. Two articles; one on " The Causes of the Decay of Mining Enterprises in many portions of the State," and the other " On the Early Development of Mining Property;" both of them suggested by circumstances which have come under my personal observation at various times.

It is a cause of much regret that the Report is as imperfect as I feel it to be. It is not presented as a complete enumeration of our resources by any means, being little more than the skeleton of what I had hoped to accomplish when I received the appointment of State Mineralogist, in March of the present year.

The following is a sketch of what the Report ought to contain, and which I earnestly hope may be accomplished during the Summer of 1867.

First. An exhaustive sketch of the Physical Geography of the State, with such information relative to its geology as can be collected during the year.

NEVADA STATE
MINERALOGIST'S REPORT
FOR 1866.

ANNUAL REPORT

OF THE

STATE MINERALOGIST

OF THE

STATE OF NEVADA

FOR 1866.

CARSON CITY:
JOSEPH E. ECKLEY, STATE PRINTER.
1867.

school in contemplation. The cost of carrying out such a project would be but trifling, and might well be left, under a limited appropriation, in the hands of the Commission proposed in the report now before the Legislature.

"It is a matter of utmost importance that an elementary mining school should be established at once in this city, where a good practical miner may in a few months acquire a fair amount of general knowledge bearing upon his business. in addition to his already acquired skill; and by which he may be enabled to form a tolerably correct judgment with regard to the principal minerals, and accomplish the simpler processes of assaying usually required in the ordinary course of prospecting. Hundreds of miners visit this city every season, and spend quite time enough here, and have sufficient leisure, to acquire an amount of information in that direction which would be of great benefit to them on their return to the mountains. The need of such a school is daily impressed upon us by the scores of miners who are constantly calling at this office during their occasional visits to the city, desiring books, papers, and other means of information which may be useful to them in their mining operations.

"Of course such a scheme as the one here suggested differs entirely from the proposed institution of a college of mines, or " polytechnic school " of high grade. where geology, chemistry, mechanics, physics, botany, natural history, mineralogy, metallurgy, mining, agriculture, surveying, &c., &c., should be taught by a competent corps of professors and lecturers. But the project here proposed need in no way conflict with the carrying out of the proposed higher grade of school. It may either be made the basis of that institution or a preparatory school for it ; or it may, at the proper time, be discontinued, and the material which may have accumulated transferred to its more pretentious successor.

"In most European mining districts elementary schools of this description have been established, generally having no connection whatever with the higher grade of mining schools. They are usually located convenient to the mines, and are resorted to chiefly by working miners, or employed for educating a class of men to become trustworthy and intelligent agents and under-overseers. An institution of this class, and located in this city under the control, at first, perhaps, of a single instructor, is one *just suited to the present and immediate wants of the great majority of our citizens ;* and it is an institution entirely within our pecuniary reach. The appropriation needed for such an institution would be very small. A moderate amount of apparatus, only, would be required, especially to start with ; and a collection of minerals for ordinary use, not necessarily complete. but such as could readily be collected from the numerous mining offices in this city, would be all that would be needed. Of course the State Cabinet should be made available, under proper restrictions. Such a school would be of incalculable benefit to prospectors ; its beneficial effects would soon be felt throughout the State, and its importance become more and more apparent as it progressed. One of its earliest effects would be to free our community, in a great measure. from the mistakes of honest ignorance, as well as from the vexatious imposition of shallow pretenders who have not the shadow of scientific acquirements, or a moiety even of practical experience, to guide them, but who still continue to bamboozle adventurers and overwhelm confiding capitalists with a weight of words and assertions sufficient to relieve them of thousands of dollars, which are worse than thrown away upon foolish or criminal mining schemes.

"There is a flourishing school now in existence at St. Etienne, in the Department of the Loire, France, which was founded in 1816, upon a similar plan to the one here suggested, and which has been advanced from an original elementary grade to one of a very high order. The annual grant upon which this school is based never reached $4,000, including about $1,200 for rent ; and yet it has succeeded in securing large collections of every kind, a fine library, chemcal laboratory, &c. The school is now under the chief direction of the Inspector General of the Department, aided by three engineers of mines, and two or three other assistants. Of course it has received private aid from time to time, to a small extent. Beyond this it has been self-sustaining. Numerous other schools which have now arrived to positions of great usefulness might also be enumerated, which have been very successfully established on very slender pecuniary foundations. We have no lack of men to place at the head of such a school from among those who have had experience in similar institutions abroad.

" We sincerely trust the Legislature will take this matter in hand, and look into it carefully from the standpoint here proposed. We feel confident that so small an amount as five or six thousand dollars, even, can be most usefully employed in this way, and made to benefit the State many a hundred fold ere that body is again called to assemble in the State Capitol."

PARIS EXPOSITION OF 1867.

The policy of having our State fully represented at this grand collection of the industry of all nations has occupied much attention on the part of His Excellency Governor Blasdel and myself. The miserable pittance of $250 voted by the last Legislature for the promotion of this object, if expended in the collection of specimens, would have left nothing for their transportation to Paris; and after much consultation as to the best course to be adopted, we finally issued the following advertisement to the miners of the State, being unable to send collectors to the various mining localities, as would have been the more effective plan :

NOTICE TO MINERS.

INTERNATIONAL EXPOSITION AT PARIS, 1867.

No more favorable opportunity for disseminating correct information abroad, as to the extent and richness of our mineral resources, will probably occur for some years; and that the advantage may not be lost to us, and that we may not be behindhand with the other States on the Pacific coast, the gift or loan of good specimens of ores and minerals from every section of the State, so that we may be able to send a collection which shall fairly represent our unrivaled wealth, and be at the same a credit to us, is hereby earnestly solicited from all who may in any way be willing to assist us in the enterprise.

The time at our disposal is limited, and the object can only be attained by the speedy and hearty co-operation of persons in every locality. The importance of the desired result will commend itself to all when it is remembered that our future prosperity depends, in a great measure, upon the introduction of large amounts of capital; and until we remove the false impressions which have most unfortunately been created abroad, we cannot reasonably expect the tide to turn in our favor. Nothing will conduce to that result more than a good representation at this coming Exposition at Paris, where the miners and capitalists of the world will be collected together, to a great extent. In the hands of a competent Commissioner, thoroughly conversant with our resources and necessities, much may be accomplished.

For our credit and benefit as a State, it is hoped that every one interested in the success of our mines will at once extend to us their cordial co-operation and support, for without it we cannot achieve anything beneficial.

Specimens may be of any size—their weight will be no objection, provided they are really valuable. They should be accompanied with a written description, giving all details which may be of interest; and if it is desired, they will be returned at the close of the Exposition. They should be sent in by the 25th day of December, 1866, and addressed "To the care of Governor H. G. Blasdel, Carson City," or to "Richard H. Stretch, State Mineralogist, 75 North B Street, Virginia City, for the Paris Exposition," by Wells, Fargo & Co.

H. G. BLASDEL, Carson City.
R. H. STRETCH, Virginia City.

It has appeared in the Territorial *Enterprise*, in Virginia, the **Reese River** *Reveille*, in Austin, and the Humboldt *Register*. Up to the date of my writing this, (December 10th) nothing has been received in response to the call though assistance has been promised. What the results will be it is impossible to say until the time approaches at which the donations should be sent in. I have also applied, personally, to a number of mining companies in Lander, Nye, and Humboldt Counties. When first appointed in the spring, I undertook, at the suggestion of His Excellency, Governor Blasdel, to devote some time in every district I visited to this object, but circumstances, already described frustrated that intention. I would recommend that the attention of the Legislature be called to this subject immediately after their convention, and that the sum of $3,000, in gold coin, be appropriated to defray the expenses of a competent Commissioner; and that, if the contributions of the State do not furnish such a collection of minerals as it is desirable to send, he be authorized to use the State Cabinet to supply deficiencies as far as may be required. I would urge on your honorable Board the necessity of a careful selection of the Commissioner, as the information possessed by him will naturally be taken as the standard of our knowledge of mining matters in Nevada; and if a suitable person cannot be found, that the cabinet be placed in the hands of the Commissioner for California. If the collection sent in from the State is inferior in its character, I would recommend that the enterprise be abandoned altogether. But, should a Commissioner be sent to the Exposition, it would be well to authorize the printing of such portions of this Report as describe the resources of the mining districts of the State, for distribution at the said Exposition, to parties engaged in mining and metallurgical operations in Europe. It should also be made his duty, while in Europe, to procure for the State Cabinet a thorough series of European minerals, and everything which could be made available for the use of our Mining School, whenever such an institution may be organized in Nevada.

PRESENT PROSPECTS OF MINING IN NEVADA.

For the condition of mining enterprises in Nevada at the present time, I may refer to the Appendix to this Report; which embodies nearly all the information now in my possession. At no time have our prospects, as a State. rested on a more secure basis, or looked better for the future than they do to-day. The doubts which hung over the probabilities of successful deep mining on the Comstock Lode in Virginia and Gold Hill, are gradually but surely being dissipated by the result of explorations made during the past year. These have been of the most encouraging character, and give promise of a permanence and richness in depth of a really flattering nature. The gradual failure of some mines which have yielded largely in the past, in no way affects the general truth of this remark. By reference to the table of Virginia mines on the Comstock Lode, it will be seen that a number of shafts have attained a depth varying from 600 to 800 feet below the croppings of the vein, and that fine bodies of ore have been developed on the lowest levels which have been opened; and that too in ground which nearer the surface was entirely unproductive. This has been remarkably the case with the Hale and Norcross, and the southern portion of the Savage claims. The former company prosecuted their explorations almost uninterruptedly for five years without success, nor was it until they had attained a depth of seven hundred feet, that the mine ever paid a dividend. At two hundred feet below the surface the North Potosi ran many hundreds of feet of exploring drifts, through the southern half of the Savage mining ground, developing nothing of value; yet, in this same ground. at a depth of nearly seven hundred feet, two valuable deposits of ore have been opened out. This circumstance is sufficient to dispel any discouragement which may be temporarily felt, at the apparent failure of some mines which in the upper works produced fine bodies of ore, but in the lower levels look less favorable. In mines like those on the Comstock Lode, where the Bonanzas are isolated in immense masses of vein matter, it must always happen, that they will vary in their productiveness from time to time, as bodies of ore are worked out or fresh ones encountered. Just as in the instances given above, ground which to-day is barren, may, at a lower level, again become productive. In other portions of the State, the prospects are equally encouraging. This is especially the case in Lander and Nye Counties, which promise ultimately to produce as much bullion as the mines of Storey County. The southeastern section of Nevada, until the spring of the present year, was almost a terra incognita, and had the reputation of being a perfect desert. Several unsuccessful attempts had been made to explore it and to reach the Colorado River by a direct southern route; but during the months of April and May, a company organized, and, accompanied by the Governor of Nevada, crossed it from west to east a little south of the Arizona line, returning in a very direct line from Pahranagat to Indian Springs, about eighty miles south of Austin. Since that time it has been traversed in every direction by prospectors, who have used the settlements at Pahranagat and the mining districts of the Toiyabe Mountains as bases of supplies, and found it to be for the most part as well supplied with wood, water, and grass, in all the portion north of a line drawn from Indian Springs to the intersection of the 37th parallel of north latitude with the 115th meridian of west longitude, as most portions of the State. South of such a line the whole region is excessively barren. The lofty mountain ranges dwindle down to low broken hills, alternating with wide desolate valleys; water becomes scarce even in the few places where it is found; wood disappears almost entirely, consisting chiefly of small mesquite bushes; and even the sparse Indian population must find it difficult to procure a living. (For details of this portion of Nevada, see Journal of Governor Blasdel's exploring party, in the Appendix.) In the eastern section of Nye County, some of the most wonderful discoveries ever made in the State have been opened up during the present summer. The reports which come in from the Reveille, Hot Creek, Silver Bend, Danville, and Northumberland Mining Districts, were they not confirmed in so many ways, would be almost beyond belief. The mines in these localities are of great extent. The veins are large, and contain a large amount of silver in combinations which are easily reduced, and have already commenced their yield of bullion, (see notices of these districts in the Appendix) and promise to become some of the most valuable property in the State.

Discoveries which promise also to be of value have been made in other portions of the State, among which may be mentioned those in Black Rock, in Humboldt County, and in Wilson's District, Esmeralda County. In every section of the State prospectors have been actively at work, with such success as to bring to light more mines than we have the means to develop, unless previous discoveries are neglected. The field for mining in Nevada is practically inexhaustible, and must be so for many centuries to come. When we look at the limited areas covered by the mines of Cornwall, in England, and those of the Hartz Mountains in Germany, and compare them with the almost unlimited extent of our own, we may realize to some degree the position in which we stand.

STATE MAP.

The materials for a good Map of Nevada are rapidly accumulating; and, considering that no successful attempt can be made to delineate the geology of the country without such appliances, I would recommend that some one be authorized to take the work in hand. There are now the following data, which, in the hands of a skillful draughtsman, would furnish a map sufficiently reliable and complete in its details to serve as a basis for a preliminary reconnoissance:

First. Maps of surveys made under the direction of the Secretary of War, by Lieut. Beckwith, in 1855.

Second. Survey of the Overland Route, made by Captain Simpson, in 1859.

Third. Survey of the California boundary, from Oregon to within a few miles of the Arizona line, by Ives and Lawson.

Fourth. United States land surveys in Washoe, Douglas, Lyon, Ormsby, and Humboldt Counties, on file in the United States Land Office at Carson.

Fifth. Survey of the Fourth Standard Parallel, from the California line to east of Austin.

Sixth. Epler and Parkinson's map of the Humboldt mining region.

Seventh. Notes of the Route from Pahranagat to the Arizona line, (thirty miles) Egan Cañon on the Overland Route, (200 miles) and Indian Springs in San Antonio mining district, (150 miles) by R. H. Stretch, in 1866.

Eighth. Surveys in Esmeralda County, by —— McBride, County Surveyor. 1865-6.

Ninth. Surveys made for the Central Pacific Railroad, during the present year, from the western to the eastern boundaries of the State.

Tenth. Private surveys and notes of the County Surveyors.

The importance of such a map will be understood by all who have carefully examined the maps of the State hitherto published, and noted their deficiencies. Instead of being compiled from the original sources, the majority of these bear evidence that they have been copied from each other, until they have lost almost all resemblance to the surveys from which they were in the first instance derived. Such a map ought not to be a rough lithograph, but a fine copper-plate production, on which minute details could be wrought out when they were known; and should be on a scale not smaller than six miles to the inch. The plates, when engraved, should become the property of the State, so that as more information accumulated, it could be added from time to time.

RAILROADS.

The present winter has seen the active commencement of railroad enterprises in Nevada. The Central Pacific Railroad has brought a force of several thousand men to this side of the Sierra Nevadas, who are busily at work grading the road in the vicinity of Crystal Peak, on the Truckee River. For notices of local roads, see Washoe and Storey Counties in the "Mining Districts of the State," in the Appendix.

In presenting this Report, I do so with the full knowledge of its many imper-
ctions, and possible inaccuracies. The manner in which I have been compelled
prepare it, has rendered this inevitable. I have studiously endeavored to
ie only such information as I had reason to believe was reliable; yet it is not
ways possible to judge certainly of its value. The Report is presented more to
low what may be accomplished, if the right means are adopted, and in the hope
iat every one who is possessed of information relative to any of the multitudin-
is branches of mining industry, will communicate it to this office, that it may
nd a place in the Report for 1867. It is also hoped that persons who may no-
ce inaccuracies in any portion of it, will make them known, in order that they
e corrected in future notices of the facts. Nor must the residents of any dis-
·ict feel that it has been slightingly passed over, if the notice of it is meagre and
nperfect. All information at my command has been impartially used, and
nything additional will be thankfully received. It is my earnest wish to see
uch measures taken, during the coming year. as will enable the incumbent of
he office I at present hold, to prepare such a Report as shall be a complete rec-
rd of everything connected with mining in the State, and to make these
nnual reports the medium of communicating to the world our present status and
·early progress.

The unexampled rapidity of the developments within our boundaries make
uch a report almost an imperative necessity, if we would not suffer in the
uture from misrepresentation, as we have in the past. It is true, that most of
hese items find their way into the daily papers, (often, unfortunately, colored by
he wishes of the writers) but they ought to be concentrated in such a manner
is to make them conveniently and readily accessible. With this object in view,
: would solicit from the Superintendents of mines and mills, papers on the cost
if mining operations, of all kinds, and any information on the points enumerated
n the first pages of this Report.

All of which is respectfully submitted,
                    By your obedient servant,
                                    RICHARD H. STRETCH.

ORMSBY COUNTY.

Ormsby County can scarcely be considered one of the mining counties of the State, though it contributes its quota to the general welfare of the mining interests. Several districts were laid out within its limits during the early days of mining in Washoe, but since 1863, very little has been done towards their development. The greater portion of the county is mountainous land, the Sierras, with their low foothills and spurs, occupying the western section, while the Pine Nut Range covers the greater portion of the eastern. In this latter range,

SULLIVAN DISTRICT

was located in the summer of 1860, and large numbers of locations were made; but little work has ever been done in the district. It lies in the mountains east of the Carson River, and west of El Dorado Cañon. Iron and copper ores are abundant. About two years ago, there was considerable excitement about reported discoveries of coal on El Dorado Cañon. Considerable work was done on the Newcastle Co.'s location, and a depot established in Virginia for the sale of the coal, which was of a dull, black color, and shaly in its appearance, being an inferior lignite, probably of Triassic age; but work has been suspended for many months. The deposit is not likely to be of permanent value. An attempt is now being made to utilize the copper ores of this section, in the manufacture of sulphate of copper, an article of great importance in the milling operations of our State. The absence of any large per centage of iron in the copper ores of some of the deposits near Carson River makes them suitable for this purpose; but greatly superior ores exist in the Peavine District, in Washoe County.

ARGENTINE DISTRICT

is located in the range of mountains to the east of Washoe Valley, and west of Virginia, and immediately north of Eagle Valley, in which Carson City is situated. The formation is principally coarse-grained granite and metamorphic state. The mines are not likely to prove of much value. They lie chiefly in the granite, the gangue being a glassy quartz, in some instances carrying iron pyrites, and stained black with other compounds of iron, assaying small quantities of gold.

Much prospecting has been done in other sections of the county. In the foothills of the Sierra, near Clear Creek, considerable work was done in 1859 and 1860, and many locations were made west of Carson, and in the foothills immediately west of the Carson River, but none of these held out sufficient inducement to warrant any extensive outlay of capital. Much of the quartz, in both these last localities, contains considerable copper and some free gold. Probably, the only active operations at present going on are the efforts being made to find the origin of the gold which exists in the neighborhood of the

Athens mine, about three miles west of Carson. The surface of the hill was sluiced off and yielded fairly, but no well defined vein has yet been encountered.

Limestone, coarsely granular, is found south of Carson and east of the Carson River, abundantly and of fine quality; but the chief support of the county is the lumber trade, and the facilities which the Carson River affords for water power. For the details of the mills, see the Table of Mills in the Appendix.

The Sierra Nevadas furnish immense quantities of pine lumber, and much of the timber used in the mines of Virginia and Gold Hill is supplied by the mills located in this county. Large quantities of logs and firewood are also annually floated down the Carson River from the forests of Alpine County, California, nearly one hundred miles distant, to Empire City, where one of the best saw mills of the State is situated. About 5,000,000 feet of lumber and 5,000 cords of wood are brought down the river in this manner every year.

For information as to the agricultural resources of the county, I would refer to the annual report of the Surveyor General. During the fall of this year, work was commenced on the U. S. Branch Mint, at Carson City, and, under the able superintendence of A. Curry, Esq., the building is progressing rapidly and satisfactorily. It will probably be completed about the autumn of 1867, and will be, when finished, the finest building in the State. The building material is chiefly sandstone, from the quarries about a mile and a half east of the town.

As in all the counties along the base of the Sierras, and indeed in almost all the counties of the State, there are many hot and warm springs. Two of considerable volume lie in Eagle Valley, the one to the east and the other north of the town. The temperature of both, as they issue from the ground, is probably about one hundred and forty degrees Fahrenheit.

DOUGLAS COUNTY

lies south of Ormsby County, along the base of the Sierra Nevada. Its resources are chiefly agricultural, though the mountains were extensively prospected, and a number of mining districts laid out within its limits. Of these, the Genoa and Eagle districts are alone worth notice, though the Blue Ridge, Camp Faulls, and Sulphur Spring districts, in the neighborhood of Eagle District, at one time claimed passing attention.

GENOA DISTRICT

was located in 1861, in the mountains west of the town of Genoa, and work was done in it up to quite a recent date; but, after the expenditure of many thousands of dollars, operations have finally been abandoned. The ore contains some copper, and resembles that found to the west of Carson City.

EAGLE DISTRICT

was located in the mountains to the southeast of Carson Valley, and several tunnels have been run to cut the veins, which crop out very boldly, at considerable depths. Of these, the principal are the Mammoth and Peck tunnels, but up to the present time they have developed nothing of particular value. Specular iron ore is abundant in the Pine Nut Mountains, in this section of the county.

Silver Mountain, Alpine, Monitor, and Markleeville lie in California a few miles west of the Nevada line, at no great distance from Eagle District, and about forty miles from Genoa.

WASHOE COUNTY

lies to the north-of Ormsby County, along the base of the Sierra, and is one of the most important agricultural counties of the State, this branch of industry taking precedence of the mining interest (see Surveyor General's Reports for 1865 and 1866). There are, however, within its limits, mining districts which claim attention, and may, at some future time, contribute to its wealth. Of these, the most important is the

PEAVINE DISTRICT,

located to the north of the Truckee River, and near the California line, on the direct road from the Truckee River to Sierra Valley. This district is remarkable for the abundance of copper ores, assaying largely in gold, which is frequently visible in the surface rock, which has undergone decomposition. Assays from thirty-four mines in this district made by W. F. Rickard, F. C. S., show an average yield in gold of 1oz. 1dwt. 3grs., and in silver of 4oz. 9dwt. 19grs. per ton, giving a value of about $25 (see Analysis of copper ores from Peavine, in Appendix). These copper ores are chiefly rich carbonates and oxides; but it is doubtful whether many of the locations cover anything more than segregated masses of ore. These can, however, be worked at a trifling cost, and will be valuable when communication with the seaboard has been effected by the Central Pacific Railroad, which will run within a few miles of the district. Wood and water are both abundant.

GALENA DISTRICT,

so named from the abundance of galena ores within its limits, lies to the west of Pleasant Valley, and is watered by Galena Creek, which finds its way into Steamboat Creek, and thence to the Truckee River. The best developed mines are in the immediate neighborhood of Pleasant Valley, lying in metamorphosed slates. Considerable work has been done on one of the lodes, an adit being driven to the lode, from which an incline has been sunk on the vein. The gangue contains a good per centage of galena, associated with mispickel, but the position of the latter in the vein is such that no difficulties arise in its separation. It is found in a thin stratum between the wall of the lode and the galena bearing gangue. Considerable ore has been extracted from the mine, and several unsuccessful attempts to work it have been made, failing probably from want of knowledge on the part of the operators. Galena Creek, only a few yards from the mouth of the adit, affords ample facilities for dressing the ore, and the vicinity of the pine forests of the Sierra Nevada reduces the cost of wood at the mine to about three dollars per cord. The lead which has been produced is of good quality, assaying about two hundred dollars per ton in silver. The property is now in the hands of men who will probably operate it successfully; and with its ample facilities it should prove a profitable investment. The prospects of this district are, probably, as good as any within the limits of the county.

CRYSTAL PEAK DISTRICT

lies higher up the Truckee River, near the point where the river makes the sharp bend to the eastward, and is partly in Nevada and partly in California. It has chiefly attracted attention as having produced the best coal which has hitherto been found in the State. It is a black lustrous lignite, retaining strongly the original structure of the wood. As so much imperfect knowledge relative to the probabilities of finding coal in Nevada is prevalent, it may be well to speak more fully of the indications in this neighborhood. The seams of coal originally discovered at this place are interstratified with thin beds of coarse sandstone or volcanic tufa, of light colors. This formation is traceable easterly for a distance of fifteen miles, being intimately associated with trachytes and basalt wherever it is found. Where it is exposed in Long Valley, north of Virginia, it contains great numbers of fragments of willow leaves, grasses, &c., remains resembling some varieties of sage-brush, and, in one instance, the elytron of a beetle, apparently the same as a species now found on the same mountains, and attached to the piñon. These remains indicate for the formation a comparatively recent date, a conclusion confirmed by the manner in which it is associated with the surrounding rocks. The rocks of the Sierra at Crystal Peak are entirely igneous or metamorphic in their character, and have been tilted into every conceivable position by the agencies which seamed them with intruded granite and basalt. Did any of the formations which are known to accompany the coalfields of Europe and the Eastern States occur in this vicinity, even though covered up by lava beds, their immense thickness, and the distortions to which they have been subjected would certainly have disclosed their presence, and they might have been recognized by their peculiar fossils. They certainly do not exist at Crystal Peak. Had the tufas and sandstones containing the so-called coal seams been formed before the elevation of the Sierra, they would have necessarily been tilted and displaced in the same manner as the associated rocks, partaking of all the flexures and faults of the mountain range near which they lie. Instead of this being the case, the stratification is nearly horizontal, or only slightly inclined. In some places the beds have been somewhat tilted, probably by the causes which finally raised them above the water level, and gave the present configuration to the surrounding country. The conclusion is almost irresistible, that whatever coal is found in the neighborhood of Crystal Peak will be confined to the small valleys in that vicinity, which, at the period when Steamboat Valley was an inland sea bounded by the Sierra on the west and the Virginia Mountains on the east, formed small arms of the lake, and collected more or less of the vegetable *débris* which during violent storms was washed down from the pine forests on the surrounding hills. There is yet another consideration to be taken into account in estimating the probable extent of the deposit. The loss of bulk during the conversion of vegetable matter into coal is equal to about three-fourths of the original mass. It becomes evident from this that an extensive bed of coal can only be found where there has been, at some remote period, most luxuriant forest growth and water sufficient in quantity to convey the *débris* to vast tracts of marshy ground favorable for decomposition. The coalfields of the Eastern States and England afford abundant evidence that they were at one time extensive tracts of swampy forests, with a tropical climate and a luxuriance of vegetation with which even equatorial forests in the present day cannot compete. On the other hand, the remains of plants found in the associated rocks at Crystal Peak do not warrant us in entertaining the belief that such conditions ever existed in that neighborhood. What we do find point rather to a scanty growth, such as is found on the hills to-day. The almost entire absence of animal remains in the beds strongly supports this idea. Where there is an abundant vegetation there is generally a corresponding abundance of animal life, which could scarcely have failed to leave some mementos of its existence. If these views are correct, as there is good reason to believe they are, no body of coal will be found in this vicinity which, from its extent or thickness, will repay the capital expended in its development. The mere fact of the formation having accumulated in a contracted mountain valley, limits its extent and value at the same time. The thin seams of bituminous matter found between the layers of tufa may have been the product of dense growths of tule and other water plants.

The chief resource of the district is the immense quantity of lumber on the Sierra Nevada, which, when the Pacific Railroad is completed through Nevada, will be of immense value, from its proximity to the line of communication.

ARGENTINE DISTRICT

lies on the western slope of the mountain range which contains the Comstock Lode, and during the years 1861, 1862, and 1863 attracted much attention. Many claims were located, and a large amount of work done on many of them; but they have all been abandoned for many months, with but little prospect of a resumption of operations.

WISCONSIN DISTRICT

was located on the west side of Washoe Valley, and contains many small ravines, which were worked as placer mines.

Mills.—The abundance of water and wood induced the erection of a number of quartz mills, which are supplied with ore from the mines of the Comstock lode, the average distance of the mills from the mines being from twelve to sixteen miles. For further particulars, see the "Table of Mills."

Wood, etc.—From present appearances, the chief dependence of Washoe County must ever be on its agricultural and lumber resources. Compared with the area of the county, it probably possesses as large a proportion of valuable land as any in the State. (See Surveyor-General's Report of 1865–6.) The whole western section of the county is occupied by the eastern range of the Sierra Nevadas, which are covered throughout their whole extent, from foot-hills to summit, with almost inexhaustible forests of pine. The greater part of the produce of the numerous sawmills finds its way to the mines of the Comstock, and furnishes return loads for the teams which are engaged in hauling ore to the quartz mills in Washoe and Pleasant Valleys.

Railroads.—The route of the Central Pacific Railroad crosses Washoe County from west to east, entering it at Crystal-Peak, on the Truckee River, and follows that stream until it debouches on the great interior desert south of Pyramid Lake. Several thousand men are at present engaged in grading this portion of the route, so that it may be ready for connection with the road on the western side of the Sierra when the heavy works near the summit shall become completed. The Virginia and Gold Hill mining districts, lying about eighteen miles south of the Truckee River, will no doubt be connected with the great highway by one or the other of the routes which have been proposed. The longest and most expensive of these, but at the same time the most valuable to the State, has been located along the eastern slope of the Washoe Mountains, running south until the divide between Eagle and Washoe Valleys is attained: then turning north, it traverses Washoe, Pleasant, and Steamboat Valleys, reaching the Truckee River by an easy grade, not exceeding seventy feet to the mile on any portion of the route. The distance from Virginia to the Truckee is a little over thirty-nine miles, not including a branch of four miles to Carson City. The cost, including equipment, would probably be about $2,500,000. It would, however, put all the principal settlements of western Nevada in communication with the seaboard by rail, at the same time placing the lumber of the Sierra and the agricultural produce of the valleys in the Virginia market at greatly reduced figures, and supplying the mills of Washoe County with ore at one-half the rates which are at present paid for freight.

Among the natural features of Washoe County, the hot springs deserve more than a casual notice. Those at Steamboat Springs, so called because when first discovered the steam as it escaped produced a noise resembling the puffing of a steamboat, are the most important. They are situated about ten miles south of the Truckee River, and cover a belt of country about a mile in length, and a quarter of a mile in width, at the foot of a range of low basaltic hills, the basalt being an extensive flow overlying granite. They are very numerous, some of them occupying narrow fissures, which emit a sound like the battery of a quartz mill. Others are still pools, from which there is a constant emission of gas and steam; but the most noticeable is an intermittent spring, occupying a small basin about two or three feet in diameter, which has been built up by the deposition of the solid matter held in solution in the water, to a height of about a foot above the bench. The rise and fall in this basin occupies about six minutes and a quarter. For about five minutes the small quantity of water in the bottom of the basin is perfectly quiescent. It then gradually begins to rise, the ebullition increasing until the water runs over the rim, when it slowly subsides, the agitation lasting a little over a minute. This formula is repeated with great regularity. It may, however, be varied by artificial means. After throwing into the basin a few ounces of soap, the waters rise and fall as usual for three or four times, when they commence to boil with unusual energy, throwing up the spray from two to eight feet, and emitting immense volumes of steam. In this way the spring will boil for hours with varying activity, sometimes partially subsiding only to gather renewed strength, until it finally comes to rest, the water at such times disappearing entirely from the basin, and not rising again for some considerable time, as if completely exhausted. Its activity may, however, be renewed by a fresh dose of soap. The quantity of the article does not seem to be material, as in one instance a piece weighing about a quarter of a pound was thrown out soon after the ebullition commenced, having lost but little of its bulk; yet there was no apparent diminution in the activity of the spring. The lapse of years has gradually covered the bench with a thick coating of siliceous matter, nearly white, which renders the springs visible at a considerable distance; and the surrounding country affords every evidence that some time or other the springs covered an area many times greater than their present extent. The ground in the neighborhood of the springs is in some places strongly impregnated with sulphur. The temperature of the chief springs is about 204° Fahr., very nearly the boiling point of water at that altitude.

Without exception, the Truckee River affords the most valuable water power in the State. With a fall varying from thirty to forty feet per mile, a large volume of water, and freedom from serious floods, it possesses unrivaled qualifications. There is no doubt but that on the completion of railroad communication between it and the surrounding mining districts, many mills will be erected along the stream, which will not only be able to compete with those in the immediate vicinity of the mines, but will beneficiate ores yielding no more than twelve dollars per ton, at a profit both to mill and mine.

The only foreign incorporation is the Washoe United Consolidated Mining Company, who have a good twenty-stamp mill on the Truckee River, at present lying idle, having been built before the mines, which were to furnish the material for crushing, had been proved of value.

LYON COUNTY

contains a number of mining districts which have, at various times, attracted much attention. At present it depends chiefly on the numerous mills employed in crushing ores from the mines of Virginia and Gold Hill. Many of the mills are located in the vicinity of Dayton, and are run wholly or in part by the water of the Carson River. For the details of these mills, see the Surveyor General's Report for 1865, and the "Table of Mills" in the Appendix. The principal mining districts are the Devil's Gate, Blue Sulphur Spring, Brown's, Indian, and Palmyra.

DEVIL'S GATE DISTRICT

is situated in the northwestern portion of the county, and is the oldest district in the county. It is remarkable as the locality of the first operations for the discovery of silver in the State. The following notice from the Report of the Surveyor General for 1865, will explain itself:

"In 1852, H. B. and E. A. Grosch, or Grosh, (sons of A. B. Grosh, a Universalist clergyman of considerable note, and editor of a Universalist paper at Utica, N. Y.) educated metallurgists, came to the then Territory, and the same or the following year engaged in placer mining in Gold Cañon, near the site of Silver City, and continued there until 1857, when, so far as I can learn, they first discovered silver ore, which was found in a quartz vein, (probably the one now owned by the Kossuth Gold and Silver Mining Company) on which the Grosh brothers had a location. Shortly after the discovery, in the same year, one of the brothers accidentally wounded himself with a pick, from the effects of which he soon died, and the other brother went to California, where he died early in 1858, which probably prevented the valuable nature of their discovery from becoming known. In the meantime, placer mining was carried on to considerable extent in various localities, principally in Gold Cañon."

At various times a large amount of work has been done on the many claims in this district. Of these, the Pride of the West, Buckeye, Gray and Cook, and others in the vicinity of the Devil's Gate, have a general course east and west, and are more auriferous than argentiferous in their character. Others, such as Kossuth, Genessee, Mount Hope, Jewel, Hawley, Daney, Charles Caney, Cayuga, etc., are true silver bearing lodes, many of them containing considerable low grade ore, which, before many years elapse, will make them valuable property. Some of this ground has already been re-located under the State law of last winter relative to the location and possession of mining claims, and will probably be held for that purpose. But little work is being done at the present time in the district, except in the vicinity of the gold bearing lodes.

INDIAN SPRINGS DISTRICT

lies northeast of, and adjoining Palmyra District. Many of the lodes in this district are very large. The croppings of the Whitman are of immense extent, but though reported to contain much valuable ore, the mill suspended operations from some cause or other, and has, I believe, been removed elsewhere. The ores from the Whitman mine bear a strong resemblance to those found in the neighborhood of Fort Churchill, in Storey County.

PALMYRA DISTRICT

lies between Sullivan and Indian Springs District, and like the latter, is located in the lofty mountain range east of the Carson River. But little work is being done in either of them.

For notices of the copper mines, found in the southern part of the county, see Esmeralda County.

The mountains in the eastern portion of the county produce large quantities of piñon, which finds a market in Drytown, Gold Hill, and Virginia.

CHURCHILL COUNTY

occupies the central portion of the State, and has, at various times, attracted much attention, from the reported discovery of rich mining districts within its limits. With regard to its agricultural resources I would refer to the Reports of the Surveyor General for 1865–6. In addition to its argentiferous lodes, many other minerals are found in abundance. Carbonate of soda occurs in large quantities near Ragtown, as a deposit from the water of two small lakes, the smaller of which dries up every summer, leaving an incrustation of considerable thickness, capable of furnishing a large supply. The larger one has a diameter of something less than a mile, and is supplied by springs which keep the water about the same level; if such was not the case, the deposit here would be equally large, as the amount of alkaline matter held in suspension is very great, probably a saturated solution. Sulphur too is an abundant article, and the Sand Spring and Humboldt Salt Beds are in this county, having an aggregate area of nearly 20,000 acres.

The following mining districts have been located in the county: Mountain Wells, Silver Hill, Clan Alpine, Desert, Augusta, Salina, Alamo, New Pass, and Ravenswood.

Hot springs are numerous in the northwestern portion of the county, and in the valley between Silver Hill and Clan Alpine Districts. In the latter locality, the remains of many others now extinct are abundant.

This county may be considered the central basin of Nevada. Nearly in its center, is the sink of the Carson River, which here spreads itself out over a wide extent of low land into a shallow lake, whose area varies with the varying evaporating qualities of the atmosphere. On the northern boundary is the sink of the Humboldt River, regulated in the same manner, the two being connected in wet seasons; and near the northwest corner is Pyramid Lake, which receives the waters of the Truckee River. The peculiar features of all these rivers is, that they flow into lakes having no visible outlet. Persons unacquainted with meteorological phenomena have on this account imagined that there must be subterranean communications to carry off the large volume of water constantly pouring into them, an idea which needs no refutation. The true explanation is that given above; and the immense capacity of the atmosphere, not only in Nevada but throughout the Great Basin, for the absorption of water, is amply illustrated by the remains of dead animals scattered over the plains. These are completely desiccated or dried up, undergoing only a partial decomposition. Were other confirmation needed, it might be found in the shrinkage of all woodwork when brought to these elevated plateaus, even though it may have been seasoning for years at or near the sea level. Barometrical observations, had we them at our command, would undoubtedly afford additional proof.

MOUNTAIN WELLS DISTRICT

is located in the central portion of the county, and has been more thoroughly developed than any other of the mining districts in the county. Large sales have been made to Eastern capitalists, and the following companies organized to operate in the district:

1st. The Silver Wave Mining Company, working the vein of the same name, have built a mill running 10 stamps, in the town of La Plata, at a cost of probably $120,000. It is not at present in operation, being another illustration of the folly of erecting reduction works before the mines which are to supply the ores have been thoroughly prospected and proved of value. Parties who-invest in a costly mill naturally expect it to pay dividends; and if it fail to do so, are apt to feel distrustful of the enterprise, when at the same time, all that may be necessary to convert apparent failure into success is the development of the mine, so as to enable a sufficient number of men to work in it to supply the mill with ore. The erection of a mill on undeveloped property is almost certain to result in detriment to any district unfortunate enough to be so situated.

2d. The Connecticut and Nevada Company purchased the Satellite and Silver Spoon Mines. In the Report of the Surveyor General for 1865, it is stated that they contemplated the erection of a 20-stamp mill. Whether this has been completed I am unable to say. The works of this company are at Averill.

3d. The Madison and Nevada Company.

SILVER HILL DISTRICT

was located in 1860, in the range of mountains northeast of Mountain Wells.

CLAN ALPINE DISTRICT.

is located in the range of mountains east of Silver Hill. The Silver Lode Mining Company has been organized to operate in this district, and was reported, last winter, to be erecting a ten-stamp mill.

AUGUSTA DISTRICT

lies immediately to the north of Clan Alpine, and about fifty miles west of Austin.

NEW PASS AND RAVENSWOOD DISTRICTS

are located in the Shoshone Mountains, about twenty miles west of Austin.

DESERT DISTRICT

is situated in the northwestern portion of the county. A 5-stamp mill was built about two years ago, and operated for some time, but has not been running during the past year. The chief drawback of the district is the almost entire absence of water, even for domestic use.

ESMERALDA COUNTY

lies in the southwestern corner of the State, being bounded on the east by the meridian of one hundred and seventeen degrees and thirty minutes west longitude. This line has never been run out, and some doubt exists as to whether the eastern districts are in this or in Nye County; but, as the probabilities are in favor of Esmeralda from such surveys as have been made, they have been included accordingly.

In variety of mineral productions, it is excelled by none in the State. Within its limits the following districts have been located:

Aurora Section.—Esmeralda, Masonic, Van Horn, Montgomery, Blind Springs, Pahdet and Thunder Spring.

Walker Lake Section.—Lake District, Walker River, Desert, Cornell.

Eastern Section.—Excelsior, Minnesota, Red Mountain, Silver Peak, Cottonwood and Palmetto.

Esmeralda County early attracted the attention of prospectors, promising mines being discovered in the vicinity of what is now the town of Aurora, in 1860, and the prosperity of the district steadily progressed, in spite of expensive litigation and extravagant mismanagement, until the summer of 1864, when, in the general collapse, Aurora suffered with the rest of the State; and but little work has been done on the mines since that time. During the past two years, however, many promising districts have been located in other parts of the county, and the future of Esmeralda looks by no means unfavorable.

AURORA SECTION, ESMERALDA DISTRICT.

Location.—Esmeralda District was located in the summer of 1860, and immediately came into prominent notice. For several years following, the operations of the Wide West, Real del Monte, Pond, Antelope, Young America and other companies attracted considerable attention; and speculation in mining property was carried to great extremes, prices of stocks ranging greatly above their actual value. Immense sums of money were expended in the erection of costly mills and amounts equally large squandered in mismanagement, which, together with a misapprehension of the true character of the deposits, finally brought the district into disrepute, from which it has not yet recovered. The shipments of bullion for the present year, even including those from the Bodie District, which are brought to Aurora for assay, are small in comparison with previous years, the total probably not exceeding $200,000. The principal mills in the neighborhood are mostly idle. Much of the work done in the district strikes a stranger as being badly planned, if, indeed, any system can be detected in it; and since ιe period when active operations ceased, the practice of allowing coasters to ⱱork in the claims, and extract whatever they can find, has tended to leave ⱷuch of the property in a bad condition for future operations, whenever they ɱay be resumed. It cannot be expected that individuals of this class, who have ↕ο permanent interest in the mine, will expend money in timbering and securing ɦe lodes ; so that their operations are, in most cases, a real detriment to the ɔlaims where they are carried on.

But little work is being done in the district at the present time, persons waiting for the result of the recent operations on the Juniata. If the crushings from this lode are successful, it may lead to the resumption of work on other claims. The Philadelphia Mining Company, an Eastern incorporation, have purchased property on Last Chance Hill, and are down with their shaft 280 feet. Their intention is to continue sinking until the dip of their veins brings them into the shaft at an estimated depth of about 470 feet. It is much to be regretted that this, which will be the deepest shaft in the district, was not located on a more promising property ; as its success will have a powerful influence, for good or evil, on the mining prospects of Aurora. Should their expectations fail to be realized, their non-success will be held up to the disadvantage ·of Esmeralda, and will doubtless deter others who might have been induced to proceed with explorations on other claims, had good pay ore been found in their lower levels. It is sincerely to be hoped that their prospects will prove brighter than their surface indications warrant. For the prospecting of the entire hill on which the Philadelphia Company's mines are situated, no better ·location for a shaft could have been chosen, as all the lodes dip towards, and must eventually be cut by it, if continued to a sufficient depth.

The number of locations in the district can be counted by hundreds, and notwithstanding the continued depression in the mining interest, upwards of forty additional ones have been made in the neighborhood of the town this year.

For the mills of the district, see the general Table of Mills for Nevada.

Geology.—The mines of Esmeralda are found in a bluish gray porphyry at the base of Mount Brawley, the quartz veins disappearing when the basalt and other rocks by which the porphyry is surrounded are reached. The greater portion of the locations are included in an area three miles north and south, by two in width, and lie chiefly south and east of the town of Aurora.

Character of Veins.—The majority of the veins have a course nearly coincident with magnetic north, and traverse a series of hills, commencing at the south with Silver Hill, and running across St. Mary's, Middle, Last Chance, Martinez, and Humboldt Hills, to the north end of the belt, the principal locations being in Silver, Middle, and Last Chance Hills.

The veins have a quartz gangue ; vary greatly in width, from one or two, up to many feet ; and may be classed under what are frequently denominated "pocket veins," or such as have the ore concentrated in bunches with barren ground between. This circumstance has operated powerfully to their disadvantage ; the loss of the ore when a pocket or chamber was worked out, creating an unnecessary amount of alarm. The dip of the lodes is to the east, varying from nearly flat to vertical. It must not be supposed from the immense number of locations, that there is a corresponding number of veins—many of the locations being on the same lode, in different portions of its extent, and others having no more foundation than a boulder, or a small slide detached from some vein located higher up the hill. If carefully and economically managed, the mines of Aurora may yet occupy a good position among the almost countless districts of the State.

Character of Ores.—The bullion obtained from the ores of this district contains a very large per centage of gold, the presence of some little antimony being the greatest drawback to their successful reduction. The mills were all constructed on the plan adopted in Virginia, and must have lost a large per centage of the assay value of the rock.

Wood—Is abundant at $6 per cord, the proximity of the Sierra rendering a supply certain, even after the immediate vicinity of the mines has been stripped of its growth of piñon.

Water—Is sufficient for all the steam machinery required in the district.

Other Resources.—Salt is found abundantly at Teal's salt marsh, a few miles east of Aurora; and copper ore of excellent quality is found southward, in the neighborhood of Mono Lake. It is principally in the form of red oxyde, occurring in large boulders in the surface drift; but though traceable for a considerable distance up the hill-side, efforts to find the vein have hitherto proved ineffectual.

LOCATIONS ON SILVER HILL.

Cleveland,	Rich,
Roman,	Gold,
Federal Union,	Star Spangled Banner,
Ringleader,	Julia Harvey,
Locomotive,	Nero,
Lady Jane,	Silver Star,
Ashim,	Confidence,
Kalamazoo,	Well,
Monte Christo,	Jack Hays,
Sacramento,	Moore,
Blue-bird,	Identical,
Geo. N. Patchin,	Dashaway,
Neversink,	Onondagua,
Pickaway,	Happy Jack,
Only Hope,	Sierra Madre,
Union Star,	Edwin Booth,
Hart,	Cosopolis,
Georgia,	North Star,
Kentucky,	Grand Turk,
Byron,	Kate Ridgely,
Gila,	Belle,
Young Antelope,	Catherine,
Miller,	Rambler,
Perseverance,	Siskiyou,
Antelope,	Church,
Constitution,	Black Swan,
Gray Eagle,	Gentle Annie,
Bennett,	Mt. Ophir,
Mayflower,	St. Louis,
Ohio,	Falls of Clyde,
Jenny Lind,	Washington,
Primrose,	Porter,
United,	Cleopatra,
Tenry Sedley,	Morning Star,

Lone Star,
Winnemuc,
Col. Sigel,
Ida,
Santa Maria,
Cape,
Democrat,
Utah,
Iowa,
Cedar Hill,
Landers,
Christiana,
Silver Hill,
Golden Harvest,
Frankfort,
Rosebud,
Esmeralda,
National,
Benedict,
Wabash,
St. John,
San Mateo,

Mariet,
Central,
Ready Pay,
Pioneer,
Sir W. Wallace,
Silver Cloud,
Lady Van,
Fulton,
Lyons,
Morrison,
Sierra Nevada,
Gov. Nye,
Butterfly,
Rob Roy,
Ben Lomond,
Sulphurets,
Buccaneer,
Hill Lode,
Niagara,
Mountain Flower,
La Platte,
Rising Sun.

MIDDLE HILL.

Capitol,
Alturas,
Tivoli,
Whang Doodle,
Winfield Scott,
Fairplay,
Liberty,
Knickerbocker,
Giascutus,
Ross,
Monterey,
Tennessee,
Yankee Jim,
Unique,
Sumner,
Extra,
Eureka,
Constantine,
Oroville,
Live Oak,
Long Island,
Alta,
Jink,
Garden City,
Granite State,
George Emmett,
Diamond,
Atlantic,
Tuscan,

Spoon River,
Amador,
California,
Strawberry,
Red Bird,
Red Jacket,
Statz,
Violet,
St. Francis,
Lily,
Saratoga,
Lord Nelson,
Temperance,
Challenge,
Great Mogul,
Texiana,
La Fayette,
Live Yankee,
Col. Clay,
Arctic,
Meredith,
Pilgrim,
Santa Cruz,
Bogus,
Mono,
Yankee Blade,
Palo Alto,
Midas,
Daniel Boone,

5

Pacific,
Bear Flag,
Rialto,
Pacific Cross,
Mayfield,
Empire State,
Keystone State,
Golden Gate,
Flora Temple,
Elkhorn,
Great Eastern,
Emily,
Kennedy,
Grafenberg,
San Francisco,
Wm. Tell,
Dominic,
Bachelor,
Margaret,
Philadelphia,
West Lake,
Bright Star,
Bay State,
Tiger,
Constantinople,
Ontario,
Minnie,
Eldorado,
Dolphin,
Maybury,
Hamilton,

Boston,
Lucerne,
Bunker Hill,
Jackson,
Breckenridge,
Senator,
Golden Eagle,
Monitor,
Louisiana,
John Adams,
St. Lawrence,
Seward.
Henry Clay,
Rock Island,
White Swan,
Aurora Borealis,
Grace,
Swike,
Sacque,
Calais,
Boz,
Muy Rico,
Downieville,
Sarah Margaret,
Mountain Brow,
Sinaloa,
Stuart,
Romeo,
Amanda,
Lucy,
Frazer.

LAST CHANCE HILL.

Pescadero,
Four Aces,
Esquimaux,
Ocean,
Collins,
Dolpheus,
Crystal,
Herald,
Enterprise,
General Jackson.
Empire,
Golden Age,
Golden King,
Caledonia,
Hornet,
Garibaldi,
Muskrat,
Green Flag,
Sea King,
Virginia,

Express,
Cayuga,
American Star,
Lady Franklin,
Know Nothing,
Forrest,
Amazon,
Vulcan,
Sam Patch,
Occidental,
Keokuk,
Lady Ella,
Last Chance,
Bamboo,
Hesperian,
Warrington,
Valparaiso,
Fanny Mestayer,
Chippewa,
San Juan,

35

estern,
khart,
onroe,
lriatic,
'ide West,
imes,
anny South,
uena Vista,
ride of Utah,
olden Head,
t. Cloud,
ueen City,
olden Spur,
ellow Jacket,
anner,
[anhattan,
'ransit,
'ugh,
lurning Moscow,
lypsey,
ciota,
lally Boran,
'ermilion,
[ontezuma,
[etropolitan,
'lora,
lolumbia,
[ary,
lulu,
l. S. Chapin,
lessie,
on,
'ulip,
ltriped Rock,
lackus,
lnnie Hewlitt,
laywood,
[llsworth,
'resno,

Roanoke,
Golconda,
Waldren,
Caspian,
Wyoming,
Silver Age,
Orisba,
Ruby,
Bloomfield,
Etna,
Almaden,
Badger,
Rising State,
Pine Tree,
Ellis,
Cordilleras,
Invincible,
Winchester,
Ocean Wave,
Vesuvius,
Lord Byron,
Ed. Everett,
Real del Monte,
Fairy Queen,
Potomac,
Indian Queen,
Gem,
Granite,
Annie,
Carrie Corwin,
Black Hawk,
Sigel,
Juniper,
City of Malaga,
Young Andalusia,
San Antonio,
J. J. Crittenden,
Heath,
Independent.

MARTINEZ HILL.

lhicago,
llue Jacket,
leather Stocking,
luttery,
[onster,
[atagorda,
[acbeth,
leven Up,
'alstaff,
lamarilla,
)omino,
lprague,

Old Dominion,
Ne Plus Ultra,
Oro,
Bald Eagle,
Kate Howard,
Boston,
Oakford,
Santa Fe,
Neptune,
St. Joseph,
Arancieba,
Kincaid.

Hector,
Cascade,
Blue Juniata,
Horatio,
Teal,
Almorcha,
Derby,
Mild Frenchman,
Maxford,
Polar Star,

Cache,
Constellation,
Jefway,
Juniata,
Rosetta,
Cayuga Chief,
Portland,
Great Basin,
Huron,
Excel.

HUMBOLDT HILL.

General Grant,
Vietra Madre,
Chicago,
Aberdeen,
Wisconsin,

Como se Llama,
Henry Smith,
Humboldt,
Chase,
Briggs.

ST. MARY'S HILL.

Chimborazo,
Great Republic,
Mariposa,
Cotopaxi,

Massachusetts,
Kate Kearny,
Marie Louise,
Ben Coten.

BODIE DISTRICT

lies west of Aurora and north of Mono Lake, but is situated in Mono County, California. The ores from this district contain even a larger amount of gold than those from Esmeralda, the bullion ranging in value up to eight dollars per ounce.

MASONIC DISTRICT

is located immediately north of and adjoining Bodie District, partly in California, and partly in Nevada.

VANHORN DISTRICT

is located southeast of Aurora, in the range of mountains east of Dexter's Station, and nearly due north of Montgomery District, in the White Mountains, but has latterly attracted no attention.

MONTGOMERY DISTRICT,

located in 1864, comprises the northern end of the White Mountain range, and lies partly in Nevada and partly in California, the principal mines being in Mono County, in the latter State. The richness of the ores attracted much attention to it on its discovery; a town was laid out, as usual, by speculators, and two small mills driven by water power were built; but in the spring of 18-- the town site was represented only by the surveyors' stakes, and the population of the district numbered less than ten individuals—reported rich strikes to be north having drawn them away by an influence which seems irresistible to our migrating prospectors.

Geology.—The White Mountain range at this point consists chiefly of metamorphic quartzose rocks, slates, granite, and syenite, but is much broken up, and has every appearance of extensive slides from the upper portion of the mountains, which have covered up the foot-hills.

Character of Veins.—At the present time, many of the original works are caved in, but the surface explorations of others exhibit a broken and poorly-defined structure, large boulders being mixed up with irregular bunches of ore. The amount of work done is not sufficient to enable an observer to arrive at a clear idea of the system of veins. It is said, moreover, that some of the works were badly planned, as in the case of the Osceola; and that the vein was lost from a misapprehension of where it ought to be found, and not because it did not exist.

Character of Ores.—The ores of this district are exceedingly rich in silver. In the Osceola it occurred in thin flakes of nearly pure sulphurets, ($25,000 per ton) but the amount was limited. Other of the ores were of a more refractory character, which induced the erection of a small smelting furnace; but it was never successfully operated, the slags being kept in too pasty a condition. After a few runs it was abandoned, and the slags were finally crushed and amalgamated in an arastra.

Wood.—Abundant.

Water.—Abundant. The town of Montgomery was located on Union Creek, north of which, a few miles, is Rush Creek, and to the south Marble and Rush Creeks—all of them capable of furnishing considerable water power. The great elevation of the White Mountains causes the snow to lie on their summits during the greater part of the year, furnishing ample reservoirs for the streams during the summer months.

Locations.—Osceola, Gorgona, Bowman & Mitchell, Mountain Queen, Brewster, Pacific, etc., etc.

Other Resources.—A fair article of *fire clay* is said to be found a few miles to the northward, in the foot-hills of the White Mountains, near McBride's Ranch.

BLIND SPRINGS DISTRICT.

Located.—The mining districts of Blind Springs and Hot Springs were located in 1865, in a range of low mountains a few miles west of Montgomery, and separated from it only by a broad valley which opens out southward into Owen's River Valley. They have been incorporated, and now form one district known as Blind Springs District; and though in California, a few miles over the boundary, really belong to the Nevada Mining Region, and as such are mentioned in this connection.

A large amount of work has been done in this district, resulting in the development of some really fine lodes. A small three-stamp mill was early erected, but the process employed is entirely unsuited to the character of the ores, and probably not more than 25 or 30 per cent. of their assay value is obtained. Extensive sales have been made to Eastern capitalists, and two companies are now operating in the district: the Sierra Blanca Company, of New York, on the Crockett and Elmira Lodes, and the Philadelphia Company on the Cornucopia. The latter company have opened their vein by five inclines, varying from two to three hundred feet in depth, and have a large amount of fine ore in sight. Under the direction of Dr. Partz, they have erected a smelting furnace for its reduction, which has produced a considerable amount of crude bullion, consisting of copper, lead, and silver; but the difficulty of finding material which will withstand the intense action of the fire has greatly retarded their progress. The best quality of English fire-brick only last five or six days' run, and cost on the ground nearly seventy-five cents each, entailing an expense entirely too heavy. The trouble, however, is in a fair way of being overcome.

The towns of Benton and Partzwick are located only a short distance apart. about three miles from the principal mines, and can obtain an abundant supply of hay and fine vegetables from the well-watered valleys to the south.

The number of locations in the district is upwards of four hundred, covering an area of four miles north and south, by three in width.

Geology.—The mountain mass consists chiefly of coarse-grained, flesh-colored granite, containing large feldspar crystals, graywacke, syenite, and fine-grained porphyritic dykes running north and south, the general strike of the formation being in the same direction, with an easterly dip. The mountains are rough and deeply cut up by transverse cañons, the slopes at the same time being steep or even precipitous; both circumstances being favorable to the exploration of the veins by deep adits, and obviating the necessity of expensive pumping and hoisting apparatus. In some portions of the range there have been numerous faults, a number of which have been met with in the course of explorations.

Character of Veins.—The belt of veins extends on both sides the range, from the summit to the valley. The following table will show their general features, the claims mentioned being selected on account of their more extensive development. It will be noticed that the normal dip of the district is to the east; those claims which have a western dip near the surface gradually resuming their true position, but showing a more broken character and less clearly-defined walls, until some depth on them is attained.

Name of Mine.	Dip.	Strike.	Width.	Remarks.
Kearsarge	75° W.	N. 15° E.	2 feet.	Walls good.
Diana	60° E.	N. 5° E.	3 "	" "
Cornucopia	35° E.	N. 10° E.	2 "	" "
Kerrick	50° E.	N. 5° E.	2 "	" "
Camanche	75° E.	N. 15° E.	4 "	" " at 120 feet, 9 feet wide.
Elmira	80° W.	N. 10° W.	.....	Broken and faulted.
Crockett	Flat W.	....	.....	" "

Character of Ores.—Near the surface, the veins produce a considerable per centage of argentiferous galena, but from the lower workings it is chiefly argentiferous combinations of copper. The ore lies in thin strata in the veins.

and from its strong dissimilarity to the gangue is readily sorted, so as to yield an assay of $500 per ton. The value of the claims in this district would be greatly increased by careful attention to the dressing of the ores, and the erection of small stamping mills, for the crushing and concentration of the poorer qualities.

Wood.—The supply of wood is abundant, at $6 per cord. Lumber is worth $70 per thousand feet.

Water.—The nearest water to the mines, is between three and four miles distant. The flat on which Benton and Partzwick are built gives a good supply, at moderate depths. The principal supply, however, is obtained from a hot spring, running from eighty to ninety inches, with a temperature of probably one hundred and sixty degrees where it issues from the ground.

Other Resources.—The district affords an abundance of good building stone, easily quarried and worked.

Carbonate of Soda—Is abundant in Adobe Meadows, about twelve miles from Benton.

Iron Ore—Occurs in large veins on the mountains to the west of the mining localities, only a few miles from town. These articles are of great value in smelting operations.

PAHDET DISTRICT

lies to the southeast of Aurora, and was discovered in the spring of 1866, by Mr. Myers, Dr. Fitzhugh, and others. The ores of the district contain considerable copper, associated with free gold, and silver in sufficient quantity to make them valuable. The nearest water to the principal locations is nearly four miles distant.

THUNDER SPRING DISTRICT

lies immediately to the south of Pahdet District. Copper is also a prevalent metal, as in the latter, very rich deposits being spoken of. No large amount of work has been done on the majority of the locations in either of these districts, the requirements of the local laws merely having been complied with, in most instances.

WALKER LAKE SECTION.

Lake District, Walker River District, Desert District, Cornell District, all lie in the Wassuk Mountains, on the western shore of Walker Lake, the first mentioned being the most northerly. In this portion of the county, though exactly in what district I am unable at present to say, one or two large veins of gold-bearing quartz have been discovered, during the present year, which promise exceedingly well, as far as developments have extended. They lie about fifteen miles east of Wellington's Station, on West Walker River, in what are known as the Tollock Mountains.

Since writing the above, the following information, relative to this subject, has been published in the " Territorial Enterprise."

WILSON'S DISTRICT.

"This newly discovered mining district lies between the east and west forks of Walker River, about eighty miles southeasterly from this city, (Virginia) and adjoins East Walker River on the west. It was discovered and located last July, by William Wilson; and at the present time, there are about thirty men prospecting and working there. It is in a rough, mountainous country; well wooded with nut pine, and watered with springs of excellent water. There appears to be one main ledge, or series of ledges, which is called the " Himalaya," running through the district; and upon this the principal part of the claims are located, and work being done. Most of the work has been done, however, within ten or twelve feet of the surface, developing veins of quartz of various width up to ten feet; the one being of a whitish, porous, soft character, easily reduced, and very rich in free gold, with no silver, or any base metals. * * * Wagons can go within seven miles on the regular stage roads, past Wellington's; and with a small outlay of capital, a road can be made directly into the mines. Not being high up in the mountains, the snows do not fall very deep; and, taking all things into consideration, Wilson District is about as good and favorably situated as any yet discovered.

"The neighborhood of Walker River is also noted for the prevalence of copper ores. Near the northern line of the county, many fine lodes of this metal and iron occur. In the absence of personal information, I quote from the Report of the County Assessor of Lyon County, in the Surveyor General's Report for 1865, the following extract relative to these mines:"

"Near Walker River, very rich deposits of copper have been discovered. It is found in well defined veins, ranging in width from two to twenty feet, tending about 15° east of north, and containing, by assay, from twenty to sixty per cent. in copper, and from fifteen to thirty dollars in gold and silver per ton. This copper belt, properly and generally known as the Walker River Copper Mines, though carelessly and indifferently explored, may safely be estimated to be twelve miles in width, commencing about thirty miles southeast of Dayton, and extending southerly beyond the limits of the county" (Lyon into Esmeralda).

"Among the most noted of the mines already discovered and located, are the Constitution, Ward & Weister, and the Peacock. The Constitution has prominent croppings, which show a ledge of sixteen or eighteen feet in width, the ore assaying from twenty to thirty per cent. in copper, with a large per centage of iron, and from fifteen to eighteen dollars per ton in gold and silver. The Ward & Weister, adjacent to and parallel with the Constitution, is about six feet in width. The ore is pure gray sulphuret, containing native copper, assaying from forty to sixty per cent. copper, and from twenty-five to thirty dollars in silver per ton. The Peacock Ledge is situated about eight miles easterly from the Constitution, and three or four miles west of Walker River. Width of lode, about four feet, yellow sulphuret ore, assaying about the same as the Constitution." "In this connection I would state that it would be difficult to obtain water within less than two miles of these mines, but that wood (the piñon pine) may be had in large quantities, at from six to ten miles of the mines."

It may be added that the Constitution has been extensively developed during the past summer by Eastern capitalists, preparatory to the consummation of a purchase, and the results have been quite encouraging. The iron found so abundantly near the surface has diminished greatly in quantity. The assays mentioned in the foregoing extract are probably greater than the general average of the vein.

The Walker River, and Walker Lake region also, abound in argentiferous galena, which, by means of cheap crushing and concentrating machinery, might be made extremely valuable; the pure galena, when separated from the quartz gangue, almost always assaying high into the hundreds. It is, however, so thoroughly mixed in most instances with the gangue that preliminary dressing is indispensable to make a profitable result.

The east and west branches of the Walker River flow through this district and irrigate large tracts of agricultural land, equal to any in the State.

EASTERN SECTION.

EXCELSIOR DISTRICT

lies about thirty-five miles east of Aurora, west-northwest from Columbus,

MINNESOTA DISTRICT

is located southeast of Columbus, and north of Silver Peak Districts. Neither of these districts are at present attracting much attention.

RED MOUNTAIN DISTRICT

is located in the high mountains east of Fish Lake Valley, the White Mountains in which Montgomery District lies being on the west. The veins are described as very large and encased in black slates, which are characteristic of the district. They crop out boldly and yield chiefly gold-bearing quartz, for the reduction of which a small 3-stamp mill was erected in 1865. It is now proposed to take the ore by tramway to Silver Peak for reduction. Wood is abundant throughout the district, the supply for Silver Peak being chiefly derived from this locality.

COLUMBUS DISTRICT

lies about fifty miles a little to the south of east from Aurora. It was located during 1865, and by the reported richness of its ores attracted much attention for a time. The number of locations made in the district is large—the veins being spoken of as well defined on the surface and of fair width, but the work on them has been of the most superficial character except in a few instances; generally nothing more than the easy regulations adopted by the miners to enable them to hold possession of their claims. This tendency to hold on to property in this condition in the hope of disposing of it at a large figure, in the meantime lying idle or prospecting for other veins, instead of developing such as they have already located and profess to believe valuable, has been the curse of this, as well as other districts.

The mills spoken of in the Surveyor General's Report for 1865, page 4, have never been erected, everything in the district being at a standstill for want of capital. The time when persons seeking investments would build mills on the faith of a few pounds of rock crushed in a mortar, or the assurance that there was an abundance of rock to keep them running, is happily nearly past, and persons can only hope to obtain the means for reduction by opening up their claims sufficiently to demonstrate the fact, so that no doubt may hang over the success of the enterprise. One mine opened up by a shaft and drifts, so that a dozen men can work in it to advantage, if it look well throughout will do more to attract capital to a district than all the "assays" and "working tests" that ever were made; and, as soon as our prospectors begin to realize this, just so soon may they expect to reap the fruit of their labor. It is often argued that these developments cannot be made without money—a remark which is true to a certain extent: for it is just as cheap to live in a settled home as to be wandering over the country, and all the machinery necessary for preliminary developments is a rope and windlass; nor should it ever be forgotten that where there is a will there always is a way. The remarks must not be taken as applicable to Columbus District in an especial degree; they are true of great numbers of districts in the State.

The town of Columbus was laid out at the eastern foot of a range of low mountains, and near the edge of an extensive salt marsh covering an area of probably forty square miles. This prevalence of salt naturally affects the water. which, though readily obtained by sinking wells, is brackish to the taste.

Wood is limited in quantity, the whole district suffering from the want of facilities for the reduction of its ores; but it is said that a fair supply can be obtained at less distance than it is brought into Virginia and Gold Hill. If prices of articles necessary for beneficiating the ores are high, the richness of the latter is a sufficient offset. Small quantities have from time to time been taken to Austin, and are said to have yielded very fine returns; the surface rock containing considerable quantities of chloride of silver.

SILVER PEAK DISTRICT

lies immediately east of Red Mountain District, and is distant from Aurora by the road about ninety miles. The district was located about the Spring of 1865, and in the autumn of the same year a ten-stamp mill was moved there from Jacobsville, Reese River, and run upon ore from the Pocotillo series of lodes. with very good success. In the Spring of 1866 the machinery required extensive repairs, and since that time no reduction works have been in operation in the district. It is reported that a wealthy company has been organized in the Eastern States to work the Pocotillo and Vanderbilt mines, and that it is their intention to erect a large mill to beneficiate their silver ores, repairing the old mill, which is intended for the reduction of gold ores from Red Mountain District. belonging to the same company. During the Spring of 1866, another New York company were engaged in the erection of a large stone mill, but they committed the common error of incurring this expense before they had ascertained the value of their mines. The exploration of these proved unsatisfactory, and the enterprise is now apparently abandoned—the heavy patent machinery which they imported from the East, lying on the ground, worth nothing more than its value as old iron.

The settlement at Silver Peak is located on the western side of a large valley, about nine miles long and seven broad, opening out on the north by a low pass to the extensive deserts round Columbus. In this valley there is an immense salt-field covering about thirty square miles, and able to furnish unlimited quantities of a very pure article of salt. On its northwestern side a hot salt spring is found, the deposits from which are exceedingly beautiful. The residents in the districts probably number less than one hundred.

Geology.—The mountains of the district consist of slates, blue limestone and yellow magnesian limestone with large intruded masses of gray granite and porphyritic dykes, the limestone in contact with the granite being frequently converted into a fine crystalline marble. The limestones contain abundant remains of sea-weeds, corals, and other fossils, which probably point to a Silurian age;

but as the specimens collected in the neighborhood have not yet come to hand. I am unable to speak positively on the point. The superimposition of the rocks is probably in the following order, the first-mentioned being the lowest : slates, granite, slates and limestones, their dip being flat to the southwest.

There are many evidences of recent volcanic action, one of the most perfect craters in the State being situated about five miles north of Silver Peak, on the road to Columbus. It rises from a low sloping bench to an altitude of about four hundred feet, the crater being probably fifteen hundred feet across, nearly circular, with a depth of about two hundred and fifty feet, the rim being perfect on all sides except the northeast, where it is broken down to the level of the flat where it is located. The surrounding country is covered with the *débris* of scoriaceous and volcanic rocks. About twelve miles north of Silver Peak there is an extensive deposit of SULPHUR dissembled through a whitish gangue, probably volcanic ashes or mud, the whole mass of the hill being cut up by thin seams of *alum*, from the thickness of a knife blade up to several inches. On the road from Red Mountain, near the summit of the range, is a cave, the sides of which produce a curling efflorescence of *saltpetre*.

Character of Veins.—The veins here exhibit many peculiarities, and probably belong to the class of contact deposits. A brief description of the Pocotillo, Vanderbilt, and Session series will give a good idea of their character. The Pocotillo series lies between slates and granite, consisting of thirteen seams of quartz, usually three or four feet thick, separated by a corresponding number of beds of pale blackish-green porphyry. The dip of the series is about 30° to the southwest, and its width on the surface 300 feet.

The Vanderbilt series has many similar features, but lies above the granite, and is capped with slates and limestone. The quartz beds are only two in number, about three feet thick, with two beds of porphyry rather less in bulk, the dip being about 20°. The precipitous character of the hill in which these deposits are found, and their elevation above the valley, combined with the flat dip, cause these beds to crop out all round the hill, denudation having carried away the lower portion.

The Sessions series consist of five bodies of quartz, dipping about 35° to the east, imbedded in yellow magnesian limestone. The quartz is traceable for a considerable distance on the surface, but the developments are not sufficient to give any information about its character in depth.

The locations in the district number about five hundred.

Character of Ores.—The following analysis of ores from the Vanderbilt is by Maynard and Tiemann, of New York:

```
Silver.............3.18 per cent.....$1322 10
Gold .............0.03      "    .... 209 28
                                     ————$1531 38 per ton.
Silica ......... ...87.83    --
Sulphur ........... 0.94     --
Carbonic acid....... 1.85    --
Oxyde of copper..... 1.66    "
Protoxyde of Iron... 3.88    "
Antimony and arsenic 0.42    "
                    ——99.79.
```

The proportion of antimony and arsenic is probably greater than the above figures in other ores.

Wood—Is brought chiefly from Red Mountain District, about ten =: distant.

Water—Is found altogether in springs, and is a scarce article. The spr: apparently rise from great depths, the water having a slight sulphur tase. : generally containing little saline matter.

COTTONWOOD DISTRICT.

The boundaries of the district commence one and a half miles north o: F: Lake Valley, running five miles easterly, then forty miles south, following :: mountains; thence west to the summit of the White Mountains; th-: northerly along the range, and easterly to the point of begir=: Partly in Nevada, and partly in California. Principal lodes are sa: : resemble those of Red Mountain, others in the foot-hills being similar to :: found at Silver Peak. This remark probably applies more to the charace: the ores than the veins. Wood and water abundant and convenient.

PALMETTO DISTRICT,

discovered during the summer of 1866, lies about forty miles to the sor: Silver Peak.

HUMBOLDT COUNTY.

The northwestern section of the county is characterized by high, basaltic table lands, cut up by deep ravines, with lofty precipitous sides. In many places large areas—sometimes several miles in length and breadth—appear to have sunk bodily below the general level of the plateau, forming valleys with rugged wall-like boundaries, varying from a few hundred to a thousand feet in height. These valleys frequently contain small lakes with strong alkaline waters, which, as they dry up during the summer months, leave incrustations of soda, magnesia, salt, etc. The lake near the Pueblo Mining District has an efflorescence of this kind, of sulphate of magnesia, several inches in thickness. The greater portion of this region is exceedingly destitute of timber, the piñon, or nut pine, being almost entirely absent, and sparingly replaced by scrubby juniper and mountain mahogany. The former is an inferior wood for fuel, but the latter is an excellent substitute for the piñon, which is considered the best firewood the State produces. This section contains the Pueblo, Vicksburg, and Black Rock mining districts.

PUEBLO DISTRICT

lies just south of the Oregon line, and about seventy miles east of the California boundary.

Located in the summer of 1863, in a range of mountains running north and south, and extending some distance beyond the Oregon line. A small mill was built during the summer of 1864, but was burnt by Indians the following year, and the settlers in the district driven out. Some few men have returned to work ; but the extent of the developments is limited, owing to the extreme isolation of the locality and the hostile feelings of the Bannock Indians who range through it.

Geology.—The central axis of the mountains is porphyry, flanked by mica and clay slates, having on the eastern slopes a dip of about forty-five degrees to the east. On the western side they are covered up by an extensive flow of basalt.

Character of Veins.—The veins lie on the east side of the range, having a strike nearly north and south, and a dip corresponding with the slates in which they are found. They are very numerous, but vary greatly in width in different portions of their extent, as is often the case with veins imbedded in slate rocks. The gangue is quartz.

Character of Ores.—Argentiferous, containing considerable copper, and some little galena.

Wood is scarce in the immediate vicinity of the mines. What there is, is entirely mountain mahogany, until the next western range is reached, which yields some juniper.

Water.—There are many small springs and streams on the eastern slope suitable for steam, but none large enough to drive machinery by water power.

NOTE.—Information furnished by Lieut. E. B. Monroe, U. S. V.

VICKSBURG DISTRICT.

Location.—Vicksburg District lies immediately south of Pueblo District, in what may be considered as the same range of mountains, although separated by a wide gap of barren land, connecting the deserts which lie on either side of the mountains. It was located in the summer of 1863. Some little work is being done in the district this year, but it has suffered from the same causes which have retarded the development of Pueblo District.

Geology.—The chief characteristic of the district is a gray granite forming the main mass of the mountain. On the western side of the range there is some gneiss, and at the southern end, slates similar to those of Pueblo, both slates and gneiss having a western. dip. These facts render it probable that the elevation of the mountains was due in one case to the irruption of the por-phyry, and in the other of the granite.

Character of Veins.—The veins lie on both sides of the range in granite, but principally on the western slope, having a strike north and south, and an aver-age dip of about forty-five degrees, though they range from nearly flat to verti-cal. They are wide, and crop out boldly for great distances. In such claims as have been opened, well defined clay walls have been uncovered.

Character of Ores.—Argentiferous, containing but little base metal, gangue quartz.

Wood scarce, but rather more abundant than in Pueblo District; chiefly mountain mahogany and aspen.

Water.—Not found in so many localities as in Pueblo District, but in larger quantities. Alder Creek, distant about six miles from the principal mines, and flowing N.N.W., has a good fall, and could furnish water power in abundance for a number of small mills. As it approaches the valley it irrigates a consid-erable extent of good hay land. On the eastern side of the range there is a large spring, suitable for heavy steam machinery. Bunch grass of excellent quality is abundant on the mountains, both in this and Pueblo Districts.

NOTE.—Information by Lieut. E. B. Monroe, U. S. V.

BLACK ROCK DISTRICT

lies south of Vicksburg District, and during the present summer has attracted a large share of public attention, though it has been known as an argentiferous locality for about two years. The accounts brought in vary so greatly that it is almost impossible to arrive at any clear idea of the district. The lodes are described by some as very large, while others speak of them as vast deposits. A large portion of the ore has more the appearance of decomposed porphyry than a true quartz gangue, but there is no doubt that good results have been obtained from some tons of the rock brought in and worked at Dall's mill, in Washoe Valley. The district is described as deficient in wood and water; both serious items in all mining localities.

SOUTHEASTERN SECTION.

This portion of the county contains by far the greater portion of its mineral wealth, and has been most extensively prospected. Four or five parallel ranges of mountains, running north and south, made up of limestones, slates, graywacke and porphyritic rocks, the former abounding in characteristic Triassic fossils, and extensively cut up by trap dykes, are bounded on the north and west by the Humboldt River. In this region probably thirty districts have been laid off containing several thousand locations, the names of which are given as far as possible under their respective districts below. Of these ranges the most important are the two lying immediately east of the Humboldt River, and known respectively as the East and West ranges. This extensive region was early settled by immigrants from the northern portion of California, and long maintained the reputation of being one of the richest mineral districts in Nevada. Various causes have tended to retard its progress in Nevada, among which has been, and by no means the least important, an inordinate desire on the part of prospectors to make new locations, instead of developing promising ones already discovered; but if carefully managed, with a thorough knowledge of what is necessary to be done to obtain the best results, it may yet contribute vastly to our wealth as a State. The resources of the county are equal to any in the State.

THE WEST RANGE.

is distant only a few miles from the Humboldt River, and contains the Eldorado, Humboldt, Prince Royal, Santa Clara, Star, Buena Vista, Indian, American, Sacramento and Echo districts. It has a length, north and south, of about fifty-five miles; the veins, which are almost innumerable, having a corresponding strike. At the extreme northern extremity is located the

PRINCE ROYAL DISTRICT:

the principal locations being near the head of Prince Royal Cañon, where a small town bearing the same name was laid out several years ago.

Whitehall,	Thompson,
Pennsylvania,	Lucinda,
Alexander,	Red Oxyde,
Louis Napoleon,	Washington,
Lincoln,	Lassen,
Williams,	American,
London,	Lily,
Honey,	Caledonia,
Humboldter,	Alleghany,
Eliza,	Clara Hunt,

Cliff,
Oregon,
Palo,
Pacific,
Boston,
Starlight,
Yankee Blade,
Fort Pitt,
Jackson,
Springfield,
Newton,
Colthurst,
Daniel Webster,
Helena,
Socrates,
Boss,

Hope,
Morning Star,
Wm. Penn,
Ophir,
Winchester,
Sebastopol,
Tom Benton,
Empire,
Blue Lode,
Baltimore,
Sallust,
King,
Davis,
Mark Antony,
Esop,
Kate.

On the western side of the range the districts occur in the order in which they are mentioned, going south from the Humboldt River.

HUMBOLDT DISTRICT

is about nine miles in length. Humboldt City is located at about its center, in Humboldt Cañon. The locations in this district are exceedingly numerous. Among them may be mentioned the following:

Enterprise,
Kentucky,
Eagle,
Pride of the West,
Faust,
Chicago,
Rising Sun,
Crittenden,
Black Hawk,
Alleghany,
Venice,
Constant,
Summit,
Washington,
Madre,
Pacific,
Santa Cruz,
Ravella,
Kankakee,
Union,
Gov. Nye,
Potosi,
Huntington,
Cape Cod,
Canada,
Cutler,
Yankee,
Folsom,

Chief,
Philadelphia,
Republican,
Davidson,
Lone Star,
Juniata,
Copes,
Manhattan,
Baslin,
Louisiana,
Golden Gate,
Oro,
Banner,
Cass,
Monte Christo,
Columbia,
Angeline,
McClellan,
West Point,
Antelope,
Halleck,
Havana,
Isabella,
Boston,
North American,
Dean,
New York,
Cleopatra,

Union No. 2,
Vinnemucca,
Octavia,
Smyles,
Cocheco,
San Francisco,
Ross,
Waldron,
Wisconsin,
Secession,
Silver Star,
Florida,
Brannan,
Melrose,
Monmouth,
Adriatic,
Western Slope,
Detroit,
Starlight,
Doniphan,
Santa Anna,
Golden Age,
Constellation,
Edward Shell,

Edinburgh,
Humboldt,
Mississippi,
Sophia,
Ed. Payne,
Bennett,
Cuba,
Henry Clay,
Annie Laura,
Down East,
Everett,
Nassau,
Sigel,
Webster,
Cooper,
Lachine,
St. Bernard,
Leidesdorff,
St. Charles,
Tom Benton,
Grattan,
Lone Star,
Garibaldi,
Mountain Top.

ELDORADO DISTRICT

comes next, with an extent of about three miles.

Owens,
Aroostic,
Champion,
Randall,
Gov. Nye,
Blue Bird,
Widow,
Sunny Side,
Banner,
American Eagle,
Jeff. Davis,
Piedmontese,
Poverty,
Galena,
Old Quaker,

Eldorado,
Twin Brothers,
Nolverine,
Snowball,
Sacramento,
White House,
Washoe,
Hunter,
Mt. Vernon,
Pride of the West,
Lincoln,
Texas Ranger,
Shasta,
Uncle Sam,
Compton.

ECHO DISTRICT

has a length, north and south, of about nine miles.

Union,
Constitution,
Banner,
Pah-Utah Chief,
Cherokee,

Stewart,
Wolverine,
Arkansas,
St. Mary's,
Abner,

7

Mountain Sprite,	Scottish Chief,
Martha,	Arizona,
Sophia,	Boston No. 1,
Erie,	Boston No. 2,
Morning Star,	Washington,
McClellan,	Winfield Scott,
Buckhorn,	Rattle Snake,
Brazil,	Mason & Dixon,
Great Eastern,	Burning Moscow,
Highland Chief,	Lemmon,
Pacific,	Ætna,
Hall,	Eclipse,
Gentle Annie,	Russia,
Gipsey,	Yolo,
Egyptian,	Sutter,
Pritchard,	Mint,
Jefferson,	Johanna,
New World,	Diadem,
Isabella,	Yankee,
Philadelphia,	Shellback,
Great Eastern,	American Eagle,
Monongahela,	Forest Rose,
Leviathan,	D. C. Broderick,
Bacchus,	Montana,
Chico,	May Queen,
Diana,	Sunflower,
Franklin,	Wenora,
Pennsylvania,	Bluebell,
Medora,	Monitor,
Humboldt,	Yellow Spring,
Chloride,	Cortez,
Madonna,	Starlight,
Evening Star,	Mayflower,
Jupiter,	Highland Chief 2.
New York,	

SACRAMENTO DISTRICT

is the most southerly on the westerly side of the range. Commencing again at the north end of the range, we have the

SANTA CLARA DISTRICT,

with a length of about eight miles. Near its southern boundary, in the cañon of the same name, is the little town of Santa Clara, once a promising location.

Magna Charta,	Tehama,
Butte,	Sally Wilson,
Kentucky,	Accident,
Rosa Mink,	Humboldt,
Siskiyou,	Wyoming.
Banner,	

STAR DISTRICT

lies immediately south of Santa Clara, and claims about four miles north and south. Star Cañon, on which is located Star City, the second town of importance in the west range, supplies water enough for considerable mill power. The Sheba Company built a mill several years ago near the mouth of the cañon. A large amount of work has been done in this district on the Sheba, Desoto, American Basin Co.'s claims, etc.; but, owing to the irregular distribution of the ore in the veins, a large proportion of it has been "dead" work. The veins occur in slate and graywacke; and one of their most noticeable features is the almost universal association in parallel series, as indicated in the list of locations given below. The majority of the ores are exceedingly rich, but their value is greatly reduced by the large amount of antimony, zinc, blende, and other base metals which they contain, rendering their successful reduction a difficult and costly operation. As in many other districts, the process of amalgamation which had been found successful in Virginia and Gold Hill, was unhesitatingly applied to these refractory ores; and, as might have been anticipated, when in those localities with their docile material to work on sixty-five per cent. of the assay value was deemed good work, failed in the desired result. The separation of silver from ores in which antimony largely predominates, has always been one of the most difficult metallurgical problems; but during a series of experiments, undertaken in the hope of discovering some method of beneficiating a parcel of exceedingly refractory ore, J. A. Phillips, the well-known author of Phillips' Metallurgy and other works, claims to have discovered a cheap and simple method of partition, which may yet be advantageously applied to the products of many mines in this and other sections of Nevada.

1. *Mammoth Series.*
Home Ticket,
Union,
Montezuma,
Mammoth.

2. *Siskiyou Series.*
Siskiyou,
Isabella,
Waterloo.

3. *Crown Point Series.*
Goliah,
Last Chance,
Crown Point.

4. *Sheba Series.*
Sheba,
Ben Franklin,
Alamo,
Yellow Jacket.

5. *Yankee Series.*
Yankee,
Slabtown,
Arch.

6. *St. Patrick's Series.*
Fisher,
Fine,
Robertson,
St. Patrick.

7. *Almira Series.*
Kitty Rose,
Almira,
Barber,
Jeff. Davis,
May Flower,
St. Bernard.

8. *Phœbe Series.*
Sir Henry Clinton,
Phœbe Walker,
Juniper.

9. *Mountain Top Series.*

BUENA VISTA DISTRICT

lies south of Star, the town of Unionville being located about its center, in Buena Vista Cañon; Fall's Mill being in the same neighborhood.

Mary Bell,	Potosi,
Fairy,	Leroy,
Julia,	Brooklyn,
St. Louis,	Golden Fleece,
Illinois,	Empire,
Lewis Cass,	Comet,
United States,	Chili,
Bell Brandon,	Peru,
Rising Sun,	Venice,
Blue Bell,	Buckeye,
Shasta,	National,
Congress,	Gov. Downey,
Silver Grey,	Alba Nueva,
Rattlesnake,	Douglass,
Golden Eagle,	Old Dad,
Alto,	Major Anderson,
Copperfield,	Col. F. Lander,
Anne Moffatt,	Delirio,
Mars,	Keystone,
Jackson,	Chameleon.
Tom Moore,	

INDIAN DISTRICT

comes next in the order south, having a length of about five miles.

Miami,	Twilight,
Moonlight,	Ohio,
Defined,	Union,
Ophir,	Jennie,
Oriental,	Alabama,
Fort Hall,	Lexington,
Steamboat,	Silver Top,
Red Plume,	Know Nothing,
Sarah,	Noyes,
Music,	Sacramento,
Eleanor,	Red Jacket,
Sam Hulse,	Spring,
May Flower,	Moonbeam,
Mayday,	Walker,
Telequaw,	Texas Bride,
Empire,	Sunbeam,
Ellsworth,	Terra Firma,
Bugle,	Foothill Gem.

AMERICAN DISTRICT

the most southerly on the eastern side of the range.

Washington,	Shasta,
Stevens,	Schmeltzer,
Henry Clay,	Barker.
Daniel Webster,	

Wood.—In the west range the supply of wood can hardly be called abundant, but at the present rate of consumption there need be no fear of a scarcity for some years to come. Its average price may be set down at from $10 to $12 per cord. It is reported that the common sage-brush, including several varieties of the genera "artemisia" and "absinthia," has been tried with successful results at Fall's Mill, at Unionville, it being found cheaper than wood at the above price. The quantity to be obtained in most localities throughout the State is practically unlimited, and can be cut and baled at a mere nominal expense. It certainly makes an excessively hot fire, burning readily even when green, but requires continual feeding, as it is very rapidly consumed.

Water, etc.—The range affords many springs and streams on both slopes, the rich bottom lands of the Humboldt River, only a few miles distant to the westward, furnishing an abundant supply of hay and vegetables for the consumption of the district. An extensive work, called the Humboldt Canal, has been projected, having for its object the irrigation of a large area of otherwise worthless land, and the supply of water power sufficient for large and heavy machinery. A large ditch, estimated to carry 6,000 inches of water, and sixty-five miles in length, has been laid out to take the waters of the Humboldt River along the foot-hills of three ranges east of the river, and terminating on the west side of the West Range, near Humboldt City. About thirty miles of this work was completed a year ago.

EAST RANGE.

The East Range is separated from the West by a valley about ten miles broad, and extends a few miles farther north than the Western, with which it is connected, at the southern extremity of the latter, in the neighborhood of Humboldt Lake. At the southern end of the range, or rather in the chain of hills connecting the East and West Ranges, are the Alabama, Pinewood and Table Mountain Districts. The Pinewood District furnishes a fine article of alabaster. Proceeding northward along the chain, we come to Cinnabar, Ohio, Columbia, Oro Fino and Sierra Districts, in the order in which they are mentioned.

SIERRA DISTRICT

is at the northern extremity of the East Range, where it approaches the Humboldt River. This district is one of the most promising in the whole of the Humboldt region, many of the most noted claims being here located. The little town of Dun Glen is the central business point, the only mill in the district being the Auld Lang Syne, which was erected several years ago.

Geology.—The stratified rocks of the district are slates, limestones, shales and graywacke, having an easterly dip, and associated with porphyries.

Character of Veins.—The amount of work done on many of the mines in this district is quite extensive, showing them very generally to have all the best characteristics of true fissure veins; clay selvages, finely polished and striated, accompanying most of them. Their general strike is north and south, though a few, as the Gem of the Sierras, run east and west. Dip, various. In width, they range from a few inches to several feet.

Character of Ores.—Some veins, as the Monroe, are chiefly gold bearing; but the majority of them produce sulphurets of silver and antimonial silver, associated with more or less copper. In some lodes, as the " Badger and Annie," the copper predominates so largely as to be the chief consideration; and on the completion of railroad communication with the seaboard, the copper interests of the county will be among its great sources of revenue.

Water.—The Humboldt Canal is intended to furnish the chief water power of the district, though locations suitable for steam mills are not unfrequent.

Wood.—The East Range can furnish a supply of wood for some years at the rate of $6 per cord.

Tallulah,
Auld Lang Syne,
Gem of Sierras,
Oro Fino,
Natchez,
Champion,
Monroe,
Valley,
Badger and Annie,
Atlantic,
Moonlight,

Great Western,
Humboldt,
Eclipse,
Independence,
Maremac,
Plata,
Crœsus,
Steamboat,
Ne Plus Ultra,
Grass Valley.

In the third range east from the river, known as San Francisco Mountain, commencing at the northern extremity, are the Harmony, Sonoma, Clear Creek, and Golconda Districts.

HARMONY DISTRICT

was located in June, 1863, by M. Milleson and party. The lodes are described as wide and cropping out boldly for considerable distances, the gangue containing a good deal of copper and iron.

Locations.—Grand Central Series, 10 lodes; Gager Series, 3 lodes; and Franconi.

NORTHEASTERN SECTION.

The northeastern section of the county is comparatively unknown, the hostile character of the Indian tribes having made it one of the most dangerous portions of the entire State. It has, however, been ascertained to contain a large extent of valuable agricultural land, Paradise Valley being described as one of the finest in Nevada. In this portion of the county, immediately north of the Humboldt River, the Winnemucca and Santa Rosa Districts have been located.

WINNEMUCCA DISTRICT

is situated in a range of mountains about twenty miles north of Dun Glen, in the East Range. The Pride of the Mountain lode is said to lie in soft metamorphic slate, having a strike north and south, and a dip of 45° to the east. The vein is described as well defined, with good selvages, and about fourteen inches thick, the ore being of a docile character.

SANTA ROSA DISTRICT

lies immediately north of and adjoining Winnemucca District. The lodes are described as large, and wood and water as abundant in the neighborhood of the mines.

SOUTHWESTERN SECTION.

The greater portion of this section, bounded by Mud Lake, Pyramid Lake, and the sink of the Humboldt River, forms the central area of the Nevada Basin, and consists of barren deserts or mountains, comparatively destitute of wood, water, and grass. It forms a portion of the broad belt of country characterized by recent volcanic action; basalt rocks, alkaline flats, hot springs, and sandy wastes, which can be traced the whole length of the State from the Oregon line far into Arizona, being continued south by the Forty Mile Desert and the dry, repulsive region east of Walker Lake, until the desolate plains to the east of Silver Peak, on which Buel's party suffered so severely in their attempt to reach the Colorado River, are attained. In the worst portion of this district, in Humboldt County, the NEW VIRGINIA DISTRICT is located, about twenty miles east of Pyramid Lake, and in the range of mountains immediately west of the Humboldt River, and only a few miles distant from it.

TRINITY DISTRICT

has been laid off about fifteen miles distant from Unionville, in the mountains west of the Humboldt River, metamorphic slate being the chief feature of its geological formation. Among the locations are the Canada, Montezuma, and Evening Star. The latter company own a small mill on the eastern side of the range; but the mine at present attracting most attention is the Montezuma, on which smelting furnaces have been erected, it is said, with good results. The lode is described as running east and west, dipping 70° to the south, with an average width of ten feet, and good striated clay selvages; the ore consisting chiefly of antimony, lead, and arsenic, averaging in value some $90 per ton in silver.

OTHER RESOURCES OF THE COUNTY.

Sulphur is found in large quantities and of good quality.

Manganese (black oxyde) is mentioned as abundant.

Salt of excellent quality occurs over large areas.

NYE COUNTY.

The mining interest of this county has shown an unusual amount of vitality during the present year; and if present appearances are not greatly deceptive, its future promises to place it second to none in the State. The discoveries in the southeastern portion of the county, among which may be mentioned the Hot Creek, Reveille, Northumberland, and Danville Districts, are spoken of by those who ought to be competent to judge, as almost reaching incredibility, and are strongly corroborated by the results which have been obtained from the samples brought into Austin for reduction.

The mining districts of the county are located in the northern, eastern, and western portions—the central section, from San Antonio to the Arizona line, being one of the most absolutely barren regions on the American continent, so far as we have any knowledge of it. It has received the name of Death Valley, but must not be confounded with the valley of the same name in California, which was known and described before white men had trod this section of Nevada. The western line of the county has never been run out, and it is somewhat doubtful whether the mining district of Silver Peak belongs to Nye or Esmeralda County, though probably to the latter, where it will be found described. For the mills of the county, see the Table of Mills in the Appendix, and for its agricultural resources, the Annual Report of the Surveyor General.

The only mining property at present attracting much attention is such as yields principally silver; but there are within its limits, especially in the north-western section, deposits of iron and copper of almost unlimited extent. Volcano District is especially remarkable for its copper lodes.

Between thirty and forty mining districts have been laid out in the county, of which the following list is as complete as the limited means at my command has enabled me to compile.

1. WESTERN SECTION.

A. Shoshone Mountains:
North Union,
Union.

B. Mammoth Range:
Mammoth.

C. Elsewhere:
Gold Mountain,
Volcano,

Lone Mountain,
Clarendon,
Pilot,
Paradise.

D. South of Silver Peak:
Adelphi,
Edmonton,
Alida.

2. CENTRAL SECTION.

† *Toiyabe Range.—A. West Slope:*
Marysville.

Hot Springs,
El Dorado,
San Antonio.

B. East Slope:
Blue Spring,
North Twin River,
Twin River,
South Twin River,

†† *Range East of Toiyabe:*
Great Basin,
Silver Bend,
Morey.

3. EASTERN SECTION.

A. Northern Portion:
Danville,
Northumberland,
Reveille,
Hot Creek,

Empire.

B. Southern Portion:
Worthington,
Pahranagat.

1. WESTERN SECTION.

B. SHOSHONE MOUNTAINS.

NORTH UNION DISTRICT.

UNION DISTRICT.

These two districts were among the first locations in Nye County, and until recently were its chief attraction. They were located in the summer of 1864, and the town of Ione laid out on the west side of the Shoshone Mountains. Ione is the county seat. The little town of Grantsville lies ten miles to the south. Ione is about fifty miles southwest from Austin, and nearly seventy miles due east of Walker Lake. Carson is distant about one hundred and fifty miles, and is best reached by striking the overland road at Middlegate. The two districts mentioned above are enumerated in their order, commencing at the north and going south. Burnes' Park District lies to the north of Union District.

Character of Veins.—The veins vary in size from one to six feet, the smaller ones, as a rule, carrying the most valuable ores. The Pleiades, one of the principal locations, near Ione, is described as about four feet in width, with a dip of 60°, a northerly and southerly strike, and very smooth walls, the incline being down at least one hundred feet. The only mine being worked in the fall of this year is the Great Eastern, which is said to yield an abundance of $60 ore, with some which will average at least $200. (*Reese River Reveille*, Nov. 22d and 23d, 1866.)

Character of Ores.—In the absence of more definite information, I make the following quotation from the *Nye County News* of Nov., 1864: "The silver ores of this region of country are comparatively free from several of the more troublesome base metals, such as arsenic, antimony, etc. They also contain but a moderate amount of lead, though some of them are pretty strongly impreg-

8

nated with iron and copper. Most of them will evidently require roasting."
As usual in the mines in the interior of the Great Basin, the ores above the
permanent water level have undergone extensive decomposition, and contain
considerable chloride of silver.

Wood is abundant and cheap.

Mills.—The principal mill is the Knickerbocker, a few miles south of Ione.
It has twenty stamps and six roasting furnaces. It is employed on ore from
the Great Eastern Mine. The Pioneer, a five-stamp mill at Ione, is idle.
There is some talk of removing it to one of the newly discovered districts in
the southeast.

B. MAMMOTH RANGE.

MAMMOTH DISTRICT

is located about ten miles west of the town of Ione, in the Mammoth Range
of mountains, near the western boundary of Nye County; indeed, some
doubt exists whether the town of Weston, in this district, is not in Esmeralda
County.

The ores of this district are similar to those of Union District, previously
described. Iron ores are abundant. A large bed or vein of magnetic iron
ore occurs near West Cañon, about a mile below Craig and McKeehan's
Station, on the Wellington road. In close proximity to the mine, is an inexhaustible supply of fuel and water.

C. SOUTHWESTERN SECTION.

(Partly in Nye and partly in Esmeralda Counties.)

GOLD MOUNTAIN DISTRICT.

VOLCANO DISTRICT.

PILOT DISTRICT.

PARADISE DISTRICT.

CLARENDON DISTRICT.

LONE MOUNTAIN DISTRICT.

The boundaries of many of these districts are ill defined, and overlap each
other; on which account I shall speak of them collectively, more especially as
they resemble each other in many of their main features.

The predominant rocks are limestones, abounding in fossil remains of many
kinds. Volcano and Clarendon Districts are remarkable for their great abundance
of copper ores, most of them containing gold and silver. In Volcano District, the
locations of copper lodes are very numerous—no less than thirty distinct lodes
having been discovered, according to reliable authorities. Unfortunately a great
portion of this section is exceedingly barren; and the isolation of the locality
will compel the owners of property to wait the time when a system of railroads

shall enable the valuable copper interests of the State to take their true place in our mining operations.

One of the most beautiful petrifactions hitherto found in Nevada, occurs in a desert in Volcano District. It is the trunk of a large pine tree, about twenty-four inches in diameter, completely silicified. The heart of the tree has a fine yellowish buff tint, while the sap is pearly white, those portions of it which had become discolored during the incipient stages of decay being glossy black. The structure of the wood is most beautifully preserved, and shows it to be allied to, if not identical, with the common yellow pine.

D. SOUTH OF SILVER PEAK.

ADELPHI DISTRICT.

EDMONTON DISTRICT.

ALIDA DISTRICT.

The latter of these districts is about one hundred and eighty-five miles south-southwest of Austin, the other two being about one hundred and eighty in the same direction. Of the character of the ores and veins I have been unable to procure any definite information.

2. CENTRAL SECTION.

† TOIYABE RANGE.

A. WESTERN SLOPE.

MARYSVILLE DISTRICT

is about thirty-five miles south of Austin.

B. EAST SLOPE.

BLUE SPRING DISTRICT.

NORTH TWIN RIVER DISTRICT.

TWIN RIVER DISTRICT.

SOUTH TWIN RIVER.

HOT SPRING DISTRICT.

EL DORADO DISTRICT.

SAN ANTONIO DISTRICT.

Blue Spring District is about forty miles south of Austin, and North Twin River District about forty-four.

about fifty miles south of Austin, is at present attracting more attention than any of the others in Nye County, on the eastern slope of the Toiyabe Mountains. As a type of the mines in this portion of the range, I copy the following description of the Murphy Mine, from the pen of J. D. Emersley, dated Austin, October 20th, 1866:

"In Ophir Cañon, Twin River Mining District, Nye County, is located the silver mine bearing this name. It crops out in crossing the cañon, two and one half miles from Smoky Valley, and about 1600 feet above the level of the latter. The course of the vein is nearly north and south, its dip being easterly, at an angle of 40°. The lode appears to be twenty feet wide, but the richest portion of it varies from three to eight feet in width. When it was discovered in June, 1864, some beautiful specimens of native silver were found in the croppings, and occasionally delicate flakes of virgin metal are seen in the seams of the quartz now being extracted. The Murphy, the Green, and the Twin ledges, three parallel locations, each of 1000 feet running northerly from the cañon, passed into the hands of the Twin River Mining Company, of New York, in August, 1865. * * * * Immediately on completion of the purchase, steps were taken to build a road from Smoky Valley to the mine. Owing to the steep and rugged nature of the ground, this was no easy undertaking; but a passable road was open in about two months, by an outlay of $5,000. Work has been prosecuted on the mine steadily for fourteen months; and though thousands of dollars have been thrown away through ignorance in mining matters of the New York agent, and mismanagement generally, yet it is now clearly demonstrated that the Murphy is a mine of immense value, and quite capable, with anything like sensible management in the future, of yielding handsome dividends, even on the heavy expenditure which has been so needlessly incurred, both on the mine and mill of the company. * * * *

The Murphy Mine can scarcely be said to be prospected yet, as it has not been penetrated to a greater perpendicular depth than seventy or eighty feet. The hoisting, by means of a whim and whipsey-derry, is through a shaft, thirty-six feet deep, at the bottom of which an incline follows the dip of the vein some fifty feet downward. In the lower level, running northerly two hundred feet, a fine body of heavy, black sulphuret ore has been exposed, which, with very little assortment, will work two hundred dollars per ton. In the south drift, a solid mass of three hundred dollar ore has been penetrated, and from the incline and upper works, good pay mineral is being taken out all the time. The Company have a fine twenty-stamp dry-crushing mill, with all the necessary roasting furnaces, pans, and settlers ready to go into operation; and, unless there is great mismanagement in the working of the ores, satisfactory account of the yield of bullion may be expected in a few weeks. About 1,200 tons of pay ore are now on the dump, and enough can be brought to the surface, from day to day, to keep the mill in steady work from this time onward. In neglecting to put hoisting machinery on the mine, considerable risk is being incurred from the probability of a heavy body of water being struck; but even in that case, the suspension of operations would be but temporary.

A great deal of prospecting has been done in the Twin River District, and no doubt some of the numerous locations will prove valuable; but hitherto nothing has been struck comparable to the Murphy Ledge. The San José, as a gold-bearing vein, yielding ore worth from one hundred to three hundred dollars per ton, is certainly fine property; and the Ophir and other lodes, giving assays of silver from fifty to one hundred dollars per ton, from the croppings, are worthy of attention. The discovery, however, of such astonishingly rich ledges as those of Hot Creek and Danville, sixty to seventy miles east of Twin River District, has, for the time being, thrown the latter into the shade, and it will probably be years before its mines generally receive the attention which they merit. A stream of pure water is running in every cañon, and wood will not exceed from eight to ten dollars a cord, for several years, so that the expense of milling is not very extravagant. Good miners are paid from four to five dollars per day, in gold, and board costs ten dollars per week."—*Scientific and Mining Press.*

The mill of the Twin River Company is now yielding good returns of bullion.

SOUTH TWIN RIVER DISTRICT

is about fifty-five miles south of Austin.

HOT SPRINGS DISTRICT

is about sixty-five miles south of Austin.

SAN ANTONIO DISTRICT,

about eighty miles south of Austin, is located in a low range of mountains, which lie across the south end of Smoky Valley. The small settlement at Indian Springs, about ten or twelve miles from the mines, is about sixty from Silver Peak, in which distance there is but one watering-place. To the south of San Antonio Mountains, an unbroken valley extends to the Amargosa, nor has it been, until recently, that the country south of this outpost was looked upon as anything but an almost impassable desert.

San Antonio District was discovered in Oct., 1863, by Robles, Fisk, and others. The formation of the district is chiefly porphyry and slate. The ores near the surface contain chloride of silver, which, in the Twilight, Liberty and Revenue Mines, is the chief value of the rock. In Potomac Hill the ores are much stained with copper, and both these and those from the Lee Mine are principally antimonial sulphurets of silver. The gangue in the Imperial, San Thomas, and others, contains a very large per centage of iron. In width the lodes vary greatly. The Lee is about four feet wide, and dips at an angle of about 40°. The Liberty is probably twenty feet wide, with a dip of 60°. The amount of work done upon these claims, though several have been followed downward to a depth of two hundred feet and upwards, has not done much towards the development of the properties, but very few feet of lateral drifts or cross cuts having been run. The Lee, Liberty, and Potomac mines are among the most prominent in the district. But little work is being done at the present time. The Pioneer Mill with ten stamps, at Indian Springs, ran for a short time; but either from a deficient supply of ore, of a grade high enough to pay for reduction, (one hundred dollars) or some defect in its arrangements, has now been idle for some months.

Wood is scarce in the immediate vicinity of the mines, but it is abundant about ten miles from the mill at Indian Springs. At this point, there is a fair supply of water. At the mines, there is a spring at San Lorenzo, and another at Potomac Camp. At San Antonio, on the south side of the range, there are fine springs, suitable for a mill, but fully twenty to twenty-five miles distant from wood. In this latter vicinity, geodes lined with quartz crystals and many forms of chalcedony are abundant. At the base of Lone Mountain, about twenty miles to the southwest, there is an extensive salt marsh, covering many square miles.

FIRST RANGE EAST OF THE TOIYABE.

MOREY DISTRICT.

Locality, 100 miles southeast of Austin.

SILVER BEND DISTRICT.

In the absence of personal information, I quote the following from the columns of the *Scientific and Mining Press* of October, 1866:

" This district is about twenty-five miles north of San Antonio, on the eastern slope of the mountain range east of the Smoky Valley. It is about eighty-five miles from Austin, in a southeasterly direction. The belt is of slate, and not over half a mile in width, there being only two or probably three main lodes within it. One of these is the celebrated Highbridge Mine, which, though purchased by the Combination Silver Mining Company, of New York, from David E. Buell at a cost of a few thousand dollars, will probably be found of greater value than even the Comstock, when an equal amount of work shall have been performed upon it. For at least a thousand feet the vein shows ore on the surface which assays from $200 up to $3,000 per ton. The ledge appeared to be only about three feet in width when discovered in May last (1866); but now, after it has been opened to a depth of twenty-five or thirty feet, a body of the richest kind of ore has been exposed, at least twenty feet wide. Mr. Buell has had a ten-stamp mill at work in the district for several weeks, and although he has no facilities for roasting the ore, and cannot work it closer than fifty per cent. of the fire assay, he is netting a hundred and fifty dollars per ton. A run of fifteen days, with five stamps, yielded over $12,000; the expenses of mining and milling being only $4,500.

" It is the intention of the Combination Company to erect a sixty-stamp mill next spring, and the Canfield Silver Mining Company, of New York, who own ground on the same lode, have secured a working capital of $350,000, and intend to prosecute their operations with the vigor which the value of the property demands."

SECOND RANGE EAST OF THE TOIYABE.

HOT CREEK DISTRICT.

" About thirty miles east of Silver Bend is the district of this name, so called because a volume of hot water, issuing from a series of springs, makes a creek of respectable proportions, at least in a country where every little rivulet is so named, and where an extraordinary creek is called a river. The belt here is much more extensive than that of Silver Bend, being at least two miles in width, and traceable ten or twelve miles. The formation is talcose slate, capped with limestone, in which ancient sea shells and coral are abundant. Where the limestone has been stripped off by the action of water, the lodes are found large and well defined; but where they crop out only through a heavy cap the walls are not generally visible near the outcrops, and the mineral appears in small seams, as if struggling to reach the surface. By the expenditure of a small amount of labor, however, the ledges are usually exposed so as to show a fine, compact body of ore, usually of high grade. The Old Dominion, one of the best locations of the district, scarcely cropped through the limestone; but now, after a few days' work, it shows fifteen feet of first-class milling ore, assaying from $100 up to $5,000 per ton. The Gazette and Keystone Ledges also showed very little mineral on the surface when first discovered, but are now esteemed of great value. The Indian Jim, on the other hand, having been laid bare by the action of the water, stands boldly out of the ground a hundred feet in height, and has probably not less than 50,000 tons of milling ore in sight. This ledge is certainly forty to fifty feet in width, and along its course shows more mineral than has ever been seen in any unprospected vein on the Pacific Coast."

" The Silver Glance and the American Hunter are also two ledges of great promise. They are wide as well as rich, and can be traced for several thousand feet. Some of the mines referred to have recently changed hands at fair prices, and several mills are likely to be built in the district during the winter and spring months. Even assuming that the amount of $100 to $200 ore, obtained without any underground mining, were all the mills would have to depend on to keep them in work, a dozen would have all they could do for the next five years in reducing it."—*Scientific and Mining Press*, Oct., 1866.

The supply of timber in the district cannot be called abundant, but discoveries recently made promise a fair supply for some years at any rate.

SOUTHEASTERN SECTION.

The discoveries in this portion of the county during the past summer, are probably the most important that have been made in Nevada since the location of the Comstock Lode, not only as regards the number of the locations, but also the size of the veins and the richness of the metal they carry. It is scarcely more than a year ago that this portion of Nevada was marked on the maps of the State as unknown desert, and to-day our prospectors have overrun it from north to south, and from east to west, discovering it to be covered by parallel ranges of mountains, and supplied with wood, water and grass in abundance. The reports which come in daily of new discoveries seem almost too marvelous for belief, but meet with such abundant corroboration that conviction is forced upon the most unwilling.

Among the districts located in this section may be mentioned the Danville, Northumberland, Empire, and Reveille.

REVEILLE DISTRICT.

The Reveille District was located in the summer of 1866 by W. O. Arnold, Monroe and Fairchild. It lies to the southwest of Hot Creek District, and is said to be not more than sixty miles from Pahranagat, in the extreme southeast corner of the State. Many of the veins are of immense proportions. The Antarctic is reported to be fifty-six feet thick; the August, seventy-three; the Crescent, one hundred and six; the Mediterranean, sixty; the Atlantic, forty; and the National, forty-five. The Orient is but five feet in width, and the Fairview from ten to twelve.

The whole of these lodes show a very large amount of chloride of silver; so much indeed as to give them a peculiar character.

NORTHUMBERLAND DISTRICT.

Speaking of this district in October, 1866, the Reese "Reveille" says: "In Northumberland District, forty distinct ledges have been discovered and located, which are generally of large size, and better defined than those of any other district in the region. The Northumberland ledge crops on the surface over one thousand one hundred feet, and in several excavations the vein is twelve feet thick, nine feet of which are well loaded with mineral."

GREAT BASIN DISTRICT

lies about fifty-five miles southeast of Austin.

WORTHINGTON DISTRICT

lies in the southeastern corner of the State, about forty miles west-northwest of Pahranagat District, in a low range of mountains, at the foot of the Shonigodit or Grass Mountains. The ores contain considerable copper and magnetic iron, though some of the veins bear more the appearance of auriferous lodes. Wood and water are abundant. The Shonigodit Range is one of the loftiest of the interior ranges of the State, many of the summits reaching 9,000 to 10,000 feet, and retaining the winter snow through the greater portion of the year. This abundance of snow supplies a number of fine streams of water, running from three hundred to five hundred inches, which could furnish almost unlimited water power. The whole range is well timbered with nut pine, and derives its Indian name from the immense amount of bunch grass which covers the entire country. There is probably no finer country in the State for stock raising than the lofty mountains in the southeastern portion of the county.

PAHRANAGAT DISTRICT

lies in the southeastern corner of the State, in latitude 37° 30' north, and longitude 115° 30' west from Greenwich. The district was located in March, 1865, by T. C. W. Sayles, John H. Ely, David Sanderson, Samuel S. Strutt, Wm. McClusky and Ira Hatch, Indian interpreter. When at Panacker City, in southern Utah, they had heard reports of a silver mountain near a lake, and being on their return from the Colorado River, prospected this section of country. On showing specimens of float rock to an old Indian, he told them that he knew where there was plenty more of the same kind, and led the party to the "Ely & Sanderson" lode. This was on the seventeenth of March, and during the next three days a large number of locations were made. At that time the want of provisions compelled them to return to Meadow Valley, about sixty-five miles to the eastward. In June of the same year, a second party arrived in Pahranagat Valley, but in July, when there were only nine men left at the mines, the Indians, who had at first been greatly frightened, mustered in such numbers, and in so threatening a manner, that the camp was again deserted, the prospectors returning to the Mormon settlements. In October, a permanent location was effected; and during the year 1866 from one to two hundred men have been in the district.

The number of mining locations on record probably reaches one thousand, extending over a belt of country five miles long by about three wide. The altitude of Logan Springs, which is several hundred feet above the level of the valley, is given by Dr. Conger at 5,855 feet.

Pahranagat District lies in a lofty range of mountains running nearly north and south, and is distant from Callville on the Colorado River, about one hundred and forty miles in a southerly direction. A good road is open the whole distance, following the Pahranagat Valley, the Muddy River and the Rio Virgen, crossing the road from San Bernardino to Salt Lake. On the Muddy River there are three flourishing Mormon settlements, numbering probably six hundred persons.

The climate enables them to raise cotton to advantage. Egan Cañon, on the Overland Stage Road, is nearly one hundred and eighty or two hundred miles north of Pahranagat, and, until the past summer, was the usual route from Austin, making the distance between the two places three hundred and fifty miles. The discoveries in southeastern Nevada made this year have, however, shown that a good road could be made, not to exceed two hundred and forty miles in length. The direct road from Virginia by way of Indian Springs, is about three hundred and fifty miles.

Geology.—The principal mines of Pahranagat lie on the southern and eastern slopes of Mount Irish, a lofty peak which probably attains an elevation of 9,000 feet. The mass of Mount Irish is a whitish porphyritic rock, the flanks of the mountain consisting of blackish limestone (abounding in fragments of crinoids and corals) overlying slates, and capped with a heavy bed of quartzite. This bed of quartzite is said to contain fossils, and in it are found the croppings of the Green Monster, and other veins. On Silver Hill and Sanderson Mountain the outcroppings of the lodes are in limestone. On the western slope of the range, crystalline eruptive rocks are abundant.

Character of Veins.—The following table of a number of veins will convey an idea of their general character. They vary greatly in width, and in the nature of the minerals they carry ; but it is impossible from the limited amount of work which had been done on them in the spring of 1866 to speak of anything but their appearance on the surface. Reports coming from this district during the summer and autumn speak very favorably of the developments which have been made since spring. The general direction of the lodes is from N.E. to S.W., frequently varying slightly from this strike either way. It is not unlikely, from the differences which the lodes present, that there may be two or three series of different ages.

SILVER MOUNTAIN.

Hatch Lode.—Dip northwest 70°, two feet wide.

Ely and Sanderson.—Dip nearly vertical, five feet wide, crops boldly, excavation five feet deep.

North Star.—Dip nearly vertical, three feet wide, crops boldly.

Eclipse.—Dip nearly vertical, five feet wide, crops boldly.

Utah.—Dip 75° southeasterly, five feet wide, traceable some distance, walls well defined near the surface.

Bay State.—Dip very nearly vertical, four feet wide, no developments. Promises well.

Illinois.—Dip nearly vertical, twelve to fifteen feet wide, but crops boldly and traceable for some distance.

New Hampshire.—Dip nearly vertical, five to ten feet wide, well defined.

M'CLUSKY MOUNTAIN.

Rio Virgen.—Dip nearly vertical, five to ten feet wide, outcrop ten feet high.

9

SANDERSON MOUNTAIN.

Antelope.—Dip vertical, one foot wide.

Darius.—Dip S.W. 70°, three feet wide, strong-looking lode.

Silver Wave.—Dip nearly vertical, two feet wide.

These locations are not by any means to be taken as the best lodes in the district in all instances. There are many others of probably greater value than many of those mentioned, and multitudes of inferior claims.

Character of Ore.—Some of the lodes carry a large per centage of galena, as many of those on Sanderson Mountain. Others are heavily laden with oxydes and decomposed sulphurets of iron, but the majority of them carry sulphurets of silver, antimonial silver, and considerable copper. The last class are by far the most important, not merely on account of the richness of the ore, but because of their superior size.

Wood, for fuel, is abundant, the entire range being well covered with piñon, which attains a large size, and would answer well for all purposes inside the mines. On the loftier portions of the mountains, pine suitable for lumber and heavy mill timbers is found in sufficient quantities for present use.

Facilities for Reduction.—A five-stamp mill has been erected at Hico Springs, about twelve miles distant from the mines, and a ten-stamp mill is reported to be on the ground. The Montauk Mining Company of New York, under the superintendence of Captain Dahlgren, have constructed a small furnace to beneficiate ores from the Silver Wave, Silver Age, and other argentiferous galena lodes. The greatest difficulty this company will have to contend with is the want of water to dress their ores preparatory to smelting.

Water is scarce in the immediate vicinity of the mines, even for domestic use, the supply being derived from small springs, so weak as scarcely to yield an overflow. The development of the mines will probably remedy this defect. In Pahranagat Valley, about twelve miles distant, the supply is ample for all the requirements of the district, both now and in the future.

Other Resources.—*Fireclay* of good quality is said to be found in Pahranagat Valley, while a superior article is reported from Meadow Lake Valley. Rock salt is found in inexhaustible quantities on the Rio Virgen, about ninety miles south of Pahranagat, on the road to the Colorado River. The deposit is said to be traceable along the side of the mountain for ten miles, and on detaching the dirty exterior coating, an article almost as clear as glass is found beneath.

Towns.—The principal settlements are at Logan Springs; Silver Cañon and Springers' Ranch in the mountains, and Hico and Crystal Springs in the valley.

Agricultural Resources.—Pahranagat Valley is thirty miles in length, and well watered by a stream which rises at Hico, near the northern end, and, after receiving several additions to its volume, debouches into Pahranagat Lake. The valley is fully capable of raising all the supplies required by the district for many years to come, the climate being mild and genial during the winter.

STOREY COUNTY.

Though one of the smallest counties in the State, the returns of the Internal Revenue officers show that Storey County, and the neighboring counties which are dependent on Storey County for the supply of ores with which to keep their mills running, as well as for a market for their lumber and agricultural productions, yield about four-fifths of the entire revenue of the State. Storey County lies near the western boundary of the State, about ten miles from the base of the Sierra Nevada, and is bounded by Churchill County on the east, Humboldt County on the north, Washoe County on the west, and Lyon County on the south.

DISCOVERY OF SILVER IN NEVADA.

"In 1857, Joe Kirby and others commenced placer mining in Six-Mile Cañon, about half a mile below where the Ophir works now are, and worked at intervals with indifferent success until 1859. On the 22d of February, 1858, the first quartz claim was located in the Virginia Mining District, on the ' Virginia Croppings,' by James Finney, generally known as ' Old Virginia,' from whom the city of Virginia and the croppings have taken their name."—*Surv. Gen. Report*, 1865.

" The discovery of rich deposits of silver ore was not made until June, 1859, when Peter O'Reilly and Patrick McLaughlin, while engaged in gold-washing on what is now the ground of the Ophir Mining Company, and near the south line of the Mexican Company's claim, uncovered a rich vein of sulphuret of silver, in an excavation made for the purpose of collecting water to use in their rockers in washing for gold. This discovery being on the ground claimed at the time by Kirby and others, Comstock was employed to purchase their claim, whereby Comstock's name has been given to this great lode."—*Surv. Gen. Report*, 1865.

The discovery proved to the top of the immensely rich " chimney" from which the companies just mentioned have taken bullion to the amount of nearly $10,000,000. Prospectors immediately flocked into the country by hundreds; locations were made on the supposed course of the lode for upwards of six miles; and in a couple of years, as if by enchantment, the towns of Virginia and Gold Hill, with a population of probably 15,000 or 20,000 persons, sprang up in the wilderness. The following mining districts have been organized within the limits of the county: Virginia, Gold Hill, American Flat, Flowery, Silver Star, Castle, Red Mountain, Nevada and Churchill. After speaking of the more unimportant districts, I will enter more into detail regarding the mining interests of Storey County, which are chiefly concentrated in the vicinity of Virginia and Gold Hill·

RED MOUNTAIN DISTRICT

lies in the northwest corner of the county, in the neighborhood of the Truckee River, and claims but little attention at the present time. It is well supplied with wood and water, and furnishes the mills of Virginia with large quantities of the former article. Distance from Virginia, about twelve miles.

CASTLE DISTRICT

lies south of the Red Mountain, and is at present entirely deserted as a mining camp. Prospecting for coal was here carried on in most unpromising localities.

NEVADA DISTRICT

lies to the east of Red Mountain and Castle Districts.

CHURCHILL DISTRICT

lies on the east border of the county, in the neighborhood of the military post of the same name. But little if any work is being done in the district at the present time. The ores are chiefly very hard, bluish-tinted, silver-bearing quartz, strongly resembling those of Palmyra District, which lies to the southward, both districts being in all probability on the same belt.

FLOWERY DISTRICT

is located a few miles to the northeast of Virginia City. The first discoveries made in this district, in the fall of 1859, were thought to be of great promise, and for several years considerable prospecting was done with only indifferent results. When the great depression of the mining interest occurred in 1864, Flowery District was one of the first to feel the change, and since that time has been entirely under a cloud. The Lady Bryan Company continued operations up to a recent date; but at the close of 1866 I am not aware that any work is being done in the district. The location of the last mentioned company is on a large vein probably three hundred feet in width, on which a depth of about three hundred feet has been attained. The lode has yielded sulphuret ores of considerable value, but the deposits have been limited in extent.

SILVER STAR DISTRICT

lies east of Virginia, in the range of mountains between Virginia and the valley of Carson River, below Dayton. The locations in this district are quite numerous, but after the first prospecting were abandoned until about a year ago, when the reduced cost of beneficiating ores made the low grade ores of the district valuable. The principal lode is known as the New Brunswick, on which the St. John, St. Patrick, St. George, and other locations have been made. A brief description of the St. John Mine will serve as a type of all. At this point the lode is about ten feet wide, dipping about 40° to the east, with a strike considerably to the east of north. The gangue consists chiefly of carbonate of lime, and is said to yield about $20 per ton at the mill. An analysis of similar ore from the Occidental Mine, probably on the same vein, a few miles farther south, will be found in the Appendix. The Occidental Mine has been successfully worked for upwards of a year, and the St. John for a somewhat shorter period

VIRGINIA DISTRICT.

GOLD HILL DISTRICT.

AMERICAN FLAT DISTRICT.

As these three districts are all of them organized on the Comstock Lode, and to treat of them separately would be but useless repetition, it will be best to speak of them unitedly.

The greater portion of the mining claims are locations on the line of the Comstock Lode; the exceptions being some few in the Virginia District, lying near the summit of the mountains west of the town, and others in Gold Hill District, east of the Comstock Lode, and characterized by a soft, black gangue, yielding chiefly gold.

Geology of the District.—The subject has been so ably handled by Baron Richthofen in his report on the Comstock vein, published under the auspices of the "Sutro Tunnel Company," that I have made the following extracts from that report on this subject, and also on the characters of the vein and its ores. They will be found well worthy of careful attention, as are all the publications issued in connection with this enterprise.*

---

* *The Comstock Lode*, its character, and the probable mode of its continuance in depth. Ferdinand Baron Richthofen, Dr. Phil. Towne & Bacon, San Francisco, 1866.

The Sutro Tunnel, to the Comstock Lode, in the State of Nevada, by A. Sutro. Gray & Green, New York, 1866.

OUTLINES OF THE GEOLOGY OF WASHOE.

"The range of the Washoe Mountains, on which the Comstock vein is situated, is separated from the steep eastern slope of the Sierra Nevada by a continuous meridional depression marked by the deep basins of Truckee Valley, Washoe Valley, and Carson Valley. Its shape is irregular, though in general a direction from south to north may be traced in the summit range. South, it slopes gradually down to a smooth table-land, traversed from west to east by the Carson River flowing in a narrow crevice, beyond which the Washoe Range continues in the more elevated Pine Nut Mountains. Some peaks in the latter have an altitude of probably more than nine thousand feet. To the west the Washoe Mountains descend rapidly and sink beneath the detrital beds of Washoe Valley and Truckee Valley, but are connected with the Sierra Nevada by two low granite ridges stretching, at right angles with its general course, across the northern and southern ends of Washoe Valley, and thus isolating its basin. To the north and east, the Washoe Range passes into a very extensive mountainous region which is but little explored; while to the southeast it disappears abruptly below one of the middle basins of Carson River. The width of the entire range is not more than fourteen miles, while its length from north to south is not determinable, on account of the scanty knowledge we possess about the northern parts of the country. The culminating point of the range is Mount Davidson, the elevation of which was determined by Professor J. D. Whitney as 7,827 feet. The altitudes of other places are: Virginia City, (B Street) 6,205 feet; Devil's Gate, 5,105 feet; while the basins to the west and south have the following elevations: Washoe Lake, 5,006 feet; Carson City, 4,615 feet; Dayton, 4,490 feet; all according to barometrical measurement by Professor Whitney.

The summit range, which extends northerly and southerly from Mount Davidson, forms the water-shed; deep gulches, marking the intense eroding action of currents in former times, though now almost entirely dry, descend from it down to the basins.

The aspect of the Washoe Mountains is exceedingly barren; so is the view from Virginia over the hilly country to the east. Yet there is a remarkable grandeur and sublimity in it. The air is extraordinarily pure and transparent, so as to allow every gulch and declivity in the slope of mountains a hundred miles off to be distinguished. The eye wanders over an unbroken desert, where barren hills alternate with wide and sandy basins. There is no beauty in this scenery, but it has a strange charm; the constant enjoyment of the distant view is a redeeming feature of life in Virginia.

At the time of the discovery of the Comstock vein, the Washoe Mountains are said to have been covered with scattered trees of the nut-pine and cedar. But since then, they have been extirpated, and Virginia depends for its supply of wood and timber chiefly on the slope of the Sierra Nevada, which, down to the before-mentioned depression, is covered with a continuous forest. The enormous consumption of hewn timber in the mines is, however, rapidly bringing about the destruction of the better part of those forests, and the supply will soon have to be obtained from a greater and greater distance. It is almost unlimited on Truckee River, at thirty miles, distance from Virginia, but this will only be made available by the construction of a railroad from that place to the mines.

The situation of Washoe in the westernmost part of the great basin, and immediately east of the steep eastern slope of the Sierra Nevada, causes it, in its geological features, to form an intermediate link between the structure of both of them, though it partakes far more of the diversified composition peculiar to the mountain ranges of the Great Basin. To the Sierra Nevada it is related by the metamorphism of its sedimentary formations, which farther east appear more regularly stratified and less altered. With both it has in common the considerable part which tertiary and post-tertiary eruptive rocks, partly of pure volcanic origin, play in its architecture. We mention in the following only the more important rocks.

Mount Davidson, the prominent central point, consists of *Syenite*, a granitic rock, which here is composed of two kinds of feldspar, (orthoclase and oligoclase) hornblende in laminated prisms of greenish black color, some mica, and occasionally epidote, but no quartz. It is probably a continuation of the granitic axis of the Pine-Nut Mountains, and forms with the *Metamorphic rocks*, which accompany it, the backbone of the Washoe Mountains. The latter rocks join the syenite to the north and south, and are intersected by dykes of that rock, thereby proving its later origin. Lithologically, they exhibit a great variety; but they may be subdivided in three distinct groups, one of which is *of Triassic age*, and was first discovered by Prof. J. D. Whitney in Eldorado Cañon, near Dayton; this is the most recent group, and its rocks are ordinarily but little metamorphosed. They are immediately preceded in age by a series of *micaceous and quartzose slates*, which usually contain some beds of limestone. Both these groups occur only at some distance from the Comstock vein. Of more importance for the latter is a third series, of *hornblendic* (uralitic) *rocks* with interstratified layers of quartzite, gray slate, and crystalline limestone, which is often accompanied by extensive deposits of very pure specular iron. These rocks form the hills which flank American Flat to the west, as well as those between Silver City and Carson. They are capped by an overflow of *Quartzose porphyry*, an eruptive rock, which, however, is of no importance, except as forming the footwall of the Justis vein.

These rocks form the *ancient series*. They partly preceded, and partly were contemporaneous with the gradual emergence of the Sierra Nevada and the Great Basin, and the entire chain of the Cordilleras, from the ancient sea, whose traces are left in saline incrustations and salt pools at the bottom of the numerous basins between the Sierra Nevada and the Rocky Mountains, which had formerly remained filled with the water of the retiring sea. The Washoe Mountains formed undoubtedly an elevated range during the long period which elapsed till the commencement of the formation of the *recent series* of rocks, which bear still closer relation to the Comstock vein than the former. These rocks are eruptive and volcanic, and belong to the latter part of the tertiary and to the post-tertiary periods.

To the first of them in age we apply the recently introduced term: *Propylite*. In Washoe the names " feldspathic porphyry " and " hornblendic porphyry " are commonly used to designate two prominent varieties of it. They are very appropriate miners' terms; but, scientifically applied, would be capable of very differing interpretation. In other countries the terms " Diorite," " Dioritic porphyry," " greenstone," " porphyritic greenstone," and " trachytic greenstone," have been applied, which confusion of names shows best the indistinctness of the external characters of the rock. Propylite has this remarkable peculiarity, namely: that it resembles many ancient rocks exactly in appearance, and yet is among the most recent in origin. It is prominent among the inclosing rocks of the Comstock vein, and, besides, *incloses several, perhaps most, of the largest and most productive silver veins in the world,* as those in the Carpathian mountains of Zacatecas and other places in Mexico, and probably several veins in Bolivia. Mineralogically, it consists of a fine-grained paste of ordinarily greenish, but sometimes gray, red, and brown color, with imbedded crystals of feldspar (oligoclase) and columns of dark green and fibrous, seldom of black, hornblende, which is also the coloring matter of the base. A peculiarity of the rock is its ferruginous character when decomposed. Probably it contains other metals besides iron. Geologically, it is an eruptive rock; but it is accompanied by vast accumulations of breccia, which is sometimes regularly stratified. The flats of Virginia City, Gold Hill, American City, and Silver City, consist of propylite; it lies, in general, east of the mountains consisting of the ancient formations, and contains several mineral veins besides the Comstock Lode. Its distribution in other countries of the world is not very general.

Several different kinds of eruptive and volcanic rocks followed the outbreaks of propylite; but only to one of them have we to direct attention in reference to the Comstock vein, as it probably caused its formation, besides taking a prominent part in the structure of the country. It is known in Petrology by the name of Sanidin-trachyte; for convenience sake we simply use the name *Trachyte.* Its essential character is the predominance of a species of feldspar, called glassy feldspar or sanidin, which, along with hornblende and mica, is imbedded in a base or paste of a peculiarly rough texture, caused by microscopical vesicules which fill the rock. It has a beautiful appearance, and presents very different colors. Several superior qualities render it of great use in Washoe as building material; all the masonry of the Gould and Curry Mill is constructed of trachyte; some laminated varieties break easily into regular blocks used for stairs and pillars. Also ordinary varieties yield easily to the blow of the hammer, and break into conchoidal fragments; it forms, therefore, an easy blasting rock—a quality which will come considerably into account for the construction of a deep adit level.

There is no doubt about the eruptive origin of trachyte. It even presents the aspect of volcanic lava, and this term has been applied to it in Washoe. The mode of occurrence shows that it has been ejected through long fissures, in a viscous or liquid state and at a high temperature. In some places, the eruptions were subaqueous, as in the vicinity of Dayton. The entire table land around that place is built up of stratified trachytic tufa. The solid trachyte rises from it in rugged mountains, which form an elevated and very conspicuous range, passing east of the Gould and Curry mill, across Seven Mile Cañon, (where, for instance, the Sugar Loaf Peak consists of it) and bending in a semicircle round to Washoe Lake. Pleasant Valley is entirely surrounded by trachytic hills; and farther north, this rock covers the country to a great extent.

Sanidin trachyte has never been found to contain silver-bearing veins, and in Washoe none occur in it, and yet it has evidently been mainly instrumental in the formation of the Comstock Lode and other veins in that region.

No geological events after that epoch are worth noticing, for our present object. Eruptions of basaltic rocks were considerable in adjoining parts of the Great Basin, but have been of little consequence in Washoe. Volcanic and eruptive activity gradually died away, and we behold now their last stages in the action of thermal springs, such as Steamboat Springs. The surface underwent but slow and gradual denudation, and the events of the volcanic period are recorded so perfectly and distinctly in the nature and association of the rocks, as to aid us greatly in explaining the mode of formation of the Comstock vein.

GENERAL STRUCTURE OF COMSTOCK VEIN.

The Comstock vein runs nearly in the direction of the magnetic meridian, (the variation being sixteen and a quarter degrees east) along the eastern slope of the Mount Davidson range, which descends at a steep grade until it abuts against the gentle slope of three "Flats," on which, at an altitude of from five thousand eight hundred to six thousand two hundred feet, are situated the towns of Virginia, Gold Hill, and American City. The outcroppings of the vein extend in a broad belt along the foot of the steep grade and immediately above the three towns. The course of the vein, as far as yet explored, is somewhat dependent on the shape of the slope, as it partakes of all its irregularities, passing the ravines in concave bends, and inclosing the foot of the different ridges in convex curves; the greatest convexity is around the broad, uninterrupted foot of Mount Davidson itself. These irregularities are of importance, as they influence the ore-bearing character of the vein.

The length to which the Comstock vein has been traced with certainty, is about nineteen thousand feet, (from Utah mine to Caledonia tunnel, south of Overman mine) while its total extent is, probably, at least twenty-four thousand feet. The most extensive explorations are between the Ophir North mine and the Overman, a distance of about eleven thousand feet; at other parts but little or only superficial work has been done. This applies particularly to the northern and southern ends, as well as to some short portions of the central part. Several mines are being worked to more than five hundred feet in depth, while some of the shafts, as those of the Mexican, Hale and Norcross, Gould and Curry, and other mines, descend to more than seven hundred feet below the outcrops. Altogether, the amount of work done up to this time is sufficient to show clearly the structure of the vein in its upper portion, and to allow well founded conclusions to be drawn in regard to those which are below the present works.

Without entering here on the question of the "plurality of veins," or the correctness of the so-called "one ledge theory," the discussion of both of which has caused expensive and bitter litigation, and retarded the development of Washoe, but at present is decided in the minds of probably everybody—we simply state in the following pages those facts which may be considered as proved by evidence.

The Comstock vein, at a depth of from four hundred to six hundred feet beneath its lowest outcrops, fills a fissure of from one hundred to one hundred and thirty and even two hundred feet in width, but contracting in places so as to allow both walls to come in close contact. Both of the latter, at that depth, descend easterly at an angle varying from forty-two to sixty degrees. Upwards, from the average depth of five hundred feet, the western wall rises to the surface with the same inclination, which, however, occasionally diminishes at upper levels to forty and thirty-eight degrees, while the eastern wall soon bends to the vertical, and gradually turns to a western dip, which at places is forty-five degrees. Its general position to the depth mentioned is, therefore, about vertical, with an inflation to the west. The vein, consequently, expands towards the surface, in the shape of a funnel. The increase in volume is especially produced by the intervention, between the vein matter, of large fragments of country-rock, broken from the walls, but usually moved only a little way downward, by sliding from their original place. The bulk and number of these fragments, or "horses," increases towards the surface, where some of them have a length of almost one thousand feet, and a width of fifty to upwards of one hundred feet. Vein matter, branching off from below, fills the spaces between the fragments, but is generally near the surface far inferior in bulk as compared with the country-rock. The width of the belt in which these branches come to the surface, and there form scattered outcroppings, is generally more than five hundred feet.

On the western side (west of the Virginia and El Dorado croppings) the Comstock vein is accompanied by a number of smaller veins, the outcroppings of which are visible on Cedar Hill, Central Hill, Ophir Hill, and Mount Davidson, and are with some of them of considerable size. They are nearly parallel to the main vein, and dip to the east. Probably they will unite in depth with the Comstock vein, which, by its relation to them, may be considered as the main vein of what German miners call a "Gangzug." The western boundary of this main vein is exceedingly well defined, by a continuous clay selvage lying on the smooth foot-wall and separating the vein-matter very distinctly from the country; but it is different on the eastern side, where the adjoining country-rock, as is often the case with true fissure-veins, is impregnated with matter similar to that which fills the fissure. It is frequently concentrated in channels running parallel to, or ascending from, the vein, but in fact forming parts of it. The well-defined east wall of its main body has, therefore, often not the same position relatively to the entire vein, and with the growing depth gained by successive explorations, the development of vein-matter east of what was formerly considered the east wall, increases.

INCLOSING ROCK.

The rocks which accompany the Comstock vein, change in its course. They are different varieties of propylite on the eastern side, throughout its whole extent. In some places the frequent and large crystals of feldspar give it a porphyritic character, which in certain varieties is rendered more striking by green columns of hornblende; at others the rock has a very fine grain, and the inclosed crystals are of minute size; again, the rock is either compact and homogeneous, or it has a brecciated appearance from the inclosure of numerous angular fragments. Also the color changes, though it is predominantly green, and the different degrees of decomposition create, finally, an endless variety. We will presently have occasion to consider the causes to which it is due.

The western country offers more differences. Along the slope of Mount Davidson and Mount Butler, from the Best and Belcher mine to Gold Hill, it is formed by syenite, which, at some places, is separated from the vein by a fine-grained and crystalline rock of black color, having the nature of aphanite, but altogether obscure as to the mode of its occurrence. It is from three to fifty feet thick, and the elucidation of its real nature may be expected from further developments. As syenite to the west, and propylite to the east, occur just in that portion of the Comstock vein which has been most explored, and where works, more than anywhere else, extend in both directions into the country, it has been generally assumed, in Virginia, that the lode follows the plane of contact between two different kinds of rock, and is therefore a contact deposit. But immediately north of Mount Davidson, where propylite extends high up on the western hills, this rock forms the western country as well as the eastern, as at the California and Ophir mines—though at the latter, metamorphic rocks and syenite are associated with propylite, on the western side. On Cedar Hill, syenite again predominates; but, farther north, propylite forms the country on both sides. South of Gold Hill, the syenite disappears from the western wall, and its place is taken to some extent by propylite, but in greater part, by metamorphic rocks of the third of the before-mentioned classes, principally quartzite and uralitic rocks. They are best exposed in the Caledonia tunnel. Nowhere have syenite and metamorphic rocks been found occurring on the eastern side.

The outcroppings of the Comstock vein do not form a continuous line, but consist rather of small and detached ranges of quartz, ordinarily protruding from the surrounding ground, and sometimes forming bold crests, which in the aggregate constitute a broad interrupted belt. The horizontal distance across the vein of the outcrops of the different branches, amounts to upwards of six hundred feet. Those of the western branches, which retain the eastern dip of the western wall of the vein, carry principally crystallized quartz of a very glassy appearance, ordinarily of white or at least light color, and comparatively pure quality. Angular fragments of the country-rock are imbedded in the quartz, and form the centers of its crystallization; they usually occur in large pieces, and not in finely-disseminated particles. Metalliferous minerals are scarce, though nowhere entirely wanting. Nothing indicates underground wealth, nor, indeed, has such been found by subsequent mining. The only exception is Cedar Hill, where native gold·was found abundantly in places; but its scarce dispersion never justified great expectations. Of this nature are the Sacramento, Virginia, and El Dorado outcrops, and others on Mount Davidson and Mount Butler. They have in several places a width of one hundred and twenty feet, besides other branches which form part of them.

In the eastern outcrops, particles of the country-rock, together with others of clayey matter and metallic substances, occur, finely disseminated through the quartz, causing thereby a marked difference from the character of the western outcrops. A certain porous structure of the quartz, evidently originating from the removal of fine particles of ore, and the brown and red coloring caused by metallic oxydes, indicate the ore-bearing character of large portions in depth; and the dissemination of native gold and silver in small pores and larger cavities, gives evidence of the presence of ores of the precious metals. Also the chloride and simple sulphuret of silver occur in the eastern outcrops. These different characters of the "Pacos" and "Colorados" of the Mexican and the "iron hat" of the German miner, continue downward to varying depths.

VEIN MATTER.

The vein matter of the Comstock lode is of a highly varied character, if we consider every substance which enters into the composition of the body of the vein, between its two walls, as belonging to it. Its chief component parts are: fragments of country-rock, clay and clayey matter, quartz, and ores.

FRAGMENTS OF COUNTRY-ROCK.

Near the surface, about five-sixths of the mass of the Comstock vein consists of fragments of country-rock, "horses," as the Cornish miner calls them; they are often of larger size, and then terminate below in a sharp edge. Their shape and size vary somewhat with the different nature of the rock of which they consist. Those of propylite, which along the whole range occur on the eastern side, and only occasionally extend throughout the whole vein where the country is of the same character on both sides, are ordinarily very much elongated in the direction of the vein, frequently to one thousand feet or more, while their breadth is far inferior, and their height is intermediate between both. At their ends they thin out gradually. Those of syenite terminate more abruptly, and their dimensions are more equal, though they are always largest in the direction of the strike of the vein. From the large "horses" every variety of size occurs down to the smallest fragments. The quartz is often so thickly filled with angular pieces as to have a brecciated appearance. Propylite is more common among them than syenite, and brecciated vein-matter is therefore prevalent in those parts of the lode where propylite incloses the same on both sides, or where, at least, it furnished the larger part of the material for the " horses." It is for this reason abundant in the California, Central and Ophir mines, and in the southern part of the Gold Hill mines.

CLAY AND CLAYEY MATTER.

Few large veins are so abundant in these substances as the Comstock vein. Clay forms the western and eastern selvages from north to south in continuous sheets, sometimes of from ten to twenty feet in thickness. Other sheets of clay divide " horses " from quartz or different bodies of the latter; and where the two walls come in close contact, they have at places a united width of from fifty to sixty feet. This clay is ordinarily tough and putty-like, and contains rounded pebbles of the adjoining rock; only where quartz is on both sides, it partakes of its nature and is more earthy and dry. But, besides, clayey matter occurs in the body of the vein to great extent, and at places takes a prominent part in the filling of the fissure. Most " horses " terminate at their lower end in a clayey substance, and continue downward, as well as in the direction of the vein, as sheets of clay. Outside of the vein, the same matter occurs to great extent in the eastern country, but scarcely, if ever, in the western, thereby giving another evidence of the indistinctness of the eastern boundary of the vein.

QUARTZ.

The differences mentioned before as prevailing in the quartz of the outcrops continue downward; but are not so conspicuous in depth, on account of the general white color of the quartz. But even there the finely-disseminated particles of the wall-rock are more peculiar to the eastern than to the western portions, and are always abundant where the quartz contains ore. At upper levels, some bodies of quartz are of a reddish color; this is where the " colorados " continue downwards. Frequently, however, this color is only due to the red clay filling the fissures of the fractured quartz. In this case it is probably produced by the percolation of the vein-matter by water, while in the former it is likely that it is connected with the original formation of the vein, as all the phenomena presented by the " iron hat." The quartz in the Comstock vein is rarely solid, and blasting is applied for its removal in but few instances. Generally, it is fractured, and at numerous places the effects of dynamical action on it are such as to give it the appearance of crushed sugar. It occurs in this condition almost always when inclosed in clayey matter, and then frequently reminds one of the waving lines of damask. But then, also, large and continuous bodies, consisting entirely of " crushed quartz," as we may call it, are occasionally met with. Such was the case throughout the larger part of the great " bonanza " of the Ophir mine.

ORES.

The principal silver ores of the Comstock Lode are: stephanite, vitreous silver ore, native silver, and very rich galena; in small quantities occur: pyrargyrite or ruby silver, hornsilver and polybasite. Besides these are found: native gold, iron pyrites, copper pyrites, zincblende, carbonate of lead, pyromorphite (both the two last named very scarce).

OTHER MINERALS.

The Comstock vein is remarkably poor in a mineralogical point of view. The ores are seldom crystallized, and specimens, which at other mines would be considered very common, are admired in Virginia as rarities. In regard to the accidental minerals the same might be said, as they do not occur in either rare or beautiful forms. Quartz is the only gangue. Carbonate of lime very seldom accompanies it, while other carbonates, as those of lead and copper, have only in a few instances been observed. Sulphates are abundant in the waters which issue from the mine, and cover the walls of the old drifts. But the only one forming an essential part of the vein, is gypsum, which occurs in a number of places; it abounds in the lowest works of the Gould and Curry mine, and was formerly found in large crystals in the Fairview. Sulphate of baryta has not yet been observed. Zeolites are limited to the northern portion of the vein, where chabasite and stilbite fill small fissures and cavities in propylitic breccia within the body of the vein.

DISTRIBUTION OF ORES IN THE VEIN—(a) NORTH OF GOLD HILL.

The ore is distributed in a different way in the northern and in the southern part of the Comstock vein. The passage between the two modes of occurrence is gradual. In the northern part the ore is concentrated in elongated lenticular masses, of which the greatest axis is not far from the vertical, but dips to the south and sometimes also to the east. Their width across the vein varies from fifteen to fifty feet. Sometimes several of them adjoin each other laterally in such way, that the westernmost one extends farther north than the one adjoining to the east, and this, again, farther than its next eastern neighbor. This is most conspicuous in the Gould and Curry and Savage mines, where, at the same time, the western bodies extend, in general, higher up towards the surface. Three or four bodies of ore, arranged in the way described, and either separated by country-rock or adjoining each other closely, may be distinguished in these mines. Their total length from the northwestern to the southeastern and lower end, is about six hundred and fifty feet; their aggregate width about one hundred to one hundred and twenty feet; while their extent downwards is not yet known. They belong to the middle and eastern portion of the vein. The ore has been exceedingly rich in the center of the different bodies, where, at the same time, it was soft, and could easily be removed, while the outer parts are hard, and consist of second-class and low-grade ores. Upwards of twenty millions of dollars have been extracted from this immense bonanza. In the Ophir and Mexican mines only one body of similar shape was found. It commenced on the surface, where it was only two feet wide, and descended to the depth of three hundred and thirty feet. It first gradually increased in width, until it reached forty-five to fifty feet, which was the maximum; then it thinned out again in its downward course, and terminated as narrow as it commenced. As it was next to the east wall, it dipped with that towards the west, near the surface; then, in its widest portion, straightened out and gradually turned to an eastern dip, with which it terminated. The length of this body was two hundred feet: it appears that about seven millions of dollars have been extracted from it, with the imperfect processes used during the first years of mining at Washoe. This deposit was accompanied to the west, at about forty feet distance, by another body of ore, which, however, had the shape of a narrow sheet, its total width being six to fifteen feet, and its length about three hundred and eighty feet. It was parallel to the western boundary plane of the former body, but extended north and south beyond its limits, though, generally, it did not reach to equal depth; in the Mexican, however, it continued downward about three hundred and fifty feet. The amount extracted was about three and a half millions of dollars. Compared with the first body, it contained a large proportion of lead and copper.

The space between the Ophir and Gould and Curry mines has yielded but very little ore. The Central mine extracted some from the continuation of the deposits worked in the Ophir, and the California found a large body of quartz extending to its lowest level, but the ore was scattered, and rarely of rich quality. The next four mines south of it, and the northern half of the Gould and Curry mine, have been unproductive: But the explorations were not extended more than a few hundred feet beneath the surface.

The southern part of the Savage mine, and the Hale and Norcross, have been almost entirely unproductive, though both of them offer good prospects for finding ore in depth. But with the Chollar-Potosi commences another rich part of the Comstock vein. On the northern line are the so-called Bajazet chimneys, two bodies of ore, separated by about eighteen feet of barren rock, each from twelve to twenty feet wide and about eighty feet long. They have been worked several hundred feet down, and their end seems not yet to have been reached. Their greater axis dips about sixty degrees to the south. With the next deposit to the south a different shape makes its appearance, which is more perfectly developed in Gold Hill, that of very long and narrow sheets of ore intercalated in the quartz and parallel to the eastern wall, or at least to a distinct clay seam which bounds the main body of quartz to the east. The Potosi deposit is about two hundred feet long, and contained rich ore to the width of from six to twenty-three feet. It commenced near the surface, and has been mined without interruption to the depth of four hundred and ninety feet. Its northern and southern boundary lines dip south. A considerable body of poor ore lies adjacent to and parallel with it, and is at present being extracted. Some narrow "chimneys" have been found in lower levels west of this body. After some interruption, the latter continues along the so-called eastern clay for a long way, and has been explored by the Chollar Company. It first made its appearance at the depth of about three hundred and eighty feet, and had at one place a width of fifty-five feet; but it soon terminated in depth. The entire length of the eastern body of ore of the Chollar-Potosi mine, excluding the Bajazet chimneys, but including some short interruptions, is about seven hundred and fifty feet; and even farther south, ore occurs along the eastern clay, but scattered, and not worth extracting at the present time. Quartz fills here the entire width of the vein from the western to the eastern wall, and in no part can its unity be more clearly recognized. It continues with a similar character in the Bullion mine, the northern part of which consists entirely of ore-bearing quartz of about one hundred and twenty feet in width. But at the levels worked up to this time it is too poor for extraction, as the ore is not concentrated in distinct bodies.

(b) AT GOLD HILL AND SOUTH OF IT.

The occurrence of ore in "chimneys," and of barren portions between them, ceases entirely at the divide between Virginia and Gold Hill. The great wealth of the mines south of it consists in the continuous ore-bearing character of the lode for a length of fifteen hundred and forty feet, from the Alpha mine to the middle part of the Yellow Jacket, and of other extensive portions farther south. The vein is by no means ore-bearing in its entire width; but the ore is concentrated in continuous sheets, the principal one of which is very near and parallel to the eastern wall, and but little interrupted in its entire length. Its widest places, which are from forty to fifty-five feet, are in the Imperial, Bacon, and Empire mines, and again in the Yellow Jacket. In most places it commenced at from one hundred and fifty to two hundred and fifty feet below the surface; and in many mines it is still worked at their lowest levels. It is wider in the three first-mentioned mines, because there united into one mass. South of the Empire it forks into three branches, the two western ones continuing in an irregular way. Besides this very extensive eastern body, there is another one in the Gold Hill mines farther to the west, which extends from the outcroppings down to from one hundred to two hundred and fifty feet in depth, and dips at an angle of fifty to sixty degrees to the west. It was worked out in the early and most flourishing time of Gold Hill, and considerable amounts were extracted, as its width was from twelve to twenty-two feet, and the ore very rich, particularly in gold. It continued in length, without interruption, for about five hundred feet. A similar body was worked out in the Yellow Jacket, the Crown Point, and the Belcher. It was not quite continuous, but at each of the three places was several hundred feet in length. Everywhere it dips to the west at about sixty degrees, and at some depth, which, as we recede from the northern Gold Hill mines, slightly but constantly increases, flattens out to the west, the bottom being nothing but clay in horizontal layers. Also its southern portion was remarkable for its high yield in gold and for its rich ores in general, but its width was here only from six to twelve feet. The southernmost continuation of this body was found in the Overman mine, where it is likewise rich in gold, but is limited in extent.

The upper portions of the Gold Hill mines are but little explored, and even at lower levels the works were never extended to the western branches of the vein. When the bottom of the first deposit was reached, and its wealth found to terminate in clay, the owners of the mines became discouraged; but explorations from that clayey bottom towards the east brought them to the place where the real wealth of their mines is accumulated, and will probably last for a long time to come. The eastern bodies were first found in Gold Hill proper, then in the Yellow Jacket, the Kentucky, and Crown Point, while the Belcher and Overman mines have not yet succeeded in finding them.

Another subject which we have to consider, in connection with the mode of distribution of the ore, is the change in its yield. It is a matter known to every Washoe miner that, in general, it has decreased. The deposits of the Ophir, and Mexican, and of the Gould and Curry, were the richest. The former yielded, at an average, one hundred and seven dollars per ton; the latter, seventy to eighty dollars, notwithstanding the imperfect processes of extraction which were formerly applied. Ores of six hundred dollars to the ton were then no rarity, and considerable shipments could be made of such as yielded from two thousand to three thousand dollars to the ton. It would now scarcely be possible to collect one ton of such ore, excepting when old works, in the highest levels, are being overhauled. Ores of three hundred to four hundred dollars are now of as rare occurrence as formerly those of fifteen hundred to two thousand dollars. The yield of the middle and low-grade ores has also considerably diminished; and, by far, the majority of the ore, which is being extracted at this day, contains on an average not more than thirty to thirty-two dollars, while the general average of all the ores will not be more than thirty-seven dollars to the ton. This decrease applies for the total amount of ore extracted; but it is equally true for every single mine. The quantity of ore extracted has remained stationary for a long time past, and is now about twelve hundred and fifty tons daily. But the methods of reduction have improved, and their expenses been diminished; therefore, ores of lower grade than formerly can now be worked profitably.

During the early period of the working on the Comstock Lode, the proportion of gold and silver changed considerably, the yield in gold decreasing constantly.

But as a greater depth is being reached, the proportion of gold is again on the increase.

As some general rules, in regard to the mode of distribution of the ore, may be observed:

1st. The ore is, in the northern part of the vein, concentrated in chimneys, dipping at an angle of sixty to eighty degrees to the south; in the southern part, it forms continuous sheets of great length, but which are comparatively narrow.

2d. These deposits of ore are inclosed in the eastern and sometimes also in the middle portion of the vein; the western branches are barren or poor.

3d. The richest and largest deposits have been found at those places where the outcrops (including those of the western branches) were most prominent, namely: at the Ophir, the Gould and Curry, the Savage, the Chollar, the Gold Hill mines, the Yellow Jacket, the Crown Point, and Belcher.

4th. In the northern part the vein is, at the levels explored up to the present time, invariably poor where it passes a ravine (as in Ophir, Central, Mount Davidson ravines, and the one which divides Mount Davidson from Mount Butler). But in the southern part, the ore continues in the ravines (Kentucky mine and Segregated Belcher.)

5th. The richest portions are south of each ravine crossed by the vein.

6th. All the chimneys in the northern part are at those places where the walls from close contact rapidly diverge to the south and cause the vein to expand.

7th. All the principal accumulations of ore are at those places where most room was given in the fissure for the deposition of quartz, and are therefore generally rare where an unusual amount of " horses " obstruct the vein (except North Potosi chimney in Gould and Curry mine).

I have dwelt on the subject of the distribution of the ore in the Comstock vein to some length, because I consider its examination as being of great importance to enable us to draw conclusions in regard to the mode of continuance of the vein in depth."

LOCATION ON THE COMSTOCK LODE.

The following table gives the names of the locations on the Comstock Lode, as far as its continuity has been ascertained with anything like certainty; the length of the individual claims, length of each claim explored, per centage of explored and unexplored ground, depth of the lowest workings, height of the top of the shafts above the level of the Sutro Tunnel, and other information.

North of the Utah, locations have been made on what is supposed to be the Comstock Lode, but the developments are unimportant; the same remark applies to that portion of the vein south of the Overman. As far as our present knowledge extends, the two claims just mentioned appear to limit the productive portion of the vein. They include a length of nearly four miles.

The length given for the Best and Belcher and Gould and Curry companies, is the amount of ground claimed. The actual amount of ground between the Sides and Savage companies is only one thousand one hundred and forty-three feet. The lengths given for the Hale and Norcross and Savage companies, are measured on the croppings. Owing to the divergence of the north line of the Savage and south line of the Hale and Norcross to the eastward, the direction in which the vein dips, the length of their claims on the lode, as depth is attained, is constantly increasing. Six feet of ground is in dispute between the Apple and Bates and Imperial companies.

TABLE OF MINING CLAIMS ON THE COMSTOCK LODE.

NAME.	Length of Claim in feet.	Length explored in feet.	Per cent. of Claim explored.	Per cent. unexplored.	Depth of lowest workings.	Height of top of shaft above Sutro Tunnel.	REMARKS.
Utah	1000	300	30	70	260	.....	Engine removed. Not working.
Allen	925	300	32	68	200	.....	Not working.
Sierra Nevada	1959	400	25	75	650	1796	
Union	500	5	1	99	80	.....	Explored by tunnel. Not work'g.
Ophir—North Mine	1200	400	33½	66⅔	} 549	1887	{ Explored through Ophir-Mexican shaft.
Mexican	100	100	100	....			
Ophir—South Mine	200	200	100	....			
Central	150	150	100		620	1898	
California	300	300	100		428	.....	Explored by tunnel and winzes.
Central No. 2	100	100	100	....	369	.....	} Explored by whim on White
Kinney	50	5	10	90	369	.....	& Murphy claim, and by the
White & Murphy	210	210	100	....	369	1954	} Latrobe tunnel. Not working.
Sides	500	200	40	60	500	1955	Not working.
Best & Belcher	250	250	100	....	469	1954	Engine removed. Not working.
Gould & Curry	1200	921	100	....	900	1800	
Savage—Old Shaft	771	771	100	....	614	1954	
" Curtis "	....	....	....	....	448	1787	
Hale & Norcross	400	400	100	....	783	1963	
Chollar-Potosi	1434	700	50	50	923	1832	
Bullion	940	450	47	53	800	1913	
Exchequer	400	....	....	100	540	1819	
Alpha	278½	278½	100	....	680	1800	
Apple & Bates	31½	31½	100	....		.....	
Imperial—Alta	118	118	100	....		1761	
Bacon	45	45	100	....		.....	
Empire—North Mine	55	55	100	....		1763	
Eclipse	30	30	100	....		1761	
French	20	20	100	....		.....	
Empire—South Mine	20	20	100	....		.....	
Plato	10	10	100	....		.....	
Bowers	20	20	100	....		.....	
Piute	20	20	100	....		.....	
Winters & Küstel	30	30	100	....	Average, 650 feet.	.....	
Consolidated	21	21	100	....		.....	
Rice Ground	13½	13½	100	....		.....	
Imperial—H. & L.	65½	65½	100	....		1734	
Challenge	50	50	100	....		1734	
Confidence	130	130	100	....		1725	
Burke & Hamilton	40	40	100	....		.....	
Yellow Jacket	943	943	100	....	560	1567	
Kentuck	93½	93½	100	....	460	1543	
Crown Point	540	540	100	....	400	1517	
Belcher	940	940	100	....	850	1585	
Segregated Belcher	160	160	100	....	500	1570	
Overman	1200	700	60	40	711	1606	
North American	2000	...?	...?	...?	300	1620	Not working.
Baltimore American	2000	500	25	75	300	.....	Not working.

PUMPING AND HOISTING ENGINES ON THE COMSTOCK LODE.

COMPANY.	Hoisting Eng's		Pump'g Eng's.		Pumping and Hoisting Eng's		REMARKS.
	No.	Horse power.	No.	Horse power.	No.	Horse power.	
Allen	....	.....	....	.....	1	30	
Sierra Nevada	1	60	1	200	.....	.....	
Ophir-Mexican	1	60	1	200	.....	.....	Total number of engines
Central	....	.....	....	.....	1	.....	on the lode, 47. The
Sides	....	.....	....	.....	1	50	estimate of the horse
Gould & Curry	2	60	1	150	.....	.....	power in many instan-
Savage (old shaft)	1	60	....	.....	.....	.....	ces can only be con-
Savage (new shaft)	3	60	1	300	.....	.....	sidered an approxima-
Hale & Norcross	....	.....	....	.....	1	.....	tion to real power of
Potosi	1	.....	....	.....	.....	.....	the engines.
Chollar-Potosi	1	.....	1	.....	.....	.....	
Bullion	....	.....	....	.....	2	.....	
Exchequer	....	.....	....	.....	1	60	
Alpha	....	.....	....	.....	1	.....	
Imperial	....	.....	....	.....	1	.....	
Empire	....	.....	....	.....	2	80	
Eclipse	....	.....	....	.....	2	30	
Winters & Küstel, consol'd	....	.....	....	.....	2	20	
Challenge	....	.....	....	.....	1	35	
Confidence	....	.....	....	.....	1	25	
Yellow Jacket	....	.....	....	.....	2	.....	
Kentuck	....	.....	....	.....	1	.....	
Belcher	....	.....	....	.....	2	.....	
Segregated Belcher	....	.....	....	.....	2	60	
Overman & Sam	2	80	2	40	.....	.....	
North American	....	.....	....	.....	1	.....	
Baltimore	.....	.....	....	.....	1	.....	

MILLS.

The number of mills running on ores extracted from the Comstock Lode is seventy-six, scattered through Storey, Lyon, Ormsby, and Washoe Counties. For information relative to their details, see the "Table of Mills" in another part of this report. The process of reduction and amalgamation employed by them varies only in minor details. They are, without exception, wet-crushing mills, the Central Mill in Virginia having recently adopted this method, and Dall's Mill, in Washoe Valley, was unfortunately destroyed by fire only a short time since. These used to be dry-crushing mills, and were employed in beneficiating the richer class of ores from the Comstock Lode. The latter mill was one of the finest in the State. The raw ore is ground and amalgamated, after crushing, in iron pans of various forms, among which may be mentioned Knox's, Varney's, Hepburn's, and Wheeler's patents. The capacity of these pans varies from 400 to 1000 pounds per charge, and the time consumed in the reduction of each charge ranges from four to six hours. In a future issue it is proposed to give figures and descriptions of the different pans, concentrators, crushers, etc., in use in the State, with the results obtained in practice, and the means by which they are attained. The mills are expected to return in bullion 65 per cent. of the assay value of the pulp, which may be taken as the average working result of the district. There is thus an annual loss of 35 per cent., or about $8,000,000. In view of this fact, would it not be policy on the part of our State Government to offer a large reward for the discovery of such improvements in the reduction of ores as would enable us to save 90 per cent. of their assay value, provided it can be accomplished without consuming the whole

of the additional 25 per cent. saved? The annual loss of gold and silver is
more than sufficient to cover the cost of the extraction of ore from the vein every
year. In the Table of Minerals Found in Nevada, under the head of "Gold,"
will be found information relative to the proportion of gold and silver in the ores
of the Comstock vein. The cost of milling the ordinary ores of the district may
be set down at $12 to $15, and the following table will show their average
yield:

COMPANY.	No. Tons Reduced	Av'ge Yield.
Hale & Norcross............................	22,626	$46 65
Savage.....................................	29,535	44 14
Crown Point	33,377	38 15
Gould & Curry.............................	*230,546	59 02
Empire.....................................	19,750	24 69
Ophir	11,163	42 50

YIELD IN BULLION OF THE COMSTOCK LODE.

Under this heading will be found three tables, viz:

First.—Table of the products of some of the principal mines in Virginia and
Gold Hill; also, showing dividends paid and assessments levied on the same.
(San Francisco Stock Reports.)

Second.—Bullion shipped from Virginia and Gold Hill, Nevada, for 1865 and
1866, by Wells, Fargo & Co.

Third.—Estimated bullion produce of Nevada for 1866.

An examination of the first table will show that eleven productive mines
yielded $11,261,741. Of this sum, seven mines produced $9,631,118, yielding
a net profit, after deducting assessments levied during the year, of $1,614,400,
or about 16¾ per cent. of the gross yield.

The other tables speak for themselves; but it should be remembered that the
dividends enumerated in the first table do not show the entire profits of the year.
Many of the valuable claims in Gold Hill are private property, and their yield
does not, in consequence, come before the public. The excess in the shipment
of bullion from Gold Hill in 1866 over 1865, is explained by the establishment
of assay offices in that place. Formerly the chief part of the crude bullion was
taken to Virginia to be melted, and then shipped from the express office in that
city.

---

* This is the average yield of ore from July 1st, 1860, to November 30th, 1866. (See
Yield of the Mine in another portion of the report.)

TABLE

OF THE PRODUCTS OF SOME OF THE PRINCIPAL MINES IN VIRGINIA AND
GOLD HILL; ALSO, SHOWING DIVIDENDS PAID AND ASSESSMENTS LEVIED
ON THE SAME DURING THE YEAR 1866.

COMPANY.	Bullion produced.	Dividends.	Assessments.
Lady Bryan........................	....	....	$15,000
Daney.............................	....	....	26,000
Sierra Nevada.....................	....	....	55,500
Ophir	$450,000	....	184,800
Gould & Curry....................	1,605,228	$252,000	....
Savage	1,805,800	360,000	....
Hale & Norcross	1,199,768	350,000	....
Chollar-Potosi	848,750	....	....
Bullion	....	....	175,000
Exchequer	....	....	32,000
Alpha............................	....	....	144,560
Imperial	910,187	176,000	....
Empire	486,778	32,400	....
Bacon	....	....	18,000
Confidence	303,920	....	78,000
Yellow Jacket	2,310,000	390,000	180,000
Crown Point......................	1,313,357	234,000	....
Belcher...........................	....	....	143,520
Overman..........................	27,953	....	208,000
Baltimore American	....	....	18,000
Totals	$11,261,741	$1,794,400	$1,273,880

BULLION SHIPPED FROM VIRGINIA AND GOLD HILL, NEVADA, FOR 1865 AND 1866, BY WELLS, FARGO & CO.

1865.	Gold Hill.	Virginia.	Totals.
January	$253,602 89	$940,152 13	$1,193,755 02
February	229,856 24	1,033,855 89	1,263,712 13
March	235,485 68	1,154,749 76	1,390,335 44
April	150,102 45	1,191,172 00	1,341,274 45
May	197,802 30	1,012,435 59	1,210,237 89
June	246,725 62	694,256 11	940,981 73
July	260,001 59	511,127 57	771,129 16
August	314,808 93	550,730 78	865,539 71
September	399,613 99	492,203 79	891,817 78
October	496,165 00	547,365 58	1,043,530 58
November	408,307 90	539,217 76	947,525 66
December	354,425 00	619,455 28	973,880 28
Totals	$3,546,897 59	$9,286,822 24	$12,833,719 83

1866.	Gold Hill.	Virginia.	Totals.
January	$432,044 28	$520,177 20	$952,221 48
February	475,491 63	492,322 91	968,814 54
March	490,123 89	705,210 33	1,195,334 22
April	413,177 17	646,987 51	1,060,164 68
May	562,074 83	648,776 71	1,210,851 54
June	673,111 40	562,938 70	1,236,050 10
July	673,385 93	595,503 77	1,268,889 70
August	672,690 14	779,276 59	1,451,966 73
September	700,940 33	643,963 97	1,344,904 30
October	726,464 08	686,517 23	1,412,981 31
November	613,779 62	739,512 30	1,353,291 92
December	666,984 70	786,438 96	1,453,423 66
Totals	$7,100,268 00	$7,807,626 18	$14,907,894 18

BULLION PRODUCED IN NEVADA DURING THE YEAR 1866.

Shipped by Wells, Fargo & Co.	Virginia City	$7,807,626 18
	Gold Hill	7,100,268 00
	Carson City	841,366 80
	Reese River	400,587 00
	Aurora	171,534 00
Shipped by other parties, say		600,000 00
		$16,421,381 98

The recent developments in Eastern Nevada warrant us in expecting much increased shipments for the coming year. The mines of Twin River, Silver Bend, Hot Creek, Reveille, and other districts have already given evidence of their productiveness, which, taken in conjunction with the reduced price of working the ores in the Reese River section, as well as in Storey County, enabling large quantities of ore to be reduced which in former years have been valueless, certainly make an estimate of $18,000,000 for 1867 as within the mark. The prospects of the State certainly never looked more flattering, or rested on a surer foundation.

Details of the consumption of materials in the Gould and Curry mine and mill for the year 1866; cost of drifting, sinking shafts, &c., &c., furnished by Louis Janin, junr., Superintendent, or compiled from data furnished by him.

These tables will be found of great interest, not only to persons in this State, but to those interested in mining elsewhere. It is hoped that this department of the report may be very greatly enlarged in future years; and while the details given are complete as far as they go, much more might be added of lasting value. (See Synopsis of Report in the early pages of this report.) As the resources of this State are developed year by year, and the prices of material vary, such a record of what has been done in the past will become more and more valuable, to say nothing of their importance as a check on extravagant expenditure, and as data from which to estimate the probable success of incipient mining enterprises. The example of the Gould and Curry, Savage, and other companies who have adopted this system, is worthy of imitation by all. I have not thought it necessary in this place to give the monthly accounts, but have tabulated the entire consumption of each article for the year.

MATERIALS CONSUMED AT THE GOULD & CURRY MINE FOR THE YEAR
ENDING NOVEMBER 30TH, 1866.

ARTICLE.	Average Price.	Quantity.	Total Cost.
Square Timbers, feet..........		1,614,145	$54,814 00
Lumber, (boards, etc.) feet.....		581,191	19,025 00
Spiling, pieces		25,071	5,959 00
Candles, pounds.............		41,460	11,206 00
Wood, cords.................		2,023	29,418 00
Charcoal, bushels............		8,020	2,696 00
Powder, kegs................		162	1,050 00
Iron, pounds.................		46,554	5,498 00
Steel, pounds................		5,682	1,412 00
Pick Handles................		1,786	798 00
Sledge Handles..............		300	120 00
Shovels.....................		405	665 00
Sledges.....................		52	320 00
Fuse, feet...................		24,478	458 00
Nails, pounds		11,268	1,497 00
Files		635	302 00
Axes.......................		33	82 50
Saws........		13	40 50
Brooms.................. ...	(See Materials Consumed at the Mill.)	73	48 00
Bolts and Nuts, pounds........		3,823	765 00
Leather, pounds.......		231	93 00
Canvas, yards...............		153	185 00
Rope, pounds...............		2,012	432 00
Lard Oil, gallons.............		439	1,367 00
Sperm Oil, gallons...........		277	831 00
Kerosene Oil, gallons.........		425	847 00
Tallow, pounds..............		3,459	518 00
Lamp Chimneys..............		154	25 00
Lamp Wicks.................		169	8 45
Hay, pounds.................	$37 50 pr ton.	37,390	703 00
Barley, pounds..............	4½c. pr lb.	25,241	1,106 00
Car-wheels	15 45	42	649 00
Axles	4 19	11	46 00
White Lead, pounds...........	....	1,300	292 00
Water	....	....	4,305 00
Sundries	....	....	8,699 00
Total....................	....	....	$156,279 45

MATERIALS CONSUMED AT THE GOULD & CURRY MILL DURING THE YEAR
ENDING NOVEMBER 30TH, 1866.

ARTICLE.	Quantity.	Cost.	Average Price.
Wood, cords...............	11,442	$168,830 00	$14 72
Lumber, feet	172,857	3,725 00	(perM)42 40
Shingles.....................	21,500	185 00	8 60
Charcoal, bushels............	5,848	1,659 00	28
Iron, pounds.................	12,639	1,698 00	13½
Gas Pipe, pounds............	450	258 00	57½
Castings, pounds.............	395,099	33,880 00	8½
Rivets, Nuts, etc., pounds......	853	175 00	20
Steel, pounds...............	1,253	315 00	25
Copper, pounds	178	142 00	80
Babbit Metal, pounds	262	120 00	46
Nails, pounds................	3,832	417 00	11
Zinc, pounds.........	172	42 00	25
Turpentine, gallons...........	25	72 00	3 00
Belting, pounds..............	2,888	2,192 00	
Packing, pounds..............	494	497 00	1 00
Rope, pounds................	893	96 00	25
Hose, pounds................	136	97 00	
Sulphate of Copper, pounds.....	87,353	17,588 00	20
Salt, pounds..	345,668	10,943 00	03
Lard Oil, gallons.............	1,360	2,487 00	1 83
Kerosene Oil, gallons..........	985	1,615 00	1 64
Linseed Oil, gallons..........	40	99 00	2 47
Quicksilver, flasks............	675	35,013 00	51 89
Cut Bolts, pounds.............	923	214 00	23
Screens, pounds	743	633 00	$1 to .75
Candles, pounds..............	2,980	819 00	27½
Axes and Handles............	71	67 00	
Picks.......................	42	20 00	50
Shovels	239	231 00	1 39
Feed, sacks.................	487	2,087 00	
Hay, bales	196	1,120 00	
Axle Grease.................	116	58 00	50
Copper Rivets, pounds.........	280	280 00	1 00
Tallow, pounds...............	10,863	1,361 00	12½
Alcohol, gallons..............	15	60 00	4 00
Brooms	189	147 00	77
Oakum, pounds..............	126	46 00	32
Sledge Handles..............	157	77 00	50
Lamp Chimneys	531	174 00	32
Hoes.......................	76	71 00	1 00
White and Red Lead.....	1,241	242 00	20
Blankets	48	347 00	8 00
Leather....................	575	246 00	42½
Stone-coal..................	9,751	714 00	(p.t'n)150 00
Water	....	6,835 00	....
Sundries	....	3,833 00	....
Total..................	....	$301,927 00	

COST OF TUNNELING IN THE GOULD & CURRY MINE—LABOR, MATERIALS, ETC.

600 Feet.

No. Feet	Price paid per foot	Total Cost of Excavation	Timber	Lumber	Spiling	Framing and Plac'g Timber	Track Iron & Screws	Picks and Drills	Powder and Fuse	Candles	Air Boxes	Totals	Cost per Lineal Foot
59	$13 00	$767 00	$146 83	$9 12	$50 40	$42 00	$13 77	$22 50	$18 60	$27 00	$12 72	$1,109 94	$16 84
46	18 00	598 00	98 72	6 84	37 80	81 50	10 89	19 00	15 05	21 60	9 54	848 44	
47	18 00	611 00	118 26	7 14	39 48	82 90	11 60	28 80	13 80	24 30	9 80	897 07	
90	18 00	1,170 00	220 24	13 68	75 50	63 00	20 28	40 75	21 90	28 35	19 80	1,673 50	
157	10 64	1,661 00	308 04	18 84	122 48	110 50	41 68	67 00	31 20	89 70	62 80	2,518 22	
204	10 54	2,151 00	402 21	24 60	110 70	143 50	55 70	86 00	44 40	118 39	82 00	3,218 50	
168	10 67	1,789 00	297 55	18 20	92 53	113 75	48 84	98 00	80 00	91 08	65 00	2,593 90	
182	11 47	1,515 00	241 72	14 78	70 20	92 50	35 45	59 00	43 87	72 93	52 80	2,198 25	
40	18 00	525 00	74 55	4 80	24 00	28 00	10 68	19 00	21 37	22 44	16 00	745 84	
938		$10,787 00	$1,908 11	$118 00	$628 07	$657 65	$248 39	$440 05	$240 19	$495 74	$330 46	$15,798 66	$16 84

400 Feet Level.

No. Feet	Price paid per foot	Total Cost of Excavation	Timber	Lumber	Spiling	Framing and Plac'g Timber	Track Iron & Screws	Picks and Drills	Powder and Fuse	Candles	Air Boxes	Totals	Cost per Lineal Foot
30	$8 00	$240 00	$73 41	$4 56	$25 20	$21 00	$7 25	$10 00	$10 65	$13 50	$6 36	$411 93	$16 08
60	10 00	600 00	146 88	9 12	67 20	42 00	14 02	15 00	16 00	24 30	12 72	947 19	
81	11 00	891 00	198 51	12 31	68 04	56 00	18 61	19 50	21 30	24 30	16 96	1,326 53	
101	11 00	1,111 50	244 72	15 20	84 00	66 00	28 20	35 75	24 00	24 30	22 00	1,650 67	
66	10 00	660 00	159 06	9 88	54 60	46 50	14 98	34 00	18 60	26 32	14 30	1,037 24	
171	12 05	2,061 00	241 50	98 16	76 20	87 00	30 86	38 00	36 00	75 60	28 60	2,772 92	
120	12 75	1,532 00	306 42	151 29	58 80	210 00	18 89	44 00	18 00	68 64	85 00	2,487 47	
101	11 79	1,191 00	222 00	63 00	48 20	56 00	20 95	41 50	17 10	46 20	82 00	1,782 95	
209	11 64	2,433 00	468 88	15 68	79 80	98 00	45 46	102 00	39 60	78 54	56 00	3,416 91	
215	11 64	2,504 00	420 19	55 44	104 22	77 25	50 57	75 00	36 87	106 58	18 10	3,442 73	
264	7 32	1,934 00	512 31	70 50	142 50	175 00	73 50	111 00	60 00	140 25	100 00	8,319 06	
47	16 49	775 00	126 89	44 85	9 00	32 90	5 21	37 00	7 50	28 26	......	1,064 04	
1465		$15,932 50	$3,120 60	$549 49	$807 26	$967 15	$322 98	$562 75	$305 12	$654 80	$387 04	$23,559 64	$16 08

COST OF SINKING THE BONNER SHAFT.

Paid for Excavation	$22,324.50
Lumber	5,460.05
Timber	9,670.67
Framing timbers	8,518.00
Placing timbers	1,570.50
Carmen	8,530.00
Extra workmen	....
Lowering pumps, etc., etc.	4,688.75
Picks and drills	2,041.50
Powder and fuse	291.00
Candles	1,054.30
Other materials	1,777.13
Cost of running machinery, keeping pumps in order, pit-men, etc.	19,817.00
	$75,738.40

Depth attained, 692.5 feet. Price per foot, $109 86-100. The shaft consists of four compartments, five feet square, and is cribbed with twelve-inch timbers. It is capable of working the mine to a depth of twelve hundred feet.

ORE AND BULLION PRODUCT OF GOULD AND CURRY MINE, FROM DATE OF
INCORPORATION (JUNE 27TH, 1860) TO NOV. 30TH, 1866.

DATES.		Ore Worked, etc., Tons.	Bullion, etc.	Average Yield per Ton.	
From	To				
1860 July 1	1860 Dec. 13 .	140½	$22,004.82	$156.62	
1860 December 14 .	1861 Dec. 13 .	300	44,221.44	147.40	
1861 December 14 .	1862 Nov. 30 .	8,442½	842,538.80	99.80	
1862 December 1 ..	1863 Nov. 30 .	48,745	3,902,912.64	80.07	1,468,800
1863 December 1 ..	1864 Nov. 30 .	66,477¼	4,798,124.90	72.18	1,440,000
1864 December 1 ..	1865 Nov. 30 .	46,022¼	2,026,172.57	44.02	618,000
1865 December 1 ..	1866 Nov. 30 .	60,417½	1,690,952.25	28.00	252,000
Total	....	....	$13,326,727.39		
From tailings .	....	....	300,143.76		
Worked—tons.	....	230,546	$13,626,871.15	$59.02	
On hand, Dec. 1,1866—tons	....	4,249½			
Total product.	....	234,759½			

WOOD, LUMBER, WATER, ETC.

Wood for fuel ranges from $14 to $16 per cord, according to the quality. The most valuable fuel is the "piñon," or nut pine, which at one time covered all the hills in the vicinity of the mines. The immense demand has long since exhausted this supply, and it is now brought from localities ten and twelve miles distant from Virginia. The teams hauling ore to the Carson River at Empire, to Washoe Valley, Galena, &c., bring return freights of firewood from the Sierra Nevada, where the quantity is practically inexhaustible; but its inferior heating properties place it in the market about $2 per cord less than piñon, and even at that price the latter is the most economical fuel, being a closer grained, harder wood, and containing a much larger per centage of resinous matter. The annual consumption of firewood in the three districts may be estimated at about 144,000 cords, worth nearly two million dollars. The cost of transporting this firewood to the place of consumption cannot be far short of $1,250,000.

The lumber used in the districts is brought entirely from the Sierra Nevada, and the annual consumption may be estimated at about 35,000,000 feet board measure, at a cost of about $1,400,000. Of this sum the freight will be about one-half, or $700,000. As by far the larger proportion of both these articles is consumed in the mines and mills of the three districts, it is evident that any means which would reduce their price would be of immense advantage to the mines; any saving in this way, of course, increasing the funds available for dividends. Not only would a direct benefit accrue in this manner, but a diminution in the expenses of mining and milling would immediately render valuable, ores which at present, from their low grade, do not pay for extraction and reduction. The completion of railroad communication between Virginia and the Sierra Nevada would immediately reduce the cost of freight one-half, leaving even then a handsome profit on the cost of transportation. The gross revenue of a railroad between the above mentioned points would not fall far short of one million dollars per annum from these two sources alone.

The amount of water in these districts is small compared with many mining localities. At some seasons of the year it is barely sufficient to keep the machinery on the lode and the mills running. Water for domestic use finds a ready sale at $40 per month for each miner's inch. The latter supply is derived entirely from tunnels driven into the mountain above the level of the chief mining works. Were it not for the high price of labor and materials, the water which the mining companies have to contend with would be considered insignificant. When a fresh body of water is encountered in mining operations, it usually runs in considerable volume for a short time, but rapidly diminishes in quantity as the original reservoir is drained. The largest quantities of water have been met with in the northern explorations on the lode. The flow in the deep adit of the Gould and Curry Company was probably the greatest in volume, but being in an adit produced little inconvenience. The Ophir and Central companies have had the greatest difficulties in this respect. The Ophir Company at one time had a stream of three hundred gallons per minute. This water was warm, and an analysis of it will be found in the Appendix.

DEEP WORKINGS.

There are now four shafts located on the Comstock Lode, admirably adapted for working to a depth of about twelve hundred feet. Of these, the Curtis Shaft, (Savage Co.) Bonner Shaft, (Gould and Curry Co.) and Chollar-Potosi

Shaft, are down to considerable depths. That of the Hale and Norcross Company is but just commenced. The first shafts put down on the Comstock Lode were uniformly started on the croppings of the vein, and reached the west wall at about five hundred feet down. The western country-rock proved so hard that when it became necessary for the Gould and Curry Company to sink a shaft for the exploration of their property below their deep adit, they selected a site lower down the hill, about two hundred feet below the croppings of the lode. Their example was followed by the Savage, Chollar-Potosi, and lately by the Hale and Norcross. The companies lying north of the Gould and Curry will ultimately be compelled to adopt the same course; and in view of late developments it would be wise policy for the companies from the Sides to the California, inclusive, to unite in such an object and sink a shaft for the joint exploration of the whole of the claims. Such a plan would entail a comparatively small expense on each company individually, and would probably convert into valuable property some twelve hundred feet of the vein which has now been lying idle for upwards of a year. In this connection the most important work yet projected is the

SUTRO DRAIN TUNNEL.

The main features of this enterprise are now so well known to the public that it is not necessary to repeat them here. A sketch of the enterprise will be found in the Annual Report of the Surveyor General of Nevada for 1866, p. 56, and the publications of the company give all the minutiæ of the contemplated operations. The selection of the Comstock Lode, and the topographical map of the country beneath which the tunnel will pass, are valuable additions to our knowledge of these mining districts. Of the immense value of the Sutro Tunnel to the mines on the Comstock Lode there can be no doubt, and it is gratifying to find that the unwearied efforts of the projector are likely to be crowned with success. Probably no mining locality possesses greater facilities for deep drainage; indeed, Nevada is admirably situated in this respect, its mineral-bearing mountain ranges being usually lofty and precipitous, with an average width at the base of from ten to twelve miles only.

LANDER COUNTY.

Lander County occupies the northeastern corner of the State, and is bounded by Nye County on the south, and Humboldt County on the west. The greater portion of the county is still comparatively unknown, the principal mining districts lying south of the Humboldt River, along the western and southern boundaries. It is a cause of much regret to me that I was unable to visit this section during the summer, and consequently must give so imperfect a sketch of its resources, but hope to be able to enter into details in a future report. This explanation is necessary to account for the many omissions I am compelled to make—a fault which certainly does not arise from a wish to do injustice to a section of the State which has claimed such prominent attention for the last three years.

I make the following extract from "Harrington's Austin Directory," relative to the discovery of silver in this section of the State:

"Early in the month of May, 1862, William M. Talcott, an attaché of the stage station at Jacob's Springs, while hauling wood from the hillside, now within the limits of the city of Austin, discovered a vein of metal-bearing quartz, and carried a small quantity with him to the station. The rock proved to contain silver, the ledge was located as a mining claim, and named the Pony, as the discoverer had formerly been a rider of the Pony Express. On the 10th day of May, 1862, a mining district was formed, including an area of seventy-five miles east and west, and twenty north and south, and named the Reese River Mining District. A code of laws was adopted, William M. Talcott was elected recorder, and the claims already discovered were recorded."

This district has since been repeatedly subdivided, and many others discovered. The following table will give the names of the majority of them:

TOIYABE RANGE,

ON THE WESTERN SIDE OF THE COUNTY.

A. Western Slope, commencing at the southern boundary and going north.

1. Washington District, 25 miles south of Austin.
2. Big Creek District, 12 miles south of Austin.
3. Reese River District, containing the towns of Austin and Clifton.
4. Amador District, 6 miles north of Austin.
5. Mount Hope District, 12 miles north of Austin.
6. Cumberland District, 15 miles north of Austin.
7. Columbus District, 20 miles north of Austin.
8. Mount Vernon District, 30 miles north of Austin.

B. Eastern Slope, commencing at the southern boundary and going north.

9. Bunker Hill District, 25 miles south of Austin.
10. Summit District, 20 miles south of Austin.
11. Santa Fé District, 20 miles south of Austin.
12. Smoky Valley District, 12 miles south of Austin.
13. Simpson's Park District, east of Austin.
14. Indian District, 15 miles north of Austin.
15. Callaghan Ranch District, 16 miles north of Austin.
16. Wall Street District, 25 miles north of Austin.
17. Cortez District, 65 miles north of Austin.
18. Yreka District, 75 miles north of Austin.

SECOND RANGE EAST OF TOIYABE RANGE.

19. Eureka District, 60 miles east of Austin.
20. Newark District, 70 miles east of Austin.
21. Diamond District, 80 miles east of Austin.
22. White Pine District, 90 miles east of Austin.
23. Cascade District, 90 miles east of Austin.

RUBY VALLEY REGION.

24. Ruby District, 125 miles east of Austin.
25. Wolf Mountain District, 120 miles east of Austin.

EGAN CANON SECTION.

26. Gold Cañon District, 160 miles east of Austin.
27. Hercules District, 150 miles east of Austin.

EXTREME EASTERN SECTION.

28. Kinsley District, 200 miles east of Austin.

MILLS IN THE COUNTY.

In the early days of Lander County the wet crushing and amalgamation of the raw ore, as adopted at Virginia, were tried at Austin with poor success. As better information as to the character of the ores, which contain considerable antimonial silver, was obtained, dry crushing and roasting of the ore were adopted, and the mills now yield a higher per centage of the assay value of the ores than is obtained in Storey County. The price charged at the mills for reduction has gradually fallen from about $75 to $45 or $50 per ton. I regret that I am unable to give a detailed list of the mills and their statistics. Quite a number of lists have been published, but they vary so greatly as to be irreconcilable. On this account I prefer to quote from the *Reveille* the number of mills at present twenty, and the aggregate number of stamps at two hundred and nineteen, which I believe will prove to be a reliable exhibit. The price of wood is about $9 per cord, and the supply abundant for some years' consumption.

NOTICES OF MINING DISTRICTS.

The chief characteristics of the Toiyabe Mountains are slates, limestone, porphyries, and granite; the latter is largely developed in the neighborhood of Austin.

REESE RIVER DISTRICT.

The mining locations in this district are very numerous. Compared with many of our mining districts, the lodes may be said to be narrow, but the high state of concentration in which the mineral is found renders many of the veins, though small, valuable property. The information at my command is of such a character that I greatly prefer, for the present, to refer to the reports on Lander County in the Surveyor General's Reports for 1865 and 1866, in which will be found many items of interest, rather than deal in comparatively useless generalities. This district is, without doubt, one of the most important in the State, and under the better system of management which has been inaugurated, will yield steadily improving returns of bullion. If not already organized, it is contemplated to establish a "Mining Bureau" at Austin, composed of men interested in the welfare of Eastern Nevada, having for its object, the check of fraudulent enterprises, with the dissemination of correct information to all who may require it. The example is well worthy of imitation. May it prove the nucleus of a State Bureau, having the same objects.

The following statistics of the product of the mines in Lander County for the quarter ending December 31, 1866, as shown by the books of the assessor, is taken from the Reese River *Reveille:*

"PRODUCT OF THE MINES IN LANDER COUNTY.

NAME.	Tons.	Pounds.	Aver. per Ton.
Diana	143	1,909	$ 91 18
Amsterdam	1	250	168 75
Buel North Star	4	1,920	336 57
Camargo	12	973	116 57
Chase	4	1,438	405 10
Enterprise (White Pine District)	1	....	111 53
East Oregon	4	779	187 65
Empire State	7	619	99 22
Ensign	1	667	66 25
Fortune Teller	4	416	177 28
Florida	13	1,900	255 60
Fenian Star	7	1,359	54 24
Fortuna	1	1,520	30 33
Farrel	3	1,453	71 12
Great Eastern	287	....	217 94
Idora	22	1,695	220 42
J. R. Murphy	1	100	251 18
Joseph Cole	1	1,350	27 85
Jacob Bradley	1	....	116 80
Keystone	2	350	194 66
Kihock	1	....	197 27
Zaidee	1	728	100 61
Lodi	7	1,019	32 54
Livermore	3	500	157 79
Mount Tenabo Company (Cortez)	....	....	....
Morgan & Muncey	4	626	25 69
Magnolia	6	1,671	338 23
Metacom	26	....	100 99
Manhattan Company	69	288	83 90
May & Davis	2	430	136 80
North River	13	1,924	56 03
Owen & Perkins	3	1,700	46 16
Providential	64	844	54 91
Pinney, Rev	6	600	51 73
Patten	2	824	200 43
Remington	6	1,500	49 63
Savage Consolidated	451	....	103 25
Silver Queen	14	1,913	38 28
Surprise	1	....	171 66
Semanthe	2	150	332 52
Timoke	79	1,138	148 41
Taylor & Passmore (Cortez)	5	982	160 43
Tunnehill (Eureka)	3	1,338	106 85
Victoria	4	1,176	91 20
Washington	12	67	479 52
Whitlatch Union	18	546	105 97
Zimmerman	5	1,278	71 75

"The above table embraces forty-seven mines, which have yielded more or less bullion during the quarter; and, with few exceptions, the ore reduced is of good grade, sufficiently so to admit its being worked here remuneratively. It will be observed that a number of mines, which were included in the previous quarters of the year, do not appear in the present list, as well as that several mines appear for the first time. According to the Assessor's returns, there are in Lander County—and mainly in the Reese River District—fully seventy-five mines which have produced bullion during the past year. As we have remarked, the ore worked is very generally of a high grade, as the average yield per ton will show. A considerable number of the mines embraced in the quarterly lists were subjected only to testing operations, and the general result must be deemed very encouraging, and their excellent character augurs well for the future of this district. In the case of the Savage mine, the average yield of the ore is less than in several quarters preceding, but is still high, being $103.25 per ton. The yield of the Washington, Chase, Buel, North Star, Great Eastern, Semanthe, Magnolia, Florida, Timoke, Idora, Metacom, Taylor, and Passmore, etc., is grand, and as most of them are pretty well developed, they may be fairly classed henceforth among the producing and paying mines of the Reese River District."

This district is one of the many in Nevada which would derive much advantage from a well-arranged system of concentration of the ores before reduction. Many of the ores are of such a character that, though rich, they do not pay for reduction by the methods at present in use. The double sorting which they undergo in the mine and on the surface makes the cost of labor for mining high, and much valuable material has to be discarded as useless, which might be fitted, at a comparatively small cost, by the use of proper machinery, either for the roasting or the smelting furnace. This remark does not apply only to the Reese River District, but to all in which the cost of reducing the ores is large, and especially to all such as produce argentiferous galena ores. Many persons in the State have tried methods of concentration, and pronounced them failures generally, from a disregard of the first principles involved in the operation. For concentration to be successful, it is necessary first to sort the "sands," as nearly as may be, into particles of the same size, so that the difference in their specific gravity (on which concentration is based) may not be nullified by the difference in their areas exposed to the action of the stream of water by which the operation is conducted. This difficulty once overcome, the after-processes are so simplified that no difficulty need be experienced in obtaining successful results. This is scarcely the place to enter into the minutiæ of concentration, even if I had time to do so; the idea is merely thrown out as one well worthy of the attention of miners in Nevada.

CORTEZ DISTRICT,

about sixty-five miles northeast of Austin, was discovered and located in 1863. The principal lode in the district is the Nevada Giant, the following description of which is taken from the Reese River *Reveille* of January 4th, 1867:

"This giant vein is imbedded in the bosom of Mount Tenabo, a lofty peak some ten thousand feet above the level of the sea, and upwards of five thousand feet above the surrounding valleys. Its base, and thousands of feet up its side to the vein, are covered with a small scrubby pine; while its summit, and fifteen hundred feet below, are overgrown with grass and shrubs. The scarred and rugged mountain looks eternal. Some three thousand feet above its base a monster vein of silver-bearing quartz cuts its face obliquely, burying itself in the mountain at one end, and penetrating into the valley at the other, after stretching out in palpable view the enormous length of eighteen thousand six hundred and fifty feet. Its width is four hundred feet. In the course of this extreme length, the leviathan is cut transversely by a number of small veins of silver mineral. We state this as of doubtful occurrence, for in the judgment of several persons who have examined the Giant they are not transverse veins, but lateral spurs or chimneys from the main vein, and generally exhibit mineral of a very rich character. This giant vein is encased in highly crystalline limestone. Twenty locations have been made on the vein, with the following names and dimensions: Commencing at its greatest point of altitude is the Chieftain—Genessee Company, 1,400 feet; Murphy Company, 800; Gill Company, 800; Taylor and Passmore, 800; De Witt Company, 450; St. Louis Company, 2,000; Meacham and Brothers, 400; Niagara Company, 400; Savage Company, 400; Nebraska Company, 1,200. Cortez Giant—Mount Tenabo Company, 4,000; Elmore Company, 200; Russell Company, 600; Continental Company, 1,000; Argentine Company, 1,000; Empire Company, 800; Conn and Brothers, 400; Traverse Company, 400; and the Anna Burr Company, 2,000 feet. The latter claim is somewhat broken, and at its termination the vein penetrates the earth, and is lost altogether. The vein disappears also at the upper boundary of the Chieftain. It has been opened at several points along its course, in every case disclosing good mineral. The Gill, Taylor and Passmore, and St. Louis locations, near the upper end of the vein, have been worked, the two latter considerably. The Cortez Giant, which lies near the center of the vein, is the most fully developed location, and has yielded a large amount of bullion this season. Some work has also been done on the Continental, situated towards the lower end of the vein, with about the same results as in the other cases specified. Of this wonderful vein there is little exact knowledge, but that it stands out upon the mountain's face, a huge, palpable fact. It will be developed; and when that day arrives, we believe the Nevada Giant will be almost universally regarded as among the wonderful mines of the world."

There is an eight-stamp mill, with accommodation for sixteen, now running in the district, with good results. The first ore crushed was from the Berlin Lode. To obtain the best results, the ores of the district will require roasting.

WASHINGTON DISTRICT,

about twenty-five miles south of Austin, on the western slope of the Toiyabe Mountains, is remarkable for the abundance of its argentiferous galena ores. Of this class are those produced by the Live Oak and St. Helena mines. The latter mine has been opened to considerable depth, and shows fine galena, associated with iron pyrites.

EUREKA DISTRICT

was located in 1864. It is well supplied with wood and water, and there are fine agricultural lands in the neighborhood.

GOLD CANON DISTRICT. (?)

This I believe to be the name of the mining district organized in the neighborhood of Egan Cañon. The following items relative to the mines in this neighborhood are taken from the "Reese River Reveille:"

The best known and developed mine is the Gilligan, belonging to the Social Company, which has been prospected by an incline to a depth of four hundred feet, and yielded before the suspension of operations $60,000 worth of bullion.

The ore was treated raw, and but a small proportion of the silver saved. Work is about to be resumed, and the tailings will be roasted.

KINSLEY DISTRICT,

on the eastern border of the State, is remarkable for the size and richness of its copper veins. It has but recently been located.

APPENDIX "A."

ON THE CAUSES OF THE DECAY OF MINING ENTER-
PRISES IN MANY PORTIONS OF THE STATE.

APPENDIX "A."

THE CAUSES OF THE DECAY OF MINING ENTERPRISES IN MANY PORTIONS OF THE STATE.

So universally have the mining districts of the State, outside of Virginia and Gold Hill, sprung into short-lived notoriety, exciting great hopes by promises of unbounded wealth, only to lapse again into obscurity, that a universal distrust of mining enterprises in those sections obtained but a short time ago. In the earlier months of our history scarcely a day passed without some new district being discovered, which, according to the reports of the fortunate locators, possessed not only an abundance of rich ores, but every requisite for their reduction; and even to-day our prospectors still come in from their adventurous wanderings through the wilderness with accounts equally promising. How comes it, then, that of all these localities which were to supply fortunes to all who were interested in them, so few have even a passing notice to-day?—and of those few, how is it that they contribute so little to the wealth of the State? Is it because the richness of the mines was exaggerated? Is it because of mismanagement in their development?—or because the character of the ores was misunderstood, and the wrong means of reduction employed?

To a State so entirely dependent, as we are, upon our mineral wealth, the inquiry into the rise and decay of these outside districts is a most important question, as upon a clear understanding of it, in all its bearings, depends in a great measure our future existence and prosperity. From it we may learn the errors into which we have fallen, and, profiting by experience, frequently introduce success where failure has attended all previous efforts.

The observations which I am about to make in this and the succeeding chapter may seem so simple, and their truth so patent to everybody, that many persons may be inclined to smile at them; nevertheless there is such an accumulation of evidence that even to-day many of the points are misunderstood, or thought of so little value, that I cannot refrain from calling attention to them, in the hope that some good may be the result, and that the true knowledge of our position may help in some degree to remove the false impressions which exist outside of our boundaries as to the extent of our resources.

The better to understand our position, it may be well to glance at the character of the population of the State, as all the efforts which have been made for the development of our resources have been colored by their salient characteristics. Possessing a large foreign element, that of American birth predominates not only largely in numbers but in the conduct of our chief enterprises, and has given to them the peculiar features of the American character. Energetic, hopeful, and self-reliant, impatient to achieve success, but at the same time undaunted by unexpected obstacles, the inventive genius of the people has been called into more than usual activity, and probably no nation in the world could

14

have accomplished in the same time what has been achieved in Nevada, under similar circumstances.

The original population of the State came from California, and had there been engaged more or less in placer mining. As a body they were ignorant of the details of vein mining, unacquainted with the appearance and characteristics of mineral lodes, and but few indeed had any knowledge of the distinguishing features of any minerals except gold, or the means of extracting them from the gangues with which they were associated. With an adaptiveness essentially American, much has been accomplished in the way of acquiring the requisite knowledge on these points; but we may undoubtedly trace to this source most of the difficulties which have befallen us. In this there is much cause for congratulation, because time will remedy the evil. It was one, certainly, which we could not avoid, however much we may regret its results; but the more widely true, practical knowledge becomes disseminated, the less will its influence be felt, and the more steadily will our material prosperity advance.

This want of knowledge, however, was not confined to the prospectors and locators of our mines. Unfortunately, during our early history, the population was sadly deficient in men with good, practical mining knowledge to take charge of the development and working of mining property; and errors in judgment on their part have been only too numerous. This evil, like the other, is in a fair way of being remedied, many of our mines being under the management of thoroughly competent men; still it is patent that many companies, and especially those organized in the Eastern States, have been put into the hands of men, energetic and thoroughly competent as far as regards business qualifications, but unfitted for the positions they occupy, in too many instances, from a want of knowledge of mining details, and ignorance of the county in which they are residing.

The causes which have led to our difficulties may then be classed under three heads:

1st. Errors in judgment by prospectors.
2d. Errors in judgment by superintendents and trustees.
3d. Swindling transactions perpetrated on foreign capital.

Let us examine them *seriatim*. The errors in judgment on the part of prospectors resulted in unintelligent prospecting.

It was natural that men without experience should make many false estimates of the treasures they had found; and thus, it happened that great numbers of valueless locations were made, without any intentional deception on the part of the locators. Having once seen silver procured from a quartz vein, not a few arrived at the illogical conclusion that all quartz veins must contain silver; and forgetting that it is but seldom that a lode is of equal value throughout its whole extent, or even thickness, a small fragment of ore, yielding a large assay of gold or silver, was regarded by many persons as establishing the value of a claim. The results of the first discoveries of silver made in our State were so flattering, and presaged for us such unbounded wealth, that capital was early found to prospect any location that could show even the remotest probability of success; and so it gradually happened that large amounts of money were expended on locations which the eye of an experienced miner would have pronounced worthless at first sight.

Again, the want of accurate information by many of our early prospectors induced them to expend work and money on useless minerals, supposing them, from their resemblance to other valuable articles, to be good property. Within a few miles of Virginia, numerous tunnels have been run in a deposit of silicate of alumina, under the impression that it was quartz; clay jasper, mixed with iron pyrites in minute crystals, was probably thought to be cinnabar and gold by the man who dug out and broke up a large quantity of the rock; micaceous red hematite, a peculiar ore of iron, deceived some one by its resemblance to some of the silver sulphurets found in the Comstock Lode ; and in many places throughout the State, volcanic rocks have been taken for coal, and extensive work projected thereon. The labor and money expended on all such locations was, of course, uselessly employed.

Expensive litigation, which, in Nevada, has swallowed up as much of the profits of the mines as has been divided among the shareholders in the shape of dividends, was, in a great measure, the result of ignorance of the structure of mineral veins. It not unfrequently happens that near the surface there are several parallel seams of vein matter which unite in depth into some main lode : this is more likely to be the case when the dip of the vein is flat, than when it approaches a vertical position. A want of familiarity with this feature induced our early miners to regard every quartz seam as a separate lode, even though running parallel with another, and at no great distance from it. The locations on these soon came into conflict ; and scarcely any claim was free from contestants. It not unfrequently happened that there were four or five companies claiming the same ground. Since the discovery of this fact, it has been customary, when veins have been found running parallel and near each other, to locate the series ; and careful attention in this way will, in most instances, obviate the risk of future litigation.

To us, who look back at these early days with the light of experience, it seems strange that costly works should have been undertaken on claims, before a careful examination of such portions of the lode as were easily accessible should have determined whether or not there was a reasonable prospect of the mine returning the outlay ; yet, such was the case in Nevada to an unlimited extent. True, it is not always easy to decide whether such will be the case, many claims with most unpromising surface indications having proved valuable property, while others, which held out most alluring prospects, have failed to realize them in depth. But this does not alter the general truth of the position. Shafts and tunnels through the country-rock, intended to strike the vein several hundred feet below the surface, were projected on the strength of a few cubic feet of rock broken from the croppings ; it being argued when the gangue on the surface carried but little or no mineral, that it was only necessary to get down on the vein to secure the prize. These works, when carried down or into the veins, certainly explored them at the place where the lodes were struck, but gave no information of what lay between that point and the surface. It would be easy to cite many instances in support of these propositions, but sufficient will occur to every reader, within his own experience, to render the task unnecessary. If the ore on the surface was not rich enough to pay for extraction and reduction, and it was thought that in depth it might improve sufficiently to be remunerative, surely it would have been preferable to follow the vein down by an incline, in which its condition could have been judged of, day by day, and foot by foot. This course would have led to the abandonment of many works before one-quarter of the money which has been expended on them had been squandered, and we should be, to-day, that much richer as a community.

These instances are brought forward not to throw discredit on the pioneers of the State, who erred from want of knowledge, certainly not from want of zeal, but merely to show the character of the work which has been expended on mining claims and its inefficient results.

But the lavish expenditure of money did not stop here. It was deemed essential to the success of a district that a mill should be immediately erected for the reduction of the ores. This is true to an extent. It is certain there can be no ultimate result in the shape of bullion without such appliances, but it was folly to provide the means of reduction before developments had shown to a certainty that the mines could yield a constant supply sufficient to keep the machinery running. But few of the mills in the outlying districts of Nevada have been able to run steadily, and their history amply confirms the truth of the foregoing remarks. The money invested in these mills would have amply sufficed to have established the reputation of districts which now hardly attract attention. It may seem strange that the excitement of mining speculation should have so subverted the judgment of men as to induce them to enter into these wild investments, without having a solid basis to work on; but the fact none the less remains to our and their loss.

Where the ores were abundant in quantity, it frequently happened that want of success resulted from other causes. It fortunately happened that the first silver ores found in Nevada were of the most docile character and easily reduced by the simplest methods; and, without pausing to think of the chemical changes that take place in the process of amalgamation, or the effect which certain minerals exercise on each other when occurring in combination, the method which had been found so efficient in Virginia and Gold Hill was applied to everything in the shape of ore producing silver or gold, no matter whether it was associated with copper, lead, antimony, arsenic. or zinc. It would be beyond the scope of this article to enter into the chemical reasons of the failures which resulted from the cause; it is sufficient for us to know in this connection that they did fail, and not unfrequently in cases where the ore would have paid well for reduction by méthods suited to its character. The error was discovered in course of time, but not before the reputation of many districts had suffered severely, and heavy expenses been incurred for the alteration of mills to suit the ores on which they were to be employed.

This expenditure of capital on objects which did not and could not yield a return in bullion, absorbed so large an amount of money that the time was inevitable when no more would be furnished, capital being shy of investments which fail to yield a speedy return or the promise of one adequate to the risks incurred. This time arrived in Nevada in the summer of 1864. It was accelerated by the wild, baseless speculation in mining stocks which had raged for two or three years previously. Faith in the permanence of a large number of our best mines was shaken from various temporary causes, and they depreciated suddenly and seriously in value, with most unfortunate results to such claims as depended for their prospective value on the richness and permanence of others more extensively developed. The crisis came rapidly. Money suddenly became less abundant than formerly. For want of the necessary funds, work was suspended on thousands of locations, the universal distrust refusing money for the further development of even promising claims, which went down in the universal crash with those which were utterly worthless. Work on many such has not been resumed from that day to this. As quickly as persons had jumped to the conclusion that all quartz veins contained silver, just as rapidly did they reach the other extreme, and decide that because one claim was worthless or looked unpromising for the time being, that all its neighbors must be so too. Of course, the blow fell heaviest on such districts as produced no bullion, being graduated according to the success which had attended mining operations in them.

The amount of capital locked up in these useless works, and thus lost to the State, can only be reckoned by hundreds of thousands of dollars. No community can suffer such a loss without being seriously cramped in its resources, and time is necessary before the losers can again be tempted into similar investments. Even good mining property requires a large amount of capital for its development, and unless we can attract it to us by unmistakable evidence that it can be profitably employed, our future will be without promise or our progress slow and unsatisfactory. Fortunately, the ill effects resulting from the above causes are dying away, and, as they were almost entirely the result of want of knowledge, time alone is necessary to enable us to avoid them in the future.

The losses which owners of mining property have experienced in Nevada, must frequently be charged to the stockholders themselves, who have often displayed, in the selection of their superintendents, a disregard of all business principles truly astonishing. Something more than a good knowledge of mercantile business is requisite in a successful mining superintendent, yet this has frequently been their principal recommendation. Mining is a vocation, just as much as the study of law or medicine, and years of practical experience alone can enable a man to master the subject in all its details. Without such knowledge, men must necessarily work in the dark and at a disadvantage; but, happily for the prosperity of the State, a better era is dawning upon us, and men of known ability, in their peculiar field, are taking charge of our principal mines.

A few words on the causes which have given us this unfortunate name abroad, may not inappropriately close these observations. The unaccountable fluctuations in the value of our mining stocks may have had something to do with it, but undoubtedly the chief source is to be looked for in the unmitigated swindles which have been perpetrated on mining companies in the Eastern States and elsewhere. It would be easy to cite many of these, some of which died in the bud, while others were carried a stage further, but not one of which ever bore fruit in the form of dividends. Without exception, they had their base in the ignorance which exists relative to Nevada, and which enables their projectors to make statements which could only be proved false at considerable expense. What this ignorance is, may best be illustrated by quoting a few instances from the "London Standard," of June 30, 1865. In the prospectus of the "Reese River Mining Company" the property of the company is said to be within half a mile of the already mentioned railway, it being apparently intended to convey the idea that a line was then in operation in the neighborhood. Speaking of the mills which it is proposed to erect on the company's property, their cost is set down at $2,500 each, for a mill capable of reducing twenty tons of rock per diem, when that sum would not cover the expense of freight, to say nothing about machinery and erection. But the depth of the ignorance which exists relative to Nevada will be best understood when such statements as the following can find believers.

The prospectus goes on to say that, in order to show the value of their property, they will mention the names of a few well known mines in the immediate vicinity, and quote the Hale & Norcross, Bullion, Empire, and Crown Point, in Virginia and Gold Hill, and the Sierra Butte, in California! Why, it would be just as absurd to quote mines in Cornwall, England, to increase the value of one in Northumberland, two hundred miles away; and yet the parallel is complete. Nor is this all: the prices of the stocks were also given, with a statement that their par value was five dollars per share, so as to lead persons to the conclusion that they were at a premium of several hundred dollars. Again and again have facts been willfully misrepresented, and property painted in glowing colors which was totally unknown, even to old residents of the localities in which it was said to be situated; and is it cause for surprise that agent after agent, sent out to examine such locations, should return disgusted with his experience, or that mining men abroad should come to look at all our professions of unlimited mineral wealth as a complete farce, if not altogether an intolerable swindle? Occasionally one of these schemes has been nursed into practical existence, and its certain failure has only intensified the distrust.

It is not often that the miners themselves are to blame for these results, which spring from the operations of the "middle men." It is to be regretted that some share of the trouble which this fraternity has brought on the community cannot be visited upon their own heads. We have sufficient mining property of the best character to employ all the capital it would be possible to secure under the most favorable circumstances, but one of these swindles, successfully carried out, can do us more injury than months of earnest work can repair.

There is yet, however, another cause. Mining property of good character has been sold to Eastern capitalists, which, under able management, would be a credit to our State, and a source of revenue to the owners; but it is no wonder that they absorb thousands after thousands of dollars without yielding a return, or that they disgust the proprietors who are looking anxiously for dividends and receive them not, so long as men are sent out to take charge of them who never saw a mine before in their lives, and never had anything to do with machinery, let alone the reduction of ores. Not one of the men who have the control of these incorporations would think of employing a man to build a house who had been brought up at a grocer's counter, or hire a book-keeper who was not acquainted with his business; yet they suppose a man can become a good mining superintendent by simple transportation to a mining camp; and when ill luck attends their enterprises, attribute it to the property on which they have been operating, instead of to the operators themselves. Their action in this matter is not alone a dead loss to themselves, but at the same time an incalculable detriment to our State: the fact of failure being patent to all, while its true cause may be known only to a few.

In all these things there is little of which we need to be ashamed. Nay, we may justly be proud of what we have achieved in the face of our many difficulties. With careful management and intelligent superintendence, we may look forward to a future of unparalleled prosperity, our resources being unequaled by any of the mining States of the Pacific Coast.

APPENDIX "B."

HINTS FOR THE USE OF PROSPECTORS AND PER-
SONS ENGAGED IN THE EARLY DEVEL-
OPMENT OF MINING PROPERTY.

APPENDIX "B."

HINTS FOR THE USE OF PROSPECTORS AND PERSONS ENGAGED IN THE EARLY DEVELOPMENT OF MINING PROPERTY.

Having thus pointed out some of the causes which have retarded our progress to a successful result in many portions of Nevada, it remains to show in what way we may avoid them in the future; and for this purpose I would suggest the following remarks on the development of mines and the reduction of ores:

When indications of a mineral deposit have been observed, the first thing to be ascertained is its extent, as accurately as may be; and secondly, the character of the ores, and the facilities which exist for their successful treatment—as on this latter circumstance the value of the property will be in a great measure dependent. If the requisite means of reduction are near at hand, and equally accessible, a lower grade of ore will be remunerative, than would be the case if costly fluxes and machinery or transportation of ore and materials to a considerable distance are unavoidable. At the same time some attention ought to be given to the rocks which are associated with or contain the mineral lodes. If a mine in any district has been proved by development to be valuable, the country rock in which it is found should be carefully noted, as it is not unlikely that wherever they occur in the same district, other mines equally good may occur in that connection. Nor is this the only advantage to be derived. If the mine is offered for sale, almost the first inquiries will relate to these matters, experience having shown that certain minerals are usually associated with rocks of a certain age and character, and that mineral-bearing lodes are more apt to be permanent in some formations than in others. The direction of the vein, with regard to the general structure of the country, should be ascertained, noting particularly whether it runs parallel to or crosswise of the various formations; nor should traces of recent volcanic action be overlooked, as in localities where the country is much broken, it is not unlikely that the veins may have been extensively "faulted" or dislocated—an accident of great importance in the successful working of mining property.

When a mineral deposit has been discovered, the first thing to be done, as before stated, is to trace it as far as possible on the surface, to ascertain if it possesses the visible characters of a true vein; or if only an isolated or "segregated" mass, whether its extent is sufficient to warrant the cost of development and the erection of works for its reduction. When the vein-stone is hard and crops out prominently, but little difficulty will be experienced: the chief point to be noted in that case being the character of the ore in different portions of the lode, so that the most promising place may be selected on which to begin the work of development. But when the gangue is soft, and the lode has been reduced by the action of the weather to the level of the ground, or has been covered up by the formation of a bed of earth, a different course must be

15

adopted. After ascertaining as nearly as may be the course of the vein, or "strike," as it is technically termed, narrow pits or trenches should be sunk, at intervals of, say one hundred feet, across the ground where it is supposed the lode ought to be found. These pits should be sunk until the rock is found unbroken, and continued until the walls of the vein have been developed. While tracing a vein in this manner, the "dip" of the vein, or its inclination to the horizon, should be taken into account; as, provided the dip be considerable, and the country through which the lode passes be rough and broken up by deep ravines, it will apparently have a very zigzag course on the surface, though really following a straight line through the district. Or yet another plan may be adopted. Starting at the point where the original discovery was made, the vein may be stripped or laid bare on the surface in the direction of its length, and in this way the character of the lode and its comparative richness at different points may be very thoroughly ascertained; and though the process may seem a slow one, nothing will be lost in the end, as the knowledge obtained by this method will be of incalculable value in all subsequent operations.

In a country where the fever for making locations rages as violently as it does in Nevada, this method of exploration has the additional advantage, and no small one, either, of defining the boundaries of the claim and obviating the risks of adverse locations and subsequent expensive litigation. This item is worthy of serious consideration, when we bear in mind how large a proportion of the profits of our mines has been squandered in this way. Even should the developments show that different claims come into conflict, it should be remembered that it is easier to come to a settlement, in most cases, while the value of the property is yet prospective, than when one or both of the locations have been proved to be valuable.

Having, by these means, ascertained the probable character of the property, and the nature of the ores, and more especially whether any changes have taken place in its composition, as is frequently the case in passing from one series of rocks to another,* the prospector is then in a position to inquire whether the requisites for reduction are within an available distance. If the ores are such as may be reduced by a simple amalgamation process, as those, for instance, carrying free gold, or some of the simpler compounds of silver, all that will be necessary is water sufficient for amalgamation and motive power for machinery. If the employment of steam be indispensable, the supply of fuel, either wood or coal, must be greater than if hydraulic power be feasible. Should the ores require roasting, as is often the case in Nevada, the supply of fuel must be greater, and within a reasonable distance, or the cost of transportation will consume the profits of the mine, unless the ores are extraordinarily rich; and in this case the items of fire clay for the lining of the furnaces, and salt for use in the roasting process, must not be forgotten. In cases where smelting must be resorted to, the item of fire clay will be still more important, as will also the quantity of fuel; and the presence of suitable fluxes, such as lime, carbonate of soda, etc., should be ascertained. These considerations are of vital importance, and ought never to be overlooked. Mines will, of course, sometimes be found where one or more of the requisites for reduction are absent, as, for instance, wood or water; and then it will be necessary to ascertain whether the ore can be cheaply sorted or "dressed" up to a grade sufficiently high to pay for its transportation to a more favored locality. This branch of mining, which forms a large item in many European mines, has apparently been but little thought of in Nevada, probably on account of the high

---

* In the Cornish mines, veins which produce copper in granite frequently change to tin lodes on passing into the "killas" or slates, and *vice versa*; and lodes in limestone producing lead, as in many Derbyshire mines, are not unfrequently barren in the associated green stones.

price of both labor and transportation. The time is rapidly coming, however, when there will be a material improvement in both these items, and the plan, if judiciously carried out, might be adopted with advantage. The preliminary explorations, when accomplished, will have supplied the data on which to found a rational method of development. The best will depend greatly on circumstances, but in all early works, one imperative rule may be given, "never lose sight of the quartz or other vein stone." If the vein crosses a rough country, and is accessible from a ravine, it will, in most instances, be the wisest plan to start from the lowest available point and run a drift on the lode, as the ground can not only be more cheaply excavated and removed by this method* than any other, but it possesses the additional advantage of exploring a large amount of ground which can all be removed by stoping upwards, and of draining all the vein which lies above the level of the tunnel. When this plan is impracticable, because the country is comparatively level, or the vein runs along a mountain side but little cut up by ravines, the choice lies between an incline and a perpendicular shaft. The instances in which the latter can be sunk within the vein are comparatively few. The dip of most veins renders an incline preferable. Inclines, as a rule, cost less to sink than shafts, besides exploring more ground, and care should be taken to commence them in the most favorable position. The question of drainage will naturally be a leading consideration. Under the latter supposition, there will not be much choice in the matter, but in a country deeply cut up by gulches, if an incline be preferred to a drift on the lode, care should be taken to avoid the ravines; for, though they offer the advantage of attaining depth more rapidly, it should be borne in mind that they are the natural water-courses of the country, and more difficulty will be experienced, as a rule, in keeping the water under control, than if the incline be started on the sides or summits of the dividing ridges. It not unfrequently happens that the convulsions which led to the formation of the ravines have broken up the country-rocks in their beds, allowing the surface waters to penetrate more readily to a great depth, and increasing the difficulties of drainage, and the cost of timbering the works, and at the same time have dislocated the veins, which present a less promising aspect to the miner. In the location of mining works, the facilities for dump and roads should also have their weight; but these considerations are of less importance in works for exploration merely, than in such as are intended for the permanent working of the mines.

If a shaft or incline be adopted, it may be carried down to a depth of about two hundred feet by manual or horse labor, if no great body of water be encountered; and at regular intervals, say every sixty or one hundred feet, cross cuts should be run to the walls of the vein, if the whole width of it be not taken out in sinking the shaft or incline. Should appearances warrant, drifts can then be started on the same levels, from which other cross cuts can be run at intervals; and in this way the character of the mine may be fully and satisfactorily ascertained.

The whole of these works may be run as small in size as a man can conveniently work in, and as cheaply as is consistent with the safety of the mine; but however well the lode may look on the surface, no special provision for the reduction of the ore on a large scale should be made until the mine has been so thoroughly prospected in this manner as to leave no doubt that ore sufficient in quantity and quality is there to warrant the erection of suitable machinery or reduction works.

If the result of these explorations is satisfactory, the property is in a good shape for future work; and if the reverse, the value of a mill or furnace, which

---

* See cost of running drifts and sinking shafts.

in Nevada are no small items, will have been saved. No necessity for these latter exists during preliminary operations where mills are already running in the neighborhood, as tests can be had from time to time if any doubt should arise as to the value of the ore. But even where no such works are in operation, and the isolation of the district makes transportation an important consideration, it would still be the wiser policy to freight small quantities of ore to some distance for experimental reduction, even though the cost should be greater than the result obtained ; or several companies might unite in the erection of small prospecting works, an arrangement which would render the cost to each but a nominal item. Beyond this nothing should be done during the early explorations. This position is abundantly proved by the value of the capital locked up in reduction works throughout Nevada; these works being erected before the development of the mines had shown the character of the machinery necessary, or demonstrated satisfactorily that there was material sufficient to keep them steadily employed.

When development has proceeded thus far, permanent machinery for hoisting and freeing the mine of water may be erected, and means for the reduction of the ore thought of. Of the former it is not my intention to speak, much judgment and skill having been expended on such works in Nevada, of which we may reasonably be proud ; but the importance of the latter calls for a passing notice.

The character of the reduction works will of course depend on the nature of the ores to be treated, and too much attention cannot be given to them before deciding on the machinery to be employed. The importance of analytical examination as a guide is far from being appreciated as it ought to be in Nevada. In the case of true silver ores, the majority of them can be successfully treated in Nevada, either by simple amalgamation of the raw ores, as in Virginia and Gold Hill, or by dry crushing and roasting, as in the Reese River District. But we have some few silver ores, as those found in the American Basin and Sheba Companies' claims, at Humboldt, which contain so large a per centage of antimony and zinc, that some other plan must be adopted. In this class, too, come all our argentiferous galena and copper ore, the whole of which should be smelted to obtain even an approach to a satisfactory result. And then the question arises whether we can do this as well at home as abroad—whether the results obtained here, when compared with the cost of reduction, are superior to those obtained in old smelting localities, where every appliance can be brought to bear, as compared with the cost of shipment and smelting.

The process of smelting is thought by many to be an exceedingly simple operation, and when thoroughly understood it may be so ; but good judgment, which can only be acquired by long practice, is essential to success. No definite rules can be laid down which will work in every instance. A general theory may be adopted, but as the composition of ores varies to an unlimited extent, so must the theoretical practice be indefinitely modified to suit the varying circumstances. Nor should it be forgotten that the very basis of the Swansea smelting operations is the mixture of different ores, so that the ingredients in one may assist the liberation of the valuable portions of the other. Ores which by themselves are difficult to beneficiate, yielding poor results at a large expenditure of labor, become remarkably docile in the presence of other materials. This fact may often render the shipment of ores preferable to reduction on the spot, their nature entailing too great a loss or too heavy an expense if worked by themselves. In all cases, however, whether smelted on the spot or shipped for treatment elsewhere, the ores will require a previous dressing to fit them for the furnace ; and this must be done at the mine or nearest locality, where water for concentration is abundant. This branch of mining has received but little attention in Nevada, but the time is not far distant when the dressing of ores for shipment will form one of the most extensive of our mining departments; and it is well worth the notice of owners of such property.

These remarks may well be closed with a few words on the impolicy of devoting a life-time to making multitudinous locations rather than endeavoring to extract from some of them the wealth which they contain. The number of locations made in the State may be set down at not far short of forty thousand, and the population at somewhere near the same figure, or at the rate of one mine to every one of our inhabitants. Looking at this fact, it is evident that not only our hands, but those of many generations after us, can find employment on the mining ground already located; yet it is doubtful if one-tenth of the property has been even partially developed. There is enough wealth already discovered in our State to make us all rich, if we will but *work* to secure the coveted prize; and the end will be obtained more quickly and a thousand times more certainly, than by scouring the country in the hope of making the "big strike" which allures too many of our prospectors.

APPENDIX "C."

CATALOGUE OF THE PRINCIPAL MINERALS
FOUND IN NEVADA.

APPENDIX "C."

AGATE.—See Quartz.

ALABASTER.—See Gypsum.

ALUM.—*Esmeralda County.*—Twelve miles north of Silver Creek, alum is found in thin, comby seams, from the thickness of a knife blade up to several inches, traversing extensive sulphur deposits in every direction.
Storey County.—Impregnating the water of springs near the Truckee River, some sixteen miles north of Virginia.

AMETHYST.—See Quartz. .

ANTIMONY, GRAY.—See Sulphuret Antimony.

ANTIMONY, SULPHURET.—An abundant mineral in the *Humboldt* mining region, occurring largely in the Sheba, American Basin, De Soto, and other mines, and usually rich in silver. It is also found in the mines of Aurora, *Esmeralda County*, and in the vicinity of Walker Lake.

ARSENICAL ANTIMONY—"Ophir Mine, Nevada. In reniform, finely crystalline, somewhat radiated masses, of a color between tin white and iron black on a fresh fracture, but grayish black from tarnishing; associated with arsenolite, calcite, and quartz." (Blake's Cal. Minerals, from F. A. Genth, Am. Jour. Sev. (2) xxxiii, 190.)

ARSENOLITE.—Reported from the Ophir Mine, Virginia, with arsenical antimony (Genth).

BLENDE, OR SULPHURET OF ZINC—Occurs sparingly in the ores of the Comstock vein, Virginia, associated with sulphuret of silver, copper and iron pyrites, galena, etc. In some of the rich ores from the Ophir and California mines, at the northern end of the lode, the per centage of zinc ranges as high as eleven to fourteen. At the southern extremity of the vein it is scarcely present (see analysis, page 135). It is abundant in the ores from the Sheba Mine, *Humboldt County*, associated with gray antimony and brittle silver ore.

BLACK OXIDE OF COPPER.—See Copper.

BORATE OF LIME.—This mineral is found quite extensively in the salt marsh of the Columbus Mining District, *Esmeralda County*, principally in layers from two

16

to five inches thick, alternating with layers of salt, and first occurring from one to two feet below the surface. It is also found in the shape of balls three or four inches in diameter, scattered about the salt deposit. It is also reported as having occurred in a thin seam near the hanging wall of one of the Columbus mines. (Dr. A. F. W. Partz, Benton, Mono Co., Cal.)

BOURNONITE.—See Tetrahedite, under heading Copper.

CALCITE, CALC. SPAR, CARBONATE OF LIME.—Abundant throughout the State in many of its crystalline forms. Granular limestone with tremolite occurs on American Flat, *Storey County*, and at Carson, *Ormsby County*, and many other localities. The Cole Tunnel and Overman mines, in Virginia, have produced good specimens of the Dog tooth spar.

CALC. SPAR.—See Calcite.

CARBONATE OF SODA.—An abundant mineral occurring as an effervescence over large areas of low valley land, and round the margin of shallow lakes as they dry up during the summer months. Also an ingredient in many waters. Many localities, as the Adobe Meadows and two small lakes near Ragtown, *Churchill County*, forty miles east of Virginia, produce it in large quantities. The latter place affords very beautiful crystallized specimens.

CARBONATE OF LIME.—See Calcite.

CARBONATE OF IRON.—See Spathic Iron.

CARBONATE OF MANGANESE.—See Diallogite.

CARBONATE OF LEAD.—See Cerusite.

CARNELIAN.—See Quartz.

CERUSITE, WHITE LEAD ORE, CARBONATE OF LEAD.—Associated in small quantities with the sulphuret, at the Pleasant Valley mines, in *Washoe County*; and abundant in *Humboldt County*, at the Montezuma claim. Massive in both localities. Occurs also in minute crystals on silver ores in the California and Potosi Mines, in Virginia.

CHALCEDONY.—See Quartz.

CHABAZITE.—Small but perfect crystals on porphyritic rocks, associated with the Comstock vein.

CHALYBITE.—See Spathic Iron.

CHALCOPYRITE.—See Copper Pyrites.

CHRYSOLITE, OLIVINE.—Good though small crystals in volcanic rocks at the south end of Carson Valley, on the Aurora road.

CHRYSOCOLLA, SILICATE OF COPPER.—See Copper.

CHLORIDE OF SILVER.—See Silver.

CHLORIDE OF SODIUM.—See Salt.

COAL.—See Lignite.

COPPER, NATIVE.—In small quantities associated with carbonates at Walker Lake, *Esmeralda County;* and with red oxyde at Mono Lake, in the same county. Also in minute crystals in decomposed porphyry at the Sierra Nevada Mine, Virginia; probably the result of the decomposition of unfiltrated cupreous water.

COPPER GLANCE, VITREOUS COPPER, OR SULPHURET OF COPPER.— Peavine Mining District, *Washoe County; Humboldt, Churchill* and *Nye Counties.* Abundant. Usually argentiferous.

COPPER PYRITES, OR CHALCOPYRITE.—Probably an abundant ore, frequently occurring with others; but as the copper mines of Nevada have been as yet but little opened, though extensive and valuable, the surface carbonates and oxydes have been in few cases penetrated. Also associated in small quantities with the silver ores of the Comstock, and other silver lodes of the State.

COPPER ORE, GRAY TETRAHEDRITE.—Occurs abundantly at the Sheba Mine, *Humboldt County;* massive and rich in silver. It is associated with the following species, which were noted from time to time by Mr. Moss, the Superintendent, and in part by Prof. Blake: ruby silver, argentiferous galena, iron pyrites, blende, cerusite, calcite, quartz with acicular antimony, sulphuret of antimony in delicate needles, and massive native silver and bournonite. Found also in *Lander County,* with the silver ores of the veins near Austin; at the Comet Lode, Veatch Cañon, south of Austin. (Blake's Cal. Minerals, page 23.)

COPPER, RED OXYDE OF.—See Native Copper. Peavine District, *Washoe County,* and *Esmeralda County,* near Mono Lake; at the latter locality in large boulders, associated with small flakes of native copper.

COPPER, BLACK OXYDE OF.—Associated with silicate of copper at the mines near Benton, *Mono County,* California.

COPPER, CARBONATES OF.—Abundant in the Peavine Mining District, *Washoe County;* near Walker Lake, *Esmeralda County;* in many localities around Carson and Empire, *Ormsby County;* in the Volcanic District, *Nye County; Humboldt County,* and many other localities throughout the State.

COPPER, SILICATE OF, CHRYSOCOLLA.—Occurs as incrustations on argentiferous copper ores, at the mines near Benton, *Mono County,* California.

DIALLOGITE, OR CARBONATE OF MANGANESE.—Occurs abundantly in the silver-bearing veins about Austin, *Lander County.* By decomposition it becomes black and discolors the upper part of the vein; but at and below the water line, with the unchanged ores of silver, it has a delicate flesh red or pink color. (Blake's Cal. Minerals, page 12.)

DOLOMITE, MASSIVE.—Dolomite, or magnesian limestone, is abundant in the mountains in the southern portion of the State.

EMBOLITE.—See Silver.

EPIDOTE (PISTACITE).—*Ormsby County.* In metamorphic slates west of Carson, crystallized and massive, and associated with magnetic iron.

EPSOM SALT (SULPHATE OF MANGANESE).—*Humboldt County.* Efflorescence round the margin of Pueblo Lake, in the northwest corner of the county.

FELDSPAR (ORTHOCLASE).—An abundant mineral in every section of the State, as a constituent of many of the rocks.

FLUORSPAR.—In finely crystallized specimens on the mountains south of Aurora, *Esmeralda County;* usually of a pale greenish tint. Occurs as cubes, octahedrons and dodecahedrons.

GALENA, OR SULPHURET OF LEAD.—An abundant mineral throughout the State. *Washoe County*—Pleasant Valley, associated with cerusite and mispickel. *Nye County*—Washington District, at the St. Helena Mine, associated with crystallized iron pyrites. *Esmeralda County*—In the vicinity of Walker Lake abundant. A chief constituent of the ores of the De Soto Mine, Humboldt County. In *Storey County* it is found largely in the Morning Star Tunnel, at the north end of the Comstock Lode, associated with copper and iron pyrites, and is present in small quantities in most of the ores from that vein—first class Ophir ore yielding as much as five per cent. of lead, while in low grade Yellow Jacket rock it is found only in traces. Lead ores in Nevada are usually contained in a quartz gangue, and are highly argentiferous, the galena after dressing ranging in value in silver from $100 to $700 per ton.

GARNET.—A common, inferior variety is abundant near Steamboat Springs, in *Washoe County.* It occurs in large masses of aggregated crystals.

GOLD.—Gold, except as it occurs in combination with silver, is not an abundant mineral in Nevada. *Storey* and *Lyon Counties* have furnished limited placers, chiefly gulch diggings, as those in Gold Cañon and American Ravine; and many of the small ravines, heading in the Sierra west of Washoe Valley, produce small quantities of gold. They cannot, however, be considered of permanent value; and, as a source of wealth, are utterly insignificant, compared with the silver mines of the State. Gold quartz veins, as the " Monroe," occur sparingly in the Humboldt region; and in the vicinity of the East Walker River, *Esmeralda County,* promising lodes have recently been discovered. The bullion from the Aurora mines is rich in gold, that from the Comstock ranging from 22 to 50 per cent. of gold, with an average of probably about 33 per cent. in value.

The following table of the relative value of the gold and silver in ores from the Comstock Lode, is compiled from assays made at the Silver State Reduction Works, by Louis Janin, Jr., during 1863 and 1864:

TABLE OF THE RELATIVE VALUE OF THE GOLD AND SILVER IN ORES FROM THE COMSTOCK LEAD.

Name of Mine.	No. of Tons.	Per centage in Value.	
		Gold.	Silver.
Mexican..............................	267^{200}	42.49	57.51
"	225^{1600}	41.17	58.83
"	398^{300}	50.68	49.32
..	395^{720}	52.00	48.00
..	$1,147^{200}$	51.25	48.75
"	26^{8}	49.26	50.74
Savage.............................	175^{750}	22.85	77.15
"	222^{450}	26.48	73.52
"	307^{800}	24.00	76.00
..	373^{1200}	24.68	75.32
..	168	33.94	66.06
"	89	32.29	67.71
Potosi	133	25.84	74.16
Uncle Sam.........................	297^{1680}	35.64	64.51
"	225^{600}	37.94	62.06
"	91^{1000}	21.20	78.80
..	82^{1000}	34.16	65.84
"	129^{1180}	31.70	68.30
Gould & Curry.....................	440	24.63	75.37

GRAPHITE, PLUMBAGO.—Found in many localities, but usually of an inferior quality. *Storey County*, in the tunnel of the Kentucky Silver Mining Company, on American Flat, associated with dark metamorphic slates. *Washoe County*, near the road from Washoe to Virginia; used at one time for making crucibles. *Ormsby County*, in the hills, east of Empire City; it occurs in large quantities, associated with limestone and iron ore, but decrepitates on exposure to heat. A purer article is reported from Austin, *Lander County*.

GYPSUM—Is reported as abundant in the vicinity of Walker Lake, *Esmeralda County*, and occurs in thin transparent folia in many of the mines on the Comstock Lode. Of these, the Fairview mine has furnished very beautiful transparent crystals, (selenite) ranging up to an inch and a half in diameter and twelve inches in length. They occurred in fissures, in a blue porphyry, interlocked from side to side. Alabaster occurs in Pinewood District, in the southern part of *Humboldt County*, in considerable quantities, massive, and in the form of stalactites.

HAYESINE.—See Borate of Lime.

HEMATITE, SPECULAR IRON ORE.—Abundant throughout the State. *Storey County*, large veins west of American Flat; *Esmeralda County*, in large veins from eight to twenty feet wide, near the east fork of Walker River; near Blind Springs, in large vein; also in *Nye County, Lander County*, and elsewhere. The micaceous variety is found on American Flat, associated with calcite.

HORNBLENDE.—An abundant mineral in many rocks throughout the State.

Not found in large crystals. Tremolite occurs in granular limestone, near Carson, and on the Divide, south of American Flat, in *Storey County.*

IODIDE OF SILVER.—See Silver.

IRON, CARBONATE OF.—See Spathic Iron.

IRON, MAGNETIC.—See Magnetite.

IRON PYRITES.—An abundant mineral throughout the State. Both the crystalline and massive varieties are common in the Comstock vein, Virginia, associated with quartz and calcite. It occurs with galena at the Santa Elena mine, Washington District, *Nye County*, and many other localities.

IRON PYRITES, MAGNETIC.—See Pyrrhotine.

IRON PYRITES, ARSENICAL.—See Mispickel.

IRON, SPECULAR.—See Hematite.

IRON, SPATHIC.—See Spathic Iron.

JASPER.—See Quartz.

KERARGYRITE.—See Silver, Chloride of.

KAOLIN.—An article of fair quality is reported near McBride's Ranch, in *Esmeralda County*, forty miles southeast of Aurora. An impure article of no commercial value occurs near the Half-Way House between Virginia and Carson.

LABRADORITE occurs in dark colored rocks from the Black Rock Mining District, *Humboldt County;* crystals small.

LEAD, SULPHURET OF.—See Galena.

LEAD, CARBONATE OF.—See Cerusite.

LEAD, PHOSPHATE OF.—See Pyromorphite.

LEAD, MOLYBDATE OF.—See Molybdate of Lead.

LIGNITE, BROWN COAL.—Not found hitherto in quantities sufficient to pay the cost of working. It has been reported from many localities in the western portion of the State. The coal from Eldorado Cañon, east of Dayton, is found in Triassic formation, and might more properly be described as a bituminous shale. The same geological formation extends southward as far as Walker Lake, in *Esmeralda County*, and produces the same article. The coal from Crystal Peak, on the Truckee River, is a deep black, lustrous lignite, retaining very distinctly the structure of the wood, *(Pinus ponderosus)* and is found in small isolated masses, resembling the compressed trunks of large trees. This is its probable origin; for the surrounding geological formation forbids the idea of coal being present in large quantities. None of these localities are likely to prove valuable, the large per centage of ash and water detracting from the heating properties of the Eldorado Cañon lignite as a fuel. Most of the other coal discoveries are based on outcrops of black volcanic rocks.

LIME, BORATE OF.—See Borate of Lime.

LIME, CARBONATE OF.—See Calcite.

MAGNESIA, SULPHATE OF.—See Epsom Salts.

MAGNETIC IRON PYRITES.—See Pyrrhotine.

MAGNETIC IRON.—See Magnatite.

MAGNETITE.—*Ormsby County*, near Carson and Empire, not in large quantities. *Nye County*, abundant.

MANGANESE, CARBONATE OF.—See Diallogite.

MANGANESE, OXYDE OF.—See Pyrolusite.

MERCURY.—Native mercury has been reported somewhere from the center of the State, but its occurrence is doubtful.

MICA.—An abundant mineral in the crystalline rocks of the State, but not occurring in crystals of any size.

MISPICKEL, ARSENICAL IRON PYRITES.—*Washoe County*, associated with argentiferous lead ores at the Pleasant Valley mines.

MOLYBDATE OF LEAD.—" Comstock Lode, in the upper part of the California mine, in the ' rusty lode,' in small yellow crystals." (Blake's Cal. Minerals, p. 18.)

NITRE.—See Saltpetre.

NITRATE OF POTASH.—See Saltpetre.

NATIVE COPPER.—See Copper.

NATIVE SILVER.—See Silver.

NATROLITE.—Found with igneous rocks at Virginia, *Storey County*, in globular, stellated and divergent crystallizations; associated with Scolecite.

OBSIDIAN.—Abundant at the extinct craters, on the islands in Mono Lake, *Mono County*, California, and near McBride's Ranch, *Esmeralda County*. Many other localities.

OLIVINE.—See Chrysolite.

ORTHOCLASE.—See Feldspar.

PETRIFIED WOOD.—Silicified wood abundant throughout the State. *Storey County*, American Flat; *Lyon County*, Dayton; *Nye County*, San Antonio, and

Volcano Districts, and many other localities. The specimens from Volcano District are exceedingly beautiful.

PISTACITE.—See Epidote.

PHOSPHATE OF LEAD.—See Pyromorphite.

PLUMBAGO.—See Graphite.

POLYBASITE.—See Silver.

POTASH, NITRATE OF.—See Saltpetre.

PRASE.—See Quartz.

PROUSTITE.—See Silver.

PYRITES, MAGNETIC.—See Pyrrhotine.

PYRARGYRITE.—See Silver.

PYRRHOTINE—Magnetic Iron Pyrites. Austin, *Lander County.*

PYROLUSITE—Oxyde of Manganese. Reported as abundant at Humboldt.

PYROMORPHITE—Phosphate of Lead. " In the outcrops of the Comstock Lode, especially in the back ledges of the Ophir ground, giving green coats and crusts to the surface of the Quartz." (Blake's Cal. Minerals, 20.)

QUARTZ.—*Silica,* abundant in many forms throughout the State.
Amethyst.—In small crystals from the mines on the Comstock Lode ; the best from Gold Hill.
Smoky Quartz.—Potosi Mine, Comstock Lode, Virginia.
Prase.—Hill near Lakes' Crossing of the Truckee River, *Washoe County.*
Chalcedony.—*Storey County,* near Virginia ; Flowery, American Flat, etc.; *Esmeralda County,* Aurora ; Walker Lake, etc., *Nye County ;* San Antonio, etc., etc.
Carnelian.—Carnelian Bay, Lake Tahoe.
Agate.—San Antonio, *Nye County,* Aurora, etc.
Jasper.—Abundant throughout the State.
Quartz—Is the predominant gangue of the mines thoughout Nevada.

RED OXYDE OF COPPER.—See Copper.

SALT, CHLORIDE OF SODIUM.—Rock Salt of remarkable purity is found in abundance in the mountains near the Rio Virgen River, in the section of Arizona recently added to Nevada. Salt occurs plentifully throughout the State, as an incrustation over extensive areas of low valley land, many salt flats covering upwards of fifty square miles. At Silver Peak, in *Esmeralda County,* a hot salt spring near the margin of the salt marsh, affords many beautiful capillary specimens. The following description of the Sand Springs Salt Beds in *Churchill County* will convey a good idea of its usual mode of occurrence.
" This basin appears to have once been the bottom of a lake, and the salt is found good even on the surface. A covering of about three inches is loose and indifferent ; but beneath this for a depth of fourteen feet, pure rock salt is

found, as clear as ice, and as white as the driven snow. Beneath, there is water, which seems to be filtered through salt for an unknown depth. The whole of this fourteen feet in thickness does not contain a single streak of any deleterious matter or rubbish, and is ready for quarrying and sending to market. Great blocks of the pure stuff can be raised the same as if it were ice or stone; on exposure, however, it crumbles sufficiently to admit of being closely packed in sacks or wagon boxes. The loose salt on the top being removed, one man can quarry and wheel out five tons a day, ready for mill use, or to offer for sale in the store."

SALTPETRE—Nitre, or Nitrate of Potash, *Esmeralda County*. Thin seams and curling efflorescence occur in a cave on the road from Fish Lake Valley to Silver Peak, near the summit of the range.

SCHILLER SPAR.—Utah Mine, near Virginia, *Storey County*.

SCOLECITE.—See Natrolite.

SELENITE.—See Gypsum.

SILICA.—See Quartz.

SILVER, NATIVE.—Occurs in many of the silver veins of the State, in thin plates and folia. Many beautiful specimens of hairy wire-silver have been taken from the mines of the Comstock Lode, in the earlier days, when operations were conducted chiefly above the water level.

Silver Glance—Sulphuret of Silver.—*Storey County*. The chief silver ore of the Comstock Lode; generally associated with native silver, gold, lead, iron, copper, etc. Abundant in the mining districts of Humboldt and Reese River. "In the large chambers of the Ophir Mine, in eighteen hundred and sixty-one, it was very abundant, in irregular masses, ramifying through the fragmentary white quartz so as to hold it together in hand specimens."

Brittle Silver Ore (Stephanite).—"Very fine crystals of Stephanite were obtained from the Ophir and Mexican Mines soon after they were opened. These crystals were from half an inch to two inches in length, but were generally imperfectly formed. They are now more rare, but have been found in nearly all the principal claims on the Comstock Lode." (Blake's Cal. Minerals, page 22.)

Polybasite.—Small crystals from the Reese River Mines.

Pronstite.—Light red silver ore, abundant in the mines of Lander County.

Pryargyrite.—Dark red silver ore—Ruby silver. Abundant in the Reese River mining districts. It is found but sparingly in the mines of the Comstock Lode; usually in the massive form. One of the most important silver ores of Nevada.

Embolite.—"Is believed to occur in the surface ores of Lander County, near Austin, and of Washington District, farther south, but has not been certainly identified." (Blake's Cal. Minerals, page 12.)

Iodide of Silver.—Reported to occur in thin crystallized films on ores from the Tesoro Mine, Austin.

Chloride of Silver—Horn Silver, Kerargyrite.—Abundant in the surface ores of all the mining districts in the southern and eastern portions of the State, usually occurring as thin flakes in the minute crevices of the gangue. It is a rare mineral in the Comstock Lode.

Xanthocone.—Reported from the Manitowoc Mine, *Humboldt County.*

SILVER, HORN.—See Chloride of Silver.

SPAR, CALC.—See Calcite.

SPAR, FLUOR.—See Fluor Spar.

SPATHIC IRON, CARBONATE OF IRON, CHALYBITE.—Benton, *Mono County,* California. Near Nevada line.

SPECULAR IRON.—See Hematite.

SODA, CARBONATE OF.—See Carbonate of Soda.

SODIUM, CHLORIDE OF.—See Salt.

STEPHANITE.—See Silver.

STIBNITE.—See Antimony (Sulphuret of).

SULPHUR.—Abundant. *Humboldt County* furnishes large quantities which might readily be purified. About twelve miles north of Silver Peak, in *Nye* or *Esmeralda Counties,* large beds occur, which are traversed in every direction by thin, comby seams of alum. This locality affords good crystallized specimens. In *Washoe County,* at the Steamboat Hot Springs, it is found, impregnating the earth in the vicinity of the springs; and many other similar localities throughout the State.

SULPHURET OF IRON.—See Iron Pyrites.

SULPHURET OF LEAD.—See Galena.

SULPHATE OF MAGNESIA.—See Epsom Salts.

SULPHURET OF SILVER.—See Silver.

SULPHURET OF ZINC.—See Blende.

TETRAHEDITE.—See Copper.

TOURMALINE.—Long, slender, black crystals occur in quartz near Empire City, *Ormsby County;* also in granite near Fuller's Crossing of the Truckee River, *Washoe County.*

TREMOLITE.—See Hornblende.

TUNGSTATE OF MANGANESE, with Tungstate of Lime, in the Mammoth Mining District. (C. T. Jackson, Proc. Cal. Acad. iii, 199.)

TUNGSTATE OF LIME.—See Tungstate of Manganese.

VITREOUS COPPER.—See Copper Glance.

XANTHOCONE.—See Silver.

ZINC, SULPHURET OF.—See Blende.

APPENDIX "D."

ANALYSES OF NEVADA MINERALS.

APPENDIX "D."

ANALYSES OF NEVADA MINERALS.

ANALYSES OF ORES FROM VARIOUS PORTIONS OF THE STATE OF NEVADA.

One and Two.

Ophir Mine—first-class ore and metal produced therefrom by the Freiberg process, by George Attwood.

Gangue	63.380	.00
Silver	2.786	41.51
Gold	.059	1.58
Lead	4.151	39.01
Antimony	.087	.00
Zinc	14.455	.56
Sulphur	7.919	.00
Copper	1.596	17.04
Iron	5.463	.17
	99.896	99.87

Three and Four.

Ore from California Mine, Virginia. No. 1, made in London; No. 2, at Swansea.

	No. 1.	No. 2.
Silica	67.5	65.783
Sulphur	8.75	11.35
Copper	1.30	1.31
Iron	2.25	2.28
Silver	1.75	1.76
Gold	.059	.57
Zinc	12.85	11.307
Lead	5.75	6.145
Loss	.25	
	100.00	100.00

Five.

Weston's Mine, near Dayton; analysis by W. F. Rickard, F. C. S.

Gold	.0016	$5 02
Silver	.0250	10 98
Peroxyde of Iron	1.6370	
Peroxyde of Manganese	.2500	
Alumina	.7750	
Carb. Lime	83.7240	
Sulphur	.0050	
Chlorine	traces.	
Silica	13.2500	
Loss	.3324	
	100.0000	$16 00

Six, Seven and Eight.

Yellow Jacket ores, second class; by W. F. Rickard, F. C. S.

	Six—white.	Seven—brown.	Eight—mixed.
Gold	.005=$30 03	.001=$ 7 52	.002=$10 04
Silver	.150= 62 83	.050= 21 99	.157= 65 98
Iron	.575	2.800	1.230
Lead	traces.	traces.	traces.
Copper	"	"	"
Sulphur	.693	.160	.457
Lime	traces.	.000	traces.
Silica	98.810	96.560	97.850
Loss	.267	.429	.304
	100.000 $92 86	100.000 $29 51	100.000 $76 02

Average of sulphur, 8.73 lbs. per ton of ore.

Nine.

Copper ore from Peavine District; by W. F. Rickard, F. C. S.

Gold	.0005	$ 2 50 per ton
Silver	.0200	7 85 "
Oxyde of Copper	34.1000	135 00 "
Peroxyde of Iron	2.3200	
Alumina	.2200	
Sulphur	1.3600	
Carbonic Acid	11.2000	
Silica	46.6600	
Water	3.8400	
Loss	.2795	
	100.0000	$145 35 per ton

Average copper from twenty-four mines in Peavine District, 17.3 per cent.
Average gold and silver from thirty-four mines in Peavine:

	oz.	dwts.	grs.	
Gold	1	1	3	per ton
Silver	4	9	19	"

Ten.

Gold quartz from Bodie, Mono County, California; by W. F. Rickard, F. C. S.

Gold...................................	.110	$767 61 per ton
Silver	.350	134 56 "
Peroxyde of Iron...........................	1.233	
Peroxyde of Manganese....................	traces.	
Sulphur....................................	.140	
Lime	.370	
Magnesia	.252	
Alumina	4.120	
Silica.....................................	93.210	
Loss	.215	
	100.000	$902 17 per ton

Eleven.

Kearsarge Mine, Owen's River Valley, California; by W. F. Rickard, F. C. S.

Gold...................................	.0015	$9 04 per ton
Silver....................................	10.5000	
Chlorine.................................	3.6955	
Lead	4.6200	
Sulphur..................................	2.3350	
Peroxyde of Iron.........................	20.0720	
Silica....................................	58.6230	
Loss	.1540	
	100.0000	$3,968 69 per ton

ANALYSES OF VARIOUS WATERS FROM STATE OF NEVADA.

One.

From Humboldt; by W. F. Rickard, F. C. S.

Specific gravity, 1.010, a slight alkaline reaction.

Chloride of Sodium...................................	716.000
Carbonate of Soda....................................	2.560
Sulphate of Lime............................	20.320
Sulphate of Soda.....................................	8.850
Sulphate of Magnesia.................................	11.520
Sulphate of Iron.....................................	traces.
Free Soda...	"
Organic matter and loss..............................	.150
Total amount of solid matter per gallon..............	760.000 grains

Two.

Water supplied to Gold Hill, Nevada; by W. F. Rickard, F. C. S.

Water slightly opaque, with faint greenish yellow tinge; gives feeble alkaline reaction, which becomes stronger after boiling.   Specific gravity, 1.0014.

Sulphate of Lime	11.85
Sulphate of Magnesia	7.63
Sulphate of Soda	.65
Carbonate of Soda	.11
Free Soda	traces.
Organic matter	traces.
Total amount of solid matter per gallon	19.74

Three.

Hot Water, from Ophir Mine, Virginia, Nevada.—By George Attwood.—Taken from a depth of 453 feet.   Temperature, 70° Fah.   Flow, 300 gallons per minute.   Entirely free from any trace of precious metals.   Mechanically suspended matter in one gallon of 70,000 grains, 14.84 grains.   Total amount of carbonic acid, 23.30 grains.   Fixed matter in one gallon, 28.07 grains, Specific gravity at 50° Fah., 1.0007.

Carbonate of Lime	4.10
Carbonate of Magnesia	2.82
Sulphate of Lime	10.01
Sulphate of Potassa	.65
Sulphate of Magnesia	2.93
Sulphate of Soda	2.67
Chloride of Sodium	.60
Silicic Acid	2.20
Alumina	traces
Loss	.27
Total amount of solid matter, per gallon	28.07

APPENDIX "E."

JOURNAL OF EXPLORATIONS IN SOUTHERN NEVADA IN THE SPRING OF 1866,

BY

HIS EXCELLENCY GOVERNOR BLASDEL,

OF NEVADA.

R. H. STRETCH.

18

APPENDIX "E."

The company, of whose explorations this journal is a record, was organized for the purpose of opening up direct communication between the settlements in Pahranagat and the towns in the western portions of the State, in the belief that some nearer practicable route than the one by way of Egan Cañon and Austin must exist. It is not proposed to give more than the outlines of the journey, and the features of the country; nor would these have been thought suitable matter for incorporation in this report, did they not set at rest some disputed points relative to the southern portion of the State, and contain information about districts which has not, as yet, met with general circulation.

Silver Peak, on the eastern border of Nye County, was selected as the starting point—Pahranagat being supposed to lie to the southeast, though its exact location was a matter of considerable doubt, some persons claiming it to be in Nevada, and others in Utah.

The company started on *April 3d*, a little after nine o'clock in the morning, numbering over twenty individuals, with a buggy, one wagon, the necessary horses, and pack train. Six miles over sandy plains brought us to low rolling hills, our course being nearly south. The highest range of mountains to the southeast still covered with snow. The low range of hills on the east of the valley, near the edge of Salt Marsh, appear similar to those around Silver Peak, which are probably of Silurian age, being banded and blotched with dark blue and brownish yellow limestone (?). At ten miles, entered the bed of a wide, deep arroya, and shortly after a contracted cañon, the mountains on either hand being made up of white conglomerates, slates, and limestones. At eighteen miles, found a small spring on the right of the road, a little up the hillside. At nineteen and one-fourth miles, another spring of moderate size, on a knoll, south of high bluffs—the spring being scarcely visible from the bottom of the cañon. Camped at spring, 21 miles from Silver Peak. The spring is in a ravine, about one mile west of the main cañon. Near it were the remains of an old Indian rancheria. Piñon timber is abundant on the mountains, which also furnish plenty of grass of good quality.

April 4th.—Night very cold, and morning stormy. Three miles of easy grade brought us to the summit of the pass, soon after passing which we entered a narrow, steep gulch, in the bottom of which several outcrops of good looking copper-stained rock showed themselves. Five miles from the summit brought us out into a narrow valley, (Alida Valley) with snow-capped mountains to the south, and two good springs among willows near the outlet of the valley. The ground round the springs much coated with alkaline efflorescence, but the water not seriously tainted. The mountains on the south of the valley are well wooded, and consist mainly of coralline limestones, of both the black and yellow varieties; mica slates, very compact and crystalline; and granite, with whitish mica. The limestones are very largely developed, and in many places are made up of small fragments, evidently detached from ancient coral reefs, and afterwards cemented together—the whole mass exceedingly full of broken corals. The dip of the entire formation about forty-five degrees to the northeast, and the strike northwest by southeast, nearly corresponding with the direction of the mountains. The range contains many lodes of quartz, from two to five feet wide, with a dip and strike common to the clay slates in which they are found. The latter overlie the metamorphosed mica slates, and are capped by the limestone. Alida Valley appears to have a good connection with Fish Lake Valley, on the west, by easy grades, and the mountains, both on its north and south sides, are but spurs of the lofty range on the east of Fish Lake Valley. The entire district is well wooded, and produces an abundance of good feed for stock. Badgers, moles, and gophers abundant.

April 5th.—Still continuing our southerly course, four miles down a narrow cañon brought us out into a broad valley, opening out to the eastward, and connecting with the desert which lies east of Silver Peak. In this valley we spent the day, looking unsuccessfully for water to the east. In that direction the prospects were far from promising. The lower portion of the valley sandy, with a smooth gravel plateau, on which an arborescent aloe grew abundantly along the foothills. Much fine volcanic *débris* scattered about the valley, which may possibly have been ejected from an extinct crater on the southern side. Some little grass near the northern foothills.

April 6th.—Followed the valley eastward twenty miles, in the hope of finding water, but without success, and returned in the afternoon to our camp in Alida Valley.

April 7th.—Ascended the mountains on the south of Alida Valley, which we called the Lookout Mountains. To the eastward, the mountain ranges appear to degenerate into broken hills. To the south, a long uninterrupted valley extended as far as the eye could reach, commencing on the south side of the mountains which bound the valley in which we had been so unsuccessful. All along the summit of the ridge remains of Indian signal fires were abundant, the stations being connected with well beaten trails, apparently long unused. Indian signs are abundant, but as yet we have seen nothing more.

April 8th.—In camp all day.

April 9th.—On again reaching the valley to the south, we struck directly across it, entering the mountains just west of the volcano mentioned above, and reaching the summit in about seventeen miles. The hills on the north side of the summit are chiefly granite, with large quantities of barren quartz; on the southern side, the country is granitic with crystalline volcanic rocks. Eight miles down a broad open sandy arroya brought us to Desert Springs, small and poor in quality. These granite mountains are destitute of timber. After leaving the summit, the grass became very scanty, and sage brush disappeared entirely, being replaced by a small bush with olive green leaves, equally uninviting. Desert Springs lie at the northern end of a long valley bounded by lofty mountains on the west, which do not, however, reach the snow line. The springs are probably one thousand three hundred feet below the level of Alida Valley. The Indians use a bulbous mass found in the head of the young shoots of the aloes mentioned on a previous page for food. It is about the size of a hen's egg, has a slightly bitter taste, and cuts like a raw potato.

April 10*th.*—Followed the valley southward for nineteen miles to Bonner Springs. It everywhere gives evidence of comparatively recent volcanic action. The banks of the arroya are bluff, showing gravel beds overlaid with ten to twelve feet of stratified mud, the whole covered with a sprinkling of volcanic scoriæ. Three miles from the springs, the valley contracts to a narrow cañon, the walls of which are the same whitish mud, the whole capped with ten to twelve feet of basalt. The mountains on either side of the valley, precipitous, barren, and destitute of timber. Bonner Springs rise in a low range of hills on the western side of the valley, and flow over a succession of benches, on which they have gradually built up a great thickness of porous rock, and are slowly, by their cementing agency, converting the gravel beds in which they sink into conglomerates. Grass, and grape vines loaded with blossoms, grow luxuriantly along the banks of the many little streams. Found a small Indian camp at this place; they appear to be living principally on ducks, which they manage to secure by damming up the water from the springs, and building small brush houses (from which they are able to shoot their game) by the small pools thus formed.

April 16*th.*—Reached Wilson's Wells, thirty miles from Bonner Springs. The last few days have been spent in the effort to find water in this direction. Some fifteen miles from Bonner Springs the banks of the arroya die out into a wide wash of coarse gravel, which bears unmistakable evidence of the immense power and volume of the torrents which occasionally pour down this valley. The mountains continue barren as ever. Wilson's Wells lie on the east side of the valley, which at this point has widened out to several miles in extent. The greater portion of it is occupied by shifting sand dunes, on which small mesquite trees manage to find subsistence. The wells are about ten feet deep, and contain about seven feet of water.

April 17*th.*—Fifteen miles still down the valley, which is again contracted to something approaching its old width, brought us to Lost Wagons; many remains of the wagons belonging to emigrants who perished here in the attempt to reach California, lie scattered round these springs. The road to-day lay across sand and dried mud flats, exceedingly heavy, the crust not being thick enough to prevent the horses breaking through into the soft alkaline earth beneath. Water at Lost Wagons strongly alkaline. Found float quartz containing magnetic iron. Judging from the *débris*, the mountains are probably limestone, slate and granite. Mines here would be absolutely valueless, from the utter want of facilities with which to work them. Lost Wagons lies at the northern end of the celebrated Death Valley, in California, which we entered through a belt of hills four miles across, and *entirely destitute of every trace* of vegetation; and skirting its northeastern margin, camped near some muddy ground, yielding a little intensely salt water. At this point, judging from the rate at which we have been steadily descending, we must be nearly five thousand feet lower than Silver Peak, or somewhere near the sea level.

April 18*th.*—After leaving the last camp, three miles brought us to good springs in the foothills, about two miles from the edge of the valley proper, and three more to a still better location, almost under the shadow of the lofty mountains east of the valley. A fine warm spring, with a temperature of about 85° Fah. The foothills consist entirely of immense gravel beds, conglomerates and soft mud banks, the mountains being made up of limestone, slates, quartzite (?) and granite. The whole formation has been tilted until it is nearly vertical, and bears evidence of immense denudation. Traces of the action of waters highly charged with siliceous matter are everywhere abundant. No wood except a few small mesquite brushes.

April 20th.—Eight miles through rough hills of soft mud, which some members of the party facetiously called " self-rising earth," from its resemblance to the crust of a loaf, brought us to Furnace Creek, and to camp at Hadley Springs, in which it has its source. The low hills on the west of Death Valley almost defy description, being so utterly unlike anything with which most persons are familiar. They consist of gravel banks, conglomerates, soft mud deposits, etc., of almost every conceivable color, except green, and are so cut up by deep, precipitous gulches as to be almost impassable anywhere, except when they begin to die out on the flat. Anything more desolate can hardly be conceived. Here and there among them small springs are found, which are traceable by the growth of inferior grass along their banks. Furnace Creek, although containing probably one hundred inches of water, is dissipated after running little more than four miles. The "wash" of gravel at the mouth of the cañon is of vast extent and thickness, consisting of *débris* from the mountains, which must have been carried down during the prevalence of tremendous storms. These "washes" are the peculiar feature of this southern country, and must be made by the bursting of water spouts, such as are of frequent occurrence in Nevada; no other agency could produce such results. When we first arrived here, the weather was intensely hot, the thermometer probably standing at 110° Fahrenheit. The mountains, entirely destitute of timber, acted as reflectors, and made the name of the locality perfectly appropriate—for it was indeed a furnace.

May 7th.—We have been in camp most of the time up to this date. During this time, we made an unsuccessful attempt to find a pass out to the eastward. Death Valley proper is about thirty miles long and ten wide, the greater portion of its area being covered with incrustations of salt. It is exceedingly destitute of vegetation, and surrounded by mountains of great height, though the fact of their not reaching the snow line attests the great depression of the valley below the surrounding country. This morning we broke camp. Our road lay through rough mountains for over twenty miles, the higher portions of the range being similar to those near Bonner Springs. The low, broken hills on each side of the cañon are made up of sandstone, shales, conglomerates, gravel beds, and mud banks on the western side of the summits, capped with basalt on the eastern slope. The color of the formation ranges from dirty white, through yellow, yellowish brown, dark brown to black, as it recedes from the center of the cañon, imparting to the country a very peculiar appearance. The gravel beds must be many hundred feet in thickness, and have sometimes been tilted in common with the shales on which they rest, while in other places they are unconformable. The conglomerates are often seamed with veins filled with compact limestone, and cutting the formation at an obtuse angle. We came to camp on the eastern side of the valley; water and grass abundant. Amargosa Valley must be two thousand feet higher than Death Valley, and extends northward as far as Silver Peak, but its water-shed is to Death Valley, with which it is connected, along the northern margin of the great Mohave Desert. It is about twelve or fifteen miles wide, thinly covered with sage brush, and large portions of it are covered with salt grass. Water is abundant a few feet below the surface, but often poor in quality.

May 10th.—Six miles across meadow and sand flats, with some small white ash timber and grape vines, brought us to a range of low coralline limestone hills, with a fine spring on the summit, in a cave thirty feet long and ten wide. Crossed Ash Creek about three miles from camp. Camped on dry flat, with water three feet below surface.

May 11th.—Ten miles across desert flats to foothills; then eight miles to hard table land, with broken mountains to the summit. Shrubby cacti abundant, taking the place of the globular varieties, hitherto predominant. Mountains, lime-stone. On the top of a high tabular hill Mr. White found a profusion of fossil shells, chiefly large conical univalves. It is to be regretted that the specimens collected have been lost on their way to Carson. Indian tracks abundant on the summit, which, to the south, rises into the lofty snow range known as the Spring Mountains. Still following the general easterly course which we have maintained since leaving Death Valley, thirteen miles brought us to Indian Springs. Water and grass scarce. Few small mesquite bushes; no other timber seen to-day.

May 12th.—Five miles to Indian Creek, over hard flat, with sage brush. Found large Indian ranch, (apparently abandoned) with remains of maize, broom corn, and squash. Mountains still limestone. Grass scarce; some small mesquite bushes and willows. Las Vegas, on the San Bernardino Road, lies forty miles down the valley to the south.

May 13th.—Thirty miles up the valley, which runs nearly north, brought us to Quartz Spring. Water, far from abundant. Indians troublesome. Road up the valley good, over hard mud flats, often destitute even of sage brush. Quartz Spring lies on the east side of the valley, in mountains made up of limestone and quartzite. Plenty of fine bunch grass.

May 14th.—Traveled ten miles up wash and through low rolling conglomerate hills, in a northwesterly direction. Some small cedar trees near the summit. Then eight miles north, across open, sandy valley, with a large alkali flat to the west, and four miles through low hills to a small spring. Water very scarce, but grass abundant. Indians troublesome. Colonel Buel's last camp, when endeavoring to reach the Colorado River, was probably about five miles from this place.

May 15th.—About four miles through low hills, and twenty-eight N.N.E.N. across a wide level valley, brought us to Hadfield's Ranch in the Pahranagat Mountains. (See Pahranagat, in Synopsis of Mining Districts.)

———

It will be noticed that the chief features of the country through which we passed are:

1st. The parallelism of the mountain ranges, which, having a direction nearly northwest and southeast near the California line, gradually swing round nearly to north and south, going eastward.

2d. The alternation with these mountains of wide valleys, sometimes covered with sage brush, but often containing wide mud flats as completely destitute of vegetation as the floor of a room.

3d. The uniform structure of the mountains, and the presence of volcanic rocks in the foothills.

4th. The complete absence of timber, the only wood being the small mesquite bushes near the springs.

5th. The scarcity of water, almost all the localities where it occurs having been noted, the omissions being such as were close to our camping grounds.

6th. The prevalence of wide gravel washes at the mouths of the cañons, suggesting, by the remains of vegetation which have been brought down, the occurrence of tremendous rain storms.

7th. The absence of mineral-bearing veinstone in the *débris*.

8th. The peculiarity of the vegetation in Death Valley, and the long valley leading to it from the north. This is dissimilar from anything else seen in the country, and disappears on crossing the mountains which bound the valley on the east.

9th. The scarcity of Indians throughout the district.

FROM PAHRANAGAT TO INDIAN SPRINGS.

May 24th.—Started with a company of nine; five and a half miles from Springer's Ranch brought us into Coal Valley, so called from supposed discoveries of that article, which, however, proved to be nothing but black volcanic rocks; and five more to the mouth of a wash in the mountains on the western side of the valley. The mountains are made up chiefly of crystalline, igneous rocks. Following up the wash through the mountains for two miles, we turned north along their western slope, and reached Pahwahcumbah Spring, about twenty miles from Springer's. Rocks near the spring principally of eruptive origin. Leaving the spring we struck out eastward across the valley, crossing the low northern extremity of the mountain in which the Worthington District is located, and reached a fine stream, after traveling twenty miles across good, though in some places sandy roads. Many of the veins in Worthington District contain copper and magnetic iron; others have more the appearance of auriferous lodes.

May 26th.—The creek on which we are camped runs about five hundred inches of water, another a few miles to the north runs an almost equal quantity, and yet another is reported in the same direction. These all rise in the Shonigodit or Grass Mountains, which are most appropriately named. The bunch grass grows thick enough to mow, and covers the mountains from base to summit. This range in many places attains an elevation of nine thousand feet, and at present is covered with snow many hundred feet down from the loftiest peaks. The boulders in the cañon show the range at this point to consist chiefly of volcanic rocks, porphyries, etc., with but few indications of quartz. Piñon timber of large size is abundant, with mountain mahogany of heavy growth on the higher mountains.

May 27th.—Following up the bed of the stream, we reached the summit in six miles, making an elevation of probably two thousand five hundred feet above the valley. There is a lower and broader pass some few miles to the southward. The whole cañon is exceedingly fertile, having in many places a broad level bottom, sometimes choked up with small cottonwood and elder trees. Camped on the summit with good feed and water. Rocks crystalline, eruptive.

May 28th.—Night exceedingly cold and windy. Six miles down a rather rough cañon brought us to Shewadzee Springs, at the western base of the mountains, which are well timbered down to the valley. Springs, three in number; water good and tolerably abundant. Indians came to camp, one of them going ahead with us. We were the first white men they had seen.

May 29th.—Five miles through the foothills brought us to a wide, sandy and gravelly valley, ten miles across which we found a small stream of only inferior water. This stream rises somewhere in the valley on the east of the Soong-up Mountains, and flowing southward, finds its way into the present valley through a wide gorge in a range of low mountains, made up at this point to a great extent of crystalline rocks. Crossing these, fifteen miles across another valley brought us to the base of the Soong-up or Rough Mountains. Good road all day, and bunch grass in abundance.

May 30th.—Three miles to Milky Springs; water muddy, but of fair quality. In five miles, over broken spurs of the mountain, we reached the summit, and three more brought us to White Rock Spring, at the western base of the mountains. This spring dries up during the summer months. It derives its name from the prevalence of intensely white rocks in the neighborhood. This range of mountains is fairly supplied with timber; the lower range passed yesterday, furnishing but little, if any.

May 31st.—Drove ten miles to Duck Springs Crossing, a low ridge about half way. Duck Springs lies just under a rough ridge which we crossed, ascending into a valley about twelve miles wide. After climbing another steep slope, and following down a ravine about a mile and a half, we came to Innyobah Springs, in wide meadows of wire grass. Rocks red, crystalline, eruptive. Wood abundant.

June 1st.—Passed several springs soon after leaving camp, and reached Indian Springs in about twenty-five miles, or somewhere about one hundred and fifty miles from Pahranagat; since this date it has often been made in four or five days. It will be seen that the whole of this section of the State is tolerably well supplied with wood and water. Grass of the finest quality is everywhere abundant.

List of Mills in Nevada.

NAME.	Motive Power.	Cords of Wood p'r Day.	No. of Stamps.	Weight of Stamps.	No. of Pans.	Nature of Pans.	Crushing Capacity per Day. Tons.	REMARKS.
STOREY COUNTY.								
Atlas............	steam	4½	15	500	8	Hepburn............	25	
Atwood..........	"	4½	16	....	26-2	Knox, Wheeler......	20	
Bay State........	"	6	23	....	14	Wheeler............	35	
Bowes's..........	"	4	20	10-600 10-700	80	Knox	25	
Central..........	"	8	18	....	4	Hepburn............	12	
Crown Point......	"	8	8	500	8	Knox	8	
Comet............	"	4½	16	....	....	Plain..............	20	
Douglas..........	"	4	10	650	26	....	16	
Eclipse..........	"	4	15	....	8	Hepburn............	25	
Empire, No. 1....	"	5½	21	650	29	....	80	
Empire, No. 2....	"	8	16	650	12	Wheeler............	82	
Empire State.....	"	8	15	....	20-2-2	Knox, Wheeler, Hepburn	15	
Gold Hill........	"	8	14	8-600 6-750	24	Knox	17	Refitting.
Granite..........	"	20	80	....	89-8	Hepburn, Varney....	100	
Gould & Curry....	"	8½	8	750	24	Knox	12	
Hoosier State....	"	8	44	600	74	Knox	?	
Imperial.........	"	5½	20	....	10	Wheeler............	80	
Land's...........	"	4	12	....	2-6	Knox, Wheeler......	15	
Mariposa.........	"	5	9	....	80	Plain..............	18	
Marysville.......	"	6	22	....	12	Wheeler............	20	
Ogden............	"	8	80	650	15	Wheeler............	50	
Pacific..........	"	8½	16	700	18	Knox	26	
Petaluma.........	"	5½	20	650	12	Hepburn............	80	
Plute............	"	8	25	....	18-8	Knox, Hepburn......	40	
Rhode Island.....	"	4	10	....	5	Varney	12	
Bigby's..........	"	8½	8	....	....	....	12	
Rogers'..........	"	5	16	750	56	Knox	28	
Sapphire.........	"	5	16	....	8	Tubs, Wheeler, Hepburn	25	
Simcoe...........	"	2½	8	500....	10	Knox	10	
Stevenson's......	"	6	20	....	....	....	26	
Succor...........	"							

Name	Power					Stamps		Remarks
Summit	"	6	90	625	11–1	Wheeler, Varney	85	
Union	"	2¼	14	10–650	14	Hepburn	14	
Winfield	"	5	18	4–500	8		30	
LYON COUNTY.								
Birdsall & Carpenter	water	9	30	650	20	Wheeler	55	
Bacon	steam	6	30	650	17	Wheeler	30	
Bartolo	"	3	8	550	8	Knox	9	
Cole & Co.	"	3	5	480	4	Wheeler	8	
Devil's Gate	"	5	8	900	10	Hepburn	14	
Daney	water	6	15	550	15	Wooden Tubs	20	
Dayton, No. 1	steam	1	20	500	6	Wheeler	20	
Dayton, No. 2	water	6	15	800	8	Varney	15	
Eagle	water		5	400	2	Knox	15	
Eastern Slope	steam	5½	16	800	6	Hepburn	20	
Excelsior	"	8	10	650	18	Knox	18	
Eureka	water		20	650	8	Wheeler	22	
Franklin	"	4	10	600	8	Knox	12	
Golden Eagle	steam	3½	10	850	25	Hepburn	18	
Illinois	"	5	20	400	5	Knox	20	
Island	"	2	19	650	11	Tubs	14	
Lindauer & Co.	st'm & water	2¼	15	480	10	Wheeler	90	Dismantled.
Metallurgical Works	steam	5	15	700	6	Wheeler	16	
Monitor	water		5	450	2	Wheeler	3	
New York & Nevada	steam	5½	20	550	17	Hepburn	25	
Ophir	st'm & water	2¼	24	600	15	Hepburn	85	
Pioneer	steam	6	15	700	15	Tubs and Wheeler	90	
Phœnix, No. 1	"	7	15	650	8	Tubs and Wheeler	19	One of these Mills
Phœnix, No. 2	"	4½	20	534	84	Tubs	28	1866.
Palmyra	"	2¼	10	650	12	Tubs	15	
Rock Point	st'm & water	6	56	650	50	Tubs and 6 Hepburn	60	
Sparrow & Trench	steam		20	550	19	Tubs and 6 Hepburn	25	
Sherman & Co.	water		6	400	2	Tubs	4	
Swansea	steam	5	14	900	22	Tubs	20	
Smith, D. L.	water		5	450	4	Tubs	4	
Sacramento	steam	5	12	750	12	Tubs	18	
San Francisco	st'm & water	8	10	650	7	4 Tubs and Wheeler	14	
Weston & Co.	steam	4	15	550	9	Wheeler	14	
Weston & Co.	water		10	450	8	Tubs	11	

LIST OF MILLS IN NEVADA—CONTINUED.

NAME.	Motive Power.	Cords of Wood p'r Day.	No. of Stamps.	Weight of Stamps.	No of Pans.	Nature of Pans.	Crushing Capacity per Day, Tons.	REMARKS.
ORMSBY COUNTY.								
Santiago	water	...	24	550	18	Wheeler, Hepb'n, Coleman	40	On Carson River, between Empire and Dayton.
Vivian	st'm & water	...	16	650	8	Wheeler	30	On Carson River, between Empire and Dayton.
Merrimac	water	...	20	1000	15	Wheeler	40	On Carson River, between Empire and Dayton.
Brunswick	"	...	8	1050	4-1	Knox, Varney	20	On Carson River, between Empire and Dayton.
Yellow Jacket	st'm & water	...	40	900	9-30	Varney, Hepburn	80	At Empire.
Mexican	water	...	44	900	12	Hepburn	75	At Empire.
Carson	"	...	15	500	5	Wheeler	20	At Carson.
Sierra	st'm & water	...	8	500	16-2	Knox, Hepburn	12	At Carson.
WASHOE COUNTY.								
Dall's Mill	st'm & water	...	60	...	...			Rebuilding.
Ophir	steam	...	72	...	24	Freiburg Barrels	50	Ophir, Washoe Valley.
New York	"	...	24	...	16	Varney	50	Washoe City.
Atchison	water	...	20	...	16	Wheeler	30	Washoe City.
Minnesota	steam ?	...	16	...	12	Wheeler	25	Washoe City.
Buckeye	" ?	...	10	...	8	Wheeler	25	Washoe City.
Manhattan	water	...	24	...	16		30	Allen Cañon.
Napa		...	...	...	...		25	Galena.
Temelec	steam	...	15	...	12	Wheeler	25	Pleasant Valley.
Washoe Consolidated	water	...	20	...	...		30	Not running. On the Truckee River.
CHURCHILL COUNTY.								
Silver Wave	steam	...	10	...	...		...	Not running.
Silver Lode	"	...	10	...	...		...	Not running.
Connecticut & Nevada	"	...	8	...	...		...	
Desert	"	...	5	...	...		...	Not running.
ESMERALDA COUNTY.								
Aurora	steam	...	10	...	20	Wakelee's	...	The first eleven of these mills are at Aurora, and have mostly been idle for some time.
Pine Creek	"	...	10	...	4-4	Wakelee's, Tubs	...	
Union	"	...	8	...	6	Wooden Tubs	...	
Antelope	"	...	8	...	16	Wakelee's	...	

Name	Motive power	No.		No.	Apparatus	No.	Remarks
Wide West	"	20		40	Wakelee's		
Pioneer	"	8		6	Wakelee's		
Gibbons'	"	4					
Independence	"	16		12	Wakelee's		Dismantled; to be refitted by the Philadelphia Co.
Napa	"	8		80	Wheeler		
Real del Monte	"	80		6			
Alturas	"	7					
Silver Peak	"	10				10	Not running.
Red Mountain	"	8					Crushes gold-bearing quartz.
NYE COUNTY.							
At Ione (1)	steam	10					Three miles south of Ione.
Knickerb'ker & Nevada	"	20					Not running. At San Antonio District.
Hunt's	"	10			Barrels.		In Philadelphia or Silver Bend District.
Buel's	"	10					
At Hot Creek (1)	"	10					Pahranagat District.
Raymond's	"	5					Twin River District.
Murphy	"	20					
LANDER COUNTY.							
Names not specified (Total, 20.)	chiefly steam	219					Chiefly dry-crushing mills.
HUMBOLDT COUNTY.							
Sheba							
Fall's							
Auld Lang Syne							Of the details of these mills I do not possess any definite information, neither am I certain that they include all the mills of the county.
Holt's							
Etna							

Lightning Source UK Ltd.
Milton Keynes UK
UKHW020726191218
334233UK00007B/675/P